0/98

I0646512

45.⁰⁰

COPS, CROOKS,
AND
CRIMINOLOGISTS

COPS, CROOKS, AND CRIMINOLOGISTS

An International Biographical Dictionary of Law Enforcement

Alan Axelrod
Charles Phillips
with Kurt Kemper

Facts On File, Inc.

AN INFOBASE HOLDINGS COMPANY

Cops, Crooks, and Criminologists: An International Biographical Dictionary of Law Enforcement

Copyright © 1996 by Zenda, Inc.

Facts On File, Inc.
11 Penn Plaza
New York, NY 10001

Library of Congress Cataloging-in-Publication Data
Axelrod, Alan, 1952–
    Cops, crooks, and criminologists : an international biographical
  dictionary of law enforcement / by Alan Axelrod, Charles Phillips
  with Kurt Kemper.
      p. cm.
  Includes bibliographical references and index.
  ISBN 0-8160-3016-2 (acid-free paper)
    1. Police—Biography—Dictionaries. 2. Criminals—Biography—
Dictionaries. 3. Criminologists—Biography—Dictionaries.
I. Phillips, Charles, 1948– . II. Kemper, Kurt. III. Title.
HV7911.A1A94 1996
364′.092′2—dc20
[B]   95-30564

Jacket design by Catherine Hyman

This book is printed on acid-free paper.
Printed in the United States of America
VB VC 10 9 8 7 6 5 4 3 2 1

Contents

Acknowledgments

The authors thank John Kelley, Nanette Maxim, and Alison Mitchell for their assistance in researching and writing this book.

Introduction

This book is intended to be neither a policemen's hall of fame nor a rogue's gallery of notorious criminals. It is an encyclopedic dictionary of major and significant figures, living and dead, who have shaped the history of law enforcement. That history involves much that is of vital concern to us today: our system of laws and the nature of what we consider crime; those who transgress those laws and how we come to terms with them; those we employ to enforce the laws; and the methods and techniques developed over time to aid in solving crimes and catching crooks. Historically, matters are not quite as simple as the morality play politicians have made of inner city despair in recent years, the one in which tough but underfunded cops fight evil, rich and ubiquitous drug-lords and youth gangs in a never-ending conflict of clear moral extremes. Such a melodrama may win elections, it may even be based on fact, but it has little to do with the history of law enforcement and a lot more to do with the refusal to face up to the social ills of poverty and unemployment, which have always been the mother and father of crime. Historically, matters are not so black and white.

Crime, simply put, is conduct forbidden by authority—by God, by tyrant, by king, by custom, or by law. Traditionally, certain acts have tended to be more or less universally considered crimes (rape, murder, and robbery, for example), while others have depended much more on the nature of the authority that outlawed them (fornication, blasphemy, and usury come to mind). Early legal codes—from that of the Sumerian Ur-Nammu in 2050 B.C. to the Judaic Ten Commandments of Moses—included, pell-mell, broad moral injunctions and specific social and economic rules. But though they held sin and crime to be one and the same, they defined transgression primarily by the injunctions against it. Even Adam and Eve had to have a rule to break, or their "crime"—eating the forbidden fruit, which gave them a knowledge of sin—would have been merely an accident and thus unpunishable. The Romans, perhaps, were the first to separate carefully the legal from the moral, crime from sin, and the Roman saying, *nullem crimen sine lege* or "[there is] no crime without a law," became the bedrock of modern legal theory, which is based on the realization that, though authority from time to time changes—people worship a different God, tyrants fall, kings abdicate, customs die out, new laws are passed—the rule of law, not necessarily its content, is essential for any society to function.

We are steeped in the traditions of secular law inherited from the Romans. If there is no crime without a law, we say, even immoral or antisocial behavior cannot be considered criminal unless it is forbidden or punishable under some law. For us, crime and illegality, not crime and sin, are synonymous, and the basic tenets of our legal system have to do not with the nature of crime, or with transgression, but with the nature of law, with the rules that define transgression. Laws should be strictly interpreted; they should be as clear and unambiguous as possible; new laws should never be retroactive. That does not mean, of course, that the law has lost all connection with morality, and indeed laws cannot long function if they contradict the general public's moral sense of right and wrong, since in the end it is the acquiescence of those governed by the law that give the law its authority. In fact, it is when our morals come in direct conflict with our legal definitions of criminal behavior that the rule of law tends to break down. Until the mid-19th century in the United States, slavery was legal, and those who opposed it actively by helping slaves to escape, like the abolitionists, or by assassinating slaveholders, like John Brown, were criminals. It took a bloody civil war to change the law, to bring it in line with the prevailing morality.

On the other hand, laws based on a morality that ignores common social practice and basic human nature define crime too broadly and make criminals of us all. The "progressive" prohibition against the sale and use of alcohol in the United States during the early decades of the 20th century is the classic example, and it is particularly instructive for what it has to say about our society's fascination with crooks. From January 1920 to April 1933, the U.S. federal government forbade, under the Volstead Act passed by Congress to enforce the recently ratified 18th Amendment, the manufacture, transport, and sale of alcoholic beverages anywhere in the country. Prohibition signaled a triumph of the religious fundamentalism that had slowly been taking command of the rural parts of the United States since before the American Civil War and whose chief beneficiary in the late 19th century was the politically narrow but incredibly focused Temperance Movement. The special-interest groups it spawned—the Women's Christian Temperance Union and the Anti-Saloon League—had by the turn of the century successfully begun to influence state and local elections in favor of "dry" candidates, and by 1916 21 state legislatures had outlawed saloons. That year, voters in congressional elections sent a dry majority to Washington, a majority that secured the passage of the 18th Amendment, which was submitted to the states for ratification in December 1917.

From the moment the Volstead Act went into effect, America became a nation of lawbreakers. The big-city ethnic neighborhoods, unlike the rural-dominated state legislatures, had, for a generation, overwhelmingly voted against various prohibition referendums. Folks in these neighborhoods began immediately to brew and bottle bathtub gin and moonshine, often with the encouragement of their friends and neighbors. Contemptuous of a law they hated, determined themselves to continue drinking, and looking to make a buck, these neighborhood bootleggers had the support of their local grocers, who supplied the necessary raw materials, and of their local former saloon-keepers, their restaurant owners and ice cream and soft drink parlor operators, who helped distribute their products. Neighborhood policemen looked the other way. Friends warned one another about raids. But the business was risky. Raids did occur. People were punished. Some even lost their citizenship.

Then, lured by the chance for big profits, the underworld moved in.

The gangsters, like those they preyed upon, were immigrants. Crime simply offered a convenient, alluring, and quick way up the ladder of success, and bright, ruthless, upwardly mobile immigrant youths, convinced that other means to wealth and the pursuit of happiness were unavailable to them, turned to crime as a profession. Such men tended to be at home with violence, and neighborhood bootlegging looked like a good, easy mark. The mobsters began terrorizing the newly illegal traffic in liquor, extorting protection money and brutalizing the uncooperative. Gangs, their members often no more than teenagers, battled each other for control, using sawed-off shotguns and Thompson submachine guns to make their points and establish their monopolies. The mainstream press, pandering to its nativist, middle-class audience, tried to make the most recent immigrants—the Italians—responsible for the crime wave that Prohibition had created in major American cities. Almost weekly, headlines announced still another Sicilian gang war or the discovery of yet another illegal warehouse in one Little Italy or another. But the first well-known mobster in New York was an Englishman, Owney MADDEN, the second a Jew, Arnold ROTHSTEIN; and the Irish and Germans, too, had their gangs in every city. Protected by their big-city politicos, mobsters poured their profits into clubs that played jazz over the machine-gun tattoo (rat-tat-tat) in the background, into the corruption of government officials wherever they found them, even into legitimate businesses. They became rich and powerful, but more to the point, they also often became modern urban folk heroes in the popular literature and films of the time.

Prohibition did not so much fail, as the classic argument goes, because it confused morality with legality, but rather because the moral authority upon which the law was based was so narrowly drawn, based as it was on the fears and fantasies of a distinct segment of the population. After all, the anti-drug laws that first went into effect about the same time are still around and have been over time immeasurably strengthened. And despite the fact that laws against the manufacture and sale of such drugs have had precisely the same effect as Prohibition did, no one today seriously dares to argue for the legalization of morphine, heroin, opium, or cocaine. Especially with the coming of "crack" to the inner city, the illegal traffic in drugs has created some of the world's largest and most profitable business cartels and led to the wholesale corruption of local governments and the near breakdown of the American justice system. Yet because the vast majority of Americans still find the manufacture and sale—if not the use—of crack and other hard drugs morally abhorrent, the crusade against them not only continues, but also remains an issue upon which politicians of all stripes apparently agree.

In short, whether or not Prohibition was a misconstrued morality, it was certainly bad politics. Resting on the demands of then powerful interest groups which represented what turned out to be a shrinking, mostly rural, constituency, it was doomed demographically. By 1920 more people lived in the big cities than on farms, and the fear of foreigners and foreign ways that had always fed the power of the bluenoses proved inadequate to sustain their crusade in the face of such massive urban growth. With more and more people openly violating the prohibition laws, those laws not only became unenforceable, they also appeared no longer to be grounded in social reality. Lacking real authority, they seemed arbitrary. For that reason there grew up in urban America the conditions for the appearance of men who resembled those historian Eric Hobsbawm once called "social bandits."

According to Hobsbawm, social bandits were peasant outlaws regarded as criminals by the ruling class or the state, but treated by common folk as heroes, champions, avengers, fighters for justice, maybe even liberators, but in any case men to be admired, helped, and supported. They appeared in every historical period and everywhere in the world where there was a society based on agriculture, including pastoral economies, and consisting mostly of peasants and landless workers who were ruled, oppressed, and exploited by someone else—lords, towns, governments, lawyers, even banks. "Such banditry tended to become epidemic," wrote Hobsbawm, "in times of pauperization and economic crisis." When rural society and village life were rent open by war, by conquest, by political breakdowns, by sudden changes in the administrative systems of which they formed small and remote parts, the social bandit appeared. Typically driven outside the law because of some personal act sanctioned by the local community but considered criminal by the distant state and its local authorities, the bandit remained a part of his community, even in a way represented it, and was certainly considered an honorable man within that community. Robin Hood was, of course, the archetypical social bandit, but so was the mostly legendary Juan Murietta, whose robberies and murders during California Gold Rush days became a form of communal protest for Mexican Americans against the oppressions of the mining industry and the racist policies of the United States. Under similar conditions in a rural Missouri ripped asunder by four years of civil war and federal occupation, even a cold-blooded killer like Jesse JAMES came to resemble a social bandit. And so would the petty bank robbers of the 1930s whom J. Edgar HOOVER put on his "most wanted" lists—Pretty Boy Floyd, John DILLINGER, Alvin KARPIS, and the like.

The gangsters of Prohibition were neither peasant bandits, nor farmboys turned bank robbers, but hard-souled urban entrepreneurs. Nevertheless, the inner-city immigrant community (what today we would call the ghetto) was structurally very similar to the oppressed villages of past times and other places; and to many in the 1920s and 1930s Al CAPONE was a fascinating figure whom more than a few held in some esteem. It was a fact Capone himself understood and of which he took advantage, playing a sort of clownish and rough-hewn neighborhood Robin Hood for the media and the public. Prohibition taught Jazz Age, urban Americans, even many who were not immigrants and who did not live in slums, what peasants the world over have always known: Laws are for those who make them. It was a lesson that in many ways endures. Certainly our fascination (and the barely clandestine admiration that forms part of the foundation for that fascination) with the urban gangster continues today, as even a cursory glance at modern movies—the immense popularity of the *Godfather* films, for example—will testify. Nor should this be particularly surprising. If—as Roman tradition has it—there is no crime without a law, then who is and who is not a crook is to a large extent a technical matter. We would do well to remember that Al Capone himself was tried and convicted and sent to prison not for the murders, the robberies, and the extortions he committed, but for failing to comply with the technicalities of the American income tax laws.

If crooks, then, have not always been, and are not always today, considered absolute "bad" guys, neither have cops always been, and are not always today, considered absolute "good" guys. There have been policemen—members of religious, military, or political forces charged with enforcing the law and wielding the authority necessary to do so—since at least Babylonian times. Early police forces grew from the personal bodyguards of rulers and warlords, and their job was to enforce the religious or political mandates of those in power. Rome under Caesar AUGUSTUS had one of the best organized of the early forces. To impose order on the mean and violent streets of a Rome inhabited by almost a million people the emperor created three orders of police within the Roman army, placed them under the command of an urban prefect, and empowered them to call upon his own bodyguard—the Praetorian Guard—for assistance. In addition, Augustus divided the city into 14 wards (*regiones*), broke the wards into precincts (*vici*), and created a corps of *vigiles*—containing seven squads of a thousand freedmen—who, under the supervision of precinct captains (*vicimagistri*), fought fires and at night policed the city.

Such military and semi-military police forces were the general rule down through the 18th century, and they developed independently around the world. The shogun, for example, who ruled feudal Japan in the

1600s, created an elaborate police force that had a military samurai warrior serving as magistrate in each of the castle cities dotting the countryside. The magistrate in turn appointed other sword-carrying samurai, *yoriki* and *doshin,* to patrol the streets. Early in the 18th century, the Russian czars created a militaristic police to enforce their edicts, and Nicholas I expanded this force into an early form of the state political police, the dreaded Okhrana. After the Russian Revolution, V. I. LENIN based his powerful and highly organized Cheka on the Okhrana, and the Cheka in turn served as a model for Mussolini's OVRA and Hitler's Gestapo. The 20th century's "secret" police forces, the NKVD, the KGB, the Japanese Thought Police, Iran's SAVAK, ad infinitum, with their powers not only to arrest and detain, but also to pronounce and control sentencing, had as their ancestors the Praetorian Guard and the samurai magistrates. They are a direct inheritance of the military origins of policing. But, tending to form in the early days of unstable regimes, they were an exaggerated form of that inheritance. All modern police forces use some of the techniques of the secret police—spies, informants, centralized operations, individual dossiers— as part of the same inheritance.

Lawmen in pre-Revolution France, for example, were basically the king's political police. In Paris the police force was run by the *lieutenant-general de police,* who—though he was officially subordinate to the minister of Paris—was appointed by the king directly and had the responsibility not only of controlling crime and maintaining order, but also of scrutinizing all the social, political, and economic activities of Parisians as well. And he could call upon the military for support at any time. Under his authority were 48 police commissioners, 20 inspectors, 50 captains (*exempts de police),* and a legion of *sentinelles*—10 brigades of 10 archers each and a watch guard of 200 horsemen and 400 foot soldiers—who patrolled the streets.

The Paris police ran the city. They built markets, a hospital for children, schools for the poor, and a veterinary college. They paved roads, put up street lights, opened state-run pawn shops, and organized the fire and river rescue services. They censored posters, persecuted Protestants, ran the state lottery, inspected drains, cleaned streets, surveyed dangerous buildings, examined prisons, reviewed theological works for signs of heresy, and issued regulations concerning dogs. In part, they directed the economy: inventorying food supplies, checking food prices, finding work for the jobless, overseeing the employment of foster mothers, forbidding wine sellers to use lead counters and milkmen to use copper containers, and at one point stopping fishmongers from selling

oysters between April 30 and September 10. They founded the Bourse, the Paris stock exchange, and established their own financial agency to encourage overseas trade. But their control over Paris and its citizens struck even deeper and was more sinister as well. In addition to the regular police force, the *lieutenant-general* controlled the *mouchards,* the secret police, a squad of irregular spies; their undercover intelligence activities, more than the preventative patrols, came to characterize the Paris police force, making it infamous.

No citizen was safe. The *mouchards*—and the force's regular inspectors—constantly gathered private information on the activities of French citizens through spies, brothel keepers, employers, and servants. They routinely intercepted and read private correspondence sent through the mail. One estimate suggested that one-fourth of the housemaids, butlers, and lackeys in Paris were in the pay of the police, tattling on their pals and their bosses, and police chief Sartine once bragged to his king, Louis XV, "Sire, whenever three people speak to one another in the street, one of them will be mine." Sartine and his ilk distilled the enormous number of tidbits they gathered into two reports, the *bulletin moral* and the *bulletin politique ou d'espionnage,* the first of which they sent each day to the king, the second of which they distributed to various political officials. Even if the information received by the king from domestic spying was based mostly on rumor and hearsay, hardly sufficient for a legitimate trial, his majesty could issue a *lettre de cachet* ordering the imprisonment of anyone he wished. Armed with such a letter, the police were allowed to detain people without charge and exercise various kinds of summary justice. The National Police, the *marechaussee,* employed similar powers throughout France. Originally established to control crimes committed by military personnel, by the time of the French Revolution they had been unleashed against civilians as well.

The French revolutionaries intended to change all that, and they failed miserably. They disbanded the king's police forces and reorganized police functions under a conglomeration of committees sitting in Paris, an arrangement that proved not merely clumsy but unworkable. In 1796, the revolutionaries had created the Ministry of Police and charged it with enforcing laws and preventing the subversion of the Revolution. Three years later, NAPOLEON Bonaparte came to power as First Consul in a coup d'etat, and Joseph FOUCHE was installed as the ministry's director. Fouche consolidated police administration into four departments, or *arrondissements,* and put a counsellor in charge of each, who operated under his direct authority with few, if any, legal restrictions. He centralized the police force itself under the office of the *prefet de police,* who had administrative but no judicial authority. He hired several hundred spies, many of them ex-convicts, whom he called the *regulators de l'opinion à Paris,* and put them to work informing on the public. Meanwhile, private individuals, the military, even the Jesuits, set up their own secret police forces, and spying became epidemic. Police agents, informers, and spies were ubiquitous, and citizens believed that even the smallest hint of discontent got back to the authorities and that a slip of the tongue could kill them. By the time Bonaparte had become the Emperor Napoleon, Fouche was the second most powerful man in France, and his ministry resembled nothing so much as the former French king's former political police. Fouche's minions not only disrupted political activities and controlled public opinion, they also attempted to shape political thought itself, and as Napoleon went off to conquer the world, corruption and injustice riddled the French police system.

Perhaps because the French police so depended on spying, they emphasized the work of individual detectives, who recruited and ran their agents. The most famous of these, Francois-Eugene VIDOCQ, in 1810 founded the Sûreté. Only in the atmosphere created by Fouche could a convict and daredevil jailbreaker like Vidocq approach the police with an offer to use his knowledge of the criminal underworld in exchange for his freedom and be given his own bureau to fight crime. Arguing that one sent a thief to catch a thief, Vidocq not only got out of jail, he also worked his way up to become chief of the criminal police. He created a network of spies and informers and waged a war against crime that was, by our lights, completely successful.

It was not so much that Vidocq's informers and the ministry's political spies were everywhere, but that French citizens *believed* they were everywhere that made the streets of Paris in the late 18th and early 19th centuries a haven of safety compared to those of London or New York. For if the French system reveals the modern cop's lineage in the palace guard, the Anglo-Saxon systems connected him with what we might call the vigilante tradition.

That tradition predated the Norman Conquest, stretching back to the habit Saxon citizens had of banding together for mutual protection in what early England called the "frankpledge." Under the private frankpledge, all adult males in a community became responsible for the good conduct of each community member. The frankpledge amounted to a social obligation, and when a citizen observed a crime, he was expected to raise an alarm, form a posse, and chase down and capture the criminal. Those who refused to do so were themselves subject to punishment. Should

no one actually witness a crime, it fell to the victim alone to investigate and identify the perpetrator to the satisfaction of his frankpledge peers. After the battle of Hastings in 1066, the victorious Normans added to the English system the office of constable. Originally a royal court position, by the end of the 13th century the constabulary had developed into a local, and rotating, office attached to individual manors and parishes. There, constables—in addition to their frankpledge obligations—became responsible for overseeing the local "watch-and-ward," a nightwatchman who guarded the town gates after dark (and eventually lit the town's street lamps), called out the time, kept an eye out for fires, and reported any untoward goings-on. Though the unpaid, part-time constables, assisted by their juniors, the watchmen, had a special duty to maintain the king's peace and to present offenders at court tests, social disorder also remained everyone's responsibility, and any citizen could arrest a crook. Generally, it was still left up to victims to investigate and prosecute crimes against them, and when they failed, they often hired "thieftakers" to track down the guilty and return stolen property.

Some of the early bounty hunters were justices of the peace and constables, but they could just as easily be private citizens who, for a fee, undertook to catch and convict thieves. The most notorious of the "common informers," as they were called, was Jonathan WILD, who turned the whole system into a racket, organizing the London underworld to steal the goods that he would then sell back to their owners. Despite its vast potential for corruption, the private reward system endured and became standardized, creating a "stipendary" police force that operated in a system employing Draconian punishments for petty offenses, hardly surprising given the prominence of the victims in the process. Over time, constables became totally subservient to justices of the peace, and the post's status grew so debased that prominent citizens refused any longer to serve, which hardly caused problems in the countryside but was of serious concern in the larger cities where those willing to take the job—the sick, the old, the poor—could hardly keep pace with sharp urban criminals. Nevertheless, the private frankpledge constabulary lasted for some 800 years and was transplanted to Australia, Canada, and the United States, where cities like Boston and New York could be as ill-policed and corrupt as London. What ultimately killed the system early in the 19th century was the industrialization that had wrenched people in ever greater numbers from the countryside and placed them in urban squalor.

Riots, for example, had been a well-established means of protest in rural England, but in the great cities of the Industrial Revolution they seriously disrupted economic life and could not be tolerated. In England, the Crown could call upon the military and the local yeomanry to put down such displays, but bringing in the military might increase the power of the king, a power Englishmen had already fought to restrict, and relying on the yeomanry worried the men of property, who did not trust them. In such circumstances, the shortcomings of the constabulary system became evident, especially its inefficiency, and soon England's political leaders and men of letters were calling for reform. As early as 1798, the West India Trading Company had created a force of marines, the Thames River Police, to curb the theft plaguing the London docks. It was England's first professional police force, its 80 permanent policemen and its thousand or so part-timers received a salary instead of a stipend and were not allowed to take private fees. The Thames River Policemen patrolled the docks openly and constantly in order to prevent crime rather than merely to track down those who had committed it. Their great success led the House of Commons in 1890 to make the River Police a publicly financed operation, but long before then it had inspired the creation—after bitter debate that raged throughout the early decades of the 19th century—of a standing police force, on the French model, in London under Robert PEEL.

Americans were as leery of standing police forces as were the Londoners. Like them, Americans saw paid constables walking among them as an infringement on their social and political life; like them, Americans worried about the potential for abuse of power inherent in a bureaucratic organization; like them, Americans did not want to ante up the taxes to pay for professionals. But by the early 1800s, U.S. cities too were burgeoning, and riot, crime, and disorder were endemic. More important to American middle and upper classes, the cities were beginning to attract foreigners—the Germans and the Irish—who with their strange beliefs and social habits not only offended the delicate sensibilities of the original English and Dutch settlers, but also threatened their hegemony. America's establishment no more trusted the immigrants than England's propertied class trusted the yeomanry, and after trying out versions of the private constabulary, the nightwatch, and voluntary citizen's groups, they responded to growing unrest by passing laws, building penitentiaries, opening asylums, and creating urban police forces. New York was the first, establishing a department modeled after the Metropolitan London Police in 1844. Then came Boston and Philadelphia. Within a decade, cities as far west as Milwaukee had police departments organized just like those of the English, with a quasi-

military command structure and no detectives, their minions charged with preventing crime and disorder as well as cleaning the streets and performing a wide variety of public services.

The one major difference between the police forces of the two countries was that in America, which lacked the unity afforded the British under a constitutional monarch, each city created its own force. The decentralization extended even further, down to the political ward and neighborhood level. The mostly high-born reformers who had created the police forces saw their function as reestablishing political and social control over urban populations plagued with ethnic and economic rivalries, but those in immediate control of the departments—ward heelers and neighborhood bosses—had different ideas, and the struggle to control the police became one of the distinguishing characteristics of American law enforcement.

The modern police system, then, was pretty much in place by the mid-1800s. The scion of a palace guard, put in place to control unruly populations whose political activities were now defined as criminal, the police were not particularly beloved by those they supposedly protected. It was just about this time, however, that the public opinion of the police began to change. A number of very popular writers—Charles Dickens, Wilkie Collins, Edgar Allan POE, and, a little later, Arthur Conan DOYLE—started to write fictional accounts about a new kind of hero, the detective. Inspired perhaps by the highly fictionalized autobiographical accounts of the French criminal-turned-detective Vidocq, all these writers had in common a fascination with what Poe would call "ratiocination," or, to be more precise, with the possibilities and potential of lucid, reasoned criminal investigation. They were writing in the age of Lydell and Darwin, during the days when scientific investigation seemed part and parcel of the progress of man, and for their heroes the practice of astute observation and solid deduction became central to the capture of criminals. Before them, people did not really think of criminal activity as involving a crime that could be "solved" the way a puzzle might be solved, through clues and clear thinking. And except for gathering into dossiers spy-spawned hearsay and gossip, the police did not much see it as a function of the detective to solve a crime by meticulously and systematically gathering evidence and carefully building a case on such evidence. In short, it was in the works of these early mystery writings that there first stirred the spirit of the science of criminology.

Criminology's roots, of course, stretch back much further than the founding fathers of the mystery story. Babylonians had pressed fingerprints into clay to record the identity of cuneiform writers as a check against forgery. The ancient Chinese, too, had used fingerprints for identification. It was the Romans who first came up with the idea of using handwriting for the purposes of comparison and identification. Medieval investigators developed methods of interrogation still used today, as well as many that would land a modern interrogator himself behind bars, including compurgation, or the questioning under oath of friends and relatives of the accused, not on the facts but on the general character of the accused. The inhabitants of Asia had long been aware of the principles behind the lie detector—i.e., the drying up of saliva under stress. They filled a suspect's mouth with dry rice, and if the accused had trouble spitting it out, judged him or her guilty. Though modern police methods were beginning to develop in the 18th century, it was really the technological advances and the emphasis on classification and observation evident in the 19th century—Peel's reforms calling for the keeping of comprehensive police records, BERTILLON's elaborate body measurements, HENRY's establishment of a classification system for fingerprints based on patterns and shapes—that laid the foundation for criminology. And in fact, both its birth and the fictional birth of a Sherlock Holmes were a reflection of the period's high opinion of science and the scientific method. It was, for example, in Arthur Conan Doyle's story "A Case of Identity" that the idea of tracing a specific typewriter by the peculiar properties of its individual type characters first appeared, some three years before the subject was broached in the technical literature.

The focus on investigatory technique and on the detective separated the police from policy, helping immeasurably the image of cops by placing on the work they did the imprimatur of science. The policeman no longer strived merely to prevent crime, i.e., to enforce the laws passed by representatives of the propertied classes, but also to investigate crime in a dispassionate search for the truth. In other words, the public and the police reached an understanding about the nature of crime itself that resembled the understanding between the reader and writer of the mystery story: that there was such a thing as objective truth; that it was possible and desirable to discover that truth; that folks have a responsibility to their fellow beings not to kill or hurt or steal from them; that if people do hurt, kill, or steal, they should be found and punished; that the finding of such people was the legitimate function of the police. Police work has since then generally enjoyed public support, whereas the laws the police are actually there to enforce do not always have that support, especially laws governing so-called "victimless" crimes.

We have now the basic historical background against which those included in this encyclopedia should be viewed. None of the basic elements of today's law enforcement field—secular laws, bureaucratic and professional police forces, and rational investigations of crime—developed in a vacuum. All of them were shaped by many of those men and women included here, and many of those included here were shaped by them, which is precisely the reason we chose them. Look for the famous Eliot NESS in the following pages not because of his colorful exploits, but because he formed the first serious interdepartmental task force to fight organized crime. By the same token, any number of notorious malefactors have been excluded, but the petty criminal Ernesto A. MIRANDA does appear, since the 1966 U.S. Supreme Court ruling in *Miranda* v. *the State of Arizona* profoundly affected the practice of law enforcement in the United States. The gangsters included changed history, and the cops, too. Salutory or infamous, the figures we have chosen have made a significant contribution to the development of the techniques, practices, principles, and philosophy of law in a world where laws change, crooks sometimes are considered heroes, cops are themselves occasionally crooked, and investigations are only as good as those who conduct them.

—Charles Phillips

A

Abberline, Frederick George (1843–1929) Scotland Yard detective-inspector who was in direct charge of the Jack the Ripper murders in London in 1888.

Frederick Abberline had built a reputation as a thorough, methodical, and conscientious Scotland Yard officer by 1888, when he was put in charge of investigating London's most infamous mass murderer, Jack the Ripper. Abberline failed to apprehend the Ripper, and he drew much criticism from the press for being insufficiently aggressive in his investigation. Some even believed that he had helped to conceal the identity of the murderer. Whether the criticisms or the accusations are justified or not, the fact remains that Abberline did provide very exacting reports of the five (out of a possible seven or even nine) murders ascribed to Jack the Ripper.

Abberline developed two theories concerning the Ripper murders. He suggested that the Ripper might be a woman, and (after his retirement) that one George Chapman (real name, Severin Klosowski), arrested by one of Abberline's protégés in 1903 for having poisoned several women to death, was Jack the Ripper. Some "Ripperologists" have suggested that Abbeline had actually discovered the identity of the Ripper—it was none other than the heir to the thone, the duke of Clarence—and had acquiesced in a cover-up mandated (perhaps) by Queen Victoria herself. This, of course, is speculation. The facts are that, in 1889, Abberline covered up a raid on a homosexual brothel at 19 Cleveland Street in London's Whitechapel district after discovering that much of the clientele were the wealthy, the noble, and the highly placed; Abberline, aged 46, abruptly resigned from Scotland Yard after closing the files on the so-called "Cleveland Street Scandal"; and that Abberline refused to talk about the Ripper case from the time of his precipitous resignation until his death on December 10, 1929.

Abrahamsen, David (1903–) A criminal psychoanalyst who has studied subjects from Richard NIXON to David Berkowitz, the "Son of Sam" killer.

A native of Norway, David Abrahamsen immigrated to the United States in 1940, just ahead of the Nazi occupation and the ravages of World War II. Having earned his doctorate in 1929 from the Royal Frederick University, Abrahamsen practiced both psychiatry and neurology in Norway. Once he arrived in the United States, Abrahamsen concentrated on psychiatry and, in particular, psychoanalysis.

In 1944, Abrahamsen published *Crime and the Human Mind*, which dealt with the rationalization of deviancy and how some individuals are able to suppress deviancy while others become engulfed by it. Perhaps Abrahamsen's most influential book was *The Murdering Mind* (1973), in which he examined in detail numerous cases of psychopathic murderers, most notably Jack the Ripper and David Berkowitz, the so-called "Son of Sam" killer. Most of Abrahamsen's information on Berkowitz came directly from the killer and was the product of Abrahamsen's analysis of Berkowitz—the first time a confessed mass murderer was ever psychoanalyzed. Abrahamsen concluded that Berkowitz and other serial killers are plagued by feelings of inadequacy, both social and sexual, and that the act of murder alleviates these feelings by releasing the emotional pressure they cause.

Abrahamsen's most controversial book was his *Nixon vs. Nixon: An Emotional Tragedy* (1977), in which he analyzed the former president of the United States without ever having met him. Abrahamsen used extensive interviews with Nixon detractors, as well as long-time supporters, and filled out his subject's childhood biography by reading Nixon's *Six Crises* memoir. The portrait Abrahamsen created was of a deeply conflicted, hard-driving, and utterly ruthless individual.

Abu Nidal (Sabri Kalil al-Banna) (ca. 1939–)
Leader and founder of the Abu Nidal terrorist organization, Sabri Kalil al-Banna—calling himself Abu Nidal—was responsible for near-simultaneous terrorist killings in the Rome and Vienna airports in 1985.

A highly successful terrorist, al-Banna has managed to keep almost every aspect of his life a secret. There are at least five different guesses as to his age and nearly as many as to even what his real name is. The youngest child of a wealthy citrus merchant from what was then Palestine, al-Banna led a privileged existence in his early childhood, enjoying a private education and a large house with servants in the town of Jaffa. All of that changed in 1947, when the United Nations declared the partition of Palestine and created the nation of Israel.

When the partition was announced, vicious fighting broke out between Arab and Jewish factions; when it escalated into small-scale warfare, conditions became very harsh for those caught in the middle. When Jaffa fell to the Israelis in April 1948, al-Banna and his family were forced to flee to a refugee camp and live in a tent.

Al-Banna would forever blame the Israelis for his fall from luxury and privilege, and it was this disrupted childhood that led to his becoming one of the most ruthless and efficient terrorists of the 1970s and 1980s.

After moving to Saudi Arabia, al-Banna worked as an electrician and fell under the influence of radical Moslem politics. Sometime in the mid-1960s, he joined the Ba'ath Party, a fundamentalist Islamic organization illegal in Saudi Arabia, and was able to make friendly contacts with the Ba'ath-dominated Iraqi government. Sometime thereafter, he joined the extremist Palestinian group Fatah, but was jailed, tortured, and expelled from Saudi Arabia for his membership. He then moved back to Nablus, Egypt, in spring 1967, only months before the Six Day War in which Israeli forces marched on the Sinai Peninsula, the Golan Heights, the West Bank, and the Gaza Strip. When Israeli tanks rolled down his street, al-Banna vowed to become active in the Islamic underground.

As a full-time terrorist, al-Banna took the name Abu Nidal, meaning "father of the struggle," and his first assignment was to set up a branch of the Fatah in Khartoum, the capital of the Sudan, where he stayed for eight months before being sent to Iraq in August 1970. In Iraq, Abu Nidal solidified his relationship with Yasir Arafat and the PLO and possibly joined the radical Black September group, which was respon-

sible for the murder of 11 Israeli athletes at the 1972 Munich Olympics.

In October 1974, a split occurred between Abu Nidal and Fatah, and he formed his own eponymous group, Abu Nidal. Over the next 15 years, Abu Nidal established formal ties with Iraq, Libya, and Syria and was apparently sanctioned by Lebanon and Libya in its most nefarious acts. In June 1982, Abu Nidal attempted to assassinate Shlomo Argov, the Israeli ambassador to the United Nations, and in April 1983, successfully assassinated Dr. Issam Sartawi, a moderate Palestinian leader. Its most infamous action, however, was the nearly simultaneous airport massacres in December 1985 in Rome and in Vienna, when gunmen walked into the two airport terminals and opened fire, killing a total of 20 people. In late January 1986, Rome police issued an arrest warrant for Sabri al-Banna, otherwise known as Abu Nidal. It is still in effect, and al-Banna is still at large.

Further reading: Melman, Yossi, *The Master Terrorist: The True Story Behind Abu Nidal* (New York: Adama Books, 1986).

Acton, Thomas C. (1823–98) Commissioner of the Metropolitan Police during the New York City Draft Riots of 1863, the worst civil disorder in American history.

A native New Yorker, Thomas Acton was forced to leave school early to make a living when his father died. However, he continued to study on his own, learning the law and ultimately gaining admission to the New York state bar. Acton never practiced privately, however, but immediately became assistant deputy county clerk, beginning a lifetime of public service. In 1860, Governor Morgan appointed Acton to serve on the board of police commissioners, a post in which he would serve for the next nine years.

The Conscription Act of March 1863, signed into law by Abraham Lincoln, incited much resentment in the North. Many persons were resentful of forced participation in the war. Others were more specifically outraged over forced participation in a war to free African-American slaves. In New York and other American cities, the immigrant laborers, who occupied the lowest rungs on the social ladder, feared that freed slaves would come north and take their jobs. Finally, the conscription system itself was inherently unjust. Any well-to-do man could legally buy his way out of conscription, either by paying a fee or by hiring a substitute. Poorer folk were in no position to do either. In this atmosphere, the first names were drawn by lot in July 1863, and New York City was thrown into chaos.

On the morning of July 13, a crowd gathered to protest the draft. The crowd swelled, and, in short order, mob rule prevailed. The Metropolitan Police were called to disperse the crowd, but they were immediately overwhelmed, and Superintendent John Kennedy was almost beaten to death. Acton assumed personal command, quickly ordering all precincts in peaceful areas to send all available men to headquarters. He commandeered any and all means of transportation to dispatch officers to the riot areas.

The riots continued for three days, during which time many African Americans were attacked and even lynched. A black orphanage was burned to the ground. Ultimately, it required the intervention of the Union Army—men who had just fought the battle of Gettysburg—to quell the disturbance once and for all. However, given his inadequate resources, Acton handled the situation brilliantly. He was able to have as many men as possible in the right place at the right time, greatly limiting the scope of the destruction and violence that might have occurred. Most notable among the police victories was the dispersal of a mob on the verge of burning Wall Street.

Acton's methods seem brutal by today's standards. He ordered his men to search out the mob and engage them, rather than simply disperse them. He directed that no prisoners be taken, but that rioters be beaten on the spot. In this spirit, one precinct commander ordered his men to "Kill every man who has a club." In context, the measures were appropriate; the city had no other means of dealing with large-scale civil disobedience. It lacked large municipal jails, and it had no vehicles to transport substantial numbers of detainees. Acton's tactics were widely studied by other police officials responsible for riot and crowd control.

Adams, Francis W. H. (1904–90)   Democratic politician and reformer; served as New York City police commissioner and helped root out corruption in the department.

After graduating from Williams College in 1925, Francis Adams attended Fordham Law School in New York City. After earning his law degree in 1928, he began working for a Manhattan law firm for which he had clerked to pay his way through school. In 1934, he was named assistant United States attorney for the Southern District of New York and that same year was promoted to chief assistant. The following year, he was named United States attorney before being named special assistant to the attorney general in the investigation of the burning of the cruise ship *Morro Castle* off Asbury Park, New Jersey, in 1934.

After returning to private practice in 1937 and serving on various civil commissions during World War II, Adams was persuaded by mayor-elect Robert Wagner to accept the position of New York City police commissioner. Adams accepted on the condition that he be given an absolutely free hand in rooting out corruption in the department. Adams set to work in January 1954, abolishing cushy desk jobs at headquarters and eliminating such units as the glee club and the departmental band, all in an effort to put more officers on the streets. Adams also instituted Operation Efficiency, a watchdog unit to observe officers on patrol. By the time he retired 19 months later, he had added some 2,000 officers to the force, and New York City saw a 13% decrease in serious crime.

Addams, Jane (1860–1935)   The founder of Hull House was a champion of the rights of women and the underprivileged, who believed that crime in poor neighborhoods could be reduced or eliminated by improving social conditions.

The youngest of eight siblings, Jane Addams was born September 6, 1860, in Cedarville, Illinois. A very bright and energetic woman, Addams attended the Rockville Female Seminary and was graduated in 1881, at a time when women were first beginning to attend college. After Rockville, she went to Philadelphia to attend the Women's Medical College, but

Civil libertarian, pacifist, and founder of Chicago's Hull House, Jane Addams helped to establish the first juvenile court in the 1890s. (Courtesy of the Chicago Historical Society)

was forced by ill health to return home in her first semester.

Due to her illness, Addams never returned to medical school. Instead she journeyed to Europe for treatment and to relieve a deep depression brought on by the state of her health and by her frustration over the fact that her horizons were limited in a society that placed little value on the achievements of women. In London, she visited Toynbee Hall, a settlement house for the poverty-stricken of London's slums. Here her spirits revived as she conceived the idea of bringing a similar house to Chicago. She returned from Europe invigorated both mentally and physically.

Back in Chicago, she was able to acquire the old Hull mansion on Chicago's south side. Her motive was twofold; first and foremost, to give enterprising and educated women an opportunity to showcase their personal talents and achieve something of importance, and second, to improve the lot of the urban poor and thereby eliminate the evils of poverty, including crime.

Hull House offered day-care, elementary education, a boy's club, a boarding house for working girls, and many other social programs. Addams also spoke out against sweatshop labor and inequities in the labor laws aimed against immigrants and the poor. She agitated against the politicizing of the sanitation department, which would often result in haphazard collection in certain areas and lead to disease.

She also strongly advocated the establishment of a juvenile court system and leniency toward juveniles, whose delinquency was evidence less of criminality than of social victimization. Addams also opposed the growing cocaine traffic in the inner city and the white slavery rings that preyed on the young daughters of the urban poor.

Addams's social activities were warmly received in most quarters, but her popularity was dimmed by her pacifism that was opposed to America's entry into World War I. The Daughters of the American Revolution denounced her as "the most dangerous woman in America," and even after her death on May 21, 1935, some accused her of communist sympathies. In the eyes of history, however, she is seen as one of the great pioneers of social reform and the humanization of the American criminal justice system.

Further reading: Addams, Jane, *Twenty Years at Hull House* (New York: The Macmillan Company, 1910).

Adonis, Joseph (born: Giuseppe Antonio Doto; alias: Joey A. Adone, Joe Arosa, James Arosa, Joe DeMio) (1902–72)   A New York Mafia boss for three decades.

Born in Montemarano, Italy, near Naples, Adonis illegally immigrated to New York with his family in

A handcuffed Joe Adonis on the right (Courtesy of the Library of Congress)

1915. He became a petty thief in the slums of Brooklyn, working his way up to the extortion of local shopkeepers. An avid womanizer and singularly vain about his good looks, he adopted the name Adonis; some say a prostitute gave him the idea, others believe he found a reference to the Greek god in a magazine. In 1922, when at least one woman failed to find him irresistible, Adonis raped her, a crime for which he was arrested but never convicted.

During the early days of Prohibition, Adonis and Charles "Lucky" LUCIANO purchased a large shipment of smuggled liquor from Waxey Gordon and parlayed the profits into a Mafia-financed bootlegging empire. Even as Adonis raked in bootlegging profits, he continued to serve Mafia boss Frankie Yale as his chief Brooklyn enforcer, while developing his own gang of bootleggers catering to the Broadway show crowd and dubbed the Broadway Mob. Adonis cultivated an image as a gentleman bootlegger, and his Broadway restaurant became not only a profitable speakeasy, but also a distribution center for bribes to local police officials and politicians, to whom waiters "served" envelopes filled with cash. Adonis became known as "Mr. Fix." Adonis was astute in sharing "his" police officials, politicians, and judges with other crime figures, so that he quickly became a figure of great power.

Adonis was careful to invest his estimated $10-million annual take in a variety of perfectly legitimate businesses, especially restaurants and, after the repeal of Prohibition, legitimate liquor distributors. He also became involved in a major distributor of automobiles and in cigarette vending machine companies. While the vending machine companies themselves were legal, Adonis stocked the machines with cigarettes hijacked by his men.

In the meantime, Adonis helped Lucky Luciano arrange for the murder of Joe "The Boss" MASSERIA, a gangster of the old school who had clearly outlived his usefulness. With Luciano's old boss out of the way, the embryonic national crime syndicate was free to grow, and Adonis claimed a place on the "board of directors" alongside Luciano. The killing of Joe the Boss was hardly Adonis's first blood. He had been involved in the deaths of at least 20 men before Masseria and would kill or cause to be killed many, many more. Among those he wished to eliminate was his own boss, Anthony "Little Augie Pisano" Carfano, strongman of the Brooklyn Mafia since the early 1920s. Rather than murder Carfano, however, Adonis convinced him to retire permanently to Florida in 1933, leaving what remained of his rackets to Adonis, including the Brooklyn narcotics traffic, which Adonis controlled from 1933 until his deportation in 1956. Adonis was also particularly inventive in his exercise of extortion. He kept tabs on those of Sicilian descent who purchased luxury automobiles, like Cadillacs. Joey A. would arrange for the purchaser to receive a phone call "suggesting" a payment to protect his home from "accidental" explosion and his children from "accidental" disappearance. Those who received the calls, because they were Sicilian, knew what the Mafia was capable of, and invariably they complied with Adonis's "requests."

Adonis became caretaker of Luciano's rackets when the latter was jailed in 1936 and faithfully saw to it that Frank COSTELLO remained honest. In the meantime, Adonis expanded into New Jersey, financing scores of lavish gambling dens inside abandoned warehouses. By the 1940s, the restaurants and casinos were bringing Adonis and his partners as much as $100 million a year. However, at this time, authorities penetrated and neutralized Murder, Inc., and Adonis began to close down this and his other Brooklyn operations, finally moving to New Jersey altogether, where he felt himself safe not only from the law, but also from covetous fellow gangsters.

In 1952, Adonis was brought before the U.S. Senate's Kefauver Committee, which resulted in his trial and conviction on gambling charges and—after a lengthy legal battle—in his deportation to Italy. On January 3, 1956, Adonis was escorted aboard the luxury liner SS *Conte Biancamano*. He set sail for his native land, occupying a suite customarily reserved for royalty. Adonis settled in a lavish villa near Milan and was not heard of again until 1972, when Italian police, making a sweep of known Mafia figures, brought him in for questioning. During the course of the interrogation, he died—according to police, of a heart attack. The disposition of his multimillion-dollar fortune remains unknown.

Allport, Gordon W. (1897–1967) Noted sociologist specializing in race relations and racial prejudice; developed seminars for police on racial issues.

Allport was born in Indiana and raised in Cleveland, Ohio, where he attended public school. He enrolled at Harvard University in 1915 and graduated with a B.A. in philosophy and economics. After a brief teaching stint in Constantinople, he returned to Harvard for his master's and Ph.D. His doctoral dissertation on experimental personality traits was the first of its kind in the United States. After receiving his doctorate, Allport again traveled abroad, this time for extended courses of study at the universities of Hamburg and Berlin and at Oxford University.

After returning to the United States, Allport accepted a position in the sociology department at Harvard, and in 1946 assumed the chairmanship of the newly created Social Relations Department. At Harvard, he began research on the nature of prejudice and racial tension both in the United States and elsewhere. In 1956 he published *The Nature of Prejudice*, considered one of the most important sociological contributions to the field, in which he argued that prejudice and bigotry can be eradicated only through education and with the passage of time.

Allport instituted a series of seminars on race relations for police departments. These, the first of their kind, would become a regular part of police training in sociological issues.

Altgeld, John Peter (1847–1902) Governor of Illinois who sacrificed his political future by pardoning anarchists convicted of throwing bombs during Chicago's Haymarket Riot.

A native of Germany, John Altgeld immigrated with his family to the United States in 1848. After working on the family's Mansfield, Ohio, farm during his youth, Altgeld enlisted in the Union Army in 1864 and served briefly in the Civil War. He returned to high school after the war, graduated, and became a teacher. In 1869, he moved west to Missouri and studied law, gaining admission to the Missouri bar in 1871.

Once he became a lawyer, Altgeld's political career took flight. He was appointed Kansas City attorney in 1872 and in 1874 was elected county attorney. He resigned after a year to move to Chicago, where he made a fortune in real estate, and in 1884 was nominated for Congress. He lost the general election, but in 1892 was elected the first Democratic governor of Illinois since the Civil War. The star of this reform-minded governor rose rapidly—until he resolved to review the convictions in the Haymarket bombings of 1886.

The so-called Haymarket Riot, one of the worst outbreaks of labor violence in United States history, had begun as a pro-labor rally in Chicago's Haymarket Square. When police moved in to disperse the crowd, someone hurled a bomb at the police line, killing seven officers and two demonstrators and wounding 130 others. Nine men were arrested—all speakers at the rally—and charged with murder. The prosecution's case was manifestly weak, failing to present any evidence identifying the actual bomber.

On May 4, 1886, a Chicago labor strike exploded into violent conflict between police and workers in what came to be called the Haymarket Riot. (*Harper's Weekly*, May 4, 1886, courtesy of the Nashville Public Library)

Indeed, the prosecution failed to connect any of the accused in any way with the act. What the prosecution did have was a judge, Joseph Gary, who, working in a public atmosphere of panic over a rash of "anarchist plots," was intent on securing a conviction. Incredibly, he allowed a relative and a close friend of one of the slain officers to serve on the jury, while he disqualified any laborers from sitting. He further ruled that the prosecution did not have to identify the bomb thrower or even prove the murders were in any way connected to the anarchist beliefs of the accused.

In a shameful miscarriage of justice, the nine were convicted, and eight were sentenced to death. Four of the condemned men were executed, and a fifth killed himself in his cell before Altgeld stepped in to review the case. In an act as memorable and courageous as the original verdicts had been infamous and cowardly, the governor condemned Gary for his conduct and pardoned the remaining defendants. It meant the end of his political career; he was resoundingly defeated in the next gubernatorial race. John Peter Altgeld, a martyr to justice, never held public office again.

Anastasia, Albert (Umberto Anastasio; alias: Lord High Executioner; The Mad Hatter; Big Al) (1903–57) Head of Murder, Inc., and the Mafia's most formidable exterminator, ordering the murder of hundreds, perhaps thousands, and personally killing 50 or more people.

Albert Anastasia and his nine brothers illegally immigrated to the United States from Italy during World War I, in 1917. Anastasia found work on the tough Brooklyn docks and within two years had become a longshoreman, working with his brother Anthony. He also joined a Brooklyn street gang, notorious for assaulting women, robbing and raping them, but he had the delicacy of feeling to change his name from Anastasio to Anastasia so as not to bring shame upon his family. (Anthony—Tony—retained the original spelling, even after he went to work as a dockside racketeer under the direction of Albert.)

Anastasia came to the attention of Brooklyn gang boss Joe ADONIS, who eventually financed Anastasia's own bootlegging operation during the early years of Prohibition. Almost immediately, Anastasia earned a reputation for ruthlessness, rubbing out at least five men in the process of claiming his Brooklyn bootleg territory. However, Anastasia's career was nearly cut short by this spate of killing when he murdered long-shoreman Joe Torino in 1920 by stabbing and strangling him—in front of several witnesses. Anastasia was arrested, tried, convicted, and sentenced to death. Consigned to Sing Sing's death row to await execution, he wangled a new trial, at which all the witnesses "mysteriously" changed their stories and, having re-

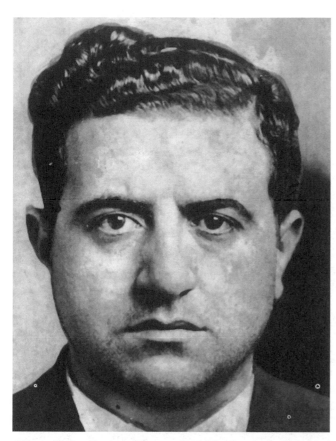

Albert Anastasia was "director" of Murder, Inc. (Courtesy of the Library of Congress)

versed themselves, suddenly disappeared. There was no choice but to release Anastasia.

After leaving prison, Anastasia went to work for Adonis as his greatly feared enforcer, primarily intimidating speakeasy owners who failed to buy his boss's goods, extorting protection money from local shopkeepers, and organizing the longshoremen into Mob-dominated unions. By the end of the 1920s, Anastasia had also begun another enterprise, assembling a group of professional killers-for-hire that would soon evolve into Murder, Inc., the enforcement arm of the national organized crime syndicate. It was Anastasia who created the vocabulary of modern gangland murder, including such terms as "contract" (an agreement to murder someone), "hit" (a reference to the victim and to the event), and "the troop" (the murderers). Anastasia's executioners included the likes of Harry "Pittsburgh Phil" Strauss, Harry "Happy" Malone, Abe "Kid Twist" RELES, Frank "The Dasher" Abbandando, Seymour "Blue Jaw" Magoon, Martin "Bugsy" Goldstein, and Allie Tannenbaum. Through Anastasia, they committed murders for the likes of Adonis, Charles "Lucky" LUCIANO, Thomas Lucchese, James V. Mangano, Louis "Lepke" BUCHALTER, and others.

Anastasia was a key figure in organized crime from its very inception and was present at the 1929 Atlantic City "convention" that is generally regarded as the event that launched the national syndicate. He was a combatant in the Castellammarese War between the factions of Joe "The Boss" MASSERIA and Salvatore Maranzano. Ostensibly allied with Masseria, it was he who delivered the final bullet to Joe the Boss in 1931, at the behest of Luciano, as fellow murderers Bugsy Siegel, Vito Genovese, and Joe Adonis watched. Anastasia was cold-blooded and utterly fearless. When Dutch SCHULTZ announced in 1935 that he wanted New York District Attorney Thomas E. Dewey dead (a proposition so outrageous that Lepke Buchalter ordered the execution of Schultz as a danger to the whole syndicate), Anastasia staked him out and reported that the job would be relatively easy. Feared as he was, Anastasia was also regarded as lacking in vision—all muscle and no brain. The Sicilian members of the Mob also distrusted him because of his devotion to Lepke Buchalter—for a time the syndicate's equivalent of the chairman of the board—who was a Jew.

In 1940, several members of Murder, Inc., indicated to authorities that they were willing to turn state's evidence, and Anastasia immediately went into hiding. Key witnesses were killed, however, and in 1942 Anastasia took the extraordinary step of enlisting in the U.S. Army. Despite his criminal record, he was accepted and, ironically enough, excelled in the service, rapidly rising to the rank of sergeant. The move not only kept him out of police hands, it also allowed him to become a naturalized citizen in 1943, thereby precluding deportation. Of course, Anastasia saw to it that his life was never in jeopardy. Although his unit was shipped overseas, he bribed his way into a position stateside, supervising a transportation center. After the war, he purchased a set of medals in a pawnshop and wove tales of heroic deeds. He also resumed direction of his gambling, narcotics, and prostitution operations in Brooklyn and New Jersey, to which state he subsequently moved his headquarters. When Luciano was deported to Italy in 1946, Philip and Vincent Mangano took over his territories. With Luciano's approval, Anastasia ordered the death of Philip Mangano on April 19, 1951, and was almost certainly responsible for the disappearance of Vincent Mangano later in the year. Thus, Anastasia was elevated to the status of Mafia Don.

He soon proved himself a dangerously impulsive leader. For example, while he was watching a television news program in 1952, he saw a story about Arnold Schuster, a private citizen turned amateur private eye, who had identified the celebrated bank robber Willie "The Actor" Sutton on a New York subway train. The robber was subsequently arrested.

Anastasia leaped from his chair, pointed to the TV, and summarily ordered the murder of Schuster. Such evidence of instability prompted Vito Genovese, Carlo GAMBINO (Anastasia's underboss), and Joseph Profaci (a Mafia family boss) to oppose Anastasia. Only the powerful Frank COSTELLO stood in the way of their toppling Anastasia. On May 14, 1957, Costello narrowly escaped death in an assassination attempt. Costello became convinced that Anastasia was behind it and, on October 25, 1957, he dispatched two gunmen to kill the Don as he was getting a shave and a haircut at his barber's.

Ancel, Marc (1902–) This French Supreme Court justice and noted criminologist led the "social defense" movement of the 1960s.

Social defense, an important movement in European criminology, sought to make the legal system responsive to human and social realities. To do this, social defense requires the subordination of that legal system to the science of criminology, defined as criminology proper (the study of the phenomenon of crime in all its aspects), criminal law (the explanation and application of the rules whereby society reacts against crime), and penal policy (the application of punishment and rehabilitation).

Although the idea of social defense existed before Marc Ancel's epoch-making *Social Defense: A Modern Approach to Criminal Problems* (1966), prior to his work, scientific criminology had relatively little direct influence on law, the application of law, and penal policy. Ancel's concept of social defense appealed to all the social sciences to participate in the understanding and treatment of criminals and criminality and, moreover, for judges, lawyers, and lawmakers to act from an understanding and appreciation of scientific criminology.

It must be further observed that, for Ancel, the "science" of criminal policy is tempered by social and psychological sensitivity, so that scientific criminology in the service of social defense is both a science and an art.

While social defense is primarily a European movement, Ancel owes much to the criminal justice system of the United States, which, early on, accepted scientific criminology and penal reform as part of its court and prison structure. Ancel's ideas sparked the modern rehabilitation movement in Europe and furthered the science of penology there.

Further reading: Ancel, Marc, *Social Defense: A Modern Approach to Criminal Problems* (New York: Schocken Books, 1966).

Anslinger, Harry J. (1892–1975) One of the first to sound the alarm against drug use, Anslinger became the first commissioner of the Treasury Department's Bureau of Narcotics.

A native of Altoona, Pennsylvania, Harry Anslinger attended Pennsylvania State University before becoming a public servant for the federal government in 1917. While working in Washington, he earned his law degree from Washington College. Anslinger held various government positions. When he moved from the War Department to the Treasury Department in 1926, during Prohibition, Anslinger became aware of the worldwide trade in alcohol and drugs. After attending seminars on smuggling and alcoholism, he was appointed commissioner of prohibition in 1929 and the following year was named the first commissioner of narcotics.

As commissioner, he spoke out virulently against drug use, promoting harsh penalties both for drug users and drug sellers. He called for "judges not afraid to throw killer pushers in jail and throw away the key!" By the mid-1930s, Anslinger saw what he called an epidemic of addiction among young people, particularly those using marijuana. He argued that the drug problem directly exacerbated the crime problem, and thereby secured passage of the Marijuana Tax Act of 1937, which essentially outlawed marijuana.

While Anslinger attacked drug use, he was quick to see the benefits of certain drugs for medicinal and military usage and, to this end, quickly stockpiled different types of drugs in the gold vaults at the Treasury building for use in the war that, by the late 1930s, had come to seem inevitable. For this foresight, he was widely lauded, and one senator had his action entered into the *Congressional Record*.

It was World War II that gave Anslinger some of his biggest ammunition against the international drug traffic. In 1942, Anslinger issued a report to Congress citing proof that Japan had violated international commitments regarding drug trafficking. He argued that Japan had been using opium as a way to enslave conquered peoples, saying, "wherever the Japanese Army goes, the drug traffic follows." He cited Korea and China as two prime examples of the "Japanese Opium Offensive." To help stop both international and interstate trafficking, Anslinger was given use of the Coast Guard, the Bureau of Customs, and agents of the Internal Revenue Service. He continued to speak out against illegal drug use until his death in 1975.

Aquinas, Saint Thomas (ca. 1224–74) Merged Aristotelian thought with Christian theology, fostering (among much else) principles of justice and individual responsibility that are cornerstones of Western concepts of crime and punishment.

Thomas d'Aquino was the son of a count and was born in his family's castle at Roccasecca, central Italy. When he was only five years old, his parents sent him to be raised by the monks of the Benedictine monastery at Monte Cassino, where his uncle had been abbot. After Monte Cassino became the site of a battle between papal and imperial troops, young Aquino moved to Naples, where he enrolled at the university. Coming under the influence of Dominicans there, he defied his family's wishes and became a Dominican friar in 1244. He then journeyed to Paris and Cologne for further study during the years 1245 through 1252 and was greatly influenced by Albertus Magnus.

From 1252 to 1259, Thomas Aquinas taught at the Dominican *studium generale*—"house of studies"—in Paris. From 1259 to 1269 he was attached to the papal court in Italy, returning to Paris in 1269. In 1272, he was recalled to Naples as head of the *studium generale* there. Two years later, while traveling to attend the Council of Lyon, Aquinas became ill and died in the Cistercian abbey of Fossanova on March 7, 1274.

Thomas Aquinas is best remembered as a moral philosopher and a theologian, with his *Summa Theologica*, composed between 1267 and 1273, standing as his masterwork. However, his writings are also acutely pertinent to modern Western concepts of crime and punishment.

Like Aristotle, Aquinas believed that the existence of a soul is unique to humanity and that it endows human beings with free will, the capacity to make moral choices. These choices cannot be regulated by natural or divine law, but must be governed by human law. Aquinas believed that fully educated men and women had no need of human law, since their education puts them into harmony with the more significant divine and natural laws. Human law, however, must exist to maintain civil order among the masses.

For Aquinas, the necessity of human law provided the basis for the concept of justice. If the object of justice is righteousness, Aquinas reasoned that justice hinges on saying that which is right. Such pronouncements must proceed from three conditions: They must arise from just inclination, proceed from some authority figure, and have a right reason.

Finally, Aquinas helped foster the modern idea of individual responsibility by extinguishing the antiquated belief in family responsibility for individual criminal behavior.

Thomas Aquinas's work provides great insight into the basis of the concepts of crime and punishment we tend to take for granted. He defined principles of free will, individual responsibility, righteousness, justice, and human fallibility. It is the recognition of the latter that both necessitates and justifies the social establishment of a criminal justice system.

Further reading: Gilson, Etienne Henry, *Moral Values and the Moral Life: The Ethical Theory of St. Thomas Aquinas* (Hamden, Conn.: Shoe String Press, 1961).

Pieper, Josef, *Guide to Thomas Aquinas* (New York: Pantheon, 1962).

Aristotle (384–322 B.C.) This Greek philosopher's ideas on criminality differed from those of his mentor Plato in that they were based on the empirical evaluation of facts and individual responsibility.

Aristotle was born in Stagira, northern Greece, to a physician, Nicomachus, well connected in the Macedonian court. In 367, Aristotle went to Athens to join Plato's celebrated Academy, first as a student, then as a teacher. After Plato's death, Aristotle joined the court of Hermias of Atarneus in 347, then went to the court of Philip II of Macedonia in 343, becoming tutor to Philip's son Alexander (the Great).

In 335, Aristotle returned to Athens, where he founded his own school, the Lyceum, or Peripatus. In contrast to the idealism of Plato's Academy, the Lyceum was devoted to the close, empirical study of nature and natural phenomena. Following the death of Alexander the Great in 323, Athens was swept by anti-Macedonian sentiment, and Aristotle hastily retired to Chalcis, where he died in 322.

The basic assumption of Aristotle's ethics is that the aim of humankind is not merely to live, but to lead a good, flourishing life exemplary of the rational nature of humanity. The "good life" is one composed of virtuous actions, which consist essentially in just actions—that is, actions lying between extremes. To be deemed truly generous, for example, one must give neither too little nor too much. Human beings, according to Aristotle, are naturally political beings, and the proper aim of the political associations (states) they form is to promote the good life for each individual. Among the steps the state must take are those to provide for justice, including the prevention and punishment of crime.

Aristotle analyzes criminal behavior in his *Nicomachean Ethics*. To begin with, criminal behavior is not the act of a sick individual, but is an act of volition stimulated by certain desires. For Aristotle, the criminal is responsible for his actions; therefore, the actions of the insane, mentally incompetant, or children, though they may be harmful, cannot be considered criminal. In the *Nicomachean Ethics*, Aristotle defines two social reactions to crime: preventative and repressive. Aristotle recognizes three types of preventative measures: eugenic, the selection of children who should be nurtured versus those who should be abandoned as incorrigible; demographic, social sanctions limiting the number of births, particularly among the poor; and deterrent, comprehensive punishment intended to intimidate the offender while deterring those who witness the punishment. Aristotle's other broad category of social reaction, repressive punishment, includes private revenge, noxal abandonment (turning the offender over to the victim's family), and atimy (perpetual banishment).

Aristotle's systematic, inductive, empirical approach to philosophy, including concepts of crime and punishment, has greatly influenced the development of Western thought and, both directly and indirectly, the formation of the modern criminal justice system.

Further reading: Bambrough, Renford, *Philosphy of Aristotle* (New York: NAL, 1963).

Aschaffenburg, Gustav (1866–1944)

Noted German psychiatrist and editor of the *Monthly for Criminal Psychology and Reform of Criminal Law*, from 1904 to 1935.

Educated in Germany and Vienna, Austria, Gustav Aschaffenburg became a leading psychiatrist during the era of Germany's Weimar republic following World War I and before the Nazi takeover. Although he had a thriving private practice patronized by a who's who of Europe's elite, Aschaffenburg's real passion was criminology. He founded the *Monthly for Criminal Psychology and Reform of Criminal Law* and served as its editor for 31 years. This influential journal gave voice to the era's leading theories of criminal behavior.

Aschaffenburg also used the pages of the *Monthly* to develop his own theory of criminal typology, which has come to be known as "multiple causation." Aschaffenburg distinguished seven classes of criminals: criminals by chance, by affection, by occasion, by consideration, recidivist criminals, habitual criminals, and professional criminals. This multiple-factor approach to criminal behavior incorporated not only elements of modern psychology, but of sociology as well and has come to be considered a classic approach to classification of crimes and criminals.

Aschaffenburg also linked alcohol consumption with crime and developed one of the first empirical studies that attempted to show the relation among alcohol, heredity, and crime rates.

Following the Nazi ascendancy in 1933, Aschaffenburg fled to the United States. The political upheaval in Germany, however, had left him emotionally drained and generally despondent. He was never able to resume his professional career and died, in obscurity, in 1944. His 1903 masterpiece, translated in 1913 as *Crime and Its Repression*, was reprinted in the United States in 1968 and rediscovered by students of criminal behavior and criminal justice.

Further reading: Cressey, Donald R., *Criminology* (Philadelphia: Lipincott, 1974).
Von Hentig, Hans, "Gustav Aschaffenburg," *Journal of Criminal Law, Criminology and Police Science*, 45:2 (July-August 1954).

Aten, Ira (1863–1953)

Texas Ranger who gained a reputation for impartiality in meting out justice.

Born in Illinois, Ira Aten moved to Texas with his family at a young age. When he was 15, Aten saw the legendary gunslinger Sam Bass ride into Round Rock where he was mortally wounded in an epic gun battle. From that moment on, Aten knew he wanted to be a Texas Ranger. In March 1883, Aten joined Company D of the Frontier Battalion, Texas Rangers. An expert marksman, he was assigned the most dangerous territory, the Rio Grande border region, which was teeming with rustlers and smugglers.

Aten performed so well that, in 1887, he was promoted to colonel of the Rangers. Two years later, he was forced to kill two rustlers in a gunfight; perhaps disturbed by having done so, he abruptly retired from the Rangers at the end of 1889. However, he quickly found himself involved in another violent showdown when he was appointed sheriff of Fort Bend County, which was in the throes of the Jaybird-Woodpecker feud between Democrats and Republicans. The feud concerned radical Republican Reconstruction policies, and it frequently turned deadly. Through skillful negotiation and minimal use of force, Aten managed to bring an end to the feud—one of the deadliest in Texas history.

Augustus (Gaius Julius Caesar Octavianus—"Octavian") (63 B.C.–A.D. 14)

The adopted son of Julius Caesar, Augustus (known early in his life as Octavian) was able to end the civil wars that ravaged Rome and return civic order through his institution of a local police force and fire brigade.

Augustus's father was an ardent supporter of Julius Caesar, who adopted Augustus following the father's death and raised him as his own. After Caesar was assassinated in 44 B.C., Augustus joined in the ensuing power struggle between Marc Antony and the Senate. Originally siding with the Senate against Antony, Augustus defeated him at Modena in 43 B.C., but then turned against the Senate and allied himself with Antony and Marcus Aemilius Lepidus to form the Second Triumvirate. After defeating Caesar's assassins in 42 B.C., Augustus and Marc Antony effectively ruled the Republic, Augustus governing the west and Marc Antony the east.

In 36 B.C., Augustus engineered the removal of Lepidus from power, then went on to clash with Marc Antony, who, with the aid of his paramour, Cleopatra of Egypt, had attempted to seize the Republic himself. Augustus defeated Antony at the naval battle of Actium in 31 B.C., and both Antony and Cleopatra committed suicide, leaving Augustus sole ruler of the Republic.

Augustus's immediate concern was the preservation of peace in the Republic, especially in Rome itself, where the civil unrest had taken a terrible toll. The city of Rome was always wary of troops stationed within its boundaries, fearful of a bloody coup or violent repression at the whim of whoever controlled those troops. Augustus, therefore, could not hope to keep a permanent body of troops in the city without invoking the wrath of both the Senate and the citizens. He was able first to establish the Praetorian Guard as his personal bodyguard, and he also deployed these troops as a police force throughout the city. To make them more palatable to the Senate and the people, he avoided assigning them a military commander, he did not issue uniforms to them, and he did not quarter them in barracks. They also were not paid nearly as well as regular soldiers.

After a minor magistrate organized a small fire-fighting force in his district, Augustus quickly moved to disband it out of fear of its growing into a hostile army, but in 7 B.C., he reorganized the city into 14 regions and took on the responsibility of establishing a fire brigade as well. A cohort of a thousand men was assigned to each region of the city and patrolled the streets at night on the lookout for fires. Since they were already making regular patrols, they also served in a police capacity as well.

Both the Praetorian Guard and the fire brigade performed admirably. But Augustus, always wary of alarming the citizens, was forced to hold back from developing a full-scale police force. He finally instituted one near the end of his reign, but even then he deliberately numbered it in accordance with the regular Praetorian units to make it look like nothing more than a continuation of that system. The so-called Urban Cohorts were organized under a more militaristic system than the previous units, however, and were given direct military commanders. They included non-commissioned officers, usually sergeants, in charge of incarceration, records and administrations, and interrogation. This system was well entrenched by the time of Augustus's death in A.D. 14 and lasted for another hundred years.

Further reading: Davies, R. W., "Augustus Caesar: A Police System in the Ancient World," in Philip John Steed, ed., *Pioneers in Policing* (Montclair, N.J.: Patterson Smith, 1977).

Augustus, John (1785–1859)   Called the father of probation, Augustus was a combination bail bondsman, probation officer, and keeper of a halfway house.

An ordinary cobbler in Boston, John Augustus happened to be in a Boston courtroom one day in 1841 when a man was arraigned for being drunk. The man struck Augustus as having a good character and, on that assumption, he bailed the man out and told the judge he would look after the man until his hearing. Three weeks later, the accused reappeared after a period of sobriety and was let off with a nominal fine. So began the career of one of America's greatest philanthropists.

Augustus would spend hours every day in the courts, seeking out people he felt were solid in character but had slipped a little. He would then arrange bail and agree to custody, while then finding the person either a job or a place to stay or just putting him or her up himself. In 14 years, he bailed out almost 2,000 individuals, accepting almost a quarter of a million dollars in bail responsibility. His efforts led Massachusetts to enact the first Probation Act in 1878, providing for a paid probation officer to do what Augustus had done on a voluntary basis for 14 years. By the turn of the century, every state in the union had a probation act.

Austin, Stephen Fuller (1793–1836)   The son of Texas colonial entrepreneur Moses Austin, this early Texas colonist is credited with creating what would become a legendary law enforcement agency, the Texas Rangers.

In 1822, following the death of his father, Moses Austin, Stephen Austin assumed control of a program to establish the first legal settlement of Anglo-Americans in Texas. This slightly built, intellectual young man immediately negotiated a treaty with the government of Mexico, which granted him virtually dictatorial powers in the region. Numerous skirmishes with the Comanche Indians led to Austin's organizing a small group of settlers to protect the territory in 1823. This body, initially financed by Austin, became known as the Texas Rangers in 1826. With the Texas war for independence from Mexico in 1835, the history of this elite law enforcement organization began in earnest as the Rangers protected settlers against marauding Mexicans. Following the Civil War, the duties of the Texas Rangers came increasingly to involve more traditional law enforcement activities.

Austin ran second to Sam Houston when the new republic of Texas voted itself a president, but he served faithfully in Houston's cabinet as secretary of state until his death in 1836.

Further reading: Barker, Eugene C., *The Life of Stephen F. Austin, Founder of Texas, 1793–1836* (1925; reprint ed., New York: Da Capo Press, 1968).

Webb, Walter Prescott, *The Texas Rangers* (Austin: University of Texas Press, 1935).

B

Baca, Elfego (1865–1945) Combining careers as a gunman, lawman, and frontier lawyer, Baca become a folk hero of the "lawless" American Southwest.

Elfego Baca was born of humble parents in Socorro County, New Mexico, and attended school in Topeka, Kansas. He returned to Socorro in 1884, where his brother-in-law, José Baca, was deputy sheriff of Frisco (now Reserve), New Mexico. The brother-in-law complained of the lawlessness of the region and especially of the crimes committed against Mexican Americans. Local cowboys used them—and their livestock—for target practice, and in one case castrated a Mexican in a saloon. Enraged, Elfego Baca "borrowed" his brother-in-law's badge, rode into Frisco, and arrested one of the offenders. The next day, 80 cowboys came to liberate him, and a titanic gunfight ensued—the kind that Western legends are made of. Single-handedly, Baca endured a 36-six-hour siege, during which an estimated 4,000 shots were exchanged. Baca killed four of his attackers and wounded eight others. Finally, he was rescued by two regular lawmen. He gave himself up, stood trial in Albuquerque, and was acquitted, emerging from the incident a folk hero.

After this, he studied law and was admitted to the New Mexico bar in 1894, practicing as a criminal attorney and serving in various local public offices, including mayor, county clerk, school superintendent, and district attorney. He also served a term as sheriff of Socorro County, and was called by many residents the best peace officer the county had ever had.

Further reading: Beckett, V. B., *Baca's Battle* (Houston: Stagecoach Press, 1962).

Crichton, Kyle S., *Law and Order Limited: The Life of Elfego Baca* (Santa Fe: New Mexican Publishing Co., 1928).

Baer, Benjamin F. (1918–91) Served on both the United States Parole Commission and the United States Sentencing Commission.

A native of Peoria, Illinois, Benjamin Baer moved to California in his youth and attended San Diego State College (now University), where he received his undergraduate degree. He continued his studies at the University of Southern California, earning a master's degree, then accepted a position as director of the Los Angeles County Probation Camp in 1942. This was his first position in corrections, and in 1954 he was named associate warden at San Quentin, California's maximum security penitentiary, serving in this capacity for six years. He left the prison in 1961, when President John F. Kennedy appointed him to the newly created Juvenile Delinquency Commission to analyze the nation's growing delinquency rate and make recommendations about curbing it.

Lyndon Baines JOHNSON, Kennedy's successor, next named Baer to the United States Sentencing Commission, a federal agency responsible for studying federal sentencing policy. In 1974, Baer was named to the United States Parole Commission and shortly thereafter became its chairman. The commission is an independent agency within the Justice Department with authority to review federal parole applications. In 1982, Baer was also named to the advisory board of the National Institute of Corrections. He served both the parole commission and the institute until his death in 1991.

Bailey, Francis Lee (1933–) One of the most publicized criminal defense lawyers of the late 20th century; defended the Boston Strangler and Patty Hearst.

A native of Waltham, Massachusetts (born June 10, 1933), F. Lee Bailey entered Harvard University in 1950 but stayed for only two years before withdrawing to enter the navy. Once in the service, Bailey transferred to the Marines, where he joined the legal staff at Cherry Point, North Carolina. Although he had no previous legal experience, Bailey was quite successful there and at the end of his enlistment was able to obtain admittance to Boston University Law School without an undergraduate degree. Bailey graduated first in Boston's class of 1960 with the highest grade point average ever recorded at the law school.

Always fascinated with the investigative applications of technology, Bailey made himself an expert in the use of the polygraph machine and undertook study at the Keeler Polygraph Institute. It was this knowledge of polygraphy that led him to his first major case, that of Dr. Samuel Sheppard, a Cleveland, Ohio, physician who had been sentenced to life imprisonment for the 1954 murder of his wife. In 1961, Bailey appealed the conviction, up through the court system to the U.S. Supreme Court by 1965. The following year, the court handed down a decision overturning Sheppard's conviction on the ground that prejudicial publicity before and during his prosecution had denied him a fair trial. This not only made a public sensation and catapulted the young attorney to the forefront of his profession, it also established a profound legal precedent that has influenced high-profile trials ever since. As a result of the appeal, Sheppard was tried a second time—the jury returning a verdict of not guilty.

Bailey lost two of his most famous cases, the trials of the Boston Strangler and Patty Hearst. When Albert DeSalvo confessed to the 13 murders attributed to the Boston Strangler in the late 1960s, there was little question of his guilt. Bailey conceded that his client had committed the murders but contended that he was insane and should be treated in a hospital and studied as an example of psychosis. The jury disagreed and found him guilty; he was later murdered in prison. In 1977, Bailey represented newspaper-fortune heiress Patricia Hearst at her trial for involvement in a bank robbery conducted by the so-called Symbionese Liberation Army, which had abducted her, but with which she then collaborated in a series of crimes. Bailey argued that Hearst had been brainwashed and was acting out of indoctrination and intimidation. Again, the jury voted to convict.

An attractive, personable, and highly articulate man, Bailey was a frequent talk-show guest during the 1970s and has written popular books about his life in the law, most important *The Defense Never Rests* (1971) and *For the Defense* (1975). In 1994–95, he became a member of the defense team in the trial of popular sports and entertainment figure O. J. Simpson, accused of slaying his ex-wife and her male friend. Significantly, one of the key issues in the trial was the publicity surrounding it—an area of concern that Bailey had pioneered with the Samuel Sheppard case.

Baldwin, Roger Nash (1884–1981) Criminologist who founded the American Civil Liberties Union in 1920.

After receiving both B.A. and M.A. degrees from Harvard, Roger Baldwin accepted a teaching position at Washington University in St. Louis in 1906. Baldwin also served as chief probation officer of the Juvenile Court in that city, where he built a reputation as the nation's foremost expert in juvenile delinquency. His book *Juvenile Courts and Probation*, written with Bernard Flexner in 1912, was the standard text in the field for many years.

Baldwin's real calling, however, came during his subsequent tenure as secretary of the Civic League of St. Louis from 1910 to 1917. Baldwin developed a passionate commitment to civil liberties, and when the United States entered World War I in 1917, he founded the Civil Liberties Bureau in an effort to preserve and defend the civil rights of antiwar protesters, "draft dodgers," and others who chose not to join in the bellicose patriotic hysteria of the period. Baldwin himself was sentenced to a year's imprisonment in 1918 for refusing induction.

The Civil Liberties Bureau became the American Civil Liberties Union (ACLU) in 1920, and Baldwin served as its director for the next 30 years until his retirement in 1950. During this span, Baldwin built the agency into the leading defender of free expression in the free world.

The ACLU continues to play a prominent, if always unofficial, role in the American justice system as the voice of civil liberties as guaranteed by the Consitution and the Bill of Rights. ACLU staff lawyers take on controversial legal cases deemed crucial in determining how the courts will define free expression and civil liberties.

After his retirement in 1950 at age 65, Baldwin spent the remaining 30 years of his life promoting his human rights agenda across the globe.

Further reading: "The Baldwin Century," *The New Republic,* 185 (September 23, 1981), pp. 6–7.

Balthazard, Victor (1872–1951) This French criminologist pioneered ballistics and the examination of hair follicles.

As a child growing up in Paris, Victor Balthazard proved himself a prodigy in mathematics, science, and technology, securing a place in the prestigious École Polytechnique. Surprisingly, in 1893 he suddenly left the academy for a military career, becoming an officer of artillery. Balthazard also took up the study of medicine during this period, particularly the new field of radium and X-ray research. When he left the army in 1904, he turned his attention solely to forensic medicine, distinguished himself immediately, and was appointed chief medical examiner for the city of Paris.

In 1909, Balthazard was confronted with a murder case that offered precious few clues. Balthazard, however, found several strands of hair beneath the victim's fingernails. After examining them, he determined that they were not the victim's, and therefore concluded that they must have been torn from the killer's head during a struggle. Balthazard measured the length and diameter of each strand, examining the roots and medulla under a microscope. From this, he was able to determine that the killer was a woman with light brown hair. When the police apprehended a suspect, Balthazard took hair samples from her and matched them with the crime-scene evidence. This marked the first time systematic hair examination had been used to identify a criminal.

Balthazard also became an adamant proponent of the science of ballistics. Although it was already well known that each weapon made characteristic marks on bullets fired from it, Balthazard argued that firearms made unique marks on cartridges and casings as well. Using microscopic examination, he demonstrated that firing a weapon exerts tremendous pressure on the cartridge, forcing it backward against the breechblock, leaving a microscopic imprint of the breechblock on the cartridge. He also showed that, in the case of semi-automatic and automatic weapons, the extractor and ejector leave similar markings on the cartridge. These discoveries greatly expanded the application and accuracy of ballistic evidence.

Barker, Dame Lilian Charlotte (1874–1955) England's first female assistant prison commissioner; laid the foundation for Britain's modern humanitarian women's prison system.

Born in Islington on February 21, 1874, Lilian Barker was educated in the local elementary school and at Whitelands College, Chelsea. She became a schoolteacher in London, soon demonstrating a particular ability with "problem" and delinquent children. In 1913, she was appointed principal of the London County Council's Women's Institute, a correctional facility. In 1915, she left this position to contribute to England's effort in World War I, first as a teacher of army cooks, then by becoming lady superintendent of Woolwich Arsenal, responsible for some 30,000 women workers. After the war, in 1919, she joined the training department of the Ministry of Labour, and in 1923 became governor of the Borstal Institution for Girls at Aylesbury. Barker revolutionized and revitalized Aylesbury, transforming it from a conventional prison into a model humane reformatory, with an emphasis on education, guidance, and rehabilitation.

In 1935, Barker left Aylesbury to become the first female assistant commissioner of prisons, with responsibility for women's prisons throughout England, Wales, and Scotland. She brought to British female prisons the same kind of reform she had brought to Aylesbury, transforming it into a system of modern facilities.

Barker, (Arizona) "Ma" (Kate) (1871?–1935) Matriarch of the notorious Barker-Karpis gang and FBI Public Enemy Number One; labeled "a veritable beast of prey" by J. Edgar HOOVER in the 1930s.

Ma Barker was born in the Ozarks around 1871 and in her youth openly expressed admiration for the exploits of her fellow Missourians Frank and Jesse JAMES. Ma Barker did not have to recruit a criminal gang; she gave birth to one. She raised her four sons, Herman, Lloyd, Arthur, and Freddie, as gangsters. After her eldest, Herman, was killed in a shootout with police, the Barker gang went underground and planned a series of bank robberies and kidnappings. During this period, Ma Barker harbored such underworld notables as Alvin "Creepy" KARPIS, Al Spencer, and Frank "Jelly" Nash. Her affiliation with Karpis led to the ransom kidnapping of millionaire William Hamm Jr. in 1933 and George Bremer in 1934.

By 1935, the FBI was in hot pursuit of the Barkers, and after a botched attempt to disguise her identity—including surgery to remove her fingerprints—Ma Barker and her youngest son, Freddie, were run to ground by FBI agents at Lake Weir, Florida. On January 16, 1935, they were killed in a gunfight with the agents.

Barnard, Chester (1886–1961) A businessman and management theorist whose work greatly influenced modern police organization.

Born to a working-class family, Chester Barnard put himself through preparatory school in Massachusetts and earned a scholarship to Harvard in 1906. He left the university one year shy of graduation to begin his business career, starting as a clerk with the American Telephone and Telegraph Company. Barnard quickly ascended the corporate ladder at AT&T to become a recognized authority on commercial telephone practices, and in 1922 he was named assistant vice president at Pennsylvania Bell, moving up to president of New Jersey Bell in 1927.

After a decade of experience in top-level management, Barnard began formulating theories of corporate management and organizational structure. In 1938, he published *The Functions of the Executive*, which identified the myriad informal organizational structures that exist within formal structures. Barnard argued that in such organizations as police forces, in which individuals subordinate their own behavior to cooperate with each other for the accomplishment of common goals, such informal structures play key roles. Indeed, Barnard showed that what appeared to be a highly formal organizational structure was really an informal network of the coordinated activities of numerous individuals rather than a structure of officially constituted authority and responsibility. *Functions of the Executive* became highly influential among police department officials and was used extensively in the restructuring of police organizations in order to bring the formal constitution of the departments into closer harmony with the actual, informal structures that prevailed.

In addition to his influential work in management, Barnard is also noted for having greatly expanded the USO (United Service Organizations) during World War II, establishing that body as a unique and enduring morale booster for America's servicemen and women.

Bartels, John R., Jr. (1936–   )   The first director of the United States Drug Enforcement Agency (DEA).

After graduating from Harvard Law School in 1960, John Bartels began working for the federal government in 1964 as assistant U.S. attorney general for the Southern District of New York. In that capacity, he began to work against the organized crime families and in 1969 was named chief of the Justice Department's New Jersey Organized Crime Strike Force. With the considerable resources of the FBI finally committed to stamping out organized crime, Bartels was highly successful in inaugurating the first significant fight against organized crime. President Richard NIXON appointed Bartels to replace John Ingersoll as head of the federal government's anti-narcotics branch in September 1973. Under the Reorganization Plan of 1973, the Bureau of Narcotics and Dangerous Drugs was renamed the Drug Enforcement Agency (DEA), and Bartels was made its first head.

As DEA chief, Bartels vowed to wage an aggressive campaign against domestic and international drug traffic. Although the DEA did enjoy a modicum of success, Bartels's tenure was quickly marked by controversy, both over DEA methods—which often barely skirted constitutionality—and his administration of the agency. Suddenly, in May 1975 Bartels was forced out as chief, ostensibly because the administration of Gerald R. Ford was dissatisfied with the agency's failure to stem the influx of illegal drugs into the country and onto the streets. Within two months after Bartels's ouster, it was revealed that Bartels had obstructed a high-level inquiry into DEA practices.

Bates, Sanford (1884–1972)   The first chief of the Federal Bureau of Prisons and an ardent advocate of rehabilitation.

A Boston native, Sanford Bates graduated from Northeastern University in that city and earned his law degree in 1906, graduating cum laude. He operated until 1929 in private practice, while also serving in the Massachusetts House of Representatives, the state senate, and on the state constitutional convention. In 1918, he reluctantly accepted the position of commissioner of penal institutions for the city of Boston.

At the city level, Bates sought to introduce a prison school for those who had no education and limited self-government for the inmates. Bates saw early on that inmates could use their time in prison as a chance to better themselves in preparation for their return to society. He also recognized that inmates with a voice in determining the conditions of their incarceration were likely to be less bitter about their experience. Although his legislative measure to coordinate the management of the four Boston prisons was defeated because he refused to employ an unqualified political crony, he shocked his political opponents by returning $25,000 of his unused budget in 1919. This impressed Governor Calvin COOLIDGE so much that he nominated Bates as state commissioner of the Corrections Department. Bates accepted and, over the next 10 years, continued to introduce reform into the penal system, including a revised parole system, new prison industries such as printing to create better prison jobs, a prison wage, and university extension courses for inmates.

In 1926, Bates was elected president of the American Prison Association, and in 1929 he accepted the superintendency of the five existing federal prisons. With the creation of the Federal Bureau of Prisons in 1930, Bates was nominated by the attorney general to the position of director, serving in that capacity until 1937.

As director of the federal system, Bates added 15 more institutions, including Alcatraz, all the while continuing to improve the system, adding libraries, social work facilities, and other ways to rehabilitate prisoners in order to provide for their successful reentry into society. Upon his retirement from public service in 1954, he continued to advocate rehabilitative services.

Battle, Samuel J. (1883–1966)   The first African-American policeman in New York City was eventually promoted to parole commissioner before his retirement.

The son of former slaves, Samuel Battle was born in New Bern, North Carolina, and attended the segregated schools there. After moving north to attend a manual-training school in New Haven, Connecticut, Battle went to work as a porter at Grand Central Terminal in New York City. He was working 12-hour days as assistant chief of the red caps when he decided he would study for the civil service exam to become a patrolman. Exhausted by his grueling schedule, Battle fought off sleep in an effort to study. Although he passed the exam in 1910, his appointment was delayed under the pretext of his having a heart condition. In truth, city authorities were wrestling over whether or not to hire a black policeman.

At length, Battle was admitted to the force and was assigned to the West 68th Street Station, where other officers shunned him. They gave him the "silent treatment" and generally ostracized him. Battle persevered, however, and maintained a polite demeanor toward his coworkers. In 1913, he was transferred to the West 135th Street Station in Harlem—at the time a community with a growing African-American population—and was well received there, so much so that by 1919, Battle was encouraged to study for the sergeant's exam. Yet when he applied to the police preparatory school for the exam, he was told that his admission was conditional on the approval of the others in the class.

While he waited for a decision, the "Straw-Hat Riot" of 1919 broke out in Harlem after a white officer shot and killed a black resident. When another white officer was cornered by the mob and was in danger of losing his life, Battle rushed the crowd and saved the officer. He was promptly admitted to sergeant's school.

He passed the exam with flying colors, but was then forced to wait until 1926 for his promotion, at which time he was finally named the first black sergeant on the New York City police force. He continued to advance, making lieutenant in 1935—again the first African American to do so—and parole commissioner in 1941, working primarily with delinquent black youths from Harlem.

In 1943, Battle was called away from this position by Mayor Fiorello LaGuardia to restore order during the Harlem Riots of that year, again precipitated by a police shooting of a black man. Battle's first directive was to order all white people off the streets of Harlem, including Mayor LaGuardia himself, to soothe inflamed emotions. After putting officers on strategic rooftops and ordering mounted units to take to the streets, he personally patrolled the area, using his high-recognition factor and prestige in the community to help restore order.

Battle worked as parole commissioner, specializing in helping young African Americans who ran afoul of the law, until his retirement in 1951. Two years before his death at his home in Harlem on August 7, 1966, Battle was formally hailed in a special Father's Day ceremony as "the father of all Negroes in the Police Department."

Bayle, Edmond (1879–1928) Pioneered the criminological study of fibers and the use of spectrophotometry in criminal investigation.

Edmond Bayle began his scientific career as a researcher at the famed Pasteur Institute of Paris. He left the institute to serve as a chemist for the French state railroads, examining soils, wood, and steel for use in constructing track. On January 1, 1915, he took a position with the Paris police as a criminal chemist and physicist.

As has been the case with so many innovators in criminology, Bayle's landmark discoveries came in difficult cases, where no other leads were forthcoming. In a bizarre 1924 murder investigation, Bayle's laboratory findings figured as the only evidence in the case. Having no other clues to follow, Bayle microscopically examined every grain of dirt and fiber on the victim's clothing and hair, discovering two mysterious red particles. When he exposed the particles to ultraviolet light, they fluoresced vividly; intrigued, Bayle measured the emission with a spectrophotometer, which gauges the intensity of light as it passes through the visible spectrum. Certain paints and dyes display unique characteristics when exposed to ultraviolet light, and such was the case with the two particles, which the spectrophotometer showed to contain rhodamine, a red pigment. When rhodamine was discovered in the suspect's basement, Bayle knew he had his man.

In addition to his work in spectrophotometry, Bayle relentlessly examined all sorts of fibers, touring textile mills to learn methods and techniques of clothing and rope manufacture, noting how some fibers twist right or left or how yarn is doubled. He created in his laboratory a veritable museum of fibers as samples, which allowed him to identify a vast array of evidence recovered from crime scenes. Realizing that cloth fibers are not only valuable as evidence in and of themselves, but also that they are absorbent and frequently hold other clues, Bayle created methods for combining fiber study with spectrophotometry to identify the origin of fibers as well as the nature of stains found on them. His data and working methods profoundly influenced forensic investigation.

Bean, Judge Roy (ca. 1825–1902) The self-styled "Law West of the Pecos" dispensed hard liquor and harder justice from his saloon/courtroom.

Originally from Mason County, Kentucky, Roy Bean left home for New Orleans as a teenager but was forced to return after getting into trouble. By

1847, however, he left home for good, journeying to Mexico, where he led the life of a bandit. After being forced out of Mexico for killing a man, Bean moved to California, first to San Diego then to Los Angeles, to join his brother Josh. Both ran into trouble there: Josh was murdered and Roy hanged—luckily for him, at the end of a defective rope, which didn't kill him but did permanently injure his neck.

For reasons of personal safety, Bean left California and settled in Mexico, where, during the Civil War, he joined a Confederate raiding company that kept more loot for itself than it passed along to the troops of the Confederacy. After the war, he settled in San Antonio, married and worked as honestly as could be expected in the postwar South.

In 1882, Bean opened a saloon in the young town of Vinegaroon, Texas, and got himself appointed justice of the peace, in part, legend has it, simply because he owned a copy of *The 1879 Revised Texas Statutes.* When lawless Vinegaroon calmed down, he moved east to the town of Langtry.

There Bean opened his Jersey Lily Saloon, named in honor of actress Lillie Langtry, and used it to sell

Judge Roy Bean boasted that he was "the law west of the Pecos." (Courtesy of the Western History Collections, University of Oklahoma)

lots of alcohol while dispensing justice. He would always announce last call before beginning court proceedings, but would frequently interrupt them if someone got thirsty and was paying cash. On the outside of his saloon/courtroom were signs proclaiming "JUDGE ROY BEAN NOTARY PUBLIC, LAW WEST OF THE PECOS," under which was another placard bearing the legend: "ICE BEER."

Not only was the manner in which Bean dispensed justice out of the ordinary, but so also was the justice. For example, on one occasion he acquitted a man of murdering a Chinese laborer because, after poring over his law books, he declared that he couldn't find any law saying it was illegal to kill a "Chinaman."

In truth, Bean had no education and didn't know any law, but he was tolerated because he was a tourist attraction on the Southern Pacific Railroad and because he was generally harmless—at least to the tax-paying whites. Indeed, in 1896, while standing for reelection, he was elected with more votes than there were eligible voters, causing the election to be given to his opponent. No matter; Bean continued to serve as if nothing had happened, and people continued to abide by his decisions until the day he died.

Further reading: Sonnichser, C. L., *Roy Bean: Law West of the Pecos* (Albuquerque: University of New Mexico Press, 1943).

Beccaria, Cesare, Marchese di (Cesare Bonesana) **(1738–94)** One of the first writers to oppose capital punishment; wrote the celebrated *Crime and Punishment*, an indictment of the excesses of the criminal justice system and the reform steps needed.

The son of a noble of modest means from Milan, Marchese Cesare Beccaria was born on March 15, 1738. Like many boys of his social station, Beccaria was expected to enter the clergy and was sent to a Jesuit school in Parma at the age of eight. Moody and mercurial himself, he bridled under the rigors of Jesuit life, protesting that it was stifling to "the development of human feelings." He left the Jesuits to study law, and by 1758 received his law degree from the University of Pavia.

Beccaria returned to Milan and joined an organization of young Milanese called "The Academy of Fists," which was dedicated to social change nurtured by the Enlightenment movement sweeping Europe at the time. One of his close associates and a moving force in the academy was Pietro Verri, who encouraged Beccaria to write. The young man's first pamphlet, on monetary reform, was well received. In 1763, Verri suggested he write a similar work on the criminal justice system. In response, Beccaria produced what many call the most important single volume ever written on the subject.

Crime and Punishment was a scathing indictment of the current state of criminal justice in Italy—and, by extension, most of the "civilized" world. His principal assumption was the Benthamite doctrine that government should create the greatest good for the greatest number. The criminal justice system did no such thing, and Beccaria harshly criticized the use of torture in punishment and interrogation, the corruption of state officials, and disproportionately severe penalties for relatively minor offenses. He argued that the penal system should exist solely to maintain law and order, not for the aggrandizement or degradation of individuals. Finally, and perhaps most radically, Beccaria was the first modern writer to speak out against capital punishment.

Beccaria's work was hailed by all thinkers touched by Enlightenment ideas, and it proved influential in the subsequent reform movement of the European criminal justice system. Beccaria was invited to Paris in 1771 to confer with the likes of Helvetius and Diderot. Shunning the spotlight, he soon fled back to Milan and his wife.

Further reading: Phillipson, Coleman, *Three Criminal Law Reformers: Beccaria, Bentham, Romilly* (Montclair, N.J.: Paterson Smith, 1970).

Bennett, James Van Benschotten (1894–1978) Director of the U.S. Federal Prison System from 1937 to 1964; responsible for major penal reforms.

Bennett was born on August 28, 1894, in Silver Creek, New York, and was raised in Providence, Rhode Island, where he attended the Classical High School and Brown University. He received his B.A. in 1918, despite an interruption for service as an aviation cadet in World War I. In 1919, Bennett moved to Washington, D.C., where he worked as an assistant investigator for the U.S. Bureau of Efficiency. By 1923, he was made chief investigator, and, after earning a law degree from George Washington University in 1926, he was assigned to assist a congressional committee investigating the federal penal system.

What Bennett's investigation uncovered was a system of 19 scandal-tainted and inhumane institutions, filled with desperate convicts and undertrained, underpaid guards. It was Bennett's reports to Congress that resulted in the formation of the U.S. Justice Department's Bureau of Prisons, of which Bennett was appointed head in 1937, after serving as its first assistant director.

Bennett earned a reputation as a fair-minded, liberal superintendent who developed and maintained a policy of rehabilitation and who insisted on treating prisoners as individuals deserving of human dignity.

Under his administration, the federal prison system instituted programs of psychiatric counseling and medical care, and he expanded the federal system to provide for short-term correctional institutions and youth reformatories as alternatives to penitentiaries for less hardcore criminals. Bennett instituted the nation's first halfway house program to facilitation reintegration from prison into society, and he created Federal Prison Industries, Inc., to oversee all industrial enterprises and vocational training for federal prisoners.

Bennett played a key role in the creation of the Juvenile Delinquency Act of 1938 and the 1948 law providing psychiatric services for mentally ill criminal offenders. In 1950, he helped pass the Federal Youth Correction Act, and in 1958 he was largely responsible for the enactment of a series of diagnostic sentencing laws. After his retirement as director of federal prisons in 1964, Bennett served as vice chairman of the American Bar Association's Select Committee on Criminal Law and served as official delegate to the United Nations Conference on Crime and Corrections in 1970.

Bennett, William John (1943–) The United States' first "drug czar"; has had a controversial political career that includes presidential aspirations.

William Bennett was born July 31, 1943, and was raised in what was then the strict Catholic environment of the Flatbush section of Brooklyn, New York, attending Holy Cross Boys' School. After moving to Washington, D.C., as a teenager, Bennett attended Williams College in Massachusetts, graduating in 1965, then attended graduate school at the University of Texas, Austin, completing his Ph.D. in 1970. A year later, he received his J.D. from Harvard University Law School.

Bennett then entered the education field and assumed a variety of teaching and administrative positions before becoming executive director of the National Humanities Center in North Carolina. As director, he adopted a distinctly conservative stance, arguing, among other things, that the "affirmitive action" hiring of minorities was reverse discrimination. In Bennett, President Ronald Reagan saw a man capable of taking the liberally inclined National Endowment of the Humanities in a new, conservative direction, and Reagan nominated Bennett for the post of chairman in 1981.

Bennett led the NEH for three years before President Reagan nominated him to replace the outgoing secretary of education in January 1985. As education secretary, Bennett enthusiastically supported the administration's conservative policies, but resigned after two years.

When George Bush succeeded Ronald Reagan in 1988, he instituted the Office of National Drug Control Policy, its head popularly dubbed the "drug czar." Bennett sought the position, and the new president obliged, naming him as one of his administration's first appointments.

The outspoken Bennett managed to offend many within the anti-drug community, including law enforcement, drug education, and treatment personnel. One of his much-touted top priorities was the drug clean-up of Washington itself. When D.C. mayor Marion Barry was convicted of cocaine use, Bennett was left supremely embarrassed. After less than 18 months as "drug czar," Bennett stepped down.

Bennett's quick exit from ONDCP did not discourage President Bush from tapping him to head the Republican Party in November 1990. Bennett accepted the chairmanship of the party, only to quit within a month. He next became a founding member and director of Empower America, set up as a GOP rival to the Democratic Leadership Council. When Empower America became a forum for the presidential candidacies of Jack Kemp and Bennett himself, many of the GOP faithful abandoned it.

Bentham, Jeremy (1748–1832)   The founder of the philosophy of utilitarianism argued that law must be used for the "greatest good of the greatest number" of people, and, with this precept, became one of the greatest reformers of English Common Law.

A member of England's burgeoning industrial upper class, Jeremy Bentham was a child prodigy, educated at Westminster and later at Oxford, where he earned a law degree and passed the bar shortly thereafter. However, he soon found the law morally reprehensible, as well as intellectually stifling. He withdrew from practice and set himself upon his life's work of social and legal reform.

Bentham's social thinking was based chiefly on the concept of hedonism. He argued that human beings are largely motivated by an attraction to pleasure and happiness on the one hand and a desire to avoid pain and misery on the other. Indeed, pleasure and happiness he accounted the "sovereign masters" governing man's conduct, and the law, he argued, should be designed to meet the end of attaining these. Crime and punishment, for Bentham, were two sides to a single equation: Individuals who impinged on another's right to happiness and pleasure should be subjected to a pain greater than the happiness they received through the commission of the crime. This theory of "useful punishment" became a founding principle in the philosophy of utilitarianism.

Bentham said that social institutions—foremost among them, the legal system—should be judged on their utility to society, that is, their ability to provide pleasure and happiness to the greatest number of people. Assuming that human beings act simply out of self-serving motives and that the ego responds only to the promise of pleasure and the threat of pain, it is likely that one's ego might demand the injury of another in order to attain some pleasurable end. To check such urges, laws must prescribe greater pain than the pleasure derived from the injury of another.

Bentham spent almost his entire life writing about legal reform, and his philosophy of utilitarianism is evident in many of today's legal codes. The abolition of torture is consonant with utilitarian theory because the pain of torture is far greater than any pleasure gained through crime and, furthermore, is random to the pleasure and not related to it. For Bentham, punishment was to fit the crime—a basic concept we take for granted today.

By the time of Bentham's death in 1832, many considered the age of reform and the age of Jeremy Bentham to be one and the same.

Further reading: Seagle, William, *Men of Law: From Hammurabi to Holmes* (New York: Macmillan, 1947).

Berger, Meyer ("Mike") (1898–1959)   Pulitzer Prize–winning crime reporter for the *New York Times* from 1928 until the 1950s; covered Al Capone's trial in Chicago and a host of New York's sensational crimes during the first half of the 20th century.

A well-respected journalist with a reputation for scrupulous fairness, Mike Berger always handled his often sensational subjects with sensitivity and consideration. Berger was nominated for a Pulitzer Prize in 1932 for his coverage of the Chicago trial of Al Capone on charges of income tax evasion. His 1950 coverage of a bizarre mass killing in Camden, New Jersey, won the journalist the prize in 1950. In typical fashion, Berger, without fanfare, donated the prize money he received to the aging mother of the Camden killer.

Further reading: Berger, Meyer, *The Story of the New York Times, 1851–1951* (New York: Simon and Schuster, 1951).

Beria, Lavrenti Pavlovich (1899–1953)   The head of the KGB—the Soviet secret police—under Josef STALIN; instrumental in helping Stalin to carry out his planned persecution of political enemies.

Lavrenti Beria was born on March 29, 1899, to a poor peasant family in Georgia, the same region in which Stalin was born. After attending local school and then technical school, Beria joined the Communist Party in 1917 and immediately took part in radical activity in Georgia and Azerbaijan. In 1921, he began studying intelligence and counterintelligence, a field he would work in on behalf of the Communist Party for the rest of his life.

In 1931, Beria was appointed to the political leadership of the Transcaucasian republics and was instrumental in their integration into the burgeoning Soviet Union. As part of his leadership program in the Transcaucasus, Beria conducted ruthless purges similar to those Stalin was ordering in Russia at the same time. With the end of the purges and show trials in Moscow, which Stalin had engineered to justify much of the mass murder he was committing, the dictator now sought a single scapegoat. The logical choice was N. I. Ezhov, the head of the NKVD, a secret police force descended from the original and greatly dreaded Cheka and the OGPU (United State Political Administration) and the antecedent of the KGB.

Stalin, impressed by the vigor with which Beria carried out his own purges, called him to Moscow and named him head of the NKVD. Beria promptly had Ezhov executed. It was under Beria that the NKVD, and later the KGB, infiltrated every aspect of Soviet society in a paranoiac extension of Stalin's personality.

Beria turned the security police into his personal fiefdom simply because Stalin allowed him to. And the true measure of his power came with the approach of World War II, when the NKVD was used as a military arm, and Beria was elevated to the rank of general commissar of state security in January 1941. With Stalin and three other men, Beria was named to the State Defense Committee and was given responsibility for domestic policy and took charge of munitions and research on atomic weapons. The secret police had now been elevated to the highest level of government and were, in fact, running the country while Stalin administered the war effort. Beria's power continued to grow. But he was soon to fall out of Stalin's favor.

At the end of the war, Stalin again purged hundreds of thousands of potential political opponents he conveniently labeled Nazi collaborators. Accordingly, Beria unleashed his security force, and when the bloodletting was concluded, true to form, Stalin sought a scapegoat. He focused on Beria, but before the KGB chief could be brought down, Stalin himself died in March 1953.

Following the dictator's death, Beria attempted to establish his own personal dictatorship. However, he was arrested late in 1953, and in a single day, December 23, 1954, was tried for high treason, found guilty of the same, and executed.

Further reading: Knight, Amy W., *The KGB: Police and Politics in the Soviet Union* (Boston: Allen and Unwin, 1988).

Bernard VII, count of Armagnac (d. 1418)

Serving for a short time as constable of France, Bernard of Armagnac was given de facto military control of Paris during the Burgundian-Orléans civil war.

As count of Armagnac, Bernard VII ruled over an influential region in the south of France in the early 1400s. When his daughter married Charles I, duke of Orléans, he became embroiled in one of France's most brutal and bitter civil wars. The houses of Orléans and Burgundy were both vying for control of the throne held by the mentally incompetent Charles VI. Bernard became an immediate enemy of the duke of Orléans, and the struggle soon developed into a personal quarrel between the two. Following the humiliating defeat dealt to France by the British at the battle of Agincourt in 1415, Bernard was named constable of France and given charge of the defense of Paris and the maintenance of civil peace in the battle's wake.

As constable, Bernard reformed the administration of justice in Paris, greatly rationalizing it. At the same time, however, he most often used his reforms to deal more swiftly and severely with Burgundian transgressors and soon developed a reputation for brutality. In the end, Bernard's reign as constable became a veritable byword for tyranny, turning many Parisians against the Orléanists and into the camp of the Burgundians. The Paris mob took to the streets in June 1418 and began a systematic massacre of the Armagnacs; an estimated 800 were purged, including Bernard, whose severed head was paraded through the streets.

Bertillon, Alphonse (1853–1914)

Called the "Father of Scientific Detection," Bertillon developed *bertillonage*, or the "Bertillon System" of applied anthropometry (the study and technique of human body measurement for use in anthropological identification) to aid in the positive identification of criminals in the days before the development of dactylscopy (fingerprint identification).

Alphonse Bertillon was born to a middle-class French family in 1853. His father was a physician by profession, but by avocation was a dabbler in statistics and anthropology. In 1878, shortly after Alphonse Bertillon took a job as a records clerk in the Paris Prefecture of Police, his father's hobbies profoundly influenced the young man's attempt to revise and rationalize the police department's chaotic recordkeeping and prisoner identification methods. Bertillon began to develop a systematic descriptive method of identifying individual prisoners in order to tag and track repeat offenders. The method, which he evolved after seven years of work, involved the application of anthropometry—the study and technique of human body measurement for use in anthropological identification.

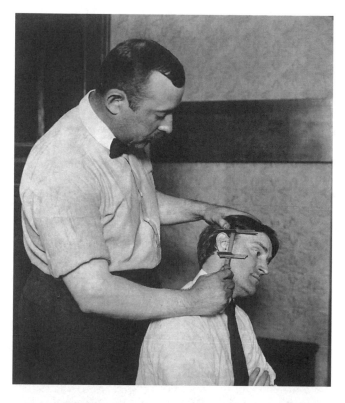
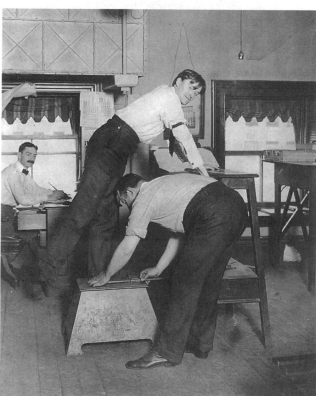

Alphonse Bertillon's "system" of criminal identification, based on measuring various parts of the body, was eventually superseded by fingerprinting, but it proved invaluable in developing and popularizing the use of scientific methods in criminal investigations. (Courtesy of the Library of Congress)

Bertillon theorized that careful, objective measurements of certain key aspects of the human body would provide positive, unalterable proof of an individual's identity. His method, which he published in 1885 as *Identification Anthropométrique* (Anthropometric Identification), depended on obtaining precise measurements of the length and width of the head; the length of the left, middle, and little finger; the length of the left foot; the length of the left forearm; the length of the right ear; the height of the subject; measurement of the outstretched arms; and measurement of the trunk (that is, with the subject seated, the distance from the bench to the top of the head). In addition to these basic measurements, Bertillon noted any distinguishing marks (scars, eye color, and so on), the shape of the nose, and, in precise detail, the shape of the ear, which included identifying no fewer than 11 unique formations: lower rim, upper rim, front rim, tragus, lobe, antitragus, cavity of the shell, rim of the shell, furrow of the rim, navicular cavity, and the starting point of the rim.

Bertillon's system gained rapid and widespread acceptance. In conjunction with *bertillonage*, Bertillon developed techniques of photographing prisoners that are still used today. Each subject was photographed full face and in profile, with his prisoner's register number conspicuously fastened to his coat. These "mug shots" he called *portraits parlés*—speaking portraits.

On February 1, 1888, in recognition of his system, the Paris police appointed Bertillon chief of the Service of Judicial Identity. He went on not only to perfect *bertillonage*, but also to develop photographic methods of documenting crime scenes and the objects involved in crimes. He also became an expert in the use of photography to certify the authenticity of documents and to identify forgeries. In 1889, he published a method of contact photography to distinguish even very careful erasures on questioned documents. In the days before ultraviolet and infrared techniques, Bertillon took conventional photographic methods as far as possible in the study of documents. His pupil and disciple R. A. Reiss carried these techniques even further.

The only blot on Alphonse Bertillon's distinguished career was his association with the infamous Dreyfus case, in which the French army captain Alfred Dreyfus was wrongfully convicted of treason and sentenced to life imprisonment on Devil's Island. The prosecution bolstered its case, which was based in large measure on a note Dreyfus allegedly wrote to a German agent, by Bertillon's scientific testimony that the treasonous document was authentic and in Dreyfus's hand. In fact, it was later demonstrated that the document was a forgery trumped up by a cabal of army officers.

Bertillon's anthropometric system rested on the assumption that the physical characteristics measured were, taken together, unique to each individual. However, in 1904, officials at the federal prison at Leavenworth, Kansas, discovered two convicts who had precisely the same measurements. This widely published discovery undermined the Bertillon system and made it clear that an even more accurate identification method was required. Increasingly, police scientists turned to dactylscopy—fingerprint identification—which gradually displaced *bertillonage*. Indeed, Bertillon himself was one of the first police scientists to embrace fingerprinting, although he maintained that it should be used merely to supplement his own system.

Whatever its shortcomings, the work of Alphonse Bertillon was invaluable in developing and popularizing scientific methods of criminal identification and crime investigation.

Further reading: Bailey, William G., ed., "Bertillon System," in *The Encyclopedia of Police Science* (New York: Garland, 1989).

Johnson, David Ralph, *American Law Enforcement: A History* (New York, 1984).

Rhodes, Henry T. F., *Alphonse Bertillon: Father of Scientific Detection* (New York: Abelard-Schuman, 1956).

Bethea, Rainey (1914–36)   The last man publicly executed in the United States.

History takes no note of the background of Rainey Bethea. He is remembered only as a young African-American man who was convicted of killing a 70-year-old white woman in a predominantly white Kentucky county. Kentucky law had been changed in 1920 to establish the electric chair as the primary means of execution, but the state maintained hanging in cases of "criminal assault," an offense subject to highly ambiguous definition.

Bethea had made a prison-cell confession, in the absence of witnesses and presumably under torture. Although he repeatedly recanted the confession, Bethea was found guilty. In the most shameful tradition of Southern white justice against blacks since Reconstruction, the county sheriff demanded that Bethea be hanged in an open field so thousands could watch. Indeed, it was estimated that at least 20,000 people gathered in Owensboro, Kentucky, the night before the execution. The entire black population of the town fled for fear of reprisal violence. During the drunken revelry that preceded the execution, there were many calls for a mass lynching.

At dawn, Bethea appeared, and the crowd alternately jeered him and cheered the hangman as he tested the scaffold. When the trap was sprung and Bethea's body jerked downward, the crowd rushed the scaffold and began looting the body, taking pieces of clothing and, in some instances, chunks of flesh. Because of the mob, it took the presiding physicians some time to reach Bethea, and when they did, they announced that he was not yet dead. At this announcement, the spectators pulled back in order to watch Bethea dangle for another 15 minutes before he died. Then they rushed him again, searching for the grand prize: the black death hood.

Biaggi, Mario (1917–) A highly decorated New York City cop who became a U.S. representative but was ultimately caught in a web of rumor, scandal, and criminal conviction.

Born in a tenement in the Italian section of Manhattan's Harlem on October 26, 1917, Mario Biaggi was the son of immigrants from Lombardy. Raised in poverty, he shined shoes and delivered laundry to supplement his family's meager earnings. After graduating from high school in 1934, Biaggi worked in a braid factory, then, in 1936, became a letter carrier and was active in the National Letter Carriers Association. He joined the New York City Police Department in 1942, beginning a 23-year career on the force, which brought him 21 citations for bravery and meritorious service, including the Police Medal of Honor for Valor, the department's highest distinction (awarded in 1960). The first citation came only 18 months into the job, when he shot and killed a suspect who tried to stab him with an icepick while Biaggi was transporting him to the station house.

Biaggi quickly rose through the ranks, but as early as 1955, his image as a hero was clouded by rumors and suspicion when he was found absent without leave during a surprise inspection. In 1959, while off-duty and in civilian clothes, Biaggi was involved in the fatal shooting of a man whom Biaggi said forced him to drive to a remote spot with the intention of killing him. Biaggi claimed that he was able to draw his own revolver and kill the would-be assassin. Some police officials remained unsatisfied with Biaggi's account, but, in the end, it was for this incident that the department awarded Biaggi its highest honor.

In 1960, at the urging of the dean of the New York Law School, Biaggi took a leave of absence from the force to earn a law degree on scholarship. He graduated in 1963 and retired from the police department two years later with a disability pension for a leg injury received in the line of duty in 1946. Although he twice failed the New York bar exam, he passed in 1966, set up a successful practice, and in 1968 easily won a seat in Congress, representing the eastern Bronx and most of Yonkers, New York. Voters—particularly the Italian and Jewish ethnic constituency living in "changing" neighborhoods—saw Biaggi as a tough

but fair-minded cop-turned-politician who represented them and their needs. Nevertheless, Biaggi was dogged by scandal and innuendo. In 1973, Biaggi campaigned for the office of New York mayor, but aborted his run after the *New York Times* reported that he had invoked the Fifth Amendment when questioned by federal investigators in 1971 concerning immigration bills he sponsored on behalf of foreign individuals. The incident that finally brought Biaggi down was the so-called Wedtech scandal of 1988, in which Biaggi and five codefendants were convicted of turning a Bronx-based U.S. Defense Department contractor, Wedtech, into a racketeering enterprise that bribed politicians to promote the company within the government. After two convictions, Biaggi resigned from Congress and dropped out of the race for an eleventh term. Remarkably, he ran again in 1992, but was overwhelmingly defeated.

Birkett, William Norman (1883–1962) One of England's most successful attorneys, both for the defense and the prosecution; established himself as a master of judicial procedure and precedent, eventually becoming a distinguished judge.

Birkett originally intended to follow his father into the Anglican ministry, but, after earning degrees in history and theology from Emmanuel College, Cambridge, in 1909, Birkett turned to the law instead. He was admitted to the bar in 1913 and rapidly developed a large and profitable practice. By 1920, his London practice included partnership with Sir Marshall Hall, one of London's preeminent private lawyers, and by 1924 Birkett was wearing the silk gown of a royal barrister.

After a brief term as a member of the House of Commons in the later 1920s, Birkett returned to the practice of law on a full-time basis and was involved in the most significant cases of the period between the two world wars. With the outbreak of World War II, he temporarily abandoned his practice for war-related work, but in November 1941 accepted a position on the King's Bench.

If anything, Birkett had an even greater impact on British jurisprudence as a judge than he had as a lawyer. Rarely does so impassioned an advocate make a good adjudicator, but Birkett's innate brilliance of judgment and mastery of procedure made him more than equal to the demands of the bench. After serving as an alternate justice in the Nuremberg War Crimes trials, Birkett was named privy counsellor and later appointed to the Court of Appeal. He retired in 1956.

Blackstone, Sir William (1723–80) His *Commentaries on the Laws of England* was the first comprehensive treatment of English common and constitutional law.

William Blackstone was born on July 10, 1723. He enrolled in Oxford University, then read law at London's Middle Temple and commenced his practice in 1746. Although he had been an excellent student, Blackstone was a poor speaker and, therefore, enjoyed little success as a trial advocate. After struggling through an undistinguished career for seven years, he returned to Oxford to teach, introducing, in 1753, courses in English law. It was a revolutionary step; the common law had not been the province of the university, but was taught only in apprentice fashion at the Inns of Court.

Blackstone's courses were very well received, and when the university was given an endowment for the study of common law, he was appointed the university's first Vinerian professor. In 1761, despite his deficiencies as a speaker, Blackstone entered politics as a member of Parliament.

It is not for his subsequent political career that he is remembered, but for the fruits of his life in academia. *Blackstone's Commentaries,* a collection of his Oxford lectures, was published in 1765–69. This comprehensive examination of the dauntingly complex system of English common and constitutional law remains remarkable for its eloquence of style and for the manner in which the lectures distilled a vastly complex subject into a logical, lucid presentation. The *Commentaries* were the basis for most legal education in England and in the United States late into the 19th century. Despite criticism from certain social thinkers, most notably Jeremy BENTHAM, who argued that Blackstone would brook no criticism of English law and took no account of the evolving social systems that underlay it, the *Commentaries* was also the basis for much legal thought in both countries and elsewhere.

In recognition of his accomplishments, Blackstone was offered the post of solicitor general in 1770, but he declined this lofty position for a humbler judgeship of the Court of Common Pleas. He served in that capacity until his death.

Blankenburg, Rudolph (1843–1918)

Blankenburg, Rudolph (1843–1918) Reform mayor of Philadelphia, Pennsylvania, who was able to eliminate much of the graft that traditionally plagued the city, especially in the police department.

Born in Germany, Rudolph Blankenburg was educated at home by his father, a German Reformed minister. After going away to school in Lippstadt, Blankenburg decided against following his father into the clergy and journeyed to the United States in 1865. He settled in Philadelphia, where he became a traveling salesman, using his talent for languages (he was fluent in five) to become a European buyer for several companies. In 1875 he founded his own company.

After his semi-retirement from business in 1909, Blankenburg became moderately involved in Philadelphia politics, serving on several municipal advisory councils, as well as the Businessmen's Good Government League. Although a Republican in national politics, Blankenburg opposed the local party because it was rife with graft and corruption. With support from many Democrats in 1912, he was elected mayor on a reform ticket, narrowly defeating the Democratic incumbent.

The first order of Blankenburg's fledgling administration was to clean up the police department, which, as in most politically corrupt turn-of-the-century American cities, was the principal source of the corruption. He named George Porter, a former military man, director of public safety. Porter in turn ousted the superintendent of police and replaced him with two other U.S. Army alumni, who set about cleaning house, dismissing personnel involved in graft schemes. The new administration also instituted police retraining programs, stressing physical exercise through a military-style regimen, issuing a new policy manual, and instituting standard proficiency exams. Perhaps the greatest innovation of this period was a three-squad rotation within a 48-hour shift instead of the two-squad rotation. This created manageable and efficient eight-hour shifts instead of the exhausting and inefficient 12-hour tours of duty.

With his new streamlined police department, Blankenburg went after vice in the city, shutting down hundreds of gaming houses and brothels. His administration all but rid Philadelphia of street-walking prostitutes and kept a tight hold on the city's liquor distributors. Despite the effectiveness of Blankenburg's administration—he claimed that he had saved the city over $5 million by cutting corruption—the Democrats regained the mayor's office in 1916, and Blankenburg retired from city politics.

Bliss, George Miles (fl. 1860s–1880s)

Bliss, George Miles (fl. 1860s–1880s) One of the most notorious bank robbers of the post–Civil War era; perfected the art of large-scale robbery in part by compromising the police.

The Civil War bred thousands of desperate men, hardened to a life of combat and willing and able to do whatever they deemed necessary to survive. One of them was George Bliss, who perfected the fine art of bank robbery. Bliss developed a device he called the Little Joker, a tiny lock pick that could be used to open almost any lock. Bliss and his gang, which became known as the Bliss Bank Gang, were so successful that the New York banking industry brought tremendous pressure to bear on local authorities to apprehend the malefactors. In response, Bliss brazenly walked into William "Boss" Tweed's office and offered a deal. If the police would turn a blind eye to his gang's activities—and even cooperate in some robberies—Bliss would cut in police and other public officials for a percentage of each robbery—generally 10%. In addition, Bliss proposed setting up a few "dummies"—phony heists—which the police could "solve," therefore making them look good. Finally, Bliss arranged to place one of his own operatives, Jim Irving, in the post of chief of detectives.

Tweed and Tammany Hall found the arrangement agreeable, and Bliss was given free rein to rob at will—most spectacularly in 1878 at the Ocean Bank, from which his gang took $2.75 million in a heist that netted the police more than $132,000 in bribes.

The Tweed Ring was so entrenched that even Tweed's arrest and imprisonment in 1873 failed to bring it down, and Bliss's career continued unabated until Thomas BYRNES was named chief of detectives of the New York Police Department in 1880. From this point, the reign of graft began to approach an end.

Boggs, John C. (1825–1909) Sheriff of Placer County, California, during its lawless boom days, Boggs was known as the "outlaws' nemesis."

Boggs was born in Greencastle, Pennsylvania, on October 18, 1825, and went to work as the manager of an ironworks when he was 20. Like many other young easterners, Boggs was lured to California in 1849 by the promise of gold. For the next three years, he worked mines in Placer, Nevada, and Yuba counties, enjoying periods of prosperity and enduring periods of poverty. In 1853, Boggs became the first watchman of Auburn, a mining camp that had been established as Dry Diggings. Like other mining settlements in the region and at that time, Auburn was racked by violent crime.

In 1856, Boggs was instrumental in the capture of the notorious highwayman Tom Bell and members of his gang. In 1859, Boggs collared another desperado, Rattlesnake Dick, followed by a series of others. Boggs ran unsuccessfully for the office of sheriff of Placer County in 1860, 1862, and 1873. Despite these defeats, he continued to fight crime as a member of citizens' committees and on his own. In the fall of 1877, Sheriff C. C. Crosby appointed Boggs undersheriff, and in 1879, Boggs was finally elected to the office of sheriff, the goal that had long eluded him.

As sheriff, Boggs was responsible for apprehending the county's first train robbers, a gang led by a miner named Ed Steinegal and gambler George H. Shinn, with accomplices John Mason, Reuben Rogers, and Henry Frazier. After Steinegal subsequently escaped

and a sympathetic jury refused to convict Rogers and Frazier, Boggs declined to run for reelection and retired from law enforcement in March 1880.

Bonaparte, Charles Joseph (1851–1921) As U.S. attorney general, Bonaparte is credited with the creation of the fledgling Federal Bureau of Investigation (FBI) in 1908.

Charles Bonaparte's father was the son of Jerome Bonaparte, Napoleon's brother. Charles's grandmother, a Massachusetts heiress, had married the emperor's younger brother in 1803, but Napoleon denounced the union, and Jerome was shipped back to France, never to see his young son or grandchildren.

Charles grew up in Massachusetts, graduating from Harvard College in 1871 and from the Harvard Law School in 1874. Entering into private practice in Baltimore, he distinguished himself as a champion of civil service reform, then joined President Theodore Roosevelt's cabinet in 1905 as secretary of the navy. The following year, he became attorney general, eagerly embarking on antitrust litigation.

In 1907, Bonaparte called for the creation of a federal bureau of investigation separate from the Treasury Department (which controlled the Secret Service, at the time the nation's only federal police agency) and under the authority of the attorney general's office. Congress rejected this proposal, deeming a federal policing agency a threat to democracy. Various members of Congress even made reference to the infamous secret police maintained by the attorney general's grand uncle, the emperor.

Despite congressional resistance, Bonaparte persisted; while Congress was adjourned in 1908, he discreetly established a force of secret police, which became the basis of the Federal Bureau of Investigation—though it was not so named until 1935.

When Congress reconvened, the debate was heated, but the legislative body did not move to abolish the new agency, which would evolve into one of the world's most prestigious investigative agencies.

Bonaparte left office in 1909 and returned to private practice until his death in 1921.

Further reading: Bishop, J. B., *Charles Joseph Bonaparte: His Life and Public Services* (New York: Harper and Co., 1922).

Lowenthal, Max, *The Federal Bureau of Investigation* (New York: Chelsea House, 1976).

Bonger, Willem Adriaan (1876–1940) This Dutch criminologist developed a Marxist interpretation of crime that identified economic conditions as the leading cause of criminal behavior.

The youngest of 10 children (his older sister was married to Theo van Gogh, brother of the great Dutch painter), Adriaan Bonger studied at the University of Amsterdam, where he subsequently became a professor. An active socialist, Bonger was concerned with the environmental conditions surrounding crime. Like his philosophical idol, Karl Marx, Bonger parted company with the then-prevailing view of the causes of crime, which stressed racial influences, and instead concluded that the social milieu, primarily its economic conditions, was the determining factor in producing crime. Although Bonger was a resolute believer in democracy and free enterprise, he nevertheless saw the socioeconomic stratification wrought by capitalism as directly linked to crime.

In 1932 Bonger published *An Introduction to Criminology* (translated from Dutch into English in 1936), which was, at the time, the most complete survey of the new science and became a standard handbook for generations of criminology students.

Bonger was also one of the first criminologists to study female crime, but perhaps his greatest contribution to the field was his commitment to the science of criminology itself. Bonger's pioneering work is credited with helping prove that sociology and criminology could be treated as genuine sciences.

In 1939 Bonger's name was regularly mentioned in Nazi propaganda as an archenemy of National Socialism. When, the following year, Hitler invaded Holland, Bonger wrote his son: "I cannot bow to this Scum which will now overmaster us." Bonger took his own life.

Further reading: van Bemmelen, J. M., "Willem Adriaan Bonger," *The Journal of Criminal Law, Criminology and Police Science*, 46:3 (September–October 1955).

Bonneville, Arnould de Marsangy (1802–94)

This mid-19th-century French penal reformer established the École Penitentiaire and is considered the European father of the concept of parole.

Trained as a jurist, Arnould de Marsangy Bonneville held numerous positions in the French judicial system, including that of imperial counselor. His work in criminology was concentrated on the reform of the prison as an institution, and he published several notable works on prison reform, the best known of which are his *Essay on the Institutions Complementary to the Penitentiary System* (1847) and a two-volume work titled *Of the Amelioration of the Criminal Law* (1855 and 1864). In these and other writings, Bonneville introduced the progressive ideas of parole, criminal reparation, pardoning power, and rehabilitation. Considered the European father of the parole concept, he was also the founder of the École Penitentiaire, a pioneering institution for the study of penology and a landmark in the worldwide penal reform movement.

Further reading: Normandeau, André, "Arnould Bonneville de Marsangy," *Journal of Criminal Law, Criminology and Police Science*, 60:1 (March 1969).

Bradley, Tom (1917–)

Five-term mayor of Los Angeles and former Los Angeles police officer who was the first African-American lieutenant in LAPD history; as mayor, he clashed with controversial police chief Daryl GATES.

Born in Calvert, Texas, Tom Bradley moved with his family to Los Angeles when he was six years old. He excelled in school and proved to be an excellent athlete, winning an athletic scholarship to the University of California, Los Angeles, and gaining a reputation as a world-class quarter-miler on the track team. Bradley left UCLA after his junior year to join the Los Angeles Police Department, where he quickly distinguished himself with a record of meritorious service. Over the course of 15 years, he climbed from beat cop to lieutenant, the first African-American lieutenant on the force.

While working the streets, Bradley also began attending law school, earning his law degree from Southwest College in 1956. Bradley believed that racist sentiment in the LAPD would prevent his rise above lieutenant, and he retired from the force in 1961 after 20 years of service to start a private law practice. Community leaders soon urged him to run for city council, and, standing for election in a predominantly white district, he easily won in 1963, beginning a political career that would span 30 years.

After an unsuccessful bid for mayor in 1969, he was elected by a 56% majority in 1973, then reelected in 1977, 1981, 1985, and 1989. However, Bradley's ability to build consensus within the increasingly diverse and economically stratified city began to diminish by his fifth term, especially as Los Angeles, with the rest of California, fell on hard economic times.

On March 3, 1991, four white LAPD officers were videotaped by an unseen witness savagely beating Rodney King, a black motorist whom they had arrested. The beating prompted Bradley to call on Chief Daryl Gates to resign—a demand Gates markedly and deliberately ignored. The subsequent trial and acquittal of the four officers on charges of brutality sparked four days of rioting, to which Gates's police force responded inadequately. (Gates, later protesting that he had maintained a continual "command presence" during the riots, was criticized for, among other things, attending a political fundraising cocktail party during the period.) Under intense pressure, Gates at last agreed to step down. But Bradley was likewise widely condemned for having failed to exercise more leadership over the police department, especially given his awareness of racial problems within the organization. He retired in 1992, after his fifth term in office.

Brandeis, Louis Dembitz (1856–1941) One of the greatest justices of the U.S. Supreme Court; championed the Fourth Amendment while serving as a harsh watchdog on government legal excess.

A native of Louisville, Kentucky, Louis Brandeis was born November 13, 1856, and grew up in a prosperous environment. When his father foresaw the economic depression of 1873, the family moved to Europe for three years, where Brandeis attended college. Returning to the United States in 1875, he enrolled at Harvard Law School, where he excelled, and he continued on to postgraduate work.

After spending a year in St. Louis in private practice, Brandeis returned to Boston and a partnership with a law school colleague. He quickly became one of the most successful lawyers in the city by specializing in litigation relating to the demands of the ongoing industrial revolution. After joining the progressive reformers, he sought to keep large industry from taking advantage of the consumer. His first target was the Boston traction franchises, then insurance companies; next, he devised a plan for savings bank life insurance. While financially successful, Brandeis contributed much of his work pro bono.

Having gained a reputation in the practice of industrial law, Brandeis accepted a case involving an Oregon statute limiting women to 10-hour workdays. In *Muller* v. *Oregon*, Brandeis introduced what was later called the Brandeis Brief, or what many at the time called sociological jurisprudence. A brief was generally reserved for citing legal precedent as a basis for one's case. Brandeis instead included only two pages of precedent and then introduced more than a hundred pages of relevant sociological information ranging from studies to opinions of experts to effects of legislation in other countries. Brandeis argued that the courts should use the same information when rendering a decision that the legislature uses when passing legislation.

The Brandeis Brief is now an accepted part of the American judicial system.

In 1912, President Woodrow WILSON drafted Brandeis—now known as "the people's attorney"—to help formulate his new administration. Brandeis argued that regulation of monopoly was not as important as regulation of competition. Wilson sought to nominate Brandeis as solicitor general, but the partisan opposition proved too great. However, in 1916, an opening occurred in the Supreme Court, and Wilson quickly named Brandeis amid a hail of political controversy but wide public support from all sorts of reform groups.

In his 23 years on the court, Brandeis became a strong advocate of the Fourth Amendment, which secured personal liberties against the state, particularly the sanctity of the home from unwarranted searches and seizures. In a 1920 case involving evidence gained from an illegal search, Brandeis argued with the majority in defining the principle of the "fruit of the poison tree," stating that all illegally gained evidence, regardless of its weight, was the poisoned fruit of a tainted search and, therefore, inadmissible. In *Olmstead* v. *Ohio*, however, Brandeis vehemently dissented from the majority decision, which upheld the government's use of wiretapping to gain evidence in federal prosecutions, declaring that to allow the government to commit crimes to secure the conviction of another "would bring a terrible retribution."

Brandeis set the standard for judicial restraint in that, while he was personally opposed to the implications and consequences of many of the decisions he handed down, he declared that his moral feelings had no bearing on questions of law. For example, Brandeis was opposed to most of Franklin Delano Roosevelt's New Deal legislation, but upheld most of it that appeared before him because the legislation was not unconstitutional. It was this uncompromising attitude of judicial restraint that frequently put him in the position of the lone dissenting vote during his 23 years on the court.

Brennan, William J. (1906–   ) One of the last liberal Supreme Court justices before the conservative swing of the court in the 1980s, Brennan was a loose constructionist and a diehard supporter of personal liberties.

William Brennan was born April 25, 1906, to a struggling immigrant family in the working-class city of Newark, New Jersey. He idolized his father, a laborer who went from shoveling coal to becoming a prominent local union and reform leader. It was from his father that Brennan received his social activist philosophy. After graduating with honors from the Wharton School of the University of Pennsylvania, Brennan went on to Harvard Law School, graduating after his father's death.

Service in World War II interrupted Brennan's career as an attorney, but after the war he became a leader in the New Jersey court reform movement and quickly rose in the state judicial hierarchy, being named to the state supreme court in 1952. His reputation for efficiently navigating the judicial bureaucracy and clearing a docket that was hopelessly backlogged prompted President Dwight D. Eisenhower to nominate Brennan to the U.S. Supreme Court in 1956, despite his Democratic affiliation. The conservative Eisenhower would later say that it was one of the worst mistakes of his administration, second only to his nomination of another judicial liberal, Earl WARREN.

Brennan quickly established himself as a loose constructionist—one who interprets the Constitution liberally—and was the architect of many of the landmark decisions attributed to the Warren Court. Brennan and Warren quickly became friends, meeting privately before sessions to discuss cases and strategy. Once a decision had been reached, Warren would delegate Brennan to circulate among the justices to facilitate a consensus. An early Brennan opinion set the tone for his influence on the court in 1956. *Cooper* v. *Aaron* reiterated federal judicial supremacy in ameliorating the South's "organized and massive resistance" to school desegregation.

Most noted for his protection of the First and Fourteenth Amendments, Brennan helped lead the court in its decision to extend freedom of speech libel protection explicitly to cover criticism of public officials as long as absence of malice could be proved. He also gained attention for upholding freedom of speech in several obscenity cases and in his decision regarding flag desecration cases, in which Brennan argued: "We do not consecrate the flag by punishing its desecration, for in doing so we dilute the freedom this cherished emblem represents."

As his tenure wore on and the liberal justices of the 1960s and 1970s were replaced by the more conservative appointments of Presidents Ronald Reagan and George Bush, Brennan found himself increasingly in the minority. Perhaps the issue Brennan is most noted for is his 1972 stand on capital punishment, which he adamantly opposed on the basis that it violates the Eighth and Fourteenth Amendments, in particular the prohibition of "cruel and unusual punishment." He was joined in this only by Associate Justice Thurgood MARSHALL, but persisted in criticizing the death penalty as arbitrary in its administration, observing that the overwhelming majority of those on death row were members of racial and ethnic minorities.

Citing his advanced age, Brennan retired in 1990, after 34 years on the court.

Briggs, Albert Martin (1874–1932) In 1917, this Chicago advertising executive formed the patriotic citizen, vigilante/anti-subversive group called the American Protective League.

Citizen activist A. M. Briggs founded the American Protective League in 1917. Inspired by a zealous patriotism and the national paranoia generated by World War I, Briggs was able to enlist, in a remarkably short time, more than a quarter-million volunteers in every state. The APL's ranks were filled with businessmen and concerned citizens who eagerly spied on their neighbors, searching for subversives, particularly German and Bolshevik sympathizers. Both the U.S. Department of Justice and President Woodrow WILSON informally condoned Briggs's organization, even though APL members routinely violated the civil rights of those on whom they focused, and some participated in lynchings.

In 1918, Briggs's APL spearheaded a roundup of "slackers" (draft evaders) and deserters in New York City. In the course of several days, over 50,000 men were rounded up by bayonet-wielding APL members, interrogated, and generally deprived of their civil rights. While most Americans deplored draft dodgers and deserters, the APL roundups turned public opinion against the organization. However, before any popular showdown could take place, an armistice was signed and World War I came to an end on November 11, 1918. Briggs officially disbanded his APL early the next year.

Briggs, Lloyd Vernon (1863–1941) Advocated legislation requiring evaluation to determine the mental competence of certain defendants to stand trial.

An exceptionally brilliant child, Lloyd Briggs studied medicine at Harvard Medical School, but had to withdraw when he contracted tuberculosis. In an effort to recover his health, he sailed for the Hawaiian Islands, where he served as a vaccinating officer during an outbreak of smallpox. Returning to the mainland, he settled for a time in California, then came back to Boston, where he began his life's work, campaigning for the humane and enlightened treatment of the mentally ill.

Briggs sought to put the treatment of mental illness on a par with that of physical illness. He wrote a state law that virtually abolished the use of restraints and isolation in both state and private mental hospitals, and he was instrumental in the creation of the Massachusetts Department of Mental Health. Perhaps his most enduring accomplishment was the so-called "Briggs Law." Passed in 1921, this Massachusetts law required a psychological examination and evaluation of all defendants who were to stand trial for any capital crime and any defendant previously convicted of a felony. The law, which served as a model for similar laws in other states, was intended to ensure the competency of all defendants to stand trial.

Bril, Jacques L. (1906–81) An innovator in the field of lie detection.

Born in New York City on September 17, 1906, Bril was educated at the University of Michigan and at Washington and Lee University, from which he received a Ph.D. (*Who's Who in America* erroneously reports an M.D.). In 1931, he founded Jacques L. Bril,

Criminology Consultants and Investigators, specializing in deception detection and serving as a consultant to the district attorneys of jurisdictions in the New York City metropolitan area.

In 1936, he was codeveloper of a type of lie detector device called the Pathometer. Subsequently, he developed the Biograph and created the so-called Bril deception test. In addition to lie-detection devices, Bril was a pioneer in electric and electronic surveillance apparatus.

Brinkerhoff, Roeliff (1828–1911)
President of the National Prison Association (forerunner of the American Correctional Association) from 1893 to 1897; a vocal and effective advocate of a strong federal role in the U.S. prison system.

Brinkerhoff was born on June 28, 1828, in Owasco, New York, the descendant of settlers who had come to America from Holland in 1638. At age 16, Brinkerhoff taught school in Owasco, then moved to Hendersonville, Tennessee, where, at 18, he was principal of a school. He studied law with a relative in Mansfield, Ohio, and was admitted to the Ohio bar in 1852, practicing until the Civil War. From 1855 to 1859, he was also publisher of the Mansfield *Herald*.

Brinkerhoff served as a quartermaster during the Civil War, then resumed his law practice and pursued other business interests in Mansfield. In 1878, he was made a member of the Ohio State Board of Charities and two years later became president of the National Conference of Charities and Corrections. A year after this, in 1883, he joined the National Prison Association, then headed by Rutherford B. HAYES, and 10 years later became the association's president, serving until 1897. Brinkerhoff was a reformer who, as a member of the Ohio State Board of Charities, called for an end to patronage in the prison system, and, during his tenure with the prison association, worked toward increasing professionalism in corrections, advocating strong federal standards and nonpartisan management policies. Brinkerhoff was also a vigorous promoter of parole, and it was in part through his efforts that Ohio passed the nation's first parole law in 1885.

Broca, (Pierre) Paul (1824–80)
This French physician and pathologist became one of the fathers of modern physical anthropology by founding the Anthropological Institute of Paris in 1859. His work in physical anthropology laid some important groundwork for the development of forensic medicine.

Paul Broca began his career in 1849 as a pathologist and surgeon in the prominent hospitals of Paris. His fascination with anatomy led to his interest in physical anthropology, the comparative study of the development of human beings, a field he helped to create. Broca was also among the pioneers of brain research, and in 1861 he demonstrated the cortical localization of the brain, identifying in particular the cortical region associated with speech, today known as "Broca's area."

A freethinker and humanist, Broca challenged the 19th-century religious and moral objections to the field of anthropology. He formed the first society of anthropology in 1859, invented some 27 instruments for the study of craniology, and published more than 223 works on the subject of physical anthropology. Broca's methodological assumptions and the practical working methods he developed helped establish a foundation for the subsequent development of forensic medicine and criminal anthropology.

Further reading: Haymaker, Webb, *The Founders of Neurology: One Hundred Thirty-three Biographical Sketches* (Springfield, Illinois: Charles C. Thomas, 1953).

Broderick, Johnny "The Boff" (1894–1966)
A legendary strong-arm detective in the New York Police Department of the Prohibition era; known to knock gangsters out cold on sight.

Johnny Broderick came from the violent Gashouse District of New York City and joined the force in 1923. "The Boff," as he came to be known, quickly established a reputation for whacking undesirables over the head with a lead pipe rolled up in a newspaper. On one occasion, the stocky Irish detective entered a movie house, located gangster Jack "Legs" DIAMOND in the audience, picked him up from in front of his seat, carried him out, and tossed him head-first into a garbage can.

Broderick's name became synonymous with the phrase "to rough up," and his partnership with fellow detective John "Dutchman" CORDES brought down many a gang during the period. In 1936, Edward G. Robinson portrayed the "Boffer" in the film *Bullets or Ballots*. Broderick's right hand was broken so many times that his X ray was used to train physicians at Bellevue, and heavyweight champion Jack Dempsey even said that Broderick was the only man he feared outside the ring.

The end of Prohibition and the gangster era also spelled an end to old-time cops like Johnny "The Boff" Broderick, who retired in 1947.

Brouardel, Paul Camille Hippolyte (1837–1906)
A diligent clinician who observed the neck tissue in cases of strangulation and developed methods for distinguishing suicide from murder in such cases.

A professor of legal medicine at the University of Paris, Paul Brouardel was one of the leading specialists in his field. Through his influence and example, the universities of Paris and Lyon became known as centers for the study of legal medicine.

Brouardel was chiefly known for his experiments regarding death by constriction of the airpipe, in order to determine whether the cause had been strangulation at the hands of another or suicide by hanging. He devised the means for distinguishing between the two modes of death by performing hundreds of autopsies in which he examined the most minute nerves and tissue in the neck and throat. Brouardel even went so far as to cut open the throats of victims and observe how certain nerves, muscles, and tissue reacted when strangled again. He published his findings in 1897, describing in detail the telltale signs of foul play versus suicide.

Although his work was eclipsed by developments in microscopic technology, continued postmortem observation, and advances in cell biology, Brouardel's work and his exacting observations raised the standards of forensic medicine and further secured its role in criminology and in the legal system.

Brown, Lee Patrick (1937–) Former police commissioner of New York City and Houston, this Atlanta-based criminal justice professor has been a prominent advocate of community policing.

Born on October 4, 1937, in Wewoka, a small town in Oklahoma, Brown had a strongly Christian upbringing. When he was five years old, his family moved to the San Joaquin Valley, California, where his father picked grapes and his mother worked as a cook. After graduating from California State University, Fresno, in 1960 with a major in criminology, Brown joined the San Jose Police Department, working undercover in narcotics and vice.

Brown then earned a master's degree in sociology at San Jose State and a Ph.D. in criminology from the University of California, Berkeley. He taught at Portland State University, where he established the school's first program in criminal justice. In 1972, Brown was made director of the criminal justice department at Howard University in Washington, D.C., and in 1975, he returned to public service as the sheriff of Multnomah County, Oregon.

Three years later, Brown accepted the post of public safety commissioner in Atlanta, Georgia. He served in this post during the horrifying series of child murders that plagued the city until 1981. The following year, Brown moved to Houston, as head of that city's police department. The new chief was asked to help rehabilitate a force plagued by incidents of racial bigotry and excessive violence. Over the next nine years Brown increased minority recruitment and inaugurated a large-scale experiment in community policing. Under this system, officers were assigned to specific neighborhoods, where they were expected to

get to know the residents and establish a cooperative, mutually beneficial exchange of information.

Believing that violence is a health issue, as well as a law enforcement problem, Brown approached the University of Texas Health Science Center and gained its cooperation in creating a Center for the Study of Interpersonal Violence.

Brown was named police commissioner of New York City in December 1989 and immediately initiated the first staffing study of the NYPD in 25 years. Despite New York's money troubles, Dinkins approved Brown's 1990 "Safe Streets, Safe City" proposal for a police expansion plan, and the city's uniformed force began to grow. In a redeployment program called "Operation All Out," on-street patrols were increased by almost 25%, and all headquarters personnel were assigned to at least one tour of street duty per week. In keeping with his commitment to a public-police partnership and to the fostering of crime-preventive, problem-solving methods, Brown established "management teams"—including both police supervisors and diverse community leaders—in each of the city's 75 precincts. The NYPD's recruitment of women and Hispanic officers increased substantially; and the entire force was trained in new, neighborhood-interactive techniques.

Brown's achievements in New York were reflected in the city's crime statistics, which, within months of his arrival, showed the first across-the-board decline in 36 years. Brown resigned on August 3, 1992, in order to spend more time with his ailing wife, Yvonne. He returned to Houston to teach criminal justice at Texas Southern University.

Further reading: Brown, Lee Patrick, *Community Policing: A Practical Guide for Police Officials* (Washington, D.C.: U.S. Department of Justice, 1989).

Brown, William P. (1918–94) His career in law enforcement spanned patrol duty, administration, the academic study of criminology—with emphasis on the relationships among law enforcement officials—the criminal justice process, and the community.

William P. Brown was born in Brooklyn, New York, on December 31, 1918, and was educated at New York University, earning his B.A. in 1944, his M.P.A. in 1948, and a Ph.D. in 1960. In 1940, he joined the New York Police Department as a patrolman, working his way through the ranks to inspector by 1962. It was during this period that he also earned his academic degrees. Brown served for a time as commander of the New York Police Academy.

Brown joined the faculty of the School of Public Affairs at the State University of New York, Albany, after his retirement from the police force in 1962, and he became one of the organizers of the university's School of Criminal Justice. His area of special expertise was in the relationships among law enforcement officials, the criminal justice process, the community, and academia, and he was appointed to many national commissions and advisory councils, including the President's Commission on Law Enforcement and the Administration of Justice, and the United States Commission on Civil Rights.

Brussel, James Arnold (1905–82)   One of the first to make use of offender profiling; used it on several highly significant cases.

A native of New York City, James Brussel was born on April 22, 1905. After attending local schools, he was admitted to the University of Pennsylvania, where he received his bachelor's degree in 1926 and his M.D. in 1929. After an internship and residency in psychiatry, Brussel went to work for the state of New York in the Department of Mental Hygiene. There he began extensive clinical research and writing, publishing his work and gaining some critical fame for his theory that the nature of the personality of a criminal can be identified by the study of his actions. The process, which became known as offender profiling, or psychological criminal profiling, had been a relatively unexplored field, and its utility had been regarded with doubt. Ironically, before Brussel's work, the most extensive use of offender profiling had been wholly fictitious. Sir Arthur Conan DOYLE's master detective, Sherlock Holmes, often made use of his keen faculty for psychological penetration to identify criminals from their actions and even to anticipate those actions. But Brussel was the first actual investigator to make systematic use of psychological profiling.

Brussel used this process quite successfully to help solve the "Mad Bomber Case" in New York during the early 1950s, and his description of the infamous "Boston Strangler" proved to be frighteningly accurate. Investigators, duly impressed, often joked that Brussel would be called to a crime scene with the most meager of physical evidence and, after scrutinizing the area for a few intense moments, walk out and yell back over his shoulder, "Look for a heavy-set, middle-aged single man, foreign born and Roman Catholic, wearing a buttoned, double-breasted suit."

The offender profiling process, further refined, is now widely accepted as a matter of course in investigative procedure and is generally used in sex crimes or offenses that feature some overt sexual activity or evidence of a psychological disorder.

Buchalter, Louis "Lepke" (Louis Bookhouse; alias: Judge Louis) (1897–1944)   One of the pioneers of organized crime in America.

Buchalter brought crime to an unheard of profit level during the 1920s. His rackets generated some $50 million in revenue each year, and, with the likes

The smiling Louis "Lepke" Buchalter was one of the founders of the national crime syndicate. (Courtesy of the Library of Congress)

of Charles "Lucky" LUCIANO, Meyer LANSKY, Frank COSTELLO, and Joe ADONIS, he formed the national crime cartel known as the syndicate—the core of organized crime in America.

He began unpromisingly enough as a common thief, so impoverished that, when he was arrested for the first time in 1913, the arresting officer noted that he was wearing stolen shoes—both for the left foot. The following year, Lepke met Jacob "Gurrah" Shapiro, who happened to be stealing from the same pushcart as he. They teamed up: The slightly built Lepke was the brains and the powerfully built Shapiro the muscle. Together, they terrorized the pushcart peddlers of the Lower East Side of Manhattan, extorting protection money from them. The pair soon earned a sufficient reputation to attract an invitation from Jacob "Little Augie" Orgen to join his gang of thugs, who were muscling in on the garment industry. The Orgen gang consisted of young men who would become the powerhouses of organized crime: Charles "Lucky" Luciano, Waxey Gordon, Jack "Legs" DIAMOND, and others.

By 1927, Lepke had become a major power in the union and protection rackets. It was time, he decided, to get rid of Orgen. On the night of October 15, 1927, Lepke, Shapiro, and Hyman "Little Hymie" Holtz (alias "Curly") machine-gunned Orgen and his bodyguard, Legs Diamond. Little Augie's body was cut in two, while Diamond was seriously wounded. (Diamond survived—to be shot on several other occasions.) The death of Orgen made Lepke undisputed king of the union rackets. Thus positioned, he set out to take over the entire garment industry, and he succeeded, gaining control of the 400,000-member Amalgamated Clothing Workers Union and thereby achieving dominion over a giant American industry. And this was only the beginning. Once in control of the garment workers he seized the Motion Picture Operators Union, and then the trucking unions.

Perhaps more than any other individual, it was Lepke who provided the impetus for the creation of Murder, Inc., the Brooklyn consortium of professional killers who hired out for killing "on contract." Working through Albert ANASTASIA, Lepke organized Murder, Inc., and some 250 other strongarm squads of "enforcers" in New York alone—perhaps another 500 squads nationwide. It is impossible to tally how many murders Lepke ordered and Murder, Inc. and the other strongarm squads carried out. Certainly, the number reaches into the hundreds. Probably, it is in the thousands.

Lepke collaborated with Lucky Luciano to eliminate Salvatore Maranzano, one of the last of the old-guard Sicilian crime bosses, when he tried to take over Lepke's union rackets. Lepke cut Luciano in on his rackets and helped him rise to a lofty position within the newly formed national crime syndicate. However, it was Lepke himself who functioned as the syndicate's "chairman of the board." His word was final and, for that, he was dubbed Judge Louis. Perhaps his most famous decree was the murder of Dutch SCHULTZ, whose threats against New York district attorney Thomas E. DEWEY put too much heat on the syndicate.

Lepke repeatedly evaded prosecution by buying off judges and juries, but, as the decade of the 1930s wore on and a crime-weary public increasingly supported reform, police pressure mounted against him. By 1937, he was under constant surveillance, and he hid out in a Flatbush, Brooklyn, apartment, which included secret rooms and hidden passageways. Finally, on August 24, 1939, Lepke decided to turn himself in to authorities via the famed newspaper and radio personality Walter WINCHELL, who arranged for no less a figure than J. Edgar HOOVER to make the arrest. Although Lepke was sentenced to 14 years at Leavenworth, he believed that the fix was in and that he would be paroled after serving a few years. The conviction, he believed, would avoid prosecution on more serious charges, including murder. The fact is that Lucky Luciano and others had set Lepke up, and in 1940 the federal government turned him over to New York state jurisdiction to stand trial for the murder of

gangster Joseph Rosen. Lepke, Hymie WEISS, and Louis Capone (no relation to Al) were convicted and sentenced to death.

Lepke fought desperately to overturn the sentence, even as he gave orders from his cell to eliminate those who had betrayed him. At least two gangland figures, Abe "Kid Twist" RELES and Moey "Dimples" Wolinsky, were murdered. But Lepke's legal maneuverings were not as effective, and on March 4, 1944, Lepke and the other two convicts walked to the electric chair in Sing Sing, Lepke reportedly assuring Weiss and Capone that "the fix is in, you'll see." At the very last moment Lepke received a stay of execution when he told the warden that he had some important information. But he said nothing new, and Thomas E. Dewey, one-time district attorney, now governor of New York, refused to grant additional stays. Lepke went to the chair without uttering another word.

Burger, Warren (1907–95)   After the retirement of his liberal predecessor, Chief Justice Earl WARREN, Burger brought the Supreme Court back to the political center, limiting the scope of some of the Warren-era decisions but without overturning them, as many conservatives had hoped.

A self-made man in every sense, Warren Burger had been born in St. Paul, Minnesota, to humble immigrant parents on September 17, 1907. While working during the day as an insurance salesman, Burger attended school in the evening, first at the University of Minnesota for two years, then at the St. Paul College of Law for another four. He graduated in 1931 *magna cum laude*. Once out of law school, Burger began practicing in St. Paul, handling corporate and probate matters, and he also began his involvement in the Republican Party. After serving as a delegate to the Republican National Convention in both 1948 and 1952, he gained the attention of Dwight D. Eisenhower and the soon-to-be attorney general, Herbert Brownell. Upon Eisenhower's inauguration as president in 1953, Brownell appointed Burger assistant attorney general in charge of the Claims Division. Three years later, he was appointed to the U.S. Circuit Court of Appeals. It was there that Burger first gained widespread notice—some would say notoriety—for his outspokenly conservative views on the Fourth and Fifth Amendments. He advocated limiting the rights of criminal defendants, while giving leeway to police and the prosecution.

Burger's reputation was exactly what Richard NIXON was looking for to make good on the promises of his "law-and-order" presidential campaign of 1968 and to capitalize on the conservative backlash over the liberal opinions of Chief Justice Earl Warren. Upon Warren's resignation in 1969, Nixon quickly nominated Burger to fill the post of chief justice. Surprisingly, after he ascended to the high court, Burger proved a disappointment to the Nixon administration and other conservatives because he did not act to overturn Warren-era decisions. To be sure, his court modified some and limited others, but it also broadened and strengthened some Warren-era decisions.

Of the many cases that came before Burger, none was more controversial than the 1973 *Roe* v. *Wade*, in which Burger voted with the majority to protect the right to abortion. When opportunities arose to overturn or at least severely limit Warren's *Miranda* decision (*see* MIRANDA, Ernesto), long a thorn in the side of the law enforcement community, Burger acted to modify it only slightly. Some of Burger's "failure" to toe the conservative line may have been due less to his convictions than to his lack of influence over his liberal court colleagues and his apparent inability to rally the allies he did have within the court. Some justices openly expressed dissatisfaction with his leadership. Burger retired in June 1986.

Burgess, Ernest Watson (1886–1966)   An advocate of parole, arguing for more accurate survey statistics and greater understanding of the system by the general public.

Ernest Burgess was born and raised in the province of Ontario in Canada and attended Kingfisher College, where he earned his undergraduate degree in 1908. From there, Burgess enrolled in the University of Chicago's School of Sociology, earning his Ph.D. in 1913. After teaching at the University of Toledo, the University of Kansas, and Ohio State, Burgess returned to Chicago, where he taught until his retirement in 1951.

It was at Chicago that Burgess became a leading advocate of the parole system. Distressed that the press habitually trumpeted the failures of parole and never its considerable rate of success, Burgess set about making a full-scale study of the system, only to discover that very little to no accurate data was available. In part, he noted, this was a failure of the system itself, in that there was no single set of criteria for a parole system; not only did parole policy vary with different offenses, it also varied from state to state and even from institution to institution. Burgess called for parole reform, which would include universal parole requirements and standards and greater accountability to enable more accurate study and evaluation.

Burns, Henry, Jr. (1930–82)   An expert on corrections and corrections reform.

A native of eastern Kentucky, Henry Burns Jr. spent several years teaching in the public schools before beginning his correctional career as director of education at the Ohio State Correctional Institution in Lebanon, Ohio. After several years, Burns left that position to return to his home state and begin work for the Kentucky Department of Corrections, where he held several positions before being named deputy commissioner in 1966.

Burns left that position the following year to begin his extensive academic career, teaching at Southern Illinois University, Pennsylvania State, and Indiana University before accepting the chairmanship of the Administration of Justice Department at the University of Missouri-St. Louis. He remained in St. Louis until 1980, when failing health forced him to step down from the faculty, but he continued to write on corrections. Shortly before his death, he published *Corrections: Organization and Administration*, the definitive textbook on correctional administration.

Further reading: Burns, Henry, Jr., *Corrections: Organization and Administration* (St. Paul, Minn.: West, 1975).

Burns, William J. (1861–1932)   Many believe Burns to have been the greatest of American criminal investigators.

Born in Baltimore to Irish immigrants, William Burns spent much of his youth as a precocious detective. When the family moved to Columbus, Ohio, and his father took the position of police commissioner, young William frequently solved the cases his father's investigators could not. In 1885, the Ohio state election was contested as fraudulent. Electoral officials were at a loss to discover who had rigged the process. Burns, only 24, not only ferreted out the culprits, but also determined the precise extent to which the election had been tainted. This case earned him instant celebrity, and he was quickly besieged with job offers.

The agency Burns finally joined in 1889 was the United States Secret Service. At the time, the primary mission of the Secret Service was combating counterfeiting. Burns quickly distinguished himself, personally solving many of the most baffling counterfeiting cases, including the so-called Brockway case, in which the counterfeiter had been operating for 25 years. During his tenure with the Secret Service, Burns did not confine himself to breaking up counterfeiting operations. For example, in 1897, he went undercover in Indiana to investigate the vigilante lynching of five criminal suspects. After three months disguised as an insurance salesman, Burns was able to make several arrests.

In 1903, Burns resigned from the Secret Service to join the Department of the Interior as an investigator. At the time, the department was embroiled in a scandalous land fraud involving the sale of western government lands for private profit. Burns relentlessly

Famous private eye William J. Burns was director of the Bureau of Investigation, which would become the FBI and a major player in American law enforcement under Burns's successor, J. Edgar Hoover. (Courtesy of the Library of Congress)

pursued the investigation, which eventually led to the indictment and arrest of several public officials, including Oregon Senator John Mitchell. Burns proceeded directly from Oregon to San Francisco with federal prosecutor Francis Heney to investigate San Francisco graft corruption under the infamous political boss Abe Ruef. It took three years, but Burns and Heney eventually put Ruef and his cronies in prison.

After dealing with Boss Ruef, Burns left government service to start the William J. Burns Detective Agency, which quickly established itself as second only to the much older Pinkerton Agency in prestige and caseload. The Burns organization—like the Pinkerton Agency—operated as a kind of private police force for big business interests against organized labor. Burns's tactics in investigating labor unions and discrediting their leaders were at times questionable, at times brutal, and at times unquestionably illegal. The most widely publicized labor case was the bombing of the *Los Angeles Times*, in which Burns successfully

implicated the Iron and Bridge Workers Union. With the success of his agency established, Burns returned to the federal government in 1921 to head the Bureau of Investigation, immediate forerunner to the FBI. This proved to be the least successful chapter of his life. The administration of President Warren G. Harding, nicknamed the "Ohio Gang," was one of the most corrupt in presidential history, and that corruption spilled over into every federal department, including Justice. The Bureau of Investigation was overrun with political hacks and corrupt appointees, and Director Burns was either stonewalled or chose to ignore the blatant acts that would result in various high-level government scandals, the most notorious and protracted of which was the Teapot Dome affair, in which federal oil leases were sold to private interests for profit.

Although Burns did succeed in prosecuting the Ku Klux Klan and brought that hate-mongering organization to the brink of extinction, this triumph was not enough to save his job. Burns resigned in 1924 and retired from public life.

Burt, Leonard (1892–1983)   This British detective commanded MI5—British intelligence—and, later, Scotland Yard's elite Special Branch, responsible for security for the royal family.

Burt was born on April 20, 1892, and educated at Totton High School, Hampshire. He served in Scotland yard's CID (Criminal Investigation Department) from 1919 to 1940, earning a reputation as a master detective in the areas of homicide, drugs, and vice and achieving promotion to chief superintendent. During World War II, from 1940 to 1946, he served in the British Army's Intelligence Corps and headed MI5, Britain's principal wartime intelligence agency. It was Burt and his Scotland Yard team who collared William Joyce, the infamous "Lord Haw-Haw," who was for Britishers what Tokyo Rose was for Americans—a traitor who made propaganda broadcasts for the enemy. Immediately after the war, Burt was credited with breaking Allan Nunn May and Klaus Fuchs, spies who conveyed atomic bomb secrets to the Soviets.

Burt's principal postwar assignment was as head of the Special Branch of Scotland Yard, responsible for protection of the royal family as well as visiting foreign dignitaries, including the likes of Yugoslavia's Tito and the Soviet Union's Khrushchev.

Further reading: Burt, Leonard, *Commander Burt of Scotland Yard* (London: William Heinemann, 1959).

Butler, Lord Richard Austen (1902–82)   As British home secretary during the late 1950s, Lord Butler was instrumental in the expansion and development of the Institute of Criminology at Cambridge University and was an important advocate of penal reform.

Richard Butler entered the House of Commons in 1929 and remained there for the next three decades. During his tenure, he held many posts, including that of acting prime minister when Winston Churchill was incapacitated in 1953. As British home secretary, Butler published a white paper entitled *Penal Practice in a Changing Society* in 1959, which advocated penal reform in Great Britain and resulted in the expansion of Leon RADZINOWICZ's Institute of Criminology at Cambridge University. Butler also called for modern, specialized detention centers for young offenders and a more generally humane legal code.

In 1965, Lord Butler retired from politics to become master of Trinity College, Cambridge University, where he continued to promote his program of reform for 13 years, until ill health forced him to retire from Trinity and public life in 1978.

Further reading: Butler, Lord Richard Austen, *Art of the Possible: The Memoirs of Lord Butler* (Boston: Gambit, 1972).

Butler, Smedley Darlington (1881–1940) A brash Marine Corps general brought in to clean up Philadelphia's police force; ran roughshod over any number of constitutional rights in his quest for "reform."

A lapsed Quaker from Pennsylvania, Smedley Butler ran away from home at the age of 16 to join the Marine Corps when that organization called for recruits during the Spanish-American War. He was dedicated to a life in the military forever after and saw action in every military conflict involving the United States, from the Spanish-American War to the Marine Expeditionary Force sent to China in 1927–29. Butler was decorated with a Distinguished Service Medal and two Congressional Medals of Honor—a very rare achievement in the history of the nation's highest military honor.

Butler's reputation as a hard-driven, incorruptible man was exceeded only by his reputation as an outspoken, impetuous sayer of the truth-as-he-saw-it. He once declared that certain unnamed naval officers were "desk admirals without ships." He was almost court-martialed when he charged Benito Mussolini, dictator of Italy, with running down a child in his car in 1930, an accusation that required a formal apology from the U.S. government and resulted in a reprimand on Butler's record. This dual reputation prompted newly elected Philadelphia mayor W. Freeland Kendrick to offer Butler the position of director of public safety—in effect, chief of police—to clean up vice and corruption and enforce Prohibition in the city.

Butler jumped at the chance and secured a two-year leave of absence from the Marine Corps. Butler sought to impart a military style of leadership to the police department, a shape-up-or-ship-out attitude. The experiment was an utter failure. While Kendrick had been elected on a reform ticket, Butler sacrificed constitutional law and due process in the name of his own program of police reform. Sworn in on January 7, 1934, he immediately ordered that the city be rid of vice within 48 hours. Two days later, 75% of the city's 1,300 saloons had been closed down, and the "48-hour drive" became a fixture of Butler's administration. He organized the "bandit patrol," consisting of uniformed thugs with sawed-off shotguns and armored vehicles busting in on any suspected criminal, the evidence or its lack notwithstanding. He once declared that the only way to reform a criminal is to shoot him. "Shoot a few of them, and make arrests afterward."

In his manner of ethical reform, he was equally high-handed. He abolished the police academy and declared that "every cop will learn his job right on the beat." He also abolished accepted procedures of promotion, and would instead swagger into a station house, single out a hard-working patrolman, and promote him to sergeant on the spot.

Celebrated as the "Fighting Quaker" and "Gimlet-Eye," Butler was nevertheless more than the mayor could take, and he asked the Marine to resign after two years.

Butler, Thomas (1913–70) A Scotland Yard detective who twice postponed retirement to track down the 15 men known to have perpetrated England's "Great Train Robbery."

Thomas Butler earned his niche in law enforcement history as the relentless "Gray Fox" who tracked down and captured all 15 men who pulled off the $7 million robbery of the Glasgow-to-London mail train on August 8, 1963. It was the largest cash heist in history. Butler's investigation and pursuit consumed a total of five years; all but one suspect was captured by 1966, and the last, Bruce Reynolds, was collared in the fall of 1968. (That year, Butler also went to Canada to recapture Charles Wilson, one of the robbers who had escaped from prison.) During this period, Butler traveled all over Europe—even getting arrested as a Peeping Tom in the south of France for scanning sunbathers with binoculars.

Born in London, Butler joined the police force as a "bobby" when he was 22. After walking a beat for four years, he became a detective and quickly earned a reputation for tenacity. His rise through the ranks was one of the swiftest in the history of the force. In

1953, he became detective sergeant, and within 10 years was detective chief superintendent.

Other high-profile cases in which Butler was involved included operations against guerrillas in strife-torn Cyprus, when it was a British colony in the 1950s, and the arrest of Rev. Dr. Martin Luther King Jr.'s assassin, James Earl Ray, in June 1968, at London's Heathrow Airport. At the end of that eventful year, Butler retired from Scotland Yard and became chief security officer of the Midland Bank. He died of lung cancer on April 20, 1970, in a London hospital.

Byrnes, Thomas F. (1842–1910) Creator of the original "Rogues' Gallery," this New York City chief of detectives was the first police inspector to have photographs taken of every suspect under arrest.

The turn-of-the-century chief believed that intimate knowledge of the law-breaking community was indispensable to detective work, and Byrnes once remarked that his trade "consists not in pursuing but in forming friendships with criminals." Certain aspects of this practice ultimately cost Byrnes his job, but he was long considered one of the greatest detectives in America, and his colorful personality dominated the investigative force of the NYPD for 18 years.

Born in Ireland, Byrnes was a child when his family immigrated to New York City. As a young man he worked as an installer for the gas company, then served two years with the Union Army during the Civil War. In 1863 he joined the New York City police department as a patrolman; five years later he became a roundsman, and in 1870 he was promoted to captain. But Byrnes really made a name for himself in 1878, after a spectacular heist took almost $3 million from the Manhattan Bank in his territory, the Fifteenth Precinct. Byrnes managed to arrest most of the perpetrators—including infamous bank robber George Leonidas Leslie—and recover much of the money. Impressed with his criminological efficiency, the department made him chief of detectives.

One of Byrnes's first initiatives was a strategic increase in police protection of the financial and gem districts on and around Wall Street in lower Manhattan. The chief installed nine detectives there—in an office paid for by local bankers and brokers, who also equipped the "station" with special telephone hotlines to their business establishments. Byrnes then sent word through the criminal grapevine that the entire area was henceforth off-limits to thieves. Any known felons who crossed the designated "death line" at Fulton Street would instantly be arrested, not to mention roughed up. The Wall Street bigwigs—suddenly free from the ministrations of vault burglars, pickpockets, and stick-up men—expressed their gratitude to Byrnes by making substantial stock market invest-

ments in his name. The chief's initiative proved strategic for his own long-term fortunes as well.

Over the next few years, Byrnes enlisted the approval of the state legislature to reorganize and centralize New York's detective division, bringing all of the city's investigators together under his direct supervision. In 1884, another bureaucratic shuffle permanently reassigned two detectives to each precinct, where they reported to their local captains. But the Central Office Bureau of Detectives—Byrnes's domain—was still 40 gumshoes strong, and its publicity-wise leader endeavored to make it the rival of Scotland Yard and the Paris Sûreté.

Byrnes and his men did indeed "form friendships with criminals," trading favors and information with burglars, swindlers, fences, gang leaders, madams, shyster lawyers, gambling operators, and crooked politicians in tough neighborhoods like Satan's Circus on the Lower East Side, Hell's Kitchen, and the Bowery. The detectives applied pressure to one lawbreaker to solicit details about another, turned gang rivalries and "professional" competition to police advantage, and generally cultivated a useful acquaintanceship with the underworld. "Provided he could benefit by peaching on his confederates," Byrnes declared, "I never met a thief in my life . . . from whom I could not find out anything I was desirous to know. There is no such thing as honor among thieves." When a prominent citizen's property was stolen, Byrnes often was able to arrange for its return the following day, simply by working his connections. Needless to say, such prompt recoveries did wonders for the chief's reputation as a sleuth.

The first American police official to experiment with Alphonse BERTILLON's anthropometric identification system, Byrnes strongly believed in the value of criminal identification methods. At nine each morning, he held a parade outside the Mulberry Street station. Every suspect arrested within the previous 24 hours would be marched back and forth before Byrnes's detectives, who were expected to point out repeat offenders and commit new faces to memory for future reference. An even better reference were the tintype photographs that Byrnes began to compile of all arrested suspects.

A huge man with muttonchop whiskers, Byrnes used any and all means to get what he needed from a suspect or informer, and he was famous for his frequent application of the third degree. Across the hall from his office was a room he called "The Mystery Chamber," a sort of showcase for the tools of the criminal trade, full of confiscated weapons, burglar's instruments, robber's masks, and other memorabilia. A hangman's rope swung from the ceiling, and the walls were papered with photos of criminals Byrnes had put away. Among these tintypes was a posed picture of the chief himself, cheerfully watching as a ne'er-do-well underwent some strong-arm persuasion while having his own portrait taken. Byrnes found the chamber an effective interrogation room, but he also invited journalists there to marvel at his collection.

The head detective shared his tintype archives with the public in September 1886, when he published *Professional Criminals of America.* Byrnes offered this volume of photographic reproductions for the use of "bankers, brokers, commercial and business men, and the public . . . to serve as a medium in the prevention and detection of crime." In addition to hundreds of mug shots, the book included methodological descriptions of the individual bank robbers, forgers, confidence men, shoplifters, and other specialists such as "sawdust men" and "horse sale fraudsters." Interestingly, Byrnes omitted some data about prominent gangsters and burglars who were still at large upon the book's publication.

In 1888, New York City created the position of chief inspector and Byrnes was given the new title; part of his job responsibility was to serve as acting superintendent when the regular official was unavailable. When Superintendent William Murray retired in 1892, Byrnes replaced him at the top. Soon thereafter, however, the Reverend Charles PARKHURST's crusade against police corruption began to heat up, and one of New York's police commissioners, Theodore ROOSEVELT, believed Byrnes to be an especially rotten apple in the department's barrel. During the Clarence LEXOW committee hearings, begun in 1894, Byrnes was one of many law enforcers asked to testify concerning Parkhurst's allegations of bribery, graft, and laissez-faire arrangements between police and illegal vice operators. When it was shown that many precinct

detectives served primarily as "bagmen"—pay-off collectors—for their captains, and that few arrests were made by investigators unless monetary rewards were guaranteed in advance (these disbursements evading the process of approval and deductions for police pension contribution that the commissioners formally required), a *New York World* reporter suggested that if Byrnes didn't know what was going on under his nose, he probably couldn't "detect Limburger cheese without eating it."

The superintendent's personal wealth also underwent scrutiny. On a salary of $5,000 a year, Byrnes had somehow accumulated over $350,000 in cash and real estate, including a rental property on Fifth Avenue. The gratitude of the Wall Street magnates had evidently served him well. Byrnes did, finally, admit to the Lexow Committee that many gambling and prostitution houses were indeed allowed by police to operate in exchange for a steady cut of the take. Byrnes declared this practice a lamentable and preventable outcome of departmental "politics"—insufficiently centralized control of all detectives under the superintendent.

Byrnes resigned in June 1895, at the age of 54. But even though the Lexow hearings had embarrassed him into retirement, he continued to defend his record. During his tenure, the former chief of detectives declared, the department's arrests had brought about convictions resulting in combined total jail terms of 10,000 years—more than Scotland Yard, the Paris Sureté, and the police departments of New Jersey put together. In his heyday, Byrnes was described by contemporary writers Jacob Riis and Lincoln Steffens as "a giant every way . . . a big policeman . . . simple, no complications at all—a man who would buy you or beat you, as you might choose, but get you he would."

C

Caldwell, Charles (1771–1853) One of several doctors of his day who discussed the relationship between phrenology and crime, Caldwell established himself as a prominent criminologist.

Charles Caldwell was born in Newark, Delaware, on May 14, 1771, to an Irish immigrant family that subsequently settled in Caswell, North Carolina, when Charles was very young. Early recognized for his oratorical talents, Caldwell seemed destined to become a minister, especially since his father had forbidden him to enter either the law or the military. He quickly tired of religion, however, and, in 1792, entered the medical school of the University of Pennsylvania, the most prominent medical school in the country.

After completing his degree, Caldwell obtained a commission as a military surgeon during the quick and bloodless 1794 Whiskey Rebellion in western Pennsylvania. Next, Caldwell campaigned for a teaching position at the University of Pennsylvania medical school; failing to obtain this, he moved to Lexington, Kentucky, to reorganize the fledgling medical school there. He put hundreds of hours and his own dollars into developing the obscure frontier school, and it eventually could claim the best medical library in the country. After 20 years, he decided that rural Lexington was not the ideal location for what had become a leading medical school and determined to start a new institution in the more urban city of Louisville. The new school fell short of the Lexington prototype. After Caldwell's advancing age compelled him to retire, the new institution declined, although it eventually recovered to become the University of Louisville.

In 1824, Caldwell published a book called Elements of Phrenology, which dealt with the "science" of interpreting the correlation between the size and shape of the brain and various traits of emotion, intellect, and character. Like other phrenologists, Caldwell theorized that criminals committed particular acts because of certain specific formations of the brain. Furthermore, he believed that such formations and the corresponding actions they tended to produce were entirely identifiable. His book became the first American textbook on phrenology. While phrenology has long since been discredited, the 1824 work established Caldwell as an early American medical criminologist.

Further reading: Caldwell, Charles, *The Autobiography of Charles Caldwell, M.D.* (Philadelphia: Lippincott, Grambo, and Co., 1855).

Callahan, John T. (ca. 1895–1976) An investigator with the early Securities and Exchange Commission who helped track down major stock-market swindlers in the turmoil of the Great Depression.

Voted All-American in football, Callahan studied at Columbia University, Fordham Law School, Oxford University, and Yale, where he graduated in 1920. He worked in private practice and on the legal staff of the Federal Trade Commission before joining the newly founded Securities and Exchange Commission (SEC) in the mid-1930s. In its Division of Trading and Exchanges, Callahan was teamed with Edward JAEGERMAN to ferret out cases of fraud, stock manipulation, insider trading, and other securities violations nationwide. Called "the Rover Boys" by magazine and newspaper reporters, Callahan and Jaegerman traveled the country pursuing the convoluted paper trails of dummy corporations, false identities, and similar financial vanishing acts. The two-man team broke up several "boiler rooms," where slick-talking telephone pitchmen sold unknown or worthless stocks to credulous, Depression-beleaguered citizens—their names compiled on "sucker lists"—across the United States.

In the following decade, Callahan helped foil an international confidence ring. The operators (from Florida, New York, and Quebec) kept Montreal headquarters as an asylum from U.S. authorities, and they fleeced investors over the long distance lines by fraudulently proffering stock in a "new," but actually ore-exhausted, Canadian gold mine. On Wall Street, shares in raw, undeveloped mineral resources became known as "moose pasture" stock because of such north-of-the-border bamboozlers.

After participating in over 500 separate investigations, Callahan retired as assistant general counsel of the SEC in 1968. He died in North Andover, Massachusetts.

Camarena, Enrique (1948–85) U.S. Drug Enforcement Agency officer who was abducted and killed by "cocaine cowboys" in Guadalajara, Mexico.

Born in Mexicali, Mexico, Camarena was raised in California and became an agent for the U.S. Drug Enforcement Administrationn (DEA). In 1980, he was sent to Guadalajara, Mexico, where he devised "Operation Miracle," a program of aerial surveillance over the marijuana fields outside the city of Guadalajara. Mexican authorities cooperated grudgingly; however, Primer Commandante Miguel Aldana Ibarra of the *federales* (Mexican Federal Judicial Police) sanctioned a May 1984 raid that netted 20 tons of marijuana.

The raid was a good show, but it barely dented the drug empire of Rafael Cáro Quintero, who thrived primarily on cocaine smuggling. In September 1984, Camarena learned that Aldana Ibarra was actually protecting the cocaine smuggling ring. Camarena's revelations resulted in a January 1985 congressional investigation of drug-trafficking corruption at the highest levels of the Mexican government. Just as the congressional reports were being printed, Camarena was abducted outside the Camelot Bar in Guadalajara. On March 5, his mutilated body, along with that of Captain Alfredo Zavala Avelar (who had flown many of the DEA surveillance missions), was found outside of Villahermosa, near the estate of Manuel Bravo Cervantes, a former Mexican legislator. When police attempted to question Cervantes, they were shot at from inside the former politician's house, a gun battle ensued, and Cervantes, his wife, and two children were slain before they could say anything to authorities.

Under intense U.S. pressure, Mexican authorities arrested a former police officer, Raul López Alvarez, who confessed to having participated in the abduction of Camarena at the behest of Cáro Quintero, in whose home the DEA agent was tortured to death. Alvarez and two others were extradited to Los Angeles, where they were tried and convicted on racketeering and

murder charges. Alvarez was sentenced to 240 years plus life in prison, and the others received similar sentences. Cáro Quintero was tried in Mexico and was sentenced to 34 years in prison on charges of smuggling weapons and making peasants work on a marijuana plantation.

Campbell, Sir George William Robert (1835–1905) One of the founders of the Ceylon Police and one of the principal architects of the British Colonial Police system.

At the age of 20, George Campbell entered public service by enlisting as an ensign in the Argyll and Bute Rifles in Scotland; he was promoted to lieutenant within a few months. The unit was disbanded in 1866, and Campbell journeyed to India, where he worked in the Bombay Revenue Society. When a native mutiny flared up against British authorities, Campbell served temporarily as assistant superintendent of police. Commanding some 400 men, he was instrumental in the suppression of the mutiny and was cited for his service.

After serving in various law enforcement positions within the British colonial system, Campbell was named to reorganize the Ceylon Police Force in 1866. Following a successful two-year beginning, he resigned from the Colonial Indian Service and entered the full-time service of Ceylon. There, he was responsible for remaking the police along the lines of the Royal Irish Constabulary. In doing so, he kept the organization predominantly military in style and discipline, but altered its mission to encompass more civilian law enforcement functions.

To strengthen morale and improve response time in cases of emergency, Campbell instituted compound-style quarters, where police officers could live with their families but still be readily mobilized. He also maintained strict but fair discipline with an equitable system of reward and promotion. In his efforts to make the police more responsive to civilian needs, Campbell issued memos on procedure and guidance and instituted proficiency exams.

By the time of his death in 1905, the Ceylon Police bore the indelible stamp of Sir George and served as a model for other colonial police organizations.

Camps, Francis Edward (1905–72) A leading figure in the history of forensic pathology, this British expert, professor, and author developed the world-famous department of forensic medicine at London Hospital Medical School.

The son of a prosperous surgeon and general practitioner, Francis Camps was born in Teddington, England, on June 28, 1905. After earning high marks at Marlborough College, Camps trained for his father's profession at Guy's Hospital Medical School, University of London. He also studied at Switzerland's University of Neuchatel and earned additional degrees at the School of Tropical Medicine, University of Liverpool. Working as a physician at Chelmsford and Essex Hospital, Camps became interested in pathology, and his subsequent consultation to the Essex County police force led him to specialize in the forensic aspect of the field.

His talent and single-minded enthusiasm for the profession won Camps a reputation as a brilliant, if haughty, professional, and his lightning speed at the autopsy table was legendary. Early in his career, Camps performed postmortems with his bare hands, and even later on—well into his eventual total of 88,000 dissections—the pathologist's brusquely impatient style demonstrated only token concern for rubber gloves and other antiseptic safety measures. Yet his shrewd and painstaking investigation of telling details was also renowned, and many of his most famous cases involved quite subtle means of identifying the badly mutilated, decomposed, or incomplete remains of grisly murders: for example, the victims of John Reginald Christie and Wills Eugene Boshears, and the ill-fated Stanley Setty, first known as the "Essex Marsh Torso."

Camps also applied his expertise to uncovering clues at the crime scenes. In the Setty case he and a police chemist found minimal blood traces in a suspect's freshly dyed rug and the cracks of his newly refinished wooden floors. Camps and a colleague had a piece of identical flooring replicated in their lab, then poured pints of fresh blood upon it, methodically measuring the seepage over several days in order to prove that the between-floors bloodstains in Mr. Hume's home were caused by carnage far more substantial than any nosebleed or other household accident. Conviction ensued.

In the lecture hall as well as in professional circles, Camps zealously championed his chosen field. He taught at numerous universities before joining the London Hospital Medical College in 1954, and there he was made professor of forensic medicine, then director of the department, and in 1970, professor emeritus. A member of many professional academies and societies, Camps was awarded the Swiney Prize for Medical Jurisprudence by the Royal Society of Arts in 1969. He served as consultant to the British Army and diverse government committees, and as scientific advisor for the British television programs, "The Strange Report" and "The Hidden Truth."

The pathologist's writings include *Medical and Scientific Investigations in the Christie Case* (1953), *Practical Forensic Medicine* (with W. Bentley Purchase, 1956, 1957, rev. 1971), and *The Investigation of Murder* (with

Richard Barber, 1966). Camps also contributed articles to several pathological and medico-legal journals and served as editor of *Medicine, Science, and the Law* (1964), *Recent Advances in Forensic Pathology* (1969), and *Sudden and Unexpected Deaths in Infancy (Cot Deaths)* (1972).

By all accounts, Camps was a forceful personality, and his idiosyncracies included a somewhat quixotic interest in offering defense testimony for minimal reward but, unlike his prosecutorial efforts, with little success. An exception was the 1960 case of the "Mummy of Rhyl"—actually an air-dried, maggot-hollowed, and literally moth-eaten corpse discovered in a long-locked rooming house cupboard. Confirming that the body may well have died of illness—disseminated sclerosis, to be exact—and not of violence, Camps and postmortem examiner E. Gerald Evans materially supported the proprietress-suspect's confession of merely stashing a deceased tenant post facto. Mrs. Sarah Jane Harvey did go to prison for 15 months—not for murder, but for her fraudulent collection of institutional funds (the unreported corpse's "rent") during the 20 years since Mrs. Frances Knight's presumably natural death.

Another of Camps's quirks was his abiding, vocal—and even, reportedly, obsessive—hatred for fellow pathologist Keith SIMPSON. But Camps's greatest personal folly was the delusion that took his own life prematurely, only months after his retirement. In great pain, and self-convinced that his affliction was terminal cancer, Camps stubbornly refused all medical attention. An otherwise treatable stomach ulcer brought him to his grave on July 8, 1972. Despite Camps's often-expressed horror that his arch-rival Simpson might be called to conduct his autopsy, no postmortem was performed.

Further reading: Camps, Francis Edward, *Camps on Crime.* (Devon, England: W. J. Holman, Ltd., 1973).

Jackson, Robert, *Francis Camps* (London: Hart-Davies McGibbon, 1973).

Canter, David Victor (1944–   ) A University of Surrey (England) professor of psychology who developed methods of psychological profiling in order to trace serial offenders, particularly killers and rapists.

Canter was educated at Liverpool Collegiate Grammar School and received his B.A. and Ph.D. degrees from the University of Liverpool in 1964 and 1969. He taught at Liverpool and at Strathclyde University, serving as a research fellow in the Building Performance Research Unit from 1967 to 1970, advising on the psychological aspects of the design of workplaces for efficiency and safety. He was appointed to the staff of the University of Surrey in 1972, becoming head of the Department of Psychology in 1987, and was the prime mover behind the university's MSc program in investigative psychology, established in 1992 to train law enforcement personnel and others in psychological methods of crime detection.

Canter established a significant reputation as a kind of latter-day Sherlock Holmes, using minute crime-scene clues to create detailed psychological portraits of some of England's worst criminals. The portraits were invaluable in helping police track down offenders, particularly those who perpetrate serial crimes. In the 1980s, Canter's work was instrumental in the capture and conviction of John Duffy, the so-called "railway rapist," who was singled out from a group of no fewer than 1,999 suspects. Using such features of Duffy's crimes as location, timing, and method, Canter was able to establish, among many other points, that he had a turbulent and childless marriage, that he had an interest in the martial arts, and that he was a semi-skilled laborer. Such information allowed police to narrow the field of suspects and focus on Duffy.

Capone, Alphonse ("Scarface") (1899–1947) Symbolized the brazen crime and deadly violence of the Prohibition Era in the United States.

Born in the slums of Brooklyn, New York, to a family that included eight other siblings, Al Capone spent virtually all of his life on the wrong side of the law. He attended school sporadically to the sixth grade, then left after assaulting his teacher and receiving a humiliating beating from the principal as punishment. From that point on, Capone never spent an honest day in his life. He began running with small-time New York City street gangs, eventually graduating to the notoriously violent Five Points Gang of lower Manhattan. As a Five Pointer, Capone learned the brutal arts of extortion, robbery, and murder, and practiced his new skills avidly.

Capone began working for his old friend Johnny TORRIO, who owned a saloon and brothel in Brooklyn. Capone served as a hired thug who mercilessly beat up those who got behind on their payments to Torrio. Next, he supervised Torrio's prostitution ring, personally beating women suspected of withholding Torrio's nightly take. By the time he was 16, Capone began tending bar and working as a bouncer at Torrio's club, continuing to assault anyone who in any way crossed his boss. At this time, in sampling the goods Torrio purveyed in the upper stories of his establishment, Capone contracted syphilis; it went untreated, and it would eventually debilitate and kill him.

By 1918, Torrio had moved his operation to the raucous city of Chicago and now asked Capone to come along, which he happily did. In the Windy City, Capone continued working as a thug and hitman for

Perhaps the most notorious criminal in history—Chicago mobster Al Capone (Courtesy of the Library of Congress)

Torrio. He gained a reputation for sadism in the discharge of his mission, and, indeed, seemed to take particular pleasure in beating victims to death. Torrio was working for his uncle, Big Jim Colosimo, Chicago's most powerful crime boss, and when Torrio suggested they begin making money off the impending prohibition of alcohol, Colosimo felt he was wealthy enough and didn't want in on the new racket. Torrio, seeing the sure profits in booze, decided his uncle had to go, and dispatched Capone to kill him. The young man committed the murder in Colosimo's own cafe and then calmly walked back to Torrio's club and upstairs into bed with a prostitute.

After Colosimo's death, Torrio arranged for all the Chicago underbosses to meet. They carved up the city, each agreeing not to trespass on the other's turf. This agreement soon broke down, mostly due to Capone's own dealings, and open warfare broke out.

After several high-level hits, Torrio himself was almost killed, prompting him to retire in fear, summarily leaving to Capone his entire operation. Capone now began a ruthless program of extermination directed against his foes. He had inherited from Torrio more than half the Chicago police force, as well as numerous aldermen, judges, and prosecutors. He was, accordingly, never worried about facing criminal prosecution. In one instance, Capone walked right into a bar, put a gun to a man's head, coolly blew off the top of his victim's skull, then calmly walked out. Of the only two witnesses who said they saw Capone do it, one disappeared forever and the other "forgot" what he had seen.

At length, Capone was opposed only by Hymie WEISS, a signatory to the original agreement with Torrio. The two waged urban warfare on one another, making liberal use of the newly developed Thompson submachine gun, which was available as government surplus by the thousands. The "Tommy gun" became a pop-culture icon of Roaring Twenties gangsterism. After eliminating Weiss in an elaborately contrived hit, Capone turned his attention to Weiss's successor in the North Side Gang, George "Bugs" MORAN. Capone masterminded an elaborate hit, hoping to kill Moran in the garage the gangster maintained as a front for his operations. Two Capone men disguised as police detectives moved in, lined up the seven men they found in the garage, then pulled the Thompsons from beneath their coats. They fired so many rounds into their victims that several men were cut in two by the gunfire. This butchery, which took place on St. Valentine's Day, went down in popular gangland legend as the St. Valentine's Day Massacre.

The "Massacre" proved a turning point in Capone's career. Not only did it fail to eliminate Moran—who was not, in fact, present in the garage—its sheer brutality finally mobilized public opinion against Capone, who had been hitherto popularly portrayed as a harmless bootlegger operating in the teeth of a greatly resented Prohibition. He was now perceived as a cold-blooded butcher. Still, Capone managed to evade prosecution until federal authorities began probing his vast "business" interests, hoping to prosecute Capone on multiple counts of income tax evasion. Before that investigation got under way, however, Capone learned that Moran had offered $50,000 for his head. Figuring that prison was the safest place for him—at least for a time—Capone actually arranged to have himself arrested in May 1929 for carrying an illegal firearm. He was sentenced to a year.

Following his release, President Herbert Hoover personally pressed the Treasury Department to put Capone away for good. After extensive investigation,

the Internal Revenue Service was finally able to prosecute Capone in 1931 for six years of tax evasion. He was sentenced to 11 years in prison and assessed $80,000 in fines and costs. By this time, the syphilis acquired from his years with prostitutes had resulted in paresis, progressively attacking Capone's central nervous system. Paralyzed and almost completely insane, he was paroled from prison in November 1939. He retired to his home in Florida where, in January 1947, suffering from pneumonia, he died of a massive brain hemorrhage.

Further reading: Pasley, Fred. *Al Capone: The Biography of a Self-Made Man* (1930; reprint ed., New York: Ayer, 1992).

Bergreen, Laurence. *Capone: The Man and the Era* (New York: Simon & Schuster, 1994).

Cardozo, Benjamin (1870–1938) One of the most significant Supreme Court justices; joined Associate Justices Harlan Fisk STONE and Louis BRANDEIS in advocating judicial restraint while at the same time establishing several important legal precedents.

A native of New York City, Benjamin Cardozo was born on May 24, 1870, and raised in the traditions of Sephardic Judaism by his parents, whose families had been in North America since the late 1600s. Graduating from Columbia University in 1889, Cardozo earned his master's degree the next year and entered Columbia Law School. By 1891, he was admitted to the bar without ever having graduated from law school. He gained a reputation as a liberal reformer and was elected to the New York Supreme Court in 1913, serving as chief justice of that body beginning in 1926.

It was on the New York bench that Cardozo earned his first renown as a justice, and some legal historians believe that his work on the state court was of greater significance than his career on the U.S. Supreme Court. In 1916, Cardozo wrote his decision in *MacPherson* v. *Buick Motor Company*, concluding that an implied warranty of safety exists between a manufacturer and a consumer, regardless of intermediate ownership by a retailer. This decision still stands as the basis for consumer-manufacturer product and liability guarantee. He later amended *MacPherson* in 1931 to include third-party owners in protection from fraud.

When Associate Justice Oliver Wendell HOLMES resigned from the Supreme Court bench in 1932, President Herbert Hoover nominated Cardozo to fill his spot. Quickly confirmed, Cardozo joined Louis Brandeis and Harlan Stone as advocates of judicial restraint, holding that the courts should follow the legislature's lead. During Franklin Delano ROOSEVELT's administration, Cardozo joined in supporting much of the New Deal legislation, most notably the

Social Security system as a congressional prerogative under the Constitution.

Two cases that particularly marked Cardozo's tenure on the court, both dealing with the Fourteenth Amendment, were *Nixon* v. *Condon* and *Palko* v. *Connecticut*. In *Nixon*, Cardozo ruled that the exclusion of minorities from party primary elections was a violation of the Fourteenth Amendment. In *Palko,* he argued that double jeopardy did not violate the due process clause when applied to the states, noting that the Fourteenth Amendment imposed only those provisions of the Bill of Rights that were "of the very essence of a scheme of ordered liberty," a decision later reversed by the court in *Benton v. Maryland* (1969), which held that double jeopordy was so fundamental that it was a requirement of due process. Much of Cardozo's significance on the federal court lay in his authority as a legal and jurisprudential scholar as well as in the clarity and gravity of his decisions.

Carlos (Ilyich Ramirez Sanchez) (1949–) A Venezuelan assassin known by his alias Carlos, he made history as the first internationally renowned mercenary terrorist. After his dramatic 1975 kidnapping of 81 OPEC oil ministers in Vienna, Carlos collected millions in ransom money and disappeared—though various sightings were subsequently reported, and he was ultimately captured in 1994.

Born in Caracas, Ilyich Ramirez Sanchez was christened with Lenin's patronymic—Ilyich—by his parents, a wealthy, zealously communist lawyer and his socially prominent wife. The youth and his younger brother, Lenin, were sent to Moscow for their secondary education, and Ilyich remained there to attend Patrice Lumumba University, then a common training ground for future military leaders of Third World "liberation" movements. Although Sanchez was eventually expelled from Lumumba, he had already made close contacts with the KGB, the West German Baader-Meinhof group, and other underground political organizations.

In 1969 Sanchez—now called Carlos—moved to London, where he accompanied his mother in the high-profile social whirlwind of diplomatic circles. Early in the 1970s, he began to travel throughout Europe and the Middle East, exploiting his fluency in several languages to forge links with activist groups as diverse as the Japanese Red Army, the Basque separatists, and the Arab *Feyadeen.* It was during this period that he acquired his second nickname, the Jackal, a reference to another violent operative who had once made an attempt on the life of French president Charles DeGaulle. Later, Frederick Forsyth's popular novel, *The Day of the Jackal,* centered on the

attempt on DeGaulle, would be loosely based on the career of Carlos, not on the earlier would-be assassin.

Various explosions, assassinations, and other political exploits—particularly those executed on behalf of the so-called Popular Front for the Liberation of Palestine (PFLP)—were attributed to Carlos and his Paris-based network, which called itself the International Terrorist Collective. As acts of political terrorism increased worldwide, the intelligence departments of a dozen nations hunted Carlos. Although a few of his associates were captured in London and Paris, and a handful of his many false passports were seized among their possessions, Carlos himself persistently eluded the authorities' grasp.

Married to another alleged terrorist, Magdalena Kaupp, Carlos continued to operate for the PFLP and was said to be the organization's premier "hit man." On June 27, 1975, he murdered a Lebanese informer and two French intelligence agents who had come to interrogate him at his Latin Quarter apartment in Paris. Once again, the Jackal vanished from the scene.

But it was on December 12 of that year that Carlos perpetrated his most spectacular crime. On the second day of an international conference in Vienna for the Organization of Petroleum Exporting Countries (OPEC), he led five accomplices in a raid that killed three people and took custody of 81 international delegates. In the name of the "Arm of the Arab Revolution," he demanded that his cadre and their hostages be given safe passage overseas. Austrian and Algerian officials negotiated the release of 41 Austrians who had been taken in the guerrilla attack, and Carlos and the remaining captives were flown to Algiers. There, on the following day, several more "neutral" delegates were let go, and the terrorists flew the plane to Tripoli. On December 30, after the shah of Iran and King Khaled of Saudi Arabia had met the guerrillas' demands with a reported $5 to $50 million in ransom money, the last OPEC ministers were released. Carlos and his men escaped into Libya, via Algiers, unscathed.

The coup earned Sanchez yet another sobriquet, "the superstar of violence," and in the aftermath, rumors flew that Libyan leader Muammer Qaddafi had personally rewarded Carlos with a $2-million-"bonus" for his successful raid. Other sources claimed that Carlos was paid by his clients with a cut of the ransom money. In any case, it was widely believed that the kidnapping operation had benefited from the support, either overt or covert, of numerous anti-Western individuals, organizations, and governments.

The following year, international authorities believed Carlos had masterminded an Air France airliner hijacking by pro-Palestinian forces that culminated at Uganda's Entebbe Airport with a successful Israeli rescue mission on July 4. In early September, West German agents reported spotting the terrorist boarding a plane for Belgrade, where his identity was confirmed and his movements surveilled. But to the angry frustration of the American, French, German, and Austrian intelligence agencies who had urged his immediate arrest, Yugoslav authorities—suddenly claiming mistaken identity—facilitated Sanchez's passage to Baghdad, thereby attracting a storm of speculation about the East European government's own potential political interests.

In the late 1980s, Carlos was reportedly heading the International Faction of Revolutionary Cells, a pro-Palestinian group and a division of the West German Revolutionary Cell organization. Carlos was captured in the Sudan while undergoing plastic surgery in 1993.

Carroll, Joseph F. (1910–91) A former FBI agent and former head of the U.S. Air Force Office of Special Investigations, Carroll was appointed first director of the Defense Intelligence Agency in 1961.

In 1940, Joseph Carroll joined the FBI, leaving the bureau in 1947 to become head of the U.S. Air Force Office of Special Investigations. The OSI was the investigative arm of the Air Force and was involved in espionage, counterintelligence, and internal review. Carroll remained at that post until 1959, when he was appointed chief of staff of the United States Air Force in Europe. In 1961, following the intelligence fiasco that had accompanied the ill-fated Bay of Pigs invasion of Cuba, President Kennedy and Secretary of Defense Robert McNamara chose Carroll to become the head of the newly formed Defense Intelligence Agency, the primary mission of which was to coordinate the activities of the intelligence community in order to eliminate duplication and improve the efficiency of Defense Department information-gathering efforts. Carroll remained at the post during the turbulent 1960s, retiring in 1969.

Casper, Johann Ludwig (1786–1864) Considered one of the first reformers in the field of legal medicine, Casper insisted on maintaining scrupulous scientific methods in its practice.

Johann Casper turned away from the more profitable avenues of fashionable Parisian medicine to dedicate himself to the postmortem examination of criminals and those touched by crime. Laboring in a morgue located in the slums of Paris, Casper worked toward the advancement of forensic pathology.

Casper brought a new thoroughness and rigor of observation to forensic pathology, and his *Forensic*

Dissection, published in 1850, expanded the field beyond its customary use in cases of strangulation and mental disorders. He provided guidelines for a thorough, methodical postmortem, demonstrating how science could be used in the service of law. Casper's uncompromising approach not only expanded his field, but secured a permanent place for forensic pathology in the science of criminology and the legal system.

Cass, Edward R. (1890–1976) Vice chairman of the New York State Commission of Corrections; served the corrections system for more than 60 years, shaping policy and representing the United States at the United Nations First International Prisons Congress in 1955.

Cass was born and raised in New York City and graduated from Trinity School, Cornell University, and the New York School of Social Work. He began his career as a director of boys' camps under the auspices of the New York Children's Aid Society and was director of the Brace Memorial Residence for Boys, a reformatory in Lower Manhattan. Beginning in 1913, he was a guiding force in the Prison Association of New York (later the Correctional Association of New York), becoming its president in 1928. In 1934, Governor Herbert H. Lehman appointed Cass to the State Probation Commission, a post he resigned two years later when he was named to the state Commission of Corrections, an office he held for 37 years.

As a representative of the United States to the First International Prison Congress, held in Geneva in 1955 under the auspices of the United Nations, Cass was instrumental in opposing a move to employ prisoners under a contract system calling for private employers to pay for prisoner labor, thereby giving prisoners an advantage over free labor. Under Cass's influence, the Geneva congress ultimately adopted a resolution favoring the American system, in which prison labor is for the use of the government only.

Cass served on numerous key legislative commissions, including the Commission to Investigate Prison Administration and Construction in 1930 and the Commission to Undertake the Study of the Sex Offender in 1948. He was also a consultant to the Prison Industries Section of the War Production Board during World War II.

Cass retired from the New York State Commission of Corrections on April 23, 1975.

Cecil, R. H. See HEWITT, Cecil Rolph.

Chamberlain, Paul (1941–) Ex-FBI agent who established a multimillion-dollar investigative consulting firm specializing in corporate kidnapping and extortion.

The son of an army master sergeant, Paul Chamberlain had planned a medical career. While his father was stationed near Los Angeles in the early 1960s, Chamberlain picked up a job as a part-time clerk in the Los Angeles FBI office to help pay for medical school. Within days of taking the job, Chamberlain abandoned medical school and made plans to join the bureau. He enrolled in the FBI Academy at Quantico, Virginia, graduated in 1965, and was posted to Tulsa, Oklahoma, and San Antonio, Texas, before being stationed back where he had started, in Los Angeles. Eventually Chamberlain was assigned to the kidnapping division, and in 1980 he was put on the Stalford case, the abduction of the four-year-old son of a wealthy Beverly Hills banker. Chamberlain recovered the boy unharmed, and the family, to show its gratitude, offered to bankroll Chamberlain's investigative consulting firm.

Chamberlain left the FBI, and with $500,000 he established Paul Chamberlain International as a one-man operation in 1981. Within 10 years, PCI had 33 full-time employees, as well as more than 50 field consultants, and was a $10 million company. Chamberlain specialized in corporate kidnapping and extortion, a field that gained significant publicity in recent years when a number of corporate executives were the targets of kidnapping schemes. Chamberlain has also undertaken sophisticated financial investigations and has consulted with his former colleagues at the FBI in numerous investigations surrounding collapsed savings and loan corporations in the aftermath of the S&L debacle of the 1980s. The distinguished British insurance underwriter Lloyd's of London has retained Chamberlain on several occasions.

Chandler, George Fletcher (1872–1964)
The organizer of the New York State Police and also its first superintendent.

A native of New York state, George Chandler attended Syracuse University for two years before deciding to pursue a career in medicine at the College of Physicians and Surgeons of Columbia University. He graduated in 1895 and stayed in New York City to practice for five years before moving up the Hudson River to Kingston. In 1906, Chandler joined the New York National Guard as first lieutenant and assistant surgeon, finally achieving the rank of captain in 1910. After graduating from officer candidate school at Fort Leavenworth in 1915, Chandler served on the Mexican border during the campaign against Pancho Villa in 1916–17. After the United States entered World War I, Chandler served as a surgery instructor in Chattanooga, Tennessee.

When a brutal murder committed in a rural area of New York in 1913 publicly demonstrated the inadequacy of local law-enforcement officials to deal with serious crime, agitation for a state police force began. After much political posturing and argument, the New York State Police was finally created in 1917, and Governor Charles Whitman named Chandler as the body's first superintendent.

Chandler immediately set about writing training manuals, designing uniforms, purchasing horses, and delineating jurisdictional lines. Although he resigned his position in 1923 to return to his medical practice, he had placed the fledgling state police on a firm footing with a solid corps of leaders and a strong group of political supporters in the state legislature.

Chenkin, George (1897–1962)
A legendary private investigator from New York City who earned his reputation through dogged determination and keen observation.

A native of New York's tough Lower East Side, young George Chenkin became interested in law enforcement when he befriended a beat cop who had a penchant for gefilte fish smothered in ketchup, a delicacy in which George's mother specialized. George never grew past five feet, five inches tall, well below the minimum standard for the New York Police Department. After a short stint in the army during World War I, Chenkin took a low-paying job as a parole officer on the Lower East Side; it was the only job he could get in law enforcement. He proved to be one of the best parole officers ever. Most officers assigned to the Lower East Side were content with the scheduled office visits of the district's myriad criminals, and even then they could not keep up with them all. Chenkin, however, chose to hit the streets, making unannounced home, work, and social-scene visits. This resulted in such an increase in convictions for parole violations that gang lords put a $5,000 bounty on his head. As a parole officer, Chenkin broke up two narcotics rings and a movie house robbery ring, and also solved several murders—some 256 cases in all.

Chenkin's successes as a parole officer led an insurance company to approach him as an investigator of insurance fraud during the late 1940s. Chenkin found the criminals a little stupider, the work a little easier, and the money a lot better. He quickly established himself as the industry's premier investigator of fraud and broke up several rings that perpetrated insurance fraud on a large scale. He also did consulting work for the police, earning a reputation as a problem solver. The Queens County district attorney became so tired of asking to borrow Chenkin that he hired him as a special county detective during the early

1950s, a unique position in which he continued to compile a remarkable investigative record.

Cherrill, Fred (1892–1964) Scotland Yard's leading fingerprint expert in the first half of the 20th century was able to match thousands of prints from memory.

Fascinated with the science of fingerprinting from the earliest days of his London childhood, Fred Cherrill studied the history of the process and revered its founders. From childhood, he knew that he wanted to become a police officer. His parents, however, had in mind for him a career as an artist, and Cherrill was enrolled at Oxford to study painting and sculpture. After a severe illness forced him to withdraw from the university for a time, he spent much of his recuperation in a hospital bed adjacent to a former police officer, who regaled him with tales of shrewd criminals and crafty detective work. This encounter set Cherrill back on the course of police work, and his parents reluctantly gave in to his ambition. In 1914, he was appointed a constable in the London Metropolitan Police Force.

Once on the job, Cherrill found that walking a beat was not nearly as fascinating as he had envisioned. He was allowed to do little investigative work on his own, but he bided his time, and in 1920 he was finally promoted to the Fingerprint Department of Scotland Yard. Although the principles of print identification were firmly established, the field was still developing as a standard investigative tool. Cherrill's work did much to pioneer the science, especially in his introduction of the single-print method in 1930. The old method of cataloging and filing prints by all 10 fingers was cumbersome and time-consuming, so Cherrill developed a system by which each print was cataloged and filed separately. Cherrill's reputation quickly grew, and he was often the star witness for the prosecution, instrumental in the solution of some of the most sensational murder cases in London at the time.

One of Cherrill's greatest assets was his ability to hold thousands of prints in his memory, often being able instantly to identify a print at a crime scene. Those he was not able to identify immediately, he usually could quickly locate in his single-print files.

During his tenure at Scotland Yard, more than 2 million fingerprints were collected. In 1938, Cherrill was promoted to bureau chief of the Fingerprint Division, a position he held until his retirement from police work in 1953.

Childs, Sir Wyndham (1876–1946) Combining legal training with a military background, Childs reformed military justice in England and went on to become assistant commissioner of police, responsible for anti-espionage and anti-terrorist operations.

Childs was born on December 15, 1876, in Cornwall, the son of a solicitor (lawyer), to whom he apprenticed. With the outbreak of the Boer War, Childs joined the army and served through the Boer period and into World War I. Early in the war, he drafted the army's Suspension of Sentences Act, which enabled offenders to be kept in the trenches rather than being sent home for imprisonment. This significantly reduced the incidence of crime in the army, since a number of men deliberately committed offenses in order to be removed from the dangers of the front.

Childs's next action in the field of military justice was in the treatment of conscientious objectors. As a military man, Childs tended to be resentful of COs, yet he also reformed the military's treatment of them, ensuring that they were neither physically coerced nor abused.

In 1921, Childs left military service to become assistant commissioner of police under Sir William Horwood. He was given command of the Special Branch of Scotland Yard, which was in charge of combating subversion, terrorism, and espionage. He reorganized this department into an effective force against Irish republican terrorists as well as postwar communists active in England. Much of his activity involved the suppression of the illegal arms trade within England. In 1927, the Special Branch staged a spectacular raid on the Russian Trade Delegation, uncovering a network of Soviet spies, which resulted in the severance of diplomatic relations between Great Britain and the Soviet Union. A 1928 operation resulted in the deportation of Prince Carol, later king of Rumania, for "plotting to obtain the Rumanian throne on English soil."

Like many police officials charged with counterespionage and political responsibilities, Childs was a controversial figure. He resigned from Scotland Yard in 1928, after seven years of service.

Churchill, Robert (1886–1958) Celebrated firearms expert for Scotland Yard and the first to introduce scientific ballistics into the Old Bailey.

An apprentice gunsmith, Robert Churchill inherited a gunmaking shop from his uncle in 1910, and he practiced gunsmithing, in one form or another, for his entire life. The shop he inherited had been known mainly for producing cheap pigeon-hunting guns, but he turned it into one of England's leading high-quality smithies. It was his intimate knowledge of firearms that led to Churchill's becoming one of the greatest ballistics experts of his time.

Shortly after he inherited the smithy, Churchill was called upon for the first time to testify as an expert witness in a case involving firearms. Afterward, he was called on with increasing frequency. Before testifying at any trial, Churchill experimented in his own shop and was usually intimately familiar with the firearm he would be testifying about. He earned a tremendous reputation, although the few mistakes he did make were compounded by his frankly obnoxious air of self-assurance on the stand.

Churchill's lasting reputation was made by a sensational murder case in 1927. When a chief constable was found murdered, and the few clues were a spent shell casing and three slugs, Scotland Yard called in the gunsmith. Just prior to the case, Churchill had ordered a custom-built comparison microscope, which allowed him to examine and compare two specimens simultaneously. This innovation proved invaluable. After comparing the recovered slugs with those of the suspected murder weapon, Churchill was able to match the two almost immediately, something that had previously taken days of tedious work. In April 1928, the case went to trial at the Old Bailey, and, for the first time, modern ballistic science played a role in a criminal prosecution.

Cicourel, Aaron V. (1928–) Offered a radical social reinterpretation of the standard models of juvenile delinquency.

Aaron Cicourel received his undergraduate training at the University of California, Los Angeles, where he also earned a master's degree in sociology. He took his doctorate at Cornell University in 1957 and went on to teach at Northwestern University before moving back to the West, where he taught in several schools of the University of California system, finally settling in at the University of California, San Diego.

Most of Cicourel's work has been devoted to deviance, and in 1968, having rethought the accepted social models for juvenile delinquency, he published the *Social Organization of Juvenile Justice*. Cicourel challenged the accepted notion that deviance is a natural and inevitable part of an ordered social structure, in the same way that such structures produce individuals who are weak, strong, rich, or poor. Cicourel conceded that deviance could not be totally eliminated, but he argued that the very aspects of society that strive to correct deviance are too often the forces that perpetuate it. Cicourel therefore argued for greater coordination among such social bodies as police, church, schools, and the family in order to redefine, prevent, and correct deviance.

Cizanckas, Victor I. (1937–80) Appointed police chief for life in Stamford, Connecticut, Cizanckas was hired to clean up the town's rampant corruption and graft.

Reminiscent of the graft charges in San Francisco under "Boss" Abe Ruef and in New York under Jimmy WALKER earlier in the century, the allegations made against the Stamford, Connecticut, police department in the 1970s seemed to grow seamier by the day. After the police chief was forced to resign, city officials looked for an outsider to clean house. They settled on the chief of the Menlo Park, California, department, Victor Cizanckas.

A lifelong law enforcement officer, Cizanckas was appointed Stamford's chief for life in 1977 in an effort to insulate him from political pressures and to show how serious the city was about cleaning out the corruption. When he reported to work, what he discovered (as he put it) "traumatized" him. Although not everyone in the department was corrupt, almost every aspect of operations was to some degree compromised. Before he could even begin his own investigation, Cizanckas's first order of business was to work with the U.S. attorney brought in to investigate— among other crimes—coercion and payoffs to gamblers and drug dealers. The new chief cited over $35 million in illegal gambling traffic that went through Stamford, saying that the corrupt practices were "not very subtle."

Cizanckas forced out many career officers who were implicated, stating that they were so inbred to the system that rehabilitation was impossible. He abolished the entire Traffic Division, declaring that "traffic was not a police function." That division had been one of the major sources for corruption, with officers taking Mafia-style cuts off the top for every streetlight or stop sign installed in "their" neighborhood and stealing hundreds of thousands of dollars in equipment. Cizanckas also hired civilians to replace police officers in jobs ranging from dispatcher to mail clerk, thereby releasing more uniformed officers for field work.

The patrolmen's union voiced serious opposition to Cizanckas and his policies, but, following extended meetings, even the union was persuaded to accept reform.

Cizanckas's life term proved all too brief. He died in his sleep in 1980, aged 43, after having served only three years. This brief span stands, however, as an example of what can be done, when necessary, to reform even deeply corrupt police agencies.

Clark, (William) Ramsey (1927–) The liberal Clark was attorney general during the administration of President Lyndon Baines JOHNSON.

Ramsey Clark was born in Dallas, Texas, on December 18, 1927 and was educated at the University of Texas and the University of Chicago, receiving from the latter institution both an M.A. in American history and a J.D. degree in December of 1950. Clark's entire family was steeped in legal tradition, and he was the son of Tom Campbell CLARK, who served as U.S.

attorney general and, later, as an associate justice of the Supreme Court. Clark practiced law privately, then went to work for the U.S. Department of Justice before fellow Texan Lyndon B. Johnson appointed him attorney general in 1967.

During his time at the U.S. Department of Justice before he became attorney general, Clark undertook several assignments, most notably in civil rights. After the riots at the University of Mississippi in 1962, Clark arrived on the campus as head of the federal forces called in to restore order. In 1963, he traveled to Birmingham when racial tensions led to violence. That same year he trekked across the South, meeting with school officials and helping work through the problems of desegregation. To Clark goes much of the credit for formulating the 1964 Civil Rights Act, and in the spring of 1965 he traveled once again to the South, this time to Selma, Alabama. Now an assistant attorney general, he served as chief officer of the federal forces sent to accompany the march from Selma to Montgomery led by the Rev. Martin Luther King, Jr.

Not surprisingly, as attorney general, Clark was responsible for administering the law-enforcement aspects of much of what was left of Johnson's "Great Society" programs, especially the prosecution of organized crime and the enforcement of civil rights law. Convinced that the Justice Department should play an active role in civil rights, he immediately upon assuming office initiated the first law suit to force a school district (in Dale County, Alabama) to comply with the desegregation plans it promised to follow when applying for federal funds. He championed legislation to make the purchase of firearms more difficult, introducing a Johnson administration–sponsored bill to regulate the importation, interstate shipment, and sale of guns. Favoring greater federal support and guidance for local law enforcement, Clark was vehemently opposed to wiretapping and bugging by police. He issued sweeping regulations denying the use of wiretapping to—and, indeed, forbidding eavesdropping of any kind by—federal agents, except in special cases involving national security. Clark was a staunch suporter of the then recent Supreme Court decision in *Miranda* vs. *Arizona* (1966; see MIRANDA).

When he had first come to the Justice Department, Clark served under Attorney General Robert Kennedy, whom President Johnson had asked to remain in office after the assassination of his brother, John F. Kennedy. Robert Kennedy and Johnson had never gotten along, and the animosity between the two men became public after Kennedy resigned and broke with the president over his escalation of the Vietnam War. A friend of Kennedy's, Clark—like some other members of the Johnson administration—grew increas-ingly distant from the president over his obsessive insistence on continuing to prosecute the war. Clark became more and more vocal in his opposition to the war after he resigned from office in 1969 at the end of Johnson's term of office. In 1972 he made a highly publicized and controversial visit to North Vietnam, and in 1974 he ran for a Senate seat from New York, but was defeated. In 1976 he failed to gain the Democratic party's nomination in the senatorial race.

In 1970 Clark published *Crime in America,* in which he revealed himself to be a loose follower of Emile DURKHEIM, a sociologist who held that America was a criminogenic society, i.e., one in which crime-inducing forces are inherent in its dominant social structures. Clark's variation on the theme held that crime in the United States lay rooted in two moral deficiencies of American society—"the apathy of affluence" and "narrow self-interest." These faults lay behind the fundamental social problems related directly to crime—poverty, drugs, abundant and cheap weapons, ineffective courts and prison systems, and the rotten relationships between police and communities. For Clark, the only solution lay in changing radically America's basic institutions, including those dealing with education, health care, housing, and race relations.

Clark continued his defiant leadership of liberal causes in 1980, when he and a group of 10 other Americans defied a presidential ban on travel to Iran to attend a conference there. In Iran, he argued for the release of the American hostages who had been taken captive and held by militant Iranian "students."

Clark, Tom Campbell (1899–1977)

As U.S. attorney general, Clark used his office to root out suspected Communists and subversives.

A native of Dallas, Texas (born September 23, 1899), Tom Campbell Clark graduated from the University of Texas in 1922 after having returned there to study law following service in the army during World War I. He was appointed U.S. attorney general by President Harry S Truman in 1945, and, during the early Cold War years, he worked closely with the U.S. Immigration and Naturalization Service (INS) to identify and deport political subversives. Not since the days of Mitchell A PALMER's infamous "Red Scare" raids of the late teens and early twenties had the Justice Department worked so closely with the INS to achieve essentially political ends. Not only did Campbell actively prosecute leaders of the American Communist Party, he drew up the first attorney general's blacklist of known subversive organizations in 1947. Many jurists questioned the constitutionality of Clark's actions.

Clark resigned as attorney general in 1949, when President Truman nominated him as an associate justice of the Supreme Court. Having already gained a reputation for his aggressive antisubversive programs and for broadening the powers of the FBI when he was attorney general, Clark did not disappoint his champions after he began sitting on the federal bench. He made his always strong anti-Communist views abundantly clear throughout the 1950s in such cases as *Irvine* vs. *California* (1954) and *Breihaupt* vs. *Abram* (1957). Not surprisingly he remained the scourge of dissenters on into the 1960s, with his frequent dissents from the liberal majority under Chief Justice Earl Warren. Though such opinions put him at odds with Warren most of the time, in one area the two men proved surprisingly compatible. Clark was an avid supporter of civil liberties. In the famed *Mapp* vs. *Ohio* (1961), he wrote the majority opinion that evidence obtained by illegal search and seizure could not be used in state courts, thus vastly expanding the constitutional protections afforded to defendants. In 1963, he again penned a liberal majority opinion, prohibiting (in *School District of Abington* vs. *Schempp*) the reading of the Bible in public schools. And in 1964, he wrote three civil rights opinions that laid the foundation for most if not all the subsequent civil rights legal battles to come, many of them championed by his son, soon-to-be attorney general Ramsey Clark.

When Ramsey Clark was appointed U.S. attorney general in 1967, the old man promptly resigned from the Supreme Court to avoid not merely the possibility but also the least appearance of a confict of interest. Tom Campbell Clark died on June 13, 1977.

Clum, John P. (1851–1932)

A U.S. Indian agent who used a reservation police force made up of Indians to control most of the Apaches in Arizona, including the legendary Geronimo.

A native of New York state, John Clum spent a year at Rutgers College in New Jersey before enlisting in the U.S. Army Signal Service, which posted him to a weather station in Santa Fe, New Mexico, in November 1871. In February 1874, he became an agent for what was then called the Indian Service at the Apache San Carlos Reservation on the Gila River. Clum's chief priority at the army-run San Carlos Reservation was to reestablish civilian control and reduce the inflammatory military presence. In order to accomplish this, he developed the concept of an Indian police force, using for this purpose the Indian scouts already in service to the army. Clum claimed to be the first to employ Indians in this manner. Although there may, in fact, have been other Indian-staffed policing organizations at this time, none were as formally constituted or as effective.

Unlike many Indian agents, who were often corrupt, incompetent, or both, Clum truly strove to improve life on the reservation. He was able to persuade the government to remove all military troops from San Carlos, and his administration of the reservation was so impressive under his Indian police that the Indian Service transferred Apaches from other reservations to San Carlos, thereby tripling its original population and greatly overcrowding it.

After his initial success, Clum became engaged in a hot controversy with the army, which wanted to reassert control over the reservations. Clum argued that the military povoked nothing but resentment and animosity on the part of the Indians, but most local whites opposed Clum's program of civilian control largely because they feared the consequences of arming a growing Indian police force. At the height of this debate, Clum proved his effectiveness by successfully capturing the elusive Apache raider Geronimo, whom he brought onto the reservation in April 1877. But this was to be virtually Clum's last official action. Sensing the futility of his cause, Clum resigned in July 1877 after his offer to administer all the Arizona Apaches was rejected.

Clum lived in various locations throughout the West until he died in Los Angeles in 1932.

Further reading: Clum, Woodworth, *Apache Agent: The Story of John P. Clum* (Lincoln: University of Nebraska Press 1978, c1936).

Hagan, William T., *Indian Police and Judges* (New Haven: Yale University Press, 1966).

Coetzee, Johann (1929–)

South Africa's commissioner of police during the final, brutal days of apartheid (government-mandated racial segregation).

Little is known about Coetzee's early life, except that he was raised in one of the rural parts of South Africa. He joined the mounted police in 1946 and subsequently joined the Security Police, an undercover force mainly responsible for infiltrating the Communist Party and other opposition groups. Coetzee was a scholarly man who was reportedly an avid student of ancient Greek philosophy and who (also reportedly) earned a Ph.D. in political science (his dissertation is said to have been on Leon Trotsky). He was an expert on international communism.

In June 1983, Coetzee was named commissioner of police, the third successive commissioner drawn from the ranks of the Security Police. The 44,000-man police force Coetzee headed was charged with enforcing South Africa's long-enduring policy of apartheid, the policy of "separate development," a rigid system of racial segregation designed to maintain white supremacy. Although it had been a de facto policy since the late 19th century, it became official government policy only when the National Party came to power in 1948.

Under Coetzee, the South African police used brutal measures to enforce apartheid and to root out and suppress its opponents. Acting under "emergency powers" granted in 1985, Coetzee's police staged pre-dawn raids on suspected urban guerrillas and made mass arrests, detaining hundreds without hearing or trial. Police seized women and children as hostages to exchange for anti-apartheid activists. The secret police in particular were feared for tactics that included torture and assassination. Under Coetzee, a so-called "Third Force" was formed, with the secret mission of eliminating—through assassination—key anti-apartheid leaders.

With the repeal of the last of the apartheid laws in 1991, Coetzee stepped down as police commissioner. He held no position in the government led by black activist Nelson Mandela.

Cohen, Louis Harold (1906–55) Coauthor of *Murder, Madness and the Law,* which was instrumental in establishing criteria for judging criminal insanity.

A native of New Haven, Connecticut, Louis Cohen was very much a product of Yale University, earning his bachelor's, master's, Ph.D., and M.D. degrees there during the late 1920s and early 1930s. Cohen was an academic and clinician, who was also frequently called upon to testify in criminal cases as an expert in legal psychiatry.

Cohen's writings stressed the responsibility of the psychiatrist not only to the mentally ill but also to society in general. He believed that the psychiatrist had an obligation to monitor the emotional well-being of society. Most significantly for the law, Cohen, with Dr. Thomas Coffin, undertook an extensive study of various cases of criminal insanity in an effort to rationalize definitions of and criteria for judging a defendant criminally insane. The product of this collaboration was *Murder, Madness and the Law* (1952), a detailed examination of the mental processes of psychotic murder through 18 case studies. Cohen and Coffin concluded that, frequently, victims of psychotic murderers were friends or family, the crime was unplanned, and it usually occurred in broad daylight with a makeshift weapon. The murder was never perpetrated for any rational gain such as money or prestige, and the murderer usually did not care about being arrested.

Cohen, Mickey (1913–76) Highly visible, prototypical West Coast gangster who served as bodyguard to Benjamin "Bugsy" Siegel.

The diminutive 5-foot 5-inch Mickey Cohen was not a major figure in organized crime, but he was

Although he was relatively small time, Mickey Cohen—shown here being interviewed, a frequent occurrence—was a flashy, high-profile California mobster. (Courtesy of the Library of Congress)

the kind of flash-dressing, hot-headed, and vulgar loudmouth that came to symbolize the gangsters of the late 1940s and 1950s. He was Bugsy Siegel's long-time bodyguard, and when Siegel was murdered at the behest of Charles "Lucky" LUCIANO and other Mob leaders, Cohen's impotent reaction was to stride into the lobby of the hotel in which he believed the killers were lodged and repeatedly fire his revolver into the ceiling.

Following Siegel's assassination, Cohen, marked for death himself, cowered inside his Los Angeles home, which was twice bombed. He transformed the home into a veritable fortress and maintained a state-of-the-art siege defense, with floodlights, alarm systems, and an arsenal of weapons, reportedly stored alongside some 200 custom-tailored suits he had made in emulation of the stylish Siegel.

Part of Cohen's high-profile identity came from his whining to the press that his underworld associates stalked, threatened, and persecuted him—though, true to the gangsters' code of silence, he refused to name names. When the luckless Cohen employed a bodyguard, the man, John Stompanato, was himself killed—not by gangsters but by Cheryl Crane, the teenage daughter of actress Lana Turner. Cohen then found himself stuck with paying Stompanato's funeral expenses, purchased the cheapest coffin available—and then presented the media with Lana Turner's love letters to Stompanato, apparently just to be mean.

Despite the threats against him, Cohen lived quite well off the gambling operations he had inherited from Siegel, but, like many other Mob figures before him, he was eventually convicted of income tax evasion. Cohen served four years in prison, only to be convicted a second time and sentenced to another 10 years. During his incarceration, he was attacked by another inmate, who fractured his skull with a pipe. Cohen recovered and was released in 1972, when he began a poorly organized and ineffectual campaign against prison abuses. He died in 1974 of a heart attack.

Colburn, Wayne B. (1907–83) As head of the U.S. Marshals Service from 1970 to 1976, Colburn rehabilitated the scandal-ridden agency and took it into a controversial confrontation with Native American protestors at Wounded Knee, South Dakota, in 1973.

Wayne B. Colburn was a career police officer who was appointed the U.S. marshal for the southern district of California in 1962. When Marshals Service director Carl Turner was forced to resign in 1969 because of charges of graft and corruption, Attorney General John Mitchell appointed Colburn to replace him in January 1970.

Colburn vigorously set about reforming the ailing agency, defining new missions for it (including judicial security, air piracy, and sensitive witness security), converting the agency to civil service status, establishing new promotion standards for personnel, and securing federal bureau status, placing it on a par with other justice department law enforcement agencies.

Colburn was largely successful in professionalizing the U.S. Marshals Service, although the fight to attain bureau status became a political football during the tumultuous Watergate years. President Nixon's attorney general, Richard Kleindienst, who had replaced Mitchell, granted it bureau status on May 10, 1973. When he was forced to resign during the Watergate scandal, his replacement, Elliot Richardson, seeking to reduce the size of the federal government, revoked the bureau status on October 17, 1973. Richardson himself resigned in protest over Nixon's dismissal of the Watergate special prosecutor, and his successor, William Saxbe, reestablished the Marshals Service as a federal bureau in May 1974. Colburn, however, never succeeded in removing the nomination of U.S. marshals from the political arena; their nomination remained the province of individual U.S. senators.

Part of Colburn's reform efforts included refashioning the Marshals Service as a "professional, semimilitary oriented law enforcement" force, and in 1971 Colburn created the Special Operations Group (SOG) within the service. SOG was an elite body of about a hundred uniformed officers whose mission was to respond in times of national emergency and civil crisis. It was SOG that evicted militant members of the American Indian Movement (AIM) from the Twin Cities Naval Air Station, which they occupied early in the summer of 1971. SOG also ended AIM's 19-month occupation of the former federal prison at Alcatraz Island in San Francisco Bay on June 11, 1971.

SOG was called to Wounded Knee, South Dakota, when AIM took over and occupied the Bureau of Indian Affairs facilities at the Pine Ridge Reservation during a 71-day standoff in 1973. An occupation and hostage situation developed at this emotionally charged site, where, on December 29, 1890, hundreds of Sioux men, women, and children had been killed by U.S. Army forces, effectively bringing to a bloody end the Sioux Wars for the Black Hills and, indeed, 400 years of warfare between whites and Indians in the New World. The Wounded Knee occupation developed into a full-scale siege, with SOG and FBI agents entrenched around the hamlet and gunfire traded nightly. Two Indians were killed, and one marshal, Lloyd H. Grimm, was permanently paralyzed by a spinal wound. Although Colburn favored retaking Wounded Knee by storm, using armored personnel carriers, Attorney General Kleindienst insisted on negotiation, and the occupation was ended on May 7. The Marshals Service was recognized for its discipline and restraint during the crisis.

After Wounded Knee, Colburn introduced additional reforms and upgrades of the Marshals Service, including government vehicles (previously, officers had used their own cars, for which they were compensated), sophisticated communications, and higher training standards for all personnel. Colburn retired in May 1976, and he died at his home in Chula Vista, California, on June 21, 1983.

Colden, Cadwallader (1688–1776) Forensic pathologist, historian, and New York Loyalist politician who urged universal standards regarding postmortem examination.

Born in Ireland while his mother was traveling there, Cadwallader Colden was a Scotsman who took a bachelor's degree from the University of Edinburgh in 1705 and went to London to study medicine. Feeling that his professional opportunities would be greater in the colonies, Colden left for Philadelphia in 1710, where he began practicing medicine and running a small mercantile business.

Although Colden would leave Philadelphia in 1718 for New York, where he was surveyor general for the Crown, it was in Philadelphia that he achieved some note in the field of medicine. The practice of postmortem examination had been steadily gaining approval in the medical and legal professions; however, there were no set standards of procedure, nor was there any legislation in place mandating such examinations in suspicious cases. Colden was one of the first to lobby for legislation, not only to require autopsies in certain instances but also to set specific procedural guidelines, including the examination of all organs.

Colden's authority in the medical field was diminished somewhat after his move to New York. As an agent of the Crown and a fierce supporter of the king, Colden faced strong opposition from patriots after the imposition of the Stamp Act. Colden retired to his estate on Long Island and died in September 1776.

Coleman, William Tell (1824–93) Important San Francisco merchant and vigilante leader during the city's turbulent 1850s.

Born in Kentucky, William Tell Coleman migrated to the West in the 1840s, settling in boisterous San Francisco in 1850, where he formed the merchandising firm of William T. Coleman & Co. San Francisco at the time was beset by rampant organized criminal activity that was allowed to thrive by corrupt public officials. After several highly publicized killings and other acts by the notorious criminal gang known as the Hounds, against whom the corrupt and ineffective police were helpless, Coleman organized and headed San Francisco's first Committee of Vigilance in 1851.

The purpose of the committee was to establish law and order in the town. Vigilance committees had long been associated with the American frontier, but most so-called vigilance committees had merely been unorganized shoot-to-kill purveyors of mob justice. In contrast, Coleman's committee sought to bring the accused to a "court" made up of other committee members. Defendants were given a trial, and either acquitted or summarily hanged.

Coleman's original vigilance committee faded soon after it was formed, but in 1856 the murder of renegade journalist James King brought a new public outcry for justice and sparked the resurgence of the Committee of Vigilance. Coleman was made president of the executive committee and proceeded to organize a group of 25 armed companies, which surrounded the jailhouse and demanded the release of two suspects in the slaying, whom the vigilantes wanted to try in their own "court." The sheriff backed down, and both men were tried and hanged.

As late as 1877, the group again reformed under Coleman, who organized more than 5,500 men, nicknamed the "Pick Handle Brigade" after the weapons they wielded. This time, the committee had as its purpose the maintenance of law and order and the protection of Chinese immigrants, who were perpetually the targets of violent racist attacks.

Coleman's activities brought him into national prominence, and there was even a movement to secure for him a nomination as a presidential candidate in 1884. Business reverses in 1886 sent Coleman into

William Tell Coleman organized San Francisco's first vigilante committee during the city's turbulent 1850s. (Courtesy of the Society of California Pioneers)

bankruptcy, and although he was obligated to pay his creditors only 40 cents on the dollar, the high-minded Coleman pledged to make good on his debts 100%. This he did by the year before he died.

Today, the idea of vigilante justice seems a manifest evil, yet for William Tell Coleman vigilante justice was based on the principle that the power of government comes from the people and that, therefore, the people have a right to seize and exercise power when duly constituted authorities fail in their duties.

Further reading: Scherers, James A., *Lion of the Vigilantes* (Indianapolis: Bobbs-Merrill, 1939).

Coll, Vincent "Mad Dog" (1908–32) As his moniker suggests, Coll was a killer legendary even in organized crime for his viciousness.

A native of New York City's notorious Hell's Kitchen neighborhood, Coll was the son of Irish immigrants. Largely uneducated, he became a pushcart thief, pilfering from neighborhood pushcart merchants, at an early age and seemingly delighted in

The press branded Vincent Coll "Mad Dog" after a mob hit he engineered resulted in the death of a five-year-old child and the wounding of other bystanders. (Courtesy of the Library of Congress)

dealing severe beatings to other boys on the slightest pretext. While still a juvenile, he was involved in a number of street gang deaths and was sent to the state reformatory at Elmira for robbery. Upon his release, he was hired by Dutch SCHULTZ as strongarm.

By 1930, Coll was no longer content with his $150-a-week salary from Schultz and demanded a percentage of the bootlegging take. The Dutchman refused, and Coll collected his brother Peter, Frank Giordano, Arthur Palumbo, and others in order to set up his own operation, boldly hijacking Schultz's beer and liquor trucks. Determined to unseat Schultz, Coll tried to hire Vincent Barrelli, Schultz's main connection to Canadian rum-runners. When Barrelli refused, Coll personally executed him, together with his girlfriend. Coll continued trying to recruit the Dutchman's personnel and to prey upon his business. In 1931 Schultz actually walked into the Morrisania precinct station in the Bronx—the borough in which both he and Coll were headquartered—and attempted to bribe the detectives into killing Coll.

The officers declined the proposition, but Dutch Schultz was by no means the only New York gangster who wanted Coll dead. Owney "The Killer" MADDEN swore vengeance on Mad Dog after Coll kidnapped his partner, George Jean "Big Frenchy" DeMange, on June 15, 1931, and held him for $35,000 ransom—at the time, an unheard of move in the world of organized crime.

It was Coll's brother Peter who fell first, the victim of Schultz's goons. Mad Dog swore vengeance, and Schultz responded by placing a $50,000 price on Coll's head. Coll and his gang struck preemptively on July 28, 1931, against one of the Dutchman's torpedoes, Joey Rao, opening up on the gunman and others with submachine guns in front of the Helmar Social Club at 208 East 107th Street. The intended targets scattered for cover, but the bullets found their mark among a group of children playing in the street. A 14-year-old girl, a five-year-old boy, and a three-year-old toddler were gravely wounded. Michael Vengali, age five, was killed.

It was the underworld itself that ratted on Coll for killing children and babies. And the newspapers were quick to hang the "Mad Dog" moniker on him. The gangster was arrested and indicted for the Vengali killing, along with Frank Giordano. Coll hired Samuel LEIBOWITZ, one of the great criminal attorneys of his day (he would become best known for his defense of the Scottsboro Boys in a sensational Southern race-related rape case), who managed to get both gangsters acquitted for lack of evidence.

That left Coll to the vengeance of Schultz, Madden, and other underworld figures, eager to do away with a loose cannon who had turned baby killer. Coll quickly moved to ally himself with Jack "Legs" DIAMOND and Vannie Higgins, enemies of Schultz and Madden, and an all-out gang war began on the streets of Manhattan, resulting in the deaths of at least 15 of Schultz's thugs and drivers.

In October 1931, Frank Giordano and Dominic "Toughy" Ordierno, who had left Schultz to join Coll and Diamond, shot and killed Joseph Mullins, whom Schultz employed as a simple handyman. Witnesses had seen the murder, however, and Giordano and Ordierno were arrested, tried, convicted, and sentenced to the electric chair. Giordano, in a bid to save his life, told the warden that he had seen Coll kill the Vengali boy, and New York governor Franklin D. Roosevelt stayed the execution in order to permit Giordano to testify. It turned out to be unnecessary. On February 7, 1932, Coll strolled out of his apartment in the elegant Cornish Arms Hotel in Manhattan's Chelsea district and went to the London Chemists' Shop to make "business" calls in the public phone booth. Abraham "Bo" Weinberg, one of the

Dutchman's enforcers, entered the drugstore with a tommy gun. Weinberg told everyone in the store to "keep quiet. Keep cool, now." He walked up to the booth and opened fire, sending 15 rounds into the body of Mad Dog Coll.

Collins, Ben (?–1906)   An Indian policeman in the Indian Territory of what later became Oklahoma; later nominated to serve as deputy U.S. marshal for the region—the first Native American so named.

Very little is known about the early life of this Native American. After serving as an Indian policeman in the Oklahoma Indian Territory, Ben Collins was named deputy U.S. marshal for the Emet, Oklahoma, area. His uncompromising approach to his position led to friction with some of the area's more prominent citizens, many of whom were involved in highly questionable business dealings. In 1905, Collins attempted to arrest Port Pruitt, one of Emet's wealthiest residents. Pruitt resisted and drew his gun on Collins, who responded in kind, fired, and wounded Pruitt. Pruitt was charged with intent to murder, but the charges were dropped, and he vowed revenge on Collins. The following year, Pruitt and his brother Orr offered a $500 bounty to anyone who would kill Collins. On August 1, 1906, one Killin' Jim Miller collected that fee when he brutally murdered Collins with multiple close-range shotgun blasts to the face and chest.

Colquhoun, Patrick (1745–1820)   One of the early "architects" of the modern police force; author of *A Treatise on the Police of the Metropolis,* published in London in 1796 and one of the founding documents of modern law enforcement.

A native of Scotland, Patrick Colquhoun immigrated to America and lived in the colony of Virginia for seven years before returning to Glasgow, where he was elected chief magistrate in 1782. In 1789, he moved to London and three years later was appointed justice of the peace. Colquhoun had a long-standing friendship with English philosopher Jeremy Bentham, and both men were interested in the pioneering work on London police reform by the Fielding brothers, Henry and John. Drawing on the Fieldings' practical experience as magistrates and on Bentham's theories, Colquhoun wrote his 1796 *Treatise on the Police of the Metropolis.*

Underscoring John Fielding's insistence on the necessity of a professional force, the book also broke new ground by redefining the role of modern police: "By the term police we are to understand all those regulations in a country which apply to the comfort, convenience and safety of the inhabitants." The concept of crime *prevention* was a radical redefinition of the role of the police, whose function traditionally had been to apprehend criminals after the commission of a crime. Colquhoun's work would have a profound influence on Sir Robert Peel, the man who established London's "New Police" in 1829.

Colquhoun was more than a theorist. In 1789, he established the Marine Police on the Thames River, and in less than a year, order was restored to this vital artery of commerce, which had been plagued by piracy. Largely due to the effectiveness of the Marine Police, the West India Company, for example, was able to report a £100,000 increase in its revenues. In 1800 the British government took over full responsibility for the Marine Police Establishment, and Colquhoun retired in 1818.

Patrick Colquhoun, who died in 1820, is commemorated on a mural tablet in St. Margaret's Church, Westminster, as "the originator of the Marine police."

Further Reading: Grant, David Yates. *A Biographical Sketch of the Life and Writings of Patrick Colquhoun* (London: 1818).

Colt, Samuel (1814–62)   Invented the revolving-chamber pistol, the famous six-shooting "equalizer" that won its first adherents in the proving grounds of Texas and the American West.

Born in Hartford, Connecticut, on July 19, 1814, Colt was the son of a well-to-do textile manufacturer and the grandson of Major John Caldwell, an early American luminary in banking, insurance, commerce, and state politics. The family fortunes suffered in the financially ruinous War of 1812, however, and Samuel was obliged to go to work at an early age. After helping out at his family's Hartford textile mill and studying briefly at a school in Amherst, the 13-year-old shipped out as a seaman.

During a voyage to Calcutta, Colt occupied his spare time by carving a rough wooden model of a new sort of pistol, one whose chamber could hold several bullets—rather than just a single shot—then align and fire them in rapid succession. When he returned to the States, he again joined the family mill, learned some chemistry pertinent to its affairs, and began to fashion working models of his innovative weapon. Although one of these early prototypes blew up, Colt persisted and refined his design.

Now 18 and anxious to raise capital for his invention, Colt hit the road as a popular lecturer—"Dr. Coult"—and gave public demonstrations of the "laughing gas" nitrous oxide, at the time a popular novelty. He traveled widely, collecting admission to his show, and in three years he was ready to obtain his first patents—in Britain and France (1835) and then in the United States (1836)—for the multi-chamber, rotating cylinder that discharged through his gun's single barrel.

Colt's pistol, and this time endorsed it unanimously. But with sales still insufficient, the entrepreneur was forced to close shop two years later. Once again, Colt applied himself to exploring new technology. Experimenting in the telegraphy business in 1843, he created the first waterproof electric cable and connected New York City with stations on Fire Island and Coney Island. Independently, he invented an underwater mine for harbor defense, foretold the development of the modern torpedo, and, using electric batteries and explosive charges, sunk ships via remote control, another prescient innovation. Once more he approached the U.S. military with his marvels; once more it short-sightedly declined them.

But in 1847, General Zachary Taylor persuaded the army to purchase 1,000 Colt revolvers for use in the Mexican-American War then under way. The inventor quickly improvised production facilities in Eli Whitney's Connecticut factory, and together they filled the army's order with Colt's latest, upgraded model of the weapon. The following year Colt was able again to establish his own plant, in Hartford, Connecticut. Now customers from all over the globe clamored for his product, and Colt's Patent Fire-Arms Manufacturing Company became the largest private armory in the world.

Colt himself died on January 10, 1862, but his widow, Elizabeth (née Jarvis), took over, and the company lived on. Colt pistols were the dominant handgun throughout the Civil War, and the "Peacemaker" revolver model, released in 1873, became the instrument of choice for settlers, townsmen, and early law enforcers of the far American West.

Further reading: Rohan, Jack, *Yankee Arms Maker: The Story of Sam Colt and His Six-Shot Peacemaker* (New York: Harper and Brothers, 1953).

Comstock, Anthony (1844–1915) A fundamentalist reformer who used his position as New York City postal inspector to lead a zealous crusade against what he defined as obscene.

A descendant of Christopher Columbus, Anthony Comstock served in the Union Army during the Civil War. He moved to New York in the late 1860s and began working with the YMCA as a crusader against obscenity. Comstock's powerful presence and knack for publicity inspired the 1871 congressional legislation commonly known as the "Comstock Law," barring the transmission of obscene matter through the mail.

Comstock accepted a nonpaying position as a postal inspector to enforce the new legislation. He personally raided illegal pornography shops, abortionists' offices, and anything else he deemed immoral in New York City. In 1873, Comstock organized the New York

Samuel Colt invented the revolving-chamber pistol, the famous six-shooting "equalizer" that helped to "win the West." (Courtesy of the National Archives)

Trusting his motto—"It is better to be at the head of a louse than the tail of a lion"—Colt formed a company in Paterson, New Jersey, to manufacture what he called his "revolver." Business was slow at first, and two U.S. Army boards advised against adopting the weapon, but the Texas Rangers became customers during their territorial campaigns. Decades before Henry Ford developed the assembly line to build his Model T, Colt made streamlined efficiency his factory's goal. Assembly-line machinery, designed and cast on the premises, allowed mass production of the weapon's fully interchangeable parts. Employees also benefited from fairly progressive management, since Colt believed that "workers who have good pay, steady employment, comfortable housing, and plenty of good entertainment and recreation, are more profitable than underpaid, ill-housed, disgruntled wage-slaves whose only diversion is getting drunk on Saturday night." Dedicated, keen-eyed supervisors inspected all output. A breech-loading revolving rifle was added to the wares.

In the winter of 1837, Colt traveled to Florida, and he made more converts there among men fighting the Seminoles. In 1840 another army board reviewed

Society for the Prevention of Vice and used his postal inspector position to spread his moral message.

Comstock's activism prompted him in 1913 to initiate a crusade against Paul Chabas's nude painting *September Morn*, touching off an unending American debate over the definition of obscenity and censorship versus the right to free expression guaranteed by the First Amendment.

Further reading: Bennett, De Rubigne M., *Anthony Comstock: His Career of Cruelty and Crime* (1878; reprint ed., New York: Da Capo, 1971).

Conlisk, James B., Jr. (1899–1984)

Superintendent of the Chicago Police Department during the urban unrest of the late 1960s; drew heavy fire from the media and liberal critics for a "police riot" during the 1968 Democratic National Convention.

The son of a police officer, James Conlisk was a native of Illinois and aspired to follow in his father's footsteps. He achieved that goal in February 1946, when he was named to the Chicago Police Department. Rising in rank steadily, he was appointed superintendent by Mayor Richard J. Daley in 1967. While Chicago was spared some of the early unrest of the civil rights movement, it got more than its share in 1968. In that year, demonstrations against the war in Vietnam and in support of the civil rights movement became increasingly numerous and intense. In this explosive atmosphere, the city hosted the 1968 Democratic National Convention.

The 1968 convention attracted a huge number of college-aged demonstrators, most of whom gathered or camped out in Grant and Lincoln parks along the city's lakefront. It is unclear exactly what Conlisk and his subordinates had planned in terms of crowd control, but it is certain that they were unprepared for the number and perseverance of the demonstrators. Demonstrators taunted police officers, who responded so fiercely that the ensuing melee was immediately dubbed a "police riot." Against a background of demonstrators' chants of "The whole world is watching," television cameras and newspaper photographers documented Chicago police officers pursuing and beating demonstrators and others—for all appearances indiscriminately.

While notables across the country denounced the actions of the police, Mayor Daley defiantly lauded their actions and argued that the demonstrators were professional agitators who had traveled to Chicago specifically to incite a riot. Any action required to restore and maintain order was justified, Daley argued, in light of the near-revolutionary activity taking place. It was later revealed that Conlisk, acting under instructions from Daley, had ordered National Guard troops (brought in to reinforce the Chicago police) to shoot to kill if necessary.

Conlisk managed to survive the political storm, mostly because he had the all-powerful mayor's backing, but in 1973, when 37 officers were indicted on various charges of graft, conspiracy, and bribery—charges unrelated to the 1968 affair—Conlisk stepped down.

Cook, David (1842–1907)

The arrest record of this western lawman peaked at just over 3,000. Cook's memoirs, published in 1897, are a compelling account of law and order in the Wild West.

Born in Indiana, David Cook went west at age 17, signing up with a Colorado cavalry regiment during the Civil War. As a detective attached to the regiment, Cook was assigned to track spies, smugglers, and deserters. The skills he demonstrated in this assignment landed him the position of city marshal of Denver in 1866, and three years later he was elected sheriff of Arapaho County. After single-handedly capturing the notorious Musgrove-Franklin Gang in 1868, Cook was appointed deputy U.S. marshal.

Cook became major general of the Colorado militia in 1873, and during his nine-year tenure in that post he quelled numerous riots, including the infamous Chinese riot of 1880.

Although his name is far less familiar than that of Wyatt Earp or "Wild Bill" Hickok, David Cook was a more impressive lawman than either and is best remembered for his 1897 memoirs, *Hands Up! or Twenty Years of Detective Work in the Mountains and on the Plains*, a classic of popular frontier literature. Cook's recollections—even where he has unduly and undoubtedly embellished them—provide insight into the life and work of the "cowboy detectives" who operated in the latter half of the 19th century.

Cook survived gunfights and ambushes, dying peacefully and of natural causes in 1907.

Further reading: Collier, William R., and Edwin V. Westrate, *Dave Cook of the Rockies* (Denver: Monitor, 1936).

Coolidge, Calvin (1872–1933)

As governor of Massachusetts, Coolidge was publicly perceived as saving Boston (and the nation) from dangerous police efforts to unionize.

Calvin Coolidge was born in Plymouth, Vermont, on the Fourth of July, 1872. After attending Amherst College, near Northampton, Massachusetts, he practiced law in that town and began his political career as its mayor. After a stint in the state senate (1912–15) and three terms as lieutenant governor, the Republican was elected governor in 1918.

During his first year in office, Coolidge was instrumental in solving several major labor disputes involving the state's firemen, telephone workers, and railway personnel. But in 1919, the Boston police strike catapulted Coolidge into national fame and popularity, a strange turn of events given his actual role in the matter. While publicly expressing some sympathy for the underpaid patrolmen, Coolidge passively supported Commissioner Edward Upton CURTIS in his outright prohibition against police union affiliation and refused on jurisdictional grounds to intervene in the strike. After the commissioner's inflammatory, permanent dismissal of the 19 police officers who had initially organized the contested union effort, Coolidge again sent mixed signals to the parties involved—mildly mentioning his hope that the officers would be reinstated, while still keeping his distance from the ever-more-heated conflict. By ignoring persistent pleas from Mayor Andrew Peters and his James Storrow–led independent citizen's committee, who begged him to help resolve the stand-off, Coolidge did absolutely nothing to prevent the clearly anticipated strike. And even after police walked out on the evening of September 9, the governor continued to avoid the political hot potato, waiting and watching as first gambling and pranksterism, then looting and rioting, took over the unpatrolled streets.

Curtis also did nothing. Wishing to break the strike and garner public support for his anti-union ultimatum, he purposely delayed until morning the deployment of his halfheartedly assembled, pitifully inadequate guard of metropolitan, state, and volunteer police, while at the same time announcing that all striking policemen—three-quarters of Boston's entire force—were now permanently fired.

Overnight, as the scenario deteriorated in several Boston neighborhoods, people across the country began to ponder the question of police unionism while envisioning a city rendered helpless against violence and crime. Finally, on September 10, Mayor Peters superseded Curtis's chain of command and summoned locally based members of the State Guard to restore order to the city, while requesting from Governor Coolidge an additional 3,000 state militia troops. These forces patrolled the streets with bayonets; though more rioting and several deaths occurred that night, by morning the city seemed to be under control.

Only on September 11, as the streets were quieting, did Coolidge finally make a move, issuing an executive order and proclamation putting himself in charge of Curtis and all replacement forces and calling out the remainder of the state militia. Despite the fact that Coolidge had acted little and late, he was given credit for resolving the civic nightmare that had shaken citizens throughout the United States.

Hailed by the press and by Washington senators as Boston's savior, an uncompromising defender of law and order, and a statesman capable of holding firm against the sweeping tide of Bolshevism that threatened the country, Coolidge went from obscurity to fame almost instantly. In the aftermath of Boston's crisis, the governor exchanged several telegrams with American Federation of Labor president Samuel GOMPERS, who had urged Coolidge to reinstate the strikers and submit their grievances to arbitration. The governor replied that he had no authority to countermand the police commissioner's orders and refused to oust Curtis from his post. Coolidge's second telegram to Gompers included a paragraph that was reprinted in newspapers across the country: "Your assertion that the Commissioner was wrong cannot justify the wrong of leaving the city unguarded. That furnished the opportunity; the criminal element furnished the action. There is no right to strike against the public safety by anybody, anywhere, anytime."

The last sentence in particular had a ring to it, and its sentiment echoed that of President Woodrow WILSON, who had described the Boston strike as a "crime against civilization." Coolidge won reelection as governor in November. The following year, he lost the Republican presidential nomination to Warren G. Harding, but rode his newfound popularity into the vice presidential nomination. With Harding's death in 1923, Coolidge became the 30th president of the United States.

Further reading: McCoy, Donald R., *Calvin Coolidge, the Quiet President* (New York: Macmillan, 1967).

Cordes, John H. F. ("Dutchman") (1890–1966)

This famous New York detective won his department's prestigious Medal of Honor twice during his 34-year career.

In 1923, New York cop John Cordes entered a cigar store during a holdup. The perpetrators had bound and gagged the clerk and put him out of sight. Cordes, suspicious, began to question the two men behind the counter. Suddenly, the pair opened fire on the detective, who nevertheless managed to wrestle one down and shoot him in the stomach. By this time a young patrolman entered the store and mistakenly shot Cordes through the face. Riddled with five gunshot wounds, Cordes survived to receive his first Medal of Honor for his apprehension of the hold-up men. But from that time on, Cordes refused to carry a revolver while on duty.

A large, athletic man, Cordes consistently arrested more individuals than anyone on the force. His celebrated capture of two kidnappers in 1927 won him another Medal of Honor. Unarmed and facing two loaded pistols, Cordes nevertheless effected an arrest. He was the first New York City police officer to be awarded the medal twice.

Aside from his skill as a police officer, Cordes was a humanitarian as well. He promised employment for anyone he arrested when they got out of prison. All they needed to do was ask, and he always came through on his promise. Cordes's generosity paid off when one ex-con for whom he had secured a position on the loading docks tipped him off as to the whereabouts of a stolen shipment of machine guns destined for the Mob.

Cordes retired in 1949 as acting lieutenant of detectives. His courage and genuine concern for victims and for the cause of rehabilitation defined the highest traditions of modern police work.

Costello, Frank (1891–1973)

Revered or reviled as the "Prime Minister of the Underworld"; with "Lucky" LUCIANO and Meyer LANSKY, developed the first national crime syndicate in America during the 1930s, in effect inventing "organized crime."

Born Francesco Seriglia in Calabria, Italy, Frank Costello immigrated to the United States at age five and settled with his family in the tough East Harlem section of Manhattan. By age 24, Frank Costello was a seasoned criminal with an impressive police record.

Costello's criminal genius lay in his recognition of the power of "greenbacks" over bullets, and throughout his career it was his ability to buy protection and purchase influence over policemen, politicians, and

Frank Costello was one of the early architects of organized crime. (Courtesy of the Library of Congress)

judges that made him the leading mobster of his day.

Prohibition did more to make the gangsters wealthy than it ever did to strengthen America's moral fiber, and Frank Costello was among the chief beneficiaries of the Volstead Act. As an importer of high-grade illegal liquor, Costello became friends with Charles "Lucky" Luciano and Big Bill Dwyer. In particular, it was Luciano's command of a criminal network that, in combination with Costello's political influence, created the first national crime syndicate in the United States. In 1933, Meyer Lansky "invested" the proceeds of the considerable Cuban casino action he controlled, and also by that year Costello virtually owned New York's Tammany Hall political bosses. This gave him tremendous clout in both the underworld—no gangster could operate without going through Costello—and on the political landscape of New York City. By the 1950s, Costello was generally recognized as the most powerful crime boss in the United States, with extensive criminal operations in Las Vegas, California, Chicago, New York, New Orleans, Havana—and Sicily, the spawning ground and headquarters of the Mafia.

Frank Costello's downfall came at the height of his power and prosperity in the 1950s, when he came under the scrutiny of Senator Estes Kefauver's committee investigating organized crime. Refusing to testify before the Senate committee, Costello was found in contempt of Congress and sentenced to a year and a half in federal prison with an additional five years tacked on for income tax evasion in 1952.

After Costello obtained early release in 1957, future Mafia kingpin Vincent "the Chin" Gigante was sent by Mafia boss Vito Genovese to assassinate him. The rubout attempt failed, but, honoring Mafia tradition, Costello refused to testify against Gigante and took the option of "retiring" early before another attempt could be made on his life.

Costello spent his remaining years quietly and was a frequent customer at Toots Shor's famous New York nightclub, where he reminisced about the "good old days." Frank Costello died of natural causes.

Courtright, Long-haired Jim (Timothy Isaiah) (1848–87)

Surly and alcoholic and one of the West's more colorful lawmen.

Raised in Illinois, "Long-haired" Jim Courtright served the Union in the Civil War as a scout in Arizona, New Mexico, and Texas under General John Logan. At war's end, he settled in Texas to farm, but he abandoned the plow when he was elected marshal of Fort Worth in 1876. After three years in Fort Worth, Courtright was dismissed for drinking too much, and he moved to New Mexico to work as marshal of Lake

Colorful Texas lawman "Long-Haired Jim" Courtright (Courtesy of the Western History Collections, University of Oklahoma)

Valley, a silver boomtown. After that, in 1883, he was hired by his Civil War commander as foreman of his ranch, responsible for keeping rustlers and squatters away. In this capacity, Courtright killed two squatters who refused to leave Logan's property. To avoid trial, Courtright fled to Fort Worth, were he established a private detective agency.

He was tracked down and arrested in Fort Worth, but before he could stand trial, he made a daring escape. Stowing away on a freight train to Galveston, Courtright made his way to South America and thence to New York. Disembarking there, he traveled north across the Niagara River into Canada before heading west all the way to the Pacific Coast. Reentering the United States through Washington state, he then returned south to New Mexico in 1886 and was successful in getting the charges against him dropped.

Courtright returned to Fort Worth and his detective agency. When his business faltered, he resorted to extorting protection money from the local saloonkeepers. One of them, Luke Short, refused to pay, a gunfight ensued, and Courtright was killed.

Cressey, Donald Ray (1919–87) Distinguished educator, sociologist, and authority in the areas of delinquency and crime, criminal justice, and corrections.

Donald Cressey's distinguished career in criminology began during his work as chief sociologist of the Illinois State Penitentiary at Joliet in 1949. He left Joliet to take a position at the University of California, Los Angeles, in 1949 and remained there for the rest of his career. During his tenure at UCLA, Cressey published several notable books on criminology, including *Theft of the Nation: The Structure and Operations of Organized Crime in America* (1969)—a harrowing account of the corruption fostered by the Mob—and *With Other People's Money: A Study in the Social Psychology of Embezzlement* (1953), which he wrote with Edwin Sutherland. In 1960, Cressey published a sweeping social analysis of America's prison system, *Theoretical Studies in the Social Organization of the Prison.*

During the administration of President Lyndon Johnson, Cressey headed up the national Organized Crime Task Force and the Commission on Law Enforcement and Administration of Justice. Cressey retired from teaching in 1986 and died the following year.

Further reading: Laub, John H., "Interview with Donald R. Cressey, March 20, 1979," in *Criminolgy in the Making* (Boston: Northeastern University Press, 1983).

Crofton, Walter Frederick (1815–97) A pioneer in the adminstration of parole, Crofton developed a system to help mainstream convicts back into society, stressing reform rather than punishment.

Commissioner of prisons in Ireland in 1853–54 and again in 1869, William Crofton strove for a better way to deal with criminals than simply locking them up in deplorable conditions for a set period of time. Administrators of Australia's prison colonies had already set out to do similar work, and Crofton's "Irish system" is generally considered an improvement on that original scheme.

Crofton developed what he called the indeterminate system—later popularly called the Irish system—by which he sought to change the emphasis of incarceration from punishment to a process of repentance and reform. The system consisted of a series of stages through which the inmate went on his way toward gaining his freedom. First of all, Crofton followed the Australians' lead by abolishing the flat sentence, which gave no hope of release until the full time had been served. An indeterminate sentence, in which time served was in some measure linked to a convict's behavior in prison, promoted better behavior and more earnest effort at repentance and self-reform.

The first stage of the Irish system was essentially solitary confinement coupled with dull labor—the most severe part of the program. The subsequent stages each granted greater degrees of freedom and greater exposure, in varying amounts, to social interaction, either inside or outside the prison walls. The final stage was an intermediate prison, or what had been called community houses or halfway houses. This provided for continued supervision, but allowed inmates the opportunity to reintegrate into society while showing penal officials that they were capable of such reintegration.

The Irish system hinged on two elements, the first being the program of good behavior. With the abolition of the flat sentence, inmates were able to earn time off by working within the program and striving for penitence, thereby earning "time off for good behavior." The second, and more crucial part, was the novel idea of parole, something that had been discussed but never put into practice in Europe. Parole motivated reform and repentance even more forcefully and directly. Crofton's Irish system is now the basis for the penal systems in most civilized societies.

Croker, Richard (1841–1922) New York City political boss who ran Tammany Hall for a time after the downfall of Boss Tweed.

Richard Croker and his family immigrated to New York City from Ireland in 1846, when Richard was four years old. He attended public school sporadically for a few years, then, aged 13, left school to work as a machine operator. A large boy for his age, Croker quickly established himself as a neighborhood tough, leading the much-feared Fourth Avenue Tunnel Gang. By the age of 21, he was following Tammany Hall politics and was hired by Tammany to "persuade" voters to toe the party line.

After a brief stint with the fire department, Croker joined the Young Democrats in 1868, a breakaway faction of Tammany opposed to the long regime of Boss Tweed. Croker claimed that his only aim was to free the city from the corrupt clutches of Tweed, and when the Young Democrats were successful in toppling Tweed, Croker was elected an alderman. Once in office, all the new aldermen pledged their loyalty to the leadership of the Young Democrats. Tweed, however, made a brief comeback and managed to legislate the alderman out of office. The Boss's return was short-lived, and he was indicted, tried, and imprisoned in 1871. Croker, in the meantime, had obtained a lucrative position in the city government. Cozying up to Tweed's successor, John Kelly, Croker was able to obtain the post of city coroner, using the position to great profit, rendering favorable opinions

in questionable cases and always for a price. During the election of 1874, a man involved in illegal election day activity was shot and killed, a crime of which Croker was accused. The case was dropped for lack of evidence. Croker was released after spending a month in jail and returned to his position as coroner.

In 1885, Croker was able to bring about the Tammany nomination of Hugh Grant as sheriff, a harbinger of his rising power. When Kelly died in 1886, Croker quickly took over the Tammany leadership, ruling the New York City Democratic Party for the next 16 years. Croker set about organizing Tammany Hall into a powerful machine that was still as crooked as ever, but that exercised tighter control over local officials through a system of patronage. In 1894, after revelations from the reform-minded Lexow Committee on the corruption of the police department, the Democrats were voted out of office. The ever-resilient Croker nevertheless managed to engineer the election of Robert Van Wyck three years later. Van Wyck proved to be one of the most corrupt of all Tammany politicians, and his excesses brought down Tammany again in 1902. With this final defeat, Croker retired to England and then to his native Ireland, where he lived the life of a country squire until his death.

Cummings, Homer (1870–1956) Attorney general under President Franklin Delano ROOSEVELT, Cummings introduced sweeping reforms of the United States justice system.

A product of the Yale University Law School, Homer Cummings distinguished himself as a hard-nosed, by-the-book prosecutor in Stamford, Connecticut, before becoming that city's mayor for three terms, beginning in 1900. In 1932, Cummings rounded up critical eastern "Establishment" support for Franklin Delano Roosevelt in his bid for the Presidency, and FDR rewarded him with the post of attorney general on March 4, 1933.

In the course of six years as attorney general, Cummings transformed the Justice Department in accordance with FDR's New Deal policies. He instituted the so-called Lindbergh Law, making kidnapping a capital offense; he made bank robbery a federal crime; and he gave J. Edgar HOOVER the authority and mandate to transform the Federal Bureau of Investigation (FBI) into the most powerful law enforcement agency in the country. Cummings also reorganized the federal prison system, developing Alcatraz, in San Francisco Bay, into the model maximum security facility for the most hardened criminals.

Cummings published two notable books on crime and justice: *We Can Prevent Crime* (1937) and, with Carl McFarland, *Federal Justice* (1939).

Cummings shared the president's ambition to liberalize the federal courts and, in particular, the Supreme Court. At the direction of FDR, Cummings secretly prepared a proposal, pursuant to an earlier idea put forth by Associate Supreme Court Justice James McReynolds, to add a judge for every judge who refused to retire at age 70 with full pay. In this way, the president would be empowered to appoint some 50 judges, including a half-dozen Supreme Court justices. This so-called "court-packing plan," put before Congress in February 1937, touched off 168 days of furious, rancorous debate before the Senate finally killed it by returning it to committee. In the long wake of the furor, Cummings retired in January 1939 to a private law practice. He died in Washington, D.C., 14 years later.

Further reading: Swisher, Carl Brent, ed., *Selected Papers of Homer Cummings: Attorney General of the United States, 1933–1939* (New York: Scribner's, 1939).

Cunninghman, Tom (1838–1900) "The Thief Taker of San Joaquin" was a lawman in the rough-and-tumble settlements of Northern California.

Born in County Longford, Ireland, on August 17, 1838, Cunningham was sent to Brooklyn, New York, when he was 10 years old to serve as an apprentice to his brother-in-law, a harness maker. In his spare time, Cunningham managed to secure an education and at age 16 set off for California, arriving in San Francisco in 1855. Settling in Stockton, he found work with a series of harness makers and in 1860 opened his own shop; he married and had three daughters.

Cunningham was a civic-minded man who joined the volunteer fire department in 1857, becoming its chief in 1865, the year he also became a Stockton city councilman. In 1871, he was nominated to run for sheriff and was elected by a large majority, taking office in 1872. Immediately after the election, many expressed doubts that the naturally gentle and soft-spoken Cunningham could handle the job, but for the next 27 years, he was involved in manhunts for some of Northern California's most notorious outlaws, including Tiburcio Vasquez, Black Bart, Bill Miner, Isador Padillo, Evans and Sontag, Jack Brady, and Sam Browning. He was so efficient at tracking and apprehending criminals that he earned the sobriquet "Thief Taker of San Joaquin."

More than a brave and dedicated lawman, Cunningham pioneered the use of scientific criminology and detection in the American West. He was meticulous and systematic in his study of the habits, methods, and motives of criminals and assembled one of the largest rogues' galleries in the United States at the time: some 42,000 photographs at the time of his retirement, representing a personal investment of $20,000. Moreover, Cunningham personally designed the San Joaquin County Jail, which was considered a model of its kind and, sporting distinctive pointed towers, was dubbed Cunningham's Castle. In addition to compiling his files and rogues' gallery, Cunningham put together a museum of crime in four rooms of the old courthouse. The museum held more than a thousand weapons and curios.

Cunningham retired from office on January 3, 1899, and died the following year.

Curphey, Theodore (1897–1986)   The first medical examiner of Los Angeles County; ordered the controversial "psychological autopsy" of Marilyn Monroe following the star's apparent suicide.

After obtaining his medical degree and passing the New York State Board examinations, Theodore Curphey began working in the county coroner's office for Nassau County, Long Island. In 1938, he was named to head the office and served in that capacity for 29 years. In 1957, the Los Angeles Board of Supervisors restructured the county coroner's office as a medical examiner's department, to be headed by a qualified physician rather than a political appointee. The supervisors hired Curphey, who became the county's first medical examiner.

Over the course of his tenure, Curphey gained many admirers as well as enemies for his refusal to bend to political pressure or "massage" high-profile investigations in celebrity-filled Los Angeles. No one, however, could fault his expertise as a physician, and he established the Los Angeles County medical examiner's office as one of the finest in the nation.

Curphey found himself in the limelight in 1962 when international sex symbol Marilyn Monroe was found dead in her Los Angeles bungalow, the victim of an apparent suicide. Because the death was believed to be a suicide, Curphey's office handled the investigation, rather than the Los Angeles Police Department, and no formal public inquest was ever held. Curphey appointed a three-member panel of psychiatrists to interview acquaintances of Monroe to determine her mental state prior to her death. This so-called "psychological autopsy" was a rare procedure at the time and drew much skeptical criticism. The investigation lasted 11 days, and the panel concluded that it was indeed a suicide. However, critics of the panel noted that the testimony the panel heard was not sworn, nor did the committee interview all the key witnesses. For example, Peter Lawford, an actor who was the last person to speak to Monroe before her death, was not interviewed. Curphey refused to comment on the case after the investigation, and it clouded his administration until he retired in 1967.

Curtis, Edward Upton (1861–1922) Commissioner of Boston's police in 1919; provoked a disastrous police strike by dismissing officers who had worked to unionize their ranks.

Former mayor Edward Upton Curtis was Boston police commissioner in 1919, when the long-suffering police of that city applied for a union charter with the American Federation of Labor (AFL) to aid in their negotiations for better wages and working conditions. The commissioner's immediate prohibition of any sort of union membership—and his rigid dismissal of 19 officers who had led the union effort—prompted Boston's law enforcers to go on strike, an event that drew national attention and, in its aftermath, was described as "a crime against civilization" by President Woodrow WILSON himself.

The son of a lumber merchant, Edward Curtis was born and schooled in Roxbury, Massachusetts, at the time a suburb of Boston. He attended Bowdoin College in Maine, graduating in 1882, then earned credentials at Boston University Law School. A Republican active in party politics, Curtis practiced law, won election as city clerk, and in 1894 successfully campaigned for mayor of Boston. While in office, Curtis restructured the metropolitan administration, creating commissioners for each city department and for the supervision of city elections, and revising the system of financing public schools.

At the end of his term, Curtis resumed his law practice but remained active in municipal affairs as a member of the Metropolitan Park Commission, then as assistant U.S. treasurer at Boston, and finally, as collector of the Port. In December 1918, outgoing governor McCall appointed Curtis police commissioner.

The lawyer and former mayor took over a troubled and unhappy department. Long hours of duty and filthy, crumbling station houses—whose maintenance happened to fall between the cracks of the city bureaucracy—meant miserable working conditions for Boston's police. Furthermore, the officers' wages had been inadequate for years; paid half as much as the average worker during the World War I period, the policemen now had to manage postwar price inflation with municipally frozen salaries. In May 1919, Curtis managed to pressure the city government for a $200 increase in the officers' annual pay. But the raise was small improvement, and Mayor Andrew Peters and the city council refused to stretch any further.

The following month, members of the thoroughly disgruntled department began to contemplate and organize an application for affiliation with the American Federation of Labor (AFL), hoping that the national union would give them greater clout for negotiation with Boston's authorities. In July the officers proceeded to file for an AFL charter under the auspices of an informal, local police fraternity, the Boston Social Club. At the time, no city law or departmental rule forbade the police from forming a union affiliation, and indeed, the AFL had already (somewhat reluctantly) granted a few such charters to the police of other cities.

But Curtis would have none of it. The commissioner was willing to act as advocate on behalf of his police force, but he had no intention of bargaining with his men through any union intermediary. Declaring that "a police officer cannot consistently belong to a union and perform his sworn duty," Curtis prohibited all personnel from membership in any outside club or organization, with the specific exception of three military veterans' groups: the Grand Army of the Republic (G.A.R.), the United Spanish War Veterans, and the American Legion. Violators of this order would be subject to disciplinary action.

The police chief's ultimatum further inflamed the frustrated officers, and when he leveled formal charges against the 19 policemen who had organized the union effort, the rank and file began to talk about a strike. Mayor Peters, now concerned about the uproar, appointed an independent citizen's committee to study police conditions and recommend a means of settling the dispute, but Curtis rejected the committee's proposal for a compromise solution. Peters and his group then lobbied Governor Calvin COOLIDGE to intervene with the unbending commissioner, but Coolidge refused to get involved in the matter, claiming no jurisdiction. When Curtis fired the 19 union leaders on September 8, the Boston police voted 1,134 to 2 to walk out after roll-call the following evening. And so they did.

Although Curtis had begun gathering a few replacement officers some time before, his volunteer and metropolitan police reserves were wholly insufficient, and in any case he assigned them to begin their patrol duty on September 10, the morning after the scheduled walkout. If Curtis intended to break the strike immediately, by leaving the city utterly unprotected for more than 12 hours—and after dark—his method failed. But if he wished to demonstrate to a fearful public the horrific potential consequences of labor organizing in the police profession, his deliberate inaction greatly succeeded. Adding fuel to the fire, Curtis announced that any and all strikers would be permanently dismissed, thereby ending the careers of three-quarters of the city's regular police force. (Some older officers who had voted for the strike did report for duty; it had been understood in advance that some men could not be expected to risk their retirement pensions at so late a date.)

The night of the walkout, public gambling and pranksterism were the first signs of disorder. But after midnight, real trouble began, and even when Curtis's volunteers began duty the next morning, their meager and largely inexperienced numbers had very little effect. A night and day of lawlessness brought looting, robbery, vandalism, and eventually rioting to the streets of Boston.

Mayor Peters finally stepped in on the afternoon of September 10, superseding the police commissioner's authority. Peters summoned 3,800 members of the State Guard to quell disturbances. Though several citizens and one patrolman were killed in confrontations that night, the militia, armed with bayonets, gradually restored peace to the city.

The next day, September 11, Governor Coolidge finally made a move, now at the panicked and disenfranchised police commissioner's request. Coolidge issued an executive order and proclamation, recouping administrative control for Curtis (though under himself) and marshaling more state troops for city patrol. Ironically, Coolidge, not Mayor Peters, was soon crowned with laurels for saving Boston from its criminal community, and newspapers across the country lauded the governor, not the hardline, anti-union Curtis, for having stood up to a "Bolshevist"-leaning police department and won.

As press reports alerted the watching and worried nation of Boston's victory over peril, the appalled president of the AFL, Samuel GOMPERS, telegraphed Coolidge and exhorted him to reinstate the strikers, submit their grievances to arbitration, and to fire Curtis for his handling of the entire matter. But Coolidge, jurisdiction-shy as ever, continued to back the commissioner's authority, and Curtis had already reconfirmed his declaration that the strikers' jobs were vacant. In a much-reprinted second telegram to Gompers, Coolidge wrote, "There is no right to strike against the public safety by anybody, anywhere, anytime." These words were stirring music to the ears of an outraged nation. By 1920, the hitherto obscure Massachusetts governor had gained sufficient celebrity and popularity from the Boston emergency's spotlight to win the Republican vice presidential nomination on Warren Harding's ticket—and, when Harding died three years later, the U.S. presidency itself.

Although Boston's police commissioner gained few friends in organized labor, Curtis did keep his job, and he proceeded to recruit new officers and begin rebuilding the city police force. In 1921 he fell ill, but insisted on remaining in office to complete the department's restoration. Ill and overworked, Curtis died on March 28, 1922.

Further reading: Curtis, Edward Upton, *Fourteenth Annual Report of the Police Commissioner for the City of Boston* (1920).

American Federation of Labor, *Report of the Proceedings of the 40th Annual Convention of American Federation of Labor* (New York: AFL, 1920).

D

Darrow, Clarence (1857–1938) One of the greatest criminal defense lawyers in American history; argued high-profile cases, including the Scopes "Monkey Trial" and the Leopold-Loeb "Thrill Kill" murder trial.

Born in Kinsman, Ohio, on April 18, 1857, Clarence Darrow attended school at Allegheny College but left after a year to transfer to the University of Michigan. Leaving Michigan after a year as well, Darrow passed the bar exam in 1878 without ever having graduated from law school. In 1887, he moved to Chicago, where he became active in the Democratic Party. He quickly established himself as a friend of labor, and, in the violent labor clashes of the turn of the century, Darrow gained early fame with his gallant but unsuccessful defense of Eugene V. Debs in 1895 during the great railroad strikes. Darrow went on successfully to represent the miners in the famous Anthracite Coal Strike in western Pennsylvania as well as left-wing labor leader William "Big Bill" Haywood on a charge of conspiring to murder the former governor of Idaho in 1907. When he became aware that some of the labor leaders he was representing were, in fact, crooked, the high-minded Darrow became increasingly disenchanted with the labor cause. Nevertheless, he then took on the strike-related *Los Angeles Times* bombing case, in which he pleaded his clients guilty in a successful bid to save them from the death penalty.

Darrow continued to represent publicly unpopular clients or clients who would not ordinarily be expected to receive a fair trial. It was said that he "represented the poor and the rich . . . but he never represented the strong against the weak." In 1917, he defended a group of Milwaukee anarchists, appealing their convictions all the way to the U.S. Supreme Court and securing the reversal of nine of the 11 convictions. In 1924, Darrow took on one of the most sensational murder trials of the 20th century, in which he introduced a landmark defense that had never been used before. Two wealthy young men, students at the University of Chicago, Richard Loeb and Nathan Leopold, both intellectually gifted but emotionally disturbed, decided that as a fitting challenge to their mental capabilities, they would execute the perfect murder. They kidnapped a small boy and bludgeoned him to death, then burned his face and genitals with acid. As it turned out, they were not nearly as clever as they thought, and they were, in fact, quickly apprehended. An outraged public demanded the death penalty in what the press dubbed the Thrill Kill case. Darrow was hired by their wealthy parents for a large sum (which was never paid) to defend the two.

As was the right of the defense, Darrow waived a jury trial and opted to plead his case directly to the bench—a bold, risky, but shrewd move in the emotionally charged climate surrounding the case. He pleaded his clients guilty, but appealed to the judge to sentence the young men to life imprisonment rather than to death. For the first time in legal history, Darrow introduced as a mitigating circumstance the concept of psychopathy—not insanity, but a state of emotional vacancy that rendered the defendants unable to comprehend moral right and wrong. Darrow successfully argued to the judge that executing the defendants would not bring back the victim, nor would they die with the realization of what they had perpetrated. Accordingly, Leopold and Loeb were sentenced to life imprisonment. (Darrow personally detested the two. Loeb was later murdered in prison while attempting to rape another inmate. Leopold was eventually paroled and dedicated his life to giving medical care to the poor.)

Only a year after the Thrill Kill trial, Darrow took on another very high-profile case. A Tennessee high school biology teacher, John T. Scopes, was arrested

One of the best-known defense attorneys of all time, the intense Clarence Darrow (Courtesy of the Illinois State Historical Library)

for teaching Darwin's theory of evolution in defiance of state law. Darrow, himself a fierce agnostic, quickly jumped to the defense, and the trial soon became a hotly reported national debate over freedom of inquiry, freedom of speech, and science versus theology. In a spectacular legal move, Darrow put the prosecuting attorney on the stand—no less a figure than William Jennings Bryan, famed orator, Populist political hero, former secretary of state under Woodrow Wilson, and a perennial presidential candidate. Darrow lost the case—though Scopes was slapped on the wrist with nothing more than a token fine of $100—but he is universally conceded to have won the debate and so humiliated Bryan that, broken by the experience, within days the Populist warrior collapsed and died. (Scopes's conviction was subsequently overturned on a technicality by the Tennessee Supreme Court; it was never heard by the U.S. Supreme Court.)

Darrow's legal career was widely publicized, in large part through his own numerous books, includ-

ing *The Story of My Life* (1932), and he is remembered as the quintessential crusading attorney.

Further reading: Stone, Irving, *Clarence Darrow for the Defense: A Biography* (Garden City, N.Y.: Doubleday, Doran & Co., Inc., 1941; reprinted in 1970).

Weinberg, A., and William O. Douglas, eds., *Attorney for the Damned* (New York: Simon and Schuster, 1957, reprinted 1983).

Weinberg, A. and L., *Clarence Darrow* (New York: Putnam, c1980 reprinted 1987.)

Daughtry, Sylvester, Jr. (1945–   )   Chief of the Greensboro, North Carolina, police department, and the second African-American president of the International Association of Chiefs of Police (IACP).

Daughtry, a distinguished chief of police, was instrumental in creating nationally accepted professional standards for law enforcement agencies. He joined the Greensboro Police Department in 1968 and was promoted to sergeant in 1973, to lieutenant in 1977, to captain in 1980, to assistant chief in 1983, and to chief of police in 1987. He was graduated from North Carolina A & T State University with a B.S. degree, and reformed the Greensboro department, creating Neighborhood Resource Centers, modernizing computer facilities, and implementing an enhanced 911 telephone emergency system. Highly active in the area of professional standards for law enforcement agencies, Daughtry served as a member of the Commission on Accreditation for Law Enforcement Agencies; under his guidance, the Greensboro Police Department became the first agency in North Carolina to achieve national recognition.

In 1993, Daughtry was elected president of the IACP, the second African American (after Lee BROWN) to serve in that post.

Davis, Katherine Bement (1860–1935)   Penologist and social worker who was the first woman to fill a cabinet post in the New York City government.

The daughter of a prominent educator, Katherine Davis was encouraged at an early age to seek educational opportunities that were rare for women in the 19th century. In 1877, she entered the Free Academy in Rochester, New York, to study chemistry, and in 1890 enrolled in Vassar College, where she specialized in food chemistry and nutrition, with particular emphasis on the relation between nutrition and social welfare.

After graduating in 1892, Davis was appointed head resident of St. Mary's Street College Settlement in Philadelphia. Her three-year tenure there confirmed her commitment to the field of social welfare and, after studying on a fellowship at the University of Chicago, with additional study at the universities of

Berlin and Vienna, she received her Ph.D. from Chicago in 1900.

Davis returned to New York state and in 1901 was named superintendent of the Reformatory for Women at Bedford Hills. Here she was an innovator in female penology. In 1912, she helped establish a diagnostic laboratory of social hygiene, which undertook the study of prisoners by sociologists, psychologists, and psychiatrists.

In January 1914, she accepted the position of commissioner of corrections for the City of New York, the first woman to hold such a high post within the municipal government. Davis vigorously reformed the system, cutting into prison drug trafficking, separating female from male prisoners, improving prison food and medical care, and establishing educational resources for prisoners. Such enlightened programs drew criticism from hard-line traditionalists, but her efforts to secure more uniform governance of prisoners were rewarded in 1915 when the state legislature passed a law establishing the New York City Parole Commission, giving it broad jurisdiction over prisoners with indeterminate sentences and those who had been reformed short of serving out their sentence.

When the tide turned against reform in 1918, Davis was swept out of office, but she continued to work for social reform until her death in 1930.

Dawson, Margaret Damer (1874–1920) The founder of the Women's Police Volunteers was instrumental in establishing a role for women as police officers in London.

Born into a wealthy family in Sussex, England, Margaret Damer Dawson grew up with an abiding love for music. She studied under well-known composers at London's Royal Academy of Music and was awarded several commendations along with her diploma. Dawson was a cultivated, compassionate, and humane person, who despised any mistreatment of the fragile and vulnerable. She worked tirelessly with several animal protection agencies and served as the organizing secretary to the International Congress of Animal Protection Societies in 1906. Her service earned her medals from the sovereigns of both Denmark and Finland.

Yet another of her activities was membership in the Criminal Law Amendment Committee, possibly the first organization in Great Britain to argue for female police officers. Although many thought the idea absurd, Dawson was given the opportunity to organize a female police auxiliary after the outbreak of World War I in 1914. When Belgium was invaded in August, thousands of refugees flocked to London and were easy prey to an assortment of shysters, con men, and criminals. Dawson organized a group of wealthy, civic-minded women who owned automobiles to meet these refugees at the train depot and shepherd them to safe havens.

As a result of this work, Dawson recognized a need for some official presence at the train depots, and she contacted Sir Edward Henry, London's police commissioner, who granted her permission to form a Women's Police Volunteer unit. These women would not be empowered to make arrests, but they would be uniformed and did command some authority. Dawson personally oversaw training for the women and was herself one of the first women on patrol. The chief duty of the WPV was a crackdown on wartime prostitution and white slavery involving servicemen and refugees.

After an internal power struggle, Dawson resigned as chief of the WPV in February 1915 and formed the Women's Police Service. This body, attached to constabulary stations, was paid rather than voluntary, and soon took on duties beyond caring for wayward children and dealing with prostitutes. Dawson was subsequently named commandant of the new force and continued to work in that capacity until her death.

Deitsch, Philip M. (1840–1903) Chief of the Cincinnati Police Department and an important law enforcement reformer of the late 19th century.

A native of Bavaria, Philip Deitsch was one of many German immigrants who settled in Cincinnati. He joined the police force of that city in 1863, achieving (presumably through political influence) almost instant promotion to sergeant within one month after joining. Two months after this first promotion, Deitsch became lieutenant. He left the force in 1873 to become an agent for the United States Revenue Service.

In 1885, Cincinnati was rocked by widespread charges of illegal voter registration. A special Committee of One Hundred was formed to investigate the fraud and uncovered more than 1,250 false registrations. Warrants were issued for the arrest of seven officials, but the police commissioners refused to make the arrests. The Committee of One Hundred turned to the state legislature for help, and in the spring of 1886, the legislature enacted a bill reorganizing the corrupt Cincinnati police. Two hundred thirty-eight of the department's 289 patrolmen were dismissed, and the city called in Deitsch to become the new police chief who would remold the department, virtually from scratch.

Deitsch instituted military-style discipline among his men, including military drill and physical training at a new police gymnasium. He introduced military-style uniforms and weapons as well, setting a paramilitary standard that would permanently influence police departments across the nation. Deitsch required rigorous medical examination of all officers and formulated a program of police training that set the standard nationally. The new chief also introduced the so-called three-platoon system, which reduced the patrolman's tour from 12 hours to eight.

Deitsch's reforms, supported and publicized by the newly founded International Association of Chiefs of Police (IACP), proved highly influential—though many historians of United States police practices have judged his emphasis on the military model as a feature of dubious value.

della Porta, Giambattista (1535–1615)   Natural scientist, philosopher, and playwright; one of the most prolific writers and theorists of the Italian Renaissance, wrote an early treatise on physiognomy.

Della Porta's 1586 treatise *De humana physiognomonia* ("On Human Physiognomy") posited that the size and shape of various physical features corresponded directly to an individual's internal character. As one example of the principle, della Porta asserted that thieves could be identified by their sharply shifting eyes, bushy brows, open and full-lipped mouths, small ears and noses, and long, slender fingers. Because of his typological description, some later writers of the positivist school considered della Porta a forerunner in criminology.

A noble-born scholar and lay brother of the Jesuits, della Porta founded the Academy of Natural Secrets in Naples and later joined the Roman Accademia dei Lincei, in which Galileo was to make his name. In 1589 della Porta published his 20-volume masterwork, *Magiae naturalis* ("Natural Magic"), which examined the wonders of the natural world with a methodology partly scientific, partly mystical. Among the author's many works were treatises on agriculture, cryptography, memory, plant and celestial physiognomy, distillation, geometry, military fortifications, meteorology, and the mechanical properties of water and steam. His theories about, and experiments with, concave and convex lenses earned him a place in the history of optics, but despite some claims to priority, he did not himself invent the first telescope.

Della Porta's philosophical, sometimes alchemical approach to natural science brought him under the suspicious scrutiny of the Inquisition, and his publications were banned for several years during the 1590s. Amusing himself with lighter efforts during this period, he penned a number of comedies, several of which were widely read and performed, even influencing the British playwrights Shakespeare and Middleton. Of all of his writings, della Porta's dramatic, optical, and agricultural works have earned most respect from posterity.

DeLoach, Cartha (Deke) (1920–   )   Assistant to the director of the FBI from 1965 to 1970; a key player in J. Edgar HOOVER's secret intelligence campaign during the civil rights movement.

Cartha DeLoach joined the FBI in 1942 after graduating from Stetson University. One of his first assignments was to investige possible Communist Party members in Ohio. A brief stint in the navy interrupted his FBI career, but after World War II he returned to the bureau and began a sharp and steady rise through the ranks of the agency. By 1950, the young agent had caught the attention of J. Edgar Hoover, who in 1959 appointed him assistant director for crime records in the public relations arm of the bureau.

DeLoach became Hoover's point man in his public and private crusade against supposed communist infiltrators in government. DeLoach himself infiltrated the American Legion, which he determined to use as a natural ally in what had become a personal war against communism. At one point, DeLoach simultaneously held the chief public relations position in both the Legion and the FBI.

During the 1964 Democratic National Convention, DeLoach was in charge of a special investigative unit that provided surveillance and wiretapping to monitor the activities of civil rights leader Dr. Martin Luther King Jr. DeLoach reported directly to Hoover and President Lyndon B. JOHNSON.

The following year, DeLoach became assistant to the director of the FBI, effectively second in command. In this position, he developed a close relationship with President Johnson and was the only member of the bureau to have a direct telephone line to the White House. DeLoach directed a secret campaign to discredit Martin Luther King through leaks to the press concerning the popular civil rights leader's alleged promiscuity. Such activities provoked sufficient outrage to prompt the president to distance himself somewhat from DeLoach, but he remained the FBI's primary liaison with the White House during the early Nixon years until his retirement from the bureau in 1970, when he accepted a lucrative offer to become an executive with Pepsico, Inc.

Further reading: Nash, Jay Robert, *Citizen Hoover: A Critical Study of the Life and Times of J. Edgar Hoover* (Chicago: Nelson-Hall, 1972).

Deringer, Henry, Jr. (1786–1868)   The inventor of the diminutive pistols that bear his name, Deringer revolutionized homicide by creating an effective weapon that could be concealed practically anywhere.

The son of Henry Deringer Sr., master gunsmith of Easton, Pennsylvania, Henry Deringer Jr. was born on October 26, 1786, and was apprenticed to a gunsmith in Richmond, Virginia, at a very young age.

By 1806, he had completed his apprenticeship and returned to Easton, where he opened a smithing shop of his own.

Deringer grew wealthy from numerous government contracts for thousands of flintlock rifles, including one $87,000 order for 6,000 rifles. While filling government orders, Deringer did not neglect the commercial gun market and manufactured a variety of weapons for a growing frontier society. His most famous and distinctive was the Deringer.

The Deringer—also spelled Derringer—a pistol of only 3½ inches in length, which a man could completely conceal in his hand, was enthusiastically received. Before effective law enforcement was commonplace in many towns, almost everyone, male and female alike, carried a weapon of some sort for protection. Deringer's pistol became the weapon of choice in saloons and brothels everywhere and for "ladies" and "gentlemen" of all kinds. John Wilkes Booth even used one to assassinate Abraham Lincoln.

Deringer failed to get a patent on the model or even a copyright on the name, so smiths everywhere copied it, altering the spelling of the name by adding an additional r—although this was not even a legal necessity.

By the time of his death in 1868, Deringer was all too aware that he had invented the "Saturday Night Special" of the 19th century, a weapon responsible for many deaths.

Further reading: Carey, Arthur Merwyn, *American Firearms Makers: When, Where, and What They Made* (New York: Crowell, 1953).

De Veil, Sir Thomas (1684–1748)

The first magistrate of Westminster, serving from 1735 to 1748; established the famed Bow Street headquarters that eventually became the birthplace of the modern professional police force.

Mid-18th-century London had no professional police force. The magistrate had officers at his disposal, but they functioned more as a buffer between the masses and government authorities than as protectors of the public and their property. Indeed, these officers were often deeply resented by the public.

De Veil, a retired army colonel who held the position of magistrate of Westminster from 1735 to 1748, was primarily responsible for neutralizing a major crime syndicate in London and enforcing the Gin Act of 1736. With funds he obtained through the questionable distribution of patronage positions, De Veil purchased a house in Bow Street to serve as headquarters for his operations. Under subsequent magistrates, most notably the Fielding brothers, the Bow Street house would become the birthplace of the world's first modern, professional police force, which

was destined to serve as a model for police organizations in many countries. In his own time, De Veil was unable to diffuse public animosity toward the magistrate and his officers—who were perceived as oppressive agents of the crown—and the Bow Street house was repeatedly ransacked by angry mobs. Despite severe "public relations" problems, De Veil remained magistrate until October 6, 1748, when a sudden illness took his life.

The colorful colonel was married four times and is known to have fathered more than 20 children.

Further reading: Fitzgerald, Percy, *Chronicles of Bow-Street Police Office* (London: Chapman and Hall, 1888).

Devery, William (ca. 1855–1919)

As chief of police in New York City, Devery proved to be one of the most corrupt police officials of the many notoriously crooked Tammany Hall administrations.

The son of a bricklayer who helped build the actual structure called Tammany Hall, William Devery soon gained the nickname "Big Bill" for his physical prowess during his days as a bartender in the rough-and-tumble Bowery. In 1878, he paid the going bribe to join the police force as a patrolman, and he quietly began to ascend through the ranks, literally paying his "dues"—but beginning to collect some as well. In 1884 Devery made sergeant, and by 1891 he was appointed captain of the First Precinct, wangling the lucrative Eldridge Street Station, which contained a notorious red light district and offered plenty of graft ripe for collection.

An agent of Tammany Hall from the beginning, Devery did his best to bring out the Tammany vote in his district by discreetly promising to protect all illegal interests in the area if the Tammany ticket was elected. Having established himself as a loyal Tammany man, Devery was appointed chief of police in 1898, following the forced and underhanded dismissal of the previous chief, a holdover from an ousted reform administration. The new post was a huge windfall for Devery because, the year before, Brooklyn, Queens, Staten Island, and the Bronx had been consolidated with Manhattan to create Greater New York—roughly the city as it is today. With these newly incorporated areas came new police districts and high-ranking offices to be bought and sold.

The chief could be found every night from 9:00 P.M. to 2:00 A.M. on the corner of 28th Street and Ninth Avenue, resting against a fireplug, gathering information from his myriad informants and dispensing favors—for handsome fees. Devery's efforts helped get Robert Van Wyck elected mayor, but Van Wyck was so outrageously corrupt himself that he could not save Devery, who was legislated—by the state—out of office in 1901. Not to be deterred, Devery promptly ran for office the following summer as district leader in Chelsea, the Manhattan neighborhood that encompassed his hallowed fireplug. As "a campaign expense," he rented nine boats and loaded aboard some 18,000 would-be constituents for a free cruise up the Hudson and a huge picnic. He won by a landslide.

The triumphant Devery had, however, committed an unforgivable sin in Tammany politics: He had become bigger than the machine itself. The following year, Tammany turned against him in his reelection bid. In 1903, he ran against the Tammany ticket for mayor and was soundly defeated. He retired from public life, a bitter, albeit very wealthy man. He once remarked, "I bought a reserved seat in the political game, and Tammany Hall made me sit in the gallery."

Dew, Walter (1863–1947)   Chief inspector of Scotland Yard's CID (Criminal Investigation Department) who won fame for his successful, 3,000-mile pursuit of one of England's most infamous murderers, Dr. Hawley Harvey Crippen, who had poisoned his wife in 1910.

Walter Dew was a career police investigator who had participated in the unsuccessful manhunt for Jack the Ripper in 1888. Promoted to chief inspector of CID by the turn of the century, Dew earned worldwide fame as the man who apprehended Dr. Hawley Harvey Crippen. Crippen had poisoned his wife, a failed singer whose stage name was Belle Turner, and then meticulously dismembered (investigators used the word "filleted") her corpse in order to facilitate cremation in the cellar grate of his London flat.

The sensational crime captured the attention not only of Edwardian England, but also of the world, for Crippen had murdered his wife in order to run off with his secretary, Ethel Clara LeNeve. After disposing of Belle—and successfully enduring Dew's questioning in the matter of his wife's disappearance—Crippen set sail with LeNeve for Canada aboard the steamship *Montrose*. The captain of the vessel recognized the couple (even though LeNeve was disguised as a boy), and telegraphed Scotland Yard. Dew boarded a faster vessel and, while maintaining constant radio communication with the skipper of the *Montrose*, overtook the slower ship at Father Point at the mouth of the St. Lawrence River off the Canadian coast. He boarded the *Montrose* and approached Crippen, announcing himself with dry understatement: "Good morning, Dr. Crippen. I am Chief Inspector Dew of Scotland Yard. I believe you know me."

The Crippen murder was Walter Dew's most famous case. Here, Dr. Hawley H. Crippen and his paramour Ethel LeNeve face justice in the dock of a courtroom. (Courtesy of the UPI/Bettmann Archive)

Belle Elmore Crippen, who was murdered and dismembered by her husband (Courtesy of the UPI/Bettmann Archive)

The Crippen pursuit was the first time in history that the "wireless telegraph" had been used to apprehend a criminal. It also did much to enhance the image of Scotland Yard as a law enforcement body to be reckoned with and gave new meaning to the expression "the long arm of the law." Crippen was subsequently tried and executed. After his retirement, Dew wrote a memoir entitled *I Caught Crippen* (1938).

Dewey, Thomas E. (1902–71) Republican presidential candidate, governor of New York, and hardnosed lawyer; earned his spurs as the special prosecutor in New York's landmark racketeering trials during the 1930s.

In 1935, young lawyer Thomas Dewey was appointed special prosecutor for the investigation of organized crime in New York. For the next two-and-a-half years, Dewey would wreak havoc on the widespread corruption in the city. His special investigative team obtained more than 72 convictions against narcotics and vice racketeers as well as against loan sharks and racketeers in the restaurant, bakery, poul-

try, and garment trucking trades. Dewey assembled one of the most effective legal staffs in the history of investigation, swore them to silence, and made an appeal to the public for information on the bad guys. With the help of accountants, private investigators, and talented prosecutors, Dewey nabbed such big fish as underworld boss Dutch SCHULTZ—who was murdered by Lucky LUCIANO to silence him—Tammany boss James J. Hines, corrupt circuit court judge Martin T. Manton, and the biggest fish of all, Lucky Luciano himself.

The story of Dewey's New York operations became national news, provoking the *Philadelphia Inquirer* to remark, "If you don't think Dewey is public Hero No. 1 listen to the applause he gets every time he is shown in a news reel." Dewey went on to become a three-time governor of New York and made two unsuccessful presidential bids (against Franklin D. ROOSEVELT and Harry S Truman) as the Republican nominee. Dewey is still remembered as the prototype prosecutor with a passion for law and order.

Further reading: Walker, Stanley, *Dewey: An American of This Century* (New York: McGraw-Hill, 1944).

As New York's crusading district attorney, Thomas E. Dewey earned a reputation as a crimebuster and was targeted for death by mobster Dutch Shultz. (Courtesy of the National Archives)

Diamond, Jack "Legs" (alias: John T. Nolan; John Thomas Diamond; John Hart; John Higgins) (1897–1931) Earned dubious distinction as the "Clay Pigeon of the Underworld" because he survived the many hits directed against him.

It is unclear just how Legs Diamond acquired his famous moniker. Some say it was because he had earned a reputation as a dancer of great skill; others believe it was a reference to the swiftness with which he repeatedly eluded pursuing police during his early days, stealing goods from delivery trucks as a member of the Hudson Dusters gang. Whatever its source, the nickname was associated with one of the gaudiest gangsters of the Roaring Twenties, who boasted to all and sundry that "the bullet hasn't been made that can kill me."

Diamond was born in the Irish slums of Philadelphia in 1897 and, in partnership with his younger brother, Eddie, soon became a petty thief. After the death of their mother in 1913, the boys' father took them to Brooklyn, which was even tougher than Philadelphia's Kensington district. The Diamonds enlisted in the Hudson Dusters, a gang of sneak thieves, and drew the attention of such underworld luminaries as Johnny Spanish, Joseph Weyler, "Little Augie" Orgen, and Nathan "Kid Dropper" Kaplan.

Not that Diamond was all that successful at his trade. He was arrested time and time again for burglary, assault, and robbery, and was repeatedly sent to the New York City Reformatory. World War I intervened, and in 1918 he was drafted. Chafing under military life, he went AWOL, was located by the military police, and sentenced to five years in Leavenworth for desertion. After serving a year and a day of the sentence, he was paroled in 1920 and found work as bodyguard to gambling czar Arnold ROTHSTEIN. Next, Diamond was employed by Rothstein associate Little Augie Orgen, who vied violently with Kid Dropper Kaplan for control of Manhat-

tan bootlegging in the wake of the brand-new Volstead Act. Diamond quickly rose in Orgen's gang and became a close associate of Charles "Lucky" LU-CIANO, Waxey Gordon, and Louis "Lepke" BU-CHALTER. Diamond and Gordon were primarily responsible for overseeing Orgen's liquor distribution rackets, and Diamond was given the assignment of eliminating Kid Dropper Kaplan. Diamond concocted an elaborate assassination scheme, inducing a young gangster named Louis Kushner to ambush Kaplan as he left a Lower Manhattan courtroom on August 28, 1923. (Kaplan's last words were the classic: "He got me.") Diamond inherited a significant portion of Kaplan's bootleg and narcotics operations, and he plunged into a life of fast automobiles, lavish hotel suites, and gaudy nights on the town. Although married, he assembled a veritable harem of showgirl mistresses. With partner Hymie Cohen, Diamond opened the Hotsy Totsy Club on Broadway between 54th and 55th streets, which became the meeting place of New York's underworld and the scene of numerous shootouts.

On October 15, 1927, Diamond emerged with Little Augie Orgen from a meeting at Orgen's Lower East Side headquarters. The two were sprayed with machine-gun fire. Orgen died instantly, and Diamond was wounded in the leg and arm. In his hospital bed, he admonished detectives: "Don't ask me nothin'! You hear me? Don't ask! And don't bring anybody here for me to identify! I won't identify them even if I know they did it!" Knowing that Lepke Buchalter was behind the shooting, Diamond sent him a message, telling him that he had no intention of interfering with his incursion into the garment workers' union. All he wanted was to maintain control of his bootlegging and narcotics operations. However, Dutch SCHULTZ believed that Orgen's empire should devolve upon himself, and he launched a war against Diamond, which stretched over the next two years. Al-

Jack "Legs" Diamond, second from left, was shot and shot so often that he became known as the underworld's "clay pigeon." (Courtesy of the Library of Congress)

though Schultz was more often on the losing end of the war, the murder of Arnold Rothstein in 1928 dried up much of Diamond's financial backing, and Diamond soon found himself locked in combat with the would-be inheritors of Rothstein's kingdom, particularly Waxey Gordon. The most spectacular battle was a shootout in the Hotsy Totsy Club on June 13, 1929. Shortly after this, Schultz and Diamond arranged a truce meeting in which Diamond agreed to relinquish his midtown beer territory in return for $500,000, which was paid, in cash, on the spot. When Schultz and his associate Joey Noe left the meeting, Diamond's men ambushed them, killing Noe. Schultz swore revenge and, unable to locate Jack Diamond, ambushed his brother Eddie instead. Somehow, Eddie Diamond survived the attack, later to succumb to tuberculosis in a New York sanitorium.

Legs Diamond, of course, now vowed to avenge his brother and launched attacks on a series of Schultz's men. Schultz retaliated in October 1929 by storming into Diamond's room at New York's Hotel Monticello and shooting up the bed in which Diamond lay with his principal mistress, Kiki Roberts. Roberts emerged unscathed, but Diamond had been shot five times. After he recovered, he sailed for Europe, traveling in England and Belgium, where he took time out to establish lucrative drug connections before returning to New York. In April 1931, after he returned to his headquarters at an inn in Acra, New York, Diamond was again the victim of a drive-by shooting. Again, he survived. In December of 1931, Diamond moved part of his operation to Albany, New York, torturing two local bootleggers, Grover Parks and James Duncan, in order to "persuade" them to cooperate. But the code of silence was not as powerful in Albany as it was in Manhattan, and Parks and Duncan went to the police. Diamond and an associate were arrested and tried for kidnapping, but Diamond evaded conviction. Diamond, his wife, and friends celebrated the victory in an Albany speakeasy on December 17, 1931, then Diamond, leaving the party, hopped a cab to the apartment of Kiki Roberts, who had followed Diamond to Albany. After spending three hours with Kiki, the drunken gangster returned to the shabby boarding house he used as a hideout. Once inside, he passed out. That is when two assassins entered the room and pumped three slugs into Diamond's head, killing him at last.

Dillinger, John (1903–34) One of numerous bank robbers active in the Depression-plagued 1930s, he gained national prominence and even semilegendary status when J. Edgar HOOVER's FBI branded him Public Enemy Number One.

John Dillinger was born in Indianapolis on June 22, 1903. He grew into a petty thief, and, when he was

America's Depression-era public was fascinated by the exploits of bank robbers like John Dillinger, shown here (tieless on the right) at Crown Point in 1934. (Courtesy of the Chicago Historical Society)

21, he was arrested in the act of robbing a grocery store. For this, he spent nine years in prison and became a hardened criminal. After his release, he organized a gang that specialized in robbing banks across the Midwest.

As bold and skillful as Dillinger was at robbing banks, he was even better at breaking out of jail, managing to do so twice. Then, in April 1934, he fell into a combined FBI and police ambush at the Little Bohemia Lodge, north of Chicago, in Wisconsin. Instead of surrendering, Dillinger fought his way out; in the ensuing bloodbath, FBI agents under the command of Melvin PURVIS accidentally killed three innocent bystanders.

As a result of the Little Bohemia fiasco, the FBI—at the time struggling to achieve full recognition as a vital agency of law enforcement—suffered a serious public relations blow, which Hoover countered by making the Dillinger case a special crusade. In a highly publicized campaign, he branded the criminal "Public Enemy Number One," instantly transforming him into a quasi-mythical figure, the very incarnation of gangsterism. Hoover dispatched Purvis to nail Dillinger once and for all, with the aid of a "confidential informant," Anna Sage. Purvis and his agents set up an ambush outside the Biograph Theatre on Chicago's Near North Side. On July 22, 1934, Sage, wearing a scarlet dress for maximum visibility (and therefore dubbed by the press "The Lady in Red"), led Dillinger out of the theater (they had just seen a gangster movie). Purvis lit a cigar to signal his agents, and the trap was sprung. At the last minute, Dillinger sensed an ambush and fled, but the FBI agents gunned him down in a hail of bullets, which wounded two women bystanders and killed John Dillinger.

Dillinger's significance for the history of law enforcement in America has less to do with his criminal activities than with the Hoover-orchestrated role he played in bolstering the image of the Federal Bureau of Investigation as the government's incorruptible force of good against evil. Even so, his stature in the public imagination was such that unfounded rumors quickly spread, claiming that the FBI had killed the wrong man and that the "real" John Dillinger had yet again escaped.

Dix, Dorothea (1802–87)   Champion of reform in the care and protection of convicts and the institutionalized mentally ill; led a one-woman humanitarian crusade across America and Europe during the first half of the 19th century.

Dorothea Dix was a schoolteacher until 1841, when she was asked to teach a Sunday school class at the East Cambridge jail in Massachusetts. It was in this decrepit prison that Dix found her calling. Disgusted with the primitive, inhuman treatment of prisoners—especially those suffering from mental illness—Dix set out on a mission of reform. Using the newspapers, Dix wrote eloquent letters to convince the public of her cause. Her notable "Memorial to the Legislature of Massachusetts," written in 1843, successfully pressured that body to enlarge the Worcester insane asylum. Dix received national attention from this Massachusetts victory, and she used it to further her cause, following the same procedure in each state she visited. Between 1841 and 1852, her efforts resulted

Prison reformer Dorothea Dix (Courtesy of the Bettmann Archive)

in modernization and expansion of facilities in Massachusetts and Rhode Island and the construction of institutions in Pennsylvania, New Jersey, and Canada, as well as reform legislation in 10 other states.

Dix successfully petitioned the U.S. Congress to create and pass a bill to raise $12 million in taxes earmarked for the care of the insane, but President Franklin Pierce vetoed the measure in 1854. Following this, Dix took her crusade to Europe, and by 1857 "The American Invader," as she was called, had succeeded in convincing several European nations to reform as well.

Dix returned to the United States in time for the Civil War and secured an appointment as superintendent of women nurses for the Union. After the war, she continued to campaign on behalf of penal inmates and the insane. In 1881, Dix retired to a residence in Trenton Hospital—an institution she had created—where she died six years later.

Further reading: Dix, Dorothea, *On Behalf of the Insane Poor* (collection of writings) (New York: Arno Press and The New York Times, 1971).

Marshall, H. E., *Dorothea Dix: Forgotten Samaritan* (Chapel Hill: The University of North Carolina Press, 1937).

Doe, Charles (1830–96)   Chief justice of the New Hampshire Supreme Court from 1859 to 1876, Doe handed down decisions challenging the existing laws on insanity and laid the groundwork for the repealing of the antiquated M'Naghten Rules.

Charles Doe's rulings on the legality of tests for mental disorder put him among the pioneers of American criminology. The so-called M'Naghten Rules were a uniform test for insanity generally accepted in mid-19th-century American courtrooms. The M'Naghten Rules were riddled with loopholes and soon became an easy defense in grave criminal matters. Influenced by the writings of pioneering medical jurist Dr. Isaac RAY, Doe believed that a jury, not an antiquated test process, should decide whether the accused is fit to stand trial. Furthermore, Doe was the first jurist to insist that the law should collaborate with science, especially in the field of criminal responsibility. It was not until the 1950s that Doe's decisions were generally incorporated into the nation's criminal justice system, but without his insight, questions of criminal responsibility may well have remained a matter for the medical profession, not the legal process, to decide.

Suggested reading: Kenison, Frank, *Chief Justice: The Judicial World of Charles Doe* (Cambridge, Mass.: Harvard University Press, 1967).

Dondero, John A. (1900–57)   One of the foremost experts on fingerprinting in the United States was also a brilliant inventor who developed several products to outwit criminals.

John Dondero earned his bachelor's degree in chemical engineering in 1923 from the City College of New York and began work as a research chemist at Chemco Powers, Inc. Seemingly destined for a career as an industrial chemist, Dondero was by chance seated across the dinner table one night from former New York City police chief and fingerprint expert Joseph FAUROT. In casual conversation, Faurot mentioned some of the difficulties inherent in fingerprinting processes, most notably the sloppiness of the ink. Dondero went home that night and began work on an inkless fingerprint pad, which he perfected within a short time.

He soon quit his job at Chemco and founded, with the former police chief, Faurot, Inc., a manufacturer of crime-detection devices, especially fingerprinting materials. Dondero became an expert on the subject of fingerprinting, conducting numerous seminars and classes on fingerprint techniques, as well as introducing and promoting the latest devices he had invented, including special stains visible only under fluorescent light, dyes that could not be removed with regular soap and water, and powders that marked stolen bills. Dondero also developed a fingerprint bank and checking account identification system for disabled persons unable to sign their names. He created the system of footprinting babies at birth, which is now virtually universal throughout the United States. He even established a system of noseprinting dogs for identification purposes. Under Dondero's stewardship, Faurot, Inc., more than doubled in size, production, and staff, becoming one of the leading manufacturers of investigative equipment in the world.

Doolin, William M. (Bill) (1858–96)

This Wild West desperado and his gang were pursued and captured by the famed "Three Guardsmen" in the 1890s.

A fierce outlaw with a fast draw and a knack for disappearing, Bill Doolin joined the notorious Dalton Gang in 1892, after fatally wounding two deputies in a barroom dispute. Doolin rode with the gang most of the year, assisting in bank robberies and train holdups. The outlaw was a no-show, however, at the infamous ambush of the Dalton Gang in Coffeyville, Kansas, that same year, and thus escaped being wiped out with the rest of the gang.

With the Daltons out of the way, Doolin was able to assemble his own gang, "Doolin's Oklahombres," which embarked on a three-year crime spree that terrorized the West. A trio of deputy marshals was assembled with the sole mission of capturing or killing Bill Doolin's boys. The three lawmen, Chris Madsen, Bill Tilghman, and Heck Thomas—christened "The Three Guardsmen"—hunted Bill Doolin across the country until, in 1896, Heck Thomas shot Doolin down.

Further reading: O'Neal, Bill, *Encyclopedia of Western Gunfighters* (Norman: University of Oklahoma Press, 1979).

Douglas, William O. (1898–1980)

The longest-serving Supreme Court justice in history was a fierce defender of individual rights as defined in the Bill of Rights.

Born into abject poverty on October 16, 1898, in Yakima, Washington, William Douglas was stricken with polio at the age of four. As if things weren't tough enough, his father died when he was six, forcing his mother to raise him and his two siblings alone. After working his way through school, he "hopped a freight and headed east," as he put it, to Columbia University Law School in New York. He arrived completely broke, but managed to work full-time and still graduate near the top of his class. His success in the classroom earned him a clerkship with Columbia alumnus and Supreme Court Chief Justice Harlan Fiske STONE.

When his clerkship was over, Douglas got a job on Wall Street, hated it, and jumped at the chance to teach at his alma mater. In 1934, the newly created Securities and Exchange Commission offered him a post, which he took; he later headed the SEC. Franklin Delano ROOSEVELT appointed Douglas to fill the Supreme Court seat left vacant by the retirement of Louis BRANDEIS in 1939, and, at the age of 41, Douglas became the second youngest man ever to sit on the high court.

Once on the court, Douglas became a vehement supporter of the Bill of Rights. He argued that the Bill was written on the basis of human existence and that to impose limitations on the rights it guaranteed was not only unconstitutional, but also inherently oppressive, something that has always been unacceptable in the United States. His unwavering support of the First Amendment angered many because he refused to impose any restrictions upon it, culminating in the obscenity cases of the 1960s, in which he argued to uphold the Constitution every time and refused to restrict the publication of "obscene" material.

Douglas sat on the court during the liberal FDR years and remained during the conservative shift under Chief Justice Frederick Vinson, then the shift back to the left under Chief Justice Earl WARREN. During the second liberal shift, the court struck down the death penalty because the ambiguity of the legislation made for cruel and unusual punishment. Douglas, a longtime opponent of capital punishment who once granted a stay of execution to convicted spies Ethel and Julius Rosenberg, argued in his opinion that such statutes must be "evenhanded, nonselective, and nonarbitrary." Any "discretionary statutes are unconstitutional in their operation." This expression of extreme liberalism provoked a short-lived movement to impeach him, but it failed, and Douglas served until 1975, when a stroke forced his retirement.

Dowbiggin, Sir Herbert (1880–1966) One of the founding fathers of the British Colonial Police, Dowbiggin was among the first to introduce the concept of the police as primarily the servants of law rather than as the instruments of government.

After attending the Merchant Taylor's School, Herbert Dowbiggin joined the Ceylon Police Force in 1901 as an inspector. The force, still administered as a paramilitary organization, was called out only to quell civil disorder. Policemen were heavily armed and engaged in guard and patrol duties most of the time. Inspector-general C. C. Longden attempted to institute reform that would develop the force along the lines of the London Constabulary, and after Dowbiggin was promoted to superintendent in 1905, he ardently supported Longden's measures. This loyalty, as well as a tireless work ethic and efficiency at his post, led to Dowbiggin's promotion to inspector-general in 1913.

Dowbiggin completed the process begun by Longden, but took it in a new direction that left his personal stamp on the force. He redefined the mission of the Ceylonese police as the detection and prevention of crime, while dealing with civil disorder was left to the colonial militia. In 1915, a Criminal Investigation Department was created, and by 1924 a photographic branch was added. While they were trained in the use of firearms, and weapons were available in the station, the officers went on patrol unarmed, carrying only a billyclub, which they swung more as an emblem of authority than as a physical threat. In 1925, a training school was developed, a forerunner of the modern police academy, stressing academics more than the previous military drill and training in the use of firearms. A Police Boy's Brigade was also instituted, helping not only with volunteer work but also serving to involve wayward boys in lawful endeavors.

Although he never left the service of the Ceylon police, Dowbiggin gained such widespread acclaim and wielded such influence over the British Colonial Police that he served on special duty, reporting to the Cyprus Police in 1926, the Palestine Police in 1930, and the Northern Rhodesia Police in 1937.

Doyle, Sir Arthur Conan (1859–1930) English novelist and short story writer who created the most famous fictional detective ever, Sherlock Holmes.

Born on May 22, 1859, in Edinburgh, Doyle studied medicine in the famed medical school of that city.

After practicing medicine in London from 1882 to 1890, he served as senior physician to a field hospital in South Africa during the Boer War in 1899-1902. He was knighted for his services.

Doyle wrote "A Study in Scarlet," his first story featuring Sherlock Holmes, for *Beeton's Christmas Annual* in 1887. It was instantly popular. From 1890 until his death—except for his service in South Africa—Doyle was a full-time writer, producing four novels and 56 short stories based on Holmes and his admiring and credulous companion, Dr. John Watson. This body of work not only elevated the detective story to the level of a legitimate literary genre, it also forever fixed in the popular imagination the image of the master detective: an intense, if eccentric investigator who based his observations on seeming trifles that allowed him to solve mysteries by brilliant deductive reasoning.

Doyle was not entirely happy with his brilliant denizen of 221B Baker Street—Holmes's London address—since the public's insatiable demand for more Sherlock Holmes stories completely overshadowed his other literary work, which included science fiction (*The Lost World* and *The Poison Belt*, 1912 and 1913) and historical novels (such as *Sir Nigel*, 1906; *Micah Clarke*, 1889; *The White Company*, 1890), as well as his historical nonfiction (*The British Campaigns in Europe*, 1912). In 1893, Doyle attempted to kill Holmes off, sparking such public clamor that he finally produced *The Return of Sherlock Holmes* in 1904. The last Sherlock Holmes book, *The Case-Book of Sherlock Holmes*, appeared in 1927, just three years before Doyle's death. Even this was hardly the end of Sherlock Holmes, who figured in an immense body of literary scholarship, unprecedented for popular fiction, spawned a veritable Holmes cult and scores of clubs and societies and, finally, numerous films—the most enduringly popular of which star the British actor Basil Rathbone in the title role.

Following the death of his son in World War I, Doyle embraced spiritualism, producing a two-volume *History of Spiritualism* in 1926–27.

Further reading: The Sherlock Holmes stories are available in numerous editions, the most extensive of which is:
Baring-Gould, William, *The Annotated Sherlock Holmes* (New York: C.N. Potter, Distributed by Crown Publishers, 1967).

Draper, Frank Winthrop (1843–1909) Medical examiner for the state of Massachusetts; wrote an influential textbook on legal medicine, and his department served as a model for the nation.

Frank Draper was born in Wayland, Massachusetts. At age 19 he enlisted in the 35th Massachusetts Volunteers and fought in the Civil War, serving until 1864, when he was discharged with the rank of captain.

Following his discharge, he attended Harvard Medical School, graduating with honors in 1869. From 1875 to 1884, Draper taught legal medicine at the university. In 1877, he became the first medical examiner of Massachusetts, replacing the corrupt coroner's office. During 30 years as chief medical examiner, Draper earned the respect of law enforcement officials, judges, and lawyers, and his rigorous attention to detail and accuracy served as a model for the nation.

In 1905, Draper wrote *A Textbook of Legal Medicine*, which became a standard text in forensic medical education.

Drummond, Thomas (1797–1840)

Founded the Royal Irish Constabulary, which brought a measure of order to the politically strife-torn countryside.

Born in Edinburgh, Scotland, Thomas Drummond attended the University of Edinburgh at the age of 13, impressing his professors with his cheerful disposition and his diligence. After taking his degree in engineering, he began work as a surveyor in Edinburgh, where he invented two instruments important to his profession, the heliostat and the limelight, both of which greatly increased the accuracy of land surveys. The brilliant limelight—also called the Drummond light—became the chief illumination of lighthouses worldwide for many years.

In 1824, Drummond arrived in Ireland to participate in the great general survey of that land. After several years of successful work, his powerful friends arranged to have him named chancellor of the exchequer. By 1835, he was appointed undersecretary at Dublin Castle, where he began his work as the chief administrator of Ireland. At this time, the Catholic majority in Ireland was subject to government persecution and discrimination, which incited frequent incidents of mob violence. The city of Dublin employed only 400 night watchmen, all Protestant, and mostly considered lazy, belligerent drunks who were otherwise unemployable. In order to help pacify the religious fervor as well as quell the political storm led by supporters of the Protestant House of Orange, Drummond disbanded the watchmen and formed the Irish Constabulary, later the Royal Irish Constabulary. The RIC consisted of 10,000 men, a mixture of Catholic and Protestant peasants—but mostly Catholics—reflecting the actual makeup of the Irish population. Drummond argued that peace in Ireland could best be kept by trusting the Irish to keep it themselves. While this policy alarmed many in the British government, it proved quite effective. Within four years, by 1839, political faction fighting had all but ceased, and Drummond had managed to put off the great religious conflagration that would ignite a century later.

du Cane, Edmund Frederick (1830–1903)

Reformed the British prison system of the 19th century, bringing it under central government control. He also introduced registration of criminals and fingerprint identification of them.

Born in Colchester, Essex, on March 23, 1830, du Cane was the son of an army major and entered the Royal Military Academy at Woolwich in 1846. He graduated at the head of his class in 1848 and was commissioned a second lieutenant in the Royal Engineers. From 1851 to 1856, he was employed in organizing convict labor on public works in Australia, and in 1863 he became director of convict prisons as well as inspector of military prisons. In 1869, he was appointed chairman of the board of directors of convict prisons, and four years later introduced a plan for the transfer of all local prisons to government control. This was finalized in 1877, and du Cane became chairman of the prison commissioners, presiding over a prison system that had been rationalized, reduced in size by 50%, and made more efficient and more humane. Du Cane introduced uniform rules of discipline and a system of useful employment for prisoners, who were assisted after release to adjust to freedom.

Du Cane also produced in 1877 England's first "Black Book," a listing of some 12,000 known criminals, including aliases and descriptions. To this was added a more fully developed system of physical description, including the use of fingerprint registration.

Duffy, Clinton T. (1898–1982)

An advocate of rehabilitation rather than punishment for criminals, Duffy was given the chance to implement his reforms at San Quentin.

Clinton Duffy was the son of a prison guard, born and raised in the shadow of California's maximum-security San Quentin prison. Duffy saw the institution not as a monument to social decay, but as an opportunity to realize that most American of ideals, the second chance. He began working at San Quentin as a clerk, working his way to the post of warden.

By the late 1930s and 1940s, San Quentin had degenerated into the model of a grossly mismanaged prison. It was the scene of numerous riots, escape attempts, and hunger strikes. In 1949, the state's attorney general fired the warden and the entire prison board, naming Duffy as temporary warden for 30 days, and at 42, the youngest warden ever of a major prison in the United States. The temporary appointment stretched into a 12-year tenure.

As soon as he was hired, Duffy set about implementing his reform plans, which had taken shape over the many years he worked in the prison. He immediately abolished corporal punishment and replaced it with a system of privileges and the revocation of privileges, making San Quentin one of the first prisons to employ such a system. He also allowed the establishment of a prison radio station and organized a night school for the inmates. Advocates of the harsh "Auburn system"—which favored a punitive approach—criticized Duffy as soft and warned that the inmates would soon take advantage of the warden's "weakness." In fact, under Warden Duffy no once ever escaped or even attempted to escape. The prison itself had become a much safer place as well. Duffy demonstrated that he could walk alone through any area of the prison without fearing for his safety. Duffy transformed San Quentin from an example of just how bad a prison could be into an illustration of the potential of humanely and rationally managed correctional institutions.

Duncan, Andrew (1744–1828) Founder of the chair of forensic medicine at Edinburgh University and one of the pioneers of the field.

A longtime professor of medicine, Andrew Duncan devoted himself wholly to the field, inspiring his son, Andrew Jr., to follow in his footsteps and eventually to replace him on the faculty.

After establishing himself on the faculty at Edinburgh University in Scotland during the 1770s, the senior Duncan was impressed by the dearth of medical knowledge applied to legal matters. To remedy the situation, he established a chair at Edinburgh in the field of "medical jurisprudence," a phrase he coined.

After Duncan lobbied officials of the Crown and patrons of the university to obtain funding, the chair was finally established in 1791. Duncan was the first professor of medical jurisprudence, although he did not occupy the chair in that field. That distinction remained for his son, who occupied it in 1807, when the department was formally created. Nevertheless, it was the lectures of the senior Duncan that introduced the field to the British Isles and went a long way in advancing the administration of English justice.

Durkheim, Emile (1858–1917) Differing radically from his colleagues in the field of sociology, Durkheim believed crime was not only normal in a society, but beneficial to it as well.

Born in Epinal, eastern France, on April 15, 1858, Emile Durkheim attended the University of Epinal and then the Superior Normal School in Paris. After completing his formal education in 1882, he became a professor of philosophy at various schools throughout France, then accepted a full-time position at the University of Bordeaux in 1887, where he taught the first course in sociology to be offered in a French university. He left Bordeaux after 15 years to join the faculty at the University of Paris, where he finally earned his doctorate at the age of 54.

Durkheim's writings on crime and criminals radically diverge from those of his contemporaries and even later sociologists. Durkheim did not attempt to determine a cause for crime, but instead theorized that crime is simply inherent in society. Maintaining that the individual is a product of society, not the author of it, Durkheim concluded that society does not respond to the actions of the individual, but rather that the individual conforms to society's norms and what it permits. In this, Durkheim did not greatly differ from many of his colleagues, but, building on these assumptions, he went on to draw radical conclusions concerning crime.

Durkheim argued that crime is not only inherent in society, but also a normal element within it rather than a pathological one. Crime is "normal" because a society without crime is impossible. Criminal acts are simply a part of the totality of society, just as birth and death are. For a society to exist without crime would require a moral and conceptual standardization of individuals within a society "which is neither possible nor desirable." He further argued that crime is actually beneficial to society. With the presence of crime, society is forced continually to evolve its legal system, whereas without crime, the law would not evolve at all.

Further reading: Lunden, Walter A., "Emile Durkheim," *The Journal of Criminal Law, Criminology and Police Science,* 49:1 (May–June 1958).

Dzerzhinsky, Felix Edmundovich (1877–1926) The director of the first political police in communist Russia gained a reputation for his ruthlessness and fanaticism in service to the party.

Felix Dzerzhinsky was born in Vilna (in present-day Lithuania, but then under Polish rule) on September 11, 1877. Little is known of his early years until he joined the Social Democratic Party of Poland and Lithuania in 1895. By 1897, he had gained a reputation for being a radical and was arrested at Kaunas that year by czarist officials and exiled to Siberia. Two years later, he escaped and returned to Poland, only to be rearrested in Warsaw. He escaped again in 1902, but this time went to Berlin. After returning to Poland to take part in the Polish Revolution of 1905–06, Dzerzhinsky was again exiled until 1912, when he returned to Warsaw and was yet again arrested and, this time, sentenced to nine years at hard labor.

With the revolution of March 1917 in Russia, Dzerzhinsky was released and quickly became an important organizer for the November uprising that would put the communists in power. In December 1917, with the help of party leader Vladimir Ilyich LENIN, Dzerzhinsky organized and led the first communist secret, or political, police, the Cheka.

Under Dzerzhinsky's supervision, the Cheka became a potent security and terror arm of the party. Its overriding purpose, as would be true of all subsequent Soviet political police, was the protection of the state against political subversion. The Cheka was mostly concerned with internal subversion and, to the end of eliminating it, employed the "machinery of repression." The party was not enjoying the breadth of support its leaders had expected, and the Cheka was needed to maintain Communist Party supremacy over various rival factions. With Dzerzhinsky's cooperation, Lenin maintained personal control over the activities of the Cheka.

In February 1918, when the Germans announced the armistice it had concluded with the Soviets, the Cheka decreed that it would execute on sight any agents operating against the state. This broad threat was intensified after an attempt on Lenin's life and the murder of another high official. Then, on September 30, 1918, a resolution was passed authorizing a "red terror" against the bourgeoisie. By now, a civil war was in full swing within Russia, and Lenin and Dzerzhinsky unleashed the Cheka to crush anyone suspected of failing to toe the party line.

With the end of the Russian civil war in 1921, many, including Lenin, felt the Cheka had served its purpose, and they wished to reform the political police. Accordingly, in February 1922, the Cheka was abolished and replaced with the OGPU, which differed little from the Cheka except that it was subject to tighter controls. Dzerzhinsky retained general supervision of the renamed and somewhat reformed force, but he did not direct its day-to-day operations as he had before, concentrating instead on economic matters. In 1924, he was named to head the Supreme Economic Council. Two years later, on July 20, 1926, he died.

E

Earp, James (1841–1926) Eldest brother of the famous Earp family, James Earp worked behind the scenes, managing the gambling and saloon interests owned by his better-known brothers Virgil and Wyatt.

Wounded in 1863 during the Civil War, James Earp never fully recovered, which is one reason that he failed to achieve his brothers' level of notoriety. Nevertheless, Earp followed his brothers throughout their careers, looking after the lawmen's often dubious interests in gambling houses and saloons. Indeed, James's wife was a prominent western madam, whose brothels were well protected by the Earp family. James Earp died in San Francisco.

Collectively, the Earp family's exploits did much to shape the popular image of the western lawman.

See also: EARP, Morgan; EARP, Virgil; EARP, Warren; EARP, Wyatt.

Further reading: Jahns, Pat, *The Frontier World of Doc Holliday* (New York: Hastings House, 1957).

Lake, Stuart N., *Wyatt Earp: Frontier Marshal* (Boston: Houghton Mifflin, 1931).

Martin, Douglas D., *Tombstone's Epitaph* (Albuquerque: University of New Mexico Press, 1951).

O'Neal, Bill, *Encyclopedia of Western Gunfighters* (Norman: University of Oklahoma Press, 1979).

Earp, Morgan (1851–82) Lawman and younger brother of Wyatt Earp, Morgan Earp was wounded by the Clanton Gang at the famous shoot-out at the O.K. Corral in 1881.

Born in Iowa, the fourth of the legendary Earp brothers (from oldest to youngest: James, Virgil, Wyatt, Morgan, and Warren), Morgan Earp could draw and shoot with the best of the West's many gunmen. His reputation landed him a series of jobs as a lawman, including the position of deputy town marshal in the violent cattle town of Dodge City, Kansas, in 1876, and "town tamer" of lawless Butte, Montana.

In 1880, Morgan joined his older brothers Virgil and Wyatt as a shotgun rider on Wells Fargo coaches out of Tombstone, Arizona. It was in Tombstone the following year that the Earp boys, along with a disreputable, tubercular dentist named Doc Holliday, violently settled a potentially reputation-ruining feud with the cattle-rustling Clanton clan at the O.K. Corral. Wounded in that exchange, which became one of the West's legendary shoot-outs, Morgan Earp survived, only to be fatally shot in the back on March 17, 1882, in Bob Hatch's Billiard Saloon by a group of Clanton sympathizers. Morgan's dying words: "This is the last game of pool I'll ever play." Brother Wyatt EARP embarked on a campaign to avenge Morgan's death.

The five Earp brothers collectively did much to shape the popular image of the western lawman.

Further reading: Jahns, Pat, *The Frontier World of Doc Holliday* (New York: Hastings House, 1957).

Lake, Stuart N., *Wyatt Earp: Frontier Marshal* (Boston: Houghton Mifflin, 1931).

Martin, Douglas D., *Tombstone's Epitaph* (Albuquerque: University of New Mexico Press, 1951).

O'Neal, Bill, *Encyclopedia of Western Gunfighters* (Norman: University of Oklahoma Press, 1979).

Earp, Virgil (1843–1906) Lawman, prospector, and older brother of Wyatt, Virgil Earp was wounded at the infamous shoot-out at the O.K. Corral in 1881.

In 1877, after serving as deputy town marshal in Dodge City, Kansas, Virgil Earp moved to the vicinity of Prescott, Arizona, to try his hand at prospecting. He was joined by his brothers, and by 1881 the Earps had established residence in Tombstone, Arizona, with Virgil serving as the town's acting marshal. That same year, the Earps fell into a dispute with the Clanton family, which climaxed on October 26 in a shoot-out at the O.K. Corral. Both Virgil and Morgan

Earp were wounded during the incident, which resulted in the deaths of Billy Clanton and Clanton allies Frank and Tom McLaury. Doc Holliday, a tubercular dentist allied with the Earps, was also wounded in the exchange.

Several months after the shoot-out, Virgil Earp was ambushed by Clanton supporters, who hit him with five shotgun blasts. Amazingly, Earp survived the assault, and brother Wyatt had him safely transported out of the territory to recuperate.

Virgil Earp returned to Prescott around 1900. He died six years later of pneumonia. He and his brothers greatly influenced the popular conception of the 19th-century western American lawman.

See also EARP, James; EARP, Morgan; EARP, Warren; EARP, Wyatt.

Further reading: Jahns, Pat, *The Frontier World of Doc Holliday* (New York: Hastings House, 1957).

Lake, Stuart N., *Wyatt Earp: Frontier Marshal* (Boston: Houghton Mifflin, 1931).

Martin, Douglas D., *Tombstone's Epitaph* (Albuquerque: University of New Mexico Press, 1951).

O'Neal, Bill, *Encyclopedia of Western Gunfighters* (Norman: University of Oklahoma Press, 1979).

Earp, Warren (1855–1900)   The youngest of the legendary Earp brothers, Warren Earp was fatally shot in a saloon brawl with cowboy Johnny Boyett.

Warren Earp did not participate in the infamous shoot-out at the O.K. Corral in 1881, but he did assist brother Wyatt in tracking down and exacting vengeance from his brother Morgan's assassins in the latter part of that year.

After the vengeance killings, the Earps were forced to flee Arizona, Warren returning to the territory around 1900, when he embarked on a career tracking rustlers as a cattle detective. Within a few months, Earp became involved in a saloon brawl with a cowboy named Johnny Boyett, who shot and killed him. Presumably, the fight was the result of persistant ill-will toward the Earp brothers.

The history—and legend—of the Earp brothers did much to establish the popular image of the 19th-century western American lawman.

See also EARP, James; EARP, Morgan; EARP, Virgil; EARP, Wyatt

Further reading: Jahns, Pat, *The Frontier World of Doc Holliday* (New York: Hastings House, 1957).

Lake, Stuart N., *Wyatt Earp: Frontier Marshal* (Boston: Houghton Mifflin, 1931).

Martin, Douglas D., *Tombstone's Epitaph* (Albuquerque: University of New Mexico Press, 1951).

O'Neal, Bill, *Encyclopedia of Western Gunfighters* (Norman: University of Oklahoma Press, 1979).

Earp, Wyatt (1848–1929)   Most famous of the Earp brothers, this lawman, gunfighter, prospector, and pimp came to symbolize the colorful, harrowing struggle for law and order in the "wild" West of the late 19th century.

Born in Monmouth, Illinois, on March 19, 1848, Wyatt Earp spent his youth in Illinois and Iowa before moving to California with his family—including brothers James, Virgil, Morgan, and Warren—in 1864. While earning a reputation as a gunfighter and gambler in the dusty gaming saloons of San Bernardino, California, Wyatt worked as a bartender and stagecoach driver. In 1868, the Earp boys moved east to Lamar, Missouri, where Wyatt married and was elected constable in 1870. Typhoid took his wife the following year, and the lawman himself was arrested for horse theft. Earp paid a $500 fine and, after a short stint as a buffalo hunter, moved to Wichita, Kansas.

In Wichita, Earp once again became a lawman, serving as a police officer from 1874 to 1876, when he was dismissed for financial misdeeds. Earp then joined his brother Virgil as a deputy marshal in Dodge City, Kansas, from 1876 to 1879. It was in this notoriously lawless cattle town that Wyatt Earp gained his notable reputation for cleaning up crime and corruption. Yet Earp's own dealings were often less than noble. He and his friend Bat Masterson earned the dubious title of the "Fighting Pimps," because they supplemented their law enforcement incomes with gambling and prostitution enterprises. Wyatt Earp had a financial interest in at least half of the brothels in Dodge.

Leaving Dodge in 1879, Earp traveled south to Texas and was involved in a bunco scheme in Mobeetie, Texas, with the outlaw "Mysterious Dave" Mather before heading to the Arizona town of Tombstone, where the other Earp brothers had settled, with Virgil Earp serving as the town's acting marshal.

Once in Tombstone, Wyatt, eager to establish himself—at least to all appearances—as a solid citizen, associated with prominent businessmen and even joined the Republican Party. He became a saloon keeper and a deputy marshal. Part owner of the infamous Oriental Saloon, Wyatt, with his brothers, either controlled or protected for profit the town's many gambling joints and whorehouses. Among the many persons with whom the Earps had questionable or outright illegal dealings was the cattle-rustling, stagecoach-robbing Clanton clan—father N. H. "Old Man" Clanton and sons Ike, Phin, and Billy. When these worthies threatened to expose the Earps in 1881, a feud developed between the brothers and the Clantons. The Earps provoked a gunfight on October 26, 1881, celebrated in history and legend as the "Shoot-out at the O.K. Corral."

At the O.K. Corral, Wyatt Earp was joined by Doc Holliday, a hard-drinking, hard-gambling tubercular

The O.K. Corral, where the Earps shot it out with the Clantons (Courtesy of the National Archives)

dentist who had a reputation as a ruthless killer, and two other Earp brothers, Virgil and Morgan. The shoot-out resulted in the deaths of three Clanton Gang members, including Billy Clanton and the McLaury brothers, and the wounding of Virgil and Morgan Earp and Doc Holliday. Nor did the violence stop with the O.K. Corral exchange. Months after the incident, Virgil and Morgan Earp were separately ambushed by Clanton men—Virgil was gravely wounded, and Morgan was killed. This provoked Wyatt to seek revenge, and he and Holliday tracked and killed Clanton partisan Frank Stillwell. Next, Holliday and Wyatt and Warren Earp hunted down and dispatched Florentine Cruz. Wyatt also probably killed Curly Bill Brocius, a cattle-rustling associate of the McLaury brothers.

Wyatt Earp's vengeance spree made him a fugitive in Arizona, which he left for Dodge City in 1883; then he moved on to Idaho and, finally, California. It was there, in 1927, that author Stuart Lake recorded the aging lawman's life in a highly sensational biography that was largely responsible for creating the legend of Wyatt Earp. Wyatt Earp died on January 13, 1929, in Los Angeles.

See also EARP, James; EARP, Morgan; EARP, Virgil; EARP, Warren.

Further reading: Earp, Josephine Sarah Marcus, *I Married Wyatt Earp: The Recollections of Josephine Sarah Marcus Earp* (Tucson: University of Arizona Press, 1976).

Jahns, Pat, *The Frontier World of Doc Holliday* (New York: Hastings House, 1957).

Lake, Stuart N., *Wyatt Earp: Frontier Marshal* (Boston: Houghton Mifflin, 1931).

Martin, Douglas D., *Tombstone's Epitaph* (Albuquerque: University of New Mexico Press, 1951).

O'Neal, Bill, *Encyclopedia of Western Gunfighters* (Norman: University of Oklahoma Press, 1979).

Eastman, George Daniel (1912–91) A police chief, a professor, and a specialist in police training, who served as a consultant to many law enforcement agencies in the United States.

Eastman was born on November 6, 1912, and was educated at the University of Washington (B.A., 1951), New York University (M.P.A., 1959), and Michigan State University (Ed.D., 1965). From 1946 to 1952, he served as chief of the Seattle Police Department. In 1952, he became director of the western region of the National Safety Council and was a consultant to the U.S. Department of the Treasury in 1954–55. He was appointed superintendent of the Port of New York Authority (now Port Authority of New York and New Jersey) police in 1955 and served until 1957, when he became director of public safety for Pontiac, Michigan, serving until 1960. From 1960 to 1963, he was associate professor of police administration at Michigan State University, then became headquarters representative of the Public Administration Service. In 1967, he was appointed professor of political science and director of the Institute for Government Research and Service at Kent State University. He retired in 1987.

An expert in professional police training, Eastman served as consultant to more than 40 U.S. cities and wrote and edited numerous books and articles on police work, including the standard *Municipal Police Administration* (1971), of which he was principal co-editor.

Eisemann-Schier, Ruth (1942–   ) An accomplice in one of the most notable kidnapping cases of the latter half of the 20th century. She was the first woman placed on the FBI's "Most Wanted" list.

A native of Honduras, Central America, Ruth Eisemann-Schier was in the United States working as a biology researcher when she met Gary Steven Krist, a career criminal who smooth-talked her into participating in his scheme of kidnapping Barbara Jane Mackle and holding her for ransom. Mackle, the daughter of a wealthy Florida real estate developer who was also a personal friend of then president-elect Richard Nixon, was kidnapped in the early morning hours of December 17, 1968, in Atlanta. The kidnappers took the girl to a wooded area in Gwinnett County, just outside of the city, and buried her alive in an oversized coffin with a small electric light, minimal food and water, and tubes to the surface to admit air. They demanded a ransom of $500,000, to be dropped in a remote location in southern Florida. When Krist went to pick up the money, he was surprised by a cop, who mistook him for a burglar. He was able to escape with the money, but not before the getaway car was discovered and both Krist and Eisemann-Schier were identified.

Shortly after midnight on December 20, the FBI received a tip as to the whereabouts of Mackle. She had survived her ordeal, but the light was dead and the food and water almost gone. Two days later, Krist was caught while attempting to flee, but Eisemann-Schier made it as far as Oklahoma. The FBI posted her on its Ten Most Wanted list, giving her the dubious distinction of being the first woman ever to make the list. In Oklahoma, Eisemann-Schier was arrested when she applied for a job under an alias.

Gary Krist was sentenced to life imprisonment, but was released on parole in 1979 under the condition that he live with his family in Alaska. Ruth Eisemann-Schier was sentenced to seven years in prison and upon her release was deported to Honduras.

Enright, Richard Edward (1871–1953)   The first New York City police commissioner to rise from the department's own ranks, Enright instituted many changes in administrative policy—and attracted considerable public controversy—during his eight-year tenure in the difficult era of World War I and Prohibition.

Born on August 30, 1871, in Campbell, New York, Enright was a telegrapher in Elmira and Queens before joining the police department in 1896. After two decades of service, he had climbed no higher than lieutenant; his outspoken presidency of the Police Lieutenants' Benevolent Association stung and irritated department superiors, and Enright was three times passed over for promotion to captain. But when John F. Hylan, who respected Enright's views, became mayor of the city in 1918, the lieutenant was made commissioner—and made history, as the position's first force-trained appointee.

Enright immediately launched a series of reorganizational campaigns. In keeping with his earlier championship of the professional rank and file, Enright solicited public donations to help rookie officers defray their equipment expenses. He mandated a day off for every six days on duty, abandoned the "shoo-fly" method of internal espionage in favor of an honor code, and lobbied the federal government to exempt his officers from the ravenous wartime draft. (At the same time, the commissioner exhorted his force to arrest civilian draft evaders and bring into custody any "enemy aliens" found on the beat.) Responding to suffragist pressure, he hired a token number of female officers. Later in his tenure, Enright made improvements to the pension system, expanded the police relief fund, and founded a convalescent home near Tannersville, New York, for the recuperation of ailing officers and those injured in the line of duty.

To better serve the metropolis itself, Enright reorganized the city's precincts and reduced their number. He opened the Missing Persons Bureau 24 hours a day, created a special city-wide division to stamp out

In 1918 career-cop Richard Enright replaced Harvard patrician Arthur Woods as New York City's police commissioner and changed the direction of the NYPD for 50 years. (Courtesy of the UPI/Bettmann Archive)

vice and illegal gambling, and revised the department's merit system—which had previously rewarded sheer volume of individual arrests—to discourage any promotion-motivated officer from harassing private citizens. Enright's aggressive efforts to purge and streamline the police department—and to replace corrupt, inefficient, and incompetent officers with fresh, young, earnest recruits—brought him into conflict with more complacent elements on the force and in the political community. But when he pressed a longtime and much-lauded vice investigator, "Honest Dan" Costigan, into unwelcome retirement, Enright stirred a storm of general public opposition as well.

Prohibition posed additional law enforcement challenges and brought increased internal affairs woes. By 1922 the city was awash with crime waves, and the police department was under grand jury and congressional committee investigations for bootleg graft and corruption. Although Enright countered public accusations with personal libel suits, the controversy remained unresolved. Two years later, Enright himself reluctantly brought charges against a host of police inspectors and captains for failing to enforce the constitutionally mandated liquor ban.

Before he retired as commissioner in December 1925, Enright initiated the International Police Conference to encourage dialogue and greater cooperation among law enforcement organizations around the globe. He made use of his position to promote the notion of universal fingerprint registration, which, he argued, would benefit the law-abiding public—in missing persons, amnesia, inheritance, life insurance, and other identification-dependent cases—as well as the police. Enright also wrote his first detective novel, *Vultures of the Dark*, in 1924, and though it was fairly well received, his hasty follow-up, *The Borrowed Shield*, met with little interest the following year.

After stepping down from office, Enright briefly attempted the publication of a pulp magazine, then entered into a business providing automatic alarm systems to retail stores. He called upon his police experience again in 1933, when he organized a law enforcement service for the New Deal's National Recovery Administration. In his last years, he directed the New York-based United Service Detective Bureau. At the age of 82, he fell at a friend's home, and the resulting spinal cord injury ended his life.

Esquirol, Jean Etienne Dominique (1772–1840)

Protégé of the great psychologist-physician Philippe PINEL, Esquirol was one of the pioneers in the field of psychiatry during the early 19th century, working to differentiate the mentally ill from criminals.

Although the Frenchman's theories were based on traditional concepts of the environmental causation of mental disease, his advanced research and methods of observation trained a generation of physicians who would become the first true psychiatrists. Esquirol focused much of his attention on the antiquated state of asylums in his native France. He was directly responsible for the planning of new asylums in Rouen, Nantes, and Montpellier, and indirectly responsible for the rational and objective treatment of the mentally ill. Esquirol helped to create the first laws of protection for the mentally ill, putting France in the vanguard of an international reform movement.

Further reading: Amdur, M. K., and E. Messinger, "Jean Etienne Dominique Esquirol," *American Journal of Psychiatry*, 96 (1939), 129–35.

Esquirol, Jean, *Mental Maladies: A Treatise on Insanity* (New York: Hafner, 1965; first published, 1845).

Evert, Anghelos (1895–1971)

The chief of police of Athens, Greece, during World War II, Evert was able to aid the Greek resistance as well as hinder German efforts to round up Jews in the area.

Graduating with a law degree from Athens University in 1930, Anghelos Evert joined the Athens police force and was named chief in 1939. When the Germans and the Italians invaded Greece, Evert was persuaded by the Greek prime minister to remain in his position and use it as a cover to aid the Greek resistance. Evert ostensibly cooperated with the occupying forces, while actually acting as a double agent. He became the liaison between the Greek resistance and Allied secret agents operating within Greece. Evert coordinated resistance attacks and warned of impending Axis raids through a secret radio he had installed in police headquarters.

Despite Evert's work, the invaders suppressed much of the resistance movement and then turned to rounding up Greek Jews. In 1943, Evert began secretly issuing false identification papers to all Jews who requested them. By the end of the war, he had issued thousands of these documents, thereby enabling many Greek Jews to avoid the Nazi death camps. For his actions, he was awarded special recognition by the Israeli government in 1969 and was saluted by an assembly of thousands of Jews, who waved their lifesaving false papers at him.

F

Fallon, William J. (1886–1927)   One of the flashiest and most celebrated defense lawyers of the 20th century was not above breaking the law himself to get an acquittal.

A graduate of Fordham University Law School, William Fallon was named a Westchester County assistant district attorney right out of school and rapidly gained a reputation as an effective courtroom orator. Going into private practice, he soon earned the sobriquet of the "Great Mouthpiece," defending (it seemed) every prominent pimp, prostitute, numbers runner, thief, gangster, and murderer in New York City.

Fallon ran up an astounding record, never losing to the electric chair even one of his more than 100 murder clients, many of whom looked hopelessly guilty.

Fallon's achievements were not always due solely to his oratorical skills and meticulous investigative technique. Often, he just plain cheated. On one occasion, for example, he had the prosecuting attorney's briefcase stolen just before presentation of evidence. Sometimes he bribed jurors, offering them $2,500 up front, then $2,500 after acquittal—though he never made the second payment. He was often brazen enough to tamper with a jury within the confines of the courthouse itself.

Fallon's specialty was hung juries—which required convincing just one juror to vote not guilty. Frequently, during jury selection, he would pick the most gullible or naive person and then direct his entire defense, including opening and closing remarks, to that one juror.

Fallon's sharp practices caught up with him, in more ways than one. In 1924, he was brought up on jury bribery charges after reporters for one of William Randolph Hearst's newspapers had him shadowed until he slipped up. Fallon conducted his own defense and won an acquittal by making Hearst the defendant rather than himself. He frequently questioned Hearst's character and even suggested sexual delinquency on Hearst's part. Fallon died three years after this triumph, on April 29, 1927, from heart disease complicated by acute alcoholism.

Further reading: Fallon, William J., *The Great Mouthpiece: A Life Story of William J. Fallon* (New York: Blue Ribbon Books, 1931).

William J. Fallon, left, with Stephen Clow, publisher, 1937 (Courtesy of the UPI/Bettmann Archive)

Faulds, Henry (1843–1930) Fingerprinting pioneer who developed practical applications for criminal identification through the use of fingerprints.

Henry Faulds was the first trained scientist to observe the phenomenon of fingerprint identification. As a Scottish physician teaching physiology to medical students in Tokyo, Faulds first encountered the ancient Japanese custom of fingerprinting documents, a symbolic gesture of good faith in that country. After collecting numerous prints, Faulds noticed the uniqueness of each individual print. Faulds realized that the unique signature of the human fingerprint might revolutionize the archaic methods of criminal identification then in use. In 1880, he published his findings in *Nature,* an English journal. Faulds's article drew fire from William HERSCHEL, a British colonial bureaucrat who had also been working on fingerprinting as a means of criminal identification. This dispute, which appeared in the pages of *Nature,* triggered a feud between Faulds and Scotland Yard, which overshadowed the importance of Faulds's observations and conclusions, which, in fact, were more thorough and scientific than Herschel's. It was not until the 1930s, shortly after Faulds's death, that his contributions to the science of fingerprint identification were officially recognized.

Further reading: Faulds, Henry, *Guide to Finger-Print Identification* (Hanley, England: Wood, Mitchell & Co., 1905).

Faurot, Joseph A. (1872–1942) Considered the "father of fingerprinting" in the United States, this young New York City police officer overcame formidable bureaucratic obstacles to gain national acceptance for fingerprint identification in the early 1900s.

The study of fingerprints was hardly new to the world in 1904, when it was first widely seen in America at the Louisiana Purchase Exhibition. The uniqueness of human fingerprints and the application of this property to criminal identification had been researched extensively in Britain by such early pioneers as Henry FAULDS, Sir Francis GALTON, and William HERSCHEL, and in Argentina by Juan VUCETICH. By the late 1800s, Scotland Yard was the hub of fingerprint experimentation.

After attending the Louisiana Purchase Exhibition, young New York police officer Joseph Faurot convinced his superior, police commissioner William McAdoo, to allow him to go to London to study this new technique. By the time Faurot returned, however, McAdoo had been replaced by a new commissioner who wanted nothing to do with fingerprint identification. Convinced more than ever of the importance of fingerprint identification, and undaunted by the commissioner's rebuff, Faurot set out to prove his theories on his own. He built up a sizable collection

of prints and, through dint of careful observation and study, made himself an expert at identification. But his expertise proved incapable of shaking the status quo.

Faurot, it seemed, needed a miracle. And he got it in 1906— while walking his beat, which included the exclusive Waldorf-Astoria hotel. There he came across a well-dressed man who nevertheless struck him as suspicious. On a policeman's hunch, Faurot arrested the gentlemen and brought him to the station. There, on his own initiative, he fingerprinted his suspect. The individual, now loudly giving vent to his outrage, claimed to be James Jones, an Englishman. Resisting pressure from his superiors to release the suspect, Faurot sent his prints to Scotland Yard. After 14 days, Scotland Yard communicated a positive identification of the man Faurot had arrested. "James Jones"—nothing more than one of many aliases—was wanted in Britain for a string of hotel thefts.

Confronted with Scotland Yard's reply, the suspect confessed, thereby vindicating Faurot's faith in fingerprinting. It would take Faurot another five years of patient crusading—and an important case—to gain acceptance for fingerprinting as legally admissible evidence. The landmark case involved a burglar named Caesar Cellar. Apprehended and tried in 1911, the suspect was convicted solely on the fact that his prints were found at the scene. The skeptical judge, who had never heard of fingerprinting, directed Faurot to leave the courtroom while 15 men inked impressions of their prints. One of these individuals put his fingerprints on a glass as well. Faurot was summoned back and given the glass, which he dusted for prints. With great drama, the young officer immediately identified the owner of the prints on the glass. Judge and jury were sufficiently impressed to find Cellar guilty. The criminal further obliged by subsequently confessing to the crime.

Faurot's star now rapidly ascended within the department. He established the police department's fingerprint bureau and rose to the rank of deputy commissioner. He retired in 1930, having been responsible for untold thousands of arrests and successful prosecutions.

Fedele, Fortunato (1550–1630) Author of one of the earliest works on forensic medicine, who was among the first to suggest autopsy when investigating deaths under mysterious circumstances.

A native of Palermo, Sicily, Fortunato Fedele first gained notoriety with the publication of his *Report on Medicine,* which was published at the beginning of the 17th century. This work not only dealt with previously published Greek and Latin material, but for the first time in European medicine also included Arabic advances in the field of legal medicine. Because of this work, Fedele is considered one of the founders of forensic medicine.

Fedele advocated investigative autopsy and carried out hundreds of autopsies himself, making detailed notes. He was able to determine, for example, how an accidental drowning could be differentiated from an intentional killing. He conducted tests on numerous persons who had died from varying causes and made copious notes outlining what the tissue looked like under different conditions and how specific irregularities might be taken as signs of foul play.

Fedele was also one of the first to discuss the subject of chronic lead poisoning caused by the use of lead water pipes.

Ferracuti, Franco (1927–   )   Advocate for the development of a discrete investigative discipline of criminological diagnosis who argues that the field should be developed along the lines of medicine and psychiatry.

Born in Italy, Franco Ferracuti attended the University of Rome, graduating cum laude in 1951 with a master's degree. He held numerous positions in criminology, including as a consultant for the United Nations on kidnapping and anti-terrorism, before returning to the University of Rome to teach criminological medicine and forensic psychiatry.

Ferracuti came to believe that criminology lacked definition as a field, largely because of the absence of a model of professional diagnosis similar to that which exists in medicine and psychiatry. Ferracuti noted that, in the two medical professions, the ailment is the first to be defined, studied, and treated, whereas in criminology the "patient"—that is, the criminal— is the primary focus, and the "ailment" is relegated to the background or even ignored completely. Ferracuti criticized the lack of standardized methods in diagnosis in criminology, a deficiency that is exacerbated by the general unwieldiness of the criminal justice system, which involves multiple interventions by such figures as the arresting police officer, the lawyer, the judge, the staff of the prison system, and, finally, the parole officer. There is little coordination among these elements and scant possibility of standardizing typology and classification among them. Ferracuti argued that, until criminology becomes a more rigorously consistent discipline with emphasis on consistent diagnosis and methods of diagnosis, its effectiveness in defining, preventing, and treating crime will continue to be compromised.

Ferri, Enrico (1856–1929)   A criminal sociologist who argued the theory of social responsibility in explaining both crime and punishment.

Born on February 25, 1856, in the province of Mantua, Italy, Enrico Ferri was admitted to the University of Bologna in 1873. In his third year of study there, Ferri began to develop his theory of social responsibility in opposition to the widely accepted doctrine of individual free will. Ferri argued at his dissertation defense in 1877—and would elaborate on this argument for the rest of his professional life—that a criminal had a social responsibility, not a moral or legal one, to be accountable to the society against which he perpetrated the criminal act. Ferri further argued that social responsibility took precedence over the so-called moral responsibility to one's own supposedly free will.

After traveling in France for a year of statistical criminal study, Ferri studied at the University of Turin for a year under the renowned criminologist LOMBROSO. Afterward, Ferri accepted a three-year appointment as professor of criminal law at his alma mater, then moved from there to the University of Siena in 1882. After Siena, Ferri began a political career that would see his election to the Italian parliament.

During his time in the parliament and after his eventual defeat, caused by his unpopular ties to the Socialist Labor Party, Ferri embarked on a series of lectures in which he expounded his theories of criminal sociology. He stressed the social responsibility not only of the criminal, but of the justice system as well. He was a firm believer in the punishment fitting the crime—something not at all universally accepted in Europe at this time. Ferri believed that society was collectively responsible for exacting a fitting indemnity from the criminal and rehabilitating him so he might again become a contributing member of society.

When Benito Mussolini came to power in Italy, Ferri was asked to propose a new penal system for the nation. He gladly accepted and went about formulating the new system according to his positivist views. Called either the Ferri Project or the Ferri Draft, the new penal code was finished in 1922, seven years before Ferri's death on April 12, 1929.

Further reading: Sellin, Thorsten, "Enrico Ferri," *The Journal of Criminal Law, Criminology and Police Science,* 48:5 (January–February 1958).

Field, Poole (1880–1948)   An explorer and prospector who was a member of the Northwest Mounted Police and one of the few lawmen in the remote Canadian Klondike.

Poole Field lived for much of his life in Aklavik, the far northern outpost of the Canadian Northwest Territories. He was a prospector and fur trapper who also served as a member of the Northwest Mounted Police, patrolling the remote Nahani Valley, where many men died in search of gold during the days of the Klondike rush. He was often the only representative of law enforcement in the region during the roaring gold rush days.

During World War II, Field was in charge of a U.S. Army Air Force supply depot at Fort Providence.

Fielding, Sir Henry (1707–54)   Best remembered as 18th-century England's greatest novelist—the author of *Tom Jones* and other books—Fielding was also magistrate for the City of Westminster from 1748 to 1754 and creator of the famed "Bow Street Runners," an early prototype of a truly professional police force.

The son of an army general and grandson of a judge on the King's Bench—England's principal criminal court—Henry Fielding was educated at Eton, where he made a lifelong friend in George Lyttleton, who became a politician in adult life and secured Fielding's appointment to the post at Bow Street.

Fielding, a writer of great gifts and one of England's most important and popular novelists, took his 1749 appointment very seriously, publishing *An Enquiry into the Causes of the Latest Increase of Robbers*, an enlightened essay that called for unprecedented police reform.

At the time of Fielding's appointment, the position of magistrate was in great disrepute. Preceding magistrates had been little more than racketeers and, if anything, protectors of London's flourishing criminal

English novelist and magistrate Henry Fielding was the creator of the "Bow Street Runners," an early prototype of a truly professional police force. (Courtesy of the Library of Congress)

element. Fielding set out to rid Bow Street—as the magistrate's headquarters building was called—of corruption. In 1752, Fielding published at his own expense *The Covent-Garden Journal*, which publicized thefts, gave descriptions of criminals, and sought to interest the populace in criminal law. The *Covent-Garden* was the forerunner of the *Police Gazette*, issued years later by Scotland Yard.

Fielding's persistent call for a professional police force went largely unheeded by a public that mistrusted the civil extension of royal power and by government officials, who simply remained indifferent to matters of public welfare. Fielding persevered, however, and in 1753 obtained a small grant from the government, which he used to assemble a force of 12 men to investigate a series of murders in London. This small body of agents is considered to be the first professional police force in London.

Henry Fielding died the following year, but his half brother John FIELDING, who succeeded him, kept the group together. First popularly called "Mr. Fielding's People," they eventually came to be celebrated as the "Bow Street Runners."

Further reading: Dudden, F.H., *Henry Fielding: His Life, Works, and Times* (Hamden, Conn.: Archon Books, 1966).

Fitzgerald, Percy, *Chronicles of Bow-Street Police Office* (London: Chapman and Hall, 1888).

Pringle, Patrick, *Hue and Cry: The Story of Henry and John Fielding and the Bow Street Runners* (New York: Morrow, 1955).

Fielding, Sir John (1721–1780)   Magistrate of the City of Westminster and leader of the famed "Bow Street Runners"—London's first professional police force—from 1754 to 1780, Fielding and his older half brother Henry are credited as the founders of the modern police.

John Fielding succeeded his half brother Henry FIELDING as Westminster magistrate in 1754. Totally blind, John Fielding (according to legend) could recognize and identify some 3,000 criminals by voice alone.

John Fielding took up where his half brother had left off, maintaining the Bow Street Runners and continuing the campaign for a major professional police force in England. John Fielding made Bow Street a genuine police headquarters, and, for the first time ever, two horses were kept at the ready outside the building in order to pursue robbers and bandits.

John and Henry Fielding proposed the introduction of such modern police methods as routine patrols to prevent crime and the maintenance of a full-time force. But it would take another half-century before their ideas were further developed and fully instituted.

Further reading: Dudden, F. H., *Henry Fielding: His Life, Works, and Times* (Hamden, Conn.: Archon Books, 1966).

Fitzgerald, Percy, *Chronicles of Bow-Street Police Office* (London: Chapman and Hall, 1888).

Pringle, Patrick, *Hue and Cry: The Story of Henry and John Fielding and the Bow Street Runners* (New York: Morrow, 1955).

Finch, Stanley Wellington (1872–1967?)

The first chief of the Bureau of Investigation (forerunner of the Federal Bureau of Investigation) concentrated his efforts on combating the white slave trade.

Finch grew up in upstate New York but went to Baker University in Baldwin City, Kansas, for his undergraduate education, then moved to Washington, D.C., where he studied at the Corcoran Scientific School. In 1893, Finch joined the U.S. Department of Justice as a clerk, moving up to bookkeeper, then special examiner, and, finally, chief examiner of the U.S. Courts. While he worked at Justice, he earned a law degree from National University (now American University) in Washington, gaining admission to the Washington bar in 1909. That same year, he was nominated to head the newly formed Bureau of Investigation, forerunner of the FBI.

Finch dedicated himself to destruction of "white slavery trafficking"—that is, organized prostitution. The problem as Finch saw it was that federal statutes made it difficult to halt the white slave trade. When Finch took office, no statute prohibited attempting to entice someone into prostitution. It was only illegal to *succeed* in the attempt. Also, it was not against the law to use the mails in connection with the trafficking, specifically to advertise prostitution. Finch successfully lobbied Congress for new laws closing the loopholes, and, so armed, he made substantial inroads into the trade. He turned next to rehabilitating victims of white slavery. With the help of John D. Rockefeller and other wealthy philanthropists, Finch set up a system of thousands of halfway houses, which was an important step in decriminalizing the victims of prostitution.

Fodere, Francois-Emmanuel (1764–1835)

One of the early leaders in providing a medical basis for the investigation and judgment of crime, Fodere was an active supporter of autopsy as well as "state medicine," or public health.

Rising to prominence in 1798 with the publication of *Treatise on Legal Medicine and Public Hygiene*, Francois-Emmanuel Fodere became the standard source of authority on the subject for the better half of the early 19th century. As a result of Fodere's work in France and the work of the many colleagues he influenced throughout Europe, numerous European nations established the office of public physician to look after the increasingly urgent hygienic needs of the cities as well as to serve as medical consultants to the courts. The public physician was thus a cross between today's public health official and the coroner.

The universities of Prague and Vienna began to offer courses on what was called "state medicine" and public health. By the time of Fodere's death in 1835, his theories on state medicine and the legal benefits of autopsy were very widely accepted and had been put to practical use.

Foreman, Percy (1902–88)

One of America's greatest and most successful trial lawyers; defended James Earl Ray—the accused assassin of Dr. Martin Luther King Jr.—and many other high-profile clients.

Born on June 21, 1902, in Cold Springs, Texas, Percy Foreman was raised in a log cabin, the son of the local sheriff. After quitting school at the age of 15, he entered law school at the University of Texas at Austin on the advice of his mother who told him that "law would be [his] best bet." Earning his degree in 1927, Foreman quickly established himself as one of the preeminent trial lawyers in the nation.

Foreman's courtroom demeanor was something out of rural folklore—with his disarmingly bumbling manner, his gaudy checkered and plaid suits, and his habit of pretending to guess at the facts during cross-examination while "accidentally" asking questions that yielded the most damning of answers. In his 60-plus years of law, involving more than 1,500 capital cases, fewer than half ever went to trial, and of the remainder he lost only 53. Only one of his many clients went to the electric chair—someone Foreman later said "deserved to die."

Foreman was given the case of James Earl Ray, the accused assassin of civil rights leader Dr. Martin Luther King Jr., only 36 hours before trial. Ray had dismissed his original lawyer after briefly meeting with Foreman, who persuaded him to plead guilty to the murder and accept a sentence of 99 years, because he was certain Ray would be convicted and get the death penalty in Tennessee.

Fosdick, Raymond Blaine (1883–1972)

Wrote two seminal books on police systems in Europe and the United States.

Born in Buffalo, New York, the son of a high school principal, Raymond Fosdick entered Colgate College in 1901 but transferred to Princeton University two years later, graduating in 1905 and taking his master's degree a year later. After clerking in a New York City law office for a time, Fosdick earned his law degree in 1908 from New York Law School. After various jobs in the public sector, including a stint as comptroller of the Democratic National Committee, Fosdick was approached by John D. Rockefeller Jr. to undertake a comprehensive study of European police organizations on behalf of one of the Rockefellers' philanthropic foundations. Fosdick spent almost all of 1913 traveling in Europe, visiting almost every major city on the Continent and in England to observe their methods of law enforcement and investigation. Upon his return to the United States, he published *European Police Systems* in 1915.

The book was highly admiring of European police departments and methods, giving particular praise to the quality of men attracted to these forces and the "elaborate training schools" in which they were educated. The book commanded such attention that Rockefeller asked him to undertake a second volume, this one on police organizations in the United States. Again Fosdick immersed himself in the task, traveling for the better part of a year to visit every city in the country with a population of 100,000 or more—72 metropolises in all. In contrast to his European study, Fosdick found much to fault among American law enforcement agencies. He particularly criticized the political scandals that plagued many departments and the prevailing lack of professionalism, which he believed was directly attributable to the dearth of educated men entering the field. As a result of Fosdick's books, the public agitated for reform. Fosdick was almost universally unpopular in American law enforcement circles, but his works nevertheless brought about much reform following World War I.

Fosdick went on to serve his country in various official governmental capacities, including as U.S. representative to the League of Nations. He was also active on the boards of directors of several nonprofit foundations.

Fouché, Joseph (1759–1820) NAPOLEON's first minister of police.

Fouché was born near Nantes, into a wealthy seafaring family, but since his health was frail, his parents decided that he should become a priest rather than a sailor. Accordingly, he was educated at the Oratory in Nantes, took minor church orders, and became a professor of logic, mathematics, and physics at the Oratory, finally gaining appointment in 1791 as prefect of the Oratory college. Although he was quiet and retiring, Fouché was also a freethinker who imbibed the revolutionary spirit of the day. He became a Freemason and an associate of Robespierre and in 1792 resigned from the Oratory to accept election to the National Convention. As a member, he quickly embraced the cause of the Left and was among those who voted for the death sentence upon Louis XVI.

By 1793, Fouché was a zealous member of the Committee of Public Safety, principal instrument of the Reign of Terror, which followed the Revolution.

His most notorious mission was as a commissioner sent to Lyon to bring that wavering city back into the revolutionary fold. This he did by means of summary tribunals and liberal use of the guillotine. When the guillotine failed to keep pace with the volume of the execution orders, Fouché and other commissioners ordered mass execution by cannon fire. Such excesses were too much even for the radical Robespierre, who declared that either his head or that of Fouché must fall. Fouché survived; Robespierre did not.

Fouché did, however, fall from his lofty position and, for a period of about five years, sank into obscurity and poverty. In 1798, the Directory appointed him minister plenipotentiary to the Cisalpine Republic (the region of present-day northern Italy), then, the next year, briefly made him ambassador to Holland. Finally, on July 29, 1799, he was appointed minister of police.

Fouché decided that he would leave what he disdainfully called the policing of "the whores, the thieves and the street lamps" entirely to his subordinates, while he himself would concentrate on using the police as an instrument for restoring equilibrium to the state. He developed a secret police force, and with it he closed down the radical Jacobin Club, but he was careful to avoid interfering with the emerging Napoleon Bonaparte and deftly stepped aside when the coup d'etat came. For this, Napoleon confirmed Fouché as minister of police.

One of Fouché's first assignments was the investigation of an attempt to assassinate Napoleon in December 1800. He went about this work thoroughly, exhibiting a flair for police science. He also waged an effective war against the bandits who were rife throughout the countryside. Fouché reorganized the police of Paris, establishing the prefecture system that survives to this day—a department answerable directly to the central government. He nationalized the provincial police as well, establishing a system of police departments and administration proportional to the population of provincial districts and towns. While citizens had good reason to be leery of Fouché, one-time apostle of the Terror, he, in fact, introduced a policy of restraint and a respect for justice, admonishing his prefects not to harass the innocent, not to detain suspects unnecessarily, and never to make arrests on mere suspicion. The former executioner of Lyon now saw himself as the advocate of a new and orderly government. The police, he believed, should serve primarily a preventive role and should not be a means of punishment for crimes committed.

Fouché served as minister of police from 1799 to 1802, then from 1804 to 1810, again in 1815—when Napoleon returned from his exile on Elba to lead France during the so-called "Hundred Days"—and finally under Louis XVIII, from July 8 to September 15, 1815. He not only established a rational administrative organization for the French police, he also laid the foundation of the ministry's intelligence resources, developing a far-flung network of informers and operatives. While Fouché forged the French police into an effective organization for fighting common crime, he also honed it into an instrument for suppressing dissent before it developed into full-scale revolt. He was the father of what French police today call *Renseignements Généraux*—General Intelligence.

Fox, Lionel Wray (1895–1960)

Chairman of the Prison Commission (Great Britain); wrote *The Modern English Prison* in 1934, a ground-breaking book on penal reform.

Lionel Fox was born on February 21, 1895, in Halifax, the son of a draftsman. He was educated at Heath Grammar School and at Hertford College, Oxford, leaving before he took his degree, to join the army at the outbreak of World War I in 1914. After serving with distinction and being decorated several times, Fox joined the Home Office in 1919 and from 1925 to 1934 served as secretary to the Prison Commission. In 1934, he was appointed deputy receiver to the metropolitan police district, and in 1941 returned to the Prison Commission as its chairman. He served in that capacity during World War II, when the prison system not only suffered from a severe shortage of manpower, but was also subject to damage from German bombs. In 1959, he was among the authors of the white paper "Penal Practice in a Changing Society," which initiated the largest prison building program England had seen in more than a century.

In 1934, Fox published *The Modern English Prison*, which advocated reforms to ensure that a prison would be less a place of punishment than an institution to promote rehabilitation. He believed that crime was not deterred by the severity of anticipated punishment, but by a would-be offender's feeling that his wrongdoing would be detected and that he would be punished. Once deterrence was removed as a justification of severe punishment, it became possible to rethink prisons as humane places in which rehabilitation could take place. The modern prison, Fox declared, should "turn the prisoners out of prison better men and women than when they came in."

In 1952, Fox published *The English Prison and Borstal Systems*, still regarded as a standard work on penology. In it, Fox proposed a wide array of alternatives to traditional prisons, including the so-called "open prison" system. Fox served on the United Nations International Penitentiary Commission and was a visiting fellow of the Institute of Criminology at Cambridge.

Further reading: Fox, Lionel Wray, *The English Prison and Borstal Systems* (London: Heinemann, 1952).

France, Johnny (1940–)

Celebrated as the "mountain man sheriff" for his 1984 capture of Don and Dan Nichols, kidnappers of world-class athlete Kari Swenson, in the Montana wilderness.

Raised by an uncle and aunt on a Madison County, Montana, ranch, Johnny France grew up to become the county sheriff. In July 1984, Kari Swenson, a world-class biathelete, was training near the Big Sky resort when she was abducted by two mountain men, a father and son named Don and Dan Nichols. Search parties were dispatched, and one of the searchers, Al Goldstein, discovered the Nicholses. Kari was chained to a tree, bleeding, having taken a .22 slug through her lung and out her back. Goldstein tried to capture the pair but was shot to death. The two mountain men unchained Swenson and left her to die. She was, however, rescued, and she subsequently recovered.

In the meantime, Sheriff France pledged that he would find the Nicholses. "I'm a mountain man, too," he said. "It will take one to catch one. I'll get them."

It took five months of dogged tracking, during which time France was constantly pressured to use more men and to speed up the search. He feared, however, that the elder Nichols, clearly unbalanced would kill his son if he were cornered, and France wanted to keep the boy alive. On December 14, 1984, he tracked the pair and managed to arrest them without incident. France continued to serve Madison County as sheriff until 1986, when he lost his bid for reelection.

Frank, Johann Peter (1745–1821)

Considered by many to be the founder of public health, Frank extended the idea of "policing" to the area of maintaining public health.

Born in Germany, Johann Frank was destined by his mother for the priesthood. After he began his advanced education in Metz in 1761, however, he became attracted to physics. After graduating at the age of 18 and having given up all notion of the priesthood, Frank went to Heidelberg to study medicine. Finishing his medical studies at the University of Strasbourg in 1766, he studied French to qualify for work in Lorraine, France. After several years, Frank returned to Baden, Germany, with the intention of working in what would come to be called the field of public health.

Frank took a special interest in the training of midwives, having lost his wife and child in childbirth. He was appointed director of the Midwives Association in Baden, and in 1773 he founded a school of obstetrics in Speyer. In 1779, the first volume of his landmark work on public health, *A Complete System of Medical Police*—as the title is usually translated—was published. In this work, he argues for the necessity of the lawful enactment of his policies as a political necessity in the process of the maturation of civilization. He developed the concept of a force of public health officials working in cooperation with police agencies and, in effect, as police themselves.

He continued to work on his *System*, eventually completing six volumes dealing with population problems and regulation, control of prostitution, public school health, sports injuries, sex education, infant and maternal welfare, and the disposal of sewage and garbage. He also published a subsequent six-volume work on *The Treatment of Diseases of Man*, a product of his years as a practical clinician. Frank returned to Vienna in his later years to finish his writings and maintain his clinical practices.

Frankfurter, Felix (1882–1965) A vocal liberal before his appointment to the Supreme Court, Frankfurter became a leading proponent of judicial restraint during his tenure on the high bench.

An Austrian immigrant, Felix Frankfurter arrived in the United States in 1894, settling with his family in New York City. Graduating from the College of the City of New York in 1902, he was admitted to Harvard Law School, graduating with honors in 1906. After a short period in private practice, Frankfurter became an assistant to Henry Stimson, the U.S. attorney for New York's southern district. After Stimson's appointment as secretary of war in 1911, he named Frankfurter to a post in the Bureau of Insular Affairs.

In 1914 Frankfurter returned to Harvard Law School as professor of administrative law, teaching there until 1939. While on the faculty at Harvard, he served in various posts in the federal government, including as legal advisor to the secretary of war and chairman of the War Labor Policies Board. In 1920, he helped found the American Civil Liberties Union, which would become the bastion of liberal legal thought and political action in the United States. Frankfurter gained national attention for his criticism of the famed SACCO AND VANZETTI anarchy/murder trial and worked vigorously to overturn their convictions.

When New York governor Franklin D. ROOSEVELT was elected president in 1932, he offered to name Frankfurter to the post of solicitor general, but the jurist declined. In 1939, Roosevelt nominated him to the Supreme Court. Although Frankfurter had a reputation as a liberal, once he became a justice, he was motivated more by a conviction that the courts must accede to the legislature in a democratic society such as the United States. He argued that the courts must defer to the wishes of the legislators and sustain

all laws with a constitutional basis. It was this philosophy that led him to uphold most of Roosevelt's New Deal legislation.

In opposition to his colleague Hugo Black, Frankfurter placed no special emphasis on the First Amendment and felt there were no constitutional absolutes. He believed that individual freedom in a highly complex society required constant fine tuning and limitation, applying an almost Keynesian economic approach to jurisprudence. Frankfurter, however, was by no means a convert to conservative thought, especially in cases of federal criminal procedure, most specifically searches and seizures. He believed that the Constitution placed fewer limits on state procedures, however, and did not hold state authorities to the same exacting standards by which he evaluated federal actions.

Forced to retire from the bench in 1963 because of poor health, Frankfurter died on February 22, 1965.

Franklin, Benjamin (1706–90) Founding father, diplomat, statesman, patriot, inventor, writer, and philosopher; the first postmaster general of the United States and, in colonial days, its first postal inspector.

Benjamin Franklin was an innovator his entire life. He invented a host of practical things, including bifocals, is generally credited with having discovered electricity in lightning, was a delegate to the Continental Congress, brilliantly engineered foreign support for the American cause during the Revolutionary War, and was an important early American writer and publisher. As a lad, Franklin was apprenticed to a printer, but soon turned to other enterprises as well. Although humble-born, Franklin was admired in polite society for his great charm and ready wit. It was said that Franklin, despite his reputation as an accomplished writer, was not entrusted with composing the Declaration of Independence for fear that he would hide some obscure joke in the middle of it.

In 1737, almost 40 years before the Revolution, Franklin was appointed postmaster for the city of Philadelphia, assigned the responsibility of overseeing individual postmasters as well as regulating all postal activity in the colonies. This essentially made him the first postal inspector of any North American postal service. Franklin personally mapped new postal routes to speed delivery, audited accounts of local offices, and instigated new accounting methods. For the first time, the colonial postal system turned a profit. Along with instituting uniform postal practices, Franklin was also charged with the law-enforcement function of controlling the rampant fraud and theft that beset the colonial postal service. Franklin was made deputy postmaster general of the colonies in 1753, continuing as de facto postal inspector. He inspected every post office in the colonies, except Charleston, and caught marauding highwaymen off guard by continually improving postal routes, a program that also sped delivery.

When the Revolution finally broke out, the Continental Congress quickly appointed Franklin the first postmaster general of the United States on July 26, 1775. He promptly created the position of surveyor of the post office, which was the forerunner of the postal inspector, the U.S. Postal Service's law-enforcement arm. Franklin served as postmaster general for just one year, but in that time he laid the foundation for the modern postal service and created an important law enforcement body within that service.

Freeh, Louis J. (1950–) A judge and a former FBI agent who was appointed by President Bill Clinton to replace William S. SESSIONS as director of the bureau.

After William S. Sessions resigned as director of the Federal Bureau of Investigation in 1993 due to what were officially described as policy differences with the Clinton administration, President Clinton tapped Louis J. Freeh as Sessions's successor. Freeh was born on January 6, 1950, in the gritty town of Jersey City, New Jersey. He took his bachelor's degree from Rutgers University in 1971 and earned his law degree (in night school) from the Rutgers Law School in 1974. A year later, he joined the FBI, and for the next six years, Freeh was assigned chiefly to investigating organized crime. He made significant inroads into Mob activities in the longshoremen's union.

Freeh moved from the FBI to the United States Attorney's Office in 1981, specializing in prosecuting Mob figures. In 1991, President George Bush appointed him to the federal bench, and in 1993 he became director of the FBI. In sharp contrast to many of President Clinton's cabinet and federal agency appointments, Freeh was seen by both political parties and by virtually all observers as an ideal nominee. He sailed through the confirmation process.

Freud, Sigmund (1856–1939) As the creator of psychoanalysis, Freud not only profoundly shaped modern theories of mind and behavior, he also postulated the existence of an "unconscious," a concept that has greatly influenced thought concerning free will, moral responsibility, accountability for one's actions, and the limits of legal definitions of guilt and innocence.

Freud was born on May 6, 1856, in Freiberg, Moravia (present-day Pribor, Czech Republic). When he was three years old, Freud moved with his family to Leipzig, Germany, and then to Vienna, where Freud came of age and made his remarkable career. It was

clear from an early age that Freud was a genius. At the age of eight, he was reading Shakespeare, which was soon followed by the Greek and Latin classics, as well as the best of French and German literature. He considered becoming a literary scholar or a lawyer, but, in the end, it was medical research that most attracted him—although he retained a deep love and knowledge of literature all his life, basing many of his theories on the insights of the great authors.

Freud began his research in what would today be called physiological psychology, producing monographs on aphasia and on infantile cerebral paralysis. His 1886 marriage to Martha Bernays prompted him to turn from relatively unremunerative research to the clinical practice of neurology. At about this time, he began working in partnership with the distinguished neurologist Josef Breuer, who had pioneered hypnosis as a therapeutic tool, particularly in cases of hysteria. Freud studied hypnosis with Breuer and with the eminent Parisian neurologist Jean Martin Charcot. Freud and Breuer developed what Breuer called the "cathartic method," whereby patients suffering from hysteria were prompted, under hypnosis, to relive some traumatic event. In many cases, this method resulted in the alleviation of such hysterical symptoms as psychosomatic paralysis, blindness, and so on. Breuer and Freud published their findings in *Studies in Hysteria* (1895), in which they spoke of their "talking cure." This work is usually considered the genesis of psychoanalysis.

Some time after the publication of their joint work, Breuer and Freud parted company over the issue of the role of sexuality in the pathogenesis of neurosis. Freud believed that it lay at the heart of *all* neurosis, ultimately concluding that sexuality is very much present from infancy—a notion that was too much for the ultimately conventional Breuer and that, in fact, outraged much of the medical profession.

Despite opposition, Freud pursued his theory. Therapeutically, his next step was to discard hypnosis in favor of what he called "free association," the stream-of-consciousness utterance of thought, which provided a window into the workings of the unconscious mind. Freud evolved an elaborate theory of the tripartite structure of mind, consisting of the Ego (the conscious self), the Id (the "It," the unconscious self), and the Superego (the internalized parental voice, which attempts to regulate both Ego and Id), that was based on his experience treating patients. But his most profound early insights came from bold self-analysis following the death of his father, toward whom (he discovered) he had highly ambivalent feelings. This led to an exploration of dreams and fantasies as further portals into the unconscious mind as it was formed in childhood. It led, too, to the conclusion that children form intensely sexual relationships with their parents and are, in fact, rivals for their love. The little boy has sexual feelings for his mother, which conflict with the role and status of his father; the little girl has such feelings for her father.

By 1900, Freud was prepared to present a comprehensive exposition of the new science of psychoanalysis. He did so that year in *The Interpretation of Dreams,* which gradually drew a band of devoted followers, including the eminent psychologists Alfred Adler and Carl Gustav Jung.

Throughout the balance of his life, Freud refined and expanded his theories, creating an entirely new field of scientific inquiry and medical treatment. Among the areas most affected by Freud's concept of the unconscious and its role in motivating actions as well as creating psychopathology, were criminology, the administration of justice, and penology. Freud's psychology greatly expanded legal definitions of insanity versus moral responsibility. It also provided a methodology for investigating crime, leading to the creation of psychological profiles of offenders. Finally, it expanded the role of penology from mere punishment to therapeutic rehabilitation aimed at penetrating to the childhood sources of aberrant behavior.

Freud's later years were marked by great suffering as a result of cancer of the jaw, which required 33 surgeries over 17 years. Recognition for his work also came with painful slowness, but in 1930 he was awarded the prestigious Goethe Prize for literature, and in 1936 he was elected to the Royal Society. A Jew, Freud was in great peril following the *Anschluss,* the Nazi annexation of Austria. Aged and ill, he moved to England, where he died on September 23, 1939.

Further reading: Gay, Peter, *Freud: A Life for Our Time* (New York: Norton, 1988).

Friedman, Elizabeth Smith (1892–1980) An American cryptologist who not only deciphered enemy codes during the two world wars, but also worked for the Treasury Department, cracking codes used by smugglers and rumrunners.

Born in Huntington, Indiana, Elizabeth Friedman (neé Smith) was educated at Hillsdale College in Michigan, earning her B.A. in 1915. Although she had majored in English, she became interested in cryptography and went to work at the Riverbank Laboratories in Geneva, Illinois, doing decoding work for the U.S. government. It was here that she met William Friedman, a fellow cryptographer, whom she married in 1917. The Friedmans relocated to Washington, D.C., in 1921, and Elizabeth Friedman went to work for several government departments, specializing in cracking codes used by rumrunners and other

smugglers. During World War II, Elizabeth Friedman joined her husband in war-related code work.

Fry, (Sara) Margery (1874–1958) British social worker and penal reformer who campaigned for the abolition of capital punishment.

Fry was born to a family of prominent English Quakers on March 11, 1874, and was educated at home until she was 17, when she went to the Roedean School and then to Somerville College, Oxford, to study mathematics. She served as librarian of Somerville from 1899 to 1904, and it was during this period that she developed an interest in young people and their problems. In 1904, she accepted a post as warden of a hall of residence for women students at Birmingham University, remaining there until 1914, when she joined her sister, Ruth, in working with the Friends' War Victims Relief Committee during World War I.

At the end of the war, she lived with her brother, the art critic and writer Roger Fry (whose circle included the so-called Bloomsbury Group of London intellectuals, among them the novelists Virginia Woolf and E. M. Forster) and became secretary of the Penal Reform League (from 1921 called the Howard League), serving from 1919 to 1926. In 1921, she became one of England's first female magistrates and the following year was appointed as the first educational adviser to Holloway Prison.

She left penal administration in 1926 to become principal of Somerville College, but she remained active in campaigning to abolish capital punishment. When she retired from Somerville in 1931, she also became active in international aspects of penal reform. Fry wrote *The Future Treatment of the Adult Offender* in 1944 and another work on penology, *Arms of the Law,* in 1951.

Fuld, Leonhard Felix (1883–1965) Author of the first comprehensive study of American police administration, lawyer and economist Fuld helped plan the New York Police Academy.

Born in New York City, the son of a merchant, Fuld graduated from Horace Mann High School. In 1902 he entered Columbia University, where he earned five degrees in the course of only seven years. For his doctoral dissertation in municipal science and administrative law, he spent two of those years scrupulously researching every aspect of law enforcement management in Europe and America, spending countless hours directly observing the daily operations of New York City's own precinct houses. The result of his labors was *Police Administration,* a wide-ranging and exceptionally readable 551-page report, the first ever of its kind. This ambitious text—published by G. P.

Putnam's Sons to widespread review and acclaim—contained strong and specific recommendations for police reform. Many of Fuld's key ideas were so incisive and progressive that they were echoed decades later by the foremost professionals and policy-making theorists in modern police history.

Recognizing the crucial importance of "individual discretion" in a patrolman's daily duties, Fuld stressed that officers should be hired as much for their intellectual and psychological fitness as for their courage and physical strength. Furthermore, he advocated offering special inducements for high school graduates and college-educated men to join the force and staff its higher ranks of service. The author very pointedly criticized any tolerance of political patronage or professional blackmailing in the employment process, though both were common practice in his era. And Fuld believed that all beginning police officers should receive an additional, occupationally pertinent and sociologically rounded course of advanced instruction during their inaugural probationary period.

After studying departmental discipline procedures, Fuld denounced the use of "shoo-fly" spies to investigate internal affairs, instead advocating the establishment of non-supervisory police inspectors. The designated officers would monitor police operations "by means of criticism of methods and not of men" and offer "general suggestions for improvements," while serving as thoroughly aboveboard watchdogs and, when necessary, reporters of police misconduct. Fuld also condemned any "rash" use of firearms in apprehending or subduing suspects, proposing that police weapons be limited exclusively to the strict defense of an officer or citizen's life. And he recommended against permanent tenure for detectives, the better to guarantee that only investigators of enduring talent, commitment, and efficiency would fulfill this critical role.

After publication of his report, Fuld worked as a civil service examiner and assisted in the planning of the New York Police Academy. He left the city for a few years after 1918, accepting bureaucratic posts in Rochester, New York, and Washington, D.C. When he left government to set up a training center for the securities salesmen of Cities Service, Fuld applied his own spare time to absorbing the pupils' coursework in financial management. The Ph.D.'s extraordinary talent for self-education served him very well again, and his subsequent stock and real estate ventures earned him a large fortune. From 1923 to 1945, Fuld gave evening lectures in economics and business administration at the Bernard M. Baruch School of City College.

Fuld's home life and habits were unusual for a man of his wealth. Until her death—from malnutrition—in 1956, he and his sister Florentine lived as near-hermits in one of his properties, a Harlem tenement where, apparently, he often undertook the janitorial service himself. He conducted a 5,000-letter-a-year correspondence entirely in longhand, largely pursuant to the benefactions of his Helene Fuld Foundation (named for his mother), which ultimately underwrote new wings, residences, and scholarship programs for over 20 hospital nursing schools around the country. Interviewed about his special concern for student nurses, Fuld vaguely remarked of their exposure to infectious diseases and denied ever having personally loved or lost his heart to any particular member of the profession. Fuld lived out his last years in a small home in Trenton, New Jersey, and, reaffirming his early interest in law enforcement education, established a fund for advanced officer training at the New Jersey State Police Academy. The philanthropist died on August 31, 1965, leaving his nursing foundation $25 million in perpetual trust.

G

Gall, Franz Joseph (1758–1828) Viennese doctor who was the first theorist and codifier of phrenology, the study of the topography of the human skull.

Gall proposed that the irregular bumps and bulges of an individual's cranium were the external expression of that person's character and inclinations. These protrusions, he believed, revealed the shape, size, and relative endowment of distinct brain "organs" that determined specific moral, intellectual, and emotional tendencies, which he called "faculties." Having formulated this theory, Gall began to examine the heads of a wide variety of in-some-way-exceptional individuals, including the inmate populations of prisons and mental asylums. The contrasts and comparisons he found among his subjects, and among the skull shapes of carnivorous and herbivorous animal species, encouraged Gall to deduce certain generalizations and draw a "map" of the cranium-molding brain. This, in turn, postulated a comprehensive overview and detailed classification of the specific components that make up the human psyche.

Born in Teifenbronn, Germany, on March 9, 1758, Gall was the son of the town's mayor, a merchant of Italian extraction. As a schoolchild at Baden and Bruchsal, Gall was impressed by the markedness and diversity of "natural gifts"—exceptional aptitudes for drawing, sports, mathematics, and so on—that he observed among his fellow students. He took special notice of classmates who (unlike himself) memorized so easily that they consistently surpassed other, more painstakingly studious pupils at recitation exercises and exams. Curious about their facility, Gall noted that all of these naturally memory-strong children seemed to have large, "flaring" eyes.

Although Gall's Roman Catholic parents wished him to pursue the priesthood, he chose to become a doctor instead. While attending university at Strasbourg, he perceived the same and other coincidences of talent and outward appearance among his academic peers, and he began to postulate a connection. Since every type of sensory capacity—sight, hearing, smell, and so on—had its corresponding organ, why shouldn't diverse mental talents and capabilities have physical correlatives as well? Man's very nature might find rational explanation through a practical investigation of these different "organs," which Gall believed resided in the brain.

In 1781 he moved to Vienna, where he finished his medical training and established a successful and prestigious private practice. Over the next decade he continued to ponder and refine his ideas on natural talents and predispositions, and in 1791 he published a treatise on the philosophy of medicine, which set forth his concept of the plurality and independence of the brain's organs. He also began to promulgate his theories in public lectures and addresses.

In 1800 Gall gained an assistant and collaborator, Johann C. SPURZHEIM. The following year, news of the pair's speaking engagements and public exhibitions prompted Austrian emperor Francis I to write Gall personally and order him to cease promoting his notions about brain endowment and moral character, which Francis believed to foster materialism, atheism, and fatalism—all inimical to the state's Catholic religion. The prohibition only further piqued public curiosity.

Despite Gall's numerous appeals and petitions, the emperor refused to rescind the ban, so in 1805 Gall and Spurzheim decided to seek an audience elsewhere. They embarked on a major tour through Germany, Switzerland, Denmark, and Holland, stopping at schools, jails, insane asylums, and other institutions to further their research, explain their theories, demonstrate Gall's practical technique of cranioscopy, and exhibit their now-considerable collection of skulls and plaster casts of skulls. In prisons at Berlin and Span-

dau, Gall did "blind" inspections of the heads of over 600 inmates, pronouncing the natural proclivities of each and suggesting which criminal offense each might have committed. Reportedly, Gall's success rate was remarkable.

Among the brain organs Gall had by now identified were those of "Combativeness" (evident in an over-size skull formation Gall deemed common among impulse killers) and "Destructiveness," which he had initially called the "Murder Organ" because it appeared to be prominent in cool, deliberate murderers, as well as in hunters and sportsmen. (Gall also noted its greater enlargement in dogs than in sheep, and its virtual absence in hares and non-predatory birds.) Other, somewhat less inherently menacing, faculties whose size and relative ratio determined their degree of influence on the composite personality were Adhesiveness (capacity for friendship), Alimentiveness and Aquativeness (love of food and drink), Acquisitiveness (which he first termed the organ for "Theft"), Conscientiousness, Conjugality, Firmness, Imitativeness, Mirthfulness, Philoprogenitiveness (capacity for parental or filial love), Secretiveness, Self-Esteem, Spirituality, and many more. In all, Gall identified 29 distinct faculties, and of these, he believed that animals shared 19 with humans.

From the outset, Gall's discussion of psychological organs and his flamboyant public demonstrations of cranial "readings" attracted scathing critics as well as enthusiastic converts among members of the orthodox scientific community. Indisputably, Gall did make several new and important discoveries about the physical structures of neuroanatomy after 1800, when he began inspecting cadaver brain specimens to support his at first strictly theoretical hypothesis. His dissections were in themselves pioneering; instead of slicing successive cross sections of the entire brain, he dismantled the organ according to its natural segmentation. Even one of Gall's most pointed contemporary critics, Pierre Flourens, recalled in 1863 his wonder and enlightenment as a witness to one of these dissections and, despite his rejection of phrenology, acknowledged Gall as "the author of the true anatomy of the brain." In his general explanation of the formal arrangement of the brain's tissues, Gall was the first to note that the organ's gray matter (site of the as-yet-undiscovered neurons) was the matrix of the nerves, and was active tissue, while the white matter (the ganglia) served as a conductive network.

Borrowing some analogies from botany, Gall pointed out the hierarchical structure of the nervous system and correctly surmised the crucial functions of the cerebral cortex and the spinal cord.

Gall's work prompted other contemporary scientists to devote further study to the brain's anatomy.

But the actual value and significance of Gall's specific laboratory observations came to be appreciated almost a century later, when subsequent physiologists began to better understand other aspects of the nervous system.

In contrast, the doctor's bump-derived guesswork about the physical locations of specific cortical functions and personality-determining traits has endured only as an interesting, anachronistic footnote to modern medical knowledge—with one exception. Gall's location of speech ability roughly corresponded to a section of the brain now known, in cases of lesion, to be linked with aphasia, or loss of verbal lucidity. In fact, one of Gall's supporting arguments for the localization of neurological functions included references to head-injury cases, in which the patients' abilities and actions were selectively affected by the site-specific trauma of their wounds.

Although Gall believed that the predispositions caused by cerebral endowment were innate, he often acknowledged that personality could be tempered or modified by environment, experience, or sheer conscious or moral effort. Furthermore, Gall never insisted that his own mapping of particular talents and characteristics would prove perfectly accurate or conclusive. Having only just inaugurated the field of study, he predicted that medical science would require much more time and additional research before authoritative precision could be won. But instead of this hoped-for, meticulous follow-through by the scientific establishment, Gall's practical method of character analysis received premature propagation—and even commercial debasement as a parlor and carnival entertainment—within his own lifetime. The doctor's hands-on approach—so proudly displayed at the cranioscopic demonstrations to which Gall himself (somewhat scandalously) charged admission—became widely popularized by a legion of pseudo-scientific, fortune-telling practitioners who found followers, or at least paying customers, in France, England, and the United States through the 1840s and later.

Nevertheless, Gall's functional, naturalistic approach to the study of human anatomy and behavior helped promote and direct the subsequent development of several disciplines, including evolutionary theory, physical anthropology, sociology, philosophy, and criminology. His influence found institutional expression in the efforts of some public policy reformers of education, mental health, and penal corrections.

Gall and Spurzheim arrived in Paris in 1807, and once again, their work was dismissed or censured by official authorities—the Institut de France rejected Gall's doctrines in 1808, and Napoleon himself dis-

couraged their influence. Gall became a French citizen in 1819, but this mattered little to the French Academy, which denied Gall's application for recognition in 1821.

However, Gall continued to attract converts among lecture attendees and an ever-growing reading audience, and he again established a lucrative, high-society medical practice; his clientele numbered the officials of 12 embassies, as well as such luminaries as Stendhal, Saint-Simon, and Metternich. Gall's intellectual adherents would ultimately include such famous names as Hegel, Bismarck, Marx, Queen Victoria, Walt Whitman, and American president James Garfield. Phrenological societies were founded in Europe and the United States, and their journals and translations of Gall's writings further popularized his ideas.

In 1826, Gall began to suffer symptoms of cerebral and coronary sclerosis. He died of an apoplectic stroke on August 22, 1828. Because his writings had been placed on the Catholic Church's prohibited Index—and perhaps also because of his openly colorful love life, which had featured many mistresses and may have produced an illegitimate son—Gall was denied a religious burial.

Further reading: Capen, Nahum, *Reminiscences of Dr. Spurzheim and George Combe and a Review of the Science of Phrenology, from the Period of its Discovery by Dr. Gall. . . .* (New York: Fowler and Wells, 1881).
Combe, George, *System of Phrenology* (Boston: Marsh, Capen, Lyon, and Webb, 1839).

Galton, Sir Francis (1822–1911)   Nineteenth-century "gentleman scientist" who advanced the study of fingerprint classification.

Francis Galton was a first cousin of Charles Darwin. Like Darwin, he became known as a scientific explorer, undertaking many and varied experiments in statistics, anthropometry, and psychology. It was his interest in his cousin's work on heredity that led Galton to the study of fingerprints. Galton consolidated the pioneering work of Dr. Henry FAULDS and William HERSCHEL on the subject and, using this foundation, established a statistical approach to the classification of individual prints. In 1893 Galton published his conclusions in a book entitled simply *Fingerprints*. The book revolutionized the taxonomy of prints and greatly simplified the complex task of classification. Knighted in 1909 for his scientific accomplishments, Sir Francis Galton died two years later in Surrey.

Gambino, Carlo (alias: Don Carlo; Carlo Gambrino; Carlo Gambrieno) (1902–76)   At the time of his death, Gambino was "Don" of the most powerful Mafia crime family in the United States and had figured as the principal model for Mario Puzo's novel

The Godfather and the Francis Ford Coppola films based on the book.

Carlo Gambino was born in Palermo, Italy, on August 24, 1902. He came to the United States as a stowaway aboard the S.S. *Vincenzo Florida* in 1921 and settled in Brooklyn. After working briefly in his uncle's trucking company, he joined the Mafia during the 1920s, functioning as a "soldier" for "Joe the Boss" MASSERIA. When Masseria was killed on April 15, 1931, Gambino deftly shifted his loyalty to Salvatore Maranzano, Don of New York. The reign of Maranzano was brief. In September 1931, he was dispatched, and Gambino and his brothers-in-law, Paul and Peter Castellano, became soldiers for Philip and Vincent Mangano.

Gambino was always an unassuming gangster—conservative and quiet rather than flashy. His rise through the Mafia ranks was slow and steady, and in 1951 he became an underboss for Albert ANASTASIA, who had allegedly ordered the death of the Manganos. Six years later, Anastasia himself was assassinated in a Manhattan barbershop—according to FBI informant Joseph VALACHI, at the behest of Gambino, who now became boss of his own crime "family." When Anastasia's right-hand man, Aniello Dellacroce, protested Gambino's ascension, Gambino "replied" by killing Armand Rava, a close associate of Dellacroce. Then Gambino offered Dellacroce the position of underboss. He accepted.

Quietly but ruthlessly, Gambino expanded his organization's power over the next several years. He forged a working relationship with Meyer LANSKY and conspired with Lansky and others to send New York policy boss Vito Genovese to prison, so that he and Lansky could assume full control of gambling in the city. Gambino closed his fist around the waterfront unions during the 1960s and 1970s, eliminating Joseph Colombo when he threatened his authority with the longshoremen.

Gambino was arrested 16 times and was convicted six times, but he managed to evade jail on all but one occasion, in 1937, when he served 22 months for income tax evasion. When federal authorities finally built up a deportation case against him in 1967, Gambino's lawyers appealed the decision to the U.S. Supreme Court, which upheld the order in 1970—though only on the grounds that Gambino had entered the country illegally. However, the aging Don suffered a heart attack that year, which effectively put the deportation order on permanent hold. Continued illness throughout the remainder of his life ended his active involvement in organized crime.

As with a number of other highly placed figures of organized crime—most notably Sam GIANCANA—Gambino was linked to covert U.S. government activity. An inmate at the Ohio Penitentiary claimed that Gambino worked with the CIA and FBI and that, in 1968, government agents offered him a million dollars to assassinate the Reverend Martin Luther King Jr. Gambino allegedly declined the assignment. Carlo Gambino succumbed to a heart attack on October 15, 1976.

Garofalo, Raffaele (1852–1934)   One of the earliest writers to deal with the criminal thought process; published his views in the landmark work *Criminology*.

Born into the Italian nobility, Raffaele Garofalo spent his life working in the law, first as a private-practice lawyer, then as a prosecutor, and finally as a magistrate. He also spent much time at the University of Naples, where he was professor of criminal law and procedure. In particular, Garofalo devoted himself to the study of the psychology and sociology of crime.

Garofalo wrote several works on crime, but is best remembered for his monumental *Criminology*, in which he postulated that crime is conducted by persons lacking two major emotional qualities: probity (concern and respect for others) and pity (revulsion at inflicting harm or displeasure upon others). The absence of one or both of these emotions creates the possibility of the criminal mind. Garofalo observed that while the absence of probity, pity, or both does not necessarily and absolutely cause criminality, criminality cannot occur unless one or both of these emotions is absent.

Realizing the ambiguity of his parameters, Garofalo defined pity and probity as relative to the morally average members of a society, which may, in fact, be well below those of superior moral perception. Thus Garofalo's psychological definition of criminality was made in relation to social norms, and he further defined a truly criminal act as one that is harmful to society. If an act is not harmful to society, it may be morally deficient, but it is not criminal.

A positivist, Garofalo rejected the doctrine of free will and concentrated on social Darwinism, stressing that crime is determined by inheritance and social conditions and can be understood only by understanding these.

Further reading: Allen, Francis A., "Raffaele Garofalo," *The Journal of Criminal Law, Criminology and Police Science,* 45:4 (November–December 1954).

Garrett Pat (Patrick Floyd) (1850–1908)   The supposed killer of Billy the Kid doggedly pursued the bandit, setting several unsuccessful ambushes before finally catching him.

Born in Alabama and raised in Louisiana, Pat Garrett left the Deep South in 1869 to take up the life of

The highpoint of lawman Pat Garrett's life came when he shot down Billy the Kid. (Courtesy of the National Archives)

a Texas cowboy. After joining in the great buffalo slaughter of the 1870s, he moved to Lincoln County, New Mexico, in the midst of the so-called Lincoln County War between Irish and English immigrant ranchers. The war also spawned the criminal career of one Henry McCarty, among whose aliases were William Bonney and Billy the Kid. Billy's acts of mayhem prompted the citizens of embattled Lincoln County to make Garrett their sheriff and assign to him the task of bringing in the Kid dead or alive. But Billy sought to head off this effort by meeting with territorial governor Lew Wallace, who promised him a pardon in exchange for information on the Murphy-Dolan faction and their part in the Lincoln County War.

Billy made good on his promise and furnished the information, but Governor Wallace never issued the pardon. After Billy broke and ran, one of the great manhunts of the American West commenced.

Pat Garrett was neither a great lawman nor even a very competent tracker. He went about his task by simply setting numerous ambushes for the Kid, most of which were triggered by a case of mistaken identity and resulted in the death of a hapless innocent who may or may not have borne a resemblance to the Kid. After several of these unfortunate killings, Garrett finally ran the Kid to ground in Fort Sumner, New Mexico. Secreting himself in the bedroom of a turncoat friend of Billy's, Pete Maxwell, Garrett gunned down the fugitive (who, Garrett's claims to the contrary notwithstanding, was unarmed) as he entered the dark room.

Many westerners resented Garrett for his underhanded and careless methods. As for the sheriff, the rest of his days were haunted by fears that partisans of the Kid would exact revenge against him. After a failed attempt at ranching and a brief stint with the Texas Rangers, Garrett was elected sheriff in 1897 in Doña Ana County, New Mexico, serving until 1901. He was next named Customs Agent for El Paso by President Theodore Roosevelt, and then returned to ranching, but once again failed to make a go of it. In 1908, after reneging on an agreement concerning his ranch, Garrett was murdered, apparently shot in the back of the head while he was urinating—although two witnesses claimed the killing was an act of self-defense, and the killer was in fact acquitted on the grounds of self-defense, despite much evidence to the contrary.

The story would have ended there, except that shortly after the turn of the century, a man named "Brushy Bill" Roberts appeared at a New Mexico newspaper office claiming to be Billy the Kid and wanted his long-overdue pardon from the governor. His story had but few holes, and he recounted things that only the Kid would have known. He even displayed bullet wounds on his back from a well-documented gunfight some thirty years before. Nevertheless, the state of New Mexico refused to accept him as Billy the Kid, and the governor declined to issue the pardon. Bill Roberts died shortly thereafter.

Further reading: Garrett, Pat, *The Authentic Life of Billy the Kid* (Norman: University of Oklahoma Press, 1954)

Utley, Robert M., *Billy the Kid* (Lincoln: University of Nebraska Press, 1989).

Gary, Elbert H. (1846–1927) President of the United States Steel Corporation who founded the National Crime Commission in 1925.

A native of Wheaton, Illinois, Elbert Gary was raised on a farm and became accustomed to hard work early in life, an experience that gave him excellent health and physical prowess. Too young to enlist at the outbreak of the Civil War, Gary attended the Illinois Institute, from which he graduated in 1864, and promptly enlisted in the army. Gary served only two months before leaving the service to teach school. After less than a year, he began reading law and in 1866 entered Union College of Law in Chicago. After graduating at the top of his class, Gary served for three years as clerk of the state superior court before entering into private practice with his elder brother.

He rose to the forefront of the Illinois bar and accepted the presidency of the Federal Steel Company in 1898. Federal Steel was backed by multimillionaire J. P. Morgan, who was so impressed with Gary that he chose him to organize United States Steel, a conglomerate composed of Federal Steel and American Steel and Wire. The resultant corporation was the largest the world had ever seen at the time.

As the head of USS, Gary quickly became one of the most powerful businessmen in the country. With that in mind, Mark Prentiss, a prominent writer and businessman, asked Gary in 1925 to use his influence to call together some of the biggest names in politics and business. The purpose of the meeting was to discuss the rising crime rate in America and to determine if there was anything that big business could do about the situation. After hearing from Richard Washburn Child and reviewing his nationwide study of crime, the group voted to form the National Crime Commission, the first such non-governmental body in the country devoted to fighting crime.

Due to his advanced age, Gary declined the chairmanship of the commission but nevertheless held sway over the group. The commission hoped to form local groups to involve private citizens in the fight against crime as well as foster a greater sense of unity among local officials, local police, and private citizens. Gary envisioned a national conference involving jurists and law enforcement officials to resolve inadequacies in the criminal justice system. He also suggested the restriction of immigration and more progressive ways of dealing with institutionalized criminals. Gary's biggest concern was reaching errant young people before they became hardened in a life of crime.

The commission was moderately successful in achieving some of its goals. Gary himself died less than two years after having established it. The Lake Michigan city of Gary, Indiana, chartered in 1906 and dominated by U.S. Steel, was named in honor of the judge and businessman.

Gates, Daryl (1926–) Chief of the Los Angeles Police Department from 1978 to 1991; praised by President George Bush and Senator Joseph Biden (chairman of the Senate Judiciary Committee) as an American hero and the nation's "top cop," but condemned by others as a neo-fascist and racist. His indisputable contribution to law enforcement was the development of the SWAT team concept.

Daryl Gates was born in Glendale, California, on August 30, 1926. The Great Depression straitened his family's financial circumstances, and while Gates managed to work his way through the University of Southern California, he was (in his words) "enticed by the $290 a month" to leave the university in his senior year and join the LAPD on September 16, 1949.

Early in his career on the force, Gates became the driver and "factotum" (his word) for the department's new reform-minded and strongly right-wing chief, William H. Parker. Parker radically restructured a scandal-ridden and demoralized department, and Gates, becoming something of his protégé, was exposed to what he called "a tutorial on how to be chief."

After 15 months as Parker's driver and assistant, Gates transferred to the Juvenile Division and then to Vice. In 1954, he was promoted to sergeant, and he steadily received promotions after that, gaining wide experience in the various divisions of the LAPD. By 1963, he was a captain and head of the department's prestigious Intelligence Division. In this capacity, he organized infiltrations of organized crime; as the sixties developed into the decade of leftist radical activism, he turned his attention increasingly to infiltrating such organizations as the Students for a Democratic Society (SDS). He was a field commander during the Watts riots of 1965 and was appalled by the department's failure to quell the mass violence. As a result of this experience, he became interested in riot control techniques and wrote two manuals on the subject.

Independently of their superiors, Gates and others, including Commander John Powers, Lieutenant Frank Brittell, and Sergeant George Morrison, began studying guerrilla warfare. They also studied the tactics of U.S. Marines fighting in the Vietnam War. By late 1967, Gates had developed D Platoon, ostensibly an anti-sniper group consisting of an elite corps of highly disciplined officers using specialized weapons and tactics and ranked in the top 25% of the department for their physical skills. Consisting of 220 men, including 60 crack marksmen formed into five-man teams, D-Platoon, as Gates later observed, would "revolutionize law enforcement agencies all over the world." To Chief Parker, Gates proposed calling D Platoon a SWAT team—Special Weapons Attack Team. When Parker objected to the word "attack," Gates, having conceived an affection for the acronym he had invented, proposed "Special Weapons And Tactics" instead. Parker agreed.

While Daryl Gates became known as the "Father of SWAT," he did not claim to have invented the tactics the team used, but merely to have provided the "opportunity to develop the unit." The concept of SWAT is quick, decisive, guerrilla-style action using a minimum of force. SWAT saw its first action at the end of 1969, and Gates gained tremendous publicity for his favorite unit almost a decade later when he volun-

teered its services during the Iran hostage crisis of 1978. (The federal government declined his offer.)

In that same year Gates, having gained a reputation for flamboyance and leadership, succeeded Ed Davis to become the LAPD's 49th chief of police. Sworn in on March 28, 1978, he saw himself as the head of an embattled department, commanding a force with fewer officers per population than in any other major American city. Combative, he became a hero to some and a villain to others. He frequently found himself at odds with his city's African-American mayor, Tom Bradley, who was outraged to discover that LAPD officers had put him under surveillance. In 1982, Gates stunned the African-American community when he answered a reporter's question about the controversial "carotid choke hold" his officers employed to restrain subjects. The reporter alluded to statistics that showed a disproportionate number of deaths among African-American suspects on whom the choke hold had been used. "We may be finding that, in some blacks, when [the choke hold] is applied, the veins or arteries do not open up as fast as they do in normal people." Gates later explained that African Americans "are vulnerable to sickle-cell anemia. They have a high level of hypertension and a high risk of heart failure. There is also a sudden death syndrome, which is far greater in blacks than in other groups." Between 1984 and 1988, Los Angeles incurred some $13 million in civil police misconduct awards.

Throughout the 1980s, Gates successfully fended off calls for his dismissal as chief. However, the beginning of the end did not come until the next decade, when, on March 3, 1991, a group of Los Angeles police officers brutally beat Rodney King, who was being arrested for a traffic violation. The incident was captured on amateur video and played nationwide to a shocked television audience. Although Gates publicly deplored the beating, he was widely blamed for having created in the LAPD the atmosphere of racism and violent reaction that made the beating possible. When the officers involved were brought to trial and, despite the video-taped evidence, acquitted, massive rioting broke out in predominently black south-central Los Angeles. Gates seemed uncharacteristically slow to respond and was roundly criticized for his handling of the situation. Shortly after the riots in the spring of 1992, he resigned as chief of the Los Angeles police department.

Further reading: Gates, Daryl F. (with Diane K. Shah), *Chief: My Life in the LAPD* (New York: Bantam Books, 1992).

Gaynor, William Jay (1849–1913) A reformer in the mold of the Progressives, Gaynor staunchly opposed abuses by New York City police as well as other violations of civil liberties perpetrated by the municipal government.

William Gaynor was born on February 23, 1849, to impoverished Irish and English immigrants in upstate New York. Originally trained for the priesthood, Gaynor attended seminary and then the Christian Brothers College in St. Louis. After declining to take his orders, he decided to receive lay instruction and traveled in Mexico and the American West until 1869, when he left the Church and renounced Catholicism as too conservative.

Returning to New York, Gaynor opened a law practice on Long Island and began a one-man reform movement that was successful enough to earn him a term as police commissioner of the city of New York. Once in public service, Gaynor continued to fight for reform and exposed corruption in municipal government and public service companies, ranging from water companies to the city's burgeoning subway system. After declining the mayoral nomination, he was elected state Supreme Court justice in 1893 and promptly sent most of Brooklyn's political henchmen to prison for numerous counts of election fraud. Although his reform views were now quite popular, he refused the gubernatorial nomination and continued his service on the bench.

In 1909, however, Gaynor resigned to become mayor of New York City. As mayor, he focused on the police department, whose abuses threatened to make the city a virtual police state. He firmly held that police must adhere to the laws they enforce in the manner in which they enforce them. Gaynor argued that no violation of civil liberties, regardless of the person or persons involved, could be tolerated.

The mayor's views were not popular with the "machine men," who had operated without any resistance for years, and Gaynor barely survived a singularly bloody assassination attempt in 1910. He again declined the gubernatorial nomination, saying that only the presidency was more important than serving as mayor of New York. Gaynor's exemplary career ended when he died suddenly on September 10, 1913.

Gerard, James Watson (1794–1874)

New York City lawyer and philanthropist who was a persuasive public advocate for the establishment of uniformed attire for members of the Metropolitan Police Department.

A native New Yorker of French and Scottish descent, Gerard graduated from Columbia University and volunteered for the Iron Grays, a company defending New York's harbor in the War of 1812. Having received an M.A. from Columbia in 1816, he was admitted to the bar and went on to establish a successful law practice. A public-minded individual, Gerard joined the Society for the Suppression of Pauperism in 1823, and the following year he helped found a House of Refuge for Juvenile Delinquents, the first such institution in the United States. The lawyer was also a firm abolitionist loudly opposed to the repeal of the Missouri Compromise. Gerard sponsored many charities, and in his later years devoted special interest to the cause of public education.

In 1853 Gerard wrote a series of articles comparing crime problems and police operations in New York City and London, which he had recently visited. Among other opinions on the contrasts he found, the lawyer highly praised the British constabulary's official dress code and suggested that New York and its law enforcers would greatly benefit by following their example. At the time, American peace officers wore their own street clothes while on duty, with only a star-shaped badge to distinguish them from ordinary citizens. The word "cop" originated from this copper badge, and though regulations required its display, the star was easily concealed whenever a low profile was desired—whether for legitimate or illegitimate purposes. Gerard argued that a distinctive uniform would lend greater moral authority and distinction to the patrolman and, at the same time, help prevent him from hiding or loafing on the job. Standardized attire would also enable civilians and other officers instantly to recognize a policeman and call on him or come to his aid in an emergency.

Gerard did all he could to promote acceptance of his proposal, writing letters, giving speeches, and consulting with city authorities. At a fancy-dress society ball given by a certain Mrs. Coventry, he donned a London policeman's uniform to publicize the notion. Soon thereafter, directors of the forthcoming Crystal Palace exhibition discussed the matter with Chief George MATSELL and determined to supply uniforms for the special police force charged with the fair's security. Public and press response to these uniformed officers was very favorable. Later that year, the New York police commissioners established a dress code for all of the regular force. At first, only the winter uniform was to be standardized citywide—a blue frock coat for the months between September and May, inclusive—while the individual wards would be free to settle the particulars for each district's summer gear.

The rank and file immediately resisted this innovation, and with considerable gusto. They argued that a dress code would restrict their independence and injure their morale. Many felt that, far from enhancing dignity, the uniform would degrade the policeman's public image by giving him the appearance of a liveried footman or other lowly servant. Worst of all, the decision was unfair, since the men themselves would be required to pay for the hated outfits. Although Chief Matsell tried to arrange for a $100-a-year wage increase to defray the expense of the uniforms, the mood of the city council, already critical of police administration under the exuberantly corrupt Mayor Fernando WOOD, was against him.

The patrolmen's protest meetings and legal appeals nevertheless proved to be in vain, and officers who refused to conform to the new ruling were fired. This—and the men's reportedly surprised admiration for the style of the coat, once it was actually introduced to them—cooled the climate of rebellion. Soon, striped trousers, belt, and neck stock were added to the winter uniform—bringing another brief round of Bronx cheers from the officers—and a standard summer costume was introduced, with white pants, vests, and Panama hats. The public, at least, greatly approved of the change.

Further reading: Gerard, James Watson, *London and New York: Their Crime and Police* (New York: G. P. Putnam's, 1853).

Gettler, Alexander Oscar (1884–1968)   Served as New York City's first chief toxicologist and "blood detective" from 1918 to 1959.

Born in Austria, Alexander came to Brooklyn with his family at age five. He received his Ph.D. in chemistry from Columbia University in 1912, and when New York City abolished the inadequate and antiquated coroner system in 1918, replacing it with the office of medical examiner under Dr. Charles NORRIS, Gettler was appointed the first toxicologist of the new agency.

For the next 41 years, Gettler developed numerous devices and procedures that became standard in the field of investigative blood chemistry. His most notable contributions were blood tests to determine if a person had died by drowning, and a landmark process for analyzing brain tissue to determine the presence of alcohol at the time of death. During his tenure in the medical examiner's office, Gettler examined more than 100,000 corpses and solved numerous cases through chemical detection. His pioneering efforts and his commitment to training and educating future toxicologists helped establish blood analysis as a vital part of criminal investigation.

Giancana, Sam "Momo" (1908–75)   Longtime head of Chicago's Mafia who was both an ally and a target of the Kennedy administration.

Sam Giancana got his start as a "wheelman"—chauffeur—for Al CAPONE. He served the same function for Capone's successors, Tony Accardo and Paul "The Waiter" Ricca in the 1940s. By the forties, he had

Chicago crime boss Sam Giancana was both a target and sometimes ally of the Kennedy administration. (Courtesy of the Library of Congress)

been arrested more than 70 times, beginning in 1925. After serving a sentence for illegally distilling whiskey during the late 1930s, Giancana invaded Chicago's ghetto-district gambling rackets, dealing death to any of the African-American policy bosses who refused to yield to the Mafia. By the mid-1950s, Giancana was promoted to "manager of operations" for the Mafia in Chicago, and by 1957 he was considered the head of the Chicago "family." He held that position until 1965, when he was jailed for refusing to cooperate with a federal grand jury investigating organized crime. Released the following year, he "retired" to a luxurious self-imposed exile in Peru, Beirut, Puerto Rico, and Mexico. During Giancana's tenure as head of Chicago's Mafia, the city saw no fewer than 79 mob murders.

Organized crime figures had, of course, a long tradition of bribing local law enforcement and government officials. Giancana went considerably further, "delivering" Chicago to John F. Kennedy in his extremely close presidential race with Richard M. NIXON. That the Kennedy administration failed to "lay off" organized crime—indeed, Attorney General Robert F. KEN-

NEDY attacked it with a vengeance—has led to theories of Mob involvement in the assassination of JFK. Giancana's involvement with the Kennedy administration may have run even deeper. Reportedly, he joined a botched CIA plot to assassinate Cuban dictator Fidel Castro. Giancana's girlfriend, Judith Campbell Exner, claimed to have served as a courier between the White House and Giancana via mobster Johnny Roselli. It has also been reported that the CIA, as a favor to Giancana, provided surveillance of comedian Dan Rowan, who was having an affair with singer Phyllis McGuire, another of Giancana's girlfriends.

Whatever Giancana's status within the government, his lifestyle was lavish, including an elegant house in the West Side Chicago suburb of Oak Park, a suite at Lake Tahoe's Cal-Neva Lodge, and another estate in Mexico, and it drew a great deal of attention from the press. And even if the gangster had cozied up to the CIA earlier, the FBI, during the 1960s, probed deeper and deeper into his dealings. This continued even after he went into semi-retirement at his villa in Cuernavaca, Mexico. In July 1974, Mexican authorities rousted him from his house, and he was extradited to Chicago, where he was brought before a federal grand jury investigating syndicate gambling operations and the murder of another Mob figure. Fearing that he would testify, the Chicago Mob arranged a hit. On June 19, 1975, two days after he returned from gall bladder surgery in Houston, Giancana was gunned down in his Oak Park bungalow.

Girard, Stephen (1750–1831) One of the wealthiest Americans of his day and a generous philanthropist, Girard left a substantial endowment to fund the Philadelphia Police Department.

Learning the sea trading business from his father, Stephen Girard became perhaps the wealthiest man in America by the end of the 18th century. After settling in Philadelphia in 1776— simply because that was where he managed to dock after evading the British fleet on patrol during the Revolution—he expanded his trading fleet to include commerce with the West Indies and French Louisiana.

A dedicated patriot, Girard almost singlehandedly salvaged the Bank of the United States in 1810 by investing $1 million in that institution to stimulate foreign investment. When the bank could not be rechartered, Girard bailed out the government by purchasing all of the buildings. Nor were Girard's contributions all financial. Earlier, when a yellow fever epidemic devastated Philadelphia in 1793, Girard volunteered to work in the hospitals and carry out the dead, including the rotting corpses that lay seemingly everywhere because others were afraid to touch them. He took up this duty when the scourge returned twice

more in the decade, both times ministering to the sick as well as to the dead.

When Girard was killed in an accident in December 1831, the city of Philadelphia mourned the loss of a generous benefactor. When his will was read, however, the city discovered just how generous he was. He bequeathed handsome sums to various private institutions within the city, and also left half a million dollars to the city itself to "provide more effectually than now for the security of the persons and property of the inhabitants of the said city by a competent police." His bequest provided for 24 full-time officers and added 120 men to the night watch. Girard's generosity gave Philadelphia the young republic's first professional police force.

Gisevius, Hans Bernd (1904–74) A chief prosecution witness at the Nuremberg trials, Gisevius had also been involved in numerous plots to assassinate Hitler.

Although he was a political conservative and an ally of the old line German nationalist stalwart Paul von Hindenburg, Hans Gisevius saw the coming dominance of the Nazis and joined the Gestapo (the Nazi secret police) in 1934. Soon disillusioned and disgusted by what he found in that organization, he began working to bring about the ouster of Gestapo head Rudolf Diels. His replacement was just as morally bankrupt, and Gisevius left the Gestapo after four months. He was transferred to the Police Department in the Prussian Ministry of the Interior, where he secretly hatched numerous plots against the life of Adolf Hitler. All, of course, failed—though, through them all, Gisevius managed to remain above suspicion.

After the outbreak of World War II, Gisevius was stationed in Switzerland as German vice consul in Zurich. From this position, he continued to work against Hitler and was in frequent contact with Allen Welsh Dulles, chief of the U.S. Office of Strategic Services (OSS). Gisevius was involved in the July 20, 1944, assassination attempt on Hitler (in which the Führer was wounded but not killed). Again, he survived the subsequent investigations, show trials, and executions.

When the war ended, and it became clear that high-ranking German officials would be held accountable for their crimes against humanity, Gisevius became a star witness for the prosecution, giving detailed descriptions of government complicity in Hitler's program of genocide against the Jews: the so-called "Final Solution."

Glaister, John Jr. (1892–1971) Succeeding his father as Regius Professor of Forensic Medicine at Glasgow University, pathology expert and textbook author Glaister made important strides in several areas of his field.

Born and raised in Glasgow, John Glaister Jr. studied law and medicine. Graduating in 1916, he served three years in Egypt with the Royal Army Medical Corps, then returned to his hometown and his father's university department, where he worked as assistant, gaining admission to the bar in 1926. The next year, noted professor Sydney SMITH was called back to Scotland from Cairo to head Edinburgh University's forensics faculty, and Glaister traveled again, replacing Smith as teacher and as medical-legal expert for the Egyptian government.

Several innovations distinguished Glaister's subsequent career. He created one of the first basic timetables for the sequence of organic changes in corpse decomposition, and from this he posited a formula to aid in determining a victim's time of death. Experimenting with the recently invented comparison microscope, Glaister led the way in analyzing hair and fiber samples, publishing a standard reference, *Hairs of Mammalia from the Medico-Legal Aspect,* in 1931. He also wrote *Medical Jurisprudence and Toxicology* and *The Power of Poison.* Glaister's legal testimony in several murder cases established new landmarks in microscopic detection and provided further reinforcement and elaboration of Edmond LOCARD's "trace evidence" theory.

In 1937, Glaister took over his father's chair at Glasgow University. He continued to serve as expert investigator and witness and contributed many articles to scientific journals. In 1964 he completed his autobiography, *Final Diagnosis,* and four years later retired from teaching, as professor emeritus.

Glaser, Daniel (1918–) A professor of sociology at the University of Southern California; writes on prisons and parole.

Born in New York City on December 23, 1918, Glaser was educated at the University of Chicago, from which he took an A.B. (1929), M.A. (1947), and Ph.D. (1954), all in sociology. Immediately following World War II, Glaser worked as a prisons officer for the United States Military Government in Germany from 1946 to 1949, then served as a sociologist-actuary for the Illinois Parole and Pardon Board from 1950 to 1954.

Following this practical experience, Glaser joined the sociology faculty of the University of Illinois, where he taught from 1954 to 1968. While he was at Illinois, Glaser directed a Ford Foundation study on the federal correctional system.

In 1968, Glaser left Illinois for Rutgers University, teaching there until 1970 while also serving on the New York State Narcotics Addiction Control Commission. In 1970, he became a professor of sociology at the University of Southern California at Los Angeles.

Glaser is best known as an expert in prison and parole theory and research. He is a strong advocate of the concepet of community corrections—an orderly process aimed at gradually reintegrating parolees back into society.

Glaser's many books include *The Effectiveness of a Prison and Parole System* (1964); *Crime in the City* (editor, 1970); *Social Deviance* (1971); *Adult Crime and Social Policy* (1972); *Handbook of Criminology* (editor, 1974); *Strategic Criminal Justice Planning* (1975); and *Crime in Our Changing Society* (1978).

Further reading: Carter, Robert M., "Dialogue with Daniel Glaser," *Issues in Criminology,* 7:2 (Fall 1972).

Laub, John H., "Interview with Daniel Glaser, March 14, 1979," *Criminolgy in the Making* (Boston: Northeastern University Press, 1983).

Glueck, Eleanor (1898–1972) and Glueck, Sol Sheldon (1896–1980) This Harvard-based criminologist couple wrote numerous works on crime and criminals and developed the controversial Glueck's Social Prediction Table in the 1950s.

Eleanor Touroff and Sheldon Glueck were married in 1922, and both joined the faculty at Harvard in 1925, Sheldon as an instructor of criminology and penology, and Eleanor as a research criminologist in the department of social ethics. Together, the couple spent over 30 years researching and publishing their findings on such topics as juvenile delinquency, recidivism, criminality, and rehabilitation.

In their best-known and most provocative collaboration, *Predicting Delinquency and Crime* (1959), the Gluecks developed a "Social Prediction Table," which they intended as a tool to help recognize and remedy the signs of incipient delinquency in children as young as two years old. Glueck's Social Prediction Table, highly controversial, was nevertheless considered a breakthrough in the early detection of delinquency.

The Gluecks' double lifetime of research in criminology produced some of the most prolific writing on the subject, and both are considered pioneers in modern research criminology.

Goddard, Calvin Hooker (1891–1955) Army doctor, ballistics expert, criminologist, ordnance historian, and editor; helped found two of the most influential institutes of modern police science.

Born in Baltimore, Calvin Goddard was the great-grandson of a U.S. congressman and the son of a writer and insurance executive. He studied at Johns Hopkins University, receiving his bachelor's degree in 1911 and his M.D. in 1915. As an assistant at the

Johns Hopkins School of Medicine, he worked with the first electrocardiograph in the nation.

In 1916 Goddard enlisted in the U.S. Army. After attending the Army Medical School in Washington, D.C., he was commissioned to the U.S. Army Medical Corps and was soon promoted to major. He served a year as assistant to the adjutant, then he was sent in 1918 to Camp Upton, New York, where he was cardiovascular consultant and, subsequently, camp surgeon. During the great influenza pandemic of 1918–19, which hit Camp Upton hard, Goddard showed that isolating the afflicted helped to contain the spread of the disease. He went on to serve in France, Belgium, Germany, and Poland. He resigned from the army in 1920, but two years later he was recommissioned in the Ordnance Reserve, serving tours in various U.S. arsenals and at the Massachusetts Institute of Technology. Goddard was promoted to the rank of lieutenant colonel in 1928.

During his first years in the military, Goddard also worked in a physician's clinic in Birmingham, Alabama, again as a cardiovascular consultant. In 1921 Goddard returned to Baltimore to take the post of assistant director of the Johns Hopkins Hospital, where he practiced and taught cardiography. Three years later he switched jobs again, becoming assistant professor of clinical medicine at Cornell University Medical College and then director of the first outpatient clinic in the nation, a department of the Cornell Pay Clinic in New York City.

Goddard had been interested in guns all his life, collecting them as early as age seven and touring their places of manufacture since the age of 15. In 1925 he made firearms the focus of a new career, resigning from Cornell University to join with Charles E. WAITE in his newly conceived Bureau of Forensic Ballistics, the inaugural institute of its type. The New York-based firm was created for specialized research and expert consultation in the realm of arms and ammunition. Almost immediately, its founding members revolutionized the field with their new techniques of firearm identification.

Among the inventions of bureau founders Waite, Philip GRAVELLE, Goddard, and others were a comparison microscope, specially fitted for the simultaneous examination of two bullet specimens, and the helixometer, an adaptation of the medical cytoscope that permitted well-lit and magnified inspection of the internal mechanism of firearms. Together, these implements allowed previously unheard-of certainty in the matching of crime slugs to the firearms that had fired them. Goddard was the first to give court testimony based on the bureau's instruments, and his premier court case gained acquittal for a wrongly accused defendant. Goddard and the new ballistics

methods were to make prosecution history in many subsequent trials, embarrassing all previous forms of conflicting and unreliable firearms testimony, and ultimately replacing them as a new standard.

Waite died in 1926, and Goddard carried on with the bureau's investigative and consulting work, lecturing widely and writing professional articles about ballistics research and its applications.

In a 1927 inquiry into the wildly controversial conclusion of the SACCO AND VANZETTI trial, Goddard brought the comparison microscope into a courtroom for the first time. His application of the new ballistics tests caused one defense lawyer and another seasoned firearms expert to reverse their stances and finally believe the defendants guilty. Indeed, many historians still refer to Goddard's test as the prosecution's only persuasive evidence of guilt. The Lowell Committee certainly agreed; their report upheld conviction and the two anarchists were electrocuted within months.

Two years later, Goddard was asked to consult on the CAPONE-related gangster killing in Chicago popularly known as the St. Valentine's Day Massacre. Authorities in Chicago were so impressed with Goddard's criminological methods that they resolved to establish a special institute with the former army doctor as head.

After three months in Europe, visiting the police laboratories and medico-legal institutes of 13 countries, Goddard made use of his overseas research to set up and then direct the Scientific Crime Detection Laboratory (SCDL) in Evanston, Illinois. Sponsored by John H. WIGMORE, and boasting 14 specialists on staff, the laboratory provided state-of-the-art services in a host of technical areas—not only firearms identification, but also fingerprinting, X-ray and ultraviolet examination, chemical analysis, graphology and document examination, serology, photography, and toxicology. Goddard and his establishment supported Leonarde KEELER's work with the "lie-detecting" polygraph, and other researchers at the lab experimented with scopolamine, a so-called "truth serum."

The new facility became part of Northwestern University Law School, and in 1931, Goddard, now a professor at the school, began to teach the world's first courses in "police science." He also founded and edited the *American Journal of Police Science* to broadcast advances in this new and thoroughly modern discipline. Thousands of law enforcers came to Evanston to learn about the new instruments and techniques. The federal government's Bureau of Investigation—soon to become the FBI, among whose first officers were many Goddard pupils—went on to establish its own laboratory modeled on the SCDL.

By 1934 the Depression had taken its toll on institutional funding, and the laboratory closed. Over the next few years Goddard began work on a still unpublished textbook for firearms identification and collaborated with others in England and America on the development of a new type of machine gun. He was recalled to active army duty during World War II, joining the Historical Section of the Army War College in Washington, D.C. By 1942 he was chief historian of the Ordnance Department, and he supervised the compilation of all wartime documentation. He was later made historical editor on a special staff of the War Department.

Goddard was transferred to the Far East Command in 1947, becoming assistant chief of the historical branch at the General Headquarters in Japan. A year later, he was appointed head of the Far East Criminal Investigation Laboratory in Tokyo, and was commissioned in the Corps of Military Police. Goddard trained Japanese police officers and handled cases from all over the region, including many pertaining to the Korean War. While visiting the Philippines—teaching a two-month course in police science to the islands' constabulary—he reviewed the evidence in an attempted assassination of the Phillippine Army's chief of staff and contributed to the solution of the crime. By this time, Goddard was a colonel.

In 1951, poor health forced the ordnance expert and criminologist to return to the United States, but after three months' leave Goddard went back to work as chief of the Historical Unit of the Army Medical Service. There he began the task of editing a 40-volume series on the medical history of World War II. Having assembled a team of specialists in each field, he helped publish several volumes before retiring in 1954, though he continued as a consultant to the project until his death. Goddard also served as military editor, from 1940 to 1955, of all articles on ordnance and military history for the *Encyclopedia Britannica.* In 1942, he became the first American editor of the *Encyclopedia.*

Among Goddard's many awards and decorations were the Order of the Crown of Italy (1946), the Legion of Merit of the United States (1951), and numerous medals for marksmanship. Goddard held memberships in countless military, scientific, historical, and criminological societies and academies.

Gompers, Samuel (1850–1924) A pioneering American labor leader, Gompers was embroiled in a landmark controversy over unionizing the Boston police force.

Samuel Gompers was born in London, and at the age of 13, he immigrated with his family to New York City. There the second-generation cigarmaker studied at night and gradually rose through his local craft union's ranks, winning its presidency in 1875. In 1881,

Gompers helped found the Federation of Organized Trades and Labor Unions; he served as its vice president for the next five years, then became the key organizer and founding president of the American Federation of Labor (AFL). As head of the AFL from 1886 to 1895, then from 1896 to 1924, Gompers was an influential voice in virtually every major labor issue to arise during this turbulent era in American capitalism.

In July 1919, members of the Boston police force—under the auspices of the local Boston Social Club—applied for an AFL charter, hoping that this affiliation would help their stalled negotiations for much-needed improvements in wages, working hours, and station house conditions. But immediately, and weeks before Gompers's union was to grant the charter in August, Boston's Police Commissioner Edward Upton CURTIS issued orders forbidding police personnel to join any outside club or organization of any type, apart from three specifically excepted military veterans' groups. If the police had felt ill-used before, they now felt stripped of a basic freedom. Furthermore, Curtis formally charged 19 police officers involved in organizing the AFL application with violation of this prohibition. When he announced the officers' permanent dismissal on September 8, the police made good on their promise to strike. They voted a walkout for the following evening.

The crisis was handled badly by city authorities. Having long refused all compromises that would have averted the strike, Commissioner Curtis had made little effort to raise, let alone effectively deploy, his volunteer and metropolitan replacement forces when the inevitable occurred. He did, however, summarily and permanently fire every striker, thereby dismissing three-quarters of the city's police department. This announcement only widened the window of opportunity now open to Boston's criminal community. Gambling, robbery, looting, rioting, and other violence took over the streets until September 10, when Mayor Andrew Peters finally intervened by calling out more than 3,000 members of the state militia. These troops, patrolling with bayonets, began to bring matters under control, though several deaths occurred that night.

On September 11, Governor Calvin COOLIDGE, who had for weeks refused all pleas from mayor and citizens to involve himself in the police dispute, issued an executive order restoring Curtis's authority—under himself —and called more State Guard troops to the now relatively quiet city. Ironically, the long-blinkered, jurisdiction-shy Coolidge was credited with saving Boston from its nightmarish episode of lawlessness, and Americans everywhere applauded his firm stand against the ignominious, perhaps communist-leaning police.

Samuel Gompers was outraged by the chain of events in Boston and alarmed by the anti-union sentiments press coverage was eliciting nationwide. For more than 20 years police forces around the country had begged the AFL for affiliation and had been refused. But in the four weeks since Boston's charter had been granted, 35 more police applications had arrived at the federation's office, a new record for any single occupational type in so short a time. While Gompers believed in a policeman's—indeed every worker's—fundamental right to strike, the AFL had in no way ordered or encouraged the action. On September 12, the union leader urged the officers to return to work, and he telegraphed Coolidge and Peters with appeals to reinstate the strikers and submit their grievances to arbitration.

The following day Commissioner Curtis publicly announced that no reinstatement would be forthcoming, and Coolidge telegraphed Gompers a reply, once again disclaiming any gubernatorial authority in the matter. The police commissioner's decisions were beyond his reach, he wrote, and Coolidge would support Curtis in "the execution of law and the maintenance of order." Gompers wired again, proposing (as others had before him) that Coolidge simply remove Curtis from his appointment as commissioner, given his unfair and intransigent prohibition of AFL affiliation—which had brought on the thoroughly preventable strike—and his purposely delayed and ineffective action after the walkout, which had endangered the entire city in the interest of discrediting the strikers and, by extension, the American union movement. Gompers reminded Coolidge that President Woodrow WILSON himself had once acknowledged the right of the Washington, D.C., city police force to bargain collectively.

Coolidge's second telegram was reprinted by journalists across the nation. He again refused to fire Curtis, who had been appointed by Governor McCall, Coolidge's predecessor, and noted that the "right of the police of Boston to affiliate has always been questioned, never granted, [and] is now prohibited." He shrugged off the reference to President Wilson and the D.C. police, because that force had remained on duty and Boston's had not. He reminded Gompers that Wilson's comments on the present crisis had characterized the Boston police strike as "a crime against civilization." But the most famous line of the telegram, and the one that helped make Coolidge a national hero, was, "There is no right to strike against the public safety by anybody, anywhere, anytime." The governor closed by saying that he wished to "join and assist in taking a broad view of every situation," and assured Gompers of his support in "every legal action and sound policy."

The deal was done. Curtis began to recruit a new police force to replace the dismissed strikers. Most American citizens, frightened by Boston's experience—and even fearful of a slide toward "Bolshevism" on the seemingly slippery slope of collective organization—approved of its final outcome.

The Boston police strike was only one crisis in the developing history of American labor relations, though its consequences for law enforcement and other public sector servants were deeply felt. Gompers continued his lifelong fight for worker-management cooperation in other areas, and he described his experiences in a two-volume memoir, *Seventy Years of Life and Labor: An Autobiography*, which was published posthumously in 1925.

Further reading: Kaufman, Stuart B., *Samuel Gompers and the Origins of the American Federation of Labor, 1848-1896* (Westport, Conn.: Greenwood Press, 1973).

Livesey, Harold C., *Samuel Gompers and Organized Labor in America* (New York: Library of American Biography, 1987).

Goring, Charles B. (1870–1919)   English philosopher and psychiatrist who wrote *The English Convict* (1913), a monumental analysis of criminal behavior and a precursor of modern research criminology.

Educated at the University of London, Charles Goring received his M.D. in 1903. He subsequently began a lifelong career as a medical officer in the English prison system. Over a 12-year period, he studied more than 3,000 convicts to produce *The English Convict* in 1913. This monumental book rejected the widely accepted positivist theories of LOMBROSO, who concluded that criminal behavior was largely a matter of inherited traits. After exhaustive study, Goring concluded that no human being is born a criminal, but that adverse environmental factors can create one.

Goring was among the first social thinkers to advocate education as a deterrent to crime. Goring's ideas, revolutionary in the early 20th century, have come to represent the most widely accepted basic assumptions of modern criminology.

Further reading: Driver, Edwin D., "Charles Buckman Goring," *The Journal of Criminal Law, Criminology and Police Science*, 47:5 (January–February 1957).

Grant, Julius (1901–91)   A renowned British forensic document examiner, Grant uncovered the forgery that, in the 1980s, was passed off as the long-lost diaries of Adolf Hitler.

Criminology owes a great debt to British chemist Julius Grant, who worked in the field of forensic science for some 50 years. As one of the founding fathers of the Forensic Science Society in 1959 and president of the Medico-legal Society, Grant built a career investigating some of the most celebrated forgery cases in history. Earlier, during World War II, Grant worked with British intelligence, developing such spy equipment as invisible ink and edible paper. He also invented forgery-proof ration books to improve life on the homefront.

After the war, Grant went into private forensic practice, specializing in document analysis and eventually the wider field of forensic science. He was frequently called upon in England and elsewhere as one of the leading expert investigators and witnesses in civil and criminal court cases. Grant became known to a broad public for the role he played in solving the notorious safecracker case of Alfie Hinds—Grant matched the wood shavings found in the suspect's trouser cuffs with those found at the crime scene—and for his crucial testimony in the Great Train Robbery case of 1963.

In 1967, Grant made world headlines by disproving the authenticity of diaries purported to be those of Benito Mussolini. He established that the paper on which the diaries were written had not been produced during Mussolini's lifetime. Even more notable was the Hitler Diaries scandal of the 1980s. After less than five hours of examination, Grant determined the so-called diaries to be a hoax, based on his irrefutable expertise in chemical paper composition. Examining the paper under ultraviolet light, he discovered the presence of optical dyes—substances that did not exist until after World War II.

Grant's last major case before his death was in 1987, when he was called upon to testify at the Israeli Supreme Court trial of accused Nazi war criminal John Demjanjuk—thought to be the sadistic death camp guard known as Ivan the Terrible. Grant provided testimony affirming the authenticity of identification documents relating to Demjanjuk. (Demjanjuk's conviction was overturned in 1993 by the Israeli high court.)

Gravelle, Philip O. (1877–1955)

San Francisco-born photomicrographic expert who invented the "comparison microscope" for ballistics examination, and the instrument became a crucial scientific and legal tool in the area of firearms identification.

Philip Gravelle was working in New York City as a textile designer and studying chemistry at night at Columbia University when he first combined microscopy with his longtime avocation of photography. The combination came to fascinate him, and in 1923 he was the first American to be awarded the Barnard Gold Medal of the London Photomicrographic Society.

Shortly thereafter, Gravelle was invited by Charles E. WAITE to help in the establishment of his Bureau of Forensic Ballistics, the world's first institute devoted to the field. Under the bureau's auspices, many advances were made in forensics. Physicist John H. Fisher adapted the medical cytoscope—a bladder and kidney probe—to create the helixometer, an instrument for lighting and inspecting the interior of rifle and pistol bores in order to study their characteristic patterns of rifling for purposes of identifying bullets fired from them. Another instrument, the micrometer microscope, was devised to take extremely refined measurements of firearm bore features.

Gravelle applied himself to related experiments. In order to examine and photograph bullets discharged from different pistols of the same make and caliber, he fired these mass-produced, supposedly identical guns into targets of absorbent cotton. He quickly confirmed Waite's working hypothesis, that the spent rounds from any firearm bore surface peculiarities unique to their source, as though every gun produced a recognizable "fingerprint" on its ammunition. Frustrated by—and distrustful of—the need to "remember" the appearance of one bullet while examining another, Gravelle created an ingenious dual-objective microscope that allowed simultaneous examination and comparison of two specimens.

The combined investigations of Fisher and Gravelle showed that even the minutest differences in the lands (flat surfaces) and grooves of a factory-produced firearm's rifling—differences produced by sharpness and other variations in the initial tool marks, or by the scratches and slivers of the individual bore's internal wear and tear—created characteristic furrows and striations in any bullet fired. With the new instruments, a murder bullet could be matched to a suspect's weapon—or contrasted, as proof of innocence—with virtually final certainty.

Another bureau cofounder, the doctor and ordnance expert Calvin GODDARD, brought these discoveries to the courtroom—and to worldwide attention—in the high-profile cases of SACCO AND VANZETTI and Chicago's "St. Valentine's Day Massacre." The previously haphazard and conflict-ridden field of ballistics became a reliable cornerstone of modern police science.

A fellow of the Royal Photographic Society of Britain and a life member and fellow of the New York Microscopy Society, Gravelle died in Newark, New Jersey, on February 3, 1955.

Gray, L(ouis) Patrick (1916–)

Acting director of the FBI during the Watergate scandal; eventually resigned under a cloud of controversy after admitting to having destroyed evidence germane to the investigation.

Born to a poor family in Houston, Texas, L. Patrick Gray studied diligently in public school and won a scholarship to Rice University in Houston. There he trained with the Naval Reserve and, after completing his four-year degree at Rice, won an appointment to the U.S. Naval Academy at Annapolis, Maryland, graduating in 1940 with an ensign's commission. During World War II, he served aboard a submarine in the Pacific.

At war's end, Gray was selected to participate in a navy postgraduate program to study law at George Washington University in Washington, D.C. He graduated (with honors) with a J.D. in 1949 and was promoted to captain in 1950. With the outbreak of the Korean War, Gray again returned to submarine duty, this time as commander of a three-sub "wolfpack." In 1958, he was named military assistant to the chairman of the Joint Chiefs of Staff, and it was here that he nurtured a passion for serving among the power brokers of the nation's government.

Attaching himself to Richard NIXON's failed bid for the presidency in 1960, Gray gained several important contacts that would keep him in the forefront of the Republican Party. When Nixon was elected in 1968, Gray was named executive assistant to the secretary of health, education and welfare. He quickly earned a reputation as a die-hard Nixon loyalist, and in December 1970 was named assistant attorney general in the Justice Department's Civil Division. This meant that he was charged with prosecuting the numerous antiwar activists who had illegally demonstrated on federal property, a program Nixon pursued with zealous vigor.

In February 1972, Nixon nominated Gray for the post of assistant attorney general under Richard Kleindienst, who had been nominated to succeed John MITCHELL as attorney general. While the confirmations were being held up in the Senate, J. Edgar HOOVER died in his sleep on May 2, 1972, suddenly leaving the position of FBI director vacant. Nixon quickly withdrew Gray's name from confirmation and named him acting head of the FBI. Gray immediately relaxed many of the strict regulations imposed under Hoover, including dress code and grooming requirements and, more important, restrictions on women's service as field agents.

After gaining reelection in 1972, Nixon nominated Gray for the permanent position of FBI director. By the time of Gray's confirmation hearings, however, the Watergate investigations were in full swing, and Gray admitted to having alerted the White House, specifically Nixon aide John Dean, to the direction of the FBI's investigation of the break-in, as well as having provided raw, unevaluated evidence to Dean, including telephone transcripts. Gray also admitted that he had permitted officials of the Committee to Re-Elect the President (CREEP) to sit in on FBI interviews of CREEP employees. Gray replied to congressional criticism by saying that the president, and, by extension, his closest advisers, had a right to be kept up to date on the investigation. Caught up in a firestorm of criticism, Gray asked the president to withdraw the nomination.

Following the hearings, Gray later admitted to Senator Lowell Weicker of Connecticut, a Watergate committee member, that Dean and John Ehrlichman, another aide to the president, had given him information taken from the files of Howard Hunt, a former aide who had helped engineer the Watergate break-in. The information detailed how Hunt had doctored State Department cables to show that John F. Kennedy had ordered the assassination of South Vietnam's president, Ngo Dinh Diem. These documents were to be used in the event that Senator Edward Kennedy might run against Nixon in the 1972 election. When the story was made public, Gray resigned in disgrace as acting director of the FBI and barely escaped indictment.

Groome, John C. (1860–1930) The first commander of the Pennsylvania State Police; quickly turned the unit into a skilled and well-disciplined force.

A native of Philadelphia, John Groome spent his entire life in the military or law enforcement. He joined the Pennsylvania National Guard, quickly rising to command his unit. At the outbreak of the Spanish American War in 1898, Groome led his entire state unit to enlist for federal service before the war was seven days old. After exemplary service in the army, Groome returned to his state unit based in Philadelphia and was instrumental in leading the National Guard during the brutal Anthracite Coal Strike of 1902.

When Governor Samuel PENNYPACKER created the State Police in 1905, he offered its command to Groome. Groome accepted on condition that the force not become a dumping ground "for political henchmen or ward politicians." Pennypacker eagerly agreed, and Groome set about building one of the first state police forces in the nation.

The mission of the force was to serve as a police unit outside of incorporated areas and to be used as a law enforcement body in place of the defense-minded National Guard, which was not specially trained in law enforcement.

Groome's adherence to a work ethic and his military background proved to be exactly what was called for in building the state police. The organization quickly gained a reputation equal to that of its commander and served as a model for other units across the country. Once the force was well established, Groome resigned in 1917 to serve in World War I and was in charge of building and administering a large POW camp at Tours, France. After the war, he was appointed warden of the Eastern Penitentiary.

Further reading: Mayo, Katherine, *The Standard-Bearers: True Stories of Heroes of Law and Order* (Boston: Houghton-Mifflin, 1918).

Gross, Hans (1847–1915)   Author of a pioneering and comprehensive textbook of investigative techniques, this Austrian legal expert and professor was one of the most influential founders of scientific criminology.

Born in Graz and trained as a lawyer, Hans Gross became an examining magistrate in 1869. Because his region's police force was mainly a peacekeeping operation staffed by former soldiers, crime detection and investigation fell to the examiner himself. Gross took this aspect of his responsibility—so crucial to the delivery of justice—very much to heart. In addition to the practical information he solicited from local officers and tradespeople, he began to study aspects of both the natural and social sciences, seeking any and all knowledge that might help better equip him for his formidable role as inspector and judge.

Gross took particular interest in ballistics, and for an unusual reason. His grandfather had been shot in the head during service in the Austrian Army in 1799, and the ball had lodged behind the soldier's eye, where it remained until his death in 1845. The missile was removed during the elder Gross's autopsy, and the object ultimately came into his grandson's possession. The nascent criminologist noticed a series of marks, even powder traces, on its surface, and young Gross predicted that such signs would eventually be used to identify firearms in criminal cases.

In 1893, Gross published the first edition of his *System der Kriminalistic,* a landmark, practical manual for magistrates, trial attorneys, and police. The book's exhaustive range of subjects included the desirable characteristics for an investigator; interrogation procedure, and the psychological influences that might affect the testimony of persons under questioning; the professional inspection of crime scenes; and the handling, collection, and interpretation of all sorts of physical evidence. Outlining the techniques of microscopy, fingerprint collection, and other modern advances, Gross also shared the results of his research with dyed liquids and showed how blood spots could be "read" for clues to determine a victim's movements. Throughout, Gross advocated a thorough, precise, and fundamentally scientific approach to crime investigation and legal deliberation, frequently cautioning the reader to guard against human error or subjective conclusions. He particularly urged law enforcers to be wary of depending on the accuracy of eyewitness recollections and suspects' testimony, encouraging judges to place greater faith in hard physical evidence instead. For this reason, Gross strongly advocated the use and coordination of experts specializing in particular scientific or technical fields. He also stressed the importance of understanding causality when investigating a specific crime, especially when considering questions of motive.

The success of the book prompted a second edition the following year, then a third, and the volume was translated into many foreign languages, becoming a truly international standard. The first English translation, titled *Criminal Investigation,* was published in 1907.

In 1902, Gross was made chairman of the department of criminology at the University of Prague; three years later he began to teach penal law at the University of Graz. The legal scholar and expert was a popular lecturer.

Gross later wrote another vanguard text, *Criminal Psychology,* and John Henry WIGMORE, the first president of the American Institute of Criminal Law and Criminology, helped arrange for its translation around 1910. Once again, Gross emphasized an analytical approach to investigative law enforcement. He wrote: "The whole business of the criminalist is the study of causes . . . The fact that we deal with the problem of cause brings us close to other sciences which have the same task in their own researches; and this is one of the reasons for the criminalist's necessary concern with other disciplines . . . In certain directions our task is next to the historians' who aim to bring men and events into definite causal sequence."

Gross's books greatly influenced the subsequent development of criminological science, including Edmond LOCARD's founding of the police laboratory at Lyons, France, and the theory of "police professionalism" espoused by Berkeley, California, police chief August VOLLMER.

Further reading: Gross, Hans *Criminal Investigation: A Practical Textbook for Magistrates, Police Officers, and Lawyers,* 5th ed., adapted by John Adam, J. Collyer Adam, and Richard Leofric Jackson (London: Sweet & Maxwell Limited, 1962).

Gross, Nelson (1932–)   Former chairman of the New Jersey Republican Committee; served as "drug czar" during the administration of President Richard M. NIXON.

A New Jersey native, Nelson Gross attended Yale University, graduating in 1953 and earning his law degree from Columbia University in 1956. Once out of law school, he was named an assistant United States attorney and in 1962 was elected to the New Jersey state assembly, serving for a year before becoming the Bergen County (New Jersey) counsel from 1963 to 1966. In 1966, he chaired the Bergen County Republican Party and served as a delegate to the 1968 Republican National Convention. It was at the convention that Gross gained national attention.

In the crucial pre-vote caucusing that occurs before a floor vote is taken on nominations, Richard Nixon was perilously close to being defeated on the first ballot. Gross held five key votes previously allotted to favorite-son candidate Clifford Chase (a stand-in for candidate Nelson Rockefeller) and gave them to Nixon, thereby denying Rockefeller the first ballot. In return for his votes, Gross was named chair of the party in New Jersey.

After suffering a stunning defeat in the 1970 senatorial election, Gross served in the U.S. Department of State as special coordinator on international narcotics from 1971 to 1973. As so-called "drug czar," Gross was the first government appointee whose sole responsibility was attacking the illegal narcotics trade. With the full support of the "law-and-order" Nixon administration, Gross used the State Department to pressure foreign governments to crack down on the production and export of drugs. Through Gross's office, the United States gave Turkey $35 million to stem production of the heroin-producing poppy seed; the funds were to be used as direct compensation to the farmers who grew the crop legally. Gross also made inroads into the Southeast Asia drug trade, confiscating over six tons of heroin in 1971.

Nelson Gross resigned from his post in 1973 amid allegations of tax fraud, perjury, and obstruction of justice. He was convicted on these charges and served four months in prison.

Grosso, Salvador "Sonny" (1935–)   As New York City detectives, Grosso and his partner Eddie Egan cracked the so-called "French Connection" heroin case, which became the basis of a hit movie and launched Grosso on a career in the entertainment industry.

Sonny Grosso was a New York City police detective working undercover in the narcotics division, primarily making drug buys and then fingering the pushers. In 1962, he transferred out of the undercover division and, with his partner Eddie "Popeye" Egan, started to go after bigger game in the drug jungle: the ultimate

suppliers or "connections." With Egan, in 1962, Grosso cracked the so-called French Connection case, making the biggest seizure of heroin up to that time: 50 kilos, worth about $32 million.

The story of the case received wide public exposure and prompted Grosso to leave the NYPD, first to serve as technical consultant on the book and movie versions of *The French Connection*, then on movie versions of *The Godfather* and *The Seven-Ups*, and on the television series "Kojak," "Baretta," and "The Rockford Files." Grosso also wrote and coproduced "The Marcus-Nelson Murders," the three-hour television pilot for the "Kojak" series. In 1980, Grosso teamed up with Larry Jacobson, a television executive, to form Grosso-Jacobson Productions, responsible for producing CBS television's reality-based "Top Cops," ABC's "Bellevue Emergency," NBC's "True Blue," USA's "Diamonds," and—perhaps improbably—the once-popular CBS children's series "Pee Wee's Playhouse."

In 1988, Grosso-Jacobson Productions became the Grosso-Jacobson Entertainment Corporation.

Grüninger, Paul (1891–1972)   Swiss police border guard who aided the escape of hundreds of Jews from Nazi-held Austria.

Following the Anschluss of March 1938, whereby Nazi Germany annexed Austria, Austrian Jews began streaming across the border into Switzerland. Enacting an anti-Semitic policy of its own, the putatively neutral Swiss government banned Jewish emigration and closed its borders to Jews in August 1938.

Paul Grüninger, a police commandant in the small Swiss border canton of Saint Gall, decided he had no moral alternative but to defy his government's order. He back-dated the passports of Jews who came through his checkpoint, so that they predated the August order. In all, some 3,600 Jews passed through Saint Gall before the German legation in Bern alerted the Swiss government, which suspended Grüninger in December 1938. The following January, he was convicted of insubordination, assessed a heavy fine, stripped of his pension, and barred from any future government employment.

In 1971, just months before his death, Grüninger was officially recognized by the Israeli government for his humanity and personal sacrifice in helping Jews escape the Holocaust.

Guttenplan, Henry L. (1918–82)   Police officer who wrote a Ph.D. dissertation that was instrumental in reorganizing the New York City Police Department.

After graduating from the City College of New York in 1940, Henry Guttenplan joined the navy and served for almost four years during World War II. He joined the New York City Police Department as a patrolman in 1944, and, over the next 15 years, rose through the ranks to become an inspector in charge of the scientific research office, coordinating the efforts of police chemists, biologists, and physicists. During this period he attended night school at New York's City College and earned a master's degree in 1959. He next set to work on a Ph.D. in law enforcement administration, completing his dissertation in 1965.

Guttenplan submitted his dissertation to the police commissioner for review. The document called for the reorganization of the scientific units of the police department, specifically the police lab, ballistics, and the bomb squad, as well as changing shift hours and merging investigative and research units to emphasize and facilitate teamwork in criminal investigations. The commissioner enthusiastically endorsed the plan and ordered the overhaul of the department, implementing most of Guttenplan's recommendations.

After retiring from the department in 1967, Guttenplan joined the faculty of Pennsylvania State University as a professor of law enforcement and corrections.

H

Hague, Frank "Boss" (1876–1956) This controversial and tyrannical political boss of tough Jersey City, New Jersey, is remembered for declaring: "I am the law.

Frank "Boss" Hague first rose to political power in 1913, elected as one of five commissioners of Jersey City, New Jersey. Serving in this capacity as the city's director of public safety, the fiery sixth-grade dropout assumed the responsibility for single-handedly reshaping Jersey City's police department. In fact, Hague was bent on transforming the department into his own private fiefdom. Under the guise of eliminating police corruption, Hague obtained the authority to fire and hire all police officers and fire fighters. This allowed him to build one of the largest and most powerful political regimes in history, and the Jersey City police force became nothing more than a tool of Hague's ambition and greed. He used the police force to create a powerful machine that catapulted him into the mayor's office in 1917.

Once Hague had consolidated his power base, he systematically took control of much of New Jersey politics. His so-called "Zeppelin Gang"—an elite detective force used to spy on internal and external Hague opponents—succeeded in suppressing all resistance to the mayor, and Hague remained secure in office for more than three decades.

Although Hague's prime motive was to attain and maintain total power, the by-products of Hague's tyrannical rule were one of the best-paid police departments in the nation, the elimination of petty graft by individual police officers, better enforcement of many laws, and, as the electorate of Jersey City perceived it, an improvement in public safety.

In 1947, Hague resigned from his $7,500-a-year-job as mayor and retired to his half-million-dollar estate in New York and his opulent summer home on the Jersey Shore.

Further reading: McKean, Dayton David, *The Boss: The Hague Machine in Action* (New York: Russell and Russell, 1940).

Hale, George (1855–?) Compiled the first American encyclopedia of police work.

Born and raised in Lawrence, Massachusetts, Hale answered the call of the West. He worked on Mississippi River steamboats, raised sheep and Angora goats on an uncle's California farm, worked a Mojave Desert silver mine, and ran his own teamster business—until a broken wagon wheel threw him headfirst down the side of a precipitous canyon. After a period of recuperation in a hospital, in 1879 Hale joined up with H-troop of the Sixth U.S. Cavalry at Fort Verde, Arizona. An excellent marksman and one of the best of a fine group of riders, he dodged unfriendly Indians on his courier routes. Next came a yearlong assignment to clerical duty. Dissatisfied, Hale sought discharge in 1882, worked for the chief quartermaster for a time, then reenlisted, signing up with General George Crook on his expedition south of the border in search of Geronimo and his renegade Apaches. When Hale returned to the Arizona Territory, he took work on a hay ranch and on a construction crew.

Ending a nine-year adventure in frontier living, Hale made his way back east and enlisted in the Fourth Heavy Artillery at Fort Warren, Boston Harbor. He taught at the camp's artillery school, but one day a premature cannon shot nearly blew him away. His enthusiasm for the military now permanently cooled, he quit the army again in 1887 and worked in a hardware store while pondering his next move.

The question of career was answered when he took the police civil service exam and scored 100%. That, plus his fluency in Spanish and his excellent military record, prompted several high-ranking authorities to recommend Hale for a diplomatic career, but the former cavalry man preferred to accept a post on the Lawrence, Massachusetts, police force.

Little else is known about Hale's personal or professional life, except that in October 1891 he began work on what would become a world-famous *Cyclopaedia.* Noting that "arguments and disputes continually arise" over the legality or advisability of any given peace officer's course of action, Hale sought to create a bible for consultation, gathering together in one book a mass of information that would otherwise require "examining a library of law volumes and public statutes, or writing to the 'ends of the earth.' " Hale did just that, sending questionnaires to city chiefs of police around the country and the world—from Chicago to Calcutta, Manhattan to Mexico City, St. Louis to Stockholm—inquiring of their duties, laws, and methods. (His preface to the published volume takes numerous jabs at certain much-queried non-respondents, while specially commending those officials who replied with clear handscript or typewriting.)

Completed with amazing speed in February of the following year, Hale's book included, among other remarkable and useful data, glossaries of crime definitions and legal terms, detailed descriptions of police rights and duties around the world, civil service regulations affecting police in some localities, and a listing of police personnel in every U.S. city with an 1890 population of 10,000 or more. Hale admitted that had he "been fully aware of the vexations and delays which would ensue, and the profanity which would be involved" in preparing such a book, he never would have taken on the task. But having done so, he earned a name for himself as a pioneering scholar in the field of law enforcement. His intention to update the volume annually, however, must have bowed to these vexations, because the first American edition was also the last.

Further reading: Hale, George W., *Police and Prison Cyclopaedia* (Cambridge: Riverside Press, 1892; Boston: W. L. Richardson Company, 1893).

Hall, (Jesse) Lee (Leigh) (1849–1911)

Known simply as Lee Hall, this Texas lawman became one of the most celebrated of the Texas Rangers.

Hall was born in Lexington, North Carolina, on October 9, 1849, and simplified his name to Lee Hall when he arrived in Texas. He became city marshal of Sherman, Texas, and a deputy sheriff, and he was named second lieutenant of the Special Force, a division of the Texas Rangers. He served with the Special Force from August 10, 1876, to February 29, 1880, soon amassing a reputation as one of the greatest of the already-legendary Texas Rangers.

Hall, quickly promoted to captain, was instrumental in putting an end to the destructive range war known as the Sutton-Taylor feud, and arrested the notorious King Fisher as well as a host of other criminals. Hall was the kind of western lawman of whom popular legends were made. His reputation was tarnished in the mid-1880s, when he was indicted for embezzlement and making false claims while he was serving as agent for the Anadarko Indians. The case was dropped, however, for lack of evidence. During the Spanish-American War of 1898, Hall raised two companies of volunteers, personally serving in the Philippines as leader of the Macahebe Scouts. He received a brevet for gallantry during this period. After his death on March 17, 1911, Hall was buried in the National Cemetery at San Antonio, Texas.

Haller, Mark (1928–)

An acute critic of police practices in the United States.

Mark Haller received his bachelor's degree from Wesleyan University, Middletown, Connecticut, in 1947. After earning a master's from the University of Maryland and a Ph.D. from the University of Wisconsin, he joined the sociology faculty of the University of Chicago in 1959 before moving to Temple University, where he remained for the rest of his career.

Haller was a student of the reform movements that marked the Progressive Period in the United States at the turn of the century. He concentrated particularly on an analysis of urban political and bureaucratic corruption, questioning the common belief that politicians were corrupt and that they forced other aspects of society to become corrupt as well. Whenever reform candidates were swept into office, their first act was to remove as many political cronies of their predecessor as possible, as if that would be sufficient to transform society. Haller said that this was analogous to removing a tumor to cure cancer. The problem, however, was that such surgery failed to attack the root disease, which permeated all social institutions. Specifically, he argued that until the professionalization of police forces was standard practice, the police would continue to be potential pawns of urban machine politicians. Using the history of the Chicago Police Department, Haller demonstrated that politics were central, not peripheral, to the daily workings of the department. Haller concluded that, until the police were permanently raised above the political fray, removing this or that politician from office served only to distribute the political spoils more efficiently.

Hamer, Frank (1884–1955)

This legendary Texas Ranger is best remembered for his ambush of the notorious bank-robbing couple Bonnie Parker and Clyde Barrow.

Frank Hamer's law enforcement career spanned two periods of Texas outlawry: the "bad man" era of the Wild West and the gangster era of the 1930s. Hamer joined the Texas Rangers in 1906 at age 22 and was immediately dispatched to clean up the boisterous oil-boom town of Doran, in which the most recent sheriff had been murdered. Hamer himself was ambushed by a local criminal, but managed to put a bullet in his assailant and went on to accomplish his mission of cleaning up the town.

Over the course of his career, Hamer would get involved in over 50 gunfights, be wounded more than 20 times, and kill at least 50 outlaws in the process—a record unmatched by any lawman (or, for that matter, gunman) of the wildest period of the Wild West.

Frank Hamer's most famous case involved the pursuit and killing of Bonnie and Clyde. It came in 1934, the year Hamer resigned from the Texas Rangers in protest over its corruption by Governor "Ma" Ferguson. Hamer was a Texas highway patrolman when he went after the outlaw couple.

Director Arthur Penn's popular movie, *Bonnie and Clyde* (1967) portrayed Hamer as bumbling and weak, but in reality Frank Hamer's 102-day tracking of the notorious couple is an example of the famous lawman's diligence and skill as a detective. Hamer took the case in the first place because Clyde Barrow had killed a fellow officer, and it was with particular determination that Hamer followed the couple through three states, traveling and sleeping in a Ford V-8—a car just like Barrow's.

Hamer's diligence paid off on May 23, 1934, when his men ambushed the couple outside of Plain Dealing, Louisiana. After the pair defied his command to "stick em up," Hamer and his men opened up on the couple and their car, riddling the vehicle and the outlaws with 187 bullets. Frank Hamer's name came to be synonymous with the best traditions of the Texas Rangers. A tough and unshakable pillar of law and order, the old Texas Ranger retired in 1945.

Further reading: Webb, Walter Prescott, *The Texas Rangers* (Austin: University of Texas Press, 1935).

Hamilton, Alexander (ca. 1755–1804)   One of the most influential of the nation's founding fathers, Hamilton, secretary of the treasury, established the U.S. Coast Guard on August 4, 1790, to combat smuggling.

Hamilton was born on the West Indian island of Nevis, the illegitimate son of Rachel Fawcett Lavien and James Hamilton. He spent most of his youth on Saint Croix as an apprentice to a clerk, and in 1772 his guardian, the merchant Nicholas Cruger, sent him to New York City. There he enrolled at King's College (now Columbia University) and was caught up in the debate that preceded the American Revolution. Hamilton soon moved from words to action, enlisting in the militia and fighting with such distinction that George Washington commissioned him an officer in the Continental Army, making him his personal aide-de-camp. Hamilton commanded a New York regiment at the battle of Yorktown in October 1781.

After marrying Elizabeth Schuyler in December 1780, Hamilton was admitted into the inner circles of New York society, became a lawyer in 1782, then assistant to Robert Morris, at the time superintendent of finance. That same year, Hamilton was elected a member of the Continental Congress, in which he became a champion of a strong federal government at the expense of the states. With John JAY and James Madison, he wrote *The Federalist Papers,* an argument for the ratification of the new constitution and one of the most influential documents in American political history.

In 1789, Hamilton was appointed the first secretary of the treasury under the new constitution. Among his many brilliant achievements in organizing the Treasury Department and generally laying the foundation of the new republic's economy, Hamilton created the United States Coast Guard, a unique arm of law enforcement intended to combat smuggling operations and to ensure that the Treasury Department received all export and import duties to which it was entitled. Founded on August 4, 1790, the Coast Guard predates the U.S. Navy as the nation's first permanent seagoing armed force.

By the time Hamilton left the Treasury Department in 1795, he had firmly established key administrative and policy foundations not only for his department, but also for the entire federal bureaucracy. Returning to private life, Hamilton resumed his law practice, taking time to serve as inspector general of the army (1798–1800) and helping to put the national defense on a firm footing.

Hamilton vigorously opposed Aaron Burr's candidacy for president in 1800, regarding him as an entirely unprincipled man. The conflict between Burr and Hamilton escalated, until Burr challenged Hamilton to a duel. The two faced off at Weehawken, New Jersey, on July 11, 1804. Hamilton, as the challenged party, claimed the right to fire first. He discharged his weapon into the air. Burr shot to kill, and the mortally wounded Hamilton died the next day, leaving a wife and seven children.

Hamilton, Mary (active 1917–1930s)   The first female police officer to serve as a field supervisor, Hamilton was director of the Women's Police Bureau of the New York City Police Department.

Entering the Missing Person's Bureau of the NYPD in 1917, Mary Hamilton had no idea she was embarking on her life's work. She began with the department as a volunteer in Missing Persons and became one of the first female officers in New York City. As an officer, she was responsible for handling most cases concerning women and children, and she dealt extensively with runaways and cases in which women felt more comfortable talking to a female officer rather than a man.

After the appointment of Ellen O'Grady as deputy police commissioner in 1918, the women's movement within the department gained momentum. By 1924, the duties that Hamilton and her fellow female officers were performing had become such a vital component of the department that the police commissioner appointed Hamilton director of the newly created Women's Police Bureau and ordered that the station house on West 37th Street be renovated as bureau headquarters. This marked the first instance in which a woman was given field command of other officers.

Hammurabi (ca. 1792–1750 B.C.) King of ancient Babylon who is best remembered for his legal code, which embodied the practice of "eye for an eye" punishment (*lex talionis*).

Although best remembered for his legal code, Hammurabi was also an effective conqueror, moving against his more powerful neighbors and firmly securing his boundaries. Hammurabi's military successes allowed him to strengthen his domestic control and implement a series of laws, known in modern times as the Code of Hammurabi, which would help define Babylon as a civilized society.

The code dealt with almost every aspect of daily life and therefore provides a vivid glimpse into Babylonian society. The code divided society into three social classes, ranging from the nobility, to citizens, to slaves, and defined each of their responsibilities with regard to the Babylonian system of justice. The wealthy could exact a greater punishment when wronged, but could be held more criminally liable when responsible for a criminal action themselves. Slaves, in contrast, could expect only slight monetary compensation for corporal offenses.

The most familiar aspect of the code is the section dealing with punishment and the *lex talionis*, the concept of an eye for an eye. Indeed, the phrase had its origin in the code, which specifies that if a man pokes out the eye of another, the offender's eye is in turn taken, in effect punishing the offending member. Thieves, for example, frequently suffered amputation of the hand that stole. The death penalty was freely imposed under Hammurabi's Code, but sometimes in

ways that strike the modern sensibility as bizarre. For example, if a man caused the death of another's child, his child—not he—would be executed.

Hammurabi's Code is among the very oldest sets of written laws in the history of civilization and is the most comprehensive ancient legal document.

Further reading: Seagle, Wiiliam, *Men of Law: From Hammurabi to Holmes* (New York: Macmillan, 1947).

Hankey, Richard O. (1915–79) A champion of police professionalism.

Richard Hankey was born in Illinois but came to California on an athletic scholarship to the University of California, Berkeley. There he earned a degree in social criminology while playing football for the Golden Bears—and also met the legendary August VOLLMER, the Berkeley police chief, professor, and guiding light of the movement to professionalize the nation's municipal police forces. When he graduated in 1939, Hankey took a position with the Berkeley department, working under his mentor, and attained the rank of sergeant before joining the army near the end of World War II.

Hankey was stationed in Germany, where he was a military government public safety officer, charged with reviving and restructuring German civil law enforcement. The experience gave him a taste for something more than routine police work, and Vollmer urged him to pursue a law enforcement career in academia. His first position was at the College of the Sequoias in Northern California, where he was the pioneering director of law enforcement training. In 1957, Hankey moved to California State College (now University) at Los Angeles, where he developed the Department of Police Science and Administration into a program of national prominence and a training ground, in particular, for the growing Los Angeles Police Department.

Hankey's final teaching position was at Linn Benton College in Oregon, where he died in 1979, having become one of the preeminent figures in the professionalization movement.

Harrington, Penny (1949–) The first female police chief of a large American city, Harrington was forced to resign and subsequently sued the city of Portland, Oregon, because of sexual harassment.

A native of Michigan, Penny Harrington attended Michigan State University in East Lansing, where she studied criminal justice. After graduating in 1964, she moved to Portland, Oregon, hoping to become a police officer there. She was initially rejected, but she spent the next several months lobbying the Portland mayor to increase the number of women on the force. Ultimately successful, she was named in 1966 to the

Women's Protective Division, which worked almost exclusively with juveniles and rape victims. After serving with the WPD for six years without advancement, Harrington filed the first of 42 formal complaints or suits against the department, demanding that the competitive examination for detective be opened to women. She won the right to take the exam, and soon thereafter became Portland's first female detective. Over the next 16 years, Harrington would become Portland's first female sergeant, lieutenant, and captain, at each stage having to file a complaint or suit and at each stage prevailing.

In 1985, Harrington was named police chief, the nation's first female chief in a large urban jurisdiction. Almost immediately, however, she ran into opposition. Although she handled her opponents deftly and made significant improvements in relations between the police department and Portland's African-American community, her restructuring of the department along gender and racial lines drew harsh criticism, particularly from the mayor, who had previously supported her. An independent commission established to review Harrington's policies found "a breakdown in morale" and "poor management style." It recommended dismissal, the mayor agreed with the recommendation, and less than 18 months after her promotion to chief, the mayor demanded Harrington's resignation.

Harrington stepped down, but filed a sexual harassment suit against the department, the mayor, and the city, claiming not only that would she never have been subjected to such a review commission if she were male, but also that the mayor failed to notify her that her job was in peril, and that she was denied due process. After a lengthy trial, the suit was dismissed.

Harrison, Harold Charles (1907–70) Established the University of Rhode Island's Laboratory for Scientific Criminal Investigation, one of the nation's foremost forensic facilities, and also developed Rhode Island's breath test for alcohol detection.

Harrison was born in Rutland, Vermont, on February 10, 1907, the son of a banker. He was educated in public schools and took his B.S. degree in 1931 at Washington and Lee University and his Ph.D. in chemistry at Cornell in 1938. He was a postdoctoral fellow at the Massachusetts Institute of Technology (M.I.T.) in 1939 and at Harvard from 1946 to 1949. From 1938 to 1941, he was also assistant professor of chemistry and spectroscopy at the New York State College of Ceramics, and from 1941 to 1944 he was chief chemist and spectroscopist with the Oregon State Department of Geology and Mineral Industries and a consultant to the Oregon State Crime Detection Bureau. From 1944 to 1946, he was in the U.S. Navy, attached to the Bureau of Ordnance.

In 1949, Harrison joined the faculty of the University of Rhode Island as associate professor of chemistry, advancing to full professor in 1956, a post he held until his death. In 1953, he established the Laboratory for Scientific Crime Detection at the university and served as its director, also until his death. The laboratory was a cooperative venture of the university and the state attorney general's office, and it conducted research in analytical chemistry and criminalistics. At the laboratory, Harrison also established a training school for law enforcement officers.

Harrison soon established a national reputation for the laboratory and himself in the field of scientific crime detection, especially in the areas of ballistics and identification through hair, paint, and dirt samples. He was instrumental in developing Rhode Island's pioneering breath test for alcohol, which became central in establishing intoxication in cases of suspected drunk driving and other crimes. Harrison appeared frequently as an expert witness in trials in Rhode Island and throughout New England, and he served on many state and national crime-detection and crime-prevention committees.

Hauptmann, Bruno Richard (1899–1936) This German immigrant was probably the most hated man in America after he was convicted of the kidnapping and murder of Charles Lindbergh Jr., the 20-month-old infant son of the nation's favorite aviator.

During the night of March 1, 1932, the German-born carpenter—who had entered the United States illegally and who had a criminal record in Germany—climbed his homemade ladder to the bedroom window of the infant son of Charles and Anne Morrow Lindbergh and abducted him. He left near the window a ransom note demanding $50,000. Over the course of the next few weeks, amid a media circus, a tragic drama was played out. Two nocturnal meetings were set up in Woodlawn Cemetery in the Bronx between Hauptmann (whose identity, of course, was not known) and a volunteer intermediary named John Condon, whom the newspapers promptly dubbed Cemetery John. Condon delivered ransom money as he had been instructed, but the child was not returned. Two months after the kidnapping, his decomposed corpse was found in a shallow grave near the Lindberghs' home.

The murder of the Lindbergh baby shocked and outraged the nation and the world, sparking the largest manhunt in the history of law enforcement up to that time. After two-and-a-half years, an alert gas station attendant recognized a marked $10 gold certificate, which had been part of the ransom money.

The station attendant noted the license plate number of the vehicle belonging to the man who had given him the bill, and police readily located Bruno Hauptmann, arresting him at home in September 1934.

On January 2, 1935, Hauptmann was put on trial. Both Charles A. Lindbergh and "Cemetery John" testified that the carpenter's voice was the one they had heard in the cemetery, but even more damaging evidence came from expert witness and "wood detective" Arthur KOEHLER, who traced portions of the wooden ladder left at the kidnapping scene directly to lumber from Hauptmann's attic. On February 13, after an 11-hour deliberation, the jury found Hauptmann guilty, and he was sentenced to death.

Electrocuted on April 3, 1936, Bruno Hauptmann had never confessed to the crime, and various persons—including his widow—staunchly maintained his innocence.

Further reading: Scaduto, Anthony, *Scapegoat: The Lonesome Death of Bruno Richard Hauptmann* (New York: Putnam, 1976).

Haviland, John (1792–1852)   British-born architect who designed the Eastern Penitentiary at Cherry Hill, near Philadelphia, in 1829; the facility became an international model for prison architecture.

A group of Pennsylvania Quakers hired the young British architect John Haviland to design a new prison in 1820. The Quakers believed that solitary confinement both day and night would foster genuine penitence—and, therefore, rehabilitation—and would also deter future crime. Proceeding from these assumptions, Haviland designed the prison at Cherry Hill like a giant wagon wheel, with relatively isolated confinement areas radiating from a central hub. The prison was the first totally self-contained facility of its kind that focused on rehabilitation, and, as such, became highly influential. The so-called Pennsylvania System served as a model for other prisons, including the federal facility at Leavenworth, Kansas, and the state penitentiary at Trenton, New Jersey.

Outside of America, Haviland's architecture made an even greater impact. International dignitaries converged on Cherry Hill during the late 1820s, and Haviland's style can be seen in prisons throughout Europe, Asia, and Africa. Belgium actually rebuilt its entire prison system based on Haviland's designs.

Further reading: Mannheim, Herman, "John Haviland," *The Journal of Criminal Law, Criminology and Police Science,* 45:5 (February 1955).

Hayes, Rutherford B. (1822–93)   Best known as the 19th president of the United States, Hayes was also the founder of the National Prison Association, forerunner of the American Correctional Association.

Hayes was born on October 4, 1822, in Delaware, Ohio, the posthumous son of a farmer. He was educated in Norwalk, Ohio, and at a private school in Middletown, Connecticut. He returned to Ohio to study at Kenyon College and, after graduation in 1842, studied law locally and at Harvard. Admitted to the bar in 1845, he began to practice in Lower Sandusky, Ohio. In 1850, he moved his practice to Cincinnati and, the following year, entered local politics. With the outbreak of the Civil War in 1861, Hayes enlisted, serving throughout the war and gaining election as a U.S. representative from Ohio afterward. He was elected governor of Ohio in 1868, serving two terms before he was nominated by the Republicans as their candidate for president in 1876. Although Hayes received fewer popular votes than his opponent, Samuel J. Tilden, the Republicans managed to reverse the electoral tally of the three southern states they still controlled under post-Civil War Reconstruction laws. The election finally had to be decided by a special congressional commission. Under a cloud, Hayes was installed in office (even friends referred to him as "Your Fraudulency") and served his term but declined to stand for reelection, turning over the candidacy to James A. Garfield.

After leaving the White House, Hayes took up a number of humanitarian and social causes, including prison reform, becoming one of the founders of the National Prison Association in 1883 and serving as its first president for the decade of 1883 until his death in 1893. During his tenure as NPA president, Hayes became a highly regarded, highly visible, and highly successful spokesman for penal reform. From 1884 to 1892 he annually addressed Congress on the subject, elaborating on the causes of crime (based on early sociological studies), advocating a list of practical reforms, and always concluding on a note of religious uplift.

The NPA and its later incarnation, the American Correctional Association, were instrumental in humanizing American prisons and in professionalizing their staffs by raising them above political patronage and corruption.

Haynes, Richard "Racehorse" (1923–)   One of the most successful and flamboyant defense attorneys of the 20th century, Haynes is best known for the stratospheric fees he commands and his ability to devastate almost any prosecution.

Somewhat of a throwback to the defense attorneys of the early 1900s, Richard Haynes brings high drama to the courtroom and deems nothing too lurid or seamy to further the defense of his client. Born in Houston, Texas, on April 2, 1923, Haynes attended the University of Houston for both his undergraduate degree and his law degree before being admitted to the Texas bar in 1956.

Although much of Haynes's notoriety comes from his impressive fees and his equally impressive ego, colleagues and opponents alike agree that he is a courtroom genius. Haynes frequently gains acquittals or, at least, hung juries in cases that prosecutors consider airtight. He freely admits that many of his clients have indeed committed the crime in question, but that it is not his place to decide innocence or guilt, only to present the facts as effectively as possible.

Perhaps his most infamous case was that of Texas multimillionaire T. Cullen Davis, who had the distinction of being the richest man ever tried for murder in the United States. Although the prosecution had three eyewitnesses who unequivocally identified Davis as his wife's murderer, Haynes gained an acquittal by calling the witnesses' testimony into question without ever attacking the substance of what they said.

Finding and exploiting the substance of "reasonable doubt" is Haynes's specialty. The attorney once described his devastating method with a homely illustration: "Say you sue me because my dog bit you. I say my dog doesn't bite; second, my dog was tied up that night; third, I don't believe you really got bit; and finally, I don't even have a dog." Prosecutors and ordinary citizens simultaneously fear, admire, and revile Haynes. When he contemplated defending Manuel NORIEGA in 1990 against drug trafficking charges, he received a letter threatening to charge him with treason. Although he eventually declined the Noriega case, many feel that Haynes—like other high-powered, high-priced, no-holds-barred defenders—is a menace to law and order. Others believe that lawyers like Haynes keep the legal system sharp and discourage the sloppiness and abuses that can send innocent people to prison.

Hays, Jack (John Coffee) (1817–83)   The traditions of the Texas Rangers were largely formed under the leadership of this famed lawman.

Born in Little Cedar Lick, Tennessee, John Hays settled in San Antonio, Texas, around 1838. According to some accounts, Hays joined the Texas Rangers about that time and, under Deaf Smith and Henry Karnes, fought raiding Indians and marauding Mexicans. In 1840 Hays was promoted to captain of the Texas Rangers and put in charge of protecting the particularly vulnerable settlement of San Antonio. That same year Hays fought the Comanches at Plum Creek; numerous other battles followed, including Enchanted Rock in 1841 and Bandera Pass in 1842.

Hays evolved as the archetypical Texas Ranger: stern, disciplined, direct, and highly effective in tactical and strategic planning. Hays was one of the hand-

John Coffee "Jack" Hays was an early Texas Ranger who did much to shape the traditions of the organization. (Courtesy of the Library of Congress)

ful of Ranger leaders who created the mystique that surrounded the organization as it evolved from its primarily military mission to one of law enforcement. By gathering about himself the best trackers, the best soldiers, and the bravest men in Texas, Hays helped ensure that the Rangers would be feared by their adversaries and respected by all who knew them.

Hays left the Texas Rangers in the late 1840s for California, where he became sheriff of San Francisco County in 1850. In 1853 President Franklin Pierce appointed him surveyor-general of California, and his most notable achievement was the survey and plotting of the city of Oakland. The Ranger in him reemerged in Nevada during the so-called Pyramid Lake War fought against the Paiutes in 1860; Hays scored a significant victory at the mouth of the Truckee River.

Hays retired from combat after the battle of Truckee and became a successful land speculator in California until his death at Piedmont in 1883.

Further reading: Axelrod, Alan, *Chronicle of the Indian Wars: From Colonial Times to Wounded Knee* (New York: Prentice-Hall General Reference, 1992).

Webb, Walter Prescott, *The Texas Rangers* (Austin: University of Texas Press, 1935).

Hays, Jacob (1772–1850)   "Old Hays," a baton-wielding "terror to evil-doers," was the high constable of New York City for the first half of the 19th century and a near-legendary figure in early American law enforcement.

Born in Bedford Village in Westchester County, New York, Jacob Hays was the son of a Jewish merchant who had fought under George Washington in the Revolutionary War. Hays received a typical school education and spent several restless years in the family business until 1798, when his father asked Aaron Burr to help situate Jacob in a more gratifying career. This Burr did, persuading Mayor Varick to appoint Hays a marshal in the city of New York. Within three years, a new mayor, Edward Livingston, had promoted him to chief of the constabulary force.

With bold physical courage, dogged tenacity, a keen memory for names and faces, and his own uniquely forbidding stare, Hays protected the peace of the young metropolis for the next five decades—his only weapon a gold-headed baton. The constable's larger-than-life personality and rough-and-ready, street-based policing style earned him a mythical reputation as far away as the capitals of Europe. Whether breaking up a gang fight or combing the docks for murder suspects, "Old Hays" was idolized by the press and made famous for getting the job done—and thoroughly—by whatever means and against whatever odds. His stunningly simple, yet unprecedented measure of pairing officers for their own protection—and as a hedge against the corruption of either—remains standard practice today.

In 1844, New York reorganized its police department and the Office of High Constable was formally eliminated, but the grateful city honored Hays himself by maintaining his title and benefits for life. The senior lawman's international renown continued to grow even then. After a Hays-escorted tour of Manhattan's seamiest neighborhoods, visiting British author Charles Dickens returned to England with a hair-raising description of the city's underside, further bronzing the chief's heroic accomplishments in vividly sharp relief.

For many years, New York mothers extorted good behavior from their children with the admonition, "You be good, or old Hays will get you!" The high constable succumbed to natural causes at the age of 78.

Hecht, Ben (1894–1964)   Crime reporter for the *Chicago Journal*, became a famous and prolific Hollywood screenwriter (*Scarface*) and playwright (*The Front Page*) by fictionalizing his experiences as a crime reporter.

Ben Hecht's flamboyant journalism and dramatic portrayal of the Chicago underworld of the 1920s helped create the popular image of the American gangster. Hecht and Charles MacArthur, his opposite number writing for the rival *Chicago Examiner*, gripped the city with their daily accounts of crime and criminals—and with their aptitude for actually solving some of the cases they reported. Best known was the mysterious "ragged stranger" case of 1920. The husband of a slain woman claimed his wife had been the victim of a robber described as a "ragged stranger." The police sought the stranger, discovering that the husband was a covert homosexual who wanted his wife dead because she had become pregnant.

Through such sensational investigative reporting, Hecht and MacArthur virtually invented yet another pop culture "type": the hard-boiled, big city crime reporter.

Hecht left Chicago for New York in 1924 to collaborate with MacArthur on several hit Broadway plays, including, most notably, the widely acclaimed *The Front Page* in 1928. In 1927, he wrote the world's first gangster movie, *Underworld*, which was directed by Josef von Sternberg. This was followed by the 1931 screenplay for *Scarface*, the title of which reportedly miffed "Scarface" Al CAPONE, who sent some of his "boys" to visit Hecht, who skillfully talked himself out of a beating—or worse.

Although Hecht is best remembered as a crime reporter and for his plays and screenplays of the 1930s, he also wrote short stories and even ventured into television drama. A passionate crusader against anti-Semitism, he wrote *A Guide for the Bedevilled* in 1944, a highly provocative analysis of the phenomenon. His 1954 autobiography, *Child of the Century*, is considered a classic.

Heinrich, Edward Oscar (1881–1953)   One of the first professional criminologists was a master of several fields and was one of the first to use ballistics extensively as a form of evidence.

Born in Clintonville, Wisconsin, on April 20, 1881, Edward Heinrich, like so many noted criminologists after him, studied at the University of California, earning his degree there in 1908. From California, Heinrich moved to Tacoma, Washington, where he gained a reputation as an able chemist who was frequently called upon by the local authorities as an expert witness. In 1917, his investigative savvy landed him the job of Alameda police chief, but he remained in that position for only a year before accepting the post of city manager of Boulder, Colorado. In late 1919, Heinrich returned to the San Francisco Bay area and began lecturing at his alma mater on criminal investigation, criminalistics, and his latest discovery, ballistics. Heinrich had noted that every rifle barrel makes its own unique impression on every bullet fired from it, thereby making it possible to trace bullets found at a crime scene—or discovered in the course of an autopsy—to the weapon used in the commission of the crime.

Heinrich participated in the solution of more than 2,000 criminal cases in his lifetime. These included the infamous 1916 Black Tom bombing in Jersey City, New Jersey, which Heinrich proved to be a German sabotage plot aimed against the United States preparations for possible entry into World War I; and the sensational sex homicide case in which silent film comedian Roscoe "Fatty" Arbuckle was accused of having caused the death of starlet Virgina Rappe.

No case was more famous in its time than his solving of the d'Autremont case, a train robbery involving a quadruple homicide. On October 11, 1923, a Southern Pacific mail train was halted by three gunmen after partially clearing a tunnel in southern Oregon. When efforts to blow open the mail car resulted in its total incineration, killing the mail clerk inside, the gunmen murdered the engineer, the brakeman, and the fuelman, fleeing into the Oregon forest, leaving behind only a pair of greasy overalls as evidence. After weeks of fruitless searching, authorities turned to Heinrich. He immediately determined that the substance on the overalls was not grease, but fir tree pitch. He then issued a shocking statement: The criminal was a left-handed lumberjack from the Pacific Northwest in his early twenties and fastidious about his appearance.

This statement was made after minute observations that turned up clues previously missed. Heinrich discovered fir needles from trees that grew only in the Pacific Northwest; the left pockets in the overalls were much more worn than the right, denoting left-handedness; and Heinrich also extracted several carefully trimmed fingernail clippings from the cuff of the overalls, revealing a personality trait of someone concerned about meticulous appearance. Finally, a single strand of hair revealed the man's hair color and age.

After further examination, Heinrich discovered a balled up piece of paper embedded in the fabric of the overalls. After carefully extracting it with tiny forceps, he noted that it was totally blurred from having undergone numerous washings with the overalls. After treating it with iodine vapor, however, he was able to discern that it was a registered mail receipt. Recovering the number, he was able to trace it to the criminals.

Heinrich died on September 28, 1953, leaving behind a legacy of minute investigation and relentless observation of the available facts that rivaled Arthur Conan DOYLE's fictional master sleuth, Sherlock Holmes.

Further reading: Eugene B. Block, *The Wizard of Berkeley* (New York: Coward–McCann, 1958)

Helldorf, Wolf Heinrich, Graf von (1896–1944) Chief of police in Berlin during World War II, Helldorf was involved in the 1944 assassination attempt against Adolf Hitler.

Helldorf enthusiastically enlisted in the German Army in World War I and was quickly given an officer's commission. In 1916, he served as commander of a machine-gun company and was awarded two Iron Crosses. After the war, he joined the vehemently nationalistic Rossbach Freikorps, battling communist insurrections in the Rhineland. In 1920, he took part in the Freikorps' rightist Kapp Putsch (an attempt to seize control of the government) but was exiled to Italy when the putsch failed. Helldorf returned to Germany when the Weimar Republic began to falter and in 1931 became an officer in the S.A., the so-called Brownshirts of the early Nazi movement.

Although he was not a singularly avid Nazi, Helldorf rose in the party hierarchy and, after Adolf Hitler was named Germany's chancellor in 1933, he was appointed to high positions in both the S.A. and the S.S. In November of that year, Helldorf was elected to the Reichstag (parliament) as a Nazi deputy, while also serving as police president of Potsdam. In 1935, he was named to that same position in Berlin.

Helldorf was not present in Berlin on Kristallnacht, November 9, 1938, and disciplined his officers for their complicity in the orgy of anti-Semitic violence. However, he was no champion of the Jews. Indeed, during most of his tenure as head of Berlin's police, he engaged in various corrupt activities, most notably the confiscation of Jewish passports, which he sold back to those from whom he had taken them for as much as 250,000 marks each.

As the course of World War II turned against Germany and Hitler appeared to many political and military insiders as unstable and incompetent, an assassination plot involving high-ranking civil and military leaders took shape. On July 20, 1944, a bomb intended to kill Hitler was planted at a staff conference. The explosion resulted only in wounding Hitler, and 14 of the conspirators were immediately arrested, including Helldorf, who admitted his complicity and said he was "fed up" with Hitler. After being tortured for several days, he was executed on August 15, 1944—like the other would-be assassins, hanged by the neck with piano wire.

Helpern, Milton Dr. (1902–77)   Remembered as "Sherlock Holmes with a microscope," Helpern served as New York City's chief medical examiner from 1954 to 1973.

After receiving his medical degree from Cornell University in 1926, Milton Helpern was befriended by Dr. Charles NORRIS, New York City's first medical

New York City's chief medical examiner Dr. Milton Helpern has been called "Sherlock Holmes with a microscope." (Courtesy of the UPI/Bettmann Archive)

examiner, who subsequently hired Helpern as his assistant in 1931. For the next 42 years, Helpern would serve in the agency, becoming its head in 1954.

One of the most prolific criminal pathologists in history, Dr. Helpern participated in over 80,000 autopsies during his tenure. His talent for "sniffing out a homicide" solved numerous crimes and secured many convictions, including that of Dr. Carl Coppolino in a sensational 1967 murder trial. Coppolino, who poisoned his wife with what he thought was an undetectable drug, had not reckoned on the skill of Dr. Helpern, who exhumed the body and found traces of the drug in the victim's brain.

Tireless in his dedication to the advancement of forensic pathology, Helpern coauthored the 1,350-page textbook *Legal Medicine: Pathology and Toxicology* in 1937, which became the standard work in the field. Dr. Helpern also pioneered investigations into deaths due to narcotics, abortion, and carbon monoxide poisoning, and he advanced the study of Sudden Infant Death Syndrome (SIDS). Helpern retired in 1973.

Further reading: "Milton Helpern, M.D.," *Journal of Forensic Sciences,* 17:4 (October 1972), 505–513.

Henderson, Sir Edmund (1821–96) Chief commissioner of London's metropolitan police from 1869 to 1886; created the renowned CID (Criminal Investigative Division) of Scotland Yard.

After serving as a leading prison official for more than 15 years, Henderson succeeded Richard MAYNE as police commissioner in 1869. At the time of his appointment the police force was in disarray, reeling under charges of rampant insubordination. Henderson stepped in and immediately began a reorganization of the police force, forming the elite Criminal Investigative Division (CID) and consolidating its headquarters at Scotland Yard. The subsequent record of the CID not only made Scotland Yard a world center of criminal detection, it also established a model for detective divisions of police agencies worldwide.

Henderson's work was disrupted by strikes and political unrest that swept the the city and brought the commissioner under fire for the way his police handled the disturbances. Finally, in 1886, a riot in Trafalgar Square set off a public safety panic that sealed Henderson's fate. He resigned under pressure that same year.

Further reading: Scoli, David, *The Queen's Peace* (London: Hamish Hamilton, 1979).

Heney, Francis Joseph (1859–1937) As special prosecutor for the attorney general of the United States, Heney prosecuted the Oregon land fraud cases and the San Francisco corruption cases of the early 1900s.

Although born in the East on March 17, 1859, Francis Heney moved with his family from New York to San Francisco when he was still an infant. In San Francisco, Heney attended public school, but dropped out to work in his father's furniture store. He enrolled in night school and took a job teaching math at a local grammar school after graduating. When he had saved sufficient funds from his teaching salary, Heney enrolled at the University of California but was dismissed in his freshmen year for fighting.

After working a while longer as a teacher, Heney moved to Idaho to become a miner. While there, he undertook the defense of a man charged with murder and, though he had no legal experience, won his acquittal. Moving back to San Francisco, he enrolled in Hastings School of Law and was admitted to the California bar in 1884. After living in Tucson, Arizona, where he served as attorney general for the Arizona Territory in 1893, he moved back to San Francisco to open a private practice.

In 1903, Heney was assigned to prosecute the Oregon land fraud cases by U.S. Attorney General Philander Knox. With the whole political machinery of the state against him, Heney revealed a conspiracy involving a U.S. attorney, a U.S. senator, and countless local politicians.

His success in Oregon helped land him the post of assistant district attorney in San Francisco in 1906, where he took on the forces of that city's infamous corruption. With the help of a U.S. Secret Service officer, Heney conducted a four-year investigation that toppled hundreds of powerful people, including the mayor and police chief of San Francisco, as well as the political boss Abe Ruef, a figure comparable to New York's Boss Tweed.

Public opinion was overwhelmingly in Heney's favor until he announced his intention to pursue those who had offered him bribes in the course of the investigation. These individuals were legion and they included prominent businessmen as well as their companies. The economic fallout of the resulting prosecutions earned Heney the public's wrath.

The trials that followed the indictments in the fall of 1908 were nothing short of high drama. The defense brought in Los Angeles attorney Earl ROGERS, and Rogers and Heney went at each other immediately on a personal level, Rogers charging Heney with cowardice and Heney accusing Rogers of being a drunk. Private detectives followed detectives following other detectives, and Heney even received death threats. Finally, on a Friday the thirteenth, no less, a man stood up in court and shot Heney in the neck.

Although Heney recovered, his stance against *all* parties in the graft hearings cost him his much-desired political career. Twice he was defeated for the California governor's seat, and once he was defeated in the California senatorial election. He retired again to private practice.

Hennessey, David Peter (?–1890)

As police chief of New Orleans, Hennessey vowed to suppress the growing Mafia in that city but was murdered, touching off vigilante action against the accused Mafiosi.

By the late 19th century, Italian immigrants had taken over control of the New Orleans docks from Irish longshoremen. As was often the case with waterfront labor, organized crime interests entered the picture. Two Italian families, the Matrangas and the Provenzanos, vied for control of the docks, and mob warfare ensued, the like of which Chicago and New York would not see for another 35 years. Within 18 months, some 40 mob murders had taken place, and the police seemed powerless.

In 1890, the flamboyant David Hennessey was elected police chief of New Orleans and vowed to bring the violence to an end. Under Hennessey's direction, the police staged a series of successful raids in the waterfront region. When Hennessey charged

Police Chief David Hennessey vowed to sweep the Mafia out of New Orleans at the turn of the century. He was murdered. (Courtesy of the Louisiana Division, New Orleans Public Library)

two of the Provenzano brothers, he announced the discovery of a secret cabal aimed at organizing and controlling crime in New Orleans. It was called the Mafia.

Hennessey reported that he had wired Rome for criminal records on numerous New Orleans Mafia members and would divulge all his findings in the Provenzano trial. The threatened exposure temporarily united the Provenzanos and the Matrangas, and the latter family ordered Hennessey's execution. The police chief was murdered on October 15, 1890.

The killing outraged the citizens of New Orleans, who demanded swift and certain retribution. A grand jury was convened, and 19 indictments were issued against members of the Provenzano family. The trial proved to be a sham: Witnesses were either bribed or threatened, as were members of the jury. Despite overwhelming evidence against 11 of the defendants, the jury voted to acquit a total of 16 of the defendants and was hung on the remaining three. The city's Italian community organized huge celebrations, osten-

A lynch mob storms the Old Parish Prison in New Orleans, March 14, 1891, seeking the Mafia killers of Police Chief Hennessey. (*Harper's Weekly*, March 28, 1891, courtesy of the Nashville Public Library)

sibly to celebrate the birthday of King Umberto I, but actually in honor of the acquittals. This served to further enflame passions. Two days after the verdicts, a mob of several thousand, led by 60 of New Orleans's most influential citizens, marched on the city jail, to which all the defendants had been remanded for final processing and to resolve any residual charges.

The mob carried a list of the 11 who had appeared most guilty at the trial, but had instructions not to harm the remaining six defendants, including the two Matranga brothers. Quickly overrunning the jail, the mob hauled two of the Mafiosi out into the streets, where they were hanged from lampposts. Seven others were lined up in the women's section of the prison and executed by firing squad. The remaining two were shot to death as they hid in the prison dog house.

Although some newspapers condemned the mob action, the majority of citizens, including the mayor, expressed their belief that the mob was justified.

Henry, Sir Edward Richard (1850–1931) Building on the discoveries of fingerprint identification innovators FAULDS, HERSCHEL, and GALTON, Bengal-based police inspector Henry was the first to devise a practical method of fingerprint classification suitable for archival storage and retrieval.

The son of a London physician, Edward Richard Henry joined the Indian Civil Service in 1873 and was posted to the province of Bengal. His intelligence and organizational skills were rewarded with speedy advancement; he went from lieutenant-governor's assistant to deputy magistrate collector to secretary of the board of revenue, and in 1891 he was made inspector general of police. Two years later, Henry introduced the BERTILLON criminal identification system to his Bengalese force, but the slow and labor-intensive method of measuring key bodily features left much to be desired. Moreover, its accuracy depended on slighter margins for human error than could be readily counted on, especially in provincial police stations. In the East, fingerprint "seals" were a centuries-old method of ratifying important documents, and Henry was aware of Herschel's investigation of the subject in the very same Indian province. He also knew of Galton's research in England, so he read with great interest the Troup Committee's 1894 report on dactyloscopy (fingerprint identification), which confirmed that no efficient system had yet been found for the orderly filing of the virtually infinite universe of individual fingerprint patterns.

On leave in England a few months later, Henry visited Galton in his South Kensington laboratory and was warmly received by the septuagenarian scientist. Remarkably free of scientific elitism or professional jealousy, Galton provided Henry with stacks of original photographs and other research material. The dactylographic novice returned to Calcutta with keen aspirations to bring order to this great organic puzzle and make fingerprinting a useful tool in the detection of crime.

Collecting and photographing thousands of additional fingerprint specimens, Henry dedicated his spare time and considerable mathematical skills to examining and analyzing fingerprint configurations. In December 1896, while riding a train, he made a sudden breakthrough in his approach to classification.

Henry had identified five basic geometric patterns—arches, tented arches, radial loops (which ran toward the thumb), ulnar loops (which pointed toward the little finger), and whorls—and had marked these groups with the initial letters A, T, R, U, and W. Subpatterns were then determined by variations in Galton's "deltas," the small triangles created by forked papillary lines, bifurcation, or the divergence of parallel lines. Now, establishing key points in these deltas, Henry etched a straight line from their "outer terminuses" to designated "inner terminuses" in the print's loop patterns. Counting the ridges intersected by this line, he added those numbers to his letter system and produced a manageable code for identifying individual print sheets.

Equipped with nothing more than a counting needle and a magnifying glass, virtually anyone could learn his simple formula, apply it, record information, and readily retrieve it. A month after devising the system, Henry initiated a practical test of his records system, pitting 10-finger dactyloscopic registration against *bertillonage* (Bertillon's method of physical identification) in the station houses of his district. By January of 1897, he was satisfied with the performance and reliability of his new method, and he sought and won the governor-general's support for its implementation throughout India as a replacement for Bertillon's anthropometry. Indeed, its success was quickly apparent. In the year 1899, and in Bengal alone, 569 repeat offenders were verified by their fingerprints; a near two-thirds majority of these would have failed positive identification by *bertillonage*.

Next, in the Charan case of 1898, Henry for the first time introduced a crime-scene fingerprint as legal evidence. Though the Calcutta court was reluctant to execute a murder suspect solely on the basis of this new technique, the authorities did convict Charan of a robbery associated with the capital crime. Encouraged, Henry began work on a single-print filing system and wrote *Classification and Uses of Fingerprints*.

News of the Bengal inspector's work traveled slowly, but in 1901, after study by the British Home Office—and with the continuing support of Galton—Henry's method was substituted for anthropometry at Scotland Yard. Henry himself was brought to London as acting commissioner of police and head of the Criminal Investigative Department (CID), and under his tutelage, new—and ultimately world-class—experts were trained. As astounding numbers of criminal identifications were made with unprecedented accuracy and speed, crime-scene fingerprints began to prove themselves in British courtroom proceedings. Within 10 years, dactyloscopy had been adopted throughout Europe and the United States, and Henry's system, with only minor refinements, is still in use today.

Knighted and many times decorated for his valuable contributions to the law-enforcement field, Henry went on to found the PEEL Training School and to develop a police-sponsored orphanage.

One day in November 1912, Henry was entering his Kensington home when he was shot at and wounded. His assailant—a man incensed by Scotland Yard's rejection of a driver's license application (he had a previous conviction for drunkenness)—was captured. Although Henry's physical injuries were to trouble him for years, the commissioner's pleas for lenient sentencing won his attacker a prison term of 15 years instead of life. Henry retired in 1918, and became an active member of London's Athenaeum.

Hepbron, James Merritt (1891–1979) Managing director of the Baltimore Criminal Justice Commission, a pioneering agency for promoting the "intelligent and efficient administration of criminal justice."

Hepbron was born on February 17, 1891, in Chestertown, Maryland, graduated from Baltimore City College in 1910, and took his law degree in 1913 at the University of Maryland. He worked for a legal publisher from 1913 to 1917, when he became a member of the Fosdick Commission on training-camp activities during World War I. After serving on the U.S. Interdepartmental Board following the war, he was appointed in 1922 as assistant director of the newly formed Baltimore Criminal Justice Commission. Two years later, he was made managing director.

Under his leadership, the commission rapidly earned a reputation as one of the country's most effective crimefighting bodies, and it served as a model for jurisdictions nationwide. In 1923, an average of one in six Baltimore criminals was apprehended and punished; by 1941, largely through the work of the commission, 90 out of 100 criminals were caught and convicted.

The commission was especially noteworthy for operating with a very small staff and an extremely modest budget. Hepbron also served as consultant to many law enforcement agencies and was a member of various commissions on juvenile delinquency, the practice of penology, and other social issues.

Herschel, William James (1833–1917) Pioneer in the science and application of fingerprinting, Herschel accidentally discovered the unique "signature" nature of individual human fingerprints.

An English colonial bureaucrat in the Indian Civil Service, William Herschel worked on a day-to-day basis with Asians, among whom was a long-standing custom of validating important agreements and other documents by means of applying one's inked handprint to the document. After years of observing this custom, Herschel began to notice what he took to be a highly interesting fact: No two fingerprints were exactly alike. Herschel began deliberately collecting prints during the 1860s. After 15 years of accumulating and studying them, he sent a letter to the prisons of Bengal, which used fingerprints as a form of prisoner identification. Officials there confirmed his hypothesis concerning the uniqueness of each print.

Herschel's findings were initially dismissed, but his research proved vital in developing the science of fingerprinting, or dactyloscopy.

See also; FAULDS, Henry; GALTON, Sir Francis; HENRY, Sir Edward Richard.

Hewitt, Cecil Rolph (1901–)

After a 25-year career with the City of London Police, Hewitt became a noted journalist and writer of books, whose pseudonyms include R. H. Cecil, Oliver Milton, and C. H. Rolph.

Hewitt was born in London on August 23, 1901, the son of a chief inspector of police. He followed in his father's footsteps, joining the City of London Police as a constable in 1921. He was promoted steadily through the ranks, making sergeant in 1925, subinspector in 1928, inspector in 1930, and chief inspector in 1938, serving until 1946, when he became a staff writer for the London-based *New Statesman*. From 1965 to 1980, Hewitt also served as director of the Statesman Publishing Company.

Most of Hewitt's books are popular, practical works on police work and crime. They include *A Licensing Handbook* (1937), *Crime and Punishment* (1950), *On Gambling* (1951), *Personal Identity* (1956), *Mental Disorder* (1958), *Commonsense about Crime and Punishment* (1961), *The Trial of Lady Chatterley* (1961, an important work on censorship, using the suppression of the D. H. Lawrence novel as an example), *Hanged by the Neck* (1961, with Arthur Koestler), *The Police and the Public* (1962), *Law and the Common Man* (1967), *Books in the Dock* (1969), *The Queen's Pardon* (1978), and two autobiographical volumes, *London Particulars* (1979) and *Further Particulars* (1986).

Hewitt believed that the punishment of criminals is not reformative, but retributive, and serves only to protect society against criminals—unfortunately, a very necessary function. He advocated greater expenditure on the "succor of individual victims and on the *prevention* of crime." He was vice president of New Bridge, for friends of released prisoners, vice president of the Howard League (for prison reform), and a member of the Parole Board for Great Britain.

Heyns, Garrett (1891–1969)

This American penologist championed the rights of inmates and stressed probation and parole over the traditions of punishment.

Born in Allendale, Michigan, on September 21, 1891, Heyns was the son of a clergyman and educator who had emigrated from the Netherlands. Heyns's early education was at public and private schools in South Dakota, Minnesota, Illinois, and Michigan and at the preparatory school of Calvin College in Grand Rapids, Michigan. He took his A.B. degree in 1915, his A.M. in 1916, and his Ph.D. in 1927—all at the University of Michigan. During this period, he taught in elementary and high school to earn tuition money. After

receiving his Ph.D., he taught at the University of Michigan and at Northern Michigan College. In 1937, he became the first educator to be appointed warden of the Michigan State Reformatory in Ionia. From 1940 to 1948, he was a member of the Michigan State Parole Board, and from 1941 to 1949, he was director of the Michigan Department of Corrections. In 1949, he returned to Ionia as warden of the State Reformatory, serving in that capacity until 1957, when he became director of the Department of Institutions of the state of Washington. He left this post in 1966 and the following year was appointed executive director of the Joint Commission on Correctional Manpower and Training, Washington, D.C., a post he held until the end of his life.

Heyns developed a philosophy of penology that stressed the possibilities of probation and parole over the traditions of punishment and retribution. In 1955, he delivered a widely publicized speech advocating the release of one-third of the nation's inmates. He believed that prison could never serve as an effective deterrent to crime, but was principally an instrument of public hostility toward offenders. The more effective deterrent, he argued, was not to confine offenders for unduly long periods, but to guide them within the environment in which they were expected to live. He called for a redefinition of sentencing, not as appropriate punishment for a crime, but as the means of efficiently effecting rehabilitation. Accordingly, he advocated much greater latitude in parole practices, governed by more adequate post-release supervision and counseling.

Hickok, (James Butler) "Wild Bill" (1837–76)

For many, the exploits of this legendary gunman and lawman personify the Wild West period of American history.

Born on May 27, 1837, in Troy Grove, Illinois, James Butler Hickok set out for the West at an early age. After serving in the abolitionist Free State Army in Kansas, Hickok was elected constable of Monticello, Kansas, in 1858. The following year, Hickok met Buffalo Bill Cody and Joseph Slade; with the latter, Hickok was employed to track down Indians who had run off horses from a western Nebraska Pony Express station.

Hickok next worked as a wagon master for the freighting firm of Russell, Majors and Waddell. In 1861, after he was badly mauled by a bear while leading a train through the Raton Pass along the Santa Fe Trail, Hickok was assigned convalescent duty at Russell, Majors and Waddell's Rock Creek station in Fairbury, Nebraska. A rancher named Dave McCanles, who lived across the road from the station, kept a mistress, Sarah Shull, with whom Hickok began

Wild Bill Hickock, frontiersman, army scout, gunman, gambler, and American legend (Courtesy of the National Archives)

Magazine article by George Ward Nichols, and became the basis of the legend of Wild Bill Hickok.

Hickok became a scout in the Union Army during the Civil War, participating in the bloody battle of Pea Ridge in Arkansas and guiding General Philip Sheridan through hostile midwest territory. After the war, Hickok settled in Springfield, Missouri, where he set up as a professional gambler and was involved in another celebrated gunfight with badman Dave Tutt in 1865. The following year, Hickok became deputy U.S. marshal at Fort Riley, Kansas, serving under the celebrated marshal, Charles Whiting.

In 1867, the first of many dime novels appeared, featuring the exploits of Wild Bill Hickok. With his reputation always preceding him, Wild Bill secured numerous law enforcement positions over the next few years, including sheriff of Ellis County, Kansas, and city marshal of the rough cow town of Abilene, Kansas. Most of his stints as a "peace officer" were brief and characterized by Hickok's heedless attitude

Dave McCanles taunted Wild Bill Hickok until the latter shot him down. McCanles died in the arms of his ten-year-old son. (Courtesy of the Western History Collections, University of Oklahoma)

a liaison. Compounding the growing animosity between Hickok and McCanles was a festering financial dispute McCanles had with the freighting company. The rancher taunted Hickok with insulting names ("Duck Bill"—in reference, perhaps, to Hickok's protruding lips—and "hermaphrodite").

At length, on July 12, 1861, McCanles called Hickok out for a fight. The soon-to-be legendary lawman hid behind a curtain until he saw his opportunity to shoot McCanles down. The sound of gunfire sent McCanles's 12-year-old son Monroe, McCanles's cousin James Woods, and a ranch hand named James Gordon running to the freight station. Monroe found the lifeless body of his father, which he cradled in his arms as Hickok shot both Woods and Gordon. Wounded, the two men fled. Doc Brink, stable hand at the station, caught up with Woods and hacked him to death with a hoe while stationmaster Horace Wellman polished off Gordon with a shotgun blast.

This episode of frontier mayhem was glorified as a heroic gunfight in a highly fictionalized *Harper's* and his quick-tempered tendency to what can only be described as psychopathic violence. What happened at Abilene was typical. On October 5, 1871, Hickok had a showdown with Phil Coe and Ben Thompson, a pair of Texas gamblers who got rowdy in the streets of the town. What should have been a simple intervention to restore order esclated into a deadly temper tantrum as Hickok asserted his authority by shooting Coe, who took three agonizing days to die.

It got worse. The marshal's deputy, Mike Williams, ran to Wild Bill's aid. Hickok spun around and fired on the running figure, killing Deputy Williams instantly.

In a characteristic gesture of what he deemed generosity, Hickok paid for Williams's funeral. That was not enough for the citizens of Abilene, who got a new marshal, one townsman observing that Hickok "acted only too ready to shoot down, to kill outright." Wild Bill himself remarked: "As to killing, I never think much about it. I don't believe in ghosts, and I don't keep the lights burning all night to keep them away. That's because I'm not a murderer. It is the other man or me in a fight, and I don't stop to think—is it a sin to do this thing? And after it is over, what's the use of disturbing the mind?"

Hickok hung up his guns, and in 1873 briefly joined Buffalo Bill Cody's famed Wild West Show in New York. Then he drifted West again, his health failing and, suffering from gonorrhea, his eyesight failing as well. In 1876, he was picked up for vagrancy in Cheyenne, Wyoming, then lit out for the gold fields of Dakota Territory but turned to gambling instead of prospecting.

On August 2, Wild Bill Hickok was being cleaned out at a gaming table in Deadwood Saloon No. 10. At 4:10 P.M., a drifter named Jack McCall approached Hickok from behind, leveled an old Colt revolver at the back of his head, and squeezed off a round.

"Take that!" he said.

Wild Bill slumped to the floor, still gripping his first winning hand of the afternoon: a queen and two pairs, aces and eights—ever after known as the "Dead Man's Hand."

Further reading: Rosa, Joseph G., *They Called Him Wild Bill: The Life and Adventures of James Butler Hickok,* 2d. ed. (Norman: University of Oklahoma Press, 1964).

Hilton, Ordway (1913–   )   A handwriting identification specialist of international reputation and one of the founders of the forensic school of document analysis.

Ordway Hilton, longtime police science editor (1941–43, 1948–72) of the *Journal of Criminal Law, Criminology and Police Science,* is one of the pioneers and most prominent practitioners of document analysis

in forensic science. In 1938, Hilton was appointed document examiner for the Chicago Police Scientific Crime Detection Laboratory, and during World War II he served as a handwriting specialist in the Naval Intelligence Service. After the war, Hilton became recognized as one of the leading handwriting experts in the world. His expert testimony has resolved many criminal and civil cases, and his dedication to the field has set the standards for his profession.

Hilton's textbook *Scientific Examination of Questioned Documents* (1956; revised edition, 1982) continues to serve as the standard handbook of forensic document studies. Hilton continues to write. In 1991 he published an important monograph, *Detecting and Deciphering Erased Pencil Writing,* and in 1992 a significant article on the analysis of signatures in the *Journal of Forensic Sciences.* Hilton also continues as an examiner of questioned documents and an expert witness in private practice and is assistant editor for questioned documents, *International Forensic Science,* Elsevier Science Publishers.

Hindelang, Michael (1946–82)   One of the first to explore the relationship between intelligence (as measured by IQ) and delinquency.

A native of Detroit, Michigan, Michael Hindelang attended Wayne State University for both undergraduate and graduate training in psychology. In 1969, he earned a Ph.D. in criminology from the University of California and accepted a position as professor of criminal justice at the State University of New York, Albany. In 1972, he established the Criminal Justice Research Center at SUNY, Albany, to provide a research training facility for graduate students.

At the center, Hindelang began a study to determine the correlation between intelligence, as measured by IQ, and deviancy. A prevailing theory held that there was a direct correlation between high IQ and criminal delinquency, regardless of the density of population (another determinant of delinquency). Hindelang's 1976 studies indicated, however, that low IQ was a good predictor of delinquency—and an even better predictor of self-reported delinquency. While Hindelang's first result ran counter to prevailing notions of delinquency, the second reinforced earlier conclusions that individuals with high IQ can more readily escape detection and punishment for delinquent acts.

Hiss, Alger (1904–   )   Subject of one of the most celebrated spy cases in American history, Hiss was accused of selling State Department secrets to communist interests.

Alger Hiss graduated from Johns Hopkins University in 1926 and went on to Harvard Law School, graduating cum laude in 1929. He clerked for Oliver Wendell HOLMES Jr. before joining the New Deal administration of President Franklin D. ROOSEVELT. In 1933, Hiss was recruited by future Supreme Court Associate Justice Felix FRANKFURTER to serve on the staff of the Department of Agriculture. Hiss moved on briefly to the Department of Justice and served also as an aide on an important Senate committee. Finally, Hiss began working for the State Department.

Hiss's star quickly rose at State, and in 1945 he was chosen to attend the Yalta Conference as a policy advisor to President Roosevelt. He was named temporary secretary general of the United Nations at the San Francisco Conference in April 1945 and was elected president of the Carnegie Endowment for International Peace the following year. It was widely believed that he was in line to become the next secretary of state.

Such speculations were shattered in 1948, when it was alleged that Hiss was a communist spy who had passed State Department documents to the "other side."

The allegations were made by one Whittaker Chambers, an admitted former communist and former editor of the *Daily Worker*, a communist newspaper published in the United States. In August 1948, Chambers, who had left the party for philosophical reasons, appeared before the House Un-American Activities Committee (HUAC), headed by freshman congressman Richard M. NIXON. Chambers claimed that Hiss was passing documents through him to the Soviets. Hiss vehemently denied the accusations and was brought before the committee to testify, where he again denied the accusations but was unable to give plausible explanations of Chambers's knowledge of Hiss's past.

In October 1948, Hiss was brought before a grand jury under charges of treason. Hiss claimed that he had known Chambers, who then called himself Crosley, only for a year in 1935 and hadn't seen him since. In his testimony, however, Chambers proceeded to give a detailed description of Hiss's life since 1935, including the layout of his house, personal habits and hobbies, eating habits, and even intimate childhood memories. Hiss admitted to traveling to New York with Chambers in 1935, but he didn't remember why. He also gave Chambers the use of his car, as well as letting him live rent-free in the back of his house.

The evidence mounted against Hiss. Chambers produced scores of official documents, both handwritten and typed, which were either signed by Hiss, written in his handwriting, or typed on his personal typewriter. Chambers claimed that Hiss regularly deposited such documents in a pumpkin patch on the property of Chambers's suburban Maryland home.

Hiss protested that most of the documents were forgeries. As for the typewriter, Hiss claimed the FBI had stolen samples from his desk, then made a machine that could duplicate the key strokes of his personal typewriter to implicate him. He also charged that Chambers was a psychopath and a homosexual, whose advances Hiss had spurned.

In the end, the grand jury lacked sufficient evidence to indict Hiss for treason, because the Constitution requires two witnesses to the treasonable act, but Hiss was indicted on charges of perjury. The first perjury trial ended in a hung jury, but the second one convicted Hiss in January 1950, and he was sentenced to five years in prison.

After several unsuccessful appeals, Hiss went to jail, still protesting his innocence. Released in December 1954, Hiss continues to protest his innocence to this day.

Further reading: Hiss, Alger, *Recollections of a Life* (New York: Seaver Books/H. Holt, 1988).

Weinstein, Allen, *Perjury: The Hiss-Chambers Case* (New York: Knopf, distributed by Random House, 1978).

Holden, Thomas J. (1896–1953)   The first man listed on the FBI's Ten Most Wanted List was a brutal bank and mail robber who killed his wife and her two brothers.

Along with Francis Keating, Thomas Holden was the leader of the St. Paul Gang, which made daring bank and payroll robberies in the late 1920s and early 1930s. The gang included such notables as Harvey Bailey, Frank "Jelly" Nash, and Verne Miller, later identified as the triggerman in Kansas City's Union Station Massacre. Arrested in 1928 and each sentenced to 25 years imprisonment for a train robbery, Holden and Keating managed to escape in 1931 with forged passes (possibly obtained with the aid of a then little-known thug, George "Machine Gun" Kelly) that allowed them simply to walk out of Leavenworth Prison. Fleeing to Kansas City, the two teamed up with the Barker-Karpis gang and resumed their career as bank robbers.

Holden and Keating, along with Harvey Bailey, were arrested on a golf course in Kansas City, but FBI agents did not realize the group was a foursome, because Nash's golf game was so poor that he was several holes behind the other three. This allowed Nash to evade capture. (Ironically, one of the arresting agents, Raymond Caffrey, would die at the hands of Verne Miller in the Union Station Massacre, as he was escorting Nash, whom he had taken into custody.)

Holden was paroled in 1947, moved to Chicago, and married. In a domestic dispute, he shot and killed his wife, then turned on her two brothers. The FBI, which had just instituted its Ten Most Wanted List, quickly put Holden at the top, the first to occupy that spot. He was tracked down in Beaverton, Oregon, where a citizen recognized him from the wanted poster in the post office. Holden, who had been living under an assumed name, was arrested and convicted of murder. He died two years later—of natural causes—in prison.

Holmes, Oliver Wendell, Jr. (1841–1935)   One of the greatest of American jurists, Holmes championed the rights of the individual over property rights during his 33 years on the Supreme Court.

Of distinguished Bostonian lineage, Oliver Wendell Holmes Jr. was born March 8, 1841, the son of a prominent physician-poet and the grandson of a Massachusetts Supreme Court justice. After a fine elementary and secondary education, Holmes attended Harvard College and graduated as the class poet in 1861. With the outbreak of the Civil War, Holmes promptly enlisted in the 20th Massachusetts and marched off to war. On three occasions at three major battles, Holmes was severely wounded; he recovered to return to the field each time. By the end of his enlistment in 1864, he had been breveted a lieutenant colonel.

After the war, Holmes entered Harvard Law School and graduated in 1866 with his law degree. He was admitted to the bar in 1867 and went into private practice for 15 years. During this period, he held various positions at Harvard and also edited the *American Law Review* with particular distinction and insight. His writing for the *Review* earned him a series of lectures at the Lowell Institute in Boston, which established him as a preeminent legal scholar. The lectures were subsequently published as *The Common Law,* which many describe as the first notable American work on legal history.

Holmes's growing reputation as a jurist and legal scholar earned him a full professorship at Harvard in 1882 and then an appointment as an associate justice on the Massachusetts Supreme Court in January of 1883. He served that body for 20 years, the last four as chief justice, writing many influential decisions. One of his more noted opinions involved the regulation forbidding civil servants to engage in political activity. Holmes, in upholding the dismissal of a police officer who engaged in political activity, commented that "the defendant has the constitutional right to talk politics, but he does not have the constitutional right to be a policeman." Holmes argued that the city may impose on an employee any reasonable conditions it so desires, as long as the employee accepts them at the time of employment.

Holmes was named to the United States Supreme Court by President Theodore Roosevelt in December

Famed jurist Oliver Wendall Holmes (Courtesy of the National Archives)

1902 and was confirmed by the Senate the following year. On the Supreme Court, Holmes consistently championed the rights of the individual and the cause of human rights over property rights. He wrote in one opinion that the Constitution calls for the principle of free thought above everything else, "Not free thought for those who agree with us but freedom for the thought we hate." Like John MARSHALL before him and Earl WARREN and Thurgood MARSHALL after him, Holmes felt that the law must continually evolve, and for that to happen, the Constitution must be interpreted liberally.

Holmes fiercely emphasized that the personal opinions of judges should not interfere with their decisions. He felt that since appointed judges were not elected officials, they had no constituents to answer to and were therefore responsible to the law only. One example of this position was his personal opposition to Prohibition but his staunch support of it in the courts simply because it was the law of the land. He also had little regard for precedent for precedent's sake. This liberal attitude caused him to reverse many a decision simply because the legal precedent set a poor example.

After serving the Supreme Court for over 30 years, Holmes, aged 91, finally stepped down from the bench at the suggestion of his fellow justices. He died two days shy of his 94th birthday and left his house, its furnishings, and his books to the United States of America, which Congress deemed a memorial to the history of the Supreme Court. He is buried at Arlington National Cemetery.

Further reading: Novick, Sheldon M., *Honorable Justice: The Life of Oliver Wendell Holmes* (Boston: Little, Brown, 1989).

Hooton, Earnest Albert (1887–1954)

Controversial Harvard anthropologist who conducted a 12-year study of criminals, published as *Crime and the Man* in 1939 and concluding that an individual's physical characteristics determine the type of crime he is likely to commit.

A professor of anthropology at Harvard from 1930 until 1954, Dr. Hooton spent his career studying body types and how they relate to certain emotional characteristics. Hooton, a confirmed positivist, believed that heredity was the key determinant in criminal (and other) behavior. Therefore, his work concentrated on drawing connections between certain inherited physical characteristics and "corresponding" patterns of behavior. Hooton offered his observations in part for their predictive value in determining who was likely to commit criminal acts and what category of acts they were likely to commit. However, he also took his assumptions to their most extreme conclusion by suggesting that the most effective way of dealing with crime and criminal behavior was by genetically interrupting the criminal cycle through sterilization and biological control.

Hooton's controversial, even inflammatory *Crime and the Man* embodied these assumptions and conclusions, causing a loud uproar within the scientific community. The book contained numerous drawings of criminals, which sought to illustrate (for example) what a criminal in any given American geographical location would look like. Typical observations include the conclusion that robbers who murder are tall and thin, while men who commit fraud and murder are tall and heavy; rapists are short and heavy, while smaller men are most likely to commit thefts and burglaries.

Today few criminologists take such anthropological typecasting seriously enough to debate it. In his own time, however, Hooton was a scientist to be reckoned with and remained a respected anthropologist who continued to publish and teach until his death in 1954.

Further reading: Jones, David A., *History of Criminology: A Philosophical Perspective* (New York: Greenwood, 1986).

Hoover, J(ohn) Edgar (1895–1972)

Director of the FBI for 48 years, Hoover, in effect, *was* the FBI, making it in his own image through decades of strong, uncom-

J. Edgar Hoover directed the FBI for half a century and built his position into one of immense personal power. (Courtesy of the National Archives)

promising leadership, public-relations savvy, and a large measure of bullying, harassment, and even blackmail.

A native of Washington, D.C., J. Edgar Hoover at first intended to enter the ministry, having been raised by his mother to read the Bible daily. After graduating as valedictorian from high school, he entered George Washington University, graduating in 1916 and then earning his law degree a year later. His first job out of college was with the Justice Department in 1917, a division of the government whose service he would not leave until his death 55 years later.

At the end of World War I, Attorney General A. Mitchell PALMER undertook a sweeping campaign of identifying and prosecuting "foreigners" who had communist ties or who had openly opposed the American war effort. Palmer chose Hoover to head the Justice Department's General Intelligence Division, which conducted raids, blatantly illegal searches and seizures, and campaigns of persecution against thousands of immigrants, most of them ultimately acquitted. Through Hoover, Palmer ordered mass arrests, which resulted in the deportation of 247 Russians in 1919, then the pair went after all communists, foreign or not. This began the series of "Red Raids," starting on January 2, 1920, in which more 2,500 people were arrested by means of tactics more suited to Lenin's secret police than an agency of the United States government. While prosecuting Palmer's program, Hoover began his lifelong practice of keeping detailed files on people under investigation. He would later expand this to maintaining files on whomever he wished.

Officially transferred to the Bureau of Investigation—precursor of the FBI—in August 1922, Hoover was appalled by its feebleness and disorganization. Rife with political corruption, the bureau employed agents who were either political hacks or outright crooks. When the scandals of the Harding administration broke, both the attorney general and the director of the bureau, William BURNS, were forced out, and Harlan Fiske STONE was appointed the new attorney general. After careful consultation with then-secretary of commerce and future president Herbert Hoover (no relation to J. Edgar), J. Edgar Hoover was named to head the bureau on May 10, 1924.

J. Edgar Hoover spent the next seven years radically reorganizing the newly renamed Federal Bureau of Investigation, firing most of the old regime and mandating rigid rules of conduct and ethics. The transformation was a monument to his administrative genius, and by the end of the decade, the FBI was staffed by highly trained, dedicated law enforcement professionals, all of whom were also qualified attorneys.

In the 1930s, Hoover concentrated the bureau's efforts on the rash of bank robberies perpetrated by the likes of the BARKER clan, Pretty Boy Floyd, Baby Face Nelson, and Hoover's personal nemesis, John DILLINGER. These were high-profile crimes in Depression-racked America, and by solving them, Hoover hoped to enhance the public prestige of his agency. With a genius for public relations equal to his talent for administration, Hoover enlisted the help of Hollywood to propagandize the FBI, encouraging the production of movies that portrayed the invincible, all-seeing, and utterly incorruptible image that Hoover came to glory in. Indeed, Hoover deeply resented anyone else taking publicity or credit from him. Any time the FBI was mentioned, Hoover wanted his name to be associated with it. He forced out several agents popular with the media when he feared that their renown would eclipse his. He forbade anyone other than himself to issue statements to the press, and he would often invite reporters to his house for a dinner that frequently would be interrupted by pre-arranged phone calls in which the director would make dramatic, split-second decisions designed to make him appear every bit the "G-Man" he wanted the press to think he was. Hoover cultivated writers who cast the FBI in a positive light and even employed some to ghostwrite publications issued under his own name.

In time, Hoover loomed larger than the FBI itself, and although many presidents would have liked to relieve him of office, none dared. Hoover, his private files bulging, simply knew too much about too many influential people. He exercised his clout with high-handed arrogance, habitually bypassing the attorney general (by law his superior) and reporting directly to the president. It was not until 1961 that Hoover was challenged by an attorney general, Robert Kennedy, and the two men quickly became bitter personal enemies. Hoover was particularly resistant to Kennedy's demand that the FBI investigate civil rights violations and organized crime. However, Kennedy generally prevailed against Hoover as no other attorney general had done before. In retaliation, Hoover began compiling files on the Kennedy brothers, carefully charting extramarital affairs and financial histories.

Hoover had files of this sort on most politicians in Washington—and everyone knew it. It was his way of maintaining power through silent, unspoken blackmail. Some administration insiders have suggested that John Kennedy would have removed Hoover from office had he been elected to a second term, but it was Hoover who took some pleasure in informing Robert Kennedy and the rest of the family on November 22, 1963, that the president had been assassinated in Dallas.

As Hoover grew older, his eccentricities became increasingly bizarre and his personal tyranny more open. He amassed his files with greater and greater zeal and wielded frankly dictatorial authority in the bureau. He summarily dismissed an agent for being ugly. He fired another for wearing a tie he did not like. And he drummed out yet another for marrying a foreign woman.

Part genius, part demagogue, and part monster, J. Edgar Hoover almost single-handedly created one of the most powerful, most respected, and most sophisticated investigative bodies in the world, while at the same time threatening many of the rights and liberties his agency was formed to preserve and protect.

Hoover died in his sleep of a massive heart attack on May 2, 1972.

Further reading: Powers, Richard G., *Secrecy and Power: The Life of J. Edgar Hoover* (New York: Free Press, 1986).

Theoharis, A. G., and J. S. Cox, *The Boss* (New York: Bantam, 1988).

Howard, John (1726?–90) An early pioneer of prison reform, Howard was sheriff of Bedfordshire, England, when he wrote *State of Prisons in England and Wales* (1777), which led Parliament to pass the first Penitentiary Act in 1779.

Englishman John Howard was an early pioneer of prison reform. (Courtesy of the Library of Congress)

After John Howard became sheriff of Bedfordshire in 1773, he was shocked by the condition of the prisons he visited. Torture, neglect, and general cruelty were rampant, and Howard became determined to reform the system. He toured the nation's prisons and campaigned for reform, finally publishing *State of Prisons in England and Wales* in 1777, which prompted Parliament to pass the Penitentiary Act of 1779, which established England's first penitentiary, subject to rules and regulations meant to enforce a standard of humane treatment of prisoners.

Howard's efforts were commemorated in the John Howard Society, a prison reform group founded in 1901 that today continues to function as an advocacy group to promote humane conditions in prisons and jails.

Howe, Samuel Gridley (1801–76)

A champion of the parole system who invented the term itself and fought diligently for the reintegration of released convicts into society.

Samuel Howe grew up in Boston, the son of solidly middle-class parents. After attending Brown University and earning his M.D., Howe set off for Greece, like Lord Byron, to aid in that nation's war against the Turks. Enlisting as a guerrilla fighter, he served the Greek forces as a surgeon. After the war, he remained to help rebuild the ravaged country, returning to the United States to gather a boatload of supplies and then sailing back to Greece to distribute them.

After six years abroad, Howe returned to Boston and to a life dedicated to philanthropy. In 1829, Massachusetts incorporated a school for the blind, and Howe was enlisted to administer it. He journeyed again to Europe to observe similar schools for the blind and returned with exemplary notes. He demanded that blind and deaf people be dealt with as socially and economically competent, and his work at the school was lauded throughout the country.

Howe also enthusiastically endorsed Horace Mann in his fight for better public schools, but perhaps Howe's most enduring contribution to the public good was in the area of prison reform. He argued that released prisoners must be reintegrated into society—not just dumped onto the streets—if they were ever to be fully functioning, contributing, constructive members of society. He coined the term "parole" from the Greek, loosely meaning "word of honor," to describe his proposal for systematic incentives to good behavior based on planned sentence reduction.

Howe championed prison reform, particularly the concept of parole, until his death in 1876.

Further reading: Howe, Samuel Gridley, *An Essay on Separate and Congregate Systems of Prison Discipline* (Boston: W. D. Ticknor, 1846).

Hume, James B. (1827–1904)

Wells, Fargo's first (and some say greatest) chief of detectives.

Born in Stamford, New York, on January 23, 1827, Hume moved to Lima (now Howe), Indiana, and then set off with his brother and friends to prospect for gold in California in 1850. He worked the gold fields for a decade, earning enough money to make a living but never growing rich. In 1860, he became deputy tax collector, then city marshal, and then chief of police in Placerville, California—a brutal mining community originally dubbed Hangtown. Hume was so effective at cleaning up the town that he was soon appointed undersheriff of El Dorado County. Although he lost his bid for election to the post of sheriff in 1865, he was reappointed undersheriff in 1867 and won local fame ridding the region of the infamous Hugh DeTell gang.

As effective as Hume was at subduing violent criminals, he was even more adept at detective work and interrogation. In 1868, he was elected sheriff of El Dorado County, but found himself the victim of party politics in the next election, was defeated, and accepted a position with the Wells, Fargo company, which was reeling under a series of express holdups. The company granted Hume a leave of absence in

1871 so that he could accept the post of deputy warden of the Nevada State Penitentiary following the "Big Break" of September, in which 29 prisoners escaped. Hume restored not only order, but also morale and discipline to the institution.

Returning to California and Wells, Fargo, Hume set about the formidable task of fighting crimes against stagecoaches and railroad trains. In 1875 alone, Wells, Fargo lost $87,000 to holdup men—a staggering sum in the frontier West of the period. Over a 14-year period (according to Hume's own report), the company lost $414,312.55. However, Hume's work resulted in the apprehension and conviction of 206 "road agents" (stagecoach robbers), 20 train robbers, and 14 burglars during this same period. Hume was instrumental in the 1883 capture, conviction, and imprisonment of one of the most celebrated of all western outlaws, Black Bart (Charles E. Boles, 1830–1917?), who had held up Wells, Fargo stages and eluded California law officers for more than eight years.

Hume was no heartless lawman. He frequently helped defend men he thought had been wrongly accused, including William Evans, who had been charged with killing a Wells, Fargo guard in 1893. Hume attempted to appear in defense of Evans, but failed to persuade the judge to hear evidence exonerating the accused. Hume then took his case to the newspapers and was vilified by fellow lawman for defending a known road agent. (Evans was eventually freed, after serving 13 years in prison.)

Further reading: Dillon, Richard, *Wells, Fargo Detective: The Biography of James B. Hume* (New York: Coward-McCann, 1969).

Hurwitz, Stephan (1901–81) This distinguished Danish jurist was Denmark's first commissioner of public affairs—ombudsman—setting the international standards for that position as an accepted institution. He was also the author of standard works on criminology.

Born in Copenhagen on June 20, 1901, Hurwitz was a lawyer and law professor (at the University of Copenhagen). He was instrumental in establishing Denmark's Court of Special Appeals in 1939; during the Nazi occupation of Denmark in World War II, Hurwitz, a Jew, worked in the underground resistance movement. He was later forced to flee to Sweden. After the war, he helped prepare the legal basis for the Danish prosecution of wartime collaborators, though he was a harsh critic of the spirit of revenge that prevailed in the postwar atmosphere. Hurwitz was a member of the United Nations War Crimes Commission.

In 1955, pursuant to a 1953 amendment to the Danish constitution, Hurwitz became the nation's first ombudsman, establishing a citizen's monitoring agency for government administrators. Largely due to the precedents he established, the ombudsman model was adopted in many countries and local jurisdictions worldwide.

Hurwitz's books include *Human Responsibility* and *Respect for the Human Individual*. His most important contribution to criminology is the standard textbook, *Criminology*, written with Karl O. Christiansen in 1948—the first book of its kind in Scandinavia and an international classic.

Further reading: Hurwitz, Stephan, and Karl O. Christiansen, *Criminology* (London: George Allen & Unwin, 1983).

I

Ianni, Francis Anthony James (1926–) Studied an Italian-American crime family from the inside and presented a detailed look at this social unit for the first time.

A native of Wilmington, Delaware, Francis Ianni left home at the age of 18 to attend Pennsylvania State University, where he earned his bachelor's degree in 1949. He received his master's degree the following year and finished his doctoral work in psychology in 1952. Ianni settled on a career in academia and accepted a position at Russell Sage College in Troy, New York, later moving to Yale University, Columbia University, and teaching positions in Ethiopia and Italy.

A man of Italian-American descent, Ianni became fascinated with the social structure of the Italian-American crime families that had come to dominate organized crime in the United States. He was able to gain the confidence of one such family, which allowed him to make an empirical field study on an anthropological, psychological, and social level—the first such study ever. In *A Family Business: Kinship and Social Control in Organized Crime* (1972), Ianni traced the origins of the Mafia, from its beginnings in southern Italy, through the lower social strata of immigrants to the United States, and up to its domination of criminal activity in American cities. Ianni demonstrated that, above all else, the syndicate was rooted in kinship and birthright, which created loyalties that transcended civil law and patriotic identification.

In the mid-seventies, as sociologists and criminologists took note of the inroads African Americans and Hispanics were making into urban organized crime, Ianni began work on a kind of sequel to *A Family Business*, completing *Black Mafia: Ethnic Succession in Organized Crime* in 1981. Here Ianni studied the rise of African Americans and Hispanics through the criminal hierarchy as well as the decline of the Italian-American mobster, mostly due to increased efforts by the Justice Department. He noted that, like the Italians before them, African Americans and Hispanics, the lowest groups in the American social hierarchy, used organized crime to climb the social ladder. When members of these two groups have ascended as high as crime can take them, Ianni predicted that they, too, would be supplanted by the next lowest group in the social model.

Inbau, Fred (1909–) Wrote the classic text on police interrogation of criminal suspects.

Born in New Orleans to a poor shipyard worker, Fred Inbau grew up determined to make a great deal of money. When his father told him that lawyers lived well, he decided he would go into that profession. After graduating from Tulane University in 1930, Inbau went to Northwestern University to earn his master's degree in law. At Northwestern, Inbau frequented the school's crime detection lab, the finest in the country at the time. Within a short period, crime detection became his passion.

After completing his law degree at Northwestern, Inbau remained at that institution and became a research assistant in the crime detection lab. In 1938 he was promoted to director, a position he held until 1941. Immediately following World War II, Inbau was appointed a full-time faculty member of Northwestern, and over the next several decades he became one of the preeminent law professors in the country, helping to make Northwestern one of the nation's top law schools.

Inbau published many books on a variety of topics in the field of criminology. In his most noted work, *Lie Detection and Criminal Interrogation*, Inbau stressed the use of psychological manipulation in questioning a suspect. In crimes involving great emotion, such as murder or physical assault, Inbau suggests offering sympathy and sharing thoughts of similar feelings to ease the suspect into admitting his guilt. Questioning a man accused of killing his wife, Inbau remarked to the suspect about how annoying it was to have a nagging wife and how he knew how the man felt because his wife did the same thing. He said that he even had similar thoughts of killing his wife and could easily see how this man had done it. Then, rather than ask the man straight out for a confession, Inbau asked him where the gun was hidden. The man quickly broke down and told him everything. *Lie Detection and Criminal Investigation* remains Inbau's most influential and enduring contribution to the field of criminal investigation.

Irey, Elmer Lincoln (1888–1948)   Crack lead investigator for the Internal Revenue Service (IRS) who led the unit that netted Al CAPONE for income-tax evasion in the 1930s.

Appointed chief of the Treasury Department's IRS enforcement branch in 1919, Elmer Irey put together one of the most formidable investigative teams in the history of law enforcement. Included in the hundred-man unit of so-called "T-men" was Frank WILSON, whose infiltration of the Capone mob helped nab the seemingly untouchable gangster. Despite death threats and attempted jury tampering, Irey's tax evasion case stood, and the elusive mobster was finally convicted in 1931.

Irey was also responsible for recording the serial numbers of the ransom money in the Lindbergh kidnapping case, an action that eventually resulted in the capture and conviction of Bruno Richard HAUPTMANN. Irey's unit participated in such celebrated tax cases as that of Lousiana's Governor Huey Long and publisher Moses Annenberg. In all, his T-men were credited with nabbing some 15,000 tax cheats in the course of his 27-year tenure, a period during which the Treasury Department enjoyed a 90% conviction rate.

In 1937, Irey became chief coordinator of the Treasury Department, where he headed all of the agency's law enforcement efforts. He retired in 1941.

Further reading: Spiering, Frank, *The Man Who Got Capone* (Indianapolis: Bobbs-Merrill, 1976).

J

Jackson, Sir Richard Leofric (1902–75)   President of INTERPOL; also headed the Criminal Investigative Department (CID) of Scotland Yard.

Born in Calcutta, India, to a family devoted to the legal profession, Richard Jackson journeyed to England as a youth to attend Eton and then Trinity College, Cambridge. After graduating from Trinity with his law degree, he was called to the bar in 1927, returning to Calcutta with the intention of practicing there. Disturbed by the unrest in India stirred by Mohandas (Mahatma) Gandhi and his independence-seeking followers, Jackson returned to England, where he began specializing in criminal law.

In 1933, Jackson was a prosecutor for the Crown, preparing cases for trial at the Old Bailey, where he built up key contacts as well as an impeccable reputation. In 1945, he was named secretary of Scotland Yard, one of the top administrative positions. After serving as secretary for seven and a half years, he was appointed assistant commissioner in charge of criminal investigation, the high-profile department of Scotland Yard.

Jackson directed a force of 1,650 inspectors to investigate all criminal activity in London and outside the city as well, when invited by local authorities. Jackson transformed his department into what he called "a well oiled machine," and the CID soon boasted an 80% conviction rate on murder cases and a 50% rate on all other criminal activity. Jackson's reputation as an effective administrator and persistent cop earned him the presidency of INTERPOL in 1960, a position he held for three years. He was instrumental in that agency's growth and stabilization as the premier world police organization. As representative to INTERPOL from Great Britain, Jackson handled all world inquiries affecting Great Britain, using any force associated with INTERPOL he deemed necessary. He retired in 1963.

Jackson, Robert Houghwout (1892–1954)   Serving as attorney general under Franklin D. ROOSEVELT and later appointed a Supreme Court associate justice, Jackson was the U.S. representative and chief prosecutor at the Nuremberg war crimes trials following World War II.

Born on February 13, 1892, in Spring Creek, Pennsylvania, Robert Jackson moved with his family to Jamestown, New York, where he completed his early education. Attending Albany Law School, a part of Union College, Jackson finished the two-year course in a single year and was admitted to the New York bar in 1913, before his 21st birthday. He began practicing law with several firms until 1934, when fellow New Yorker Franklin D. Roosevelt appointed him general counsel for the Bureau of Internal Revenue. Two years later he was transferred to the Department of Justice, and in 1938 he was appointed solicitor general.

His record as solicitor general was outstanding, winning 38 of 44 cases before the Supreme Court. The president moved him up to attorney general in 1940, a position he held for barely a year before Roosevelt appointed him to the Supreme Court. As an associate justice of the high court, Jackson was somewhat controversial for his stand that the arguments of the justices over cases should be carried on in a public forum. Opposed to the principle of judicial activism, he was a proponent of strict construction.

In May 1945, Jackson took a leave of absence from the court to serve as the U.S. representative and chief prosecutor at the epoch-making Nuremberg war crimes trials. His first task was to participate in the creation of an International Military Tribunal to define the charges and trial procedure acceptable to the four victorious powers. He also was responsible for drafting indictments and amassing evidence for the prosecution. He offered the opening statement for the prosecution, which was considered masterful at the time and was instrumental in the guilty verdicts of 19 of the original 23 defendants who stood trial, including the death sentences for Hermann Goering, Julius Streicher, Joachim von Ribbentrop, Alfred Jodl, Martin Bormann, and seven others. After his service at Nuremberg, Jackson returned to the Supreme Court bench, serving until his death on October 9, 1954.

Jaegerman, Edward C. (ca. 1913–80)   An attorney and leading investigator with the U.S. government's Securities and Exchange Commission (SEC), Jaegerman helped track down the con artists and stock swindlers who preyed on credulous investors throughout North America in the post-Depression era.

Having graduated at the top of his class at Yale University and Yale Law School, Jaegerman was invited by then-chairman William O. DOUGLAS to join the SEC in 1936, just three years after the commission was created by Franklin D. ROOSEVELT. Over the next three decades, Jaegerman served there as senior trial attorney, director of the Office of Special Investigations, and chief investigative counsel. During the 1950s, the securities sleuth was awarded a Rockefeller Fellowship for a year of study at Oxford.

Shortly after arriving at the SEC, Jaegerman and John T. CALLAHAN were made the investigative team for national and international cases under the jurisdiction of the Division of Trading and Exchange. Dubbed "the Rover Boys" by a 1938 *Fortune* magazine reporter, they traced financial dirty dealing wherever it led, from fly-by-night "bucket shops" and phone swindlers' "boiler rooms" to the plush boardrooms of such Wall Street high-rollers as Alexander Guterman, Walter F. Tellier, and "boy wonder" Earl Belle. Many times, their searches led north of the border to Canada, where stock-trading hustlers and "moose pasture" hucksters tried to evade the reach of U.S. authorities. One of Jaegerman's last major busts was the Texas Gulf Sulphur case, another Canadian investigation and a landmark instance of insider trading. Some of the company's chief officers had exploited their inside knowledge of a mineral discovery (not yet announced to their shareholders) to profit from trade in its stock. Untangling the Wall Street paper trails and international phone syndicates of major high-finance finaglers, Jaegerman and Callahan participated in over 500 cases.

In 1968, after 32 years of service, Jaegerman left the SEC and joined the Wall Street firm of Charles Plohn & Company. Perhaps ironically, the company was forced to disband later the same year following accusations of regulatory violations. As one of the managing partners, Jaegerman himself was subjected to SEC scrutiny. Various charges were filed against

him by the State of New York, but Jaegerman was cleared of these in a trial that brought a host of financial luminaries—some of them former SEC officials—to testify in his defense.

Jaegerman died of a heart attack at his home in New York City in February 1980.

James, Frank (1843–1915)   The name of Frank James is linked to that of his brother Jesse JAMES, whose gang was the most famous outlaw outfit in the Wild West.

Alexander Franklin James—better known as Frank James—and his brother Jesse were born in Clay County, Missouri, where they grew up in a climate of intense conflict over the issue of whether Missouri was to be a free or a slave state. With the outbreak of the Civil War, Frank James joined the brutal guerrilla outfit of William Clarke Quantrill, whose activities on behalf of the Confederate cause often involved outright murder and robbery. Younger brother Jesse followed Frank's lead by joining a related guerrilla group led by "Bloody Bill" Anderson.

Following the war, the James boys used the skills they had acquired as guerrilla raiders to embark on a

Frank James not only survived his career in crime, he escaped conviction and lived to write his highly profitable life's story. (Courtesy of the National Archives)

career of crime, beginning with a bank robbery at Liberty, Missouri, on February 13, 1866, in which a bystander was murdered. (For the balance of the James Boys' career together, see Jesse JAMES.)

A few months after the death of Jesse at the hands of Robert Ford on April 3, 1882, Frank James gave himself up to Missouri authorities. He was indicted and tried on a charge of murder, but was found not guilty. He was transported to Huntsville, Alabama, where he was tried for robbery and also found not guilty. Returned to Missouri to stand trial for armed robbery, he was yet again acquitted. The fact was that, notorious as the James brothers were, public sentiment in their favor made it impossible to find a jury that would convict Frank James. With his "martyred" brother, he was seen as a latter-day Robin Hood. In the words of the "Ballad of Jesse James," "He took from the rich and he gave to the poor."

Frank James, set free, lived a quiet, somewhat reclusive life until his death in 1915.

James, Jesse (Woodson) (1847–82)   The exploits of this legendary outlaw are deeply ingrained in the folklore of the Wild West.

Reverend Robert James left his young family in Clay County, Missouri, in 1850, to embark on a mission to save souls in California. He died that year, however, leaving three-year-old Jesse and seven-year-old Frank and their mother to fend for themselves amid the growing violence of a western border state on the eve of civil war. The subsequent struggle over secession in the 1860s drenched the Missouri earth in blood, and a 17-year-old Jesse joined a Confederate guerrilla outfit led by "Bloody Bill" Anderson—infamous protégé of the even more infamous William Clarke Quantrill—which ambushed and massacred Union soldiers and pro-Union civilians during the Civil War.

The organizations of Quantrill and Anderson were, in effect, schools for outlaws. Jesse was severely wounded toward the end of the war when he tried to surrender to Union forces. Once mended, however, he and his brother Frank (who had served with Quantrill) formed a gang of outlaws with Cole Younger (another Quantrill alumnus) and his brothers, James, Bob, and John.

The James-Younger gang is thought to have first struck a bank in Liberty, Missouri, making off with $17,000 on February 13, 1866. During the period of 1866 to 1882, the James brothers, leading various others, were responsible for at least a dozen bank robberies, seven train heists, four stagecoach robberies, at least 11 murders, and a lucrative ripoff of the Kansas City State Fair, in which a little girl was seriously wounded by one of the gang's wild shots.

As the state fair wounding demonstrated, the James Gang was a group of ruthless, careless, and vicious outlaws. However, to many westerners who felt themselves victimized by big government and the Eastern Establishment, Jesse James and his "boys" assumed the status of latter-day Robin Hoods (not that they ever gave anyone anything they took). The popular press collaborated in the creation of this image and also magnified the gang's exploits, making it seem as if every crime committed in the West and Midwest was of their authorship.

The popular image of the James boys was further enhanced by an 1875 episode involving the famed Pinkerton Detective Agency, which had been hired by the railroads to pursue the gang. Acting on a tip, Pinkerton agents surrounded Jesse's home and tossed a bomb through the window. The agents did not succeed in flushing out the gang, but the bomb gravely injured the outlaws' mother, who lost an arm, and their half-brother Archie, whose injuries proved fatal. In the 1870s, it was easy to despise the giant, unfeeling, and omniverous railroad conglomerates, and the bombing thrust the public's sympathy all the more squarely with the Jameses.

On September 7, 1876, the James-Younger Gang met with disaster during a bank robbery in Northfield, Minnesota. A bloody shootout left three gang members dead and Bob Younger gravely wounded. The crippled gang fought its way out of town (killing a citizen in the process), then proposed to finish off Bob Younger, so that they could move faster. Cole refused to abandon his brother, the Jameses moved on, and the Youngers—Bob, Cole, and Jim—were captured.

Frank and Jesse managed to escape, living incognito for some three years in Nashville, Tennessee. By this time, a $10,000 reward had been offered by the governor of Missouri for the capture of the James brothers, and Jesse had reconstituted his gang, replacing the Younger brothers with Robert and Charles Ford. The $10,000 reward proved too sweet for Robert Ford. On April 3, 1882, as the story goes, he shot Jesse (who had assumed the alias of Thomas Howard) in the back of the head—while the outlaw was straightening a picture in the parlor of his home in St. Joseph, Missouri.

The following day, the *Kansas City Journal* ran a headline that read "GOODBYE, JESSE," and Ford's deed was reviled in a popular ballad about "the dirty little coward who shot Mr. Howard and laid poor Jesse in his grave."

Further reading: Settle, William A., *Jesse James Was His Name* (Columbia: University of Missouri Press, 1966).

Jay, John (1745–1839)   The first chief justice of the United States Supreme Court, Jay was instrumental

Instrumental in the political battle to enact the U.S. Constitution, John Jay went on to become the country's first chief justice. (Portrait by John Wright, courtesy of the New-York Historical Society)

in the enactment of the principal legal document of the nation: the Constitution.

The idea of justice in America today would not exist without the contributions of New York lawyer and lifelong public servant John Jay. Born in New York City on December 12, 1745, John Jay attended Kings College—now Columbia University—graduating in 1764 and gaining admittance to the bar in 1768. It was not long before the young lawyer was swept up in the gathering tide of revolution, and Jay became a delegate from New York to both the First Continental Congress, 1774, and the Second, in 1775. It was at these convocations that he first made his mark as a significant legal mind with a unique talent for arbitration.

John Jay became chief justice of the New York State Supreme Court in 1777 and delivered a compelling speech during the opening session in September, affirming his commitment to impartiality and his passion for law and order. Jay's early decisions were fair but harsh. He believed that "lenity was cruelty," whereas a severe application of statute best served humanity in the long run. He advocated speedy trials and public notification of verdicts as a means of deterrence.

In 1777, Jay was elected president of Congress, and, the following year, he was appointed special emissary to Spain. In 1781, along with Thomas Jefferson, John Adams, and Benjamin Franklin, Jay was chosen to go to Paris to negotiate the peace treaty with Britain that would end the War for Independence. After his return, Jay served as secretary of foreign affairs from 1784 to 1790.

Despite his acomplishments as a treaty negotiator and a shaper of the fledgling nation's foreign policy, John Jay is best remembered as one of the authors of the *Federalist Papers,* which produced some of the most compelling political arguments in history in defense of the Constitution that was proposed as a replacement for the weak Articles of Confederation.

The significance of John Jay's advocacy on behalf of the Constitution—and, in particular, his work on the *Federalist Papers* (he wrote numbers 2, 3, 4, 5, and 64 under the pseudonym "Publius") is momentous. Jay and the other *Federalist* authors, James Madison and Alexander Hamilton, defined the federal system as we know it today. The battle over ratification of the Constitution turned on the New York vote, which was generally opposed to the federalist system, and it was Jay who bridged the differences that would have barred ratification.

President George Washington appointed Jay the first chief justice of the Supreme Court of the United States in 1789. As chief justice, Jay presided over many cases that set essential precedents for United States law and established the judicial branch as a powerful element in the new government. Jay's leadership laid the foundation for the work of his successor, John MARSHALL, the so-called "father of judicial review."

Further reading: Morris, Richard B., *John Jay: The Nation and the Court* (Boston: Boston University Press, 1967).

Jebb, Joshua (1793–1863)

England's first surveyor-general of prisons and the first chairman of the Directors of Convict Prisons.

Born on May 8, 1793, in Chesterfield, England, Jebb was trained for a military career at the Royal Military Academy at Woolwich and was commissioned a second lieutenant in 1812. He first saw action in North America, during the War of 1812. In 1837, while he was still in the army, he received his appointment as surveyor-general of prisons, acting primarily as a consultant on the construction of prisons. In this capacity, he designed county and borough prisons and was one of the creators of a "model prison" at Pentonville, of which he was made commissioner in 1841.

Jebb was instrumental in abolishing the policy of "transporting" convicts (that is, exiling them to colonial prisons), replacing it with a more humane system of prison treatment in England. Under Jebb's direction, felons were subjected to a period of strict separation at Pentonville, then transferred to one of several prisons more closely integrated with the community so that they could be employed in public works. (Jebb designed one such prison, Portland.)

In addition to his work in civil penology, Jebb was appointed in 1844 a member of a royal commission to report on the punishment of military crime. The commission recommended the establishment of prisons exclusively for military prisoners, and Jebb was appointed the first inspector-general of military prisons, a post he held concurrently with his civil duties. In 1850, when a unified board was created to replace the disparate bodies that had previously governed England's prisons, Jebb was named to its chairmanship, and, under his direction, the English prison system continued on its increasingly progressive course.

Jeffreys, Alec (1950–)

British scientist who discovered the forensics breakthrough of DNA "fingerprinting" in 1985.

Alec Jeffreys, acting research fellow at the University of Leicester, England, is an expert in genetics whose work in the field of DNA "fingerprinting" is changing the practice of forensic science. In 1985, Jeffreys introduced DNA fingerprinting, a process that, in theory, allows the forensic investigator to identify positively any individual from the minutest trace of body tissue or fluid, such as saliva or semen. So convincing was Jeffreys's demonstration that, within two years, both the United States and Great Britain had incorporated DNA fingerprinting techniques into their legal systems.

Despite the initial and dramatic success of DNA fingerprinting, Jeffreys's process was time consuming and did involve a significant element of subjective evaluation, giving the results some margin of error. Defense attorneys immediately began to challenge these shortcomings and were successful in the late 1980s in defeating a DNA-based prosecution. It should be noted, however, that defense attorneys have successfully used DNA fingerprinting themselves, most notably in appealing and overturning a number of long-standing rape convictions.

In 1991, Jeffreys developed Digital DNA Profiling, a far more efficient technique for identifying the signature DNA strands. The new method not only shortens the identification process, but also successfully addresses the earlier problems of accuracy and has, indeed, revolutionized the field of forensic medicine.

Like the pioneers of traditional fingerprinting (dactyloscopy), Henry FAULDS, Francis GALTON, and Joseph FAUROT, Alec Jeffreys doubtless will face battles with status quo bureaucracies. Nevertheless, his ongoing development of DNA fingerprinting technology has already established him as a highly significant figure in modern forensics.

Further reading: Thompson, Dick, "A Trial of High-Tech Detectives," *Time*, 133 (June 5, 1989), p. 63.

Johnson, Lyndon Baines (1908–73)

Hoping to push through his "Great Society" program, which included sweeping legal and criminal reforms, President Johnson instead saw his presidency—and his visions of a Great Society—overshadowed and consumed by the war in Vietnam.

A self-made man, Lyndon Baines Johnson was the son of a cattle speculator, attended a small state teachers college, and took his first job as a secretary to a Texas congressman. In Washington, Johnson quickly received attention from such major players as fellow Texan Sam Rayburn, later speaker of the House, who urged Johnson to pursue a political career. In 1935, Johnson was appointed by President Franklin Delano ROOSEVELT as the Texas state administrator for the National Youth Administration. Working for the NYA, Johnson began to build the network of congressional contacts that would later make him one of the most powerful majority leaders ever. The beginnings of this base put him in Congress for the first time in 1937 on a strong New Deal platform. He developed a personal relationship with FDR, and the president was soon his mentor and hero. By 1955, Johnson had risen to Senate majority leader, and for the next five years, he manipulated Congress as no one since John Quincy Adams had. He knew every weakness, strength, need, ambition, and quirk of every senator, and he played this knowledge like a master. Despite the opposition of the Eisenhower administration, he was able to push through the Senate much liberal legislation, including the civil rights acts of 1957 and 1960.

After failing to win the 1960 Democratic presidential nomination for himself, Johnson was named as John F. Kennedy's running mate to win support from the South and the West. Johnson hated his term as vice president, and there were rumors that he would be dropped from the ticket in 1964. The subject was rendered moot, however, by Kennedy's assassination in Dallas on November 22, 1963. Johnson vowed to follow JFK's policies, stating, "Let us continue." True to his word, he pushed Kennedy's civil rights bill through Congress as well as his $11 billion tax cut aimed at reviving the economy. He also added the first legislation of his own, an antipoverty measure. After vintage Johnson massaging of both houses, the measures sailed through.

With this legislative victory behind him, Johnson began his own program, the Great Society, one that he hoped would be favorably compared with the

New Deal of his idol, FDR. In 1964, he declared "an unconditional War on Poverty," earmarking $1 billion for the Office of Economic Opportunity to make the poor and criminally reformed employable. Further boosted by his own election in 1964 and a huge Democratic majority in both houses, Johnson went on to pass a phenomenal 69% of his legislative program.

In the second phase of his Great Society, the president sought vigorously to oppose crime. In March 1965, he sent a special message to Congress, vowing to attack crime in three ways: by increased federal law enforcement efforts; by greater assistance to local law enforcement; and by a comprehensive study of crime in modern America. In July, he formed the Commission on Law Enforcement and Administration of Justice to complete the comprehensive crime study, which addressed everything from causes of crime to arrests and rehabilitation. After introducing his anticrime legislation in the summer of 1965, he also formed the National Crime Commission to help implement his legislation as well as act on the forthcoming report from his presidential Commission on Law Enforcement and Administration of Justice.

The end of 1965 appeared to mark the end of Johnson's legislative effectiveness, as the war in Vietnam became a seething vortex that consumed the administration's resources. Johnson was forced to compromise his Great Society, because the nation could not afford both a war and a comprehensive social program. In the meantime, his vast congressional capital all but disappeared in the face of a growing antiwar movement. Realizing he could no longer be the new FDR and that the country sought a change, Johnson addressed the nation on television on March 31, 1968. He announced an end to the bombing of North Vietnam, called on Hanoi to come to the peace table, and then stunned the nation with his announcement that "I will not seek and will not accept the nomination of my party for another term as your President." The Great Society remained, in large part, an unrealized dream and the sweeping anticrime legislation an abortive effort.

Johnston, James A. (1876–1954) The first warden of Alcatraz helped develop that prison into the harsh, brutal dungeon popular legend has painted it.

After growing up in Brooklyn, James Johnston moved to California, where he finished his education and was admitted to the California bar in 1919. Prior to his admission to the bar, however, he had served as warden at California's maximum security Folsom Prison for a year. From Folsom, he went to San Quentin, the state's other maximum security prison. There he gained a reputation as a reformer, abolishing corporal punishment and the demeaning striped uniforms, as well as establishing honor camps for the inmates. Johnston stayed at San Quentin until 1925, when he left to pursue a private law practice.

With the increase in gangster activity and kidnapping during the twenties and early thirties, the Federal Prison Bureau sought to establish a place where ruthless, hardened criminals could be deposited without hope of escape. They found their dungeon in Alcatraz Island, a desolate pile in the middle of San Francisco Bay. An old army prison, the island was a mile and a half from the mainland and surrounded by some of the coldest and strongest near-shore ocean currents in the country.

In 1934, Johnston was tapped as warden over the objections of some who wanted a tougher man. Johnston's own associates likewise urged him to decline the appointment, saying that it would tarnish his reputation as a reformer. But Johnston accepted the position and stunned his assoicates by modeling Alcatraz on the brutal "Auburn system." It was a style of administration that the prison would retain until its closing in 1963. For the first four years of Johnston's administration, rigid silence was imposed on the convicts while in the cell blocks, at work, or in the dining area. Any violation of regulations brought time in solitary confinement—"the hole," a dank cell that was never lit and had no bed. It was once revealed that a particular prisoner had spent seven years in such inhuman isolation. When asked how much longer the prisoner would remain there, Johnston replied, "As long as necessary for discipline."

The most trying period of Johnston's tenure at Alcatraz was the 1946 riot, the so-called Battle of Alcatraz, in which six inmates were able to gain control of a cell block and hold nine guards hostage in an attempt to escape. The guards were locked up in cells, and when it appeared that the escape attempt would fail, the inmates began shooting them. To end the riot, Johnston proposed a frontal military attack on the cell block, complete with grenade-throwing marines. When the director of prisons expressed concern over the safety of innocent inmates, Johnston replied, "There are no innocent inmates in here."

In the end, two guards were killed and 14 wounded, along with four inmates who were either killed or wounded.

Two years after the Battle of Alcatraz, Johnston retired from the place known forever afterward as "The Rock."

Jones, Frank (1856–93) Gunslinging Texas Ranger who made a name for himself by the age of 18.

While hunting for a gang of Mexican horse rustlers one day, Jones's posse was ambushed and two of the lawmen were killed. Alone in the chase now, the

Flamboyant Texas Ranger Frank Jones (Courtesy of the Western History Collections, University of Oklahoma)

teenager went on to cut down two of the culprits and bring the third home. The young lawman's heroic reputation continued to grow. Captured with three Rangers—after three others had been killed—by another gang of thieves, Sergeant Jones managed to wrest away an enemy's rifle and shoot all five rustlers dead. Jones prevailed in stand-up gun duels, sought and seized long-"wanted" men, and after one saloon shoot-out, locked up an especially nefarious killer called Tex Murietta.

In 1891, now a captain, the Ranger went after robbers of a Southern Pacific train. Trailing the gang's hoofprints through rough country on both sides of the Rio Grande, Jones and his men kept pace for several days. A lookout's last-minute warning sent the robbers in flight from their home camp, but Jones and company recovered the railroad plunder, plus a herd of stolen cattle. The captain's subsequent chase, crisscrossing the river, left the felons horseless in dense canebrakes, and these Jones continued to beat and burn for three days before withdrawing. Reporting the manhunt's details to his commander, Jones wrote, "If we had not found the robber camp we would have been without rations for several days. I demolished their roost entirely and am satisfied hunger will drive them from the River . . . Now Genl [general] I wanted you to know through me . . . Of course I would not cross into Mexico where there are settlements and would be any danger of stirring up international trouble. You would do me a favor by stating this matter to [Texas] Gov Hogg as it really is as he might hear through the papers of my crossing . . ." A few weeks later, Jones telegraphed General Mabry that he and several deputies had now caught three of the robbers—north of the border, after all. A fourth robber, badly wounded, shot himself dead during the chase.

As it happened, two years later, Jones finally met his own death on what was technically foreign soil—Pirate Island, a six-mile-wide strip of brushland formed by a change in the course of the Rio Grande and officially under Mexican jurisdiction. Six weeks earlier, Jones had requested a large posse for a mission in El Paso County, which he knew adjoined this former riverbed where the numerous and notorious Olguin family gang stayed. But only five men rode with Jones on June 29, 1893, and one of them, a deputy sheriff, had writs for two Olguin arrests. The Ranger and his group pursued the cattle rustlers back and forth across the no-man's-land near Pirate Island, until the outlaws made it to cover in a small adobe settlement. Wounded themselves, the Olguins kept firing from the windows and doors, and they hit lawman Jones in the thigh. Another Ranger asked, "Captain, are you hurt?" He replied, "Yes, shot all to pieces." Another bullet struck his breast, and he pronounced his last words: "Boys, I am killed."

Further reading: Webb, Walter Prescott, *The Texas Rangers* (Austin: University of Texas Press, 1935).

K

Kalven, Harry, Jr. (1914–74)   With colleague Hans ZEISEL, Kalven was coauthor of the first comprehensive study of juries.

Harry Kalven earned his undergraduate and law degrees from the University of Chicago and was admitted to the Illinois bar in 1939. He served as an instructor and, eventually, as a full professor at Chicago, where he was an ardent and liberal advocate of the First Amendment. In the late 1960s, he defended "blue" comic Lenny Bruce in a First Amendment free speech case before the Illinois State Supreme Court.

In addition to freedom of speech, Kalven was also extremely interested in the work of juries and the jury trial system. Little study had been devoted to the nature of juries, even as late as the 1960s and 1970s. With Hans Zeisel, a colleague at Chicago, Kalven undertook the first comprehensive study of juries and the process of an American jury trial.

Kalven and Zeisel's study is a valuable contribution to the American legal system. More jury trials occur in the United States than in all other countries combined, and many had claimed they are time-consuming and expensive. Kalven and Zeisel determined that jury trials take little more time than bench trials and that 80% of juries that reach a verdict reach the same verdict a judge would have rendered. They also noted that, in some cases, juries perform better or worse than judges because they can go outside the law to reach a decision—something that is sometimes more, sometimes less, equitable.

Karpis, Alvin "Creepy" (1907–79)   "Public Enemy Number One" and a particular nemesis of J. Edgar HOOVER, Karpis was arrested in person by the FBI director in May 1936.

A Canadian citizen by birth, Alvin Karpis spent more time in U.S. prisons than he did living in his homeland. During one of these stays Karpis met Freddie Barker, youngest son of Arizona "Ma" BARKER. Together they formed the infamous Barker-Karpis gang, which was involved in numerous bank robberies and kidnappings in the Midwest—most notably, the 1933 kidnapping of beer magnate William Hamm, for whom they received $100,000 in ransom. Two years later, Freddie and "Ma" Barker were killed in an FBI ambush in Florida, leaving Karpis in sole possession of the dubious title of Public Enemy Number One.

In April 1936, a senator from Tennessee criticized J. Edgar Hoover for unerringly avoiding the personal dangers of bloody confrontations with gangsters. To make matters worse for Hoover, Karpis complained loudly that the director had ordered his agents to murder an innocent old woman in "Ma" Barker. An outraged and defensive Hoover vowed to capture "Creepy" Karpis and put all agency resources on the case. At last, during May 1936, FBI agents tracked and cornered Karpis in New Orleans, and Hoover flew down personally to arrest him.

Tried and and sentenced to life imprisonment, Karpis served 26 years in Alcatraz before being moved to McNeil Island Penitentiary. He was paroled and deported to Canada in 1969, where he published his memoirs in 1971, then retired to Spain, dying there in 1979.

Keeler, Leonarde (1903–49)   A polygraph pioneer who opened up the first private lie detection agency in 1938.

While he was a student at Stanford University, Chicago-born Leonarde Keeler met polygraph inventor Dr. John LARSON and became his junior collaborating partner in developing the lie detector, with the encouragement of the progressive chief of the Berkeley, California, police, August VOLLMER. Later, working at the penitentiary in Joliet, Illinois, Keeler tested over 500 criminals in order to perfect the polygraph device and the methodology of interpreting its results. His success landed him a position as chief psychologist and polygraph examiner at the Scientific Crime Detection Laboratory of Northwestern University, Evanston, Illinois, in 1929.

Two years later, Keeler obtained the first patent for the Keeler Polygraph, an improved version of Larson's original. The device was first tested in 1935, in a Wisconsin court. Keeler also sought an opportunity to test his device on Bruno Richard HAUPTMANN and other suspects in the famous Lindbergh baby kidnapping case. He was denied access to Hauptmann, but made the most of the considerable publicity the polygraph issue nevertheless generated. Keeler went on to become a millionaire as the foremost practitioner of scientific lie detection in the United States.

During World War II, Keeler was personally responsible for screening employees of the Manhattan Project—the program that created the atomic bomb—and for interrogating key German POWs. The inventor's Keeler Polygraph School, established in Chicago in 1948, was responsible for training both civilians and military personnel in polygraph technique. Keeler died of heart disease in 1949 in Sturgeon Bay, Wisconsin.

Further reading: Block, Eugene B., *Lie Detectors: Their History and Use* (New York: D. McKay Co., c1977).

Kefauver, Estes (1903–63)

A reform senator from Tennessee who gained national prominence as the head of televised Senate committee hearings on organized crime.

The son of parents who could trace their roots back to the Revolution, Estes Kefauver was born in Madisonville, Tennessee, on July 26, 1903. He grew quickly and was big for his age, even as a youngster physically dominating any room he entered. He enrolled at the University of Tennessee, where he was instantly popular, polite to all, and full of good-natured pranks. He pledged the Kappa Sigma fraternity, starred on the football team, set several records as captain of the track team, edited the school newspaper, and served as student body president. After graduating in 1924, he entered Yale Law School, earning his degree in 1927.

Kefauver joined a private practice and promptly learned the intricacies of law and research the hard way, by losing his first two cases. He also became interested in politics, winning a special election for the open Third District congressional seat. In Washington, as in the law, he paid his dues and learned the ropes, not speaking much his freshman year but making contacts and keeping his constituents informed via the now famous Kefauver letters. Re-

Senator Estes Kefauver headed a Senate committee to investigate organized crime and staged a series of televised hearings that stunned the nation. (Courtesy of the National Archives)

elected to Congress four times, he decided to run for the Senate in 1948, but failed to garner support from the Tennessee machine that had helped him initially. Despite this, he defeated the machine, won the Senate seat, and greatly enhanced his reputation among his constituents.

By 1952, he was the senior senator from Tennessee and wielded considerable influence on Capitol Hill. He headed the Senate Special Committee to Investigate Crime in Interstate Commerce, commonly called the Kefauver Committee. The proceedings were televised live nationally, the first such broadcast, and they gripped the nation, making Kefauver's name a household word. The committee of five heard testimony from over 600 witnesses, ranging from the lowliest of hoods to major crime bosses such as Joe ADONIS and Frank COSTELLO. There were sensational disclosures made that ruined the careers of several prominent men, not the least of whom was New York City's Mayor William O'Dwyer. More important, the committee brought organized crime to public and governmental attention and made significant investigative inroads into it, forcing the FBI (which had steadfastly denied the existence of the Mafia) into committing its substantial resources to the fight against "the Mob."

Further reading: Moore, William H., *The Kefauver Committee and the Politics of Crime, 1950–52* (Columbia: University of Missouri Press, 1974).

Kelley, Clarence Marion (1911–   )   The first permanent director of the FBI to succeed J. Edgar HOOVER overturned many of Hoover's policies and brought the FBI out from its secretive past.

Born on October 24, 1911, in Kansas City, Missouri, Clarence Kelley attended the University of Kansas, earning his bachelor's degree in 1936. He continued in law school at the University of Kansas City (later absorbed by the University of Missouri), graduating in 1940. Four months later, he became an FBI field agent.

Kelley's early FBI career was undistinguished, though competent. He was transferred from field office to field office on a routine basis with the exception of his World War II service and a stint at the FBI Academy in Quantico, Virginia. Kelley became disenchanted with many of Hoover's policies, particularly when he was posted in Birmingham, Alabama, at the time of the intense civil rights activity there. While the city's infamous police chief, "Bull" Connor, attacked civil rights marchers with police dogs, the word from Washington to the FBI field office was to stay out of it. Soon after this experience, Kelley resigned from the FBI to accept the position of Kansas City's chief of police.

In Kansas City, Kelley was responsible for making the police force one of the most modern in the country. He also earned a reputation for civil rights reform, working to integrate a force that was more than 95% white. Kelley made significant strides in enhancing the force's image in the community, especially the African-American community. Despite such efforts, he was criticized for using excessive force—and instigating a "police riot"—during the civil disturbances that followed the assassination of Rev. Martin Luther King Jr.

Despite the events of 1968, Kelley's record in Kansas City made him a solid choice as successor to L. Patrick GRAY, who had resigned as acting director of the FBI following his implication in the Watergate scandal coverup. Richard M. NIXON quickly nominated Kelley in 1973, who remarked during his Senate confirmation hearings that he would resign before he would bow to political pressure.

During his five-year tenure at the bureau, Kelley did much to reform the institution. He began by issuing a copy of his Senate confirmation speech, along with his directives for the future of the bureau, to every officer in the field. The document also included his direct-line phone number; in the 48 years Hoover was director, the only time a field officer ever contacted him directly was to tell him President Kennedy had been killed. Kelley changed the direction of the bureau, removing it from political influence and stressing the quality and significance of investigations rather than mere quantity. For example, FBI policy would now dictate that crimes involving a threat to human life would take precedence over property crimes, even though solving the more numerous property crimes might make the bureau look better statistically. Kelley reorganized the top levels of the bureau, seeking to add new blood to balance the holdovers from the Hoover years. He established a rational system of internal review.

Kelley retired in 1978 at the age of 67.

Kemmler, William (1861–90)   The first criminal to be executed by electric chair was an ax-murderer from Buffalo, New York, who had slaughtered his common-law wife in the rage of a drunken quarrel in March of 1889.

Electrocution as a method of capital punishment was slated for debut in 1890, and its inauguration took place amid the legal and propagandistic cross-campaigns of the two founding giants of commercial electricity, George Westinghouse and Thomas Edison. On August 6, 1890, with confidence in a celestial hereafter, William Kemmler faced the chair almost amiably, seemingly pleased with the unique place in earthly history he was to gain in a few minutes' time.

Born in Philadelphia on May 9, 1860, Kemmler grew up illiterate and at some point found work as a huckster; in this profession he sometimes used an alias, John Hart. Leaving a wife and child in Pennsylvania, Kemmler ran away with another woman, Tillie Ziegler, and the two shared an apartment in Buffalo, New York, for a year and a half. Hard-drinking and ill-tempered, the couple frequently disturbed their neighbors with raucous and foul-mouthed late-night battles. But on March 28, 1889, the neighbors heard far more alarming sounds. Kemmler had taken a hatchet to Ziegler. The police arrived, the man was caught red-handed, and Ziegler died at the scene soon thereafter.

As he was hustled off to the station, drunk and swaggering, the murderer told police that Ziegler deserved to be killed. Finding him guilty on May 10, the trial judge pronounced that Kemmler deserved to be executed. Thanks to a recent change in New York state's criminal justice system, the sentence would be imposed by electrocution.

This innovation had first been proposed about 10 years earlier by a Dr. Alfred P. Southwick, a Buffalo native. The state senate appointed a commission in 1886 to study the matter, and the opinions of lawyers, judges, and medical experts were solicited. In June of 1889, a bill was passed adopting the new method and retiring the hangman's noose. Controversy quickly followed the decision, however, with lawyers contesting its constitutionality—as a potentially "cruel and unusual punishment"—and some scientists questioning the lethal efficacy of electrical shock. The Medico-Legal Society explored the issue with a series of animal experiments, and the group affirmed the idea's workability.

But the most determined battle was waged between two pioneers of modern electricity. Thomas Edison—advocate of low-tension, direct-current (DC) power—had for some time contended that his system was safer for the home consumer than the less expensively installed alternating current (AC) system since developed and marketed by his rival, George Westinghouse. Edison's business interests would be indirectly but well served by any public demonstration of AC's lethal power, so when New York City technician Harold P. Brown got involved in the execution controversy and himself undertook the design of an electric chair that would use AC current, Edison contributed laboratory resources to Brown's project and experiments.

Naturally, enough, when Brown's test electrocutions of various farm animals, large and small, at Edison's New Jersey laboratory were reported in the press, George Westinghouse objected strenuously, beginning with a letter to the editor of the *New York Times* in which he pointed out his competitor's prejudicial motives for supporting Brown's efforts. Soon Brown had attained a contract to build three chairs for the state, and Westinghouse endeavored to block the inventor from using his company's AC equipment in these lethal devices. But since Brown had purchased his dynamos from a dealer, fair and square, Westinghouse had no legal right to restrict their use. So Westinghouse and his associates did their best to challenge the chair's capacity to administer instant, painless death, and publicized examples of shock victims who had survived as much as 1,000 volts, the voltage most experts now agreed would be sufficient for the state's purposes.

When Kemmler turned out to be the first capital conviction under the new law, Westinghouse hired W. Bourke Cockran, the nation's best defense lawyer at the time, to mount an appeal campaign on Kemmler's behalf. Brown, Westinghouse employees, and even Edison took the witness stand to argue over the scientific evidence of AC's speed and deadliness, and Cockran aggressively pursued the "cruel and unusual" constitutional protection. But though Westinghouse spent $100,000 along the way, Cockran's legal efforts were for naught. The state Supreme Court ruled that electrocution was the means of exactly the same punishment—death—as any other form of execution, all of which necessarily inflicted at least some momentary pain. Kemmler's fate was now carved in stone.

The procedure, held at Auburn prison, was less than perfectly performed, though Kemmler himself encouraged the guards to tighten the fit of his headpiece and straps to "be sure that everything is all right." He also wished the 25 witnesses good luck in the world, asserted that he was going to "a good place," and remarked that the newspapers had "been saying a lot of stuff" about him that wasn't true. After the 17-second application of approximately 1,500 volts, administered by electrodes in the chair's headgear and back, witnesses, including 14 physicians, two of them designated officials, declared Kemmler dead, and the machine was turned off. But after another half-minute, Kemmler's chest showed slight spasms, and the horrified authorities reapplied the current for 70 seconds more. As a result, the chair began to smoke, and the subsequent autopsy showed some burning "and desiccation" of tissue "like overdone beef." Reporters had been barred from attending the event, but newspaper accounts characterized the chair's trial as a grisly disaster.

In his report to the governor, official physician Carlos F. MacDonald disputed the press descriptions. Though admitting "certain defects of a minor character," he called the experiment a success. He pointed out that even if Kemmler's death had not been instantaneous, he had certainly been rendered unconscious quickly, and his death was therefore painless. MacDonald even mentioned Eadweard Muybridge's recent experiments with motion-study photography as a proof that the human brain's ability to sense pain is far slower than the power of electricity to stun. He referred to a series of photographs in which a bucket of ice-water is shown streaming down an unsuspecting woman's back before subsequent pictures show her more or less gradually reacting. MacDonald did have several technical and administrative recommendations for improving future executions, however, and suggested that, next time, all equipment should be independently built for the purpose to "cause no injustice to any electrical lighting company."

Further reading: MacDonald, Carlos F., M.D., *Report on the Execution by Electricity of William Kemmler, Alias John Hart* (Albany, N.Y.: Argus Company, 1890).

Kendall, Amos (1789–1869)   U.S. postmaster general from 1835 to 1840; established the first federal police force within the executive branch of the federal government: the Office of Inspection.

A journalist by trade, Amos Kendall was a strong supporter of Andrew Jackson, helping him to victory over Henry Clay. Old Hickory rewarded Kendall's service in 1835 with an appointment as postmaster general and asked him to reform what was then a fledgling agency. By the next year, Kendall's reforms had eliminated the agency's staggering debt and had established an efficient administrative policy.

Kendall also moved vigorously to fight the variety of criminals who used the nation's mails to swindle the gullible with an array of phony schemes and contests—especially lotteries—and others who used the mail to traffic in pornography. In addition, postal facilities were plagued by theft, highway robbery, pilfering, and internal corruption. In 1836, Congress enacted legislation reorganizing the Post Office and authorized the postmaster general to hire full-time special agents. Kendall used the new law to organize the special agent force into an Office of Inspection, which became the first executive-controlled formal police force in the federal government. Kendall returned to journalism in 1840 where he remained a prominent voice in American politics.

Further reading: Kendall, Amos, *The Autobiography of Amos Kendall* (Boston: Lee and Shepard, 1872).

Kendrick, W. Freeland (1874–1953)

A reform mayor of Philadelphia who did not have the administrative wherewithal to carry out his reforms.

A self-made man, Freeland Kendrick attended public school through the elementary grades before going to work in the steam laundry business. By 1910, he owned his own company, distributing mineral water. A moderately successful businessman, Kendrick made a much greater name for himself as a member of various Masonic orders. By 1918, he had been named Imperial Potentate of the national Shriners organization and worked diligently with the Shriners in originating the idea for the Shriners Hospitals for Crippled Children, which now help hundreds of thousands of children every year, free of charge.

His reputation with the Shriners and his experience as Philadelphia receiver of taxes for 12 years made him an apt dark-horse candidate for the mayoralty race. With the help of Republican political boss Edwin Vare, Kendrick was able to win the 1923 Philadelphia election on a reform platform. Kendrick's first attempt at reform was directed against the city's notoriously corrupt police department. He appointed a former Marine Corps general, Smedley D. BUTLER, as director of public safety. The appointment looked promising, but proved disastrous. Butler's Prohibitionist zealotry and military tactics became an embarrassment to the

mayor, who was forced to ask for the general's resignation after less than a year.

Kendrick quickly saw that he lacked the vision and tenacity to be a successful reform politician, and he stepped down after the 1928 election, returning to business.

Kennedy, Robert Francis (1925–68)

Attorney general in his brother John's administration, Kennedy took on organized crime with a vengeance unprecedented in the Justice Department.

A member of America's "royal family," Robert Kennedy was born November 20, 1925, the third of Joseph P. Kennedy's four fated sons. Graduating from Harvard in 1948, Kennedy moved on to law school at the University of Virginia, earning his law degree in 1951. Right out of law school, Kennedy became an attorney in the criminal division of the Justice Department. When his brother John decided to run for the U.S. Senate in 1952, Robert resigned from the Justice Department to run his brother's campaign. After the election, Robert returned to Washington to serve on several influential Senate committee staffs (including the legal staff serving Senator Joseph McCarthy and the House Un-American Activities Committee), and in 1957 he was named chief counsel to the Select Committee on Improper Activities in the Labor or Management Field. It was here that he first locked horns with Mob-connected Teamster union leader Jimmy Hoffa.

Many have called the Kennedy-Hoffa clash a "blood feud" far more intense than the relation of "cop" to "criminal." Kennedy went after Hoffa with such zeal that his campaign assumed the proportions of a personal vendetta. Hoffa was the president of the International Brotherhood of Teamsters. Initially, Kennedy and his committee were unable to tie anything to Hoffa, but that only strengthened his resolve to nail him. When JFK ran for president, Robert again ran his campaign. When JFK was elected president, he named his brother attorney general.

As head of the Justice Department, Robert Kennedy again went after Hoffa, setting up the labor and racketeering subdivision of the Organized Crime Section—known to Justice staffers as the "Get Hoffa Squad." Eventually, Hoffa was indicted for extorting money from teamsters, and when that trial resulted in a hung jury, he was indicted for bribing one of the jurors. On this charge he was convicted and subsequently convicted again for embezzling funds from the Teamster Pension Fund.

Hoffa was by no means Kennedy's only target. After disposing of the labor leader, he turned his attention against the Mafia itself. Only once in the entire history of the FBI under J. Edgar HOOVER did the nation's top federal law enforcement agency admit to the existence of the Mafia, and that was in a report that was recalled, destroyed, and denied within 24 hours of its release. For Kennedy to wage war against the Mob, he would need Hoover's resources. Officially, as head of the Justice Department, Kennedy was Hoover's superior. But functionally, the FBI director recognized no higher authority in law enforcement than himself. It was a difficult and delicate task to secure Hoover's cooperation, which, at length, was grudgingly forthcoming. However, to the day he died, Hoover denied the existence of the Italian Mafia.

In sharp contrast to Hoover, Kennedy believed that organized crime, embodied principally in the Mafia, was a cancer growing on society, and he felt justified using any means to bring it down. First of all, Kennedy had to bring together all 27 federal agencies involved in the war against organized crime, from the Coast Guard to the Federal Communications Commission. This had never been done before and was a signal achievement of Kennedy's term as attorney general. Under RFK, federal prosecution of organized crime increased from 19 cases in 1960 to 687 in 1964.

Robert Kennedy's relentlessness was felt through all levels of federal law enforcement, and many federal agents said they had never worked under a more dedicated top-ranking official. He frequently went into the field and was well briefed on the minutiae of cases, discussing the smallest details with the frontline officers. His attitude created a high level of morale, which in turn helped achieve the incredible success of Kennedy's campaign against organized crime.

More controversially, Kennedy was not above using illegal methods to win. He frequently authorized the use of illegal wiretapping of known Syndicate members, not for evidentiary purposes, which he knew would be inadmissible in court, but simply for surveillance and intelligence. Even his supporters admitted to outlandish harassment of known Syndicate members. One of his associates compared his zealotry against organized crime to the conduct of the Spanish Inquisition.

While Kennedy's record was impressive, following his brother's assassination on November 23, 1963, he never again personally met with his Organized Crime Section. Some who were with him on that day say that Bobby Kennedy's passion and fire died with his brother. More accurately, after the assassination, Kennedy directed his energies toward furthering the civil rights movement then building to a crescendo. He stayed on as attorney general under Lyndon Johnson until 1964, when he resigned to run for the Senate, representing New York. As a liberal senator, he continued to work for equal justice for minorities and made several trips to the rural Deep South and the

West, exposing the plight of African Americans and migrant farm workers. He inherited his brother's voting base of youth, the underprivileged, and minorities, and it was with this support that he decided to run for president in 1968. On June 6, 1968, while exiting the Ambassador Hotel in Los Angeles after speaking to supporters following his California primary victory, Robert F. Kennedy fell, like his brother, to an assassin's bullet.

Further reading: Navasky, Victor S., *Kennedy Justice* (New York: Atheneum, 1971).

Newfield, Jack, *Robert Kennedy: A Memoir* (New York: New American Library, 1988).

Kennedy, Stephen P(atrick) (1906–78) One of New York city's most popular police commissioners; resigned in 1961 over the issue of higher pay for his men.

Stephen P. Kennedy was born and raised in Brooklyn, dropped out of high school, and worked as a longshoreman and salesman—and was also an amateur boxer—before joining the police force at the age of 22. By age 36, he had made captain, and then studied in night school for 10 years to earn his law degree from New York University. During this time, he advanced to inspector and headed the department's elite Waterfront Squad. In 1954, he was advanced over 21 chiefs and deputy chiefs, who outranked him, to become chief inspector. The next year, he became police commissioner.

Kennedy quickly earned a reputation, with the public as well as the men and women he commanded, as a leader of great integrity. This was put to the test in 1961, when, in a showdown with Mayor Robert F. Wagner, he stepped down as commissioner rather than give up his demand for better pay for his officers. The issue was a $600 pay differential between police and fire personnel; firefighters were permitted to hold second jobs, while police officers were not. Ironically, the ban on moonlighting had been instituted by Kennedy himself, who believed that cops could not afford outside loyalties.

Kersta, Lawrence George (1907–) Audio engineer who developed voiceprinting technology, a new addition to the forensic arsenal.

Born in Roselle Park, New Jersey, on December 22, 1907, and trained in physics and electrical engineering at Columbia University, Kersta, working as a Bell Laboratories scientist during the early 1960s, developed "voiceprint" technology. He was approached by law enforcement officials eager to evaluate voiceprinting as a potential tool for criminal identification. The resulting experiments yielded an astounding 99% rate of success in identifying the speaker through the use of audio spectrograph technology. Convinced of the commercial possibilities of his own device, Kersta left Bell Labs in 1966 and formed his own company, Voiceprint Laboratories.

Voiceprints are based on a key assumption analogous to that forming the basis of fingerprinting. A voiceprint, like a fingerprint, is characteristic of and entirely unique to the individual. Even attempts to disguise one's voice or to imitate that of another will not alter the essential voiceprint pattern.

As was once the case with fingerprinting (see FAULDS, Henry), voiceprinting has been slow to achieve acceptance in law enforcement and legal circles and even within the scientific community. However, voiceprints have been used to identify anonymous telephone voices and have been successfully introduced as evidence in courtrooms. The forensic future of the technology seems assured.

Killinger, George Glenn (1908–) Earned renown as one of the nation's foremost educators in the field of correctional administration.

Born on March 13, 1908, in Marion, Virginia, Killinger earned an A.B. from Wittenberg College (now University) in 1930 and a Ph.D. from the University of North Carolina in 1933, specializing in clinical psychology and neural anatomy. He first became involved with the United States criminal justice system in 1937, when he served as a U.S. Public Health Service clinical psychologist at the federal reformatory in Chillicothe, Ohio. In 1938, he became director of education and assistant associate warden (in charge of individualized treatment) at the U.S. penitentiary in Atlanta, Georgia. In 1943, he returned to the U.S. Public Health Service to aid in the war effort, then became chairman of the Army Clemency and Parole Board during 1946–48. Following this, from 1948 to 1958, he was chairman of the United States Board of Parole, continuing to serve as a member from 1958 to 1960, when he joined the faculty of Florida State University, Tallahassee, as professor of criminology and corrections. This was followed in 1965 by an appointment at Sam Houston State University, Huntsville, Texas, where Killinger was director of the Institute of Contemporary Corrections and the Behavioral Sciences from 1965 to 1977; in 1968, he was named Piper Distinguished Professor. In 1977, he was appointed chairman of the Texas Board of Pardons and Paroles.

Killinger wrote a wide variety of books on approaches to corrections, including *Penology: The Evolution of the American Correctional System* (1973), *Corrections in the Community* (1974), *Issues in Law Enforcement* (1975), *Probation and Parole* (1976), and *Introduction to Juvenile Delinquency* (1977).

Further reading: Killinger, George Glenn, and Paul F. Cromwell Jr., *Corrections in the Community: Alternatives to Imprisonment* (St. Paul, Minn.: West Publishing Co., 1974).

Kirk, Paul Leland (1902–70)   One of the leading criminologists in the United States after World War II; pioneered the process of the scientific analysis of physical evidence.

The son of a newspaper editor and publisher, Paul Kirk was born in Colorado Springs, Colorado, on May 9, 1902. After attending local public schools, Kirk went east to Virginia to attend Randolph-Macon Academy, then attended Ohio State University, graduating in 1924. Kirk continued his schooling, earning his masters degree from the University of Pittsburgh in 1925 and his Ph.D. in biochemistry from the University of California in 1927.

As a doctoral candidate, Kirk was a teaching assistant and then later a research fellow, working his way up the academic ladder until he was named a full professor of biochemistry in 1945. In the meantime, one of Kirk's first students, who had taken Kirk's first laboratory courses on microanalysis, was hired by the state of California to establish the first statewide scientific crime lab in the United States. When his old student came looking for a technical adviser, Kirk offered his own services in 1937.

During World War II, Kirk worked on the Manhattan Project, which developed the first atomic bomb. After the war, he returned to his work in criminalistics, opened his own consulting firm, and was recognized as one of the leading criminologists in the state until his death. After working closely with the Berkeley chief of police, Kirk helped establish the School of Criminology in 1950 at the University of California, Berkeley.

Kirk's reputation was such that the police chief of Chicago hired him to restructure completely that city's crime lab. In the meantime, as the adviser to the state of California's crime lab and one of the field's leading consultants, Kirk was frequently called to testify as an expert witness. In the sensational trial of Dr. Samuel H. Sheppard on charges of having murdered his wife, Kirk testified that, based on entry wounds, the killer was left-handed, whereas Sheppard was right-handed. The doctor was convicted; but, based in part on Kirk's testimony, the conviction was overturned 12 years later. In another celebrated case, Kirk was able to identify an ex-convict through expert handwriting analysis.

Kirk developed a comprehensive but highly portable microchemical crime laboratory, which became standard equipment for many police departments. His many books include *Density and Refractive Index: Their Applications in Criminal Identification* (1951), *Crime In-*

vestigation: Physical Evidence and Police Laboratory Inter-science (1953), *Fire Investigation* (1969), and, with Lowell W. Bradford, *The Crime Laboratory* (1965). Throughout his varied career, Kirk continued to serve as professor of criminalistics until his retirement in 1967.

Koehler, Arthur (1885–1967)   This "wood detective" traced wood samples from the ladder used in the Lindbergh baby kidnapping to suspect Bruno Richard HAUPTMANN.

As chief wood inspector for the U.S. Forest Service, Arthur Koehler had earned a formidable reputation among law enforcement officials in the Midwest, who frequently called on him to analyze particular samples of wood products associated with crime scenes. Koehler became known to virtually the rest of the world in 1935 when he served as the key witness for the prosecution in the trial of Lindbergh baby kidnapper Bruno Richard Hauptmann. Over the course of 18 months, Koehler traced the origin of lumber used to make the homemade ladder found propped against the baby's bedroom window. Koehler traced the lumber across three states and queried more than 1,500 mills until he learned that the wood had been shipped to National Millwork and Lumber Company of the Bronx, New York—the very firm that employed Hauptmann. Even more damaging evidence emerged when Koehler was able to identify one of the steps on the ladder as a piece of wood from Hauptmann's attic.

Koehler's testimony sealed the fate of Hauptmann, who was convicted and executed for kidnapping and murdering the Lindbergh boy. Over the years, the Lindbergh trial has been subjected to much review, both official and unofficial, particularly by those who believe in the innocence of Hauptmann. However, no investigator has ever been able to impugn the testimony and conclusions of Arthur Koehler.

Kohler, Fred (1869–1933)   A reform chief of the Cleveland (Ohio) Police Department whom Theodore ROOSEVELT called the best chief in the country.

Kohler was a tough street cop in Cleveland who was tapped by reform mayor Tom Johnson in 1903 to serve as chief of the corrupt and scandal-ridden police department. Kohler focused his department on apprehending serious offenders. With regard to minor criminals, he applied what he called the Golden Rule ("Do unto others . . ."), releasing them without charge. This controversial approach earned Kohler a national reputation—some saw it as anarchic and whimsical, while others saw it as an efficient means of concentrating police and judicial efforts against truly dangerous criminals—and it also earned him the sobriquet of "Golden Rule" Kohler.

Within the department he ran, Kohler created considerable dissension, since he represented an anti-Irish clique. However, he had the support and acclaim of many prominent citizens and national figures, especially Theodore Roosevelt, who had been New York's reform-minded police commissioner long before he became president of the United States. Roosevelt praised Kohler as the best chief in the country.

Kohler's reputation, as well as his civil service rating, kept him in office even after the mayor who had appointed him was defeated. In 1912, however, he delivered a speech before the International Association of Chiefs of Police (IACP), decrying the failures of the correctional system. The chief's many critics, ever vigilant, discovered that the speech had been wholly plagiarized, and Kohler was publicly embarrassed. When he was caught in an extramarital affair the following year, he was dismissed (ironically enough) by another reform mayor, Newton D. Baker (who later became President Woodrow Wilson's secretary of war).

Kohler hardly dropped out of public life. He was popular enough to be elected mayor of Cleveland in 1921, serving until 1923, after which he became sheriff. After his death in 1933, investigators discovered over a half-million dollars in a safe deposit box registered to Kohler—presumably the proceeds of graft.

Kraepelin, Emil (1856–1926)   German physician and educator who has been called the "father of modern psychiatry."

Emil Kraepelin dedicated himself to the study and classification of clinical psychiatric disorder syndromes. He introduced much of the clinical terminology that is still generally in use, including manic depressive psychosis, paranoia, and catatonia.

Kraepelin devoted much of his early career to forensic psychiatry, and his methods of research endure today as one of his most significant contributions to the field. Kraepelin held numerous professorships in Germany, including at the universities of Tartu (1890–1904), Heidelberg (1904–26), and Munich. The latter appointment resulted in a celebrated series of *Lectures on Clinical Psychiatry* in 1904. The lecture "Morbid Personalities" developed his system for the investigation and classification of criminal disorders.

The so-called Kraepelinian School continues to influence forensic psychiatry, particularly in the United States.

Further reading: Kraepelin, Emil, *Emil Kraepelin, Memoirs* (Berlin: Springer-Verlag, 1987).

Kretschmer, Ernst (1888–1964)   German psychiatrist who developed the "constitutional theory," relating physique to patterns of behavior, including criminal behavior.

Ernst Kretschmer was a biopsychological theorist whose tremendously popular *Körperbau und Charakter (Physique and Character)*, first published in 1921 and reaching 26 editions by 1955, postulated a direct link between a person's physique and his behavior, especially as behavior is manifested in two different types of mental disorder: manic depressive psychosis and schizophrenia. Kretschmer based his conclusions on a study of 260 psychotic patients.

Criminal behavior, Kretschmer concluded, corresponds to four basic physical types. The asthenic (thin) type is most likely to perpetrate petty thefts. The athletic (tall and muscular) type is most likely to commit violent crimes. Pyknics (short and fat) tend to engage in deceptive crime. Finally, dysplastic individuals, who combine the traits of the other three physical types, are most likely to commit offenses against morality.

Kretschmer's theory gained wide acceptance for a time, with profound consequences for the diagnosis of mental illness—and, by extension, for the scientific identification of criminal "types"—since, for those practitioners who accepted his theory, physical appearance came to assume as prominent a role in classifying mental disorder as did a patient's emotional state and purely behavioral symptoms. With modification, the constitutional theory still retains a degree of influence in psychiatry, and whatever the theory's specific shortcomings, Kretschmer himself was responsible for helping to establish psychiatry as a permanent and legitimate medical specialty.

Krogman, Wilton (Marion) (1903–78) One of the first criminal anthropologists in the United States; pioneered the forensic study of skeletal bones as a means of victim identification.

During the 1940s and 1950s, Wilton Krogman emerged as a leader in the emerging field of criminal anthropology. Krogman's ability to identify badly decomposed corpses through his extensive study of skeletal bones and skulls soon became well known in the law enforcement community. The full-time professor of physical anthropology at the University of Pennsylvania Medical School was virtually buried in bones shipped to him by police agencies from around the world. Using the methods of physical anthropology, Krogman was often able to reconstruct the corpse, determine its sex, and even speculate as to the cause of death.

Krogman's discoveries opened new avenues in the field of criminal investigation and fostered the growth of the field of criminal anthropology.

L

Lacassagne, Jean Alexandre Eugène (1844–1921)
An early and important authority on many aspects of forensic detection; made a pivotal discovery that effectively launched the development of modern ballistics.

Born at Cahors, France, Lacassagne studied at the Military Academy in Strasbourg and then earned his credentials as a military surgeon. While serving as an army surgeon in North Africa, he gained an intimate knowledge of gunshot wounds, and he began to devote himself to the promising young science of forensic investigation. His advocacy of criminal identification research and record keeping—for example, in his lengthy essay on the value of tattoos in criminal investigation—anticipated the later work of BERTILLON. Lacassagne's treatise *Précis de medecine* (*Medical Abstract*, 1878) earned him a newly created chair in the department of forensic medicine at the University of Lyons.

Two of Lacassagne's most often quoted sayings were "One must know how to doubt" and "A bungled autopsy cannot be revised." Before rubber gloves or refrigeration techniques had begun to improve the unenviable working conditions of the forensic pathologist, Lacassagne's meticulous investigations of the human corpse resulted in many useful discoveries: the initial cooling rate of body temperature after death, the onset pattern of rigor mortis, causes and interpretations of post-circulatory blotching, and other revealing clues to be found in even thoroughly decayed flesh or skeletal bone. Lacassagne was also the first to explore the correlation between crime-scene bloodstain configurations and the particulars of their originating assault.

But it was in 1889 that he made his most catalytic contribution to criminological history. Examining the furrows on the surface of a murder bullet, he proposed that the marks could be matched to the gun from which it had been fired. Indeed, his hypothesis was accepted as legal proof when he identified a bullet's seven etched marks as corresponding to the seven-grooved rifling in the barrel of a suspect's weapon. Later, GRAVELLE's invention of the comparison microscope permitted far more sophisticated investigation of such evidence of ballistic "fingerprinting," but it was Lacassagne who first proposed the technique.

Another landmark in the scientist's career was his preparation of an in-depth psychological study of the so-called "French Ripper," in 1898. Joseph Vacher had used an insanity defense in his trial for the gruesome sex murders of several children, and, at the court's request, Lacassagne spent five months studying the mentality of the accused. When the esteemed criminologist reported that Vacher's purported madness was only a pretense, the "Ripper" was sent to the guillotine.

Lafarge, Marie (born Fortunée Capelle) (1816–1852)   On January 25, 1840, an elegant, somewhat literary Frenchwoman named Marie Lafarge was arrested. The charge—poisoning her husband with arsenic. Her murder trial stirred an emotional nationwide controversy, and her conviction made history as the first major case to hinge on a toxicologist's report.

Born in 1816 in Picardy, Marie Fortunée Capelle was the daughter of a baroness and a colonel who had been a favored member of Napoleon's Old Guard. Marie's maternal grandmother was believed to be the illegitimate offspring of the duke of Orleans—the king's father, Philippe Egalité—and his mistress, Madame de Genlis. This noble—yet ignoble—lineage placed the young Mademoiselle Capelle on the shadowy margins of the French aristocracy. Expensively schooled, trained in the social graces, and accustomed to the comforts of the upper classes, Capelle was nevertheless constrained from true membership in the haute monde, and her prospects for a brilliant marriage were dimmed by the lingering tarnish of her illegitimate forebears.

Orphaned as a teenager, Marie made the rounds of various well-to-do relatives, writing several essays that were published in the Paris press and attracting the attention of author Alexander Dumas, with whom she began to correspond. When she reached the age of 24, her aunt, Madame de Garat, registered her with a Paris matrimonial agency. This application, which Marie abhorred as beneath her, produced the suitor Charles Joseph Pouch Lafarge. Supposedly the rich owner of a prosperous ironworks in the south of France, Lafarge looked good enough on paper; indeed, the agency's references included beautiful drawings of his enormous, palatial estate, a former monastery in the Gothic style.

These persuaded Marie to consider the match, but when she met Lafarge, his poor education and thoroughly oafish manner revolted her. Still, her aunt's wishes prevailed, and the two were married within two weeks of their introduction. Marie's dismay with her groom's bad manners, displayed throughout their journey south, turned to horror upon their arrival at the dilapidated mansion—Gothic, yes, but a virtual ruin—at Le Glandier.

The new bride locked herself in a room and composed a letter to her husband, begging him to free her from the marriage, assuring him that he could keep her $20,000 dowry, and promising that she would take upon herself all the disgrace for the failed union. She declared that she had another lover, who had secretly followed the newlyweds to Correze province, and she further claimed to have arsenic in her possession, with which she would kill herself if Lafarge refused her abject plea for an annulment.

But Lafarge's mother, another inmate of Le Glandier, interceded with Marie and ferreted out the truth: There was no lover, and there was no arsenic. At his mother's prompting, Lafarge improved his etiquette somewhat, and he mollified Marie with (mostly empty) promises to renovate the broken-down estate. Soon, Marie was writing letters to her aunt, pretending happiness with her lot and characterizing herself as a grateful bride and a grande dame deeply admired by local society.

But now Marie did obtain a quantity of very real arsenic from the local pharmacist, explaining that she needed it to exterminate the scores of rats who scampered freely throughout the manor house.

In fact, her husband's forge was nearly bankrupt, and Lafarge had applied to the matrimonial agency only in order to catch a rich wife who could bail him out. In December 1839, as he prepared for a business trip to Paris—bringing Marie's warm letters of intro-

duction and supplication to her wealthiest acquaintances, from whom he planned to borrow additional funds—Marie persuaded Lafarge to join her in making out their wills, leaving everything to each other in the event of death. He tricked her, however, and wrote another will, naming his mother as sole beneficiary.

After her husband had left, Marie continued to feign matrimonial tenderness and asked her mother-in-law to bake some of Charles's favorite cakes to send to him in Paris. When he received the package on December 18, however, there was one large cake, rather than six small ones, in the box. Lafarge ate a piece and was violently ill within hours. Still seriously ailing, he returned to Le Glandier on January 3, 1840, the same day that Marie bought an even larger quantity of arsenic from the druggist. Impressed by his wife's loving concern and seemingly limitless devotion, Lafarge insisted that she be his only nurse.

His condition worsened, and his mother and other household members began to get suspicious.

Spying on Marie at her husband's bedside, the in-laws even caught her adulterating Lafarge's food with a white powder, but she claimed this was only orange-blossom sugar to settle his stomach. Surprised by his relatives on another occasion, Marie herself drank a glass of water she had dosed with the powder. Lafarge's family reported their misgivings to the iron-master's doctors (and began to collect his leftovers for examination), but by the time one of his physicians confirmed that the symptoms might indeed be those of poisoning, Charles was too far gone.

He died on January 14. Lafarge's mother called the local police, who came the next day. Within a fortnight, Marie was arrested, charged with murder, and taken to jail in Brive. Marie protested her innocence, and her aunt hired the best attorney in Paris to represent her.

As word of the scandal spread, Marie's childhood friend Madame de Léautaud came forward and accused Marie of having stolen a diamond necklace while visiting at her home some months before the marriage to Lafarge. Although police had suspected Marie during their first investigation of the jewels' disappearance, at the time, de Léautaud's family had defended Marie's honor and had prohibited any further inquiry. Now, Marie's possessions at Le Glandier were searched, and the necklace was indeed found among them. She was tried, in absentia, and convicted for the theft; her sentence was two years in prison. There she awaited her next appointment with the law. Meanwhile, throughout France, the plight of this fallen noblewoman prompted impassioned debate about her guilt or innocence, and legions of supporters clamored to her defense. At Montpellier prison, Marie received 6,000 letters of support, as well as numerous marriage proposals and gifts of money, perfume, gourmet delicacies, and wine. Many citizens saw Marie as a wronged woman, even a political martyr—a gentlewoman framed in a revolutionary, anti-royalist conspiracy.

The murder trial began in late 1840 and lasted 17 days. The first group of chemists to examine the physical evidence, which had been less than perfectly handled by local doctors and police, could find no arsenic in Lafarge's bodily remains, nor in the leftover soups and puddings his family had submitted to the authorities. But when the esteemed toxicologist Dr. Mathieu ORFILA was called in from Paris, he ordered that Lafarge be exhumed and new tissue samples taken and carefully prepared for testing with James MARSH's highly sensitive arsenic detection technique. Orfila's more expert—and more accurately controlled—handling of the Marsh test produced sensational results: He confirmed the poison's presence in the ramains as well as in all contested materials. Even the throngs of "Lafargists" gathered outside the courthouse were silenced by this news.

Marie was found guilty and sentenced to exposure in the Tulle pillory, followed by a life term at hard labor. Her top-flight lawyers' requests for appeal were denied, but because of her tenuous royal lineage, King Louis Philippe reduced her sentence to life imprisonment only.

In jail at Montpellier, Marie wrote her memoirs, penned a tragedy titled *The Lost Woman*, and corresponded with former supporters and defense attorneys (one of whom, long and deeply enchanted, proposed marriage) and her longtime pen pal Dumas. A decade passed, and she became ill with tuberculosis; in 1852 Napoleon III granted her request for release from prison, and she sought recuperation at a spa in the Pyrenees. She died within six months, having never confessed to the crime that had brought her fame.

Landesco, John (1890–1954) One of the first to study organized crime as a social condition rather than simply as isolated criminal behavior.

As both a student and a professor at the University of Chicago, John Landesco became a member of the Chicago School of Sociology, a center of American sociological, penological, and criminological thought throughout the first half of the 20th century. Landesco looked to the neighborhoods of Chicago itself for the subjects of his study, focusing on the sociology of Prohibition and the beer wars of Chicago's tough South Side.

Few American law enforcement officials looked on organized crime as anything more than ethnically based violence. Landesco argued that its social roots ran deep into prevailing social and political structures. Simply arresting and convicting the current offenders,

Landesco argued, only served to make room for more to take their place. What caused organized crime was not the people who practiced it, but a social system that reinforced and rewarded it, a system consisting of everyone from local merchants to local politicians to the local police chief. Landesco pointed out that organized crime was not strictly a criminal endeavor, unrelated to other things. Quite the contrary, it became extensively involved in the life of neighborhoods by "defending" locals against outsiders and by employing—albeit illegally—hundreds of people. Organized crime became involved in elections, either by committing its significant resources to a particular candidate or by simply helping to commit election fraud. Most of all, it became involved in the legal system itself, paying off judges and police officers. Using Chicago as an example, Landesco demonstrated that organized crime is as much a social institution as the police and law courts created to fight it.

Landsteiner, Karl (1868–1943) A Nobel Prize winner who identified the four blood groups—a major contribution to medicine that also created a whole new method of crime detection and investigation.

Growing up in Vienna, Austria, Karl Landsteiner earned only average grades in school but was able to gain admittance to the University of Vienna, where he studied medicine. Earning his degree in 1891, he worked in immunology and serology, quickly becoming one of the leading figures in these fields. In 1901, he made his landmark discovery of the four basic blood groups, each incompatible with the other three. This immediately saved thousands of lives by making blood transfusion a safe and effective procedure. It also provided criminal investigators with a method of typing blood samples in order to help determine the identity of criminals as well as crime victims.

Landsteiner went on to establish the viral nature of poliomyelitis, then left Vienna following World War I. After living for a short time during 1919 in the Netherlands, he immigrated to the United States. In New York, Landsteiner continued his work with blood, and, collaborating with Dr. Alexander Wiener, discovered the presence of the Rh factor in human blood, further enhancing the safety of blood transfusion and, incidentally, making blood an even more unique and reliable form of identification in criminal investigations.

For his work on blood typing, Landsteiner received the Nobel Prize in 1930.

Lange, Johannes (1891–1938) This criminologist's controversial *Crime As Destiny*, published in 1931, studied the case histories of criminal twins in order to explore the role of heredity in crime.

In 1929, Dr. Johannes Lange, physician-in-chief at the Munich-Scwabing Hospital and departmental director of the German Experimental Station for Psychiatry at the Kaiser Wilhelm Institute in Munich, studied 13 pairs of twins in which the brother or sister was a criminal. In 10 out of the 13 cases, the other twin was a criminal, too. Lange concluded that a person of a certain constitution, put in a certain environment, will become a criminal—and has no free will in the matter.

Together with Heinrich Kranz, Lange developed a typology of criminal twins, which spelled out what the two believed to be the causes of criminal behavior—genetics and environment, to the virtually complete exclusion of volition. While many believers in "indeterminism" rejected Lange's conclusion, the work of Lange and Kranz stimulated and became the model for additional studies of crime and the criminal twin.

Further reading: Lange, Johannes, *Crime As Destiny: A Study of Criminal Twins,* tr. Charlotte Haldane (London: Allen and Unwin, 1931).

Lansing, Robert (1864–1928) U.S. secretary of state from 1915 to 1920; established the first State Department Bureau of Secret Intelligence in 1916.

An expert in international law, New York lawyer Robert Lansing established the American Society of International Law in 1906 and, the following year, founded the *American Journal of International Law,* of which he served as editor until his death in 1928. Lansing's demonstrated talents brought him to considerable prominence, and, in 1915, President Woodrow Wilson appointed him secretary of state to replace William Jennings Bryan, who had resigned in protest over what he considered the bellicose direction of Wilson's foreign policy.

In contrast to Bryan, and like Wilson, Lansing was willing to prepare for possible American participation in the Great War. One of the steps he took was to create the Bureau of Secret Intelligence in 1916. The agency, headed by a special bureau chief and funded through a secret account, advised the secretary on matters of intelligence and security. The bureau outlasted the war, and by 1921 its staff had grown to 25 men. The agency evolved into the modern State Department Office of Security, which today investigates prospective State Department employees, defends State Department offices and facilities against security breaches, and enjoys a high degree of executive privilege, granting it great investigative latitude in the name of national security.

Lansky, Meyer (1902–83) One of the principal architects of organized crime in the United States.

Meyer Lansky's genius for organization created the basic structure of the national crime syndicate beginning in the 1930s. (Courtesy of the Library of Congress)

Born in Grodno, Poland, on July 2 or 4, 1902, Meyer Lansky (Maier Suchowljansky, alias Morris Lieberman; Meyer Lamansky; Little Meyer; Meyer the Bug; Charlie the Bug; Meyer the Lug) immigrated to the United States with his family, settling on Manhattan's Lower East Side. Unlike so many other gangsters, Lansky was a bright student who avoided the street gangs that were a fixture of tough neighborhoods like his. Then, on October 24, 1918, Lansky was walking home from work, carrying his metal toolbox. Hearing a woman screaming in an abandoned building, he rushed in to discover the woman, naked, with a 14-year-old boy, likewise naked, and another man beating her. She was a prostitute, he was her pimp, and he told her that he would "rip up" her face if she ever took on another non-paying customer. The 14-year-old tried to attack the pimp with a knife but was repeatedly pushed aside. At last, Lansky took a monkey wrench from his toolbox and knocked the pimp down. At that point, the police entered, arrested Lansky and charged him with assault. The case was

LARSEN, HENRY ASBJORN   157

dismissed when the pimp refused to press charges. As Lansky walked out of the court, the pimp introduced himself as Salvatore Lucania—later to become infamous as Charles "Lucky" LUCIANO. The 14-year-old introduced himself, too. He was Benjamin "Bugsy" Siegel. The trio would later become inseparable and, among them, created the nucleus of modern organized crime in America.

First, Lansky and Siegel established a floating crap game, which proved so profitable that Jacob "Little Augie" Orgen made the pair members of his labor racketeering gang, financing their games and giving them protection in return for 35% of the take. After about a year, weary of paying Orgen, Lansky hired his own thugs to protect the crap games; on August 14, 1920, the gang proved its mettle against invading gangsters, badly beating them. This incident drew Luciano's attention, and he invited Siegel and Lansky to participate in a conference about creating a "combination," whereby young racketeers would pool their interests and organize the rackets in New York and, ultimately, the entire nation.

Lansky seized on the idea and developed it into a complex and highly profitable business organization. Essentially, Lansky outlined a scheme whereby profits would be pumped into legitimate as well as illegal activities. Lansky predicted that the old-time gangsters would end up destroying one another in gang wars. The few who survived the wars could be eliminated later.

Luciano, Siegel, and Lansky went into business stealing cars, altering them, and selling them. Lansky used the income from this operation to "grow" his business, hiring a new breed of gangster, professional killers, which he used or hired out—at a price—to other gangs. The idea was not only to make money but also to encourage potential rivals to kill one another. The enterprise came to be called Murder, Inc., a group of contract killers. Lansky's confederates in the creation of Murder, Inc., were Lepke BUCHALTER, who became director of the "company," and Albert ANASTASIA, Lucky Luciano's personal enforcer.

Lansky evolved into a combination corporate tycoon and ruthless dictator, making shrewd business decisions one minute and extracting (on pain of death) absolute subordination and loyalty from his "associates" and "employees." Largely at Lansky's instigation, crime interests set up national relationships at a national crime convention held in Atlantic City, New Jersey, in 1929. All the luminaries were in attendance: Al CAPONE, representing Chicago; Charles "King" Solomon, from Boston; Abner "Longy" Zwillman, New Jersey; Johnny Lazia, Kansas City; and Frank COSTELLO, Joe ADONIS, and Lucky Luciano from New York. Lansky elaborated the hierarchy of the evolving

syndicate, setting up not only a national network but also an international banking system that allowed for the laundering of billions of dollars. His boldest international move came in 1936 when he established a relationship with Cuban dictator Fulgencio Batista, securing a vast gambling franchise in that country in return for cutting Batista in on the profits. Next, Lansky dispatched Siegel to the West Coast to organize syndicate rackets. The end result was the development of Las Vegas, Nevada, as a gambling mecca beginning in the mid-1940s.

In New Orleans, Lansky secured the cooperation of governor and political boss Huey Long to create and distribute slot machines to businesses throughout the city. And Lansky's relationship with the government became even broader during World War II, when he persuaded Luciano to cooperate with the U.S. Navy by providing security along the docks of New York. Lansky also prevailed on his friend and associate to provide the navy with Sicilian contacts who helped the Allies in their invasion of Sicily. This cooperation secured Luciano's parole in 1946.

Lansky was loyal to his friends, but responded without mercy when they failed him. He did nothing to prevent the 1947 execution of Bugsy Siegel when the Mob suspected him of embezzling funds from the Flamingo casino in Las Vegas. "I had no choice," Lansky drily observed.

By the early 1960s, Lansky was organizing gambling operations offshore, in Bolivia and Venezuela, and in Hong Kong and Haiti. Fearing that he was about to be charged with income tax evasion, Lansky fled to Israel in 1970, but that nation soon revoked Lansky's visa, forcing him to return to the United States to face charges. Astoundingly, he managed to avoid conviction—probably by exercising influence at the highest levels of government. His last decade of life was marked by chronic ill health, and he succumbed to a heart attack in 1983. He was 81.

Larsen, Henry Asbjorn (1899–1964) Commanded the largest police beat in the world, stretching from the Yukon to Northern Quebec and covering more than three million square miles.

Born in Fredrikstad, Norway, Henry Larsen was one in a long line of seafaring men in his family. After serving in the Norwegian navy, he began working for the Norwegian merchant marine and trained at the nation's navigation school, where he earned his mate's certificate. After immigrating to North America in the mid 1920s, Larsen joined the Royal Canadian Mounted Police in April 1928, taking command of the *St. Roch,* a police vessel.

After he was promoted to superintendent, Larsen, using the *St. Roch* as his flagship, commanded what was effectively the largest police beat in the world. It extended from the Yukon to Northern Quebec and encompassed more than three million square miles. In 1942, he sailed the *St. Roch* north and west through the Northwest Passage to Halifax, Nova Scotia. After his tour of duty was completed in Halifax, he sailed south past the United States and through the Panama Canal, taking 82 days to reach the coast of Vancouver. In doing so, Larsen became the first man ever to circumnavigate the entire North American continent, earning far more note as a sailor than as a seaborne policeman.

Larson, John A. (1892–1965)

A former police officer, educator, and practicing psychiatrist; invented the polygraph ("lie detector") in 1921.

Working under the direction of August VOLLMER, the University of California, Berkeley's famed professor of criminology and chief of the city of Berkeley's "scientific police department," Dr. John A. Larson, an educator and former cop, developed the first polygraph machine, or "lie detector," in 1921. Larson and his assistant, Leonarde KEELER, moved to Illinois in the 1930s, where they worked for the Department of Criminology at Northwestern University and at the penitentiary in Joliet. Larson, with Keeler and George Harry, wrote the groundbreaking *Lying and Its Detection* in 1932. It was Keeler, however, who perfected the polygraph and its application, while Dr. Larson went on to become a celebrated psychiatrist, who was associated with prominent institutions across the country.

Further reading: Block, Eugene B., *Lie Detctors: Their History and Use* (New York: D. McKay Co., c.1977).

Lattes, Leone (1887–1954)

Developed a simple procedure, still in use today, to determine blood type from dried stains.

After completing his medical studies at the precocious age of 18, the German-born Leone Lattes spent several years in postgraduate study at various German universities, including the University of Munich, where he studied under Max Richter, the noted serologist. As a result of his work with Richter, Lattes became fascinated with agglutinogens, the substances in the body that determine blood type and compatibility with transfused blood.

Lattes made his contribution to forensic science in a rather bizarre fashion. In 1915, a man came to him with a partially stained shirt. He begged for help with a very delicate problem. His wife claimed that he had been cheating on her and was convinced that the blood on the shirt was that of another woman. The beleaguered husband protested that it was his own blood. Lattes first took a blood sample from the man

and then set about typing the dried stain. He cut out the stained part of the shirt and weighed it, then cut out an identically sized unstained piece of shirt cloth and weighed it. He knew that dried blood weighed a fifth as much as whole blood. Accordingly, he added the appropriate amount of water and waited for a solution to form. After several hours, all the blood settled out of the shirt and left a perfect sample, ready for typing. The sample was indeed from the man's own blood, and Lattes not only saved the fellow's marriage, but also established a new and highly valuable method for investigative criminology.

Laurie, Sir Percy (1880–1962)

Assistant commissioner of the Metropolitan Police (London) who transformed the mounted police into an effective specialized force for riot and crowd control.

Sir Percy Laurie was born on November 5, 1880, and was educated at Harrow, afterward joining the Royal Scots Greys in 1902 and becoming adjutant in 1909. He served with great distinction during World War I, receiving many decorations and a brevet promotion to major. After the war, he joined Scotland Yard, becoming assistant commissioner in 1933, in charge of the mounted branch. Laurie demonstrated the effectiveness of a mounted police force in efficiently managing crowds and neutralizing riot situations. The techniques he developed, which involved the disciplined use of dressage to coax crowd compliance, were adopted by police forces worldwide.

Laurie retired in 1936 but became assistant chief constable to the War Department constabulary in London at the outbreak of World War II in 1939. In 1940, he was made provost marshal of the United Kingdom. In 1943, however, Laurie was convicted of fraud in obtaining a food ration book. Although the conviction was overturned on appeal, Laurie resigned as provost marshal.

Lavater, Johann Casper (1741–1801)

The founder of physiognomy, a forerunner of phrenology, developed a controversial theory that claimed to link facial features with criminal and other types of behavior.

A Swiss clergyman, Johann Caspar Lavater was part of an 18th-century backlash against the passion for reason and rationality that dominated the age. He and like-minded theorists sought to reveal the divine nature of human beings by demonstrating the mystical-metaphysical interrelation of mind and body.

Lavater's major work, *Essays on Physiognomy, 1789-1798*, was based on the assumption of a metaphysical relation between the physical and mental-emotional aspects of one's being. The *Essays* include detailed discussions of how a person's appearance reflects his internal disposition. As Lavater put it: "There must be a certain native analogy between the external varieties of the countenance and form, and the internal varieties of the mind."

Lavater's theory has stood neither the test of time nor the triumph of rationality, although a number of later psychologists and psychiatrists have developed theories drawing correlations between physique and psychological, behavioral, and criminal characteristics. Nevertheless, Lavater's work had a significant influence on his age and influenced a generation of young scholars, who would advance these early theories to develop new sciences such as phrenology, psychology, physical anthropology, and criminology in the years to come.

Leary, Howard R. (1912–94)   One of New York's most controversial police commissioners, serving during 1966–70, a period of social turbulence and the exposure of police corruption.

Leary started his career in law enforcement as a foot patrolman on the streets of Philadelphia in 1940, working his way up through the department while earning a law degree in night school. In 1963, he was named commissioner of the Philadelphia Police Department, leaving that post in 1966 to head up the NYPD.

Leary was a progressive commissioner who introduced such key innovations as the 911 police emergency phone number and the city's first computerized dispatch system. Sensitive to the needs of New York's diverse ethnic communities, he instituted programs to recruit more African-American and Puerto Rican officers, and he increased the size of the entire force. However, Leary's department was beset by scandals and other pressures. During his tenure the investigative commission headed by Whitman Knapp uncovered rampant and routine corruption, including intimidation and bribe taking, throughout the New York Police Department. The result was a public outcry against Leary, as well as the mayor who had appointed him, John V. LINDSAY. The commission itself concluded that both officials did bear some responsibility for failing to act promptly against corruption. In addition, New York was rocked by social violence during this period, including racial violence and violence between Vietnam War protestors and police at Columbia University. For their part, the police suffered from low morale and a perception that they were unfairly criticized for performing their duties.

Leary, whose relations with City Hall grew increasingly strained in the course of his tenure, abruptly resigned in 1970, neither citing any reason for the resignation nor providing a formal letter of resigna-

tion. He briefly became an executive with the Abraham & Straus department store company and then with Holmes Protection, a private security agency. In 1972, Leary accepted an appointment as professor of criminal justice at Trenton State College (Trenton, New Jersey), retiring in 1982.

Leguay, Jean (1910–89)   An official of the Vichy government in unoccupied France who was subsequently tried on two counts of crimes against Jews during World War II.

Following the Nazi defeat of France and the establishment of the collaborationist Vichy government in 1940, Jean Leguay was appointed deputy police chief for the Vichy regime and served in that capacity until the Allied liberation of Paris in 1944. Despite his collaborationist ties, he rejoined the French civil service in 1955, then left the public sector to become a top executive in a major cosmetics firm.

Leguay's postwar life took an abrupt turn in 1979, however, when he was charged with having ordered and supervised the roundup of almost 13,000 French Jews, including some 4,000 children, whom he herded into the Paris velodrome during July 1942 for deportation to Nazi death camps. Leguay was arrested and held briefly, during which time he never denied involvement in the deportations, but said what so many others charged with war crimes had said before him: He was following orders.

Leguay was released pending trial on the charges. The trial failed to materialize. However, in 1986, a second set of charges were filed—this time for Leguay's alleged involvement in a second roundup of 444 French Jews in August 1942. The chief prosecutor in the case, Serge Klarsfeld (who had been instrumental in the conviction of former Gestapo leader Klaus Barbie) alleged that Leguay had *personally* persuaded German authorities to include children in the deportations, as well as adults. This case failed to go to trial before Leguay died in 1989 of liver cancer.

Leibowitz, Samuel Simon (1893–1978)   A master of the criminal jury trial and one of the best defense lawyers of his time, winning greater access to the legal system for African Americans and also defending Al CAPONE.

Samuel Leibowitz was born on August 14, 1893, and immigrated with his family to the United States from Jassy, Rumania, at the age of four. After attending New York City public schools, Leibowitz enrolled in Cornell University Law School, graduating in civil law in 1916 and passing the New York state bar in 1917. Fascinated by criminal law, Leibowitz took a clerk's position in a civil law firm, but spent his spare time studying criminal cases. He began offering his services free of charge to penniless criminal defendants and quickly earned a reputation as a scrupulously well-prepared defense attorney.

Leibowitz believed that the secret of criminal defense lay in jury selection. Few defendants could afford to pay their lawyers for the time necessary to research and select a jury that would be sympathetic to the defense, whereas the prosecution, with all the resources of the state, could afford to do so at will. The clients Leibowitz eventually attracted, however, could afford to invest in jury selection.

Leibowitz's reputation soared when he took on Al Capone as a client in the mid-1920s, successfully defending him four times, and then defending many of his "associates" as well, including Benjamin "Bugsy" Siegel, Vincent "Mad Dog" COLL, and "Pittsburgh" Phil Strauss. His reputation made him the first choice of Lucky LUCIANO, seven members of the infamous Murder, Inc., gang, and Bruno Richard HAUPTMANN, the accused kidnapper-killer of the Lindbergh baby. Leibowitz declined to take on any of these men as clients, and all were convicted, including Hauptmann, who was subsequently executed. Of the 140 capital punishment cases Leibowitz did defend, only one client went to the electric chair.

While Capone was Leibowitz's most celebrated client, the attorney's most momentous case was that of the "Scottsboro Boys," a group of nine black men from Scottsboro, Alabama, charged with raping two white women in 1931. Originally, all were convicted and eight sentenced to death. The International Labor Defense, a communist-backed labor organization, provided an attorney who appealed the convictions to the Supreme Court and secured a new trial on the grounds that the defendants had not been afforded adequate legal counsel. The second trial resulted in another set of convictions.

At this point, Leibowitz traveled to Alabama to carry out new appeals—pro bono—for all nine men. Failing with the Alabama courts, he took the case once again to the Supreme Court, this time arguing that African Americans could not receive a fair trial in the South because they were denied the right to serve on juries. The Supreme Court agreed and ordered another retrial, forcing Southern governors to open jury selection to African Americans. In response, the state dropped charges against four of the defendants and retried five, handing down convictions but not imposing the death sentence. All were eventually paroled.

In 1940, Leibowitz was elected to the bench of Kings County Court in Brooklyn, the highest criminal court in New York state. There, he took on the legal corruption rampant in Brooklyn, especially on the police force. Leibowitz retired from the bench in 1970.

Lejins, Peter P. (1909–) Earned international acclaim as an expert in criminology.

Peter Lejins was born on January 20, 1909, in Moscow, Russia, and came to the United States to study at the University of Chicago as a Rockefeller fellow in the 1930s. He was naturalized as a U.S. citizen in 1940. He earned his Ph.D. in sociology from the University of Chicago in 1938, having earlier earned degrees in philosophy and law from the University of Latvia, in Riga, Latvia. He had also undertaken postgraduate study at the University of Paris.

In 1941, Lejins joined the sociology department of the University of Maryland and subsequently became director of the Division of Criminology within the department. From 1969 to 1979, he was director of the Institute of Criminal Justice and Criminology at the university.

Lejins served as a member of the U.S. delegations to the International Congresses on the Prevention of Crime and the Treatment of Offenders, which were held at The Hague in 1950, Rome in 1955, London in 1960, and Stockholm in 1965. President Lyndon B. JOHNSON appointed him to a six-year term as U.S. correspondent to the United Nations in the area of social defense. In addition, Lejins served on many important councils, boards, and committees in the area of criminology, criminal justice, and corrections and was a consultant to federal and state governments. He served as the chief editor of the *Journal of Research in Crime and Delinquency* for 1968 and contributed many articles, reports, and book chapters in the area of criminology and corrections.

Lenin, Vladimir Ilyich (1870–1924) The founder of the Russian Communist Party and the leader of the Bolshevik Revolution of 1917, Lenin consolidated his rule as the first head of the Soviet state through ruthless oppression by a force of secret police.

A product of a liberal middle-class upbringing, Vladimir Lenin, whose original name was Vladimir Ulyanov, grew up with a fierce compassion for his country and its people. When his older brother was executed for treason in 1887, Lenin, already a political liberal, took the road of revolution. He read radical philosophers such as Karl Marx and Friedrich Engels and finished his education at the University of Kazan, where his radicalism took root in the politically fertile soil of the university. His activism caused his expulsion, but, undaunted, Lenin enrolled in the University of St. Petersburg and earned a law degree.

Lenin practiced law for only a short time following his graduation in 1891 before devoting his attention full-time to revolutionary activity. He revised Marxist theory, later called Leninism, to raise the political consciousness of the urban proletariat, on whom (he believed) the success of any revolution depended. After being exiled in 1895 for his activities, he left Russia in 1900. While abroad, Lenin wrote copiously, defining his views of the capitalist exploitation of labor and calling for a social democracy that would lead to a classless society.

With the outbreak of World War I, Lenin seized upon the mass discontent created by the war and Russia's disastrous military performance in it to instigate rebellion following the March 1917 abdication of Czar Nicholas II. A failed uprising in the summer of 1917 forced Lenin into exile again, but he returned almost immediately to lead the famed October Revolution, which placed the Bolsheviks in power and made Lenin the new head of state. As leader, he moved swiftly to crush resistance and lingering support for the fallen imperial government. One of czarist Russia's most hated intitutions was the secret police, which was charged with detecting subversion and, often, brutally suppressing it. Ironically, Lenin created the Cheka, a new secret police force that, under the ruthless Feliks DZERZHINSKII, was given license to operate more brutally and with even less restraint than had the czar's police.

When the Russian civil war ended in 1921, many, including Lenin, felt that the Cheka had served its purpose and wished to reform the political police. In February 1922, the Cheka was abolished and replaced with the OGPU, which actually differed little from the Cheka except that it was subject to somewhat tighter regulation than the original organization. Like the Cheka, however, the OGPU was essentially an instrument of the state terror and intimidation. By the time of Lenin's death on January 21, 1924, the Soviet political police system he had founded was firmly entrenched and, in its final incarnation as the KGB, would figure as a powerful and always-dreaded reality of Soviet life until the fall of communism in 1991.

Further reading: Knight, Amy W., *The KGB: Police and Politics in the Soviet Union* (Boston: Allen and Unwin, 1988).

Leonard, V(ivian) A(nderson) (1898–1984) The author of numerous texts on police subjects and a pioneer in police education.

Vivian Anderson Leonard joined the Berkeley (California) Police Department in 1925 under the progressive leadership of Chief August VOLLMER, a pioneer in scientific methods of police work. Vollmer set Leonard to work on developing radios for patrolmen, and in 1938 Leonard published his first classic work, *Police Communication Systems.*

In 1934, Leonard left the Berkeley Police Department to become executive secretary to the chief of the Fort Worth Police Department, soon becoming superintendent of records and identification. In 1939,

he left the Fort Worth department to work on his master's degree, which he received from Texas Christian University in 1940. He subsequently earned a Ph.D. from Ohio State University.

In 1941, Leonard founded the Department of Police Science and Administration (now the Department of Criminal Justice) at Washington State University, serving as its chairman until 1957 and continuing as a professor until 1963, at which time he was appointed professor emeritus. During his long career as a police academic, Leonard wrote 28 books, including *Police Organization and Management,* which appeared in its sixth edition in 1982.

Further reading: Leonard, V. A., and H. W. More, *Police Organization and Management,* 6th ed. (Mineola, N.Y.: Foundation Press, 1982).

Levine, Lowell J. (1937–) One of the innovators of odontology; developed the process of teeth imprints for identification.

A native of New York City, Lowell Levine attended Hobart College in upstate New York before receiving his DDS from New York University in 1963. After beginning his own practice, Levine also took on the responsibilities of clinical associate professor of forensic medicine at NYU's School of Medicine, specializing in odontology, or forensic dentistry. Levine argued that dental records could be as conclusive for identification as fingerprints. As with fingerprint identification, however, dental identification required comparison of the evidence to known records. Without an existing dental record for comparison, even the best bite mark was useless. To facilitate comparison, Levine developed a process of taking bite-mark imprints. The process went well beyond dental X rays, which show only dental structure. His method also showed angle of incidence—the characteristic angle of a bite impression—which greatly extended the usefulness and accuracy of odontology by identifying a dental trait unique to each individual.

Levine has held numerous positions with law enforcement agencies, including the New York State Police Forensic Sciences Unit, the New York Chief Medical Examiner's Office, and the U.S. Department of Justice. He also worked on the Josef Mengele investigation, which searched for the notorious Nazi concentration camp medical "experimenter." Levine's landmark accomplishment in the field of odontology came in 1973 in the case of *People* v. *Milone,* in which the defendant was convicted of rape and murder almost exclusively on the strength of a bite mark on the victim's thigh.

Lewis, Nolan Don Carpenter (1889–1979) A leading psychologist and neuropathologist; cowrote

one of the definitive works on pyromania as a psychological disorder.

Born in Cloudersport, Pennsylvania, on November 22, 1889, Nolan Lewis was admitted to the University of Maryland in 1910, graduating from that institution in 1914 before going on to study medicine at Johns Hopkins University in Baltimore for four years. Lewis undertook a year of postgraduate study at the University of Vienna in neurology and psychiatry, returning permanently to the United States in 1918.

From 1920 to 1924, Lewis was professor of experimental pathology at George Washington University, and in 1936 he was appointed professor of neurology at Columbia University. He quickly became one of the most respected psychiatrists in the country and was appointed a psychiatric consultant at the Nazi war crimes trials in Nuremberg. He also did special research on Nazi medical experiments and the medical effects of the atomic bombing of Hiroshima.

In an area most germane to law enforcement, the academic highlight of Lewis's career was the publication of *Pathological Firesetting*, written with Dr. Helen Yarnell. The authors established a set of four characteristics that pyromaniacs share: a resentment of authority; the urge for destruction; an inability to show resentment; and extremely poor sexual adjustment. Lewis and Yarnell argued that pyromaniacs cannot help themselves, even though they know the harm and damage they cause. Perhaps the most compelling argument made in *Firesetting* is that pyromania responds well to treatment. Of the 138 pyromaniacs studied who were receiving care, not one was continuing to set fires.

Lexow, Clarence (1852–1910) The self-interested chairman of a committee to investigate corruption within the New York City Police Department.

Born of well-to-do parents, Lexow had the benefits of a European education at the universities of Bonn and Jena, then returned to New York City to enroll in Columbia Law School. Graduating in 1874, he was admitted to the bar in 1881, establishing a practice in Rockland County, New York. There Lexow became interested in state politics and joined the Republican Party. After an unsuccessful bid for the U.S. Congress, he was elected to the state senate in 1893.

During his first term in Albany, Lexow became involved in the investigation of the New York City Police Department. The Reverend Charles PARKHURST, president of the Society for the Prevention of Crime, made repeated and well-documented charges against the police. At length, the chamber of commerce asked the state legislature to investigate. Republican leaders in the house quickly agreed, more intent on exposing Democratic Tammany Hall's control of the ballot box

than reforming corruption. Lexow moved for the appointment of a special investigatory commission and was named its chairman. This he did in an effort to promote his own political agenda rather than out of any desire to serve as a crusading reformer.

The Lexow Committee, as it was called, was quickly drowned in evidence and testimony. Many police officers, in detailing corruption, implicated themselves as well as others. The commission established that the going rate to purchase a position on the force was $300, that monthly shakedowns were standard procedure for the operators of gaming houses, saloons, and brothels, and that these ranged from $100 to $500. Any time a new captain was transferred into a district, he immediately took a "transfer fee" from all the establishments, on top of the monthly shakedowns. As part of the patronage, higher-ranking officers would transfer captains frequently as a way for them to make more money.

Scores of indictments were issued as a result of the committee's work, and many men were dismissed. A reform administration was elected, ousting the Tammany politicians who had created the police monster. However, Lexow stopped there. He did not pursue the problems to their roots, nor did the committee make any enduring, forceful recommendations. In the end, Lexow suggested a bipartisan police commission to oversee future activity, but that idea was rejected.

As for Lexow, he was ultimately unable to parlay his halfhearted reformer role into future elected office. Within four years, the Tammany politicians were again in control, and the police department returned to its corrupt practices.

Lindbergh, Charles A. (1902–74) The 1932 kidnapping of the infant son of famed transatlantic flier Charles A. Lindbergh and his wife, Anne Morrow, occasioned the biggest, most elaborate, most bizarre, and most highly visible criminal investigation of the early 20th century.

In May 1927, Charles Lindbergh made his epic solo flight from New York to Paris, instantly becoming a national hero and international celebrity. The aviator, reserved and even shy by nature, valued his privacy and sought the seclusion of a rural New Jersey estate, where he and his wife, Anne Morrow Lindbergh, could raise their new son. Tragically, on the night of March 1, 1932, 20-month-old Charles Augustus Lindbergh Jr. was abducted from his crib.

Mrs. Lindbergh and the baby's nurse, Betty Gow, had put the infant to bed. Some time between the hours of six and ten, the kidnapper entered the child's bedroom through a window, using a handmade wooden ladder. When Gow checked on the child after 10 P.M., he was gone. Lindbergh had contacted the authorities before finding a ransom note near the window, which demanded $50,000 for the return of the child.

The press, learning of the kidnapping, went wild, and the privacy-hungry Lindberghs, now grief-stricken, were subjected to the torment of a media circus. Although the ransom money was paid, the baby was never returned, and, two months after the disappearance, his decomposed corpse was found in a shallow grave near the Lindbergh home.

The investigation—an epic manhunt of unprecedented proportions—dragged on for two years, during which time the Lindberghs were subjected to unremitting media attention and the blandishments of numerous con men and crackpots, well-meaning and otherwise. After some enlightened investigative work by "wood detective" Arthur KOEHLER and Ellis PARKER, authorities located and arrested Bruno Richard HAUPTMANN, a German-American carpenter. Largely on the strength of physical evidence, Hauptmann was convicted and executed following a trial in the small New Jersey town of Flemington.

The Lindberghs, to whom a second son had been born, convinced that their homeland was no longer safe for their family, sought refuge in Europe but never fully recovered from the tragedy.

The Lindbergh case promoted several legal and investigative reforms, most notably the act of June 1932, officially called the Federal Kidnapping Statute but popularly known as the Lindbergh Law, making kidnapping a federal offense, placing investigation under the jurisdiction of the FBI, and classifying it, with murder, as a capital crime.

Further reading: Fisher, Jim, *The Lindbergh Case* (New Brunswick, N.J.: Rutgers University Press, 1987).

Lindsay, John V. (1921–)

As mayor of New York City, Lindsay bucked the concerted opposition of the police and law-and-order advocates to establish a civilian review board to oversee police activity.

John Lindsay was raised in wealthy circumstances in New York City and educated at Yale University. He joined the Young Republicans as an enthusiastic supporter of Dwight D. Eisenhower's candidacy for president, and in the early 1950s worked for Attorney General Herbert Brownell. Lindsay decided to run for office on his own in 1958 and was elected to the House of Representatives from Manhattan's exclusive East Side "Silk Stocking" district. Once in Congress, to the surprise and dismay of some of his constituents, he became one of the most liberal Republicans in the House.

Having earned a liberal reputation, Lindsay was able to defeat the Democratic machine in 1965 and capture the New York City mayoral race. His attempt to play both sides of the political fence grated on his own party, and he was defeated in the Republican primary when he ran for reelection. Undaunted, Lindsay withdrew from the Republican Party, switched to the Liberal Party, and was elected by a plurality of votes in 1969.

As a mayor, Lindsay was most noted for his ability to keep civil unrest to a minimum during the tumultuous 1960s when other U.S. cities were in flames. Although he was able to maintain law and order within the city, Lindsay was constantly at odds with traditional law-and-order advocates because of his close ties to young radicals and minority activists. When he attempted to impose a civilian review board on the police department, conservative elements responded by charging that he would appoint black militants, flaming liberals, and young college radicals if successful. At first able to defeat Lindsay's proposal in a popular referendum, police labor interests and others were unable to halt a compromise between the mayor and the police commissioner, which created the civilian review board.

Although he was somewhat of a liberal media darling, Lindsay failed in his brief presidential campaign of 1972, withdrawing shortly and returning to his duties as mayor.

Liszt, Franz von (1851–1919)

A German criminologist and one of the founders of the International Union of Penal Law in 1889.

Professor Franz von Liszt is considered one of the "fathers" of the German criminal-sociological school, which gained worldwide attention in criminology circles toward the end of the 19th century. The "Marburg School," as it was often called, promoted the then revolutionary idea that criminal law must take into account and accommodate the new sciences of criminal anthropology, penology, sociology, psychology, and statistics. This "synthetic combination," as Liszt termed it, is necessary for the full comprehension of the sociology of the criminal. To promote this new school of thought, Liszt, with Adolphe PRINS and Gerard Hamel, formed the International Union of Penal Law in 1889, which was committed to exploring the sociological and anthropological aspects of crime.

The seeds of the modern concepts of conditional sentences, indefinite sentencing, and control of crime were all planted by the union, and Liszt wrote several influential works addressing such subjects, including, most notably, a *Textbook of German Criminal Law* in 1881.

Further reading: Ellis, Havelock, *The Criminal* (Boston: Longwood, 1977).
Garofalo, Raffaele, *Criminology*, tr. Robert Wyness Millar (Monclair, N.J.: Patterson Smith, 1968).

Livingston, Edward (1754–1836) An American philosopher, diplomat, and penologist; wrote the progressive System of Penal Law for the state of Louisiana.

Edward Livingston was a native New Yorker whose father had fought in the American Revolution. A brilliant legal thinker, Livingston served as an aide to General Andrew Jackson during the battle of New Orleans at the conclusion of the War of 1812. He remained in Louisiana, and was commissioned to codify the state's statutes. In 1824, he produced his *System of Penal Law,* one of the most progressive 19th-century works in penology. The "Livingston System" condemned capital punishment, supported separation of prisoners before trial, and promoted the concept of rehabilitation rather than mere punishment. Livingston also fostered the idea that criminal behavior is learned, not inherited—a forward-thinking notion that would come to dominate 20th-century criminology.

Old South conservatism barred enactment of Livingston's reforms, but his ideas nevertheless influenced future generations of penal reformers. Livingston left Louisiana to join the Jackson administration as secretary of state from 1831 to 1833 and then as minister to France from 1833 to 1835.

Further reading: Hall, Jerome, "Edward Livingston and His Louisiana Penal Code," *American Bar Association Journal,* 22 (1936).

Locard, Edmond (1877–1965) The founder, in 1910, of a celebrated police laboratory in Lyons, France, Locard was its director for over 40 years, contributing much to the advancement of scientific techniques in criminal detection.

Edmond Locard provided modern criminology with one of its essential tenets: "Every contact leaves a trace." Locard's research, writings, and court testimony in the areas of microscopic evidence, fingerprint analysis, graphology, and document examination supported and promoted the practical application of this "trace" theory and gained Locard himself international attention and respect.

After studying at the Dominican College in Ouillins, Locard earned degrees in both medicine and law at the University of Lyons, where he became a disciple of professor and pioneering forensics expert Alexandre LACASSAGNE. After a stint as Lacassagne's assistant, Locard was hired to set up a new laboratory to serve the Technical Police of the Prefecture of the Rhône, and in the course of his work there he began to extrapolate his mentor's ideas, applying them in new and fruitful areas of inquiry.

In 1912, Locard's investigation of a strangulation murder demonstrated the inestimable value of the microscope in revealing "trace" evidence of criminal contact; he showed that the fingernail scrapings of suspect Emile Gourbin contained not only skin remnants that might have been dug from his ill-fated paramour's neck, but also matchable particles of the specific cosmetic powder that the victim had worn on her face and throat. Presented with this evidence, Gourbin abandoned his previous alibi and confessed to the fatal crime of passion. In the same year, Locard published the first segment of his *Traite de criminalistique,* a monumental and wide-ranging treatise that he was ultimately to conclude, with a seventh volume, in 1940.

Among Locard's many technical accomplishments were refinements in the newly established study of fingerprints, the invention of "poroscopy" (a system to identify and compare skin pore patterns), an advanced expertise in handwriting analysis, and innovations in the laboratory examination of ink and other chemical elements in disputed documents. Teaching at the Lyons Department of Criminalistics of the Faculty of Law, Locard also founded and directed the Institute of Criminalistics and lectured in experimental psychology. He served as technical advisor to the International Criminal Police Commission, as vice president of the International Academy of Criminal Sciences, and as consultant in over 10,000 court cases, including the World War I trial of the notorious female spy Mata Hari.

Locard's writings shared the details of his most celebrated assignments, and the criminologist also authored works in other, non-professional areas of interest, including stamp-collecting, music, botany, and cuisine. After handing on the directorship of the Lyons police laboratory to his son, Locard continued to conduct research and write until his death at age 88.

Lohman, Joseph D. (1910–68) A noted criminologist and sociologist; instrumental in developing community relations and race relations programs within local police departments.

Joseph Lohman was born and raised in New York, then went west to the University of Denver, where he earned his undergraduate degree in 1931. A year later he received his master's degree from the University of Wisconsin and then became a graduate fellow at the University of Chicago. After serving on various university faculties as well as in several municipal positions, Lohman became a research sociologist for the state of Illinois. He also served as cochairman of the San Francisco Commission on Crime.

After settling in northern California, Lohman became dean of the School of Criminology at the University of California, Berkeley. There he continued his research into the relationship between race and crime.

He advocated programs to conduct research into the causes and effects of crime, declaring that, in the absence of proper information, crime could not be prevented only reacted to. He also began offering courses in race relations to police departments to help them deal more effectively with the rising racial tensions in the country. He offered his first race relations seminar to the Chicago Police Department, stressing that the police must subordinate their personal feelings in a professional manner. He showed that much racial unrest was the result of police overreaction and that seldom was an act of escalation initiated by minority civilians, but rather by the police, who tended to feel that a swift and harsh action was necessary to quell violence. Lohman's views were quickly incorporated into training texts and distributed to officers in many cities.

Lombroso, Cesare (1836–1909)

The most prominent criminologist of his time; classified criminals as "atavistic" and "degenerate" in comparison to society as a whole.

Cesare Lombroso was born November 6, 1835, in Verona, and, although he was a Jew, he was able to attend the public school administered by the Jesuits. After coming to the attention of a noted physician, who persuaded him to attend medical school, Lombroso entered the University of Pavia in 1852 at the age of 18, then transferred to the University of Padova in 1854 for a year, and then studied for a year at the University of Vienna in 1856, before finally earning his degree from Pavia in 1858. He then earned an additional degree in surgery from the University of Genoa in 1859.

Lombroso's writings and theories were, he freely admitted, an adaptation of those who had come before him. Much that is attributed to him is, in fact, an advancement of previous theory. Lombroso developed the concept of atavism, the idea that criminality was the result of a biological throwback to an earlier stage in evolution. He put forth the idea of the "born criminal," later modified by Enrico FERRI, arguing that criminality was the product of heredity. Lombroso further refined his typology of the criminal mind by proposing the categories "insane criminal" and the "epileptic criminal." The insane criminal was mentally deficient through atavism—a pathological, antisocial "throwback" to supposedly primitive behavior—and therefore susceptible to criminal behavior, and the epileptic criminal was similarly susceptible because of epilepsy. Lombroso further defined the criminal mind by offering the "occasional criminal," which was in turn broken down into the "pseudo criminal" and the "criminaloid." The pseudo criminal, socially normal in all other aspects, involuntarily commits petty crime, without the intent to harm society, while the criminaloid is inherently abnormal, his behavior due to abnormal socialization rather than hereditary defect. Neither variety of occasional criminal is subject to atavism.

Lombroso sought to create more than just theory on paper, and he looked for practical applications wherever possible. His postmortem work on the brains of criminals was the beginning of clinical criminology. Much of Lombroso's clinical work consisted of autopsy, and his extensive examinations of the human brain were meticulous. His work provided the basis for the methodology of cadaver identification later adopted by most agencies involved in legal medicine.

Further reading: Lombroso-Ferrero, Gina, *Criminal Man, According to the Classification of Cesare Lombroso* (Montclair, N.J.: Patterson Smith, 1972).

Wolfgang, Marvin E., "Cesare Lombroso, *The Journal of Criminal Law, Criminology and Police Science*, 52:4 (November–December 1961).

Lucas, Charles (Jean Marie) (1803–89)

A French penal reformer during the early 19th century.

In 1828, Charles Lucas published the first volume of a three-volume work entitled *The Penitentiary System in Europe and the United States.* Not only was this one of the first critiques of capital punishment, the landmark book is also credited with the creation of what Lucas called "Penitentiary Science."

In 1830, Lucas was appointed inspector general of French prisons, remaining in this position until his retirement in 1865. During his tenure, Lucas published *Reform of Prisons; or, Theory of Imprisonment,* which won further acclaim for its revolutionary stance focusing on the criminal and society rather than on the crime itslf. Lucas saw the extension of liberty during the 19th century as creating a social climate conducive to crime. Only by rehabilitating the criminal, he believed, could crime be reduced.

Lucas's work has been cited as a forerunner of international penal reform, including the 1958 United Nations adoption of the "minimal rules"—the international standards for the treatment of inmates.

Further reading: Normandeau, André, "Charles Lucas," *The Journal of Criminal Law, Criminology and Police Science,* 61:2 (June 1970).

Luciano, Charles "Lucky" (1897–1962)

One of the founders of modern organized crime in the United States.

In collaboration with Meyer LANSKY, Louis "Lepke" BUCHALTER, Joe ADONIS, Frank COSTELLO, and others, "Lucky" Luciano created the national crime syndicate of the early 1930s, which continues to operate today.

Charles "Lucky" Luciano was one of the founding fathers of modern organized crime. (Courtesy of the Library of Congress)

He was born Salvatore Lucania on November 24, 1897, near Palermo, Sicily. He immigrated to the United States in 1906, settling on Manhattan's Lower East Side. In 1907, mere months after his arrival, he was arrested for shoplifting. It was the first of his many early arrests for theft, but in 1915 he was brought in for dealing in heroin and was sent to prison for a year. Offered a deal by the prosecutor—freedom in exchange for information—he stood by the Sicilian code of silence, *omerta,* and for this was made a full member of the infamous Five Points Gang upon his release from prison a year later.

As a Five Pointer, Luciano was trained in the fine art of strongarm tactics and general mayhem. He also met the likes of Johnny TORRIO, James "Big Jim" Colosimo, Frankie Yale, and Al CAPONE. When Luciano was not doing dirty work for the Points Gang, he gambled, winning so often that he was dubbed "Lucky."

By 1920, Luciano had earned enough money to establish his own extortion operation, peddling protection to bordellos and enforcing his "requests" by sending a small army of goons to beat up prostitutes and madams. By 1925, Luciano controlled vice in Manhattan. His methods of enforcement had escalated from beatings to murder: Pimps who refused to pay were summarily executed—usually by means of Luciano's trademark icepick. Very soon, no one refused to pay. It was estimated that Luciano controlled more than 5,000 prostitutes.

By the end of the decade, Luciano had become a millionaire and lived in high style, first at the elegant Barbizon Plaza and then at the even more lavish Waldorf-Astoria. Moreover, Luciano exercised great prudence with his million-dollar-a-year income. In contrast to Al Capone, he was meticulous about reporting earnings to the Internal Revenue Service, thereby precluding prosecution for income-tax evasion. (He always claimed to have made $22,500 on wagers and paid taxes on this amount.)

Luciano had grown up in the same neighborhood as Meyer Lansky and Benjamin "Bugsy" Siegel. The three formed an unholy alliance that became the very core of modern organized crime in the United States. By all accounts, the idea of criminal activity organized on a massive national scale originated with Luciano and was elaborated brilliantly by Lansky. Those gangsters who would not cooperate with the scheme, Luciano argued, had to be eliminated. This included, preeminently, Jack "Legs" DIAMOND.

In 1929, even as Luciano was formulating his plans, he was working for Joseph MASSERIA and was inspecting a load of freshly smuggled heroin for his boss when he was ambushed, thrown into a car, savagely beaten, taken to Brooklyn, slashed on the face and throat with a knife, and stabbed in the back with an icepick. Luciano was then dumped on Huguenot Beach, Staten Island, where he was left for dead. A cop found him and he was rushed to a hospital. Questioned by detectives, he once again observed the code of silence, claiming he had been the victim of "an accident."

Although Luciano knew that Diamond was behind the attack, he bided his time. On December 18, 1931, Diamond was shot to death in an Albany, New York, boarding house. Perhaps it was the work of Dutch SCHULTZ, enemy to Luciano as well as Diamond, or perhaps it was the work of Luciano himself. In the meantime, however, Luciano was embroiled in the so-called Castellammarese War of 1930-31 between factions aligned with Salvatore Maranzano and those allied with Masseria. Although Luciano was part of the Masseria organization, he secretly met with Maranzano and agreed to set up Masseria if Maranzano would call off the war. Accordingly, on April 15, 1931, Luciano took Masseria to a Coney Island restaurant, ate, and then initiated a card game. Luciano retired to the men's room, at which point Albert ANASTASIA, Vito Genovese, Joe Adonis, and "Bugsy" Siegel walked into the restaurant and gunned down Masseria. Then Luciano moved preemptively against Maranzano, sending a hit squad to kill the self-proclaimed Boss of Bosses on September 10, 1931.

Luciano rushed into the vacuum he himself had created, combining the forces of Maranzano and Masseria, along with the non-Italian gangs in New York. In a grand scheme, the various rackets were quickly divided up. Dutch Schultz, a loose cannon, was given more latitude and allowed to maintain his own territories. But in 1935, Schultz at last went too far, publicly threatening to kill District Attorney Thomas E. DEWEY. Such boldness threatened the organization Luciano and the others were building. Luciano ordered the death of Schultz, who was gunned down in a Newark, New Jersey, restaurant.

By this time, Lucky Luciano was confirmed as the Boss of Bosses—the most powerful man in organized crime. He lived in high style, consistently evading arrest and prosecution. Indeed, he seldom left his luxurious quarters at the Waldorf, controlling his far-flung operations from his suite. However, to avoid police and federal wiretaps, he habitually used a public phone in a drugstore at 49th Street and Seventh Avenue to communicate his special orders. The death of Schultz prompted Dewey to direct his attention toward Luciano, whom he dubbed "Public Enemy Number One." The heat became so intense that the gangster retreated to Hot Springs, Arkansas. But New York prosecutors were able to convince former madams, who resented having paid off Luciano for so many years, to testify against him, and the gangster was extradited from Arkansas to stand trial in New York. He was convicted on multiple extortion charges and sentenced to 30 to 50 years in prison.

Luciano was twice denied parole—in 1938 and in 1942—but in that year, the great luxury liner *Normandie* burned and capsized at a pier on the Hudson River, where it was being refitted for use as a troop ship. The navy suspected sabotage and looked desperately for a way to prevent future mishaps. Luciano's name came up as a man who had a lot of influence on the waterfront. Navy agents visited the gangster in prison, and he accordingly arranged for security. The following year, agents returned to prison, seeking Luciano's aid in contacting Mafia dons in Sicily to cooperate with the impending Allied invasion. That any "deals" were made has been officially denied; however, Luciano was released from prison when he came up for parole in 1945—on condition that he accept deportation to Italy. He sailed on February 10, 1946.

In Rome, Luciano resumed the lush life, but he did not long endure exile. He traveled to Havana, Cuba, in February 1947, where he met with Lansky, Costello, and other syndicate leaders to create a scheme to control gambling in the free-wheeling city, splitting profits with the corrupt dictator Fulgencio Bastista. It was at this meeting, too, that Luciano voiced his displeasure over the immense cost of the Flamingo casino Bugsy Siegel had just built in Las Vegas with the syndicate's money. Suspecting Siegel of skimming, Luciano ordered the murder of his old friend and associate.

In the meantime, the United States pressured Batista to send Luciano back to Italy, where officials barred his return to Rome and exiled him to Naples. There he lived in ostensible retirement, though he still exercised considerable control of organized crime in the States, working through Costello and Lansky. Luciano participated in funding a worldwide drug-trafficking network and then began working with a Hollywood producer to create an epic film version of his life story.

On January 26, 1962, Luciano drove to the Capodichino Airport in Naples to meet a film producer who had flown in from the States, when suddenly he was struck by a heart attack. He died, instantly, on the field.

Lynch, Charles (1736–96) The man whose surname quite possibly gave us the term for execution without benefit of trial, Lynch meted out summary justice during the American Revolution.

The son of a Quaker planter in Lynchburg, southern Virginia, Charles Lynch was a member of the Virginia House of Burgesses, like his father before him. Having sworn oaths in the Burgesses, he was disowned from the Quakers "for taking solemn oaths, contrary to the order and discipline of the Friends." His ouster did not damage his political popularity, nor did it diminish his political fervency. In the face of mounting British repression, Lynch became an ardent patriot and was a signer of the non-importation agreement.

At the outbreak of revolutionary hostilities, Lynch's Quaker upbringing kept him out of the army, but he performed a valuable wartime service nevertheless. The war brought a breakdown in colonial law enforcement and jurisprudence, and banditry was rampant, particularly horse thievery. With three other respected men from Lynchburg, Lynch formed an ad hoc court to hear crimes and grievances. Lynch's court had no legal authority, but most everyone quickly came to regard it as the law in the region. Cases were heard before the four justices. Accusers were required to give testimony in the presence of the accused, and defendants had the right to subpoena witnesses. Anyone acquitted was immediately released and was given the right to sue his accuser for false arrest. Those convicted of horse thievery were immediately taken out in back of the "courthouse," tied to Lynch's oak tree, given 39 lashes, and hung by the thumbs until an "oath of liberty" was extracted.

After the war was over, many Tories sought redress from this rogue court and brought suit before the new state courts. The state of Virginia promptly issued a proclamation that, although the court was not warranted by law, it had acted out of necessity with fairness and without excess. It exonerated Lynch and his colleagues, and the proclamation became known as Lynch's Law. Since then, "lynching" and "lynch law" have come to signify any form of summary punishment by a "lynch mob" (sometimes called "Judge Lynch"). Mob action called "lynch law" usually culminates in a hanging. Some authorities believe that the modern term "lynch" originated not with Charles Lynch, but with the vigilante actions of William LYNCH.

Lynch, G(erald) Roche (1889–1957) This British medical detective was a master toxicologist who was instrumental in solving numerous criminal cases.

As head of the department of pathological chemistry from 1926 to 1954 at St. Mary's Hospital in London, Dr. G. Roche Lynch spent virtually his entire career in the forensic laboratory. He was closely affiliated with Scotland Yard's Criminal Investigative Division (CID), and Lynch became one of the most often called upon expert witnesses in London's courtrooms.

Lynch's dedication to detail and his uncanny knack for detecting poison in the blood of victims placed his testimony beyond question, even to the most diligent defense attorneys. Lynch served as president of the Medico-Legal Society of Great Britain and the Society of Public Analytical Chemists. He also represented the Home Office in scientific crime investigative in both England and Wales.

Lynch died suddenly at age 60 in Slough, England.

Lynch, William L. (1724–1820) The man whose name, many claim, is the origin of the term "lynching," Lynch and a group of vigilantes summarily punished anyone they felt had broken the law.

A native of Pittsylvania County, Virginia, William Lynch was the leader of a vigilante committee formed to purge the county of certain criminals against whom the law had failed to deal adequately—or, at least, to the satisfaction of Lynch and his confederates. In September 1780, Lynch and several townspeople en-

tered into a written agreement vowing to mete out the corporal punishment they deemed appropriate for whatever crime was committed.

Although it is unclear exactly what kind of record Lynch and his fellow vigilantes ran up, it does appear that most, if not all, of those accused were guilty of some sort of crime. Hanging was not specifically mentioned in the compact, but when a death sentence was pronounced—which was often—hanging was the method of choice, carried out by positioning the condemned man on a horse and putting the victim's head in a noose, the other end of which was tied to a tree limb. The horse was then stampeded, leaving the victim to hang.

There is dispute as to whether the term "lynching" and associated phrases and forms of the word derive from the actions of William Lynch or those of his older, 18th-century fellow Virginian, Charles LYNCH.

Lynds, Elam (1784–1855) The inventor of the Auburn prison system was a borderline sadist who claimed prisoners were "cowards" and needed to be "broken" before they could be reformed.

A native of upstate New York, Elam Lynds served in both the local militia and then in the federal service of infantry for almost 10 years before becoming principal keeper of the Auburn (New York) prison. At Auburn, he enforced stern military-style discipline on the inmates. He demanded silence at all times and made the prisoners march everywhere in lockstep—an eerie sight, especially when coupled with the silence. During meals, Lynds enforced a rigid system under which inmates were allowed to make only certain prescribed movements and had to ask for seconds or to be dismissed in a certain manner. Any variance from these regulations brought harsh punishment.

Lynds was a firm proponent of solitary confinement, a condition so deplorable to the inmates that they referred to it as the "hole," a name that continues to this day. Indeed, Lynds would have preferred solitary confinement for most prisoners on a full-time basis, but when he tried it, too many men attempted suicide or went insane, so he contented himself with employing the method only as a punishment for those who broke his stern regulations. Auburn was, however, the first prison with single-occupancy cells, in which ordinary prisoners spent less than half their day.

Lynds liberally beat prisoners who broke any regulations, declaring that the lash was the most effective way of maintaining discipline.

After several years at Auburn, where he was largely praised for the admirable discipline he maintained, as well as the orderly manner in which the prison was conducted, Lynds took 100 inmates in 1825 to the

Hudson River town of Ossining, New York, and built what would become Sing Sing Prison, founded on his own "Auburn system." After returning to Auburn in 1838, he was dismissed for his excessive methods, only to be recalled by authorities at Sing Sing a short time later. When he was finally dismissed from that institution in 1844, his career was over, but the legacy of his system remained almost intact for another century, and some of it still continues to this day in some institutions and under certain circumstances.

M

MacCormick, Austin H. (1893–1979) As New York City corrections commissioner, MacCormick uncovered scandals and brutal conditions in the city's Welfare Island Prison.

Although a native of Ontario, Canada, Austin MacCormick grew up in Boothbay Harbor, Maine, where his family had moved shortly after his birth. Graduating in 1915 from nearby Bowdoin College with a degree in English, MacCormick wrote his senior essay on prison reform and the work of Thomas Mott os-BORNE, a renowned American penologist. The paper drew some attention well beyond the university, and MacCormick was hired as a research assistant to investigate Maine's prison system. Like Osborne, MacCormick had himself committed to the state penitentiary as a forger and spent a week as an inmate. Upon his "release," he wrote a searing article on the conditions and treatment of the inmates.

After earning his graduate degree from Columbia University in 1916, MacCormick worked under Osborne, who was commissioned by the U.S. secretary of the navy to study the naval prison at Portsmouth, New Hampshire. Again MacCormick went inside as an inmate and again found deplorable conditions. Osborne was named commanding officer of the prison and MacCormick his executive officer. Together, the two put into practice their theories on prison reform and satisfactorily restored some two-thirds of the inmates to active duty.

MacCormick's greatest triumph came in 1934, when New York's Mayor Fiorello LaGuardia named him city corrections commissioner. The penitentiary on Welfare Island had been declared unfit for human habitation, with most inmates receiving insufficient and inadequate food and water and suffering confinement in dungeon-like conditions, while others, mostly gangsters and other wealthy inmates, lived in comparatively grand style. MacCormick reformed the prison, ensuring adequate nutrition, removing special inmate privileges, isolating troublemakers, instituting a program of outdoor physical fitness, and offering vocational opportunities to the inmates. His work was a model of prison reform and reclamation.

Maconochie, Alexander (1787–1860) This pioneering penologist introduced humanitarian principles into the notoriously cruel prison system of 19th-century Britain.

Maconochie was a Scot who served at the Tasmania and Norfolk penal islands off the Australian mainland from 1837 to 1839 before being appointed governor of Birmingham Borough Prison, where he served from 1849 to 1851. Maconochie wrote numerous books on the subject of penal reform, including most notably, *Thoughts on Convict Management* (1838) and *Norfolk Island* (1847). These works, in which the reformer appealed for humane treatment of convicts, earned Maconochie more criticism than admiration during his own time, but today he is remembered as one of the pioneer voices of penal reform.

Further reading: Barry, John Vincent, "Alexander Maconochie," *The Journal of Criminal Law, Criminology and Police Science,* 47:2 (July–August 1956).

Madden, Owen (alias: Owney; Owney the Killer) (1892–1964) Born in Liverpool and bred in West Side Manhattan's Hell's Kitchen neighborhood, Madden was one of the city's most feared gunmen before Prohibition.

A native of the slums of Liverpool, England, Owney Madden immigrated to the United States with his family in 1903, joining the Gopher Gang of Hell's Kitchen when he was only 11. By the time he was 23, he had already killed five men, mostly in warfare

Between 1911 and 1914, Madden built the Gophers into a terrific and violent force, staffed by the toughest gunmen in New York, including Tanner Smith, Chick Hyland, Bill Tammany, and Eddie Egan. Warfare with the Hudson Dusters and other rival gangs was continual and bloody. On November 6, 1912, Madden was shot eight times by Dusters and left for dead. Questioned by police in the hospital, Madden replied simply: "Nothing doing. The boys'll get 'em. It's nobody's business but mine who put these slugs into me!"

In 1914, Madden "stole" one Freda Horner from Patsy Doyle, a prominent Duster. This heated up the war, resulting in action and retaliation, culminating in Madden's murder of Doyle.

This time, a case *was* made against Madden, who was sentenced to 20 years in Sing Sing, but was paroled nine years later, in 1923. He was freed into a gangland scene that had very much changed, mainly due to the growing dominance of the Mafia and the criminal opportunities presented by Prohibition. Madden joined Dutch SCHULTZ's gang as an enforcer, then left Schultz in 1931 to become a professional boxing promoter, managing to rig Primo Carnera's title fights to elevate him to heavyweight champion. When Madden had decided that Carnera had outlived his usefulness, he commissioned fighter Max Baer to beat him senseless on June 14, 1934.

Owney Madden retired from the rackets shortly after this and moved to Hot Springs, Arkansas. He lived there quietly until his death in 1964, leaving an estate of some $3 million.

Madsen, Chris (1851–1944)   One of the legendary "Three Guardsmen," along with Heck THOMAS and Bill TILGHMAN, who helped rid the Oklahoma Territory of the notorious Bill Doolin Gang in the 1890s.

Chris Madsen lived an adventurous life. Born in Denmark, he served a stint in the French Foreign Legion before catching "gold fever in the 1870s and immigrating to the American West. Madsen became a deputy in the Oklahoma Territory around 1880. He joined fellow lawmen Bill Tilghman and Heck Thomas in the 1890s for the express purpose of capturing Bill Doolin's gang of criminals, who were terrorizing the Oklahoma Territory. Popularly called the "Three Guardsmen," the trio entered the ranks of the West's legendary lawmen. Madsen personally killed Doolin accomplices Tulsa Jack Blake and Red Buck Waightman in 1895.

In 1898, Madsen joined Teddy Roosevelt's Rough Riders and went to Cuba to fight in the Spanish-American War. He survived a bout with yellow fever in Cuba, and served in the Rough Rider unit until 1907.

Owen Madden had two nicknames: "Owney" and, more to the point, "the Killer." (Courtesy of the Library of Congress)

with the rival Hudson Dusters gang, and had become boss of the Gophers. The young Madden divided his time between terrorizing and shaking down West Side shopkeepers and womanizing. His reputation as a lethal maniac was well deserved, as he once killed a man on a trolley car because the man had approached one of his girlfriends. Madden boarded the car, found his man and, in front of the other passengers, shot him, then paused to ring the conductor's bell and exited. Although the police arrested Madden, no witnesses dared to appear against him, and the case was dismissed.

Deputy marshal Chris Madsen, one of Oklahoma's famed Three Guardsmen (Courtesy of the Western History Collections, University of Oklahoma)

Madsen returned to law enforcement in 1911, when he was appointed U.S. marshal in Guthrie, Oklahoma. He retired in 1922 and lived another 22 years, dying at age 92.

Malpighi, Marcello (1628–94) Among the very first to identify "varying ridges and patterns" on human fingertips, Malpighi helped develop the science of dactylology—fingerprint identification.

Born at Crevalcore near Bologna, Italy, Marcello Malpighi enrolled at the University of Bologna in 1646 and studied medicine, graduating in 1653. After moving to the University of Pisa and then back to Bologna, Malpighi embarked on an amazing career of research, which included, among other things, the discovery of the capillaries in the human circulatory system and the basis of histology.

The concept of human fingerprints as unique to each individual is an old one, dating back at least to biblical times, when important documents were "signed" with a thumbprint in clay to preclude forgery. Even as a criminal investigative tool, it dates at least to classical Rome, when a bloody palmprint was used as the chief piece of evidence in acquitting a murder suspect. However, dactylology—the systematic science of fingerprinting—did not make any serious advances until 1686, when Malpighi, an expert microcopist, discovered slight but fundamental differences in every fingerprint specimen he examined. Moreover, Malpighi identified "the varying ridges and patterns"—the loops and whorls—that would form the scientific basis for fingerprinting more than two centuries later.

Although Malpighi's discovery was original, he offered no commentary on its origins or on its possible applications. His few lectures on the discovery generated little interest.

Mandelbaum, "Marm" (Fredericka) (1819–94) A colorful and infamous fence, whose New York City brownstone was a hub of criminal activity in the 1800s.

From 1854 to 1884, Prussian-born Fredericka Mandelbaum was the queen of New York City's underworld. Her elaborate dinner parties were attended by thieves and judges alike and—for both—were the highlight of the social season. She was affectionately called "Marm" on account of her maternal qualities, but the press branded her more frankly "Ma Crime." Mandelbaum operated a sophisticated fencing operation, which channeled into the hands of New Yorkers stolen goods from all across America and throughout Europe. Mandelbaum even trained promising young thieves in the art of larceny.

At last, in 1884, Peter B. Olney, one of York's rare incorruptible district attornies, enlisted the aid of the PINKERTON detective agency to infiltrate Marm's organization. After four months of preparatory work by Pinkerton operatives, Olney ordered a raid on Mandelbaum's premises. What Olney's men found was a veritable treasure trove of art, antiques, and jewels. Marm was duly arrested, but, after posting bond, escaped to Canada—reportedly with more than a million dollars in cash—and remained there until her death in 1894. Now permanently beyond the reach of the law, her body was returned to New York City for burial.

Mann, James Robert (1856–1922) An Illinois congressman who sponsored legislation in 1910 (the Mann Act) that had a profound influence on the role of federal law enforcement agencies, especially the FBI.

James Robert Mann was twice a valedictorian, first at the University of Illinois (1876) and then at the

Union College of Law in Chicago (1881). He became the attorney for Chicago's affluent Hyde Park commissioners during the 1880s and was subsequently elected the Republican congressman from that district in 1897. He would serve in Congress for the next 25 years.

As a congressman, Mann participated in much of the progressive legislation of the turn of the century. In the field of law enforcement he is best remembered for his 1910 White Slave Traffic Act, better known as the Mann Act. Introduced as the result of a tabloid news report claiming that a Chicago criminal couple had imported as many as 20,000 women and girls to supply their brothel, the Mann Act made it a federal crime to transport women in interstate commerce for immoral purposes.

After heated debate over whether the federal government should be involved in the policing policies of individual states, the bill passed. The job of enforcement was given to the then little-used Bureau of Investigation. Although the Mann Act proved relatively ineffective in curbing prostitution, it became the first national assignment for the Bureau of Investigation, which therefore, to some degree, owes its continued existence and subsequent expansion to Congressman Mann's legislation.

Mannheim, Hermann (1889–1974) One of the greatest scholarly criminologists ever, Mannheim escaped Nazi persecution to continue his work in England.

Born in Berlin on October 26, 1889, Hermann Mannheim was sent to eastern Prussia for schooling in Tilsit until he was 19, when he left to study law and political science at the universities of Munich, Freibourg, Strasbourg, and Königsberg, completing his education in 1911. He began his legal career that year and, the following year, was awarded his juris doctor degree from Königsberg for his thesis on criminal negligence.

During World War I, Mannheim served as an artilleryman on both the eastern and western fronts until his legal qualifications came to the attention of command authorities, and he was appointed judge of court martial in 1917. At war's end, he returned to various legal pursuits and in 1925 was appointed lecturer at Berlin University. His star also began to rise in the courts, first as a magistrate, and then, in 1931, when he was promoted to the highest court in Prussia. By 1933, he had reached the pinnacle of both the judicial and academic world, holding the titles of high magistrate and full professor.

In 1934, after Adolf Hitler and the Nazis came to power, Mannheim was stripped of his professorship and was about to be reduced to a low municipal court before he resigned from the bench and fled to England. After spending a year learning the language

and establishing himself in London, Mannheim was appointed honorary lecturer at the London School of Economics in 1935. The following year he was awarded a fellowship at London University to pursue full-time the research that would catapult him to the top of his profession.

His first published work in English, *Social Aspects of Crime in England Between the Wars* was the first comprehensive critique of English criminal statistics in nearly half a century. By the early 1940s, Mannheim had established criminology as a separate subject in the academic curriculum, and in 1946 he was appointed reader in criminology, the first designated British university reading post in the field. He held the position until his retirement in 1955.

In 1949, Mannheim was responsible for the establishment of criminology as a separate field of study for undergraduates for the first time in any British university, shortly followed by postgraduate work and a Ph.D. program in the discipline.

Even after his academic retirement, Mannheim continued to write and publish extensively. He died at the age of 84, considered by many the father of modern English academic criminology.

Marsh, James (1794–1846) A chemist employed at the Royal British Arsenal in Woolwich, England, Marsh invented an extremely sensitive laboratory test for detecting minute traces of arsenic in a given sample of food, fluid, or postmortem human tissue. His testing method and apparatus helped increase the scientific sophistication of medico-legal poisoning investigations and determined the outcome of several notable murder trials.

Marsh was born on September 2, 1794, but little is known of his early life or his early career at the Woolwich arsenal. When the Englishman was 42, the nearby town of Plumstead called on him (as the only qualified chemist in the area) to deliver an opinion in a possible case of arsenic poisoning. Using then-current, German-devised methods, Marsh tested the autopsized intestines of the victim, an elderly and famously evil-tempered local patriarch, as well as the coffee alleged to contain the poison. He reported to the inquest that both clearly showed evidence of arsenic. But, at the murder trial, jurors found Marsh's description of yellow precipitates, ammonia solvents, and other laboratory materials too arcane to follow; his testimony meant nothing to them since they couldn't "see" the arsenic themselves. As a result of this antipathy to scientific details, the jury acquitted the defendant as spectators cheered. (Ten years later, the accused grandson finally did confess to the poisoning, by that time having been deported to a penal colony for subsequent crimes of blackmail and fraud.)

This courtroom experience incensed James Marsh, and the following year, he began work on developing a new laboratory test, one that would render any arsenic trace plainly visible, even to the layman. He based his approach on the 18th-century experiments of the Swedish scientist Karl Wilhelm Scheele, who had converted arsenic to the related gas called arsine. Marsh created a reaction between zinc and hydrochloric acid to produce hydrogen, which then bonded with any arsenic present in the sample and escaped from the solution as arsine. Having designed an apparatus—a U-shaped glass tube with a pointed nozzle at one end—that allowed him to control the reaction and to ignite the gas upon release, Marsh then held a porcelain bowl to the arsine flame and collected the precipitate (shiny metallic flakes, called "mirrors") that was, in fact, the extracted arsenic itself. By repeating the process, even the most infinitesimal trace of the poison could be rendered evident this way.

Marsh wrote a report describing his breakthrough test and special apparatus, and his article was published in the *Edinburgh Philosophical Journal* of October 1836. In Paris, world-famous toxicologist Mathieu OR-FILA and other prominent scientists seized upon Marsh's discovery and began their own series of experiments. Orfila contributed several practical refinements to the extremely delicate procedure. Demonstrating that even the tiniest trace of arsenic contamination in commercially produced analytical reagents could render a misleading positive result, he recommended that all reagents should be tested and proven arsenic-free before use in a poison investigation. In 1840, Orfila's expert application of the Marsh test decided one of the most frenzied controversies of the day, the murder-by-poison trial of Marie LAFARGE. Her subsequent conviction made criminological history as the first major murder case to turn on a toxicologist's report.

At the Woolwich arsenal, Marsh carried on with his work in artillery technology and electromagnetism. At some point he became assistant to a certain Faraday (no relation to the scientist Michael Faraday) at the Royal Military Academy, also in Woolwich. He held that position, at a very modest salary, until his death in London on June 21, 1846.

Marshall, John (1755–1835) The fourth chief justice of the United States Supreme Court was a great jurist who not only established the authority and scope of the court, but also largely determined the shape of American constitutional law.

Marshall was born in Prince William (now Fauquier) County, Virginia, on September 24, 1755. Born and raised near the frontier, he received little educa-

tion. After fighting in the Revolution, he studied law, opened up a successful practice, and became active in Viriginia state politics, serving in the state's House of Delegates (1782–90, 1795–96) and becoming a leading Federalist. In 1797, Marshall came to national prominence when President John Adams sent him to France as a negotiator in the infamous XYZ Affair. Partly on the strength of the popularity he won in this role, Marshall was elected to the House of Representatives in 1799, and the following year Adams appointed him secretary of state. In January 1801, just two months before Adams left office, the outgoing Federalist president appointed Marshall chief justice of the United States.

Marshall's installation on the high court was one of a number of "midnight appointments" Adams made. The most momentous of these turned out to be that of a relatively minor official, William Marbury, whom Adams had appointed justice of the peace for Washington, D.C. Although made before Adams left office, the appointment had not been "distributed" when Jefferson entered the White House. Jefferson, an anti-Federalist, declined to distribute this and other appointments Adams made under the Judiciary Act of 1801, a piece of legislation designed by Federalists to curb what they saw as Jeffersonian radicalism. Marbury petitioned the Supreme Court for a write of mandamus, which would order the distribution of the commissions. Despite his own Federalist affiliation, Marshall had no wish simply to oppose the president. However, neither did he want to weaken the Supreme Court by seeming to back down before Jefferson. Instead, he declared that Marbury was indeed entitled to the commission, but the Supreme Court could do nothing to force its delivery, because the Federal Judiciary Act of 1789, allowing writs of mandamus to be requested from the Supreme Court, was unconstitutional. The 1803 case of *Marbury* v. *Madison* was the first in which the court declared an act of Congress unconstitutional. It established the cardinal principle of judicial review by the federal courts over acts of the other two branches of government, firmly establishing the authority of the Supreme Court.

Marshall's subsequent decisions were marked by the same force of intellect. They were characteristically colored by his Federalism and tended to enhance the preservation of private property rights, federal power, and the prestige of the court. *Fletcher* v. *Peck* (1810) and *Dartmouth College* v. *Woodward* (1816) limited the states' authority to impair contracts and established the sanctity of private property rights. *McCulloch* v. *Maryland* (1819) prohibited the states from taxing a federal entity, the Bank of the United States, and the court upheld the right of Congress to establish such a federal entity by interpreting the "implied powers" clause of the Constitution in the broadest possible manner. *Cohens* v. *Virginia* (1821) and *Gibbons* v. *Ogden* (1824) established the unity of the federal court system and established the primacy of federal authority over that of the states when federal and state interests clashed.

Perhaps Marshall's most sensational moment came in 1807, when he presided over the treason trial of Aaron Burr, whom he found not guilty on the grounds that the government had established only Burr's apparent *intention* of committing treason and had not provided evidence of the *act* of treason.

Marshall served as chief justice from 1801 until his death in 1835. He participated in more than a thousand decisions, of which he wrote half. He was also the author of a five-volume biography of George Washington (1804–07).

Further reading: Baker, Leonard, *John Marshall: A Life in Law* (New York: Macmillan, 1974).

Beveridge, Albert J., *The Life of John Marshall,* 2 vols. (Boston: Houghton Mifflin Co., 1916–1919).

Marshall, Thurgood (1908–93)   The first African-American justice of the U.S. Supreme Court; helped shape the judicial history of American civil rights as chief of the legal-defense section of the NAACP.

Born in Baltimore on July 2, 1908, Thurgood Marshall was educated at Lincoln University, graduating in 1930, and receiving his law degree from Howard University in 1933, number one in his class. He returned to Baltimore, where he practiced law, specializing in civil rights litigation, and in 1940 was appointed chief of the legal-defense section of the National Association for the Advancement of Colored People (NAACP). He argued a total of 32 landmark cases before the Supreme Court and won 29 of them, the most important of which being *Brown* v. *Board of Education of Topeka, Kansas* (1954), which forever changed American civil rights law by overturning the doctrine of "separate but equal," which held that racial segregation was constitutional, provided that the separate facilities established and maintained were equal. Marshall successfully argued that racial segregation created educational facilities that were inherently *unequal,* because they failed to provide the same social experiences and opportunities. The case led not only to desegregation of schools, but also, ultimately, to the desegregation of all public facilities.

In July 1965, President Lyndon B. JOHNSON appointed Marshall solicitor general of the United States, and in June 1967 he nominated him to the Supreme Court. Marshall became one of the high court's great liberal voices, rendering liberal opinions not only in cases involving African-American civil rights issues, but also on abortion and the death penalty. Both

hailed and reviled for his often harsh frankness, he retired from the court in 1991 because of ill health.

Further reading: Goldman, Roger, and David Gallen, *Thurgood Marshall: Justice for All* (New York: Carroll & Graf, 1992).

Martinez, Bob (1934–)   Director of the Office of National Drug Control Policy during the latter half of the administration of President George Bush.

A lifelong resident of Florida, Bob Martinez was born on December 15, 1934, in Tampa and attended the University of Tampa, graduating in 1957. Despite an absence of political experience, he ran for mayor of Tampa in 1979 and won, serving eight years before he began his successful campaign for Florida's governorship, where he served from 1987 until he was defeated for reelection in 1991.

After being nominated by President George Bush as director of the Office of National Drug Control Policy and confirmed by the Senate in March 1991, Martinez vowed to increase emphasis on treatment and education over imprisonment. In contrast, as Florida's governor his policy had stressed punishment; under his leadership, the incarceration rate for first-time offenders increased by over 27%.

As federal "drug czar," Martinez proved ill-suited to deal with the myriad of agencies involved in drug enforcement, including the FBI, the DEA, the Justice Department, and even the CIA and National Security Council in international drug matters. Martinez forced out many of his own top aides, replacing them with people who had no experience in the drug war. Indeed he gained such little respect for his agency that, in 1992, when John Sununu was forced to step down as White House chief of staff and found himself in need of an office, Martinez was evicted from his to make room.

Under Martinez, the federal government promised $99 million in funding for drug education and rehabilitation, contingent on states matching the federal contribution. In the recession-plagued early 1990s, few states could come up with the necessary funds.

Martinez stepped down as drug czar in 1993, with the inauguration of President Bill Clinton.

Masseria, Joseph (Giuseppe; alias: Joe the Boss; Don Joe) (1879–1931)   An old-fashioned Mafia don, head of the New York Mob from 1920 to 1931.

Masseria was born in Sicily and fled to the United States in 1903 to escape a murder charge in Palermo, where he had been a Mafia enforcer. In New York, he became an enforcer for the Morello Gang, Sicilian immigrants who terrorized the merchants of the Lower East Side with extortion demands. Masseria functioned essentially as a gangland "soldier" for 10

Joe "The Boss" Masseria headed New York's Mafia from 1920 until he was gunned down in 1931. (Courtesy of the Library of Congress)

years until, in 1913, he moved boldly against the Morellos and, slowly and steadily, one murder at a time, assumed leadership of the Morello crime empire by 1920.

In 1922, Peter "The Clutching Hand" Morello moved to retake the Morello empire, launching a concerted attack against Masseria and his men. He contracted with professional killer Umberto Valenti (who had already murdered 20 or more men at the behest of the Mafia) to eliminate Masseria. Valenti ambushed the gangster, emptied two revolvers at him and his two bodyguards, killing the bodyguards but missing Masseria. Valenti's target ran down the street and ducked into a hat shop with Valenti in pursuit. The would-be assassin fired more than 10 shots at Masseria, who deftly dodged between the counters. Valenti finally left when he heard the approach of police. From that moment on, Masseria was dubbed the "man who dodges bullets."

He came to control all bootlegging on the Lower East Side and employed such budding luminaries of organized crime as Charles "Lucky" LUCIANO and Joe ADONIS, whom he dispatched to eliminate Umberto Valenti. Soon the other young gangsters, who would eventually create the national crime syndicate—criminal activity organized on a hitherto unheard of scale—joined Masseria's gangs. Frank COSTELLO, Albert ANASTASIA, Vito Genovese, Carlo Gambino, and Thomas "Three-Finger Brown" Lucchese all worked for Joe the Boss. And his crime empire seemed rock solid until the late 1920s, when Salvatore Maranzano, a Sicilian Mafia chieftain, arrived from Palermo, backed by money from Sicilian Mafia chief Don Vito Casio Ferro. Maranzano intended to topple Masseria, take over his empire, and expand operations to include all of New York. He meant to become the "boss of bosses" in New York.

On October 17, 1929, Maranzano abducted Masseria's top lieutenant, Lucky Luciano, who was tortured, beaten, slashed, and left for dead. From his hospital bed, Luciano observed the Mob's code of silence, refusing to reveal to authorities the identity of his assailants, but vowing to "take care of those guys in my own way." However, other Masseria thugs were not as loyal as Luciano and flocked to Maranzano, and a full-scale gangland war developed.

The fact was that Masseria was not the kind of boss to inspire loyalty—except through threats. He was reluctant to share the wealth with his subordinates, and, ultimately, Luciano was persuaded to move against Masseria as well as Marranzano. With Adonis, Costello, and others, he laid plans to take over all the Italian and Sicilian rackets in New York.

Luciano and the others escalated the Mafia warfare throughout 1930 and 1931, watching as potential rival after potential rival eliminated one another. On April 15, 1931, Luciano arranged a meeting with Masseria at a favorite restaurant. Joey the Boss, as was his custom, ate gluttonous portions of antipasto, linguine, lobster, and cream pastries. Following the meal, as the restaurant emptied out, Luciano ordered a pot of coffee and a deck of cards. The two began a friendly game of pinochle. Luciano excused himself to go to the men's room, leaving Masseria alone with a few restaurant employees. Vito Genovese, Albert Anastasia, Joe Adonis, and Benjamin "Bugsy" Siegel walked into the restaurant, drew their revolvers, and opened up on Masseria, planting six fatal shots in his body. Anastasia delivered the superfluous coup de grace—a shot to the back of Masseria's head. Luciano then emerged from the restroom and calmly called the police, explaining to them that "As soon as I finished drying my hands, I hurried out and walked back to see what it was all about."

Masseria's murder went down on the books as un-solved.

Masterson, Bat (Bartholomew) (1853–1921)

One of the legendary gunfighters of the Wild West; wielded great power as a Dodge City lawman until he was driven out of office for excessive violence.

The most famous of the three Masterson brothers, all of whom were lawmen in Ford County, Kansas, Bat had been born and raised on a farm in Quebec, Canada. After a time, his family moved to New York, then Illinois, then various locations in Kansas before finally settling in Wichita. After working on the rail-road for a year with his older brother Ed MASTERSON, Bat turned to buffalo hunting and was in the party that invaded Indian lands in 1874 and was attacked by 500 Comanche and Kiowa Indians at the battle of Adobe Walls. Bat and the 34 other hunters managed to hold off the Indians long enough to escape.

After a brief stint in Texas as a scout, a period during which he was almost fatally wounded in a gunfight, Bat came to the rough-and-tumble cattle town of Dodge City, Kansas, as a deputy marshal in 1876, but left after a year, only to return in 1877 as sheriff of Ford County. As sheriff, Bat was a high-

Bat Masterson made his reputation as a colorful western lawman, then moved back east as a newspaper sportswriter. (Courtesy of the National Archives)

profile and violent lawman, who relied heavily on his gun and his quick draw, which were enough to intimidate almost anyone. He actually killed only one man in a "draw-down" gunfight. This is not to say that he didn't kill several other men in the line of duty; indeed, he never went into a situation without his gun drawn, and once it was drawn, he hated to put it away without using it.

By 1880, when Bat came up for reelection as sheriff, many citizens were tired of the excessive violence he brought to the task. There were also disturbing questions regarding his alleged misuse of public funds. Masterson was defeated and left Kansas alto-gether, teaming up with Wyatt Earp in Tombstone, Arizona, as a professional gambler. Brother Jim MAS-TERSON called him back to Dodge City in 1881 to help him deal with A. J. Peacock, the troublesome business partner with whom he owned the Lady Gay Dance Hall. Bat provoked a gunfight that resulted in the wounding of a bystander and the nearly fatal wounding of a Lady Gay bartender. Bat was fined $10, and he and Jim left town.

After he left Kansas, Bat Masterson served as a lawman in various western towns, mostly in Colo-rado, but when a call for help came from Dodge City, Bat responded. When one of his friends felt he had been unfairly run out of town, Bat rounded up Wyatt EARP, Doc Holliday, Luke Short, and a host of other famous gunfighters to stamp out the forces of reform in Dodge City.

Never willing or able to stay in one place for long, Bat continued to roam the West until he was kicked out of Denver by the gaming authorities in 1902. He journeyed to New York, where he became a sports journalist and died in 1921, without having returned to the West for almost two decades.

Further reading: DeArment, Robert K., *Bat Masterson: The Man and the Legend* (Norman: University of Oklahoma Press, 1989).

Masterson, Ed (Edward J.) (1852–78)

In sharp contrast to his trigger-happy and far more famous brother Bat MASTERSON, lawman Ed Masterson was a model of restraint who almost never pulled his gun in the line of duty.

The oldest of the three Masterson brothers, who would all eventually work in law enforcement, Ed was a much more successful peace officer than either Bat or Jim MASTERSON because he seldom resorted to violence to restore order. He always went into a potential gunfight situation with his six-shooter holst-ered and almost never was forced to draw. More often than not, the perpetrator was drunk, and Ed was able to talk him into putting his gun away and coming in quietly to sleep it off.

Ed succeeded Wyatt EARP as marshal of Dodge City. Having served under Earp as deputy marshal, he earned the admiration of the townspeople for his nonviolent ways—a measure of respect denied both to Earp and brother Bat Masterson.

Unfortunately, Ed Masterson's term as marshal lasted barely four months. During this period he introduced such progressive reforms as community service assigned in lieu of jail time, and he cleared Dodge City of tramps and vagrants. But the marshal was killed on April 9, 1878, in a gunfight.

Masterson, Jim (James P.) (1855–95)   The youngest of the three Masterson brothers, Jim resorted to his gun more often than even his trigger-happy brother Bat MASTERSON and was, consequently, a faster draw.

Like his other two brothers, Jim Masterson went into law enforcement in the state of Kansas, particularly Ford County, which included the infamous cattle town of Dodge City. When he was unable to find work as a sheriff or a deputy, Masterson worked as a bartender in Western saloons, an occupation that involved at least as much fighting as law enforcement did. Whether behind a badge or a bar, Jim Masterson most often settled the disputes that came his way with his gun.

During one such altercation, Jim shot and killed one of his own bartenders, and both he and brother Bat, who had also taken part in the gun battle, were forced to leave Dodge City.

Jim was not forced out of law enforcement, however, roaming around Kansas and picking up work wherever it could be found. By the late 1880s, he was named U.S. marshal for Ford County. By 1889, he was serving as deputy sheriff in Ingalls, Kansas. In truth, he was nothing more than a hired gun, brought in by the town's business interests to participate in the bloody feud with the town of Cimarron over which would be the county seat. After moving on to the Oklahoma Territory and participating in several range wars there, Masterson fell into the bottle and died of alcoholism in 1895.

Mather, Cotton (1663–1728)   Forever linked with the Salem Witch Trials of 1692, Mather was a devout Puritan minister and prolific author on a wide range of subjects.

Cotton Mather was born February 12, 1663, in Salem, Massachusetts, the eldest son of Increase Mather. After some home schooling, Mather attended the Boston Latin School before entering Harvard University at the age of 12. Hoping to follow his father into the clergy, Mather graduated in 1678 with a degree in theology, but he was afflicted with a severe stammer, perhaps brought on by overly intense training at too early an age. Fearing his career in the pulpit was over before it began, Mather turned to medicine instead, but his impediment soon disappeared, and he was preaching by 1680.

Joining his father at the Second Church of Boston, he earned his master's degree from Harvard in 1681 and began to write copiously on subjects ranging from theology to history to morality to science to medicine. Among the subjects that fascinated him most was that of witches and Satanism—not an unusual obsession in the late 17th century.

In 1688, when a girl from Boston claimed to be a witch possessed by the devil, Mather studied the case diligently, inviting the girl into his home so that he could study her more effectively. The subject of witches and the devil figured with increasing prominence in Mather's sermons of this period, and many later historians have suggested that Mather was in large measure to blame for creating the atmosphere in which the Salem witchcraft hysteria developed.

When several girls claiming to have been possessed by a West Indian slave began having seizures, Salem—with Mather apparently taking the lead—entered into its self-fulfilling prophecy. Officials rounded up hundreds of suspected witches, male and female. Those who were accused, tried, and found guilty of being witches were executed if they continued to protest their innocence. Some 19 persons were hanged, and one old man perished under torture designed to extract a confession; he was pressed to death beneath a heap of stones. Others, who confessed, were jailed and supposedly healed.

While Mather actively supported the hunting and prosecution of witches, he opposed the executions and renounced the manner in which the trials were conducted. They were based on hearsay and lacked firm evidentiary rules. Mather, a true believer in the reality of witchcraft, nevertheless wanted to see the trials conducted according to rules applicable to any criminal case.

After several girls who had previously claimed to be possessed renounced their earlier confessions, public opinion turned to revulsion, and there were official admissions that innocent people may have been executed. Mather, unlike his fellow colonial worthy Samuel Sewall, was largely unrepentant and, therefore, became a convenient scapegoat for the hysteria of an entire population. The Salem episode destroyed the minister's political aspirations and sharply reduced his theological influence on a New England that was already rapidly turning away from strict Puritanism.

Matsell, George (1811–77)   A pioneering chief and commissioner of the New York City Police Department.

George Matsell's parents immigrated to the United States from Ireland in 1800, settling in New York, where his father opened a book store and eventually apprenticed young George. After working for a time with another bookseller, Matsell opened a shop of his own. In 1840, he became a police magistrate and quickly realized that the city had outgrown the watch system then current. Organizing a small squad of men under himself, Matsell began making regular night patrols, particularly along the river fronts, where he and his men made several arrests and were able to prevent crimes before they occurred. Matsell's efforts showed the direction police reform in New York and the United States needed to take: intervention in and prevention of criminal acts. In 1844 the Municipal Police Act was passed, giving the police force greater responsibility for protecting the growing city. Mayor William F. Havemeyer quickly nominated Matsell as chief of the new department.

Matsell proceeded to carry out the provisions of the act, improving patrol methods and enforcing rigorous discipline. The new system was quickly put to the test by the infamous Astor Place Riots and the election disturbances that were a fixture of New York City politics. Matsell pushed for a special river police to protect the estimated $350 million worth of property associated with the harbor and waterways. In 1857, the state legislature passed the Metropolitan Police Act, supplanting the Municipal Police Act and establishing a police commission to run the department. The ensuing battle for control over the police department resulted in a change in administrations, and Matsell lost his job.

When Mayor Havemeyer was reelected in 1871, he again nominated Matsell to a position with the police, this time as superintendent of police. Shortly thereafter, he was appointed a police commissioner, being elected president of the board of police commissioners in July 1873. When Havemeyer was again voted out of office, Matsell went with him, this time for good, returning to the private law practice he had in the meantime established.

Mattick, Hans Walter (1920–78)   A criminologist and educator.

A native of Germany, Hans Mattick moved to the United States with his family as a small child, settling first in rural Michigan and then in Chicago. He earned both his bachelor and master's degrees from the University of Chicago and in 1950 took his first position in the criminology field, as a research sociologist for the Illinois Parole and Pardon Board. At the same time, he was appointed lecturer in sociology at the University of Indiana.

In 1955, Mattick was appointed assistant warden of the Cook County Jail in Chicago and concurrently assumed a teaching post at the University of Chicago in 1957. Mattick conducted a study of unemployment and compensation for the Illinois state treasurer, then served for six years as director of the Chicago Youth Development Project of the Institute for Social Research at the University of Michigan. In 1972, he settled in Champaign, Illinois, as professor of criminal justice and director of the Center for Research in Criminal Justice at the University of Illinois. He remained at the university until his death in 1978.

Maudsley, Henry (1835–1918)   Professor of medical jurisprudence at University College in London; published *Responsibility in Mental Diseases* in 1874, which challenged the long-cherished belief that insane persons act without motive.

After serving as medical superintendent of the Manchester Royal Lunatic Asylum and editor of the *Journal of Mental Science*, 33-year-old Henry Maudsley was appointed to the faculty of University College, London. During his tenure at this institution, Maudsley devoted himself to studying the causes of mental diseases, including criminal insanity.

Maudsley's influence on forensics can be traced to his numerous writings on the subject, including the landmark *Responsibility in Mental Diseases* (1874), which sought more sharply to define responsibility for criminal acts committed by those judged insane. While Maudsley was primarily a materialist, who believed that mental disease was based in organic disorder, he also stressed the role of environment in bringing about criminal behavior.

After his death in 1918, the London University school of medicine was renamed the Maudsley Hospital, where it remains today as a symbol of the doctor's genius.

Further reading: Walk, Alexander, "Medico-psychologists, Maudsley and The Maudsley," in R. M. Murray and T. H. Turner, eds., *Lectures on the History of Psychiatry* (London: Gaskell, 1990).

May, Luke S. (1886–1955)   Popularly called the American Sherlock Holmes; brought an unusual mixture of expertise in the physical and natural sciences to his knowledge of criminology in order to solve hundreds of varied cases.

A native of Hall County, Nebraska, Luke May attended public schools and a local business college before entering Gordon Academy in Salt Lake City,

Utah. He left Gordon at the age of 17 and embarked on what would be his life's work: criminal investigation. He established a private investigation agency in Washington state and offered his clients expertise in electrical and mechanical engineering, handwriting analysis, and forgery detection, using the new technique of investigation with ultraviolet light to determine if a document had been tampered with.

Operating out of his home, May was frequently called upon by local police departments stumped by this or that case. May believed that no one committed a crime without leaving a clue to his or her identity, and he was an avid advocate of fingerprinting, even developing his own classification system. He was also an expert in microanalysis, insisting that everything found at a crime scene be saved, preserved, documented, and examined—usually with the aid of a microscope. In one case, May was able to match a tree branch found at a crime scene to the knife of an accused man. He studied the microscopic marks left by the knife that had been used to cut the branch.

May's tenacity and his knowledge of biology helped crack perhaps his most bizarre case. When a woman was found dead with no external marks or wounds, an autopsy concluded that she had suffered a broken neck. With no clues to point to a suspect, local authorities called in May, who reviewed the evidence, concluding that the body should be exhumed. May personally supervised a second autopsy and noted that the neck had not been broken at all and that there was a strange discoloration about the mouth. Knowing that ammonia discolors the skin after death, May performed tests and determined that the woman had died of ammonia poisoning. Next, he searched the woman's house and came up with a startling piece of evidence. The woman's brother-in-law, an invalid who had been staying with her and her husband, had left a series of cryptic astrological notes and signs. After hours of studying and deciphering, May discovered that the man had written instructions to his nephew to commit a whole series of murders, including that of the woman. He was able to control the young man through hypnosis and ordered him to kill his stepmother. The boy was sentenced to life in prison, and the invalid Svengali was hanged.

Mayne, Sir Richard (1796–1868) One of the founding fathers of Scotland Yard; appointed in 1829 by Sir Robert Peel as co-commissioner of the newly formed Metropolitan Police force of London, an agency he would head for 39 years.

An Irishman educated at Cambridge, Richard Mayne received an M.A. degree in 1821, after which he entered into a career as a lawyer in northern England. In 1829, Home Secretary Sir Robert Peel appointed the young lawyer as the first co-commissioner of the "new police" of London along with Charles Rowan. This was the beginning of professional law enforcement in London and, insofar as other cities looked to the British capital, in the world.

Rowan and Mayne carried out the program Peel had mandated, a program of preventative law enforcement—at the time, a radical idea. Rowan's retirement in 1849 left Mayne to deal alone with London's rising urban violence. Police operations during the Hyde Park labor riots of 1866 brought charges of police brutality, and Mayne himself admitted to having mishandled the situation. The Hyde Park affair tarnished an otherwise thoroughly distinguished career. The Crown and the people forgave Mayne, who remained police commissioner, but he never forgave himself. Richard Mayne, deeply dispirited, died two years later.

Further reading: Browne, Douglas G., *The Rise of Scotland Yard* (Westport, Conn.: Greenwood Press, 1973).
Wilkes, John, *The London Police in the Nineteenth Century* (London: Cambridge University Press, 1971).

Mayo, Katherine (1867–1940) An influential writer on criminal justice and law enforcement and an ardent proponent of a state police system for New York.

The daughter of a goldminer who scoured the world, looking for the elusive mother lode, Katherine Mayo traveled the nation and the globe with her family, observing, as she did so, much of the world's injustice and inequity. Charged with a passion for exposing such conditions to the public, Mayo began writing, selling her first sketch to the original *Life* magazine in 1892. After securing a staff position at the *Saturday Evening Post* in 1906, she began work on her first book, about the abolitionist John Brown, opponent of the greatest injustice of all.

Much of Mayo's life was spent in research, which often turned into a cause. Such was the case with the New York State Police. While visiting a friend in rural Bedford Hills, New York, she heard about a man who had been robbed and killed by itinerant laborers. With no police force for miles and the locals fearful of the known killers, nothing was done to apprehend them. Mayo promptly began agitating for a rural police force, and, in so doing, learned of a similar force in New Jersey. She studied the New Jersey organization and gathered information for *Justice to All*, her first book about the need for a state police force. The foreword was written by Theodore ROOSEVELT.

Indeed, Roosevelt ordered a copy delivered to every member of the New York legislature before a vote was taken on a proposal to create a state force. The measure passed, and Mayo earned the name of "mother of the state police."

She continued to write about injustices, including the Hindu practice of child marriage brokering in India and political corruption in the Philippines, books that may or may not have influenced policies of foreign nations regulating these practices, but which the governments of Great Britain and the United States used toward justifying long delay in granting these countries their independence.

Mayo died in 1940 while writing a book about the world narcotics trade.

Further reading: Mayo, Katherine, *Justice to All: The Story of the Pennsylvania State Police* (1917; reprint ed., New York: Ayer, 1971).

McCulloch, Hugh (1808–ca. 1890) Secretary of the treasury under Abraham Lincoln; founder of the modern Secret Service.

Descended from wealthy Scottish immigrants, Hugh McCulloch was raised in Kennebunkport, Maine, the son of the largest shipbuilder in New England. McCulloch's father was barely able to afford to send him to college after the British nearly destroyed his business in the War of 1812; however, McCulloch did attend Bowdoin College for one year before becoming a teacher. After taking an interest in the law, he moved to Fort Wayne, Indiana, to begin practicing. Within two years, he was offered the position of branch manager at the State Bank of Indiana and took it, remaining in the financial field for the rest of his life.

In Indiana, McCulloch's reputation as a genius in financial management skyrocketed. When the bank was rechartered as the Bank of the State of Indiana, he was given control over all 26 branches and their combined $6 million capital. In 1863, Treasury Secretary Salmon P. Chase appointed McCulloch as comptroller of the national currency. Two years later, when Chase's successor, William Pitt Fessenden, stepped down as secretary himself, Lincoln nominated McCulloch to fill the position.

The largest problem immediately facing McCulloch was the rash of counterfeit bills in circulation. A Treasury Department study showed that fully one-third of all bills in circulation were counterfeit. When a series of operations involving part-time officers failed to show results, McCulloch determined that only a separate, full-time federal force could stanch the flow of illegal bills. He introduced the concept of the Secret Service to the president at Lincoln's final cabinet meeting. Lincoln approved the measure, and that very night he was assassinated at Ford's Theater.

In the chaos that followed the president's murder, much of the federal government's business was tabled, including the establishment of the new force, but McCulloch persevered and President Andrew Johnson approved his plan later in 1865. William WOOD was quickly named as the Secret Service's first chief in July, and, within a single year, the problem of counterfeiting was under control, with more than 200 major counterfeiters behind bars.

McDonald, Hugh Chisholm (1913–) Former civil chief of the Los Angeles County sheriff's office; the inventor of the Identi-Kit system for criminal identification.

Born in Hopkins, Minnesota, McDonald attended the University of Southern California, the University of Michigan, and Stanford University. He joined the Los Angeles County Sheriff's Department as a deputy in 1940. The very same year, he was sent to Europe to search for certain individuals among the growing number of wartime vice and black market operators. Because few of these opportunistic felons had established any prewar criminal records, fingerprints helped little in tracking them down.

Following BERTILLON's principle of the *portrait parle* ("speaking portrait"), McDonald began turning eyewitness descriptions into rough sketches of the wanted suspects. To expedite his drawing process, he decided to create a number of transparent templates, each bearing a characteristic nose, mouth, chin, and so on. Now his witnesses could instantly choose among a variety of prefabricated elements, and McDonald, superimposing the transparencies and inking in any additional details his informers recalled, could form a composite likeness to aid in his search for the mystery suspect.

Between 1942 and 1946, McDonald served in the U.S. Army's military intelligence department, where he achieved the rank of major. When he returned to California, McDonald took his composite portrait idea to the Townsend Company of Santa Ana. Within a few years, and after further consultation with officials of the California Department of Justice, Townsend began marketing a refined and patented version of McDonald's field pack to police departments around the nation. In a box resembling an oversize index card file (4.5" × 7" × 10"), the Identi-Kit's 525 standardized and coded transparencies provided a wide range of types for every individual facial feature, including 102 pairs of eyes and 25 types of mustache and beard. Mixed and matched, these could produce 62 billion different combinations, according to McDonald. Ears (rarely noted by crime victims) could be added after the fact, and any moles, scars, or other unusual marks could be drawn in with wax pencil to provide additional distinguishing details.

One of the Identi-Kit's greatest assets was its numbering system. Before faxes and other advancements in telecommunications had made the transfer of images routine, detectives in one city could alert another city's police department of a wanted man's Identi-Kit code, and the remote officers could immediately prepare the same composite sketch from their own station-house copy of Townsend's transparencies. Identi-Files were established next, to store the particular Identi-Kit composites of known criminals, and these were useful for quick cross-reference. Another interesting advantage of the Identi-Kit system earned appreciation later on: The portraits could be broadcast on television news reports and reach a wide audience without posing the legal risks that exhibiting photographs of hunted—but unconfirmed—suspects sometimes did.

Great Britain was the first foreign country to adopt the system, and McDonald himself provided a training seminar for 31 police chiefs. By 1960, the same year McDonald was made chief of detectives in Los Angeles County, the patented service had police force subscribers in many nations around the world.

From 1947 to 1970, McDonald also worked part-time for the United States Central Intelligence Agency (CIA), and in 1968 he left the L.A. sheriff's office to become president of World Associates, a private security company. He served in that post until 1973, when he accepted the directorship of security at the Hollywood Turf Club. Also in 1973, McDonald published his first novel, a mystery titled *The Auditorium Affair*. The former detective followed this with several more documentary-style novels: *Hour of the Blue Fox* (1975), *Appointment in Dallas* (1975), *Five Signs from Ruby* (1976), and *Two Words from Kiev* (1976).

McDonald, William Jesse (1852–1918)

One of the Texas Rangers' most celebrated captains, known as a "man who would charge hell with a bucket of water."

Born in Kemper County, Mississippi, on September 28, 1852, McDonald moved with his family to Rusk County, Texas, in 1866. At age 16, McDonald was tried for treason following a conflict with the post–Civil War military government, but was acquitted. He graduated from a commercial college in New Orleans in 1872 and went into the grocery business until he was appointed deputy sheriff of Wood County, Texas. In this capacity he soon established a reputation for what biographer Ries Jarrett (*Handbook of Texas*) called

"fearless law enforcement, expert marksmanship, and lightning quick disarming of his opponent."

In 1883, he moved to Wichita County, where he was in the cattle and lumber business and where he became deputy sheriff, special ranger, and a deputy U.S. marshal. Once again, his law-enforcement work earned him a powerful reputation, and in 1891 Governor Stephen Hogg appointed him captain of Company B, Frontier Battalion of Texas Rangers. McDonald brought law and order to the free-wheeling Panhandle and in 1905 served as personal bodyguard to President Theodore ROOSEVELT when he toured the region.

In 1907, Governor Thomas M. Campbell appointed McDonald a revenue agent, and in 1912 McDonald served as bodyguard to another president, Woodrow WILSON. Wilson subsequently appointed McDonald U.S. marshal of the northern district of Texas. McDonald died of pneumonia on January 15, 1918.

Further reading: Paine, Albert Bigelow, *Captain Bill McDonald, Texas Ranger: A Story of Frontier Reform* (New York: J.J. Little and Ives, 1909).

McGranery, James Patrick (1895–1962)

As United States attorney general, McGranery used immigration and naturalization laws to fight organized crime by deporting foreign-born criminals.

Raised in Philadelphia, James McGranery attended Catholic schools before moving on to work as an apprentice printer. At the outbreak of World War I, he served in Europe in the 111th Infantry Division and as a Signal Corps balloon observer. After the war, McGranery returned to school, entering Philadelphia's Temple University in 1920 and becoming active in local politics. Earning his law degree from Temple in 1928, he was admitted to the bar and stepped up his political activity.

In 1928, McGranery headed Alfred Smith's Philadelphia campaign for the presidency and was elected to the Pennsylvania Democratic Central Committee. He made several bids for elective office, but was unsuccessful until 1936, when he was elected to the U.S. House of Representatives, being returned to his seat three times. While in the House, he became an ardent supporter of the New Deal. In 1943, he was named assistant attorney general, and in 1946 he was appointed to a federal judgeship.

On the bench, he gained a reputation as a firm jurist, and, impressed by his actions and ethics, President Harry S Truman appointed him attorney general in April 1952. There was immediate concern over this appointment, however, as various scandals within the Truman administration were currently being investigated by the Justice Department, and many feared

McGranery would sweep them under the carpet. True to form, however, McGranery actively prosecuted all those involved and managed to save face for the administration in so doing.

One of McGranery's major concerns as attorney general was the rise in organized crime, especially that perpetrated by naturalized immigrants. He decided to use the Smith Act—which provided for the deportation of immigrants engaged in illegal activity and which had already been used to deport hundreds of accused communists during the post–World War I Red Scare—to fight organized crime. Almost 50 high-ranking organized crime figures were deported during McGranery's tenure, including Frank COSTELLO and Thomas Lucchese, the ranking figures in their respective Mafia crime families.

McKay, Henry D. (1899–) McKay conducted groundbreaking, detailed, firsthand research into juvenile delinquency.

Like his future colleague Clifford R. SHAW, McKay was a farm boy and the product of a large family. He was born in December 1899 on a farm in Hand County, South Dakota, the fifth in a family of seven children. After attending public schools, he attended Dakota Wesleyan University, earning a B.A., then went to the University of Chicago in 1923 for postgraduate study. In 1924, he left the university to teach at the University of Illinois, returning in 1926 and studying sporadically until 1929. He left without completing his Ph.D.

Beginning in 1926, McKay worked at the Institute for Juvenile Research, which was created in 1926 from what had been the Chicago Juvenile Psychopathic Institute. There he met Shaw, and the two collaborated on groundbreaking studies of juvenile delinquency, which included the collection of a library of autobiographical narratives from delinquents, a geographical study of the distribution patterns of delinquency, and a pioneering community-based program of prevention called the Chicago Area Project (CAP).

McKay was the only major research scholar to make a contribution to two of the nation's important early "crime commission" reports: the National Commission on Law Observance and Enforcement (the so-called Wickersham Commission) in 1929 and the President's Commission on Law Enforcement and Administration of Justice in the early 1940s.

Further reading: Shaw, Clifford R., and Henry D. McKay, *Juvenile Delinquency and Urban Areas: A Study of Rates of Delinquency in Relation to Differential Characteristics of Local Communities in American Cities* (Chicago: University of Chicago, 1942, 1969).

McNally, George (1906–70) Director of White House communications for two decades; also worked to destroy a Nazi counterfeiting plot during World War II.

A native of Brooklyn, New York, George McNally attended the University of Notre Dame before enlisting in the U.S. Navy as a seaman. In 1935, he joined the Secret Service and worked in the counterfeiting division, specializing in locating counterfeiting operations. In 1941, he was assigned to protect President Franklin D. ROOSEVELT, and the following year he left the Secret Service to join the army. Because of his experience, McNally was assigned to the Signal Corps and stationed at the White House, where he was in charge of communications.

Near the end of the war, U.S. intelligence uncovered a Nazi plot to flood Europe with counterfeit currency of the Allied nations in an effort to create a massive panic that would cripple the Allied war effort in a way German bombs and bullets had failed to do. In response to the discovery of the scheme, McNally was quickly transferred to Europe, where he worked with Scotland Yard to root out the counterfeiters. In one seizure, investigators confiscated almost $100 million in bad notes. A conservative estimate after the war placed the amount of money counterfeited at half a billion dollars.

After the war, McNally returned to the White House, where he became director of communications, responsible for keeping increasingly peripatetic presidents in constant contact with the White House, wherever they might be traveling. When Soviet premier Nikita Khrushchev visited the United States in 1958, McNally arranged a communication link to the Kremlin, making possible what was then the longest-distance-ever direct-dial call. When President Eisenhower visited India the following year, McNally installed the first telephone ever seen in the Taj Mahal.

McParland, James (1844–1919) A celebrated Pinkerton detective who infiltrated and brought down the secret Irish-immigrant, terrorist labor union known as the Molly Maguires.

In 1871, when the Philadelphia and Reading Railroad hired the famous Pinkerton Detective Agency to investigate the Molly Maguires, a violent group of Irish labor agitators active in eastern Pennsylvania, Allan PINKERTON chose a young operative named James McParland for the job. The result was one of the most successful and most dangerous undercover operations of the century.

For two years, McParland posed as an Irish vagrant named James McKenna. McParland managed to penetrate the secret organization in 1873, all the while sending reports back to the Pinkerton Agency, which ultimately included the names and addresses of more than 400 Molly Maguires. The operation culminated in the arrest of many of the men and the eventual conviction of more than 60 Molly Maguires, including 19 men who were hanged for murder. McParland's work effectively ended the Molly Maguires and placed his name in the history books as a great detective or ethnic traitor, depending on which history you were reading.

The Irishman went on to head up the Denver office of the Pinkerton agency, where he worked with noted western detective Charles SIRINGO.

Further reading: Pinkowski, Edward, *Forgotten Fathers* (Albuquerque, N.M.: Sunshine Press, 1955).

Melville-Lee, W. L. (1865–1955)   British barrister and proponent of a professional police force; a leading voice in the early 19th-century debate over preventative law enforcement.

W. L. Melville-Lee was both a barrister and an army officer, who developed an interest in police work and sought appointment to a high police post. However, a serious polo injury prevented his achieving his goal, and he contented himself with service as an important Victorian-era commentator on the role of the police, stressing in particular the superiority of the trained constable over the more casual, often corrupt, and usually inefficient watchman. Melville-Lee emphasized the need for foot-patrol constables of high moral character and a commitment to public service. These men were to be assigned a regular beat with the object of becoming familiar and respected figures in the community, ever vigilant to prevent crime rather than waiting to pursue criminals after the fact.

While Melville-Lee failed to attain a police post himself, he did serve with distinction as an army counterintelligence officer during World War I.

Further reading: Melville-Lee, W. L., *A History of Police in England and Wales* (London: Methuen, 1901).

Mendoza, Corine (1952–   )   Heralding an era of a more ethnically representative urban law enforcement establishment, Mendoza became only the fourth Hispanic woman to reach the rank of sergeant in the Chicago Police Department.

Raised in Chicago's predominantly Hispanic Pilsen neighborhood, Corine Mendoza was about to receive an associate degree from Chicago City College in 1979 when she heard about promising opportunities for women in law enforcement. She passed the city's entrance exam and was admitted to the police academy shortly before she graduated from the City College program. When she entered the force, it had been only four years since women were assigned patrol duty, and many male officers were skeptical. But from 1980 to 1984, Mendoza proved herself in a high-risk assignment undercover in the Chicago subway system.

Mendoza next worked for a year in community relations, mostly with the Police Explorers, a Boy Scout program aimed at involving teenage boys and girls in law enforcement. Mendoza encouraged ethnic minority youths to consider police work as a career. She also returned to the academy to teach courses on cultural awareness and racial and ethnic sensitivity.

Returning to the street, she served with the narcotics division and was promoted to detective in 1989. Mendoza was promoted to sergeant in July 1990.

Merton, Robert K. (1910–   )   One of the foremost American sociologists of the 20th century; developed a model for crime and deviancy based on societal expectations.

Robert Merton grew up in a tough South Philadelphia neighborhood, where he imbibed many of the values of the street. However, he also had an intense love of books, which earned him a scholarship to Temple University in 1927. Merton became a sociology major during his sophomore year. After graduation in 1931, he earned a graduate fellowship to Harvard and did extensive research there for his doctoral dissertation, which he completed in 1936. Merton remained in Cambridge for two years before accepting a position as associate professor at Tulane University in New Orleans. He taught there for two years, finally moving to New York's Columbia University. There he remained for the balance of his long and distinguished academic career, becoming professor emeritus in 1979.

It is a mark of the early stature of Merton's work that he was named to the Columbia position. At the time, the field of sociology was sharply divided between two camps, the empiricists and the theorists. Although Merton considered himself a theorist, his work and reputation gained him acceptance by both groups.

Merton developed theories on the effect of social expectations on deviant behavior. His argument was an adaptation and extension of Emile DURKHEIM's theory of anomie, which related deviancy to a breakdown of social standards. Merton argued in an article subsequently called "the most frequently quoted single paper in modern sociology" that crime and deviancy result from the inability of all individuals in society to achieve equal success and happiness. He followed this article with another concluding that, within an individual, culture approves certain objectives and certain means to achieve those objectives. When undue emphasis is placed on the objectives rather than the means of achieving them, the result is deviancy. Thus Merton's theories put the onus of crime and deviancy on the values of society rather than on the individual, codifying the chief assumptions on which all liberal theories of criminality are based.

Miller, Richard William (1936–) The first FBI agent ever charged with espionage.

Miller was born in a working-class neighborhood of Los Angeles and was educated at public schools and at a local junior college. He later enrolled in and graduated from Brigham Young University, from which the FBI recruited him in 1964, partly because of his fluency in Spanish. He compiled an undistinguished record as an FBI agent and, indeed, was frequently criticized for being overweight (at 5 feet, 10 inches, he weighed in at more than 200 pounds) and for generally mediocre job performance.

Miller was given a low-priority assignment interviewing Soviet emigres. In 1983, one of those he interviewed was Svetlana Ogorodnikova. A sexual relationship developed between Miller and Ogorodnikova, who subsequently proved to be a Soviet agent. In the course of their affair, Miller gave her a classified FBI manual on operational methods.

Miller was arrested in 1984 and, during the next six years, was tried three times on charges relating to the case. He claimed that he had been conducting a secret one-man effort to infiltrate a Soviet intelligence network operating in Southern California and that by infiltrating the network, he hoped to redeem his lackluster FBI career. The jury at his first trial deadlocked, with a majority favoring conviction; a second jury convicted Miller, but the conviction was overturned on appeal because the judge had improperly allowed the results of lie-detector tests to be admitted as evidence. The third trial resulted in conviction on October 9, 1990. On February 4, 1991, the portly FBI agent was sentenced to serve 20 years in a federal prison. Ogorodnikova was also convicted of espionage in a separate trial and was sentenced to an 18-year term.

Miller, Wilbur R. (1944–) A criminal historian best known for his work comparing the rise of the New York and London police forces.

A native of Iowa City, Iowa, Wilbur Miller was educated at the University of California, Berkeley, earning his bachelor's degree in 1966. Leaving Berkeley for postgraduate study, Miller enrolled at Columbia University, where he earned both his master's degree and his Ph.D. in history. After a six-year tenure at Princeton University, Miller accepted a post on the history faculty of the State University of New York at Stony Brook.

Miller wrote an important history of moonshining, *Revenuers and Moonshiners: Enforcing Federal Liquor Law in the Mountain South,* in 1991, and a seminal comparative study of New York's and London's police forces, *Cops and Bobbies: Police Authority in New York and London.* Observing that both forces draw on English traditions, Miller explored the implications of the different paths of development each department took. London's police, the first modern police force in a nation with representative government, was an elitist organization based on England's vaunted institution of civil service. Because of this, the police were traditionally more responsible to the government than to the public at large. In marked contrast, the development of the New York police was tied to a system of political cronyism. This accounts not only for the extensive corruption that plagued the New York police during its early days, but also for the perception that, while the London force is an extension of the national government, the New York department is an aspect of the life of the neighborhood.

Milton, Oliver. See HEWITT, Cecil Rolph.

Miranda, Ernesto (1940–76) The case of *Miranda* v. *Arizona* occasioned the landmark Supreme Court ruling that an individual must be advised of his rights at the time of his arrest.

The son of Mexican immigrants, Ernesto Miranda was born in 1940 in Mesa, Arizona. By the time he was 14, he had committed his first felony, grand theft auto, and at 16 he attempted his first rape. After his release from prison, Miranda moved to California, where he was arrested at least three times in eight months on charges ranging from Peeping Tom activities to armed robbery. California authorities sent him back to Arizona, where he joined the army in 1958 to make a new start. Within a year, however, he was discharged as an "undesirable" and was arrested again on several occasions on various charges. By the time he was 21, Miranda had been charged with numerous felonies and misdemeanors and had spent most of his adolescence in custody.

In the early sixties, Miranda met a woman, had a child with her, and lived with her in Mesa, Arizona. Although unmarried, the couple bought a home, which provided the first real family life Miranda had ever known. Miranda got a job at United Produce in Phoenix and was an excellent worker, receiving high praise from his superiors. It had been two years since his last arrest, the longest he had gone without running afoul of the law since the age of 14.

His "straight time" ended on March 13, 1963, when he was arrested for the rape and kidnapping of Lois Ann Jameson. Taken into custody, Miranda was put in a lineup. The victim failed to identify him positively, but the police told him that he had been identified. After that, he was taken into an interrogation room, where, after two hours of questioning, he confessed to the rape. While the confession was not beaten out of him, nor was any undue physical coercion exercised on Miranda, he was not permitted to consult an attorney.

Miranda was quickly convicted of rape, despite his lawyer's argument that most of the evidence against him was inadmissible, because the defendant had been questioned without being apprised of his rights or provided with the legal counsel that would have preserved his Fifth Amendment right to freedom from self-incrimination. *Miranda* v. *Arizona* was argued all the way to the Supreme Court in 1966, where the conviction was overturned on a 5–4 vote, led by Chief Justice Earl WARREN, who wrote in his decision that all individuals must be notified of their constitutional rights before being questioned, including the right to have an attorney present during any questioning, and that they must be informed that any statements they might make could be used against them in court.

The "Miranda decision" was assailed by law enforcement advocates nationwide, who declared that the interrogation room was the domain of the police alone and that this decision would severely hinder attempts at bringing criminals to justice. While the original decision was modified under the more conservative Warren BURGER court, the fundamental import of the decision remains in force.

As to Ernesto Miranda, he was retried and once again convicted, and served a prison term until 1972. After getting into an argument over a poker game in Phoenix in 1976, he was stabbed to death in a bar. Upon his arrest, Miranda's assailant was issued the by-then standard "Miranda warning," advising him of his right to remain silent and to consult an attorney before any questioning.

Misner, Gordon Eugene (1927–) An important and ardent advocate of police reform.

Originally from Denver, Colorado, Gordon Misner began his academic career at San Francisco State College in the late 1940s before receiving his master's degree from the University of California in 1952 and his Ph.D. in criminology in 1967. Misner has taught at San Jose State College; the University of California, Berkeley; and at the University of Missouri, St. Louis. Concurrently, he held various positions with local governmental agencies in which he always advocated police reform. This gained increased attention during the late 1960s, in a climate of dissent on the one hand and strident calls for "law and order" on the other.

Misner has called for increased police professionalism, including a policy of accepting only candidates with college degrees as potential officers. Many objected that this was an overt attempt to exclude the less advantaged and minority applicants from the police force, but Misner argued that police work, like any other profession, requires a better than average understanding of the field; that is, the officer should know more about the law than the people he is enforcing it upon. Misner has also argued that increased professionalism will, of itself, bring a heightened sense of ethical and moral obligation to police work, thereby limiting the corruption that seems to pervade police departments.

In enacting reform, Misner has not put the responsibility on police administrators and personnel alone, but has demanded that reform of political leadership be included; without it, effective long-range planning and policy development cannot succeed.

Further reading: Misner, Gordon Eugene, et al., *Criminal Justice Studies: Their Interdisciplinary Nature* (St. Louis: C. V. Mosby, 1981).

Mitchell, John (Newton) (1913–88) Attorney general under President Richard M. NIXON, Mitchell was a law-and-order advocate but was himself brought down in the Watergate scandal that toppled the Nixon administration, costing Mitchell his freedom, his profession, his marriage, and his reputation.

A native of New York City, John Mitchell attended Fordham University, receiving his law degree from there in 1938. After working for a New York law firm specializing in municipal bonds, Mitchell served three years in the navy as a commander of PT boats during World War II. He returned to the law practice as a partner shortly before his firm merged with Richard Nixon's; as chance would have it, Nixon and Mitchell had adjoining offices. The two became close friends, and when Nixon announced himself as a candidate for the presidency in 1969, he chose Mitchell as his campaign manager.

Upon his election, Nixon nominated Mitchell as attorney general, although Mitchell had earlier denied that he would be a part of the cabinet. As attorney general, Mitchell followed Nixon's lead in promoting a conservative law-and-order program. He was especially harsh on campus demonstrations against the war in Vietnam, the activities of black militants, and anything that smacked of leftism or communism. Against the advice of almost everyone in the legal community, he decided to prosecute the Chicago Seven (who were charged with inciting a riot in Chicago during the 1968 Democratic National Convention)—as well as proceed with an indictment against

Daniel Ellsberg, a former employee of a CIA-run "pacification" program in Vietnam, who had leaked the "Pentagon Papers" to the *New York Times*, detailing the sordid history of U.S. involvement in Vietnam. Mitchell reaped the greatest wrath from civil liberties advocates over his use of wiretapping and the so-called "no-knock" policy.

The Supreme Court had earlier authorized the use of wiretapping in criminal cases, but the previous attorney general, Ramsey Clark, had refused to use it except in cases of national security. Mitchell vowed that he would use wiretapping extensively in criminal proceedings, especially against crime syndicates and what he called "social subversives," which included campus activists, black militants, and antiwar protesters. Of the campus activists, he said, "The thing to do is to get them into court." Similarly, the "no-knock" policy allowed police—with warrants—to enter buildings unannounced. Mitchell's hard line also advocated an automatic sentence of life imprisonment for anyone convicted of three felonies.

Mitchell's own life began to unravel, however, when the break-in of the Democratic National Committee headquarters at the Watergate Hotel was investigated. Mitchell continuously and steadfastly denied any involvement in the scandal, but was implicated as having approved the original break-in as well as having communicated with Nixon staffer G. Gordon Liddy over the scope of the entire "dirty tricks" campaign (as the tactics used by the Committee to Re-Elect the President [CREEP] were collectively called). Mitchell was indicted twice for his role in Watergate, and in 1975 he was convicted of obstruction of justice, perjury, and conspiracy. He was sentenced to two and a half to eight years in prison, but he did not begin serving time until 1977, after the courts heard a series of appeals. He would eventually serve only 19 months, securing release on parole in January 1979. He is the only attorney general ever to serve a prison sentence.

Mitchell's outspoken wife, Martha, left him in 1974, ostensibly over the scandal, claiming publicly that Richard Nixon was behind the whole affair, that he had authorized everything, and that he had deliberately allowed her husband to take the fall for it. Mitchell was disbarred in New York and disgraced as one of the masterminds of Watergate. Until the day he died in 1988, John Mitchell protested his innocence.

Further reading: Woodward, Bob, and Carl Bernstein, *All the President's Men* (New York: Touchstone, 1987).

Monsieur New York (ca. 1822–?) Known only by his pseudonym, Monsieur New York earned a reputation as the most artful public executioner in the United States.

The public has generally shunned executioners, and, for that reason, practitioners of the art jealously guarded the secrecy of their identity. Once an executioner's identity was discovered, he generally left the job and, indeed, left town. Such was the case in New York City in the early 1850s, when a man, known only as George and subsequently dubbed Monsieur New York by the local press, approached the New York sheriff about a current job opening.

The only thing known about him was that he had worked as a butcher's assistant and his professional idol was Jack Ketch, the legendary high executioner of Great Britain. Following a successful exhibition of his skills, Monsieur New York was hired and quickly earned local fame as a consummate practitioner of his craft, always inflicting a swift and (as far as anyone could tell) painless death.

Monsieur New York earned $100 per execution, plus expenses—this at a time when a common laborer was paid at the rate of a dollar a day. Monsieur New York plied his trade into the 1880s, then retired without ever suffering revelation of his identity.

Montesquieu, Charles Louis de (1689–1755) A leading French philosopher of the Enlightenment who helped define the period, especially with his two works on social justice and government.

A member of the French nobility, Charles Louis de Montesquieu received a progressive education at the Oratorian College de Juilly in 1700, then returned to his native Bordeaux, where he studied law, being admitted to practice in 1708. After practicing for a short time in Paris, Montesquieu's father died, and the son returned once again to Bordeaux and eventually inherited the castle, the barony, and the presidency of the Parlement of Bordeaux upon the death of his uncle.

The practical application of law interested Montesquieu far less than the theory and intent of law, the sociological effects of law, and the spirit of law. Motivated by such interests, Montesquieu sold his presidency of the parlement and devoted himself to writing on philosophy and the philosophical implications of law. His first work, which was not only a biting social commentary but also a runaway "bestseller" in Europe at the time, was *The Persian Letters*, a satirical consideration of various French mores and institutions written in the form of letters from three Persian travelers in Europe. In the book, Montesquieu discussed the need for law as a vehicle of human virtue, by which he meant all that is morally good and transcendent of current evils. *The Persian Letters* also contain a narrative demonstrating that law not based on virtue, but imposed from the outside, cannot create a viable society.

In 1748, Montesquieu finished his most famous, and perhaps his greatest work, *The Spirit of the Laws*, a philosophical and sociological discussion of contemporary French jurisprudence. In the book, he redefined law as "the necessary relationships which derive from the nature of things." He argues that the relationship between laws and their form of expression—government—is defined in answer to a people's physical environment and their basic social needs. He discusses how criminal law has been abused by the ignorance of both legislators and citizens alike. Montesquieu argued that legislators must adjust law to suit social conditions at the time, while citizens must work within the laws for social change.

Montesquieu's works, particularly *The Spirit of the Laws*, greatly influenced the coming of the French Revolution not only by pointing out the social injustice of the current legislative arrangement, but also by advocating the need for judicial review to preserve individual rights against tyranny.

Moran, George "Bugs" (1893–1957)   One of the most feared practitioners of organized crime in the United States.

George "Bugs" Moran was born in rural Minnesota of Polish parents, but changed his name to the Irish-sounding Moran after he moved to a tough, predominantly Irish neighborhood on the North Side of Chicago when he was a teenager. His "change" of nationality gained him entry into the Irish street gangs, and by the time he was 17, Moran was a burglar and armed robber. His first arrest came in 1910. Although he was arrested many times subsequently, he was not convicted until May 24, 1918, when he was sent to Joliet State Prison for armed robbery. Paroled on February 1, 1923, he returned to his former street gang, which had come under the control of Charles "Dion" o'BANNION, the most powerful bootlegger on the North Side.

Not only did O'Bannion, Moran, and other gang members control politicians and police officials, they also muscled in on the bootlegging operations of Johnny TORRIO and Al CAPONE of the South Side, hijacking their liquor trucks and invading their speakeasies.

When O'Bannion was killed in 1924, Moran became second-in-command of the North Side gang, serving under Earl WEISS. Moran was among those who ambushed Torrio and his wife on January 24, 1925, in a botched assassination attempt intended to avenge the death of O'Bannion. Following this, Weiss, Moran, and the other members of the North Side gang waged

George "Bugs" Moran was the intended target of the infamous St. Valentine's Day Massacre. (Courtesy of the Library of Congress)

war against the Genna Brothers (who had provided two of the men who killed O'Bannion) and New York gangster Frank Yale, an ally of Capone. On September 20, 1926, Weiss and Moran dispatched a task force of 10 cars with heavily armed gangsters who fired thousands of rounds in a drive-by shooting attack against the Hawthorne Inn, Capone's Cicero, Illinois, headquarters. In retaliation, Capone ordered the killing of Weiss, who was gunned down on October 11, 1926, in front of Holy Name Cathedral.

Moran now inherited the mantle of the North Side, swearing eternal vengeance on Capone. Nevertheless, a two-year lull in the war ensued as Moran prospered from his liquor and gambling operations. He and Capone agreed to a truce and divided the city along Madison Street, the artery that separates the North Side from the South. During this period, Moran even became a celebrity, the darling of the Chicago press. Police, judges, and juries were routinely bought off by him.

In 1929, Capone began to invade Moran's territory, and Moran collaborated with one Joseph Aiello, who plotted to murder Capone. Moran offered $50,000 to anyone who would kill Capone. When Aiello killed Pasquilino Lolordo, a Capone associate, Capone personally killed Aiello and then launched the single most famous hit in gangland history.

On St. Valentine's Day, February 14, 1929, Capone dispatched a hit squad, disguised as police officers, to murder Moran and his entire gang in the Clark Street garage that served as their headquarters. Seven men were cut to pieces by submachine-gun fire, but Moran was not present. The massacre did serve to frighten Moran badly. He checked himself into a hospital, flanked day and night by bodyguards.

The St. Valentine's Day Massacre brought two results: the rapid decline of Moran's gangland power in Chicago and a turn of public opinion against Al Capone, who had been treated hitherto as a colorful outlaw. Moran did continue to control Chicago's 42nd and 43rd wards through the early 1930s and crowed loudly when Capone's conviction in 1931 for income tax evasion sent him to prison. In 1936, Moran rubbed out "Machine Gun Jack" McGurn, chief perpetrator of the St. Valentine's Day Massacre, but by 1940, "Bugs" Moran was no longer a major criminal power.

The aftermath: Chicago, St. Valentine's Day, 1929 (Courtesy of the Illinois State Historical Library)

His gambling operations had been absorbed into the larger crime syndicate, and Moran supported himself as a common burglar. Shortly after World War II, he and two small-time thieves, Virgil Summers and Albert Fouts, robbed a bank messenger of $10,000. Arrested, tried, and convicted, they were sent to prison. Moran died, of natural causes, in the federal penitentiary at Leavenworth in 1957. Buried in the prison cemetery, he left an estate valued at less than $100.

More, Saint Thomas (1478–1535)   Possibly one of the first criminologists anywhere, setting forth far-seeing theories of crime and punishment in his celebrated *Utopia*.

Born into London's privileged society on February 6, 1478, Thomas More was educated at St. Anthony's and, later, Oxford, where he served as an assistant to Archbishop John Morton, who opened many doors for More. After launching a successful legal career in London, More turned to the theories of humanism, a movement led by the scholar Erasmus, later a friend of More's and a fellow at Oxford. By the time More entered Parliament in 1504, he was a firm believer in Christian humanism.

After a brief flirtation with the priesthood, More felt he could best serve Christianity through a lay profession. With the help of Erasmus, he helped found a model educational community for children at Chelsea, on the outskirts of London. By 1515, More began contemplating what would eventually become his magnum opus, *Utopia*, a book about an ideal community located on an island not only free from the contemporary societal ills but also offering answers to those ills. In *Utopia*, More advocated the abolition of capital punishment and proposed what was then an extraordinarily radical idea that punishment does not effectively deter crime. Only positive measures to alleviate the social conditions under which crimes are committed will prevent crime. This belief was diametrically opposed to the prevailing notion that harsh punishment could eradicate crime altogether. Like most 20th-century criminologists, More, in the 16th century, believed that the prevention of crime requires scrutiny of what gives rise to crime in the first place. More looked at the marked increase in crime in England and cited an array of social causes of crime—social problems that could be made to yield to social solutions. More's analysis marks one of the first serious efforts to identify the social causes of crime.

Tragically, More's humanist views, especially those concerning King Henry VIII's break with the church in Rome, created tension between him and the king, tension that ultimately resulted in his being executed in 1535 for treason, ostensibly because he would not support the king on an issue of religion.

Morel, Benedict (1809–73)

German-born, French psychiatry pioneer who introduced the concept of "degeneration," clinically described the symptoms of schizophrenia, and formulated a legal definition of insanity.

Physician-in-chief at the Mareville and Rouen asylums in France, Benedict Morel became recognized as the most important expert on insanity in the 19th century. Subsequently, he traveled throughout Europe diagnosing patients as well as criminal defendants. Morel was the first to publish a survey of psychiatry in Europe and the United States. He also introduced the idea of "degeneration"—a term he used to define deviation from the norm caused by such external agents as alcohol, stress, and infection.

Had Morel confined his research and writing to "degeneration," he would have been a profound influence on a generation of psychiatrists and on the legal system worldwide. However, Morel's work went far beyond this central concept. He was the first physician to recognize and describe the symptoms of schizophrenia, and his work on the subject influenced the work of the pioneering Italian criminologist LOM-BROSO.

Toward the end of his career, Morel concentrated on a field his earlier work had already greatly influenced: the legal implications of insanity. Morel's work in this area would be further developed by his contemporary, Victor Magnum.

Morgagni, Giovanni Battista (1682–1771)

The founder of pathological anatomy, who theorized through extensive autopsy that the site of pathology was the organ, not the so-called "humors," or body fluids. The establishment of modern pathology laid the foundation for forensic medicine.

Born in Romagna, Italy, on February 25, 1682, Giovanni Morgagni began his medical studies at Forli, then continued them in Bologna in 1698, graduating in 1701. In 1704, Morgagni was appointed head of the Italian Academy of Investigation, which he modeled after the Paris Royal Academy of Sciences and was thereby able to attract Europe's top scientists and physicians to Italy. In 1707, Morgagni moved to Venice to study chemistry for two years and then returned to Forli in 1709 to practice medicine.

In 1711, Morgagni was named to the staff at the University of Padua, and by 1716 he had earned the honor of being made first professor of anatomy, a position he held until his death. It was at Padua that Morgagni developed his concept of pathological anatomy and the importance of the organ in disease.

He theorized that fatal disease attacked the organs, causing lesions that brought about a breakdown in the organ. His theory would be greatly expanded in the years following his death on December 5, 1771, to trace the pathological site to the tissue and, finally, to the cell. Furthermore, Morgagni put pathology on a footing that enabled the eventual development of forensic pathology.

Moritz, Alan Richards (1899–?)

This Harvard pathologist was one of the creators of modern forensic medicine.

As professor of legal medicine at Harvard University in the 1940s, Alan Moritz was instrumental in the development of a separate curriculum for forensic pathology. Moritz believed that the growing demands of the criminal justice system called for the discipline of legal medicine to focus more sharply on pathology and death case investigation. In 1955, Moritz outlined his measures for reform in *The Journal of the American Medical Association*. By organizing forensic medicine into an autonomous field of medicine instead of simply as a part of the medical school curriculum, Moritz created the basis for the profession of forensic pathologist.

Morris, Robert H. (1802–55)

Mayor of New York in the 1840s; boldly overhauled the city's antiquated and ineffective police force, restructuring city government to do so.

As a young New York City lawyer, Robert Morris served as assistant district attorney from 1827 to 1833, when he was elected to the state legislature. In 1838, Morris was appointed recorder of the city of New York. During his tenure in this office, he became involved in a famous dispute with Governor William H. SEWARD over the legality of search and seizure. One James Glentworth, a partisan of William Henry Harrison, attempted to influence the presidential election of 1840 by illegally sending a number of voters from Pennsylvania to New York to vote for Harrison in opposition to Martin Van Buren. Morris, as New York's recorder, publicized documentary evidence against James Glentworth, which he had seized from the home of a Mr. Pierce. Seward protested that Morris had violated the search and seizure laws of the state, and although Morris responded with a brilliant defense based on the concept of probable cause—today central to police search and seizure operations—he was nevertheless dismissed from office by the governor. The public, however, sided with Morris, and in 1841 elected him to the first of three terms as mayor of New York.

Mayor Morris quickly set about reorganizing the city's outmoded and ineffectual police force. His reform measures included abolishing patronage-ridden City Council control over the police and putting the force under direct executive control. Nor did Morris narrowly restrict his reforms to the police. He introduced the concept of municipal federalism into New York City government, subordinating city ward government to a strong central municipal government and establishing the foundation for formal police precincts. With wards and precincts subordinate to the central government, patronage and favoritism in appointments, especially appointments to the police department, were greatly reduced.

In 1845, Morris was appointed postmaster of New York, and in 1852 he became a justice of the Supreme Court of New York, presiding on the bench until his sudden death three years later.

Morrison, William Douglas (1852–1943)

This noted British prison chaplain wrote two books, *Crime and Its Causes* (1891) and *Juvenile Offenders* (1900), which introduced the study of climate as a contributory cause of criminal behavior.

Reverend William Douglas Morrison was chaplain in Her Majesty's Prison Service from 1883 to 1898. His experience as chaplain led him to embark on a lifelong study of the social conditions surrounding criminal offenders. Concentrating on the character of the perpetrator rather than the particular offense, Morrison developed a theory relating climate to crime, concluding that excessive heat or cold were major contributors to particular types of criminal activity.

By focusing on the environmental conditions surrounding criminal activity, William Morrison became one of the pioneers of the social reform movement that came to dominate the field of criminology in the 20th century. His work earned him an appointment as rector of St. Marylebone in London in 1908, a position he held until his death in 1943.

Further reading: Robin, Gerald D., "William Douglas Morrison," *The Journal of Criminal Law, Criminology and Police Science*, 55:1 (March 1964).

Mossman, Burt (1867–1956)

Armed with a genius for catching cattle rustlers, Mossman was the first leader of the Arizona Rangers, which put an end to cattle rustling along the Mexico-Arizona border.

A native of Aurora, Illinois, Burt Mossman did not move west until he was 15, when he settled with his family in New Mexico. He began working cattle ranches and was made foreman of one at the age of 21. By the time he was 30, he was superintendent of the Hash Knife Ranch, which covered over two million acres of northern Arizona and was inhabited by some 60,000 head of cattle in the waning days of the open range.

Burt Mossman: first leader of the Arizona Rangers and archnemesis of cattle rustlers (Courtesy of the Arizona Historical Society)

Cattle rustlers were a plague throughout Arizona and New Mexico. They operated with impunity in the vast rangelands, which offered an infinite multitude of hiding places and, worse, strategic spots from which to launch an ambush against pursuing posses. By 1901, the Arizona legislature had grown weary of the plague and authorized the establishment of an outfit to deal solely with the rustling problem. Governor Nathan Oakes Murphy persuaded Mossman to head up the newly formed Arizona Rangers, 26 intrepid men.

Working with stealth, savvy, and boundless stamina, the Rangers set about curtailing the rustling business. Soon, the rustlers began to speak of the Rangers in mythical terms, because their presence was always felt. After establishing the Rangers as a viable force, Mossman stepped down as their leader, but not before he had hunted down one last criminal, Agostine Chacon, wanted for the murder of 52 American and Mexican citizens. After preparing a clever ruse, Mossman was able to lure Chacon across the border onto U.S. soil, where he surprised and arrested him.

Chacon was subsequently tried, convicted, and hanged.

Mossman returned to the ranching business. By the time he retired in 1944, he had charge of more than a million head of cattle.

Further reading: Miller, Joseph, ed., *The Arizona Rangers* (New York: Hastings House, 1972).

Muir, Richard (1857–1920)   One of the greatest prosecuting attorneys for the English Crown at the turn of the 20th century; among the first prosecutors to use fingerprints successfully as evidence in a court of law.

One of 15 brothers and sisters, Richard Muir was born in Greenrock, Scotland, in 1857 to a ship broker. Richard's father initially intended for his son to study the business and then take it over upon his death. Accordingly, Richard was apprenticed in various commercial ventures to expose him to the mercantile trade, but by 1881, it had become evident to the elder Muir that his son was not interested in pursuing the brokerage trade, and Richard was packed off to London in search of adventure.

His ambition was to join an acting troupe, but one of his older brothers persuaded him to go to law school instead. At King's College he compiled an exemplary record, quite a feat for someone who had never attended public school. Hoping to gain an advantage in whatever profession he chose, Richard took up shorthand and quickly became renowned for his accuracy. He was awarded a job on *The Times* (London) in 1886 and was frequently called upon to record important political speeches. Even after he had successfully established himself as an attorney, he continued to hold his position at *The Times*.

As a lawyer at the Old Bailey, Muir built his own reputation as well as that of the Bailey, which was frequently derided for its commitment to securing a guilty verdict rather than discovering the truth. Muir's investigative preparation was his stock in trade, and nowhere was it more evident than in two landmark cases. The first was the Stratton case, involving two brothers accused of robbery and a brutal double murder. The lone piece of damning evidence against the defense was a single fingerprint found on the victim's money box. The science of fingerprinting—"dactyloscopy"—was in its infancy at this time, and fingerprint evidence was not considered admissible in English courts of law. Undeterred, Muir spent hours at Scotland Yard learning the science and tracked down everyone with expertise in the process. After careful demonstration to the jury, Muir was able to use the fingerprint evidence to convict the two brothers, successfully refuting every aspect of the defense's cross-examination of the process.

The other landmark of Muir's legal career was the Crippen murder case, in which a man stood accused of murdering his wife and disposing of the body. The rotting corpse that was found was completely unidentifiable, except for a disintegrating piece of material from the corpse's pajamas. Muir tracked down every clothing and fabric merchant in London in order to locate the seller of the pajamas. The shopkeeper not only positively identified the cloth, he also personally remembered that Mrs. Crippen had purchased the garment. With this testimony, Muir won the case.

Further reading: Felstead, Sidney Theodore, *Sir Richard Muir: A Memoir of a Public Prosecutor* (London: John Lane, 1927).

Murton, Thomas O. (1928–90)   Fearlessly exposed the scandalous practices of the Arkansas prison system and inspired the 1980 Robert Redford movie *Brubaker*.

Born and raised in Oklahoma, Thomas Murton planned on being a farmer and earned a degree from the University of Oklahoma in animal husbandry. While he was at the university, however, he also took some criminal justice classes and became interested in the criminal justice system, particularly the American penal system. It is unclear just when Murton formally entered penology, but when Alaska was admitted as a state in 1959, he went north to help Alaska develop its penal system.

After returning from Alaska, Murton taught penology at Southern Illinois University. In 1968, he was offered a position by Arkansas governor Winthrop Rockefeller as the state's first professional penologist and was named superintendent of the Cummins State Prison Farm and administrator of the Tucker Prison Farm. What Murton found on his new assignment disgusted him. Both Tucker and Cummins were throwbacks to the hardline and inhumane Auburn prison systems of the turn of the century. Brutal solitary confinement and corporal punishment were meted out on a daily basis. He discovered inmates who had been locked in dark solitary confinement for months, even years. Beatings were administered with large leather straps, and an old crank telephone magneto was used to administer electric shocks to the genitals. He quickly abolished all forms of corporal punishment and released those in solitary confinement.

Murton discovered even worse atrocities. An inmate confided to him that guards, under orders from prison "trusties" (inmates with special privileges), occasionally murdered inmates, then buried them in the yard. Murton exhumed the bodies of three inmates in a remote section of the prison and said that he believed as many as 200 inmates were buried in and around the prison yard. At this point, Governor Rockefeller accused Murton of creating a "sideshow" and fired him. A police investigator was called in and ruled that the bodies were from an old graveyard.

Despite the fact that many who have investigated the story believe the bodies were indeed those of murdered convicts, Murton was effectively black-balled in the penal community, unable to find work in the field even after earning his Ph.D. in criminology. His story inspired the fictionalized account of a rural reform prison warden in the critically acclaimed Robert Redford film *Brubaker* (1980).

N

Napier, Sir Charles James (1782–1853) After conquering the Indian province of Sind, Napier developed a police force based on the Irish constabulary system, which was designed to dovetail with the occupying military force.

A sickly child from a well-connected family, Charles Napier was plagued by ill health throughout his life. As if to compensate, he threw himself unstintingly into his work. At the age of 12, he was commissioned an ensign in the 33rd Regiment in Ireland, only to be promoted to lieutenant a few months later and transferred to the 89th Regiment. This began a lifelong career in the military, which included campaigns against NAPOLEON during the Continental Wars, in which, severely wounded, he was captured and then issued a personal parole by the great French commander, Marshal Ney.

After rising to the rank of commander, Napier was sent to India in 1841 and ordered to take the province of Sind, located on the west coast of the subcontinent. After unsuccessfully attempting to deal with the various ruling emirs through diplomacy, Napier marched troops across the Indus and occupied the regions in question, blowing up a formidable enemy garrison in the desert. After taking control of the area, Napier was named the military administrator of Sind. He immediately set out to establish an organization capable of administering the new colony.

After setting up all branches of a civil government, careful to give the population as much self-rule as was "prudent," Napier established a police organization strongly based on the Royal Irish Constabulary. The force was structured along military lines, but was completely separate from the British Army. Realizing that the missions of civil police and military personnel were quite different, Napier stressed that the two forces must remain independent of one another. However, when necessary, the police were used in concert with the military, often as skirmishers. Quelling small-scale civil disorder was the province of the police, as were criminal matters.

Napier instituted a chain of command and created three different police units for greater efficiency. The province of Sind was divided into districts, with each district having a commander and mounted, rural, and urban police units. Mounted police were responsible for patrols, rural units stood guard duty and provided general support, while urban units were in charge of crime detection and prevention. Each district captain was responsible to the chief commissioner, who was in turn personally responsible to Napier. Napier's genius for organizing a colonial police force was an example of the kind of administrative talent that preserved the British Empire throughout the 19th century.

Napoleon I (1769–1821) Emperor of France and one of the greatest military minds of all time; also developed a comprehensive and equitable legal system and established the foundation of the French police system.

Born on the island of Corsica just off the Italian coast, Napoleon Bonaparte attended a French military school from 1779 to 1784 but was scorned by the faculty and his fellow students as an Italian interloper. He continued his studies in solitude and, after additional study at the Military Academy of Paris, was commissioned a second lieutenant of artillery in 1785. Young Bonaparte became active in revolutionary politics, joining the Jacobin Club. During the wars of the Revolution, Napoleon gained promotion to brigadier general after his characteristically brilliant rout of the British at Toulon in December 1793. The next year, in Italy, Napoleon was named artillery commander of the French Army.

With the fall of Robespierre and the Committee of Public Safety in 1794, Napoleon was briefly imprisoned from early August to mid-September as an accomplice in the Terror, but was soon released and returned to military duty. After dispersing insurrectionists outside the National Convention ("with a whiff of grapeshot"), he was rewarded with full command of the Army of the Interior. It was in this position that Napoleon established himself in the minds of the French people as a great military hero. In less than a year, he defeated the Austrian and Piedmontese forces, driving the former completely out of Italy and gaining huge tracts of land for French occupation, before finally advancing on Vienna itself and dictating the Treaty of Campo Formio. He next proposed an invasion of British India through Egypt. The Egyptian phase of the campaign was a triumph, but Napoleon ultimately returned to France without having reached India.

With his popularity soaring and with support for the Directory—revolutionary France's legislative body—eroding, Napoleon staged a coup on November 6, 1799, and was named first consul of France, a position he turned into a dictatorship. After defeating the Austrians again, a grateful nation elected him First Consul For Life in August 1802. Two years later, Napoleon crowned himself emperor.

Although France was at peace for only 14 months during Napoleon's 15 years in power, the emperor was an able civil administrator who established many reforms that served to stabilize post-Revolution France. In 1804, he promulgated the Code Napoléon, which codified both civil and criminal law and helped consolidate certain democratic gains of the Revolution by establishing personal liberty and freedom of conscience as well as equal justice before the law. Many feel that the Code was Napoleon's greatest single accomplishment, exceeding all of his military victories.

As part of his program of legal reform, Napoleon also developed a national police force, including the reestablishment of the Paris Police Force—that city having been without formal police protection since the beginning of the Revolution. Napoleon centralized civil government—including the police—by establishing an administrator, accountable to the emperor, over each of France's 98 departments. Within each department, every community numbering 5,000 inhabitants or more was given a police commissioner, who was accountable to Napoleon himself. The emperor also developed a police reserve and kept a highly trained army unit, the Gendarmerie, available for civil use if necessary. Within a very short time, Napoleon had established a system of police control over civil affairs without involving the military and without sparking the civil unrest to which his nation was prone. The systems Napoleon established were so effective that they ensured lasting reform. To this day, French law rests largely on the Code Napoléon, which also continues to exert an influence on the laws of the state of Louisiana, once part of Napoleon's colonial holdings, and governed by French-trained officials even after the Louisiana Purchase of 1803.

Neagle, David (1847–1926) Neagle was involved in one of the most important Supreme Court decisions in history, which Theodore ROOSEVELT used to define his "stewardship theory" of the presidency.

Born in Boston, David Neagle moved west to San Francisco when he was very young and left school at the age of 13 to work as a miner on the Pacific Slope. While still a teenager, he became a proficient miner—as well as a gunslinger, gambler, and saloon keeper. In 1880, Neagle was named deputy sheriff of Tombstone, Arizona, in the midst of the EARP-Clanton feud, and Deputy Neagle soon gained a reputation for fairness and objectivity. After the Earp faction had been forced out of town, Neagle was named city marshal, but he lost his bid for election as sheriff.

After moving around to other boomtowns as a hired gun/lawman, Neagle returned to San Francisco, where he became involved in one of the most bizarre cases in California history. A dispute began over whether a woman named Sarah Hill had actually been married to William Sharon, a millionaire senator from Nevada, and thus entitled to support and a portion of his assets. The dispute continued even after Sharon died and Hill remarried a man named David Terry. When a court decision was handed down against the Terrys, a fight broke out in the courtroom, during which Terry pulled a knife. Neagle happened to be one of the men in the room who subdued him, but a struggling Terry vowed revenge against the judge, Stephen Field, who was also an old political enemy of his.

Terry continued to make threats against Field, and Neagle was appointed special U.S. marshal to protect the judge. In August 1889, an altercation erupted between Field and Terry, and Neagle intervened, killing Terry. Neagle was initially charged with murder, but was freed after a habeas corpus hearing. The state appealed the habeas corpus decision to the U.S. Supreme Court, claiming it had jurisdiction over homicide cases and that no statute authorized marshals to protect judges. The Supreme Court upheld the dismissal, however, declaring that Neagle had acted as a lawman, the word *law* meaning "any obligation fairly and properly inferable" from the Constitution.

Theodore Roosevelt used this precedent—*In re Neagle*—to define his own celebrated stewardship theory of the presidency. As to Neagle, he passed into obscurity, but many legal scholars describe the case as among the most relevant utterances of the court on the extent of executive authority under the Constitution.

Nepoté, Jean (1915–)
One of the founders of INTERPOL; played an important role in developing that organization into a worldwide anti-crime force.

Born in Normandy, France, at the height of World War I, Jean Nepoté attended school in Rouen before earning his law degree from the University of Lyons. After graduating from law school, he entered government service in 1935 in Lyons at the Rhône Prefecture. After a five-year tour in the military, he was appointed commissioner of the French police force in 1941, serving the general secretary in unoccupied France. Active in the anti-Nazi French Resistance, Nepoté was awarded the Croix de Guerre after the war and appointed to a position at the Police Judicial Headquarters in Paris. By 1946, he moved to the General Secretariat of the fledgling International Criminal Police Commission (INTERPOL) in Paris, doing much to help establish and professionalize the organization.

Due to the devastation of the war, particularly in central and southern Europe, the criminal records of many European police forces had been destroyed. INTERPOL sought to discover lost records or build up new ones in order to maintain an international criminal database. Nepoté played a large role in this effort, representing INTERPOL at international meetings and serving as a consultant to the United Nations.

In 1958, Nepoté was named deputy secretary-general of INTERPOL, and five years later he was named secretary-general. He has also been named to the French Legion of Honor as well as made a member of the National Order of Merit. After 40 years of service to the law enforcement community, Nepoté retired in 1978.

Ness, Eliot (1903–57)
A special agent for the Prohibition Bureau of the United States Department of Justice, Ness headed a small team of corruption-proof investigators who became famous as "The Untouchables." Their explicit mission was to harass, distract, and financially cripple Chicago mobster Al CAPONE by disrupting any and all of the liquor-related operations that were the mainstay of his criminal empire.

Ness was born in Chicago on April 19, 1903, the child of Norwegian immigrants. The wholesale baker's son was raised to appreciate grand opera and Shakespeare, but when the teenage Ness discovered Arthur Conan DOYLE's Sherlock Holmes stories, he found an inspiration like no other. When his older sister married Alexander Jamie, an FBI agent, Ness gained an acquaintance with the real-life world of crimefighting. He went to college for commerce and

In Chicago, Eliot Ness headed a special force of "corruption-proof" federal agents dubbed "The Untouchables" before becoming Cleveland's director of public safety. (Courtesy of the Western Reserve Historical Society)

business administration, but, still driven by his dream, the tennis-playing student also took a course in jujitsu and, coached by Jamie, learned marksmanship at the Chicago police pistol range. He graduated from the University of Chicago in 1925, then paid some professional dues as an investigator for the Retail Credit Company, checking consumer ratings and scrutinizing insurance claims.

Ness was 26 in 1929, when the Justice Department added him to the staff of the Prohibition Bureau. Illegal booze was everywhere in Chicago, and Ness soon realized that the bureau, like the city police force, was involved in the gangsters' bootleg economy. Bribery, payoffs, and other forms of graft rewarded the more enterprising non-enforcers of the Volstead Act, while the Capone mob's gunpoint threats and cautionary beatings kept any nobler-minded officers quiet. But public opinion was beginning to turn against the legendary gangster, despite the people's thirst. The St. Valentine's Day Massacre of that year painted—in blood and gore—a far less romantic picture of Capone and his henchmen.

Surrounded by corrupt colleagues, Ness thought of himself as "a white knight" on a "broken-down" steed, but he took his own high horse—and a strategic idea—to his brother-in-law Jamie, now a member of an anti-racketeering civic group called the "Secret Six." Jamie helped Ness gain approval for his plan, which was to assemble a small, tightly knit, courageous, and squeaky-clean enforcement squad with "no Achilles' heel." Ness reviewed hundreds of FBI and Chicago Police Department personnel files, and he finally settled on nine men, all in their twenties, whose dedication to law enforcement was beyond fear and above reproach. These straight arrows also brought useful talents to the team; they were experts in motor vehicle operation, wiretapping, and marksmanship. Ness and his men got to work, revoking the carte blanche Capone's liquor business had so long enjoyed.

Over the next six years, they cost "Scarface" Al a considerable fortune. They busted stills and speakeasies, much to the amazement of managers whose police payoffs were suddenly useless. They shut down breweries, which kept Capone scrambling to start up new ones elsewhere. They broke up transport systems and seized the trucks. And thanks to advance invitations from Eliot Ness, Chicago's newsmen were there to report on every move his "Untouchables" made. Sometimes reporters got in the way at the scene, but the inconvenience was nothing compared with the public message Ness was sending, to the world in general and to Al Capone in particular. The nine-man squad confiscated warehouses full of hooch, bundles of illegally earned cash, and whatever account books they could find. The latter two items were especially important, because the Internal Revenue Service (IRS) was in the process of building the income tax evasion case that would finally send Capone himself to jail.

Ness never met Al Capone, and his Untouchables played no direct role in the mobster's arrest, but the

Frank "The Enforcer" Nitti was the successor to Al Capone and a principal target of Ness's Untouchables. (Courtesy of the Library of Congress)

damage they dealt to his alcohol business distracted the kingpin while others infiltrated his syndicate and the IRS accountants closed in.

Capone was convicted in October 1931, and for a while, before disbanding, the Untouchables harassed his successor, Frank Nitti. Ness was named chief investigator of the Prohibition forces for all of Chicago. In 1933 the FBI sent him to Cincinnati, to wipe out moonshine production in the hills of Kentucky, Tennessee, and Ohio. Narrowly avoiding ambush by hillbilly stillkeepers, Ness later recalled that "those mountain men and their squirrel rifles gave me almost as many chills as the Capone mob."

Ness was then called to Cleveland to head the Treasury Department's Alcoholic Tax Unit, and in 1935, the city asked the celebrated Untouchable to investigate its police department's rampant corruption. As director of public safety for six years, Ness fired scores of bribetakers and drunks on the force, and sent several highly placed officers to jail. He also shut down the gambling, liquor, and prostitution outlets of Moe Dalitz and the Mayfield Road Mob, and personally survived numerous shootings, assaults, and an attempted frame-up. Among his more cheerful accomplishments were founding the Cleveland Police Academy, restructuring the town's traffic bureau, and establishing a Cleveland Boys' Town.

During World War II, Ness directed the Social Protection Department of the Federal Security Agency. From 1941 to 1945, this job meant combating venereal disease among soldiers by cracking down on prostitution at every military base in the United States. The navy awarded him its Meritorious Service Citation in 1946. After the war, Ness finally left public service. He and his family moved to Coudersport, Pennsylvania, and Ness became president of the Guaranty Paper and Fidelity Check corporations. He also began to write an account of his Chicago gangbusting days, which later provided the basis for motion pictures and a television series. On May 16, 1957, shortly before *The Untouchables* went to press, Ness died of a heart attack at age 54.

Further reading: Ness, Eliot, *The Untouchables* (New York: Julian Messner, 1957).

Newman, Donald J. (1926–90) A nationally recognized authority on plea bargaining, parole, and prison conditions.

A native of Janesville, Wisconsin, Newman served in the army during World War II before attending the University of Wisconsin, where he received bachelor's, master's, and doctoral degrees in sociology. From 1953 to 1960, he taught sociology at St. Lawrence University, then returned to the University of Wisconsin, where he taught law and social work until 1967.

In that year he became professor of criminal justice at the State University of New York, Albany. In 1977, Newman was appointed dean of the School of Criminology at SUNY, Albany, but stepped down in 1984 because of illness.

As an academic, Newman was influential in developing the concept of criminal justice as a unified discipline encompassing police agencies, prosecutors, the prison system, and parole. He argued strongly against efforts in various jurisdictions to abolish parole, holding that the parole system not only reduced critical overcrowding in prisons, but also allowed for the supervised reintegration of offenders into society. In the area of plea bargaining, Newman was wary, pointing to three dangers. He feared that career criminals could manipulate plea bargaining as a way of reducing their sentence and thereby preserving their "careers." He saw the plea bargain as an inducement for an innocent person, who feared a long prison term if wrongfully convicted, to plead guilty. Finally, he was critical of plea-bargain arrangements that sent criminals to short-term prison facilities lacking rehabilitation programs. Newman was also an authority on the older criminal.

Newman was the author of several books, the most important of which include *Conviction: The Determination of Guilt or Innocence without Trial* (1966), *Introduction to Criminal Justice* (1975, 1978), *Elderly Criminals* (1984), and *Older Offenders: Perspectives in Criminology and Criminal Justice* (1988).

Niceforo, Alfredo (1876–1960)   Italian criminologist, sociologist, and statistician who developed the ideas of "deep ego," "superior ego," and "residues," important psychological concepts that significantly broadened the statistical sociological approach to the analysis of criminal behavior.

A disciple of the legendary Italian criminologists Cesare LOMBROSO and Enrico FERRI, Alfredo Niceforo became a master statistician and educator who held teaching posts in Naples, Brussels, and Rome. Like his mentors, Niceforo was a positivist, who believed criminality, like all human behavior, could be traced to specific, quantifiable causes. However, Niceforo also drifted from the individual cause-and-effect approach of orthodox positivism to embrace more expansive statistical methods. Niceforo believed that, in order to understand the criminal, it was necessary to understand "normal" people and the social environment that produced them. Achieving this understanding required broadly based statistical analysis, and Niceforo therefore became one of the first Italian social scientists to conduct extensive empirical research.

Three of the theories with which Niceforo is most closely identified are the concepts of "deep ego," "superior ego," and "residues." Niceforo identified "deep ego" as the subconscious antisocial impulses present in all individuals and harking back to a primitive stage of human development. "Superior ego," in contrast, is formed by a person's interactions with society. Finally, "residues" are constant features of personality that are exhibited by individuals in all societies.

Niceforo successfully incorporated psychological theory and statistical studies of social phenomena into the field of sociology and criminology, an achievement that had a profound effect on the subsequent study of criminal behavior.

Nixon, Richard Milhous (1913–94)   Elected president on a law-and-order platform, Nixon himself grossly violated the law by authorizing the Watergate break-in and other illegal activities in the course of his 1972 reelection campaign, ultimately forcing him to become the first president in U.S. history to resign his office.

Growing up in California, Nixon put himself through college before going off to World War II to serve in the navy. Following the war, Nixon began his stormy career in politics by winning a seat in the U.S. House of Representatives. His vicious, seemingly personal attacks on Alger HISS, a suspected communist sympathizer and turncoat, earned him a reputation as a tough anti-communist, an image he relished. Nixon won a bitter fight for a Senate seat from California amid torrid rumors of dirty campaigning. His hard line on communism and his high profile in California, a state with a wealth of electoral votes, prompted Dwight D. Eisenhower to choose him as his running mate in his successful presidential bid of 1952.

When rumors were circulated about Nixon's financial improprieties, specifically his dipping into a campaign slush fund, many felt that he would be dropped from the ticket. Without the approval of the campaign managers, Nixon went on live national television and detailed his entire financial history, including—almost tearfully—how the family had accepted their dog, "Checkers," as a gift. The Eisenhower camp was mortified at this display; however, the public responded to the "Checkers Speech" with overwhelming sympathy and support, and Nixon was retained as an asset rather than a liability.

In 1960, Vice President Nixon won the Republican nomination and faced John Kennedy in the closest presidential election ever. After the election, he returned to California and lost the gubernatorial race in a landslide, emerging from this contest with a threat that the press would no longer have "Dick Nixon to kick around." In 1968, however, Nixon reappeared and ran for president on a law-and-order platform, pledging as well to stop the immensely unpopular war in Vietnam. Elected, Nixon stepped up federal efforts to suppress the now widespread and sometimes violent demonstrations against the war. He also pushed a strong and sweeping anti-crime bill through Congress. But he was repeatedly frustrated by a liberal Supreme Court dominated by appointees from the Kennedy and Johnson administrations.

The law-and-order president fell afoul of the law in the summer of 1972, in the course of his reelection campaign. Five "burglars" were discovered at the Democratic National Committee headquarters in Washington's Watergate Hotel, having broken in with high-tech surveillance equipment. Dismissed and disavowed by the White House as a "third rate burglary attempt," the break-in was destined to consume Nixon's second term. The press—in particular *The Washington Post*—exposed a complex, multimillion-dollar "dirty tricks" campaign directed against the Democrats, ranging from break-ins to blackmail to hiring prostitutes in order to engineer incriminating photographs.

In the end, through the course of publicly telecast congressional hearings, Richard Nixon was caught red-handed by his own office tape recordings, which he had crudely attempted to erase, leaving huge gaps in the middle of conversations. He could not destroy all the evidence, however, and the information on the tapes was sufficient not only to ruin his presidency but also to show him as personally bitter, petty, and paranoid. After the House Judiciary Committee voted to recommend impeachment proceedings, Nixon resigned in a nationally televised speech on August 8, 1974. He is the only president ever to resign before the end of his term. He was saved from potential criminal prosecution by a pardon ("for crimes he committed or may have committed") issued by President Gerald Ford.

Further reading: Ambrose, Stephen, *Nixon: The Education of a Politician, 1913–1962* (New York: Simon and Schuster, 1987).
———, *Nixon: The Triumph of a Politician, 1962–1972* (New York: Simon and Schuster, 1989).
———, *Nixon: Ruin and Recovery, 1973–1990* (New York: Simon and Schuster, 1991).
Emery, Fred, *Watergate : The Corruption of American Politics and the Fall of Richard Nixon* (New York: Times Books–Random House, 1994).

Norfleet, J. Frank (1864–?) After being swindled in an investment scam, Norfleet devoted his life to catching the crooks, becoming the nation's most celebrated bounty hunter.

A cattle rancher in Dallas, Texas, Frank Norfleet was an honest and hard worker who had the misfortune of meeting up with a band of swindlers one day in the St. George Hotel in Dallas in 1920. When Norfleet found the wallet of one of the men—it was actually planted there—he returned it and was offered a $100 reward. Norfleet politely refused, whereupon the man, one Joe Furey, claiming to be a wealthy investor, pledged to invest the reward money in Norfleet's name. The following day, the group again approached Norfleet, announcing his investment had done well, and presented Norfleet with $3,000. They told him to keep the money, profit from the $100, but to return the following day for an update on his investment.

He returned, only to be informed that his investment had reached $200,000. What was now needed was $45,000 from Norfleet as a security for the initial investors before he could collect his money. After much haranguing, Norfleet complied, liquidating his bank account and mortgaging his ranch. Furey and his gang, of course, summarily disappeared.

Norfleet turned to the Dallas Police Department, and then the Pinkerton and Burns detective agencies in succession, all to no avail. Furious, he vowed to hunt the men down himself—and the pursuit took him over 40,000 miles across the United States, Mexico, Canada, England, and Germany. He ruthlessly hunted the men down one by one and turned them over to the authorities. The last caught was Furey himself, the leader. After tracking him to Jacksonville, Florida, Norfleet was granted an arrest warrant and then closed in on Furey in a restaurant. Norfleet tackled his object and then wrestled with Furey right there in the restaurant. When authorities arrived, Norfleet showed them the arrest warrant and took Furey back to Dallas, where he was prosecuted.

After settling back on his ranch, Norfleet realized that he missed the thrill of the chase, so he set up as a professional bounty hunter, eventually bringing over 500 criminals to justice.

Noriega, Manuel Antonio (1938–) The only head of state ever convicted of felony charges by the United States government, in a case that tested the limits of federal jurisdiction.

Born in Panama City on February 11, 1938, to a poor family, Manuel Noriega joined the Panama Defense Forces at the age of 22. Gaining promotion in the PDF after attending military schools in Panama, Peru, and the United States, Noriega helped suppress a 1969 coup attempt against the Panamanian president, General Omar Torrijos. For his efforts Noriega was named chief of Torrijos's intelligence forces, a position Noriega exploited to assure his ascendancy through the ranks of the Panamanian military and political hierarchy.

In 1981, Torrijos was killed in a plane crash—believed by many to have been engineered by Noriega—and within two years, Torrijos's successor, Ruben Paredes, retired, clearing the way for Noriega to head the PDF and the Panamanian government, beginning in 1983. Although ruled by a civilian government, real control of Panama lay with the PDF, and now Noriega controlled both the military and the civil government. Over six years, Noriega forced the removal of four civilian presidents who attempted to implicate him in numerous illegal activities, including drug-trafficking, kidnapping, and murder. Human rights violations under the Noriega-controlled PDF abounded, and all who openly opposed Noriega were incarcerated as political prisoners.

Noriega was tolerated by the United States because he was a valuable intelligence asset. In the early 1970s he provided intelligence information on Central America to then-CIA director George Bush. As Noriega assumed total control of Panama, President Ronald Reagan found Noriega useful in his plan to aid the Contra rebels in Nicaragua, in which Noriega was used as a clearing house for laundered drug money earmarked for the Contras in exchange for U.S. aid to Panama. Noriega also continued to supply information to the United States concerning Fidel Castro, so detailed and accurate that then-CIA director William Casey actually flew to Panama on occasion to meet with Noriega.

As the drug problem in the United States grew out of control and George Bush was dogged with accusations of impropriety during his election campaign of 1987-88, Noriega's mounting criminal record became intolerable. By 1987, all military and economic assistance from the United States to Panama was cut, and Panamanian assets in U.S. banks were frozen. Upon his election, President Bush assailed his former ally, calling for his ouster. In December 1989, Noriega publicly declared that a state of war existed between Panama and the United States. On December 16, a U.S. soldier was shot dead by PDF troops. On December 20, 1989, the United States invaded Panama, principally to arrest Manuel Noriega and make him stand trial on racketeering and drug-trafficking charges.

As a mission to arrest one man, the invasion was tragically clumsy, with thousands of Panamanian citizens killed. But Noriega was finally captured by American GIs on January 20, 1990.

The trial of Noriega began in Miami in the fall of 1991. The majority of prosecution witnesses were criminals of Noriega's stature—or worse—and were given immunity to testify. According to testimony, Noriega laundered drug money in Panama and used Panama as a clearinghouse for cocaine on its way to the United States. In 1983, on an official visit to the United States to meet with then-vice president George Bush, Noriega arrived in a plane that was loaded with cocaine for distribution in the United States.

The defense tied its case to the U.S. government's complicity with Noriega as a vital CIA asset. The defense attempted to subpoena hundreds of top-secret documents and photographs from various agencies, including the CIA, the National Security Council, the White House, and the Drug Enforcement Agency, but Federal Judge William Hoeveler rejected most of the requests as inadmissible, allowing the release of only 700 documents. While damaging to the U.S. government—and especially embarrassing to Presidents Reagan and Bush—this line of defense did little to help Noriega. On April 10, 1992, the former dictator was convicted on eight counts of cocaine trafficking, racketeering, and money laundering, and sentenced to 40 years in federal prison. It was the first time in American history that federal troops were used in a military operation to capture a defendant in a civilian criminal case—and a head of state, no less. It was also the first time a head of state was convicted of criminal charges in the United States.

Further reading: Dinges, John, *Our Man in Panama: How General Noriega Used the United States* (New York: Random House, 1990).

Norris, Charles (1867–1935) Appointed New York City's first medical examiner in 1918; created the prototype for American investigative pathology.

In 1918 New York City passed its controversial Medical Examiner Bill, effectively ending the archaic and inefficient coroner's system. The new legislation set up what is now the generally accepted protocol of criminal investigations nationwide, and Dr. Charles Norris was appointed as the city's first chief medical examiner.

A graduate of Columbia Medical School, Norris also studied in Europe with the famed pathologist Eduard von Hofmann, thereby securing the credentials that established him as the leading figure in American forensic medicine. After returning in 1904 from study abroad, Norris served as professor of pathology at New York's Bellevue Hospital until his appointment as the city's medical examiner in 1914.

During his tenure as chief medical examiner, Dr. Norris achieved celebrity status. His crime-solving techniques were in themselves often unprecedented, and his personal style was flamboyant; Norris customarily rode to the crime scene in a chauffeur-driven limousine. He used his public visibility to build his agency into an indispensable component of the police department and transformed the field of investigative pathology from merely a means of ascertaining the identity of crime victims to a means of apprehending the criminal. Norris imposed demanding standards on the young physicians he recruited as assistant medical examiners, and in 1934 he established the Department of Forensic Medicine at the New York University College of Medicine. But it was the doctor's crime-solving feats that captured the public's attention and made Norris the subject of many popular stories and news accounts.

O'Bannion, Charles Dion (alias: Deanie) (1892–1924)   His charming and pious manner belied a reputation as one of the most vicious killers of Prohibition-era Chicago.

O'Bannion was born in Aurora, Illinois, and moved with his parents to nearby Chicago in 1899. O'Bannion's father was a drunk who neglected his family, often leaving them in dire financial straits, and by 1902 O'Bannion had joined the Little Hellions, a kind of junior division of the Market Street Gang. Escaping from the police on one occasion, the youthful O'Bannion badly injured his leg, forever stunting its growth. Even this he used to his criminal advantage, however, actually exaggerating his limp in later life as a trademark that somehow had the effect of intimidating rivals. Another trait of youth that O'Bannion carried with him into adulthood was piety. Even while he was operating as a petty thief, O'Bannion was an altar boy and also exercised his fine Irish tenor voice in the church choir. He would continue to be an avid churchgoer—even as he racked up some 25 murders, all of which he committed personally.

Although his priest envisioned a church career for the boy, O'Bannion became a member of the Market Street Gang by the time he was a teenager, engaging in robbery and burglary and, as a distribution agent for William Randolph Hearst's *Chicago Examiner,* intimidating street-corner vendors and newsboys into selling only his employer's paper. The so-called Circulation Wars between rival newspapers in Chicago from 1910 to 1920 helped create the foundation of organized crime, which would greatly expand with the introduction of Prohibition. As a circulation "enforcer," O'Bannion established a network of political and police protectors and also earned the affection of such newspapermen as Charles MacArthur and Ben HECHT, who began to write stories about him as a shady, yet colorful character. Indeed, O'Bannion was

multifaceted, working in his spare time as a singing waiter at McGovern's Saloon and Cafe on North Clark Street.

It was at McGovern's that O'Bannion met his wife—as well as much of the Chicago underworld, including George "Bugs" MORAN, Earl "Hymie" WEISS, Vincent "The Schemer" Drucci, Samuel J. "Nails" Morton, Louis "Two Gun" Alterie, Frank and Peter Gusenberg, Ted Newberry, and Willie Marks. With O'Bannion, these men would become the key figures in the North Side Gang, the principal rival organization to Al CAPONE's South Side Gang.

O'Bannion was ruthless in amassing power and in gaining dominance of the North Side trade in illegal booze, but he was also a genius at public relations. Not only did he have powerful politicians on his side, he also had the press, and he had the people themselves. O'Bannion donated huge sums to local charities and orphanages, and he loaned money to jobless men. He built a reputation for delivering votes to "cooperative" politicians, through persuasion, fraud, and intimidation. Personally, O'Bannion was both charming and fearsome, always carrying two revolvers and practicing his marksmanship—which was formidable—every day. The final element of O'Bannion's success as a Prohibition-era mobster was, quite simply, the quality of his product. While other bootleggers were producing semi-poisonous rotgut, O'Bannion's distilleries made high-quality beer and liquor. Even his rivals recognized the difference, and Johnny TORRIO and Al Capone continually sought to purchase a wholesale portion of what O'Bannion made. O'Bannion delighted in turning them down with a polite, "You dagoes can go to hell!"

Indeed, O'Bannion took pleasure in baiting his South Side Italian counterparts, deliberately provoking ethnic animosity. He self-righteously condemned the Italians' prostitution activities as deeply

Chicago crime boss Charles Dion "Deanie" O'Bannion, shown here with his wife, charmed the press and public, had a passion for flowers and gardening, and was a vicious killer. (Courtesy of the Illinois State Historical Library)

immoral, and while it is true that O'Bannion did not run whorehouses, he did make a fortune from liquor and gambling, killing anyone who got in his way. It was also true that O'Bannion was personally abstemious, a teetotaller who never gambled and who was always faithful to his wife. Moreover, the Schofield Flower Shop on North State Street, in which O'Bannion purchased a controlling interest, was not just a front for his criminal activities. The thug was actually passionately fond of flowers and flower arranging.

The apex of O'Bannion's career in crime was marked by a 1924 banquet in the ballroom of the Webster Hotel. Not only O'Bannion's criminal colleagues were present, but police officials, politicians, and labor leaders as well. Far less cozy was O'Bannion's relationship with Torrio and Capone. The leaders of North and South Side crime ultimately defined their territories and vowed to cooperate, but it was clear they hated and distrusted one another, and friction between the Irish and the Italians was frequent and violent. At last, in 1924, O'Bannion informed Torrio that he was thinking of retiring and that he was willing to sell him a controlling interest in his much-coveted Sieben's Brewery for $500,000. Torrio

immediately delivered the cash, and, on May 19, 1924, Torrio, accompanied by O'Bannion, made a tour of inspection of the brewery. Suddenly, squads of police rushed in and arrested all of the gangsters. It was a setup. Both Torrio and O'Bannion were soon bailed out of jail, but Torrio was now stuck with a padlocked, useless brewery—for which he had paid $500,000. Torrio ordered O'Bannion's execution, and, on November 10, 1924, his men assassinated O'Bannion in his own flower shop.

The funeral was one of the most lavish the city had ever seen, with more than 15,000 filing past O'Bannion's $10,000 bronze and silver casket. In attendance at the funeral, Capone gloated to Torrio, but Torrio had second thoughts. They were well-founded. The killing of O'Bannion touched off the most violent gang warfare Chicago had ever seen.

Ohlin, Lloyd E. (1918–   )   Sociologist specializing in criminology and penology who has done extensive work on parole board decisions and parole statistics predictions, and is best known for developing programs to combat juvenile crime.

The third of four sons born to Swedish immigrants, Lloyd Ohlin was raised in Belmont, Massachusetts, in well-to-do circumstances, thanks to his hard-working father's successful bakery business. After graduating from high school in 1936, Ohlin was admitted to Brown University, where he took a keen interest in sociology and psychology and declared them as his major and minor, respectively. The department chairman specialized in criminology, and Ohlin became greatly interested in the field as well. After graduating in 1940 with honors, he enrolled at Indiana University to study for a master's degree in criminology. After completing his master's work and serving a short stint in the military, Ohlin accepted a position with the Illinois Parole and Pardon Board as a researcher for parole prediction as well as an interviewer of candidates for parole. In 1953, he left the parole board to become director of the Center for Education and Research in Corrections at the University of Chicago, where he continued his research into parole policy and outcomes.

In 1956, Ohlin was appointed professor of sociology at Columbia University, where he shifted his emphasis from adult corrections to juvenile delinquency. He produced numerous studies on juvenile crime, the most important of which was the work he undertook under the auspices of the Ford Foundation. The resulting survey he developed created a Mobilization for Youth program, which instituted the method now predominant in dealing with juvenile offenders: community service rather than incarceration. Ohlin developed a vigorous juvenile justice reform program, which stressed service in the community and the use of positive reinforcement to instill a sense of individual value and worth. The Mobilization for Youth program was so successful that President John F. Kennedy endorsed it and adopted it nationally.

Okamoto, Kozo (1948–) The only surviving member of the group that opened fire on hundreds of people in Israel's Lod Airport was sentenced to life imprisonment but was later released.

Very little is known about Kozo Okamoto before 1972, when he became one of the most despised of international terrorists. Okamoto apparently became involved in terrorism through his brother, who was killed several years before the attack on Lod in a failed hijacking attempt of a Japanese airliner. Kozo Okamoto studied agriculture at Kagoshima University in Tokyo in 1971, where it appears he met an Iraqi revolutionary who put him in touch with the Japanese Red Army terrorist group. After being recruited to show a propaganda film at the university, Okamoto was flown to Beirut and then to Montreal, New York, and Paris, cities in which he also presented the film.

When Okamoto returned to Beirut in early May, he was told that four Japanese would take part in a military operation. On May 30, Okamoto and two others arrived in Rome, from which they promptly flew to Tel Aviv. Upon arriving at Tel Aviv's Lod Airport (since renamed Ben-Gurion Airport), they went to the baggage claim area, pulled hand grenades and machine guns from their luggage, and opened fire on the hundreds of people gathered there, killing 26 and wounding 76 more. Among the dead were 12 Puerto Ricans on a pilgrimage to the Holy Land and the leading biophysicist in the world, an Israeli professor. Two of the terrorists were killed in the attack, and Okamoto was captured when he ran onto the tarmac and tried to blow up a waiting plane. Following the attack, the Popular Front for the Liberation of Palestine claimed credit for the operation, which they had "contracted out" to the Red Army in retaliation for the deaths of two Black Septemberists three weeks earlier in a failed hijacking attempt.

During his trial, Okamoto continually claimed full responsibility for the attack and demanded the death penalty. When given a chance to speak, he stated that the "slaughter of human bodies is inevitable . . . I would like to warn the entire world that we will slay anyone who stands on the side of bourgeoisie." Okamoto was found guilty, but was denied the death penalty and given life imprisonment, the Israelis apparently fearing that an execution would confer martyr status on Okamoto. (The only man Israel has ever executed is Nazi war criminal Adolf Eichmann.)

In 1985, when Palestinian liberation forces captured three Israeli soldiers, they demanded and received the release of over a thousand imprisoned Palestinian prisoners, including Okamoto. Japan strongly protested the release and issued a warrant—still outstanding—for Okamoto's arrest under a statute that permits the government to prosecute Japanese citizens for crimes committed abroad. It is believed that Okamoto is currently living in either Libya or another Arab country.

Older, Fremont (1856–1935) A crusading journalist who helped put an end to the corruption rife in the San Francisco municipal government at the turn of the century.

A native of Appleton, Wisconsin, Fremont Older moved west to San Francisco in 1873, but did not remain there for long as he moved from one western newspaper to another. After roaming from California to Nevada and back again several times, he finally returned to San Francisco and settled there in 1884, working for the *San Francisco Bulletin*. By 1895, he had become managing editor of the *Bulletin* and used his position to expose injustice and corruption.

Older first called the Southern Pacific Railroad onto the carpet for its policy of kickbacks and discrimination against the small farmer. The railroad would give bulk discounts and/or rebates to the large shippers while freezing out small producers, who simply couldn't afford to ship their product. In biting editorials, Older took the railroad to task and lobbied officials in Washington, D.C. The practices of the Southern Pacific and other railroads were made illegal during the progressive administration of Theodore ROOSEVELT. But Older's greatest fight was yet to come.

San Francisco at the turn of the century was under the thumb of political boss Abe Ruef, as powerful and ruthless as Boss Tweed ever was in New York City. Like almost everyone else in San Francisco, Older knew that Ruef controlled all levels of the municipal government. The trouble was, he just couldn't prove it. In the wave of Progressivism that was sweeping both nation and state, Older found the support he needed to attack Ruef and the system. He persuaded President Roosevelt to assign U.S. Special Prosecutor Francis HENEY to San Francisco in an effort to smash the corrupt government.

What followed was one of the largest graft probes in American history. Heney and Older went after not only the corrupt officials, but also those who bribed them. The entire episode consumed almost four years and, although Older was not involved in the actual investigations and subsequent trials, he was instrumental in keeping the fight in the forefront of the public's attention, exposing every dastardly deed of the opposition as it became known and, most important, securing financial backing for the years of costly investigation.

In the end, Ruef and all his men were brought down, and San Francisco was in a sense remade. Older continued to use his position at the *Bulletin* and, later, at the *San Francisco Call* to fight whatever injustices he saw.

Further reading: Davenport, Robert Wilson, *Fremont Older in San Francisco Journalism: A Partial Biography, 1856–1918* (Los Angeles: University of California graduate thesis, 1969).

Oldfield, George (1924–85) Chief constable in charge of the infamous "Yorkshire Ripper" investigation.

During World War II, Oldfield enlisted in the Royal Navy as soon as he was old enough, serving through 1947 before joining the police force of West Riding. Oldfield was assigned to the Criminal Investigative Division and soon earned a solid professional reputation, due in no small part to his solving several high-profile cases, including a terrorist bus bombing that killed several military personnel. Oldfield was named assistant chief constable in 1976. It was while he held that position that a series of ghastly murders took place in West Yorkshire during the late seventies.

The unknown serial murderer was dubbed the "Yorkshire Ripper" by the press because, like Jack the Ripper, the late-19th-century terror of London, he targeted prostitutes, whose throats he viciously slit. Oldfield immersed himself in the case, as if he had an intensely personal stake in it. Despite this, no significant leads developed, and Oldfield was humiliated when he was misled by hoax tapes purportedly made by the killer. Critics of the police charged that Oldfield's obsessive handling of the case actually hindered the investigation, and when the killer, Peter Sutcliffe, was eventually apprehended, it was revealed that he had been interviewed and released by the police no fewer than six times. Indeed, by the time of the arrest, in 1981, Oldfield had been reassigned due to ill health—most likely brought on by the Ripper investigation.

O'Meara, Stephen (1854–1918) Boston police commissioner from 1906 to 1918; instituted policies to protect the police from being corrupted by political influence.

Born in Charlottetown, Prince Edward Island, Canada, on July 26, 1854, O'Meara came with his parents to the United States in 1864. In 1872, he became a reporter for the *Boston Globe*, and in 1891 was made editor-in-chief, becoming publisher in 1896. O'Meara

was appointed the first commissioner of the Boston Police Department in 1906. During his tenure, O'Meara sought to establish public confidence in the department by instilling ethical guidelines designed to protect the police from political influence. O'Meara also promoted high standards of integrity and honesty within the department and improved working conditions and pay for patrolmen. The commissioner was on the verge of settling a labor dispute with police leaders when he died in 1918. His successor, Edward Curtis, proved ineffective, and the great Boston Police Strike occurred the following year.

Further reading: Harrison, Leonard Vance, *Police and Administration in Boston* (Cambridge: Harvard University Press, 1934).

O'Neill, (William Owen) Buckey (1860–98) One-term Arizona sheriff O'Neill never had to kill a rustler or a desperado to earn a name as one of the best lawmen the Old West ever had.

Son of an Irish-born Civil War veteran and Treasury Department employee, O'Neill was raised in Washington, D.C. He went west to seek his fortune, and at the age of 19, he reached Phoenix, Arizona, on the back of a burro. He entered the newspaper trade as a typesetter for the Phoenix *Herald*, then took jobs as editor of the *Arizona Gazette* and as a reporter for the Tombstone *Epitaph*. A devoted gambler, O'Neill picked up his nickname at the faro tables in Phoenix, where he often managed to beat the odds—or "buck the tiger."

During these years, O'Neill's peacekeeping career also began. It started the day that 12 Texas cowpunchers decided to have some fun at the local townfolks' expense—by shooting at their heels and running them up trees. The Phoenix city marshal threw O'Neill a deputy's badge, and the pair went after the rowdies. They stopped the trouble, all right: The marshal shot two of the pranksters stone dead, while O'Neill brought two down by less lethal means. Thereafter Buckey helped out when needed.

The newsman moved on to Prescott, Arizona, in 1881, and after a stint as editor of the *Miner*, he became owner and editor of a cattle rancher's paper called *Hoof and Horn*. He also worked as a court reporter, and in 1886 his interest in town politics was rewarded with a post as probate judge. Two years later O'Neill was elected sheriff for Yavapai County.

His efforts became legendary, but his casualties remained few. In March of 1889 four cowboys robbed an Atlantic and Pacific train at Cañon Diablo, then headed north with their bounty of jewelry and cash. O'Neill and his deputies took to the chase, their manhunt lasting three weeks. The sheriff wanted prisoners, taken alive, and he and his posse tracked the bandits for over 600 miles. When the smoke from the last shootout had cleared, all four were deposited neatly in the Kanab, Utah, jail.

After his term as sheriff, O'Neill invested in an onyx mine and explored the Grand Canyon, finding copper there. He also prospered through development of the Bright Angel Trail and a railroad link to the canyon. A fervent Populist, he twice ran for Congress and lost, but he did prevail in his bid for the mayor's office in Prescott on New Year's Day of 1898. Even before war with Spain was declared the next month, O'Neill had already started to raise a militia outfit, and his role in raising and organizing troops for the First United States Volunteer Cavalry Regiment— soon to be famous as the Rough Riders—was commended by Lieutenant Colonel Teddy ROOSEVELT. O'Neill served as captain of Troop A, which, preparing for the war at a base in San Antonio, had to break their own mounts, wild broncos roped in from the big Texas range. Fortunately, the men from Arizona knew horses and guns, and with Buckey as their drillmaster, they even learned how to make their bowlegs march. He worked them night and day. On one rare evening off, O'Neill and Roosevelt had their first conversation. As Teddy later recalled, this Rough Rider named Buckey discussed the literary realism of Balzac, much to the Harvard-trained New Yorker's astonishment.

Less than a month later, they set sail for Cuba. Leaning on the ship's railings during their friendly discussions, Roosevelt grew ever more impressed with the Prescott captain. Later, the 26th president mentioned O'Neill in several nostalgic accounts. In one, he recalled, "Buckey O'Neill . . . alone among his comrades was a visionary, an articulate emotionalist . . . he was less apt to tell tales of his hard and stormy past than he was to speak of the mysteries which lie behind courage, and fear, and love . . ."

Captain O'Neill led Troop A bravely in a June 24 skirmish at Las Guasimas. But on the first of July, 1898, the former gambler gazed over the tall grass where his men crouched, and a sniper's bullet caught him in the mouth, taking his life at San Juan Hill. O'Neill's body was later moved from its Santiago, Cuba, grave to be buried with full military honors at Arlington National Cemetery. In Prescott, Solon Borglum's famous monument to the Arizona Rough Riders is often linked with the memory of Buckey O'Neill.

Further reading: Herner, Charles, *The Arizona Rough Riders* (Norman: University of Oklahoma Press, 1970).

Keithley, Ralph, *Buckey O'Neill: He Stayed with 'Em While He Lasted* (Caldwell, Ohio: Caxton Printers, 1949).

O'Neill, Kenneth William (1916–88) Longtime director of the New York City Police Department's bomb squad.

A native of New York City, Kenneth O'Neill went to college at Fordham University, where he earned a bachelor's degree in chemistry in 1938. In 1941, he joined the New York Police Department, serving in various capacities before his knowledge of chemistry drew him to the department's nascent bomb squad, which he helped to develop into one of the nation's best. In 1958, O'Neill was named director of the bomb squad, a position he would hold for the next 18 years. During this period, he earned a master's degree in chemistry from Hunter College in 1963.

O'Neill seemed to thrive on the nerve-testing danger of the job. Explaining his apparent nonchalance, he observed: "If it worries you, you wouldn't be here in the first place." O'Neill's bomb squad was an elite group of only 12 men, each one hand-picked. Yet the squad averaged nearly 3,300 cases a year.

Orfila, Mathieu Joseph Bonaventure (1787–1853) Nineteenth-century chemist, professor, and author; considered the father of modern toxicology.

Born on the Spanish island of Minorca, young Orfila adjusted his career aspirations at age 15, when a seasick voyage made it clear he would never prosper as a sailor. He turned to medicine instead, and his success at universities in Valencia and Barcelona earned him a grant to carry on with his studies in Madrid and Paris. But the onset of French aggression in the Iberian Peninsula made 1807 a bad year for a man of his citizenship to arrive in Paris. Orfila was fortunate to receive the sponsorship of a chemistry professor named L. N. Vauquelin, who accepted him as a student and vouched for his political harmlessness to the enemy alien–wary authorities. Orfila graduated in 1811 and began to lecture in chemistry. He was made professor of medical jurisprudence eight years later, and in 1823 he took over Vauquelin's senior chemistry post on the faculty of medicine. In 1830 Orfila became dean.

The chemist wrote textbooks on several medical subjects, but his most significant effort was known as *Traite des poisons* (1813). Translation of its full title best demonstrates the volume's scope: *A General System of Toxicology, or a Treatise on Poisons, Found in the Mineral, Vegetable, and Animal Kingdoms, Considered in Their Relations with Physiology, Pathology, and Medical Jurisprudence.* Arranged by class of poison—corrosive, astringent, acrid, narcotic—this extensive catalog described the chemical properties, symptoms, physiological actions, and medical treatment for each individual type. Furthermore, Orfila detailed all known methods for detecting each poison's presence and determining its quantity in persons both living and dead. More generally, Orfila described the processes and findings of major toxicological laboratory experiments and notable clinical cases.

The book immediately became the comprehensive bible of its field, and Orfila followed up with a shorter, exclusively treatment-oriented manual for practical use by physicians. One of that text's more precocious observations concerned the dangers of lead to professional house painters.

Orfila's gift for arranging and compiling known data was matched by his exactitude and thoroughness in forensic investigation. Before his time, postmortem chemical analyses, if conducted at all, were confined to the contents of the victim's stomach and intestines. Observing that fully systemic absorbtion of a poison was crucial to its toxicological effects, Orfila was the first to point out that, since the alimentary tract is technically external to the body, all internal organs—the heart, liver, and so on—should be tested for toxins as well. This innovation established a fundamental tenet of modern practice.

Among the first to note and master James MARSH's new and extremely sensitive apparatus for testing even infinitesimal levels of arsenic, Orfila prompted refinements in laboratory procedures to safeguard the accuracy of test results. For example, he discovered that certain commercially prepared chemical reagents used in the test were themselves tainted with minute quantities of arsenic, rendering false-positive results. He therefore urged that all agents be pretested for purity before any Marsh conclusions were sought.

As it happens, arsenic turned out to be a fairly widespread environmental substance, in minute quantities, and its ubiquity was exacerbated by an arsenic treatment of wheat seed then common. When another scientist reported positive Marsh test results in the bones of people who had died of known, certain, and entirely non-toxicological causes, Orfila puzzled over the arsenic's origins in those cases, but wasted little time before conducting extensive control experiments to solve the practical criminological dilemma this posed. Orfila was pleased to find that when arsenic did naturally occur at trace levels, its concentration could be found *only* in bones, so the accuracy of Marsh results with internal organs would remain entirely sound in any poison inquiry. Finally, having satisfied himself that arsenic contaminants discovered in graveyard earth could not normally permeate a coffin, Orfila nevertheless recommended discretion, including testing soil samples, whenever exhumed evidence was examined.

Naturally enough, it was Orfila who was called to the hugely public and controversial murder trial of 1840—the case of Marie LAFARGE—and he was welcomed by both sides as the ultimate and final authority on the much-debated (and somewhat previously bungled) physical evidence. Performing his expert ministrations behind guarded courthouse doors, witnessed by all other investigating experts heretofore involved with the case, Orfila painstakingly tested against every potential variable that might affect the results either way. His conclusion of poisoning stunned the defense lawyers and LaFargist mobs, not to mention the tranquil LaFarge herself, who broke down and sobbed for two days. The jury's conviction was swift.

Other trials followed, and other experiments. Having in so many ways revolutionized the scientific detection of murder-by-poison, Orfila was much lauded by his peers and successors, and he was decorated several times by King Louis Philippe. The modern world's first toxicologist died on March 12, 1853.

Orwell, George (Eric Arthur Blair) (1903–50)

Best known as the author of the dystopian novels *Animal Farm* and *1984*, Orwell was an officer in the Indian Imperial Police in Burma and became a brilliant critic of the totalitarian police state.

George Orwell was the pen name of Eric Arthur Blair, who was born in Motihari, India, on June 25, 1903. His parents worked in the colonial Indian Civil Service, and, after a painful and lonely education at Eton College in England (recounted in various autobiographical writings), Orwell joined the Indian Imperial Police in Burma in 1922. This experience found later expression in the 1934 novel *Burmese Days*, which is a scathing portrait of the British colonial police system and the way in which the Crown's colonial subjects were treated by it. Orwell's firsthand knowledge of police in the service of the state doubtless also furnished intellectual material for his masterpiece, *1984*, his 1949 vision of life in a totalitarian police state. Some of the most brilliant—and chilling—parts of the novel are, in effect, bleakly satirical analyses of the terrorist tactics of a state political police force, which included a special unit known as the Thought Police. In Orwell's world, privacy and freedom of thought—let alone freedom of expression and action—were made impossible by a system of electronic spying devices directly linked to a quasi-mythical political leader dubbed Big Brother. (From every wall, posters proclaimed, "BIG BROTHER IS WATCHING YOU!")

Orwell's first book was the autobiographical *Down and Out in Paris and London* (1933), which recounts Orwell's life as a drifter in Depression-ridden Europe. Orwell published three other novels, *A Clergyman's Daughter* (1935), *Keep the Aspidistra Flying* (1936), and *Coming Up for Air* (1939), as well as two major works of documentary non-fiction, *The Road to Wigan Pier* (1937), a study of the lives of the miners in the Lancashire town of Wigan, and *Homage to Catalonia* (1938), chronicling his experiences fighting for the Loyalists in the Spanish Civil War.

After leaving the colonial police, Orwell became a socialist, but this soon developed into a distrust of all autocratic government, left or right. Orwell's most popular books, *1984* and the fable-like satire *Animal Farm* (1945), embody this distrust. It was these two works that brought Orwell his first real fame and his only significant financial success as a writer. Unfortunately, the writer's last years were marked by illness, and he succumbed to tuberculosis on January 21, 1950.

Further reading: Orwell, George, *Burmese Days* (New York: Harcourt Brace Jovanovich, 1977).

Osborn, Albert (1858–1946)   The first to develop fundamental principles for document examination, Osborn was instrumental in securing the admission of documents into court as scientific evidence.

A native of Sharon, Michigan, Albert Osborn attended public schools before enrolling at Colby College in Waterville, Maine. After graduating, Osborn set about creating the field of document examination. He founded the American Society of Questioned Documents and subsequently served as its president. When Osborn launched his career, most forms of uncertified documentation were inadmissible as evidence in court. Osborn set out to determine and establish guidelines for making certain documents admissible.

In 1922, he published *Questioned Documents,* the first work of any kind on the subject. It set out how documents could be altered or forged and then detailed how to determine the fakery. His work dealt mostly with handwriting forgery, but he also included chapters on forgeries relating to ink and paper and forgeries relating to typewritten documents. Osborn's work on handwriting included everything from tracing to pen position and pressure to size, spacing, and slant. *Questioned Documents* and Osborn's subsequent works were instrumental in securing the admission of uncertified documents into court, thereby greatly enlarging the range of evidence available to prosecuting attorneys and defenders alike.

Osborne, Thomas Mott (1859–1926)   A controversial prison reformer who was forced to resign as warden of Sing Sing Prison due to public protest over the system of convict self-government he had instituted.

The son of a wealthy manufacturer of agricultural implements, Osborne traveled widely as a youth and was educated at Harvard, graduating cum laude in 1884. He headed his father's firm until 1903, when it was sold to the International Harvester Company. Local politics greatly interested Osborne, who served on the Auburn, New York, school board (1885–91, 1893–95) and as the city's mayor (1903–06). Osborne also developed an interest in prison reform, and in 1906, addressing the national Prison Association, he declared (quoting Britain's Prime Minister William Gladstone), "The prison must be an institution where every inmate must have the largest practical amount of individual freedom, because 'it is liberty alone that fits men for liberty.' "

In 1913, his philosophy was put to a practical test when he was appointed chairman of the newly created state commission for prison reform. Osborne took the assignment seriously. He served as a "convict"— incognito—for a week at the Auburn prison. He published his experience in *Within Prison Walls* (1914), and was confirmed in his belief that prisons crushed individuality and destroyed "manhood." During the week he had spent locked up, a fellow prisoner had suggested a plan for limited inmate self-government, which Osborne instituted as the Mutual Welfare League when he was appointed warden of Sing Sing in 1914. The league was a system of self-government designed to give prisoners a sense of corporate responsibility, which, it was hoped, would greatly aid in their rehabilitation.

Osborne was unsparing in his criticism of political interference with prison administration in general and with his administration of the Mutual Welfare League in particular. His enemies mounted a campaign that resulted in his indictment on charges of perjury and neglect of duty. The case was dismissed, and Osborne was reinstated as warden of Sing Sing, but he resigned in 1916. From 1917 to 1920, he served as commanding officer of the Portsmouth Naval Prison, a post he left in 1920 to lecture and write on prison reform. He founded the Welfare League Association, an aid society for discharged prisoners, and the National Society of Penal Information, a clearinghouse for data on prison conditions. The two organizations later merged as the Osborne Association.

Oswald, Russell G. (1908–91)   Chief of the New York State Penal System; presided during the 1971 Attica Prison riot, the worst in this country's history.

A native of Racine, Wisconsin, Russell Oswald attended the University of Wisconsin at Madison and then earned a law degree from Marquette University. After serving in the navy during World War II, Oswald began work in public assistance agencies, then served as police commissioner of Racine, director of the Wisconsin Bureau of Probation and Parole, and, later, director of the State Division of Corrections. In

1955, he went to Massachusetts to become commissioner of that state's correction department, where he sought to institute a measure of reform, stating that "no case is hopeless."

In 1970 he was named commissioner of correctional services by New York's Governor Nelson Rockefeller at a time when prison security was being called into question as riots erupted all over the country. While Oswald later contended that it was a planned revolutionary act, the Attica Prison uprising of September 1971 appears to have been a spontaneous reaction to poor conditions, news of other incidents across the country, and unusually well unified inmate leadership orchestrated by the Young Lords, the Muslims, and the Black Panthers. After attacking several guards in a reprisal for a perceived unfair punishment to fellow inmates, the rioters managed to gain control of a guard's keys and within 20 minutes had control of the main cell blocks and the intersecting corridors and had seized 40 hostages.

Over three-fifths of the inmate population joined the uprising, and Oswald was immediately dispatched from Albany to deal with the riot. The inmates demanded better conditions, the removal of the warden, and total amnesty for all involved. Oswald made several concessions, but refused to relieve the warden or give general amnesty. It was this last point that would lead to the bloody finale of the confrontation. When it became evident that neither side would budge, Oswald ordered 1,500 heavily armed troops to retake the grounds by storm, four days after the initial standoff. In the ensuing melee, 29 inmates and 10 guards were killed.

State officials claimed that the dead guards had their throats cut and had been emasculated by the convicts, but autopsies showed no such mutilation and determined that all had been killed by gunfire—which, it was further determined, had originated with the incoming troops (the inmates had not been able to gain control of the prison's guns). Worse, after the guards reestablished order, they took savage revenge on the surviving inmates.

Lawsuits and allegations erupted immediately and continued to swirl long after Oswald resigned under a cloud in 1973. To this day, Attica remains synonymous with horrific brutality.

P

Palmer, A. Mitchell (1872–1936) A fervent anti-Communist who, as attorney general, formed an investigative unit—under a young J. Edgar HOOVER—to fight radicalism.

A descendant of an old Quaker family, A. Mitchell Palmer was born May 4, 1872, in Moosehead, Pennsylvania. After graduating with honors from Swarthmore College in 1891, he decided to pursue a career in law and worked as a legal stenographer while studying law on his own. Without ever attending law school, Palmer was admitted to the Pennsylvania bar in 1893. By the turn of the century, he was recognized as one of the leading attorneys in the state.

It was his reputation that allowed him to journey into public life, and in 1908 he successfully sought a seat in the Sixty-first Congress, serving until 1915. As a member of the House, Palmer introduced legislation favorable to women's suffrage and was on the powerful Ways and Means Committee. After failing to gain a vacant Senate seat in 1914, Palmer plunged into local politics, serving as delegate to two Democratic conventions and working as a member of the Democratic National Committee for eight years. It was his power brokering at the 1912 convention that eventually secured the nomination for Woodrow WILSON, after Palmer declined the nomination himself.

In return for his support, Wilson offered Palmer the cabinet post of secretary of war, but he declined on the basis of his Quaker background. After a very brief stint as a judge of the U.S. Court of Claims, Palmer served as chairman of the Democratic Executive Committee during the presidential election of 1916. After America's entry into World War I, Wilson named him alien property custodian under the Trading with the Enemy Act. Palmer's chief task was to remove German influence and interests from American business. Toward that end, he confiscated over $700 million worth of property and interests, which he promptly auctioned off on behalf of the government.

When the attorney general's position became vacant, Wilson quickly called on Palmer to take the post. Palmer's tenure as attorney general was a short but tumultuous one. He dedicated himself to fighting the "Bolshevik" radicalism that he perceived as rampant in postwar America. The campaign was given particular urgency by a rash of "Bolshevik" or "anarchist" bombings, including an attack on Palmer's own home on June 2, 1919. In July, Palmer created a new division within the Bureau of Investigation (which later became the Federal Bureau of Investigation) called the General Intelligence Division, headed up by a young Department of Justice zealot named J. Edgar Hoover. The GID's mission was simple but purposefully ambiguous: to stamp out radicalism anywhere and everywhere.

With the country gripped by a "Red Scare"—in part generated by the attorney general and his ilk—Palmer, essentially a xenophobe, gave Hoover broad directives and plenty of latitude in his search for radicalism, so much latitude that some of Hoover's agents were charged with brutalizing the subjects of their investigations. Hoover claimed that revolutionary activity began in this country with the labor unions, specifically the International Workers of the World (IWW), a radical organization filled with recent immigrants. It was against the IWW and other unions that Palmer and Hoover concentrated their efforts. During this period, Hoover began to compile his secret intelligence files on persons either under investigation or persons Hoover simply wanted information on.

Only 11 days after GID's formation, Palmer sent Hoover a memo directing him to engage in the widest possible effort to detect sedition and to secure "evidence which may be of use in prosecutions" now or "under legislation . . . which may hereafter be enacted."

With the end of Wilson's administration early in 1921, Palmer resigned from the cabinet and did not seek reentry into public life on a national scale, in part due to the number of enemies he had accumulated as alien property custodian and attorney general. He did remain active in local politics, however, and continued to serve his party until his death in 1936.

Further reading: Lowenthal, Max, *The Federal Bureau of Investigation* (New York: William Sloane Associates, 1950).

Parker, Ellis (1873–1940) Famous rural detective who crossed the line while investigating the LIND-BERGH baby kidnapping in the early 1930s, and ended up behind bars.

Ellis Parker was celebrated in the press as the "cornfield Sherlock Holmes." As chief of detectives in rural Burlington County, New Jersey, his ability to solve crimes made him one of the nation's top police officers. Although most of his career was exemplary of some of the most exceptional detective work of the time, Parker's blundering and even monomaniacal investigation of the Lindbergh baby abduction erased four decades of honorable service and landed the detective in jail.

Despite substantial physical evidence, Parker was convinced that the principal suspect, Bruno Richard HAUPTMANN, was not the kidnapper of the Lindbergh baby. He believed that Paul Wendel, a disbarred lawyer from Trenton, was the real culprit. Blinded by his zeal and working against the big city investigators, Parker kidnapped Wendel and extracted a confession from the terrified and bewildered former attorney. However, the mounting evidence against Hauptmann made it clear that Wendel had had no part in the crime. His confession was ruled to be a result of kidnapping, intimidation, and torture, and Ellis Parker was himself charged with kidnapping. Ironically, Parker was convicted on June 23, 1937, under the newly enacted "Lindbergh law." Sentenced to six years in federal prison, Parker, broken in mind and spirit, died halfway through his term.

Parker, Isaak Charles (1838–96) The infamous "Hanging Judge" of Arkansas gained a reputation for his unquenchable and sadistic thirst for the death penalty.

A native of Ohio, Issak Parker moved to Missouri to practice law after having earned his law degree in the Buckeye state. In 1871, he was elected Republican congressman from Missouri, during the Republican-controlled Reconstruction period, serving until 1875. That year, President Ulysses S. Grant appointed Par-

Judge Isaak Parker earned the epithet of the "Hanging Judge." (Courtesy of the Western History Collections, University of Oklahoma)

ker to a federal judgeship in the Western District of Arkansas, including Fort Smith and the Indian Territory. In his first six-week session, Parker tried 91 defendants, 18 for murder, 15 of whom were convicted. He sentenced eight to life in prison, one was shot trying to escape, and the other six he hanged.

Parker's term on the bench would span 21 years, and over that time, he would sentence 172 men to be hanged, 88 of whom were actually executed. He watched every one of them die. Regarding those who escaped the sentence he imposed, Parker was vituperative, blaming presidential pardons and the actions of other judicial officials for hindering his efforts to mete out justice.

Parker openly admitted to "leading" juries, declaring that "Juries need to be led. If they are guided, they will render justice." Consequently, his conviction rate was greater than five to one.

Some historians claim Parker was an out-and-out sadist, pointing to elements of ritualism he habitually employed. For example, when sentencing a man to hang, he would always say and do the same thing: "I do not desire to hang you men. It is the law." Then he would lower his head and weep. He would also weep as he watched. And he always watched.

In the later years of his tenure on the bench, he arranged several multiple hangings, directing the construction of a scaffold made to accommodate six felons at once.

At length, the legal community had had enough. In 1889, the U.S. Supreme Court allowed appeals from the Indian Territory, the region that gave Parker most of his defendants, overturning 30 of the 46 convictions it reviewed. In 1895, Congress removed the Indian Territory from Parker's jurisdiction, but the Hanging Judge died the next year, before the transfer could officially take place. When Parker's death was announced in the Fort Smith jail, pandemonium broke loose as the inmates cheered.

Parker, William Henry (1902–66) Los Angeles police chief from 1950 to 1966, Parker gained national attention as an effective crimefighting administrator and as a leading proponent of professionalism in law enforcement, although he and his force also attracted frequent criticism from civil rights activists.

Parker was born in Lead, South Dakota; his grandfather had been a frontier lawman instrumental in drafting the state's first constitution, and his father was superintendent of Homestake, the largest gold mine in America. In his mid-twenties, Parker left the Black Hills and headed to California, where he joined the Los Angeles Police Department in 1927. The rookie officer studied law by night and earned his LL.B. in 1930 at the Los Angeles College of Law. But by then Parker was committed to law enforcement, not law practice, so he furthered his professional credentials with additional police training courses offered at several institutes around the country. Parker rose quickly through the ranks of the LAPD, passing one examination after another and gaining valuable experience at every departmental level.

He enlisted during World War II, and the armed forces sponsored him to study the Italian language and overseas administration at Harvard University in preparation for European service with the Military Government branch. Parker saw a great deal more than administrative action, earning a Purple Heart for wounds received in the Normandy D-Day invasion. He participated in the liberation of Paris and won the Croix de Guerre with Silver Star from the Free French Government. He helped restore civil authority in Sardinia and was honored with the Italian Star of Solidarity. At the war's end, Parker went to Germany and helped establish new police systems for Munich and Frankfurt. He was discharged near the end of 1945 with the rank of captain.

The much-decorated hero returned home and rejoined the LAPD. During this period, the average tenure of a police chief in that city was only 18 months, and in 1950, after a vice scandal had shaken yet another administrator out of office, Parker was promoted to the top. As it turned out, he stayed there for the next 16 years.

Parker made many changes in the department. He campaigned throughout the community to improve the image of his force and foster greater citizen cooperation with the police. The highly educated chief set a minimum IQ of 110 for new recruits, and he encouraged all of his officers to pursue additional academic study even as they served. Parker established the Internal Affairs Division and coauthored the Board of Rights procedure, which separated and protected the department's disciplinary process from political influence. Parker founded the Bureau of Administration, and its divisions of intelligence, planning, and research became models of their kind, as did the impressive and functional new police administration building he helped design.

In 1949 a new radio show about crimefighters debuted, and when the popular series moved to television in 1952, "Dragnet'"s tough chief closely resembled Parker, who, with his staff, regularly provided technical background and advice for the program. Parker also received another, more official form of acknowledgment in 1952: The Kefauver Crime Investigation lauded him for his exceptional success in keeping his city's crime statistics low. A few years later, the chief's philosophy of police professionalism was expressed in an essay collection titled *Parker on Police*. Edited by O. W. WILSON and published in 1957, this influential volume was read by officers and administrators across the nation.

Having garnered praise as a tough crimefighter, Parker gained mixed reviews as an outspoken political conservative, and he was sometimes seen as "shooting from the lip." The chief deplored America's liberal shift during the 1960s and was especially critical of the Supreme Court's civil liberties decisions under Chief Justice Earl WARREN, whose "legal idealism" he considered "a social danger." In 1962, a group of 30 Los Angeles ministers accused Parker of racial bigotry and discrimination and called for his dismissal. Parker countercharged that the religious leaders were using the "big-lie technique" to discredit him and undermine his department's work.

Three years later, in August 1965, rioting erupted after a state highway patrolman chased an intoxicated driver into the low-income, primarily African-American Los Angeles district of Watts. As bystander reports spread to other residents, crowds gathered to protest police brutality, and soon street confrontations with the LAPD became violent. Ultimately, the National Guard was called to the scene. Over the course of six days, 36 people were killed and 900 were injured. More than 4,000 people were arrested. Property damage from looting and vandalism was estimated at more than $200 million. All of America watched the developing firestorm.

In the aftermath, Parker's crude description of crowd psychology exacerbated a public outcry against his department's handling of the riots: "One person threw a rock and then, like monkeys in a zoo, others started throwing rocks." Speaking for concerned citizens across the country, Martin Luther King Jr. declared "a unanimous feeling that there has been police brutality." A Civil Rights Commission delegation reviewed the Watts conflagration but leveled no specific charges of excessive use of force by city officers.

Parker refused to step down, as demanded by his critics, but he did take a leave of absence for health reasons a few months later. He underwent heart surgery at the Mayo Clinic to remove an aortic aneurism. On the evening of July 16, 1966, Parker attended a Second Marine Division Association testimonial dinner honoring himself and two other Los Angelenos, comedian Joe E. Lewis and actress Betty Hutton. On his way back from the dais, where he had accepted a plaque commending him as one the best police chiefs in the nation, Parker collapsed, and by the time he reached the hospital, he was dead of heart failure.

Further reading: Wilson, O. W., ed., *Parker on Police* (Springfield, Ill.: Charles C. Thomas, 1957).

Parkhurst, Charles H. (1842–1933)

A civic crusader who exposed rampant corruption in the New York City Police Department.

Little is known of Charles Parkhurst before his foray into New York City's corruption fight at the end of the 19th century. He spent some time preaching in New England before moving to New York in 1880 to become pastor of the Madison Square Presbyterian Church. He did little to attract attention until he assumed the presidency of the Society to Prevent Crime in 1891. The SPC was a civic organization with clerical leadership intended to curtail the city's rampant vice. The following year, Parkhurst devoted a sermon to corruption in the city's police department, attacking municipal government in general and Tammany Hall specifically, denouncing the politicians as "a lying, perjured, rum-soaked, and libidinous lot."

The fiery sermon was printed in full in the *New York World* the next day, and it set the entire city abuzz. Most people turned against Parkhurst as a religious zealot. Indeed, many saw the reverend as nothing more than a crusading publicity seeker, and

even Governor Theodore ROOSEVELT had occasion to call him a "dishonest lunatic." Parkhurst was summoned before a grand jury to substantiate his claims, and when he could not, he was given a severe reprimand and a lecture on slanderous statements. Undaunted, Parkhurst hired private detectives to help him gather evidence about police corruption. He and one of the detectives then penetrated the seamiest venues of New York's vice community, everything from small-time saloons and gaming houses to the most notorious of the city's bordellos. Returning to the pulpit on March 13, 1892, Parkhurst again lashed out at the police and municipal government, but this time he was armed with all sorts of evidence to back his claims. His now substantiated claims led directly to the formation of the LEXOW Commission, which was detailed to investigate the police.

While the Lexow Commission and a subsequent commission found numerous instances of wrongdoing, which resulted in the dismissal of numerous officers and officials, corruption as an institution was scarcely diminished. Parkhurst was successful in forcing corrupt police chief William DEVERY out of office, but this did little lasting good. Tammany politicians found themselves out of office for a single term; they and then returned to rule the city for another 35 years.

Peel, Sir Robert (1788–1850)

Founder of Great Britain's Conservative Party and three times prime minister; while serving as home secretary, established the London Metropolitan Police, generally regarded as the first modern police force and one that served as a model of professionalism for police forces worldwide.

Born February 5, 1788, to a wealthy cotton manufacturer, Peel entered Parliament as a Tory in 1809 and served as chief secretary for Ireland from 1812 to 1818. A staunch conservative, he was ardently opposed to the admission of Roman Catholics to Parliament, a stance that earned him the nickname "Orange Peel."

During the 1820s, Peel served as home secretary and adopted as a central goal of his administration the reform of England's judicial system. From 1825 to 1828, Peel shepherded through Parliament reforms that consolidated 278 confused, vague, overlapping, and contradictory major laws into eight succinct and comprehensive "Acts." While he reformed the laws, Peel also sought to reform the police. At this time, there was no national police force in Great Britain, not even a network of municipal forces. Peel wrote to the duke of Wellington, England's prime minister: "Just conceive the state of one parish, in which there are eighteen different local boards for the management of the watch, each acting without concert with the others! . . . I really think I need trouble you with no further proof of the necessity of putting an end to such a state of things."

Although Peel's grand ambition was to create an effective police force on a national scale, the people of Great Britain were almost universally opposed to such a force, which smacked of totalitarianism. Peel, therefore, concentrated on London and its environs, which were plagued by crime that overwhelmed the 350 to 400 men who made up a loosely constituted body of constables and watchmen—the best organized of which were the famous Bow Street Runners, established in the 18th century by the magistrate (and great English novelist) Henry FIELDING.

Peel obtained the necessary legislation to create a 1,000-member, unified Metropolitan Police force for London and, even more important, established the principles on which it would operate. These principles form the foundation of most modern police forces in Europe and North America. Peel decreed that the police would be under government control; that their basic mission would be the prevention of crime and disorder, not just the pursuit of wrongdoers and investigation of crime; that the success of a police force is ultimately dependent on public approval and that, therefore, the effective police officer must be helpful, civil, courteous, trustworthy, and publicly perceived as all of these things; that the police be a disciplined body organized along military lines, yet clearly distinct from the regular military; that police officers be trained professionals; that they serve a probationary period; that police strength be strategically deployed by time and area; and that police officers prosecute their mission vigorously, yet apply only the minimum force necessary to do so.

Peel's Metropolitan Police Act was passed by Parliament on June 19, 1829. The areas under its jurisdiction were Westminster, Holborn, Finsbury, Tower Hamlets, Kensington, Hammersmith, Ealing, Acton, Brentford, Deptford, Greenwich, parts of Surrey, and all of Southwark. Central London—the district still known as the City—was left to its own well-established authorities. Peel chose a distinguished retired military officer, Colonel Charles ROWAN, a veteran of Waterloo, and a civilian barrister, Richard MAYNE, to head the new police department, which they did brilliantly.

The mark of Robert Peel's reforms is evident today not only in the general principles he established, but also in many of the trappings of law enforcement. His officers wore blue uniforms, at once betokening a military-style discipline and comportment, yet clearly setting them apart from the scarlet-garbed English soldier or militiaman. Headquarters was established at 4 Whitehall Place, with a rear entrance opening on Scotland Yard. Since this was the way most officers entered and exited, Metropolitan Police headquarters quickly became known as Scotland Yard. The new police officers were almost immediately nicknamed for their founder. They were popularly called "Peelers" or, even more widely, "Bobbies."

For the first year or two of its existence, the Metropolitan Police met with controversy and opposition. But by the early 1830s, public opinion turned in its favor, as people recognized the force as an effective deterrent to crime and took pride and pleasure in a band of professionals who treated them with courtesy and respect. As early as 1844, the police department of New York City was copied directly from the London force, and Chicago, Philadelphia, and Boston soon followed suit. By 1870, the main features of the London Metropolitan Police were in general use throughout the United States and much of Europe, as well as in most British municipalities.

Aside from his establishment of the Metropolitan Police, the balance of Peel's political career was controversial. He turned away from his former anti-Catholicism and, with the duke of Wellington, pushed through Parliament the Catholic Emancipation Act of 1829, thereby alienating his fellow Tories. To redeem himself with the Tories, Peel opposed the Whig parliamentary reform bills of 1831–32, then served a brief term as prime minister during 1834–35, and founded the Conservative party. As a Conservative, Peel served two more times as prime minister, during 1841–45 and 1845–46. In this phase of his political career, he became increasingly conciliatory, seeking to bridge the gaps between the conservative and liberal points of view and becoming increasingly sympathetic toward Ireland.

Peel was fatally injured in a riding accident and died on July 2, 1850.

Further reading: Bailey, William G., ed., *Encyclopedia of Police Science* (Detroit: Gale Research, 1990).

Gash, Norman, *Mr. Secretary Peel: The Life of Sir Robert Peel to 1830* (Cambridge: Harvard University Press, 1961).

Repetto, Thomas A., *The Blue Parade* (New York: Free Press, 1978).

Peist, William (1948–) A turncoat cop who supplied information to Mafia crime boss John Gotti.

An aspiring gourmet chef, William Peist won admission to the Waldorf-Astoria's two-year training course for apprentice chefs. He immediately distinguished himself and won "Best Pastry Chef" honors. After he completed the course, the Waldorf offered him a job as banquet chef, which Peist took. After a few years, he decided to begin a new career, in law enforcement, which he saw as more exciting than creating pastries. He was appointed to the New York City Police Department in September 1974, but was laid off nine months later during a city fiscal crisis.

One night, while Peist was out with his cousin, Peter Mavis, he helped to apprehend two youths who were attempting to set fire to an apartment. The incident received news coverage, which helped Peist get back into law enforcement in various capacities until October 1979, when he was rehired by the New York Police Department.

Peist secretly served as an informant for the department's Bureau of Internal Affairs, charged with monitoring police misconduct and corruption. During this period, Peist was involved in a car accident that resulted in the amputation of his leg. He was off-duty when the accident occurred, but he was on his way to the office to retrieve some files, so he applied for line-of-duty pension compensation. While the status of his pension claim was being decided, Peist was assigned to office work in the Intelligence Division, whose primary responsibility was to monitor organized crime.

Finally, Peist's claim was rejected by the department. Presumably, this created bitterness and resentment on his part. Whatever his motive, Peist began passing confidential information to the Mafia at the behest of Peter Mavis. Mavis was heavily in debt to Mafia underboss Salvatore Gravano and offered him information on police investigations in return for forgiveness of gambling debts. For three years, from 1990 to 1992, Peist leaked information, which helped crime boss John Gotti avoid criminal conviction so often that he was christened the "Teflon Don." An FBI wiretap on Gotti and his associates tipped the police to the presence of a "mole" within the law enforcement community. Their only clue was that the informant had a cousin named Pete, which led to Mavis and, through him, to Peist.

Peist was arrested, charged with, and convicted of racketeering and obstruction of justice. With his mole gone, Gotti was subsequently convicted of racketeering and conspiracy charges.

Pellicano, Anthony (1944–) A famous Los Angeles–based private investigator, Pellicano has earned a reputation for being exceedingly successful, but critics have called him a bully and a braggart.

A native of Chicago, Anthony Pellicano began his career as a debt collector and soon realized that he was very good at finding people who did not wish to be found. Accordingly, he founded Anthony Joseph Pellicano Investigative Consultants. The agency earned a reputation for getting results, but also drew allegations of intimidation and illegal practices.

Pellicano specialized in acoustics analysis, quickly becoming one of the foremost experts in the field, most notably working with the Warren Commission's investigation into the assassination of John F. Kennedy. Pellicano concluded that recorded sounds some assumed to be additional shots fired at President Kennedy were actually backfires from the motorcycles present.

In 1983, Pellicano moved his agency to Los Angeles and landed the high-profile case of independent automaker John DeLorean, charged with cocaine distribution. Pellicano's expert testimony that the prosecution's phone conversations and taped interviews were inconclusive proved to be the turning point in the trial and secured DeLorean's acquittal. With that, Pellicano's star rose with Hollywood celebrities, who were impressed with his discretion and alacrity.

Perhaps his most highly visible client to date has been pop star Michael Jackson, accused in 1993 of sexually molesting a 13-year-old boy. Through intense investigation, Pellicano attempted to demonstrate that the accusations were contrived attempts at extortion. In December 1993, Pellicano withdrew from Jackson's defense team, and his involvement with the Jackson case ended.

Penn, William (1644–1718) The first law reformer in Britain's American colonies; devised the "Great Law" for his proprietary colony of Pennsylvania and made the criminal justice system there more humane.

A prominent Quaker, William Penn, with his followers, looked to the new colonies as a way to escape the harsh social and religious persecution in England during the latter part of the 17th century. Penn secured a proprietary charter from King Charles II and established Pennsylvania in March 1681. From the start, Penn planned to make the colony a place of tolerance, of both social and theological differences. To this end, he issued the Great Law, a stern rebuke of the harsh codes born of English Common Law.

The Great Law first and foremost did away with any religious crimes. The only transgressions it recognized were criminal. Penn also all but eliminated the death penalty. In England at the time, there were 33 offenses that could draw capital punishment. In contrast, under the Great Law, only premeditated murder merited such a punishment. Penn also abolished such means of public humiliation as confinement in the stocks, or pillory, and flogging. Penn's system was the first in the colonies to do away with imprisonment as a form of degradation and humiliation and to put the inmate to hard labor as compensation for—and in proportion to—the crime.

It was in prison reform that Penn's measures were the most humane. British jails, usually run by private contractors, were dungeons, breeding disease and violence. Frequently, English prisons became brothels, the incarcerated prostitutes allowed to ply their trade among other inmates, with the jailer taking a cut of the profits. Penn's prisons were run by the government and adequately funded. No longer were inmates required to pay their own room and board, and those who believed they had been wrongfully imprisoned were not cut off from the outside world but could seek recourse.

Penn's far-seeing reforms were not to last. As the tolerant colony grew and Anglicans came to outnumber the original Quaker settlers, a so-called Anglican Code, based on the harsh system of the mother country, displaced the Great Law. Nevertheless, a tradition of institutional and asylum reform had been established in Pennsylvania, and it would bear fruit in the early years of the American republic.

Pennypacker, Samuel Whitaker (1843–1916)
Governor of Pennsylvania; pushed approval of a state police force through the legislature to help deal with rural crime and the famed Anthracite Coal Strike.

After a nomadic beginning in which he dropped out of school and then worked various jobs throughout southern Pennsylvania, Samuel Pennypacker enlisted in the 26th Pennsylvania Emergency Volunteers, called out in July 1863 to meet the Confederate invasion at Gettysburg. Pennypacker served admirably in combat, and although his enlistment ran until 1865, he was released for service when Lee's forces were expelled from Pennsylvania.

He decided to study law some time after his discharge and attended law school at the University of Pennsylvania, gaining entrance to the state bar in May 1866, two months before his graduation. After gaining a reputation for morality and fairness in private practice, he was appointed to a state judgeship in 1889, serving until 1902, when he decided to run for governor. He ran on a reform ticket, promising to reduce the amount of legislative red tape. True to form, after his election he cut the amount of legislation in half during his first year in office.

His main concern during that first year, however, was the increasing ferocity of the Anthracite Coal Strike in western Pennsylvania. The strike cost the state millions of dollars in lost revenue, lost wages, higher coal prices, and almost $1 million alone in maintaining the National Guard presence to keep the peace—something at which it was not very successful. Mindful of the rising costs and violence and recognizing the problem of law enforcement in rural areas, Pennypacker proposed a statewide police force to be called out for emergencies such as the strike and to protect citizens living in rural areas, which lacked municipal police departments.

After ramroding the bill through the legislature, Pennypacker signed it into law in May 1905. The Pennsylvania State Police became one of the first such bodies in the nation and served as a model for other forces subsequently formed around the country. Many refer to Pennypacker as the father of the state police.

Pepper, Augustus Joseph (1849–1935)
With William WILLCOX, helped establish British pathology, including its application to the field of forensic investigation.

European pathology and forensic medicine were well established by the turn of the 20th century, and Scotland's University of Edinburgh was the world's first university to offer it as a discipline in its own right, but the field was generally looked upon as alchemy—or worse—throughout England. The reason for such suspicions was that English pathologists had yet to demonstrate the usefulness of the field, and, in any case, they were confronted by a time-honored tradition of the coroner, whose office had, since the Middle Ages, dealt with all suspicious deaths. Since the coroners were employees of the Crown, they tended to be fiercely protective of the prerogatives bequeathed them by tradition.

Pepper, along with Willcox and, later, a newcomer named Bernard SPILSBURY, worked at the prestigious St. Mary's Hospital in London, where, with other colleagues, they studied the science of pathology and gained a limited local reputation for their research. When the well-publicized and hideously brutal Crippen murder case came before Scotland Yard, investigators there quickly appointed the St. Mary's crew as Home Office pathologists to deal with the case.

Crippen, called on to explain the disappearance of his wife, claimed that she had left him, but authorities soon found a mutilated and decomposed body buried near the Crippen house. The head, arms, and legs had been severed, the bones removed, and the genital region mutilated to make the identity—even the sex—of the victim unidentifiable. The only piece of evidence was a cloth vest and a small patch of skin. Pepper, with the aid of Spilsbury, was able to determine that the skin was from the abdominal region by extracting pubic hair from the outside and identifying microscopic remains of abdominal muscles. The case hinged on the acceptance of the forensic evidence by the jury. Crippen was convicted, and the skill with which Spilsbury and Pepper had detailed their findings helped establish forensic medicine in England.

Peter, Gabor (1906–93)   Brutal founder of the Hungarian Secret Police, he was ultimately purged from the Communist Party and sentenced to life in prison.

Joining the Hungarian Communist Party in 1931 when it was an illegal organization, Gabor Peter was the kind of young zealot that the communists were looking to recruit. During World War II, he actively supported Soviet communism and its Moscow leadership against the forces of Hitler's Germany. When the Red Army entered Hungary near the war's end, he traveled to Moscow for communist education, returning to Hungary after 1945, with the men who would soon become the nucleus of Hungary's secret police organization.

The State Security Authority, as the Hungarian secret police was known under Peter, represented the very pinnacle of the Hungarian communist government's system of internal control. It was, in fact, the terror arm of that government. At its zenith, the State Security Authority consisted of more than 50,000 men and women, whose sole responsibility was to gather information on and punish fellow citizens suspected of disloyal acts.

Peter's star quickly fell in the early 1950s, when Moscow-led anti-Semitic purges swept through communist-bloc governments. A Jew, Peter was arrested in 1954 and sentenced by a military tribunal to life in prison for "crimes against the state and the people." The following year, Peter was publicly blamed for heightening the tensions between Hungary and Yugoslavia, in a further government move to discredit him. He was paroled in 1959 and worked, in total obscurity, as a tailor and librarian until his death in 1993.

Peters, Ewald (1914–64)   Personal security chief to West German chancellor Ludwig Erhard; committed suicide when he was arrested for Nazi war crimes committed during World War II.

Peters was born Ewald Czempiel in Silesia, today part of Poland, into the family of a small grocer. He studied law at Leipzig University, but dropped out when his father died. After working briefly in a bank, he joined the criminal police in 1935. Soon afterward, he joined the Nazi Party and, in 1940, changed his Polish-sounding name to the more Germanic Peters. During the war, Peters was a member of the Einsatzkommando, an SS-related unit created to help carry out the "Final Solution," Adolf Hitler's program of genocide against the Jews.

At the conclusion of the war, Peters, arrested by the U.S. Army, was ultimately cleared of implications that he had been involved in war crimes. He taught school for a brief period, then worked as an accountant; finally, in 1952 he returned to the federal criminal police force and was transferred to the secret service

squad in 1956. Peters worked his way up through the ranks of the secret service, becoming Ludwig Erhard's personal security chief. During this time, however, investigators were following up allegations concerning Peters's membership in the Einsatzkommando, including accusations that he had been involved in the murder of some 12,000 Jews. On January 30, 1964, Peters was arrested. He committed suicide in his jail cell on February 3.

Petrosino, Joseph (1860–1909)   An early fighter against the Mafia in New York City, Petrosino was assassinated in Sicily while on a secret mission to investigate the organization.

Joseph Petrosino, an Italian-born American New York City detective, was killed during an early investigation into the Sicilian roots of New York's Mafia. (Courtesy of the UPI/ Bettmann Archive)

Born in Salerno, Sicily, Petrosino immigrated to Manhattan's "Little Italy" with his family when he was six years old. After obtaining a grade-school education, he became a street sweeper, advancing to foreman and attracting the attention of a local police inspector, who suggested that he join the force. Petrosino at first declined, but, becoming aware of the growing influence of the Mafia wherever Italian immigrants lived, he reconsidered and joined on October 9, 1883. After walking a beat for some years, he was promoted to detective and began an intensive investigation of the Mafia and how it operated in the cities of the United States. He was appointed to head a handpicked group of detectives called the Italian Squad that worked secretly and undercover to gather information on the Mafia. By 1896, the Italian Squad had become a 50-man unit under Petrosino's personal command.

The unit made many arrests, but Petrosino was well aware that the source of Mafia power lay not in New York, nor anywhere else in the United States, but in Sicily. He thus secured approval for a secret mission to that country to gather evidence against Mafiosi in America. Petrosino left late in February 1909 and began his investigation, only to be gunned down in Palermo on the night of March 12. More than 200,000 people—most of them Italian Americans—lined the streets of Manhattan on the mile-long route of the funeral of one of the American Mafia's first enemies.

Pickert, Heinrich A. (1886–1949)

Detroit's tough commissioner of police during the sit-down strikes of the 1930s.

Heinrich A. Pickert was a hero of World War I, who received a Purple Heart (he was subsequently named commander of the Order of the Purple Heart) and a personal citation from General John J. Pershing. Following the war, he continued to serve in the National Guard, ultimately becoming commander of the Michigan National Guard, with the rank of brigadier general. In 1929, President Herbert Hoover appointed Pickert collector of customs, a post he left in 1934 to become Detroit's commissioner of police.

As commissioner, Pickert modernized the department, introducing a standard of three-minute police response time to any part of the city and 24-hour police patrol in radio-equipped cruisers.

During the Depression, the nation was swept by a wave of so-called sit-down strikes, in which workers, protesting low wages and poor working conditions, essentially took over and shut down plants by occupying them—"sitting down" and refusing to move. In 1937, the United Auto Workers, seeking to force General Motors to recognize the union, staged a nationwide sit-down strike at GM plants, including those in Detroit. The action at GM sparked what Detroit's Mayor Frank Couzens called an "epidemic" of sit-down strikes throughout the city, not only in auto factories, but in factories of all kinds and in department stores and other businesses as well. Some of these were orderly labor demonstrations, but others amounted to near riots. The courts granted injunctions against such actions, but they were largely defied. Commissioner Pickert responded vigorously—at times brutally—and earned himself a national reputation. To some he was a hero who restored order to a city on the verge of civil revolt; to others, he was an anti-labor fascist. Pickert stepped down as police commissioner in 1939.

Pileggi, Nicholas (1933–)

As a New York City journalist, Pileggi specialized in crime reporting and wrote *Wiseguy: Life in a Mafia Family*, a full-scale biographical study of a typical Mafia criminal, which was the basis of the 1991 Martin Scorsese film *GoodFellas*.

Nicholas Pileggi was born on February 22, 1933, in Brooklyn and was raised in the Bensonhurst section. As Pileggi put it, "What the Vatican is to the Roman Catholics, Bensonhurst was to the Mafia." Growing up in the neighborhood, he became fascinated with the lives of lower-level and middle-level members of the Mob. In 1956, he became a reporter for the Associated Press, working the New York City crime beat until 1968, when he became contributing editor of *New York* magazine. His first book was *Blye, Private Eye* (1976), a "real-life" look at the decidedly unglamorous business of private investigation. His second book, *Wiseguy: Life in a Mafia Family* (1985), explored the life of Mafia operative-turned-informer Henry Hill, a chilling account that became the basis of *GoodFellas*, a 1991 film by Martin Scorsese, with whom Pileggi cowrote the screenplay.

Further reading: Pileggi, Nicholas, *Wiseguy: Life in a Mafia Family* (New York: Simon and Schuster, 1985).

Pinchot, Gifford (1865–1946)

This Pennsylvania governor attempted to disband the corrupt private police system in his state during his two terms in the 1920s and 1930s.

Gifford Pinchot is best remembered for his contributions to forestry and his role in creating a national forest policy for the United States. Before he entered into national service, however, he was a two-term progressive governor of Pennsylvania, and he is justly credited with having initiated the process that would eventually disband the unregulated and widely abused practice of private policing.

First elected in 1923, Pinchot immediately began to revoke the commissions of the majority of the 6,000 members of the Coal and Iron Police of Pennsylvania.

Essentially "company police," whose principal activity was strike breaking and the violent intimidation of would-be labor organizers, these private officers committed widespread civil rights violations.

Pinchot's early actions curbed some of the abuses, but they were more important for simply focusing attention on the problem and shifting public sentiment from fear of "subversive" labor activity to outrage at un-American strongarm private police tactics. Pinchot easily won election to a second term in 1931, and was able to fire every member of the Coal and Iron Police. The governor then created the Commission on Special Policing in Industry, which investigated the Coal and Iron Police, producing a piercing indictment of it and calling the state's rural mining company towns "curious feudal states."

Even Pinchot's sweeping reforms were only partially successful. Coal and iron interests cut deals with local sheriffs and deputies, in effect making them members of a quasi-official private police force. However, Pinchot's efforts cast the first stone in the battle over private policing in America's industrial towns of the early 20th century.

Further reading: U.S. Congress Committee on Education and Labor, *Private Police Systems* (Washington, D.C.: Government Printing Office, 1939).

Pinel, Philippe (1745–1826) One of the founders of modern psychiatry, Pinel radically changed the way mentally ill patients were looked upon and treated, differentiating them from the criminals with whom they were customarily grouped.

Born to two generations of physicians in St. Andre, France, near Toulouse, on April 20, 1745, Philippe Pinel wanted to break with family tradition and become a minister instead of a physician. He studied at the Faculty of Theology in Toulouse in 1767, but soon fell under the influence of the Encyclopedists, a group of French scholars responsible for the 35-volume *Encyclopédie* (1751–77), especially Rousseau. Pinel withdrew from seminary school in 1770 to enroll in the college of medicine, receiving his degree in December 1773. The following year, Pinel traveled to Montpellier, where he served what amounted to a residency for four years.

In 1778, Pinel journeyed to Paris, basking in the Enlightenment thought of France on the brink of revolution. During his years in Paris, Pinel wrote various articles concerning medicine, especially mental health, for publications in and around Paris. Pinel in particular appealed for the humane treatment of the mentally ill, who, he pointed out, were not criminals and yet were treated so cruelly.

The French Revolution created a climate in which Pinel's radical ideas were welcome, and he was named director of the Paris insane asylum in August 1793. Pinel boldly released the inmates from their chains and shackles. He worked to make the asylum surroundings pleasant and comfortable, encouraging contact with friends and family members, ensuring that patients were allowed physical exercise, and carefully regulating the use of the opiate drugs that were formerly prescribed heedlessly. Pinel's humane approach not only differentiated the mentally ill patient from the common criminal, but also did much to influence later prison planners and administrators, who sought to introduce a greater degree of humanity in the treatment of incarcerated criminals as well.

Pinel continued his medical career by establishing a classification of diseases modeled on the phylogenetic classification of animal and plant life established by the Swedish naturalist Carolus Linnaeus. Pinel also developed a systematic classification of mental illness, which further enhanced his argument that the insane suffered from disease rather than demonic possession or criminal tendencies. Pinel went beyond classification to develop theories of causation.

Pinel continued to champion the cause of humane treatment for the mentally ill until his death.

Pinkerton, Allan J. (1819–84) Chiefly remembered as the world's first professional private detective.

A native of Glasgow, Scotland, Allan Pinkerton was the son of a police officer but chose to apprentice himself to a cooper. After affiliating himself with a political organization deemed subversive by British authorities, Pinkerton was forced to immigrate to the United States in 1842, where he moved to Dundee, Illinois, on the Fox River, not far from Chicago. There he resumed his trade as a barrel maker. While gathering timber along the banks of the Fox for barrel staves, he came across a band of counterfeiters, whom he later helped to arrest, thereby gaining instant local celebrity. Because he moved about the countryside so frequently, the residents of Dundee persuaded him to become a part-time deputy sheriff. After early success in local law enforcement, Pinkerton soon gave up barrel making and moved to Chicago to pursue his new profession. In 1850, he was named the first detective of the Chicago Police Department, assigned mainly to combat counterfeiting in the area, but he also took other assignments, including the rescue of two kidnapped girls from Michigan. By 1854, he was named deputy sheriff of Cook County and special agent of the Chicago postal system.

Even while he served the citizenry of Chicago, Pinkerton opened the Pinkerton Detective Agency, the first agency of its kind and one that would rapidly become the world's largest and best-known private

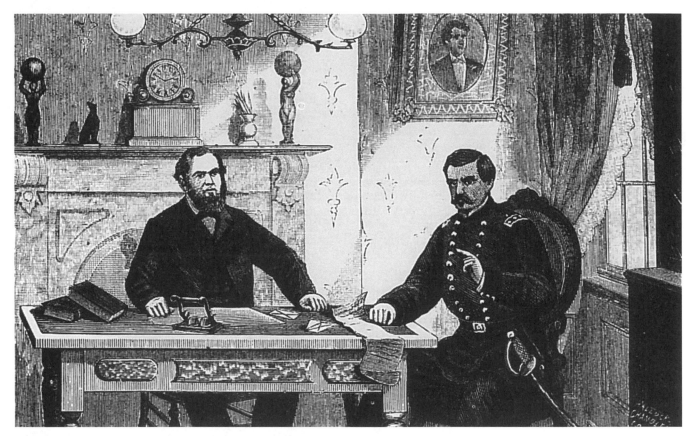

Allan Pinkerton, who ran what would become his detective agency as counterespionage organization for the North during the American Civil War, meets with the ever prevaricating Yankee general George McClellan. (authors' collection)

investigative agency and police force. Pinkerton continued to work for public law enforcement, but the nation's expanding railroads turned increasingly to Pinkerton to combat robbery as well as organized labor activity, and the detective devoted himself solely to his agency by 1860. While working for the Illinois Central Railroad, Pinkerton became acquainted with its lawyer, Abraham Lincoln, and with its president, George McClellan. Upon Lincoln's election, Pinkerton learned of a plot to assassinate the president-elect in Baltimore on the way to his inauguration in Washington. It is uncertain if such a plot existed—though the hostile climate and unrest in Maryland on the eve of the war did pose a likely threat to the president-elect—but Pinkerton successfully spirited Lincoln out of the city under cover of darkness and in disguise, without incident.

Pinkerton's association with George McClellan led to the detective's appointment as chief of military intelligence for the Army of the Potomac when McClellan served as commander of that force during the Civil War. When McClellan was named general in chief of the entire Union Army, he appointed Pinkerton as his chief of military intelligence. Pinkerton's

achievements in this endeavor were not nearly as successful as his civilian record. He consistently grossly overestimated enemy troop strength, usually by two-thirds to double the amount, a fault that fed General McClellan's own tendency to overcaution and inaction. Pinkerton was also unskilled at analyzing and interpreting military intelligence, and he failed miserably in alerting McClellan to Confederate movements in the fall of 1862, which climaxed with the battle of Antietam. He was, however, far more successful at counterespionage and was instrumental in smashing the Washington-based Confederate spy ring of Rose O'Neal Greenhow and others.

When President Lincoln relieved McClellan as general in chief following Antietam, Pinkerton relinquished his intelligence post (though he continued to ferret out the fraud and corruption rampant during the war) and returned to Chicago. He expanded his agency, opening offices in New York and Philadelphia. Following the war, armed robbery became an increasingly serious problem for the railroads, and Pinkerton found steady work combating the infamous Jesse JAMES, the Younger brothers, the Dalton Gang, and the like. Pinkerton earned the distinction of a personal death threat from Jesse James after Pinkerton agents mistakenly opened fire on what they thought was the gang's hideout. Instead, they had killed James's eight-year-old half-brother and shot his mother, inflicting a wound that necessitated the amputation of her arm. The incident provoked a considerable measure of public outrage against Pinkerton.

Next, Pinkerton turned his attention to the burgeoning labor problems in the latter half of the century. During the coal wars in western Pennsylvania in the late 1860s and early 1870s, an Irish labor group called the Molly Maguires made life difficult for management, which called in Pinkerton. A Pinkerton agent infiltrated the group, and the detective was able to deliver several leaders for trial, conviction, and execution. Over the next two decades, the methods of Pinkerton's men in labor disagreements grew increasingly violent, and the name Pinkerton became synonymous with anti-labor and pro-management strongarm tactics. Most of the violence perpetrated by Pinkerton agents occurred after the death of Pinkerton himself in 1884.

Pitt, Sir William (1759–1806) Reform-minded prime minister of England; sponsored the Police Bill of 1785, which introduced the idea of a full-time professional police force in Great Britain and Ireland.

The son of William Pitt, First Earl of Chatham, the "Younger Pitt" rose to become prime minister in 1784 at age 25. The following year, Pitt commissioned his solicitor general, Sir Archibald Macdonald, to create the groundbreaking Police Bill, officially titled a "Bill for the further prevention of Crimes and for the more speedy Detection and Punishment of Offenders against the Peace in the Cities of London and Westminster, the Borough of Southwark and certain parts Adjacent to them." The bill consolidated diverse policing organizations operating in the London area and established the first full-time professional police force.

Unfortunately, the far-seeing legislation was defeated in Parliament, which shied away from yielding police powers to the Crown. Subsequently, Pitt's government sought to implement the Police Bill in Dublin, where civil unrest was growing. The result was the Dublin Police Act of 1786. Impending war with France distracted Pitt and Parliament from consummating this (as well as other) domestic reforms, and the bill languished, ultimately failing to pass. Nevertheless, Pitt's efforts toward the creation of a professional police force did much to revise 18th-century concepts of law and order in London, Ireland, and, ultimately, the rest of the urban world. Pitt's unfinished work would serve as a precedent for Sir Robert PEEL's epoch-making Metropolitan Police Act of June 19, 1829.

Place, Martha (1848–99) The first woman sentenced to die in the electric chair.

Martha Place was a spinster for most of her life and lived quietly with her mother. In 1894, at the age of 46, she left home to work as a housekeeper for William Place in New York City. Place married his housekeeper, but it soon became evident to her that his motive had been economy rather than love: One didn't have to pay one's wife to cook and clean. Feeling trapped, Place tried to save enough money from her household allowance to leave. In the meantime, she began to direct her growing rage against Place's teenaged daughter, Ida, whose clothes she destroyed.

On February 7, 1898, Mr. and Mrs. Place fell to arguing about finances. Place left. Then Ida threatened to leave—for good. Martha Place followed the girl into her room, threw acid from her husband's photographic supplies into her face, blinding her, then suf-

Martha Place was the first woman to be executed in the electric chair. (Courtesy of the UPI/Bettmann Archive)

Martha Place marches to her execution. (Courtesy of the UPI/Bettmann Archive)

focated her with a pillow. Martha Place then mutilated the girl's body. She packed her belongings—and waited for her husband's return. When he walked in the door, she attacked him with an axe, wounding him. He ran into the street and summoned the police.

Place was tried, convicted, and sentenced to death in the brand-new electric chair installed in Auburn Prison. The execution took place on March 20, 1899, and Place earned the dubious distinction of being the first woman to die in the electric chair.

Plato (ca. 428–347 B.C.)   One of the greatest of the ancient Greek philosophers; influenced many aspects of Western thought, including criminal justice and jurisprudence.

Plato was born in Athens to a distinguished Athenian family and was destined for a political career. But the repressive reign of the so-called Thirty Tyrants and the execution in 399 of his teacher, Socrates, prompted Plato to retire from Athenian political life and to leave Athens itself. The young Plato traveled to Italy and Sicily, then returned to Athens in about 387 B.C. and founded his Academy, devoted to research and instruction in philosophy and the sciences.

When Dionysius, the ruler of Syracuse whom Plato had met during his travels, died in 367 B.C., the philosopher was invited to return to Syracuse to tutor the new ruler, Dionysius the Younger. Plato went, but the project proved a disaster. After a second visit to Syracuse in 361 B.C., Plato returned to his Academy.

Among Plato's many writings, his *Republic*, composed some time after he founded the Academy, is his most ambitious and, indeed, his masterwork. Presented in the form of a dialogue among Socrates and his students, the *Republic* begins with a discussion on the nature of justice and develops a vision of an ideal political community and the education appropriate to the rulers of such a community. Justice is defined as a principle of each thing performing the function most appropriate to its nature, a principle of the proper adjudication of being and activity. Reason is the faculty suited to rule, to determine what is just, but reason, ideally, is to be coupled with the temperance born of the harmonious rule of the happily unified individual and society.

In its more narrowly legal sense, justice, for Plato, is grounded in the equation of law with morality. Any act against morality is, therefore, an act of criminal behavior. Plato wrote that man is by nature corruptible; therefore, laws must be created to deter his natural tendency toward immorality or criminal behavior. In *The Republic* and *The Laws*, his longest and last work, Plato outlined four classes of criminal offenses (those against religion, the state, persons, and personal property) and four types of criminal responsibility (voluntary, involuntary, accidental, and mixed). The latter occurred when passion overmastered reason and led to violence. Punishment, Plato asserted, must suit the class of offense and the type of responsibilty. Plato proposed an extensive code of penal laws based on the principle of "social utility." Essentially, healthy individuals are those who create a healthy society. A healthy society cannot tolerate the presence of sick—that is, criminal—individuals. For the good of a healthy society, the sick person, the criminal, must either be cured or eliminated.

While Plato does discuss crime and punishment, his overriding theme is education, and it is education that creates healthy individuals and, therefore, prevents criminal behavior.

In *The Republic* and *The Laws* can be found much of the basis of Western principles of jurisprudence and criminology, which are founded on essentially Platonic notions of the role of the individual in society and the responsibility of society toward the individual.

Further reading: Bosanquet, Bernard, *Companion to Plato's Republic for English Readers* (London: Rivington's, 1906).

Buchanan, Scott, *The Viking Portable Plato* (New York: Viking, 1948; many later editions).

Strauss, Leo, *The Argument and the Action of Plato's Laws* (Chicago: University of Chicago Press, 1975).

Plummer, Henry (1837–64) This bandit's depredations throughout the rugged mining country of the American West inspired hundreds of tales based on his life as well as one of the largest vigilante campaigns in American history.

A native of New England, Henry Plummer moved west to California in 1852 at the age of 15. There he bought into a partnership running a bakery. After a few years, he moved to Nevada City, California, and became the town sheriff at the age of 19. While in office, he gunned down a man who accused him of sleeping with his wife. Plummer, a handsome,

smooth-talking man, was sentenced to 10 years in prison for the killing, but managed to finagle a pardon after serving only a year.

After his release, Plummer resumed his career of womanizing and simultaneously launched a new career in crime. He became the leader of a gang of "road agents"—stagecoach robbers—and, in the course of one robbery, committed another murder. After bribing his way out of a conviction, Plummer made his way to Oregon and thence to Washington, where he killed at least one more man. Moving next to Idaho, Plummer notched a fourth killing on his gun handle before settling in Lewiston, Idaho, where he worked in a gambling hall and recruited young men for his new gang of thieves and road agents. The Idaho gang christened themselves the Innocents, and they terrorized the region with a series of violent robberies, which involved several murders. In response, locals formed a "vigilance committee"—a posse of vigilantes—which Plummer joined and in which, remarkably enough, he quickly rose to a leadership position. Needless to say, the Innocents went unapprehended.

In the fall of 1862, Plummer moved his band to the brutal mining town of Bannock, Montana, where he ingratiated himself with enough citizens to gain election as sheriff. In the meantime, his gang stepped up the pace of their depredations, and Plummer ostentatiously erected a gallows on Main Street, vowing to hang the lot of them. In all, it is believed that Plummer personally murdered at least 15 people, and the Innocents are said to have been responsible for at least 102 murders.

Plummer was finally caught in his "big lie" near the end of 1863. The discovery sparked the formation of a mass vigilante movement, which succeeded in rounding up Plummer and most of his Innocents. Bannock citizens made use of the gallows Plummer had built, executing (without benefit of trial) dozens of accused gang members, including Henry Plummer himself. Plummer's career and the vigilante retribution that followed it were chronicled in Thomas J. Dimsdale's *The Vigilantes of Montana*, a sensational but remarkably good-humored book that generated considerable popular support for vigilantism.

Further reading: Dimsdale, Thomas J. *The Vigilantes of Montana* (1866; reprint ed., Norman: University of Oklahoma Press, 1953).

Poe, Edgar Allan (1809–49) One of the most important of America's 19th-century writers, Poe not only transformed the short story into an important literary form, he also invented the modern detective story and was therefore instrumental in shaping the popular image of the eccentric but infallible sleuth.

Poe was the son of a pair of impecunious touring actors, who died before the boy was three years old. Young Poe was adopted by John Allan, a well-to-do Richmond, Virginia, merchant. Although his childhood was outwardly uneventful, he suffered from a sense of Allan's never having fully accepted him as a son, and he grew up lonely. After study in England from 1815 to 1820, Poe enrolled briefly in the University of Virginia in 1826, but was forced to leave after amassing a large gambling debt, which Allan refused to cover. Moreover, Allan blocked his return to the university and saw to it that his engagement to Sarah Elmira Royster, his Richmond sweetheart, came to an end.

Like many other young men without means, Poe enlisted in the army—though by this time he had also begun dabbling in literature and published at his own expense a book of Byronic verse, *Tamerlane and Other Poems* (1827). At length, too, he and Allan were reconciled, and the latter secured for Poe an appointment to West Point. Poe engineered his own dismissal from the military academy after only six months, but not before he had convinced fellow cadets to pay for the publication of *Poems by Edgar A. Poe* (1831).

Poe moved to Baltimore, where he lived with a widowed aunt, Maria Clemm, and her daughter, Virginia. He turned from poetry to fiction as a more lucrative way of earning a living by writing. His first short stories were published in 1832 by the *Philadelphia Saturday Courier*, and his 1833 "MS. Found in a Bottle" won a $50 prize from the *Baltimore Saturday Visitor*. Poe, his aunt, and Virginia Clemm moved to Richmond, Virginia, in 1835, where Poe became editor of the *Southern Literary Messenger* and married the 13-year-old Virginia.

Using his editorial position, Poe published fiction—including the first of his truly gothic horror classics—and some of the most important literary criticism produced in the 19th century. Although Poe was successful by literary standards, his growing alcohol abuse prompted his dismissal from the journal.

He moved next to New York City (1837), then to Philadelphia (1838–44), and again to New York (1844–49), desperately seeking to establish himself as a literary journalist. While he repeatedly failed to secure a sufficient livelihood, he continued to develop as a critic, lyric poet, and short story writer. In 1841, he wrote "The Murders in the Rue Morgue," which is generally considered the first detective story. Along with others—especially "The Gold Bug," "The Mystery of Marie Roget," and "The Purloined Letter," all of which Poe dubbed "tales of ratiocination"—"The Murders in the Rue Morgue" was the beginning of a new and tremendously popular literary genre, the progenitor of many works of fiction and, later, movies, radio plays, and television programs.

The central character in most of Poe's detective fiction was Monsieur C. Auguste Dupin, who, like Sherlock Holmes after him, was a reclusive and almost supernaturally rational being, possessed of prodigious powers of observation and analytical reasoning, who solved the most baffling crimes through a combination of minute attention to seemingly casual clues and a penetrating grasp of human nature.

While the detective genre would prove highly profitable for many later writers, Poe continued to struggle in semi-poverty, and in January 1847 his beloved wife Virginia succumbed to tuberculosis—Poe being unable to afford adequate medical treatment. Although he continued to write and lecture—and even became engaged to the fiancée he had lost in 1826—Poe was absorbed in melancholy and drank heavily. In 1849, he was found, semicomatose, in a Baltimore gutter. Taken to a hospital, he never fully regained consciousness, dying on October 7 of "congestion of the brain"—most likely acute alcohol poisoning.

Further reading: Editions of Poe's fiction are numerous; see also; Wagenknecht, Edward C., *Edgar Allan Poe: The Man Behind the Legend* (New York: Putnam, 1963).

Pound, Roscoe (1870–1964) One of America's greatest legal scholars, Pound sought to reform the justice system by trying to make it more socially responsible.

A native of Lincoln, Nebraska, Roscoe Pound was born October 27, 1870. He attended the University of Nebraska, Lincoln, where he originally studied botany, receiving his degree in that field in 1888. He stayed at Lincoln to earn his master's the following year, again in botany. After receiving his master's, Pound decided to study law and was admitted to Harvard Law School, only to leave after a single term, return to Nebraska to complete his Ph.D. in botany, and then pass the Nebraska state bar exam without having graduated from law school.

After a brief stint as botany professor at Nebraska and as director of the Nebraska Botanical Survey (during which time he discovered a new species of lichen, which was named *Roscoepoundia* in his honor), Pound gave up his botany career to accept a position at Northwestern University as a professor of law. After a short time at the nearby University of Chicago as well, Pound joined the faculty of Harvard in 1911, serving as dean of the law school for 20 years, beginning in 1916. Pound stayed at Harvard until his retirement in 1947 at the age of 77.

Pound's writings reveal his strongly held belief that law should espouse social responsibility. He believed that jurists had neglected the true intent of law, which, as he saw it, was to resolve the conflicting interests that continually hamper a law and order society. He argued that the thrust of law needed to move away from the adjustment of conflicting individual interests to the adjustment of conflicting social interests. Pound believed that the individual should not be the main concern of law, but rather society as a whole.

By the time of Pound's death in July 1964, his ideas on social responsibility were beginning to take hold beyond the classroom and to influence some court decisions in the 1950s and 1960s.

Further reading: Schwartz, Bernard, *Some Makers of American Law* (Dobbs Ferry, N.Y.: Oceana Publications, 1985).

Prentiss, Mark O. (1874–1948) Principal organizer of the National Crime Commission and one of the first civilian activists to declare a war on crime and back up that declaration with a force of politicians and businessmen.

A native of Minnesota, Mark Prentiss was a successful author and businessman, who, like many citizens, prominent as well as humble, was alarmed at the proliferation of crime that marked the Prohibition era of the 1920s. Despairing of any definitive action from national and state governments, Prentiss resolved that the interests of commerce would have to take matters into their own hands. In August 1925, Prentiss convinced the distinguished Judge Elbert GARY to come to his New York offices to preside over an informal meeting of powerful men from the region to discuss the problem and decide on a course of action.

The main focus of the meeting was to meet with Richard Washburn Child, who had just completed a nationwide survey on crime. He presented his findings and recommendations to the august gathering, which included the likes of George Silzer, governor of New Jersey; Franklin D. ROOSEVELT; and Al Smith, governor of New York and perennial presidential candidate. After lengthy discussion, Smith suggested the formation of a New York State Crime Commission as well as a revision of New York's outdated criminal code. Prentiss suggested that the New York idea be taken to the national level as a National Crime Commission.

The purpose of the NCC was to assist in the formation of local crime commissions and to act as a centralized body in a national fight against crime. It would gather statistics and organize studies not only to fight crime, but also to develop more vigorous programs of prosecution and tougher prison sentences. In 1925, Prentiss wrote a popular article entitled "War on

the Growing Menace of Crime," which detailed the deficiencies of the American criminal justice system as well as the epidemic growth of crime. This article did much to galvanize public opinion in favor of the commission, which enjoyed considerable prestige and a moderate success in mounting a nationally based fight against organized crime.

Prichard, James Cowles (1786–1848) An early psychiatrist; Prichard wrote *Treatise on Insanity* in 1835, which introduced the controversial concept of "moral insanity."

In 1806, the young English physician James Prichard joined the medical faculty of the renowned University of Edinburgh. During his tenure at Edinburgh, Prichard developed an interest in the nature of human races and in the human mind. In 1808, he published an ambitious five-volume work entitled *Researches into the Physical History of Mankind,* which would become a major reference source for 19th-century anthropologists.

Prichard served in prestigious positions at Saint Peter's Hospital and the Bristol Infirmary, and in 1835 received an honorary doctorate from Oxford. That year his *Treatise on Insanity* was published, a work in which he presented his thesis of "moral insanity," a theory that certain forms of madness are morbid perversions of the natural feelings. Prichard's conception of "natural feelings" anticipated both Darwin and Freud, in that expression of these feelings, a universal inheritance of nature, would be repugnant and even criminal in civilized society. Prichard also broke with conventional thought on the nature of madness by theorizing that the disorder was not the result of any basic defect in the subject's intellect, but was, rather, a perverted state of his feelings. It was this revolutionary idea that most deeply divided fellow physicians and the legal community. For jurists, the implications were particularly disturbing: If a person commits a criminal act from an impulse that is by definition irresistible, can he justly be held responsible for the crime?

While the perplexing question Prichard's work raised was not fully addressed by courts or the medical profession during his time, the foundation for a close alliance between medicine and law had been laid. Whatever controversy Prichard had provoked, he remained a highly respected physician and in 1845 was appointed "Commissioner of Lunacy"—essentially superintendent of all institutions for the insane—for the city of London.

Prins, Adolphe (1845–1919) A Belgian penologist and one of the founders of the 1899 International Union of Penal Law.

As inspector general of Belgian prisons, Adolphe Prins was responsible for many penal reforms, including individualization of punishment with the object of reducing recidivism. Prins's advanced thought on penology anticipated the modern social defense movement, the post-World War II school led by Marc ANCEL. Prins, believing that the classical idea of moral responsibility was inadequate, helped spark the coming revolution that based penology on the principles of sociology. In his 1895 work *Les doctrines nouvelles de droit penal*, Prins outlined a sociological analysis of the archetypal criminal. Prins was also a believer in the application of physical anthropology to criminology.

Prins was the cofounder, with Franz von LISZT, of the International Union of Penal Law.

Further reading: Ellis, Havelock, *The Criminal* (Boston: Longwood, 1977).

Garofalo, Raffaele, *Criminology*, tr. Robert Wyness Millar (Monclair, N.J.: Patterson Smith, 1968).

Purvis, Melvin (1903–60) A legendary FBI "G-man," Purvis netted such gangsters as Baby Face Nelson, Pretty Boy Floyd, Verne Sankey, and John DILLINGER before a feud with FBI chief J. Edgar HOOVER prompted his resignation from the bureau.

Melvin Purvis left his South Carolina law practice in 1927 to become an FBI agent. Five years later, he was promoted to head of the office in Chicago—a hotbed of Prohibition-era gangsters and the toughest division in the agency. Purvis was immediately inundated with cases and criminals. He drew fire for his handling of the kidnapping of millionaire brewer Adolf Hamm—in which the wrong gang was nabbed, accused, and subsequently acquitted—and for the bloodbath at the Little Bohemia Lodge; while attempting to apprehend John Dillinger there, FBI agents accidentally killed three innocent bystanders.

Undiscouraged, Purvis successfully regrouped his forces, and by 1935 "G-men" under his command had apprehended "public enemy" Verne Sankey and had killed both Baby Face Nelson and Pretty Boy Floyd. In 1934, Purvis accomplished what he had failed to do at the Little Bohemia Lodge. With the aid of "confidential informant" Anna Sage—whom the tabloids dubbed "The Lady in Red"—Purvis and his agents ambushed and killed the elusive John Dillinger as he emerged from Chicago's Biograph Theater.

Purvis was responsible for capturing or killing more criminals the FBI identified as "public enemies" than any other federal agent. Acclaimed by the press and public, Purvis found himself in a personality conflict with J. Edgar Hoover and resigned from the FBI in July 1935.

The name and reputation of Melvin Purvis lived on in several popular portrayals of the FBI, including the popular "Untouchables" television series and a 1958 autobiography, *American Agent*, which also highlighted his feud with Hoover. Following his resignation, Purvis returned to practicing law in Florence, South Carolina, until February 29, 1960, when he took his own life.

Pusser, Buford (1938–74) Sheriff of McNairy County, Tennessee, who was celebrated as a rural crimebuster in the 1972 movie *Walking Tall*.

Buford Pusser was born and raised in McNairy County, Tennessee, left to join the Marines, and subsequently returned to find his home county rife with gambling, prostitution, and moonshining. He successfully ran for the office of county sheriff in 1964 and began a one-man campaign against the forces of crime, becoming famous throughout the South for personally smashing gambling and distilling equipment with a pickax and habitually carrying a—quite literal—big stick. Pusser's efforts drew at least seven serious attempts at assassination, in which he was knifed, beaten, and even thrown from a window. Characteristically, he retaliated in kind, and he was often criticized for brutality.

In 1967, he and his wife, Pauline, were driving near New Hope, Tennessee, when they were ambushed and sprayed with .30-caliber ammunition. Pauline Pusser was killed instantly, and Buford Pusser suffered severe facial wounds, which required 14 operations to repair. Undaunted, he continued to serve as sheriff but was defeated for reelection in 1970—admired by many, but (as one Tennessee newspaper put it) too strongly disposed to "overkill in the pursuit of justice."

W. R. Morris wrote two books about Buford Pusser, *The Twelfth of August: The Story of Buford Pusser* (1971) and *Buford: Story of the "Walking Tall" Sheriff, Buford Pusser* (1983). In 1972, *Walking Tall*, a motion picture based on Pusser's exploits and starring Joe Don Baker, met with great popular success in a nation of angry Middle American filmgoers fed up with crime and criminals. In 1974, hours after signing a movie deal for a sequel to *Walking Tall*—in which he himself would star—Pusser was killed in an automobile accident.

Q

Quetelet, Lambert Adolphe Jacques (1796–1874)
One of the first men to make a scientific study of crime
from a sociological viewpoint, Quetelet formulated
mathematical norms for social behavior.

A native of Ghent, Belgium, Adolphe Quetelet was
forced abruptly to end his schooling at the age of 17
when his father died. Quetelet accepted a position
teaching mathematics at a local secondary school in
Ghent, but leaned toward the arts rather than science.
Only when a professor from the new University of
Ghent encouraged him, did Quetelet devote himself
to science, although he continued to dabble in poetry
until he was 30.

Quetelet quickly threw himself into the world of geometry and statistics, making a widely acclaimed and
original contribution with his doctoral thesis on plane
geometry. After receiving several academic honors, including various chairs and professional memberships,
Quetelet began writing in earnest on statistics and
mathematics. Sometime during the late 1820s, it occurred to Quetelet to apply his statistical theories to social phenomena, including crime, and he published
Recherches sur le penchant au crime aux différents âges in
1831. His work analyzed such issues as differences in
the age-specific crime rates for men and women, for
various countries, and for different social groups.

He looked at the commission of crime in a fresh
light, proposing that crime was not inherent in the
individual but was, rather, a culmination of specific
cultural and environmental factors, which could be
quantified, studied, and modified. Quetelet laid foundations for statistical sociology and for the application
of statistics to criminology.

Further reading: Sylvester, Sawyer F., *Adolphe Quetelet's
Research on the Propensity for Crime at Different Ages* (Cincinnati: Anderson Publishing Company, 1984).

R

Radzinowicz, Sir Leon (1906–) Formerly Wolfson Professor of Criminology at Cambridge University; the author of the classic four-volume *History of the English Criminal Law and Administration* (1948–68).

Born in Poland, Radzinowicz came to England and was appointed assistant director, then director of criminal science at Cambridge University, serving there from 1946 to 1959. In 1959, he was made Wolfson Professor of Criminology at the university and was concurrently director of the Institute of Criminology, an organization he had founded. He served as director until 1972.

Knighted by Queen Elizabeth II in 1970, Radzinowicz is recognized as one of the leading criminologists of the 20th century. Radzinowicz emphasized is on the prevention of criminal behavior, and his long association with the United Nations has produced landmark work in the area of probation and international collaboration in criminal science. No geographic boundary has restricted the criminologist, who has traveled the globe in the interest of penal reform.

Among Radzinowicz's voluminous writings, the four-volume *History of the English Criminal Law and Administration* stands out as a landmark resource in the field of criminology. Other central works include *In Search of Criminology* (1961), *The Need for Criminology* (1965), and *Crime and Justice* (three volumes, 1971).

Retiring from his academic and administrative positions in 1972 to devote more time to writing and lecturing, this "father" of modern criminology remained an active voice in the field.

Further reading: Hood, Roger, ed., *Crime, Criminology and Public Policy: Essays in Honour of Sir Leon Radzinowicz* (New York: Free Press, 1975).

Ragen, Joseph Edward (1896–1971) An American penologist who was a reform-minded warden of the Illinois State Penitentiary at Joliet, known as the "world's toughest prison."

Ragen was born in Trenton, Illinois, on November 22, 1896, the son of a local sheriff and judge. After receiving an education in the public and parochial schools of Carlyle, Illinois, Ragen went into business with his father as a livestock dealer, then served as deputy sheriff in Clinton County from 1922 until he was elected sheriff in 1926. After serving as county treasurer from 1930 to 1933, Ragen became warden of the Illinois State Penitentiary at Menard, and in 1935 was named Illinois state superintendent of prisons. In 1941, he became supervising director of areas including Chicago and Milwaukee for the U.S. Department of Justice, in charge of supervising control of enemy aliens during World War II. After serving in this capacity for 18 months, he became warden of the Illinois State Penitentiary at Joliet, serving until 1961, when he was appointed director of the Illinois State Department of Public Safety, from which he retired in 1965.

It was at Joliet that Ragen made his major impact as a penologist and prison reformer, combining firm discipline with progressive programs of rehabilitation, vocational training, and educational programs that included coursework accredited at the college level. Ragen eliminated the so-called barn-boss system, a hierarchy of power among convicts, and he set prisoners to work beautifying the grounds of Illinois state prisons, not only transforming the surroundings into gardens, but also producing a quarter-million plants annually for sale. Ragen also introduced the policy of permitting prisoners to volunteer for medical research, and he received special commendation for his system's contribution to work on hepatitis and malaria.

Randolph, Ross V. (1907–89) Director of corrections for the state of Illinois, Randolph was instrumental in reforming Illinois' corrections policy.

Ross Randolph was born and raised in Hazen, Arkansas, and attended Illinois State Normal School, graduating in 1929. He went to work as a principal in the Illinois public school system, serving in that capacity until the mid-1930s, when he became attracted to law enforcement. Just before the outbreak of World War II, Randolph was elected deputy sheriff of DeWitt County, Illinois, and subsequently was appointed director of education at the Illinois State Penitentiary in Pontiac.

After serving for a brief time as assistant superintendent of parole supervision for the state, Randolph left Illinois for Washington, D.C., and a position with the FBI. In 1965, he returned to the state, becoming director of the Illinois Department of Public Safety. In this capacity, he was instrumental in developing a state-of-the-art correctional facility in Vienna, Illinois, as well as setting state policy on discipline, cleanliness, and morale throughout the correctional system.

Ray, Isaac (1807–81) A pioneering forensic psychiatrist of the 19th century; the author of the landmark *Medical Jurisprudence of Insanity* (1838), which served for many years as the authoritative work on the subject of insanity and its legal ramifications.

Isaac Ray was born in Beverly, Massachusetts, and received his medical degree from Bowdoin College, Maine, in 1827. Dr. Ray subsequently opened up a private practice in Portland, Maine, where he remained until 1831, when he removed to Eastport and began to develop his growing interest in legal medicine.

In 1835, Ray published his first work in the field of psychiatric jurisprudence, "Lecture on the Criminal Law of Insanity," which addressed the growing controversy over concepts of insanity and criminal responsibility. In 1838, Ray further developed his views on the subject in *Medical Jurisprudence of Insanity*, which was destined to see publication in five editions and served as the 19th century's central authority for the legal definition of insanity. The acceptance of Ray's work in both the medical and legal communities brought international recognition to this New England physician. In 1841, Ray was appointed head of the Maine Insane Hospital, where he remained for four years before becoming superintendent of the prestigious Butler Hospital, Providence, Rhode Island, in 1845.

Ray retired in 1867 and moved to Philadelphia, where he continued to lecture and to testify in legal cases as a medical-psychiatric expert witness until his death in March 1881.

Recently discovered correspondence of Charles DOE, chief justice of New Hampshire's Supreme Court from 1859 to 1876, reveals the influence of Ray's ideas on Doe's landmark "New Hampshire Rule," which overturned the archaic "M'Naghten Rules" as the legal standard for determining a defendant's sanity.

Further reading: Overholser, Winfred, "Isaac Ray," *The Journal of Criminal Law, Criminology and Police Science*, 45:3 (September–October 1954).

Reckless, Walter Cade (1899–1988) An American sociologist who developed new theories of delinquency.

The son of a Philadelphia textile worker, Walter Reckless's first passion was music, and he hoped to become a concert violinist. When an automobile accident took off part of a finger on his bowing hand, he reluctantly gave up his dream and enrolled in the University of Chicago in 1917, initially majoring in history. Unsure of what direction to take, he accepted a graduate assistantship in the sociology department and participated in the department's study of vice in Chicago.

Reckless spent many nights playing his violin in numerous Chicago roadhouses, observing delinquent behavior and the rules of conduct that surround such activity. His observations led directly to his doctoral dissertation, *Vice in Chicago*. After earning his Ph.D. in 1925, Reckless was offered a position in the sociology department at Vanderbilt University in Nashville, Tennessee. There he was given the opportunity to develop a criminology/corrections program from the ground up, appointing faculty, setting curriculum, and establishing standards.

Reckless remained at Vanderbilt for 16 years before moving to Ohio State University in 1940, where he taught until his retirement in 1969. At Ohio State, he designed a program similar to the one he had initiated at Vanderbilt. He also developed his model of the dynamics of delinquency. Working with Simon Dinitz and others, he conducted the celebrated "good boy-bad boy" survey, which emphasized the role of a positive "self-concept" as a buffer against delinquency. Reckless argued that both external and internal factors acted as buffers against delinquency, including respect for parents, friends, and property. He concluded that delinquency is avoided only when the clash between positive and negative buffers is overcome.

Reid, John Edward (1910–82) Lawyer who founded the John E. Reid and Associates Laboratory for Lie Detection Services in Chicago in 1947.

Born in Chicago on August 16, 1910, and educated at Loyola and DePaul universities in that city, John E. Reid operated the nation's largest polygraph (lie detector) laboratory. Not only was his firm influential in the technology and methodology of polygraph examination, but also Reid's dedication to the integrity of the polygraph examiner led to strict ethical guidelines for industry-regulated certification.

Reid was a member of the Chicago Crime Commission and coauthor of *The Polygraph Technique*. In 1944, he patented a more accurate and sensitive blood pressure detection device to be used with the polygraph equipment.

Further reading: Block, Eugene B., *Lie Detectors: Their History and Use* (New York: D. McKay Co., c.1977).

Reinemann, John Otto (1902–76) A leading criminologist, probation director, and researcher into the causes of juvenile delinquency.

Born in Frankfurt am Main, Germany, on October 10, 1902, Reinemann was educated at the local gymnasium and received law degrees at the University of Frankfurt (LL.B., 1924; LL.D., 1926). He also attended the University of Munich during 1922 and studied criminology and political science at the University of Pennsylvania during 1943-47.

In Germany, Reinemann served as a public prosecutor and public defender and as a city solicitor in Berlin. While serving in this capacity during the late 1920s, Reinemann became interested in reforming the criminal justice system, particularly in the area of juvenile delinquency. He became very active in a number of German youth movements, including several World Youth Peace conferences, which led to his dismissal as city solicitor in 1933, after the Nazis came to power. In 1934, after receiving a scholarship from Pendle Hill, a Quaker center for religious and social studies in Wallingford, Pennsylvania, Reinemann immigrated to the United States. Later in the year, he was appointed district supervisor of the Juvenile Division of the Philadelphia Municipal Court. From this time until 1948, he was involved with the Juvenile Division and was responsible for training court staff.

In 1948, Reinemann became director of probation for the Municipal Court, a position he held until his retirement in 1969. From 1969 to 1972, he was a consultant to the Citizens' Crime Commission of Philadelphia. Reinemann also taught from 1940 to 1955 at the Public Service Institute of the Pennsylvania Department of Public Instruction, specializing in corrections. From 1961 to 1970, he was an instructor at the Law Enforcement Studies Center of Temple University, specializing in juvenile delinquency. He also lectured on this subject at other universities, including the University of Pennsylvania and the University of Florida.

Reinemann was the author of a groundbreaking 1945 study of juvenile delinquency entitled *Where Do Philadelphia's Delinquent Children Live?* The report was given nationwide coverage and had a significant influence not only on the criminal justice system, but also on urban planners and public housing policy makers.

Reinhardt, James Melvin (1894–1974) Professor of criminology at the University of Nebraska; wrote about the infamous Starkweather case (subsequently the basis of two popular films) and was the first police educator ever named to the National Police Hall of Fame.

Born in Dalton, Georgia, on October 5, 1894, Reinhardt was educated at Berea College (B.A., 1923), the University of Chicago (1923–24), and the University of North Dakota (M.A., 1925; Ph.D., 1929). He taught in several universities and colleges before being appointed professor at the University of Nebraska. He was a consultant to many law enforcement agencies, including the FBI, and wrote extensively on sociology and criminology, with particular emphasis on juvenile delinquency and on the psychopathology of crime. His most influential book was *The Murderous Trail of Charles Starkweather* (1960), which chronicled the career of a youth who (while his girlfriend watched) randomly killed 11 persons in Nebraska and Wyoming in 1958, which helped shape contemporary views on the nature of psychopathic and sociopathic murder. Two motion pictures were later loosely based on the book, *Badlands* (1973) and *Natural Born Killers* (1994).

Further reading: Reinhardt, James Melvin, *The Murderous Trail of Charles Starkweather* (New York: C. C. Thomas, 1960).

Reiser, Martin (1927–) An expert on police psychology who became the first psychologist ever employed full-time by a police department in this country.

Growing up in Philadelphia, Martin Reiser attended the local Temple University beginning in 1946 and—with the exception of a four-year tour of duty in Korea with the Air Force—stayed there until 1961, when he received his doctorate in clinical psychology. After graduation, Reiser moved to California, where he secured a position in the state hospital at Camarillo, staying there for only a year before moving on to the San Fernando Valley Child Guidance Clinic. It was his work on stress, conducted while he was at that institution, that drew the attention of the Los Angeles

Police Department, which offered him an appointment in 1968 as the department psychologist—the first such appointment ever made by a police department in this country.

As department psychologist, Reiser had many duties, including counseling officers and their families, teaching and research within the LAPD, management consultation about specific crime situations, and, finally, hostage negotiation. One of the problems Reiser identified and dealt with specifically was post-shooting trauma, or post-traumatic stress syndrome. Previously associated only with war veterans, PSTS involves recurring psychological abnormalities related to a stressful occurrence, such as a shooting incident, in which an officer has had to fire on a subject. By 1974, only a very small number of agencies nationwide had implemented a formal counseling service to deal with this increasingly recognized problem.

Reiser also dealt with the problem of stress among non-field personnel, most notably middle management, who seemed to be the most adversely affected. Noting that they faced stress from both above and below them in the management hierarchy, Reiser concluded that personality traits go a long way toward determining an individual's stress level. Anxiety-prone individuals or those who take on excessive responsibility are more susceptible and tend to manifest medical conditions that can accompany stress, including diabetes, high blood pressure, and heart problems.

Reiss, Albert John, Jr. (1922–) Undertook the first ever study of police brutality in the United States.

A Wisconsin native, Albert Reiss attended Marquette University in Milwaukee, earning his undergraduate degree in 1944 before continuing on to the University of Chicago, where he took a master's and Ph.D. in sociology. After a short period as instructor at Chicago, Reiss accepted a position in the sociology department of Vanderbilt University in Nashville, where he began to study criminology. After a brief tenure at Vanderbilt, he moved on to teach at the universities of Iowa, Wisconsin, Michigan, and at Yale, where he stayed for the remainder of his academic career.

While at Yale in 1971, Reiss completed the first study in the United States of undue police violence, or police brutality. Riding with police officers in Chicago, Boston, and Washington, D.C., he discovered an abuse rate of 22.6 per 1,000 white civilians and 41.9 per 1,000 African Americans (figures that are probably conservative, since the abuse noted occurred when an observer was present). Reiss's work was important in documenting what had been a frequent, but largely anecdotal charge against police agencies nationwide:

that officers were guilty of brutality, which was often racially motivated. Perhaps most important, the study motivated police departments themselves to become aware of the issues of brutality and ethnic and racial sensitivity.

Reles, Abraham (alias: Kid Twist) (1907–41) Dubbed the "canary who couldn't fly," Reles's testimony exposed Murder, Inc., and was followed by his fatal "fall" from a Coney Island hotel window.

Raised in the slums of Brownsville, Brooklyn, "Kid Twist" Reles, together with Phil "Pittsburgh" Strauss, Frank "the Dasher" Abbandando, Charles Workman, Harry "Happy" Maione, Emmanuel "Mendy" Weiss (no relation to Hymie WEISS), Martin "Bugsy" Goldstein, Vito "Chicken Head" Gurino, and Louis Capone (no relation to Al CAPONE), formed the nucleus of a professional gangland death squad that, under the direction of Albert ANASTASIA, would come to be called Murder, Inc. Reles was the "street

Abraham "Kid" Reles "sang like a canary" to officials investigating Murder, Inc. (Courtesy of the Library of Congress)

boss" of Murder, Inc., and personally killed at least 30 men.

Reles was arrested in 1940 on charges that included robbery, assault, possession of narcotics, burglary, disorderly conduct, and murder. By this time, he had been arrested on 42 occasions and had served six prison terms—though never for a major crime. Faced with imprisonment for the rest of his life, Reles gave the police and district attorney an earful. He "sang like a canary," exposing Murder, Inc., in detail. In a single stroke, in Brooklyn alone, 49 gangland murders were instantly solved. Reles traded immunity from prosecution for the full story behind Murder, Inc. A series of arrests followed, and Murder, Inc. dissolved. For more than a year, Reles appeared as the star witness for prosecutor Burton Turkus in mobster trial after mobster trial. His testimony helped convict Louis Lepke BUCHALTER and Emmanuel Weiss for the murder of Joseph Rosen, sending Lepke—"chairman of the board" of the national crime syndicate—to the electric chair.

During this period, Reles was held in protective custody on the sixth floor of the Half Moon Hotel in Coney Island, Brooklyn. Although he was under constant surveillance by six uniformed police officers, he "fell" out of his window during the early morning hours of November 12, 1941. Just how this happened has never been explained, and theories range from suicide to accident to practical joke: Reles may have climbed out the window using bed sheets tied together, intending to run back upstairs to scare his guards sitting outside the room. Others believe that officials were bribed to admit hitmen into Reles's room in order to wreck the case against Anastasia.

Reno, Janet (1938–)   The first female attorney general of the United States.

A native of Florida, Janet Reno was greatly influenced by her brilliant and strong-willed mother, a woman who reportedly could "wrestle alligators one minute and recite poetry the next." Reno was admitted to Cornell University in 1956, graduating in 1960 with a degree in chemistry. From there, she went on to Harvard Law School, one of only 16 women in a class of more than 500. Even with a degree from Harvard, however, she was denied several legal positions because she was a woman. She eventually joined a small firm in Florida, then became a partner in her own firm in 1967.

In 1971, Reno received her first political appointment when she was named staff director of the Judiciary Committee of the Florida House of Representatives. The following year she was defeated in her bid for a seat in the state legislature, but in 1973, she served as counsel to the state senate's Criminal Justice

Committee for the Revision of Florida's Criminal Code. The same year, she took a job in the state's attorney's office of the Eleventh Judicial Circuit of Florida. She was given what was considered a dead-end job in the juvenile division of the prosecutor's office, but within two months had completely reorganized the division and made it one of the most successful arms of the state prosecutor's office. Reno was so impressive in the juvenile division that her supervisor, who was stepping down, petitioned the governor to appoint her his successor as state's attorney. The governor complied, and Reno became the first woman to head a county prosecutor's office in Florida. She was subsequently elected to the office by a margin of 74%, even though she ran as a Democrat in a Republican county. Reno quickly became one of the most respected civil servants in Florida and gained a sufficient national reputation to prompt President Bill Clinton to nominate her as attorney general in February 1993; she was swiftly and unanimously confirmed.

Almost immediately, Reno was faced with a difficult and tragic case: the siege of the Waco, Texas, compound of the so-called Branch Davidians, a well-armed religious cult led by a man calling himself David Koresh. Koresh and other zealots barricaded themselves in the compound. When it was stormed by Alcohol, Tobacco and Firearms agents, the cult members opened fire, killing four ATF officers and wounding others. After negotiations failed to bring a peaceful resolution to an armed standoff, Reno ordered the ATF and FBI to assault the compound in force. Koresh and his followers responded by setting fire to their own building, immolating themselves. Eighty-six cult members died, including 17 children. When the national media sought to fix blame for the debacle, Reno immediately stood up, acknowledged full responsibility, and absolved President Clinton of any fault. Asked if she had consulted the president before authorizing the assault, she responded: "It was my job to make the decision, not the president's."

Rios, Ariel (1954–82)   This U.S. Bureau of Alcohol, Tobacco and Firearms (ATF) agent was one of the first casualties in the federal government's "War on Drugs" in south Florida.

Growing up in New Haven, Connecticut, Ariel Rios attended the John Jay College of Criminal Justice in Manhattan and graduated in 1976. After college, he began working for various state and local law enforcement agencies in New York before he became an officer in the Bureau of Alcohol, Tobacco and Firearms in December 1978. Rios was quickly assigned to undercover work in Connecticut, usually collaborating with the Connecticut State Police and other state law enforcement agencies.

After the Reagan administration instituted its "Just Say No to Drugs" campaign in the early 1980s, the federal government generally stepped up efforts to wage a "War on Drugs." In 1982, the ATF selected 55 top agents, Rios among them, to work undercover in Miami, the point of entry for many illegal drugs coming into the United States. The ATF agents would work under Vice President George Bush and a combined federal task force designed to seek out the major drug kingpins of south Florida.

On December 2, 1982, Rios and another agent were sent undercover to buy a large shipment of cocaine. The operation went sour, they were fired upon, and Rios was killed. The agent was given numerous posthumous citations and became one of the first—and, to the media, most visible—federal law enforcement casualties in a brutal and ongoing war against the illegal drug trade.

Rizzo, Frank L(azarro) (1920–91)

Controversial, much-admired, and much-reviled nightstick-wielding former Philadelphia police chief and two-term mayor; a dominant force in the politics and policies of the City of Brotherly Love for more than four decades.

Not since the likes of New York's notorious "Clubber" WILLIAMS, had a cop stirred more passionate controversy than Frank Rizzo. The son of a policeman, Rizzo joined the Philadelphia force in 1943, rising quickly through the ranks and becoming police commissioner during the socially turbulent 1960s. As police commissioner in an economically beleaguered and ethnically changing city, Rizzo quickly earned a reputation as a maverick—or a loose cannon—whose controversial words and deeds brought both praise and criticism. Typical of the Rizzo style was the time in 1969 when the commissioner abruptly rose from a black-tie dinner, tucked a blackjack into his cummerbund, and led his men into the streets to quell one of the era's many race-centered urban riots.

How tough was Frank Rizzo? He once remarked to a newspaper reporter that he was "going to make Atilla the Hun look like a faggot." Assailed with charges of police brutality, racism, strongarm rule, and general tyranny, Rizzo nevertheless continued to command a loyal following, particularly among Philadelphia's white residents. Supporters were quick to point out that, during Rizzo's tenure as police commissioner, Philadelphia, an economically disadvantaged city, had the lowest crime rate among the nation's 10 most populous urban centers.

In 1972, Rizzo, running as a law-and-order Nixon Democrat, was elected mayor of Philadelphia—the first top cop ever elected to that office. He brought to city hall the same highhanded and outspoken attitude he had brought to police headquarters, gaining international attention during a visit to Rome, when he advised Italian police on how to break up a mob. Come to Philadelphia, the mayor told an official, so he could learn how to "spaco il capo!"—bust a head.

For many Rizzo was a national embarrassment, exemplifying the ugliest excesses of American urban politics. Nevertheless, Philadelphians returned Rizzo to city hall in 1975. Following this second term, Frank Rizzo and the Rizzo style fell out of favor. He returned to politics as a Republican in 1991, but died while staging his comeback.

Further reading: Hamilton, Fred, *Rizzo: From Cop to Mayor of Philadelphia* (New York: Viking, 1993).

Rogers, Earl (1870–1922)

One of the most successful defense lawyers of the early 20th century, Rogers turned cross-examination into a veritable art form.

Born in Buffalo, New York, Earl Rogers moved west with his family shortly after his birth, only to return to the state as a young man to attend Syracuse University. After studying at Syracuse for a time, Rogers returned to the West Coast to take a job as a reporter for a Los Angeles newspaper. It was while covering the trial beat that Rogers became interested in law. He began to study criminal law on his own and, without having attended law school, passed the California bar exam.

Beginning in civil practice, Rogers soon found it boring and changed to criminal law, which was particularly lively in the Los Angeles of the late 19th and early 20th century. Early in his career, Rogers set a tone of ethical and professional responsibility by refusing to be kept on retainer by any corporation or person as "house counsel."

With the exception of defending Clarence DARROW against charges of jury tampering, Rogers never represented anyone famous, nor did he champion a cause of great social moment or argue a case before the Supreme Court. His fame rests on his most impressive acquittal record and his ability to persuade jurors and conduct masterful cross-examinations. He was a dramatic lawyer, sometimes reenacting the crime and reconstructing the scene—once even pulling the murder weapon on a witness, just to get his reaction. In another case, he had the entire intestinal cavity of a murder victim admitted as evidence.

Rogers's greatest brilliance came in his absolute mastery of cross-examination. At the time, the process was not as rigid as it is today, and judges allowed the attorney great leeway. Even given these broad parameters, Rogers played fast and loose with cross-examination, often asking a question not germane to the case, simply attempting to discredit the witness. His favorite was: "Aren't you in fact in the pay of the district attorney?" After a denial, he would ask the witness, "Are you sure?" The jury might or might not remember the answer—but they would certainly remember the question and assume it had some basis in fact.

On another occasion, Rogers asked an eyewitness to identify the culprit in a crime. The witness automatically pointed to the person sitting next to Rogers—the customary seat for the defendant. In fact, Rogers had planted his assistant there and had seated the defendant in the gallery.

If Rogers had one failing, it was drink—though many a fellow lawyer observed that a defendant was better off with Earl Rogers drunk than with any other lawyer sober. Rogers's habits of high living bankrupted him, and when he finally succumbed to an alcohol-related illness, it was said he bummed a quarter for a drink minutes before his death.

Further reading: Kornstein, Daniel J., *Thinking Under Fire: Great Courtroom Lawyers and Their Impact on American History* (New York: Dodd, Mead, 1987).

Rolph, C. H. See HEWITT, CECIL ROLPH.

Roosevelt, Franklin Delano (1882–1945) FDR's New Deal policies greatly expanded the federal government's role in law enforcement and in police reform; his National Labor Relations Board made it possible for police to unionize.

Franklin Roosevelt's concern over crime in America dated back to his mid-1920s tenure on the National Crime Commission. Once elected president in 1932, Roosevelt made Attorney General Homer CUMMINGS his point man on crime policy, which the president characterized as a "war on crime." But so far as the public was concerned, it was the young director of the FBI, J. Edgar HOOVER, who emerged as the prominent figure in law enforcement during the Roosevelt administration. FDR strongly supported Hoover, who, in turn, helped the president both publicly and privately in maintaining his political power. The New Deal also funded a national police academy in 1935 under the jurisdiction of the FBI. In 1940, as Europe's war clouds loomed over the United States, Roosevelt gave the FBI the unprecedented responsibility of coordinating domestic security during wartime.

Roosevelt's New Deal changed the face of the American criminal justice system. It consolidated crime fighting data, making access to such information much more efficient, and also paved the way for the development of future federal law enforcement agencies such as the Drug Enforcement Agency (DEA), the Bureau of Alcohol, Tobacco, and Firearms (ATF), and the Central Intelligence Agency (CIA). The labor legislation that was part of the New Deal included the National Labor Relations Board, which made it possible for police officers to unionize without compromising their sworn duties as civil servants.

Further reading: Davis, Kenneth, *FDR: The New Deal Years, 1933–1937* (New York: Random House, 1979).
———, *FDR: The New York Years, 1928–1933* (New York: Random House, 1979).
Freidel, Frank, *Franklin D. Roosevelt: A Rendezvous with Destiny* (Boston: Little, Brown, 1990).
Miller, Nathan, *F.D.R.: An Intimate History* (New York: Doubleday, 1983).

Roosevelt, Theodore (1858–1919) New York City police commissioner, governor of New York, and president of the United States—in all capacities a leader of the Progressive movement and a champion of reform.

A member of an old-money family (they considered the Rockefellers and the Vanderbilts upstarts), Theodore Roosevelt graduated from Harvard in 1880 and studied law before being elected to the state assembly at the age of 23. The following year he unsuccessfully sought the post of speaker of the statehouse, and by the age of 28 had lost the race for New York mayor. While serving in the statehouse in 1884, he headed a state legislative commission to investigate the New York City police department. In 1889, he became the first United States Civil Service commissioner, charged with maintaining civil service regulations within the New York police department. After a moderately successful term in this post, Roosevelt became one of four New York police commissioners in 1889. As a commissioner, he set out to reform the much-maligned department in an effort to extricate it from its continual involvement with Tammany Hall politicians. He brought a military style of discipline and administration to the department, consolidating regional control in a central headquarters, hoping to diminish the power of neighborhood captains. He completely overhauled the recruitment process and initiated firearms training. During his tenure, he promoted 130 officers and appointed 1,700 rookie cops, injecting desperately needed new blood into a department mired in the old-boy network.

The state's Republican leadership, led by Thomas Platt, grew tired of Roosevelt's posturing and arranged for him to be named assistant secretary of the navy in 1897 to get him out of New York. At the outbreak of the Spanish-American War, Roosevelt organized and led the Rough Riders regiment at the battle of San Juan Hill, where he may or may not have personally inspired a frontal assault. After the war, legend established, Roosevelt returned with such acclaim that Platt could not avoid giving him the Republican gubernatorial nomination in 1899. Winning the election, he filled the post for only a year when the national Republican leadership hoped to tame him as Platt had three years earlier. They thought they had the answer by having him elected vice president of the United States, a certain dead end for any politician—or so it was thought. Senate Majority Leader Mark Hanna of Ohio exploded, "You idiots, he's only a breath away from the Presidency."

Hanna was proven correct when William McKinley was assassinated the following year and Roosevelt became president.

As president, Roosevelt continued on his bold course, not caring whom he offended as long as he did it with style, bristling when it was suggested that he should tone down his act, and uttering his trademark exclamation of approval: "Bully!" He embodied the Progressive agenda, proclaiming himself "Teddy the Trust-Buster" by going after such big guns as Standard Oil and the western railroads. He demanded a fair shake for labor and put the federal legislature and judiciary behind it.

Stepping down in 1908, he designated William Howard Taft his successor, but Taft proved unsatisfactory after one term, and Roosevelt ran for president again in 1912 on the third-party Bull Moose ticket. Surviving an assassination attempt, he finished second in the race, still the best third-party finish in American presidential politics.

Critics claim Roosevelt was more flash than form, but he did take a stand against corruption and the dictatorship of big business, and he made several social advances through his Square Deal domestic program.

Further reading: Chessman, G. Wallace, *Theodore Roosevelt and the Politics of Power* (New York: Library of American Biography, 1987).

Miller, Nathan. *Theodore Roosevelt: A Life* (New York: Morrow, 1992).

Rothstein, Arnold (alias: A.R.; The Big Bankroll; Mr. A; Mr. Big) (1882–1928)   Known as "Mr. Big," Rothstein earned legendary status in the world of organized crime as the man who fixed the 1919 World Series.

New York City gambler Arnold Rothstein mastered the art of making big-time money from organized crime without getting his hands dirty. Dubbed "Mr. Big" and "The Big Bankroll," Rothstein's modus operandi was to fund criminal operations—to invest in crime—while remaining sufficiently distant from the nefarious deeds to avoid prosecution himself. His specialty was fixing sports games—on which heavy wagers had been laid—financing bootlegging operations, controlling organized labor rackets, and bankrolling high-stakes burglaries. (Nick Arnstein, the gangster husband of singer-comedienne Fanny Brice,

For a long time, Arnold Rothstein controlled much of New York's illicit gambling empire, having earned his greatest fame, as the man who "fixed" the 1919 World Series. (Courtesy of the Library of Congress)

was jailed for big-scale Wall Street mail bond robberies Rothstein had backed.)

Rothstein was the son of prosperous Jewish immigrants who settled in New York. His father was a prominent merchant with a reputation so spotless his associates called him Rothstein the Just. His son showed early promise as a businessman, too. He was a brilliant student with a particular aptitude for mathematics. However, he applied his genius not to mercantile finance but to gambling and was forever calculating odds on wagers. This was no idle obsession, for he proved at a young age to be a phenomenally successful gambler, betting on anything and everything, and quickly amassing a fortune, which he used to open his own gambling den in Manhattan's Tenderloin district in 1912. By 1919, Rothstein was a multimillionaire who owned a number of nightclubs and gambling resorts. It was in that year that he pulled off his single boldest project, bribing eight players on the Chicago White Sox to throw the World Series.

The so-called Black Sox Scandal rocked the nation. Baseball was, after all, the American Pastime—pure and innocent, savoring of mom and apple pie. But, like anything else, it could be bought. And it was. In 1920, Rothstein was summoned to testify about the scandal. Harassed by reporters, Rothstein remained calm—then delivered a virtuoso performance before the grand jury. "Gentlemen," he declared, " what kind of courtesy is this? What kind of city is this? I came here voluntarily and what happens? A gang of thugs bar my path with cameras as though I was a notorious person, a criminal even!"

It worked. Rothstein handily escaped indictment.

Always posing as a very lucky gentleman gambler, Rothstein opened up more and more clubs and casinos, admonishing his employees always to "Treat the sucker right. He is paying your salary. His stupidity is our income. You must never insult him, just cheat him with a smile."

By the middle of the 1920s, Rothstein extended his operations to drug smuggling on an international scale, employing Charles "Lucky" LUCIANO and Jack "Legs" DIAMOND to do most of the dirty work. As he distanced himself from his own operations, Rothstein also always tried to avoid violent confrontation and destructive gang warfare. He assiduously worked to arbitrate disputes between rivals and, in effect, became the organized underworld's first "judge," so skillful and respected that he actually commanded high fees (as much as $500,000) for performing services as an arbiter.

Like other high-rolling gangsters, Rothstein invested heavily in politicians and police officials and became a central source of seed money for schemes that could not be financed conventionally. By 1928, it could accurately be said that Arnold Rothstein was New York City's single most powerful citizen. Yet it was also at this time that his fortunes seemed suddenly to decline. He became ill and nervous, and—most uncharacteristically—suffered a series of disastrous gambling losses. In an effort to recoup, he convened an epic poker game at the Park Central Hotel, which drew the nation's richest gamblers during September 8 through 10, 1928. Rothstein lost in excess of $320,000, rose from the table, and promised to "pay off in a day or two." With that, he walked out the door. The next night, while dining at Lindy's delicatessen, he was heard to say, "I don't pay off on fixed poker."

Despite the insistence of George "Hump" McManus, to whom he owed the most, Mr. Big refused to pay up. In the meantime, he continued making big bets, including a half-million dollars on the presidential election of 1928, wagering that Herbert Hoover would beat Governor Al Smith of New York. On November 4, 1928, he was summoned to the Park Central. An hour after Rothstein arrived, a bellman found him, shot in the gut. He was rushed to the hospital. In the meantime, detectives traced a trail of Rothstein's blood to the room of "Hump" McManus, whom they arrested.

Rothstein, on his deathbed, repeatedly refused to name his attacker. In response to police questions, he smiled and raised his finger to his lips. McManus and another gambler, Nathan Raymond, were charged with the murder. Raymond was released after producing an alibi, but McManus was held for trial. He was acquitted for lack of evidence, the defense suggesting that Rothstein had shot himself out of despair over his losses.

Roughead, William (1870–1952)

One of the first to write in the "True Crime" genre, producing works based on specific crimes and their ensuing trials.

A native of Edinburgh, Scotland, William Roughead earned his law degree from the University of Edinburgh at the turn of the century. Roughead, who was interested enough in writing to secure admission to the Society of Writers, began to practice law. While preparing for his first trial, he ran across an array of very seamy and highly interesting trial records. Since these were matters of public record, Roughead decided to recast the accounts in fictional guise and publish them. The resulting series of books was snapped up by enthralled readers, who, appalled by the crimes, nevertheless hungered after every detail.

Although Roughead continued to consider himself a lawyer, he seldom practiced because he was either researching old trials or observing ongoing ones for his latest book. He would produce more than 40 sensational volumes before his death.

Despite his public success, his work was not initially well received by professional colleagues, who felt that Roughead had prostituted the legal establishment and that sordid sagas of murder or brutal assault were, in any case, matters best forgotten. That attitude changed drastically with the advent of World War I, which redefined death and brutality. One writer of the period noted, "Having been commanded for four long years by every clergyman and civil magistrate to kill as many people as possible, it is not strange if human life has, for some of us, lost some of its value." In this atmosphere, a popular 20th-century literary—or subliterary—genre was born and nurtured.

Rowan, Charles (1783–1852)

First co-commissioner (with Richard MAYNE) of the Metropolitan Police force of London; considered one of the founding fathers of Scotland Yard.

A wounded hero of the Waterloo campaign, Charles Rowan was chosen by Prime Minister Sir Robert PEEL in 1829 to lead—with Irish barrister Richard Mayne—the "new police" of London. Together, the two commissioners pioneered the concept of preventative law enforcement—the prime mission of the modern police force—and Rowan is especially remembered for his definition of the police officer as a servant of the people, not an oppressive master.

By establishing a police agency run along military lines, Rowan fostered discipline and loyalty, qualities conducive to effective police work and anathema to corruption.

Further reading: Browne, Douglas G., *The Rise of Scotland Yard* (Westport, Conn.: Greenwood Press, 1973).

Wilkes, John, *The London Police in the Nineteenth Century* (London: Cambridge University Press, 1971).

Rumford, Benjamin Thompson, Count (1753–1814)

American-born British scientist who is significant in the history of penology for his establishment of a model system of workhouses for the poor.

Benjamin Thompson, who was also known as Count Rumford, was born in Woburn, Massachusetts, on March 26, 1753. A Loyalist, Thompson moved to London in 1776 at the outbreak of the American Revolution. He worked in the British Colonial Office, experimented with improving gunpowder, and was knighted in 1784. In that year he was appointed aide-de-camp to the elector of Bavaria. There he reformed the Bavarian Army, abolished mendicancy in Munich, and established workhouses for the poor. These actions served as models for all of Europe and even the United States, establishing the humane separation of the poor from criminals and separating penology from institutions devoted to social welfare.

In recognition of his services to the army and to the poor, the elector made Thompson a count of the Holy Roman Empire in 1791. However, Rumford is best remembered by history for his scientific work on the nature of heat. He showed that the prevailing belief that heat was a fluid was incorrect, and he demonstrated that heat is a form of mechanical motion. His research led to the development of the Count Rumford stove, which greatly improved home heating and cooking equipment.

Thompson helped found the Royal Institution, endowed the Rumford medals of the Royal Society and the American Academy of Arts and Sciences, and also endowed a professorship at Harvard University. He died in France on August 21, 1814.

Rush, Benjamin (1746–1813)

An important statesman during the American Revolution and the young republic's preeminent physician; often called the "father of American psychology."

Philadelphia-born Benjamin Rush received his M.D. from the University of Edinburgh in 1768. He returned to the United States to become the most famous physician and educator of the early national period. One of the signers of the Declaration of Independence, Rush also served as General George Washington's chief of medical services during the American Revolution. Following the Revolution, in 1791 he became professor of medicine at the University of Pennsylvania, and in 1812 published the first American work in the field of psychiatry: *Medical Inquiries and Observations upon the Diseases of the Mind*. For more than 50 years, Rush's book would be the standard text in American psychiatry. He also wrote extensively on the influence of such physical factors as climate and food on an individual's mental—or "moral"—faculties.

Rush produced two works relating directly to crime and punishment: *Medical Inquiries* was the first work on medical jurisprudence written in America, and his 1787 "Enquiry into the Effects of Public Punishments upon Criminals and upon Society" attacked Pennsylvania's practice of inflicting humiliating public punishment on wrongdoers. Demanding that "crimes should be punished in private, or not punished at all," he also took the progressive position that "the only design of punishment is the reformation of the criminal." His advocacy of rehabilitation as a principle of penology was particularly farsighted.

Further reading: Hawke, David Freeman, *Benjamin Rush: Revolutionary Gadfly* (Indianapolis: Bobbs-Merrill, 1971).

Ryan, Edward James (1899–1978)

One of the first to propose the use of dental records as a means of identification, Ryan designed a universal chart showing unique dental characteristics.

Little is known of Edward Ryan's early career other than that he operated a small private dentistry practice in Chicago between the two world wars. In 1937, he published an article in the *Journal of Criminal Law and Criminology* proposing the use of dental charts as a fifth method of identification by the United States Department of Justice (along with fingerprints, photographs, aliases, and nicknames). In the article he laid out a standardized dental chart he had developed, which marked every individual aspect of a person's dental structure. This chart, readable by all dentists, could be used in several ways when other forms of identification were not available.

In 1938, Ryan published another article, in *Scientific American*, which further extended his arguments. He stated that teeth marks were as unique as fingerprints and that such habits as biting fingernails, chewing earpieces of glasses, and even sucking the meat out of crab legs leave marks that are valuable and viable clues. He pointed out that teeth are shaped and positioned so differently that, while someone may have the same formation of teeth or the same deformity, the 32 (or fewer) teeth of no two people will produce exactly the same bite plate. The science of dental identification was born.

Rynning, Thomas H. (1866–1941) Long-lived and legendary western lawman who served as a captain in the Arizona Rangers and superintendent of the territorial prison at Yuma.

An orphan from Beloit, Wisconsin, Thomas Rynning began a lifetime of wandering at the age of 12. Moving west, he made his way to Texas, working as a teamster and a cowboy. In 1885, he enlisted in the army and was stationed with the Eighth U.S. Cavalry, which was soon transferred to Arizona. With the cavalry, Rynning saw action in the final "pacification" campaign against the Navajos and against Geronimo. In 1891, Rynning left the army to join Buffalo Bill Cody's Wild West Show, entertaining as a "real-life" cowboy and Indian fighter. He also began working with Southern Pacific Railroad track crews, laying right-of-way all over the Southwest between Los Angeles and west Texas.

When war with Spain broke out in 1898, Rynning reenlisted in the army as part of Teddy Roosevelt's Rough Riders. At war's end, he was discharged and accepted a captain's commission in the Arizona Rangers in 1902. In 1907, he was appointed superintendent of the territorial prison in Yuma, transforming a crude and brutal western stockade into a reasonably modern and efficient prison.

S

Sacco, Nicola (1891–1927) and Vanzetti, Bartolomeo (1888–1927)   In 1921, the Massachusetts criminal trials of accused anarchist murderers Nicola Sacco and Bartolemeo Vanzetti sparked a worldwide political sensation, and even today their names evoke controversy over whether justice was served.

Nicola Sacco was a shoemaker in a South Stoughton, Massachusetts, factory, and Bartolomeo Vanzetti was a fishmonger. The two lifelong friends had emigrated from Italy together in 1908. Together, in 1917–18, they evaded the World War I draft by going to Mexico until after the armistice. They also had similar political interests as would-be revolutionaries and anarchists.

In the period following World War I, much of the world, including the United States, was swept by a wave of radicalism, and in 1919, anarchists attempted to blow up dozens of U.S. political leaders. Political panic ensued, and federal authorities, spearheaded by Attorney General A. Mitchell PALMER, cast a wide net to bring in every known radical in the country. The so-called Palmer Raids brought in thousands of suspects and unleashed a plague of illegal searches and seizures. The raids also enflamed a public paniced with visions of violent, swarthy aliens bent on the overthrow of government and the massacre of innocent citizens.

In this charged atmosphere, a robbery was committed on Christmas Eve morning, 1919, in Bridgewater, Massachusetts, some 30 miles south of Boston. A gang of "foreign-looking men" stopped the payroll truck of the White Shoe Company. Two men got out of an Overland automobile; when the payroll driver refused to hand over the money, the hold-up men fired at the payroll truck. The driver of the payroll truck returned fire. The robbers jumped back into the car and took off. That vehicle was later found in a Bridgewater garage, and its owner was identified as a Mr. Boda.

He remained at large until April 15, 1920, when, at 3 P.M. in South Braintree, Massachusetts, Slater and Morill Shoe Company paymaster/cashier Frederick A. Parmenter and guard Alexander Berardelli moved almost $16,000 from one company building to another.

Each man carried a money bag. Two "foreign-looking" men loitered near the fence separating company buildings. They blocked Parmenter and Berardelli. One of the men shoved a revolver into Berardelli's ribs and fired several times, killing him. The two "foreign-looking men" picked up his money bag. In the meantime, Parmenter, walking behind about 10 paces, dropped his bag and sprinted across the street. The gunmen fired two bullets into his back and killed him, collected his bag, then jumped into a Buick getaway car, which police recovered two days later. Detectives identified tire tracks leading away from the recovered Buick as having been made by the Overland car implicated in the Bridgewater crime.

On May 5, 1921, Boda, Sacco, Vanzetti, and a man named Orciani went to the Bridgewater garage to collect the Overland car. Johnson, the garage owner, stalled them, and called the police. The men got nervous, and Boda and Orciani left on a motorcycle, while Sacco and Vanzetti left on foot. The police launched a search, and an officer apprehended Sacco and Vanzetti on a streetcar that evening. Sacco had various anarchist leaflets in his possession and a flyer for a speech Vanzetti was going to make.

The pair was charged with carrying concealed weapons, to which they pleaded guilty, and they were held on suspicion of having committed the Bridgewater and Braintree robberies. Sacco could prove he was at work on December 24, 1919, but had no alibi for April 15, 1920. Sacco was charged only with the South Braintree crime, but Vanzetti, who lacked any alibi, was charged with both.

On June 22, 1920, Vanzetti was tried first for the Bridgewater crime and, convicted on highly questionable evidence, was sentenced to 10 to 15 years' imprisonment. On May 30, 1921, Sacco and Vanzetti were tried together for the Braintree killings. The judge, Webster Thayer, was an arch-conservative. The prosecutor, Frederick Katzmann, announced his intention to "crucify those damned God-hating radicals!" And the defense attorney, Fred Moore, was a rumpled and belligerent radical from California, whom the conservative jury found "repulsive." Although liberals throughout the country rallied to Sacco and Vanzetti's support, even offering better legal counsel, Moore refused aid.

The 37-day trial was a bewildering circus of claims and counterclaims, beset with witnesses who gave conflicting and self-contradictory testimony. On July 14, the jury returned a guilty verdict, and Sacco screamed out: "*Siamo innocenti!* They kill an innocent man! They kill two innocent men!" On November 1, 1921, Thayer sentenced the pair to death. The judge was heard to say: "Did you see what I did with those anarchist bastards?"

Appeals and stays of execution were filed over the course of seven years, but pleas for retrial on the basis of false identification failed repeatedly. Massachusetts state buildings were picketed by thousands demanding a new trial, pardon, clemency, or parole, and an international army of liberal writers, journalists, and world leaders appealed on the men's behalf, including: Heywood Broun, Edna St. Vincent Millay, Dorothy Parker, Robert Benchley, George Bernard Shaw, John Galsworthy, John Dos Passos, Katherine Anne Porter, and even Italy's Benito Mussolini.

Responding to a deluge of petitions and letters, Governor Alvan T. Fuller of Massachusetts appointed an independent committee to reinvestigate and report to him, so that he could decide the matter of clemency. The committee, led by President A. Lawrence Lowell of Harvard University, found that, although Thayer was biased, the jury's verdict could not be challenged and agreed that defendants were guilty.

In the meantime, on November 18, 1925, a Portuguese gunman named Celestino Madeiros—of the infamous Joe Morelli gang—confessed to participating in the Braintree robbery and claimed that Sacco and Vanzetti were not involved. Judge Thayer, as the original trial judge, had the authority to reopen the case on the grounds of newly discovered evidence, but he declined, and the Massachusetts State Supreme Court refused defense requests to overturn Thayer's verdict. On April 5, 1927, Thayer confirmed the death sentence, and on August 3, 1927, Governor Fuller refused clemency. As demonstrations erupted around the world and bombs were set off in New York and Philadelphia, Madeiros (who had been condemned for another murder), Sacco, and then Vanzetti were electrocuted at Charlestown prison at midnight on August 23, 1927. The Boston funeral procession was attended by tens of thousands of mourners.

The Sacco and Vanzetti case was the defining moment for many American liberal thinkers. It radicalized many in the generation between the wars, and it prompted many others to mistrust the criminal justice system, which henceforth seemed vulnerable to political influence and motivation. Those who questioned the criminal justice system found support in the 1970s when an underworld informant revealed that the crime had indeed been committed by the notorious Morelli gang, five Mafioso brothers from Brooklyn who moved to New England during World War I.

Further reading: Young, William, and David Kaiser, *Postmortem: New Evidence in the Case of Sacco and Vanzetti* (Amherst: University of Massachusetts Press, 1985)

Sanchez, Illyich Ramirez See CARLOS.

Sanger, William (1819–72)   New York City physician who conducted the first extensive study of prostitution, between 1855 and 1857.

Dr. Sanger was the first resident physician of New York City's indigent and convict hospital on Blackwell's Island (present-day Roosevelt Island) in the East River. In his position, Sanger saw many sufferers of venereal disease, which led him to study prostitution. In 1859, after two years of research, Sanger published his *History of Prostitution: Its Extent, Causes, and Effects Throughout the World,* an analysis of what the doctor deemed humankind's greatest "social evil." Sanger estimated that between $4 million and $7 million was spent on prostitution in New York City alone each year.

Concluding that attempts to eradicate prostitution would prove futile, Sanger proposed a program for regulating the practice, restricting it to certain areas and hours and subjecting prostitutes to rudimentary medical examination. New York failed to adopt the program, but the Union Army did follow Sanger's recommendations during its occupation of Nashville, Tennessee, and other Southern cities during the Civil War. While Sanger's work received little practical application, his study provided valuable contemporary insight into the "oldest profession" and remains a principal source of information on 19th-century prostitution.

Further reading: Bullough, Vern and Bonnie, *Women and Prostitution: A Social History* (Buffalo, N.Y.: Prometheus Books, 1987).

Hill, Merilynn Wood, *Their Sister's Keeper: Prostitution in New York City, 1830–1870* (Berkeley: University of California Press, 1993).

Savage, Edward H. (1812–93) Boston police chief from 1870 to 1878, Savage wrote the world's first book-length history of a police department in 1866.

One of the most popular heads of the Boston Police Department during the 19th century, Edward Savage was an idealist who advocated crime prevention and rehabilitation long before such concepts became commonplace in law enforcement. Savage also had a particular interest in the concept of probation, and, following his tenure as Boston's police chief, he became the city's first probation officer. Savage's ideas on rehabilitation were instrumental in the founding of the National Prison Association in 1870 and, eventually, in the establishment of the International Association of Chiefs of Police.

Of all his achievements, Savage is best remembered for his landmark police history, *Police Records and Recollections; or, Boston by Daylight and Gaslight for Two Hundred and Forty Years.* Originally published in 1866 (an illustrated edition appeared in 1877), Savage's book is a revealing look at 18th- and 19th-century American law enforcement and is a highly readable history of the sensational crimes committed in Boston, especially during the early Victorian era.

Edward Savage died in 1893, while still serving as a probation officer for the city of Boston.

Further reading: Harrison, Leonard Vance, *Police Administration in Boston* (Cambridge: Harvard University Press, 1934).

Savage, Edward H., *Police Records and Recollections; or, Boston by Daylight and Gaslight for Two Hundred and Forty Years* (Montclair, N.J.: Patterson Smith, 1971; reprint of 1866 ed.).

Scarborough, George (1859–1900) Deputy U.S. marshal in El Paso, Texas, and later a private range detective who was fatally wounded hunting down cattle rustlers. He was one of the most celebrated of the West's range detectives.

The son of a Louisiana Baptist preacher, George Scarborough moved to Texas with his family at a young age and lived the life of a Texas cowboy. In 1885, he was elected sheriff of Jones County and around 1890 became deputy U.S. marshal for the El Paso region of Texas. In June 1895, Scarborough was involved in an attempt to retrieve cattle rustler Martin Morose from Mexico for prosecution on cattle rustling charges. In an attempt to lure Morose over the Rio Grande and into the United States, Scarborough and two others inadvertently killed him—in Mexico and outside of U.S. jurisdiction. The following year, Scarborough got into an argument with his close friend John Selman during the early morning hours of Easter Sunday. Selman had accused Scarborough of looting Morose's body, and the two went into an alley to argue. Scarborough killed Selman, yet escaped conviction. He was, however, forced to resign as deputy marshal and moved west to Deming, New Mexico, to work for the Grant County Cattlemen's Association as a range detective. In an effort to track down Harvey Logan and other rustlers in the area, Scarborough was wounded in the leg on April 5, 1900. The leg was amputated, but Scarborough died five days later.

Schindler, Raymond Campbell (1883–1959) A former Burns Agency private investigator who started his own company and earned a national reputation as a great detective.

Born in Mexico, New York, Raymond Schindler was raised there and in Milwaukee, Wisconsin, where he was graduated from high school. He worked as an insurance salesman and a typewriter salesman before leaving Milwaukee for a gold mining venture in northern California. When that failed, he found himself in San Francisco in the aftermath of the 1906 earthquake and became an insurance investigator. His work so impressed his employer that he came to the attention of William J. BURNS, the private investigator who had been hired by the U.S. government to investigate the graft and corruption rampant in San Francisco. Schindler rose quickly in the Burns organization and in 1910 was sent east to manage a Burns office in New York and to open a chain of other offices. Two years later, he established his own firm, R. C. Schindler, Inc., which subsequently became the Schindler Bureau of Investigation.

Schindler was instrumental in solving many high-profile cases, ranging from the 1911 murder of 10-year-old Marie Smith in Asbury Park, New Jersey (in which he was able to provide evidence acquitting a wrongfully charged suspect and incriminating the guilty party), to a spectacular one-man "sting" operation that netted bribe-taking Atlantic City supervisors, to the 1943 acquittal of Count Alfred de Marigny, wrongfully accused of having bludgeoned to death Sir Henry Oakes in the Bahamas. In the latter case, Schindler was able to demonstrate, in court, that a fingerprint of the defendant had been deliberately transferred to the scene of the crime.

In addition to his work for private clients, Schindler served the federal government as a counterespionage investigator during both world wars. He died in North Tarrytown, New York, on July 1, 1959.

Further reading: Hughes, Rupert, *Complete Detective: Being the Life and Strange and Exciting Cases of Raymond Schindler, Master Detective* (New York: Grosset & Dunlap, 1950).

Schneider, Albert (1863–1928) The inventor of a forerunner of the polygraph (lie detector), Schneider was also an expert microscopist, who combined scientific expertise with criminology.

Taking his medical degree from the College of Physicians and Surgeons in Chicago in 1887, Albert Schneider later earned several other scientific degrees, including a Ph.D. from Columbia in 1897. He embarked on a lifelong career as a teacher of science in the departments of pharmacology and bacteriology at Northwestern University, the University of California, and the University of Nebraska, and he served as dean of pharmacology at the University of the Pacific.

In his academic work, Schneider established himself as a true wizard of microanalysis. He was able to apply his expertise in pathology, bacteriology, botany, and cell structure to the fields of criminology and police procedure and became adept at identifying the types of forensic evidence that would be admissible in court and that, more important, would sway a jury without drowning them in incomprehensible scientific fact.

Dr. Schneider was also the first researcher to assert the relationship between mechanics and brain waves as electronic impulses. He developed a device to chart electrical activity in the brain, which he was able to correlate with the physiological changes accompanying stress, including the telling of lies. His device was a forerunner of the modern polygraph.

Schober, Johann (1874–1932)   Twice chancellor of Austria, Schober was also the chief commissioner of the Austrian police and helped to found the organization that would evolve into INTERPOL.

A lifelong Austrian public servant, Johann Schober began his career in law enforcement in the capital of Vienna. After Austria had endured the chaos of World War I, Kaiser Karl, the nation's last Hapsburg ruler, appointed Schober to head the Central Bureau of Police in the waning months of the war. His administrative skills and his great talent for law enforcement allowed Vienna and Austria as a whole a greater measure of security than might well have been expected among a war-weary and vanquished people. With the disarmament of the Austrian Army and with thousands of bitter and unemployed soldiers roaming the streets and the countryside, Schober's police were the only remaining, effective governmental force.

Unable to rebuild after the war, Austria turned to Schober as chancellor in 1921, a position he grudgingly accepted, feeling unqualified but responding to the call of his countrymen. Concluding a reconciliation treaty with Czechoslovakia in 1921, he did much to begin the process of healing after the war, diplomatically, financially, and emotionally. Ousted in 1922 due to hostility from pan-Germans, who believed in the unification of Germany and Austria, Schober returned to his work with the police force. In 1923, he called an International Criminal Police Conference, hoping

to revive an idea that had been born before the war. The conference was held in Vienna and was an overwhelming success under Schober's leadership. Little did he dream that the conference would evolve into INTERPOL (but only after another devastating world war).

In 1929, his country again called for his service as chancellor. He again concluded a reconciliation treaty, this time with Italy, which absolved Austria of the remainder of its war reparations. A year after concluding a controversial customs union pact with Germany, which many feel was partly responsible for the spread of the Great Depression in those two countries, Schober died of sudden heart failure.

Schultz, Dutch (born: Arthur Flegenheimer, or Fleggenheimer) (1902–35)   One of New York's Prohibition-era beer barons and an early contender for leadership in the world of organized crime.

Born Arthur Flegenheimer in the Bronx, Dutch Schultz dropped out of school in the fourth grade and joined the Bergen Gang, an association of pickpockets and thieves who preyed on small shops. His career in crime was interrupted in 1919, when he was convicted of burglary and sent to prison for 15 months. Like so many others, he emerged from prison not only unrepentant, but also hardened in a life of crime.

Using the proceeds from burglaries, Schultz bought a large Bronx saloon and declared that he was henceforth to be called Dutch Schultz—the name of a gangster legendary in the Bronx as the leader of the 19th-century Frog Hollow Gang. Using his saloon as headquarters, Schultz gathered about him the worst of the borough's criminal element: Joey Rao, George and Abe "Bo" Weinberg, Jules "Julie" Martin, Abe Landau, and Bernard "Lulu" Rosenkrantz, among others. He opened up more saloons, from which he purveyed liquor and beers, ranging from good imported stuff down to his own home brew—generally acknowledged as the worst in the Bronx. The quality of the product notwithstanding, Schultz's bootleg empire engulfed the Bronx and spread into Manhattan, Schultz liberally gunning down whatever rivals presented themselves. He also branched out from liquor into other rackets, especially numbers—or policy—which was very popular in Harlem, the Manhattan neighborhood adjacent to the Bronx. By the end of the Roaring Twenties, Schultz was making many millions from bootlegging, numbers, and, finally, illegal slot machines.

Schultz became one of the underworld's principal employers, hiring the likes of Jack "Legs" DIAMOND and Vincent "Mad Dog" COLL as his allies and enforcers. Diamond, however, had aspirations of his own, formed a rival gang, and began routinely hi-

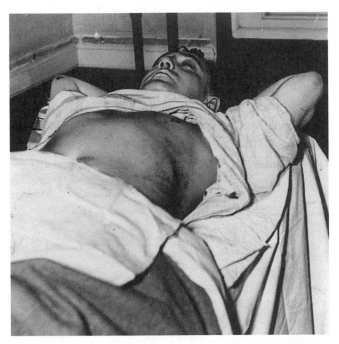

When New York booze baron Dutch Schultz decided the mob should kill the city's gangbusting district attorney, Thomas E. Dewey, even the hoodlums thought he was out of control. They made sure that it was he, not Dewey, who wound up dead. (Courtesy of the Library of Congress)

jacking Schultz's beer trucks. A full-scale gang war erupted between the two, culminating in Diamond's death in a cheap Albany, New York, rooming house on December 19, 1931—the victim of Schultz's gunmen. Earlier that same year, "Mad Dog" Coll and his brother Peter had also started muscling in on Schultz's operations, intimidating saloon owners into taking their product rather than Schultz's. Coll went a step further and invaded the numbers racket as well, loudly boasting that he meant to take over the entire Schultz empire. It was during an attempt on the life of Schultz lieutenant Joey Rao that Coll wounded several children and killed one, thereby earning the title of "Mad Dog," conferred by the press. At last, in June 1931, Schultz and bodyguard Danny Iamascia thought they spotted the brothers Coll in an alley and opened fire. After Iamascia was fatally wounded, Schultz discovered that his two adversaries were not the Colls but New York detectives. One of them managed to collar Schultz, who pulled out $18,600 from his pocket and offered it as a bribe. The detective responded that he would "shove that dough down your throat!" He knocked the Dutchman to the ground and started to stuff the wad of bills into his mouth. Although Schultz was booked on murder and other charges, his lawyer soon engineered his release. Schultz succeeded in doing away with Coll the following year, dispatching Abe and George Weinberg to

assassinate Mad Dog as he was making phone calls in a drugstore booth.

The beer baron's troubles were not over, however. Unable to nail the gangster on murder and racketeering charges, the state of New York went after him for tax evasion. Dixie Davis, Schultz's sleazy but skillful attorney, wangled a change of venue for the trial to a small town in upstate New York. Under Davis's direction, Schultz hired a public relations firm to enhance his image, and he began donating huge sums to local charities. In effect, Dutch Schultz purchased the goodwill of the town from which a jury was selected, and, in the anti-tax climate of Depression-ridden upstate New York, he was acquitted.

Schultz's conflicts with other gangsters and his absence from the city had taken their toll. Charles "Lucky" LUCIANO and Vito Genovese had moved in on many of his operations, partly with the aid of the Dutchman's most trusted lieutenant, Bo Weinberg. When Schultz returned to New York City, he ordered Weinberg dead, but he also realized the futility of going to war with Luciano and Genovese. Instead, he moved out of New York and to Newark, across the Hudson in New Jersey. Schultz was accepted by Luciano and the others as a member of the national crime syndicate and was given a place on the "board of directors." However, he soon proved uncooperative and dangerously selfish. The last straw came when he threatened to kill New York district attorney Thomas E. Dewey, who in 1935 was waging an intense campaign against the rackets that remained under the Dutchman's control, especially the illegal slot machines.

Schultz demanded that the syndicate bring about Dewey's death. "It will bring down the heat on all of us," Lucky Luciano protested, and the rest of the "board" concurred. Schultz defied the others and vowed to do the job himself, whereupon the "board" voted to kill Dutch Schultz. They commissioned the syndicate's chief enforcer, Albert ANASTASIA, the founder of Murder, Inc., to do the job. On October 23, 1935, Schultz was gunned down in the back room of Newark's Palace Chop House. The assassin was Charles "The Bug" Workman, a Murder, Inc. "employee."

Schwarzkopf, H. Norman, Sr. (1895–1958) First superintendent of the New Jersey State Police, from 1921 to 1936; gained international celebrity as the chief investigator of the sensational LINDBERGH baby kidnapping case of the early 1930s.

A West Point graduate and U.S. Army officer, H. Norman Schwarzkopf Sr. specialized in police organization, first in Europe for the army and then as head of New Jersey's first state police force. His tenure witnessed the sensational crime of the March 1, 1932, kidnapping and murder of the 20-month-old son of national hero Charles Lindbergh. The high profile of this case catapulted the 37-year-old Schwarzkopf into the national spotlight. The two-year manhunt Schwarzkopf directed, during which agents were sent as far away as Europe to question suspects, ended with the arrest of a journeyman carpenter named Bruno Richard HAUPTMANN.

Schwarzkopf testified at the trial, which resulted in Hauptmann's conviction and execution. The state police leader's celebrity landed him a stint as commentator on the popular radio program "Gang Busters" until the outbreak of World War II, when he was recalled to active duty with the army and sent to Iran. There Schwarzkopf trained and organized a military police force of more than 20,000 men.

In 1951, Schwarzkopf became administrative director of the New Jersey Department of Law and Public Safety, where he spearheaded an investigative force looking into waterfront crime. Schwartzkopf retired five years later, after a remarkable career that is sometimes overshadowed by the events of 1932. His son and namesake, H. Norman Schwarzkopf Jr., achieved celebrity at least equal to that of his father when, as a four-star general, he served as field commander of U.S. and "coalition" forces in the 1990–91 Persian Gulf War against Saddam Hussein's Iraq.

Scott, Peter D. (1914–77) This British physician was a leading forensic psychiatrist and served as an advisor to police on the management of criminal sieges involving the taking of hostages.

Born in London and educated at the Bromsgrove School, at St. Catharine's College, Cambridge, and at the London Hospital Medical School, Scott served as a surgeon with the Royal Navy during World War II. He joined the staff of Maudsley Hospital after the war and turned increasingly from surgery to psychiatry. He was with Maudsley from 1946 until his death, but he held joint appointments with other organizations, including the Stamford House Remand Home for Boys and with the British Home Office, in the capacity of forensic psychiatrist and advisor in hostage situations.

Scott did not conduct much original scientific research, but he was instrumental in developing the systematic classification of criminal behavior, including a fourfold classification of psychopathic behavior; a classification of homosexuality (in 1957, when homosexual behavior was treated as a crime in England); and a classification system for criminal sexual perversion. Toward the end of his career, Scott addressed such criminal behavior as child abuse and parental murder of children. Additionally, Scott was an advo-

cate of prison reform, believing that offenders as well as society were better served by prisons modeled on hospitals for the mentally ill rather than as places of incarceration and punishment.

Sealy, Lloyd George (1917–85) The first African American to hold several high posts in the New York Police Department, Sealy was instrumental in calming racially inflamed areas of the city.

A native New Yorker, Lloyd Sealy was born in Manhattan and was raised in Brooklyn. As an African American, Sealy was a member of a very small minority in his high school, but he was nonetheless elected student body president during his senior year. After being admitted to Brooklyn College in 1935, he graduated with a bachelor's degree in sociology and began working with the General Accounting Office of the federal government in Washington, D.C. After a short term as a railway mail clerk, Sealy joined the New York City police force in 1942.

Although Sealy was very well educated, eminently qualified, and generally liked, he encountered much overt discrimination. He was immediately assigned to walk a beat in the nearly all-black Brooklyn neighborhood of Bedford-Stuyvesant. After five years on that beat, he was promoted to sergeant—but only to work in the youth division. During this period, he also went back to college and received a law degree from Brooklyn Law School. After making lieutenant in 1959, Sealy was promoted to captain in 1963. When riots broke out in Harlem the following year, Sealy was given command of the Harlem district, encompassing 11 precincts in the area. In September 1966, he was jumped two promotions in rank to become assistant chief inspector, at that time the highest post ever held by an African American within the department.

In 1969, Sealy left the New York City Police Department to accept an associate professorship at Manhattan's John Jay College of Criminal Justice, where he taught until his death in 1985.

Seavey, Webber S. (1841–1915) The first president of the International Association of Chiefs of Police.

Webber S. Seavey was chief of the Omaha, Nebraska, police department in 1892, when, with Chicago police superintendent Robert McLaughrey, he circulated a letter to the chiefs of police departments throughout the United States and Canada. The November 18 document called for the organization of an association "composed of the General Superintendents and Chiefs of Police . . . of cities having a population of 10,000 or more." He argued that such an organization would be "the means of elevating our

American police system to a much more proficient and high standard." This would be "the greatest stroke which has ever been made in this country against crime."

Organized the following year in Chicago, during the World's Columbian Exposition, the National Police Chiefs Union (renamed in 1902 the International Association of Chiefs of Police, IACP) worked to develop efficient cooperation among the nation's police agencies and to establish uniform standards of professionalism. The organization went on to become a highly influential voice of the American law enforcement community.

Seavey was a native of Maine, who went to Wisconsin at age 16 as a woodcutter. In 1859, he joined the Colorado gold rush, then enlisted in the 5th Iowa Cavalry at the outbreak of the Civil War in 1861. From 1866 to 1873, he was a clerk on a Mississippi River steamboat, then served as city marshal of Santa Barbara, California, from 1874 to 1879. Seavey's quest for adventure took him next to the South Sea Islands, where he lived as a trader for six years, before returning to the United States and accepting the position of chief of the Omaha police department in 1887.

Sellin, (Johan) Thorsten (1896–1982)   One of the premier analysts of the juvenile criminal justice system in the United States.

A native Swede, Thorsten Sellin was born October 26, 1896, but at the age of 17 left his homeland with his family to move to Canada. He came to the United States for his higher education, earning his bachelor's degree from Augustana College in Rock Island, Illinois, and a master's in sociology from the University of Pennsylvania in 1916. He stayed at the university for his doctoral work, completing his dissertation in 1922.

Sellin held a number of positions, ranging from high school teacher to college professor to public servant, but throughout his career he conducted extensive research on criminology in the United States, particularly as it applied to juveniles. One of his most famous studies—and one of the more disturbing—demonstrated the discriminatory bias of the juvenile criminal justice system. While Sellin reported a high rate of crime among non-whites and individuals from the lowest socioeconomic bracket generally, arrest and prosecution rates were even more alarming. Fewer than half of offending white juveniles were actually arrested, whereas more than 68% of the non-whites were. Sellin showed that police officers were more likely to give a white juvenile a warning and let him go than to do the same for a non-white.

Sellin wrote several works on the relationship of sociology to crime, most notably *Culture Conflict and Crime* (1938), which addressed the criminal and delinquency problems created by a culturally divergent society.

Further reading: Laub, John H., "Interview with Thorsten Sellin, April 27, 1979," in *Criminology in the Making: An Oral History* (Boston: Northeastern University Press, 1983).

Serpico, Frank (Francisco Vincent) (1936–)   The paradigmatic "honest cop," who courageously exposed widespread corruption in the New York Police Department.

Frank Serpico was raised in the tough Bedford-Stuyvesant section of Brooklyn and early in life conceived the ambition to become a New York cop. He attended night school at Brooklyn College, then graduated from City College, taking a job as a private investigator until 1959, when he joined the NYPD.

Serpico worked chiefly as a plainclothes detective. He became the object of much hatred and many threats from his fellow officers because of his tireless efforts to bring a halt to the rampant corruption he encountered. His vendetta against crooked cops can be traced to the earliest days of his career, when he saw a beat cop shake down his own brother, who was a grocer. While training for detective work, he heard complaints from fellow students that the 30 days they spent in "plainclothes school" meant that they missed "the nut"—payoffs. The longer Serpico spent on the force, the more corruption he encountered—and the harder he tried to bring it to the attention of his superiors. He was ignored, told to "forget about it," or threatened.

Finally, six months after he testified against a plainclothes officer accused of perjury for denying that he had accepted graft, Serpico was shot in the face while arresting a narcotics suspect. While in the hospital, he received a card on which the phrase "With sincere sympathy" was embossed. Handwritten next to it was, "that you didn't get your brains blown out you rat bastard. Happy relapse."

Frank Serpico had had enough. Along with Sgt. David Durk, he told his story to the *New York Times*, charging that Mayor John V. Lindsay's police department liaison officer, Jay L. Kriegel, Investigation Commissioner Arnold G. Fraiman, and First Deputy Police Commissioner John F. Walsh had failed to investigate his report on police taking bribes in the South Bronx. The articles that resulted from Serpico's revelations prompted the mayor to appoint a special commission under Whitman Knapp. During the course of 11 months, the Knapp Commission uncovered spectacular and widespread corruption. Serpico was one of the commission's star witnesses.

In 1971, Serpico collaborated with author Peter Maas to produce a best-selling book about his experiences on the force. In 1973, the book became a hit film starring the young Al Pacino.

Serpico retired in 1974 and moved into a small chalet in Switzerland, living on his $12,000 annual NYPD disability pension and the very substantial profits from his book and the sale of movie rights. The gunshot wound to his face left him hard of hearing and subject to vertigo. Bullet fragments still lodged in his brain, if moved, could cause death or paralysis.

Sessions, William S(teele) (1930–) Director of the FBI under Presidents Reagan and Bush.

William Steele Sessions was born in Fort Smith, Arkansas, May 27, 1930. He was a clergyman's son, who grew up in Kansas City and decided to make a career in the U.S. Air Force. However, after serving from 1951 to 1955, he retired with the rank of captain. He earned a B.A. (1956) and law degree (1958) from Baylor University and was admitted to the Texas bar in 1959, setting up a private practice in Waco, Texas, in which he prospered for 10 years.

In 1969, Sessions left the private sector and moved to Washington, D.C., as chief of the government operations section of the criminal division, U.S. Department of Justice. Two years later, President Richard M. NIXON appointed him U.S. attorney for the Western District of Texas, and in 1974 President Gerald Ford appointed him a district judge. As judge, he served in El Paso from 1974 to 1980, then moved to San Antonio as chief judge of the Western District.

Sessions was a moderate Republican, but he earned the respect of his more conservative constituents for being tough on criminals, both as a prosecutor and as a judge. In 1987, President Ronald Reagan named him director of the Federal Bureau of Investigation, succeeding William H. WEBSTER. Pressure from Congress prompted President Reagan to direct Sessions to investigate charges of discrimination against African Americans and Hispanics within the FBI. The results of the investigation were issued in a report of February 28, 1989, early in the Bush administration, and Sessions forthrightly concluded that such discrimination did indeed exist. He pledged to revamp the affirmative action policies of the bureau.

Sessions continued to serve as director of the FBI through the administration of George Bush, but, despite having been sworn to a 10-year term, he resigned over policy differences early in the administration of Bill Clinton, who nominated Louis FREEH to replace him.

Seward, William Henry (1801–72) New York governor, senator, statesman, and Lincoln's secretary of state (who negotiated the purchase of Alaska from Russia), Seward was also responsible for the 1845 legislation that created the first professional police department in the United States.

The murder of a young woman named Mary Rogers (fictionally immortalized by Edgar Allan Poe in his short story "The Mystery of Marie Roget") initiated the process that would establish the first professional police force in the United States, modeled on the most advanced ideas already in operation in London's Metropolitan Police.

William Seward, stalwart, anti-slavery Whig governor of New York, used the Mary Rogers tragedy to introduce legislation that became law in 1845. The new force was decidedly primitive by modern standards; police officers wore no uniforms, and the department was subordinated to the lowest level of local government. Nevertheless, New York's department led to the development of the Chicago police department in 1851 and the Boston and Philadelphia departments in 1854.

Seward went on to become U.S. senator in 1849 and Abraham Lincoln's secretary of state during the Civil War. To police officers, Seward's legacy—his early commitment to professionalism in the maintenance of law and order—is invaluable.

Further reading: Taylor, John M., *William Seward: Lincoln's Right Hand Man* (New York: HarperCollins, 1991).

Shanklin, James Gordon (1910–88) Directed the FBI's investigation of the Kennedy assassination in Dallas and was accused of having destroyed evidence.

A Kentucky native, J. Gordon Shanklin earned a law degree from Vanderbilt University before joining the Federal Bureau of Investigation in 1943. He was variously posted in El Paso, Pittsburgh, and Honolulu before being assigned as special agent in charge of the Dallas office in April 1963.

In September 1963, the Dallas FBI office came into possession of a letter from Lee Harvey Oswald, who was then under investigation for his numerous connections with pro-Castro Cubans and the Soviets. The letter was filed away by Shanklin's agents until after the assassination of President John F. Kennedy on November 22, 1963. Apprised of the existence of the letter, Shanklin ordered it destroyed—in order to avoid charges of having failed to follow up on a potentially dangerous man. The Oswald document made no mention of the president, nor did it contain any threats. However, the fact that it was destroyed cast grave doubts on the impartiality of the FBI's investigation in Dallas. The act also became yet another in a seemingly endless series of irregularities and unanswered questions in the assassination and its investigation, which have led many to suspect conspiracy and cover-up.

Shaw, Clifford R. (1895–1957) A distinguished sociologist specializing in the study of juvenile delinquency and its prevention.

Clifford Shaw was the fifth child in a large Luray, Indiana, farm family of 10 children. His early schooling was interrupted because he was required to work on his father's farm, but, when he was 15, Shaw left to study for the ministry. Religious study served only to turn him away from religion, and he broke off his studies to join the U.S. Navy in 1917. After World War I, he completed his B.A. at Adrian College and then entered graduate school in sociology at the University of Chicago, supporting himself as a part-time parole officer for the Illinois State Training School for Boys from 1921 to 1923. He left the university in 1924 without completing his Ph.D. and became a probation officer at the Cook County Juvenile Court, serving until 1926.

While Shaw taught criminology at the George Williams College and the Central YMCA College, he also conducted important research in juvenile delinquency at the Institute for Juvenile Research, which was created in 1926 from what had been the Chicago Juvenile Psychopathic Institute. Shaw worked at the newly constituted institute with his colleague, Henry D. MCKAY. Together, they produced studies during the 1930s and early 1940s that were considered extremely important contributions to criminological thought in their day and are still highly regarded. Their work includes an extensive collection of autobiographies of delinquents, research into the geographical distribution of delinquents, and the creation of a pioneering prevention program called the Chicago Area Project (CAP).

Further reading: Shaw, Clifford R., and Henry D. McKay, *Juvenile Delinquency and Urban Areas: A Study of Rates of Delinquency in Relation to Differential Characteristics of Local Communities in American Cities* (Chicago: University of Chicago, 1942, 1969).

Sheridan, William Patrick Henry (1861–1934) Celebrated for his photographic memory, this legendary detective could remember men's faces decades after he had seen them.

A native of New York City, William Sheridan attended the College of the City of New York before dropping out to work for Western Union as a telegrapher. After being promoted to accountant, he left Western Union to join the New York Police Department in December 1886 as a patrolman. Within six months, he made detective and began a distinguished career as one of the nation's very best criminal investigators.

Sheridan continued his rapid rise through the departmental hierarchy, being promoted to lieutenant in 1907 before retiring from the force in December 1909. When William J. BURNS—later head of the fledgling FBI—sought to create a nationwide private detective agency to compete with the famed PINKERTON Agency, he enlisted Sheridan as a partner, and the two formed the Burns and Sheridan Detective Agency in September 1909. Burns's desire for continual expansion, mostly to keep up with the huge accounts he landed nationwide, was too much for Sheridan, who sold his interest to his partner early in 1911.

After dissolving the partnership, Sheridan set up his own detective agency in New York City and became a favorite of his old colleagues on the force because of his uncanny ability to identify criminals he had seen perhaps only once.

Further reading: Caesar, Gene, *Incredible Detective: The Biography of William J. Burns* (Englewood Cliffs, N.J.: Prentice-Hall, 1968).

Sherman, Lawrence W. (1949–) An important modern advocate of police reform.

After graduating magna cum laude from Denison University, Lawrence Sherman went on to receive advanced degrees from the University of Chicago, Cambridge University, and Yale University. At Chicago's famed School of Sociology, Sherman devoted himself to criminology and the study of police and their actions. After earning his master's degree from Chicago, Sherman returned to his home state of New York to work as a research program analyst for the New York Police Department. The following year he moved to Kansas City as a consultant to an innovative patrol program.

It was shortly after his patrol experiments in Kansas City that Sherman undertook a detailed study of police in an attempt to categorize systematically their responsibilities and actions. He described his findings under three general categories: the nature of police work, the character of police officers, and the structure of police organizations. Sherman found that the independent actions of individual police officers had a direct influence on the administration of the criminal justice system. He further argued that police are molded less by social background than by occupational socialization, which creates a distinct subculture. Finally, Sherman noted that police organizations are based on military, non-democratic models within a democratic society. Taken together, Sherman argued, many of the elements that make up the fabric of American police work are fundamentally opposed to the values of American society at large and, therefore, are bound to create friction when the need for imposing order clashes with the democratic liberties of the individual.

Sickles, Daniel Edgar (1825–1914)   The subject of one of the most talked-about murders of the 19th century—and the first to plead not guilty by reason of "temporary insanity."

After studying law at the University of the City of New York (now New York University), Daniel Sickles was admitted to the bar in 1846 and was quickly caught up in the politics of Tammany Hall. The following year he landed a seat in the state legislature, then became secretary to the U.S. legation in London. While he was in London, he married Teresa Bagioli, the daughter of an old friend and 16 years his junior. Sickles returned from London in 1857 and was elected to Congress that same year.

Sometime after he moved to Washington in early March of 1858, Sickles met the district attorney for the District of Columbia, Philip Barton Key, son of Francis Scott Key, who wrote the verses to "The Star-Spangled Banner," and nephew of Supreme Court Chief Justice Roger B. Taney, author of the Supreme Court's inflammatory Dred Scott fugitive slave decision. Key and Sickles quickly became friends. In the meantime, Sickles's congressional duties kept him apart from his young wife for extended periods. By May 1858, Teresa Sickles and Philip Barton Key had become not-very-discreet lovers.

Soon, it became apparent that all of Washington knew of the affair—save Dan Sickles. Key would parade in Lafayette Square in front of the Sickles's home and wave his handkerchief when he and Teresa were to meet for their almost daily trysts. When the weather was agreeable, the pair were wont to make love in the Congressional Cemetery. When the weather turned cold, Key rented a house on Fifteenth Street, only three blocks from the Sickles home. The affair continued for 10 months, until Sickles received a letter in late February detailing the relationship. (The letter was signed "R.P.G."; its sender has never been identified.)

After contemplating the letter for a few days, Sickles confronted his wife, flew into a rage, screaming and gesturing wildly about the room, and forced her to write a letter of confession, including a graphic description of the affair. Sickles took Teresa's wedding ring from her and broke it, then went to another room, where he was heard sobbing hysterically all night. (That Sickles himself was notorious for his own numerous marital indiscretions seemed hardly to matter, either to Sickles or to society at large.)

The next morning dawned bright and cold in Washington. By 11 A.M., Key, unaware of either the "R.P.G." letter or of Sickles's confrontation with Mrs. Sickles, appeared as usual in Lafayette Square. It was reported that Key paraded about the Square for more than two hours, when Sickles finally saw him and was propelled from a state of uncontrollable grief to one of uncontrollable rage. He armed himself with two derringers and a revolver, walked across the street to the Square—directly in front of the White House—and screamed at Key: "You have defiled my bed!" and "You have dishonored my house!" With that, Sickles pumped three shots into Key's chest and attempted to put a fourth in his skull when the gun misfired.

Washington was scandalized, but public opinion was solidly behind Sickles. Immediately following the murder, President James Buchanan, a close friend of Sickles, intervened in two remarkable ways. First, a White House page ran to the president to tell him what he had just witnessed. Buchanan, assuming the page had been the only witness, quickly gave him some money from his own pocket and lied to the youth, telling him that, as a witness, he would be summarily jailed and held without bond until the trial. The page left Washington immediately. Second, Buchanan personally named the prosecutor for the case, Robert Ould, who had alarmingly little trial experience and was Key's assistant in the district attorney's office—a connection that hardly made him impartial.

In the meantime, Sickles hired a formidable team of eight defense attorneys, including future secretary of war Edwin M. Stanton, who (many speculate) was included in the defense team at the behest of the president himself. Sickles pleaded not guilty, despite the fact that the murder had been witnessed by as many as 15 people. It was not until the fourth day of the trial that one of the defense lawyers, James T. Brady, a renowned specialist on the subject of criminal insanity, introduced the concept of an "irresistible impulse." Although the insanity defense was well-established, dating at least as far back as 14th-century English common law, no one had ever suggested that a man could be *temporarily* deranged to the point of criminality. The defense argued that Sickles's learning of the affair was tantamount to his walking in on the two lovers, and the resulting rage was uncontrollable. Experts identified Sickles as what today would be called a manic-depressive, and witnesses testified to his history of mercurial emotions.

The defense strategy worked, as Judge Thomas Crawford instructed the jury to "say what was the state of Mr. Sickles's mind as to the capacity to decide the criminality of the homicide," admonishing them that "if any reasonable doubt existed as to the clarity of Sickles's mind at the time of the murder, they must vote to acquit." The deliberations took only 70 minutes, and the verdict came back not guilty, setting a precedent in American jurisprudence that many prosecutors regret to this day.

As to Sickles, he continued his political career and became a general in the Civil War, known as much for his boldness in the ballroom as on the battlefield.

Further reading: Swanberg, W. A., *Sickles the Incredible* (New York: Scribner's, 1956).

Simon, Dr. Carleton (1871–1951)

Deputy police commissioner of New York City from 1920 to 1926; pioneered the study of eyeprints—the patterns of retinal blood vessels—as a means of criminal identification.

Before his appointment as New York City deputy police commissioner, this European-trained physician worked as a psychiatrist and criminologist, gaining recognition as the chief pathologist in charge of dissecting the brain of Leon Czolgosz, assassin of President William McKinley. As deputy police commissioner, Dr. Simon was in charge of the narcotics division and achieved some success in counteracting the growing drug trade in the city.

Leaving his post as deputy commissioner after six years, Simon embarked on the study of eyeprints— the patterns of blood vessels in the human retina— largely in response to recent attempts by such criminals as John Dillinger to alter their fingerprints. Like fingerprints, eyeprints are unique to the individual, but the only way to alter them would be to blind oneself. Dr. Simon developed the first eyeprint classification and eyeprint identification procedures in America.

In addition to his work in New York and on eyeprint identification, Simon served as criminologist for the International Association of Chiefs of Police.

Simpson, Cedric Keith (1907–85)

A pioneer in forensic dentistry and the first postmortem investigator to define and legally prove "battered baby syndrome," Simpson was one of the leading medico-legal pathologists of this century.

The son of a doctor, Cedric Keith Simpson was born in Brighton, England, and attended grammar school there and in Hove. Next, he earned gold medals and other prizes at Guy's Hospital Medical School, from which he graduated in 1930. After gaining another medical degree in pathology (1932), he was given an immediate teaching post; he stayed with Guy's pathology faculty until 1937.

Simpson later stated that he entered his field—some might say paradoxically—to avoid witnessing the pain and suffering common to other branches of medicine. Squeamish with the living but not the dead, he soon made a specialty of forensic detection. He began lecturing at London University in 1937, became its first full professor of forensic medicine in 1962, and retired as professor emeritus 10 years later. Between 1958 and 1964 he earned several additional degrees and honors in pathology and medical jurisprudence— MRCP, DMJ, MA Oxon, FRCP, and FRC Path—and lectured at Oxford University (1961–63).

Sir Bernard SPILSBURY was Britain's greatest forensics authority when Simpson began his career, but the latter proved his own name and gained his share of newspaper headlines. In 1942, a workman securing a war-bombed London chapel prised up a stone slab in its cellar and found a near-skeletal corpse hidden below. Simpson was called to the scene. His examination showed that the victim had suffered from a fibroid tumor when living and that her body had been dismembered, quicklimed, and burned before burial, events he estimated as occurring some 18 months earlier. Police records showed that a fire-watcher's wife had gone missing 15 months prior, and it turned out that her husband, Harry Dobkin, had been employed by the solicitors' office next door to the Baptist church. Simpson's forensic investigation continued. Although the corpse's lower jaw was now missing, its upper jaw was intact and bore the signs of extensive dental repair. Mrs. Dobkin's sister was contacted, confirmed her sibling's affliction with a minor tumor, and put Simpson in touch with the missing woman's former dentist. Dr. Barnett Kopkin checked his records, and he drew a chart of Mrs. Dobkin's upper jaw; it matched the corpse's exactly. Harry Dobkin was tried and hanged for his wife's murder some months later. And odontology—forensic dentistry— was added to the forensic investigator's arsenal.

Six years later Simpson presented another form of dental evidence when he helped prove another murderer guilty by the teeth marks he had left on his victim's breast.

Simpson's textbook *Forensic Medicine* was published in 1947 to great acclaim; several editions later, it won the 1958 Royal Society of Arts Swiney Prize for the best medico-legal work of the preceding decade. The short but thorough textbook, intended for both doctors and lawyers, contains chapters covering signs of death (including "What to do with a dead body"); blood stains and grouping; firearm wounds; asphyxia; infanticide; and sexual offenses; among many others. In his preface, Simpson assured his readers that "No pains have been spared to give the subject its vivid colours in life."

More high-profile investigations followed for Simpson, including a challenging victim identification case in the notorious 1949 "acid bath murders" of John George Haigh. And in 1964, Simpson pinpointed a time of death by noting the specific larval stage of the blue-bottle maggots infesting a corpse. He had long studied and collected insects pertinent to his field, and as he later wrote, these larvae were "mature, even elderly, fat, indolent, third-stage maggots, but they were not in pupa cases." Having included time for the blue bottles to alight on the body, Simpson's June 16 death estimate identifed the missing victim and even zeroed in on a suspect. The pathologist's court testimony, corroborated by a noted entomologist (appearing for the defense), helped send the karate-trained murderer—a debtor of the victim, who had met with him on June 16 exactly—to life imprisonment.

In 1965 Simpson made history in the first successful prosecution of a baby batterer, a crime the pathologist had long sought to bring to medico-legal attention.

Editor of the first two series of *Modern Trends in Forensic Medicine* (1953, 1967), Simpson also coedited and edited the eleventh and twelfth editions of *Taylor's Principles and Practice of Medical Jurisprudence.* Other writings include *A Doctor's Guide to Court* (1962, 1966) and over 200 scientific and popular articles, the latter under the pseudonym Guy Bailey. His autobiography, *Forty Years of Murder* (1978), was a British best-seller for several months after its publication.

A president of the Medico-Legal Society (1961–63) and a founding member and president (1966–67) of the British Association in Forensic Medicine, Simpson lectured widely and served as advisor to several British and foreign scientific committees, academies, societies, and examining boards. He received honorary doctorates from universities in Ghent and Edinburgh, and was created a Commander of the British Empire in 1975.

In 1983, Simpson refused to perform a postmortem on a suspected AIDS victim, causing a public controversy little diminished by the Department of Health's endorsement of his decision. A brain tumor took his own life on July 21, 1985.

Siringo, Charles Angelo (1855–1928) Cowboy, author, and top Pinkerton detective who led an adventurous life in pursuit of badmen across America.

Outlaw Butch Cassidy considered Charlie Siringo the best of the Pinkerton detectives. An itinerant cowboy, Siringo joined the agency in 1886 after having spent the first portion of his life on the range and after having written his first book about it, *A Texas Cowboy.* Siringo was not a "company man," preferring to work alone and outside the city. If maintaining his professional freedom meant that he had to turn down promotions within the Pinkerton organization, so be it, but his talent for tracking outlaws made him a favorite of Allan PINKERTON.

In 1892, in what would come to be called the Coeur d'Alene Affair, Siringo infiltrated an Idaho mining

Charles Angelo Siringo was the Pinkerton Agency's star western operative. Shown here (unmounted) with cowboy actor William S. Hart. (Courtesy of the Kansas State Historical Society)

union and uncovered widespread corruption and crime. Siringo narrowly escaped being found out, but the risks he took paid off in 18 convictions.

Siringo became more famous for tracking Butch Cassidy and his Wild Bunch. Fed up with the inability of state and local authorities to apprehend the train robbers, railroad officials hired Pinkerton, who, in turn, assigned Siringo to the case. Siringo later reported that he pursued the bandits over 25,000 miles, ultimately causing them to flee to South America.

Charlie Siringo retired at a time when the last of the Western outlaws were becoming extinct. He wrote a book about his experiences, *Cowboy Detective*, in 1912, which was heavily censored by the Pinkerton legal department because of its often unflattering depiction of the agency. In response, Siringo published another book at his own expense, *Two Evil Isms: Pinkertonism and Anarchism*, a remarkable Progressivist criticism of the dichotomy Siringo saw threatening America: corporate power (embodied in the Pinkertons, in effect a private army hired by high-rolling industrialists and railroad magnates) on the one hand and lawlessness on the other.

Charlie Siringo died in Hollywood much as he had lived: alone.

Further reading: Horan, James David, *Desperate Men: Revelations from the Sealed Pinkerton Files* (New York: Putnam, 1949).

Morn, Frank, *"The Eye That Never Sleeps": A History of the Pinkerton National Detective Agency* (Bloomington: Indiana University Press, 1982).

Siringo, Charles A., *Texas Cowboy; or, Fifteen Years on the Hurricane Deck of a Spanish Pony, Taken from Real Life* (Lincoln: University of Nebraska Press, 1979, c.1885).

Voss, Frederick, *We Never Sleep: The First Fifty Years of the Pinkerton Men* (Washington, D.C.: Smithsonian Institution Press, 1981).

Slaughter, John (Horton) (1841–1922) Rancher and lawman who served as a lieutenant in the Texas Rangers and as sheriff of Arizona's outlaw-infested Cochise County—which included the town of Tombstone.

After serving as a private in the Confederate Texas Cavalry during the Civil War, John Slaughter returned to Texas, joined the Texas Rangers, and became a lieutenant in the organization. In the 1880s, Slaughter left the Rangers and went into the cattle business, building one of the largest cattle operations in the Southwest when he purchased the San Bernardino land grant in 1884 to control almost 40,000 acres of pasturage.

Despite his enormous success in ranching, Slaughter returned to law enforcement in 1886 when he was elected sheriff of Cochise County, Arizona. He re-

Texas Ranger John Slaughter became sheriff of Cochise County, Arizona, which included the lawless town of Tombstone. (Courtesy of the Arizona Historical Society)

mained sheriff for four years, during which period he "cleaned up" the outlawry who habitually congregated in Tombstone.

Slaughter continued to prosper in the ranching business, further building his empire and establishing a reputation as a fearless and effective lawman.

Further reading: Erwin, Allen A., *The Southwest of John Horton Slaughter* (New York: Arthur H. Clark Co., 1965).

Small, Len (1862–1936) Notorious as the "Pardoning Governor" of Illinois, Small took bribes in exchange for the release of convicted felons—more than 8,000 of them—during his two terms from 1921 to 1929.

The year he was elected governor, Len Small was indicted for embezzling more than $600,000 from the state treasury. He was acquitted after some crafty jury tampering by his underworld cohorts Walter Stevens, "Jew Ben" Newmark, and "Umbrella Mike" Boyle. Several years later, the three would be pardoned by Governor Small as a token of his appreciation.

Perhaps no other public official in American history was as corrupt as this Republican from Kankakee. In a joint conspiracy with state's attorney Robert Crowe and Chicago mayor William Hale Thompson, Small repeatedly solicited bribes for pardons and split the take with Crowe and Thompson, both of whom contributed, revolving-door fashion, to securing convictions in the first place. When the volume of pardons began to reach into the category of the absurd—over 8,000 in eight years—Small's regime at last began to crumble. In what came to be known as the Pineapple Primary of 1928 ("pineapples," or hand grenades, were used by Al CAPONE's pro-Small hoodlums to intimidate voters), an enraged electorate finally put an end to the Small-Crowe ticket. Small was nominated again in 1932 but was soundly defeated by a margin of more than a half million votes.

Perhaps surprisingly, Small was never convicted of any crime. Indeed, newspaper obituaries were generally respectful when the former governor died on May 17, 1936, in his native Kankakee.

Smith, Bear River Tom (Thomas) (1830–70) The tamer of Abilene, Kansas, Smith earned the reputation of a courageous lawman who would rather fight you with his fists than shoot you down with a gun.

Little is known of Thomas Smith's early life other than that he was born in New York City. There is reason to believe that he served as a New York City policeman for several years and may have been involved in quelling the New York City Draft Riots of 1863. Some historians claim, however, that he had moved west by the outbreak of the Civil War. In any

"Bear River Tom" Smith was a tough New York City cop who went west to become marshal of Dodge City, Kansas. (Courtesy of the Kansas State Historical Society)

event, by the end of 1865, he was working for freighting companies in Colorado, Utah, and Wyoming.

In 1868, Smith was working end-of-track construction for the Union Pacific in a place called Bear River, Wyoming. The townsmen formed a vigilance committee to oppose the hell-raising antics of the railway workers, and friction quickly developed. When the vigilantes captured three rowdy railway workers one night and hanged them, Smith rallied the other workers and stormed into town. After cornering the vigilantes in a store and setting the jail on fire, a truce was apparently called, but, for reasons not understood, Smith shot and killed a citizen, thereby sparking a riot that resulted in the deaths of 14 men and the wounding of others, including Smith. Cavalry troops were required to restore order, and Smith earned the nickname "Bear River Tom," which he would carry with him for the rest of his life. Smith not only escaped punishment for his actions, but was also made end-of-track marshal by Union Pacific.

In 1869, the year the Union Pacific and Central Pacific were joined as the nation's first transcontinen-

tal railroad, Smith left the railroad business and entered into law enforcement full time. That year, he assumed the marshal's position in Kit Carson, Colorado, where he earned high praise and universal respect. In Kit Carson, he also earned a reputation for using his fists rather than his gun. When the mayor of Abilene, Kansas, was looking for a sheriff to put a lid on his violent cow town, Bear River Tom showed up and was given the job. He began by banning handguns within the town limits of Abilene, and he set an example by relying solely on his fists to enforce the law, successfully facing down armed men, although he was unarmed himself.

Within only a few months, Abilene was a much quieter and safer place. But the career of Bear River Tom Smith was not destined to last long. In November 1870, Bear River Tom volunteered to serve an arrest warrant on a local homesteader wanted for murder. The wanted man and his partner shot Smith as he approached them. For good measure, they also attacked the marshal with an axe, nearly decapitating him.

Abilene immediately lapsed into its former violence, and Bear River Tom Smith was replaced as town marshal by Wild Bill HICKOK, as liberal with his guns as Tom had been restrained with.

Smith, Bruce (1892–1955)   "I don't care if a rookie thinks the Duke of Wellington is a man, a horse, or a smoking tobacco . . . What counts is a man's character." So said this Brooklyn-born, world-renowned law enforcement consultant, the originator of "uniform crime reporting" and the author of several important treatises on police operations in the United States and abroad.

Son of a banker and realtor, the mischievous young Smith gained a reputation for mayhem while attending Wesleyan University. He was ultimately expelled for the satirical use of a stopwatch during a longwinded chaplain's sermon. At Columbia University, where he earned a B.S. in 1914, Smith came under the wing of Professor Charles A. Beard, the director of the New York Bureau of Municipal Research. Two years later, after earning an LL.B. and a master's in political science, Smith joined Beard on the bureau's staff. He was assigned, somewhat against his natural and professed inclinations, to study the police department of Harrisburg, Pennsylvania.

With the entry of the United States into World War I, Smith left his post and became an officer pilot in the U.S. Army Signal Corps Aviation Service. In 1919, his tour of duty complete, he rejoined his former employer, though the bureau was now called the Institute of Public Administration. In 1921, he was made manager of the nonprofit research organization, and he held that title for the next seven years.

Surveying police departments in nearly 50 cities across 15 states, Smith developed a thorough knowledge of law enforcement administration. Recognizing its chronic challenges—internal corruption, political manipulation, and the infinite array of other "environmental" obstacles to successful crime prevention and apprehension—he formulated practical proposals for meeting them. Over time, he collaborated with the National Crime Commission, numerous state crime commissions and associations for criminal justice, the Scientific Crime Detection Laboratory, and dozens of other institutions and boards seeking improvements in the field.

Smith urged better selection and more pertinent instruction of rookie officers, as well as changes in disciplinary and promotion procedures. To maximize effective use of police talent and training, he recommended freeing officers from routine office duties, hiring civilians to fill those positions instead. Smith advocated police independence from all political interference and from any bureaucratic links to the Civil Service Commission.

Around 1928, Smith began to consider the potential value of standardizing police methods in the defining and booking of criminal offenses, and he directed a committee of the International Association of Chiefs of Police to consider the matter. An extensive comparative study of European police procedures ensued, and *Uniform Crime Reporting* (1930) appeared as the new decade dawned. Well persuaded of standardization's advantages, the FBI promptly adopted this system. In time, police agencies across the nation also did so.

A host of individual city governments consulted Smith to overhaul or streamline their police forces: Chicago, Baltimore, San Francisco, Pittsburgh, Providence, and Philadelphia, among others. Several times over the course of his career, Smith was asked to reorganize a particular city's police—those of New Orleans and St. Louis, for example—only to be called back again, years or even decades later. Discovering that his earlier suggestions had been ignored, eroded, or entirely undone by entrenched interests or the forces of inertia and corruption, Smith would restate and add to his original report.

Although Smith once wrote, "Rarely does a major piece of police work receive the accolade of general approval," his own work certainly did. Internationally acknowledged as America's foremost expert on police operations, Smith lectured at Harvard, Columbia, Yale, and Chicago. He was a visiting faculty member at the FBI National Police Training Academy from its founding in 1935 until his death, and an executive board member of the American Institute of Criminal Law and Criminology from 1930 to 1942. The author of *Rural Crime Control* (1933) and *Mobilizing Police for Emergency Duties* (1940), he developed police mobilization programs for the states of New York, New Jersey, and Virginia. He was chairman of the committee to revise New York state's code of criminal procedure (1933–39) and of the American Bar Association's committee on police training and merit systems (1943–44), and he also chaired and advised on many city police chief selection committees and scores of other commissions and panels.

Having been made secretary of the Institute of Public Administration in 1940, Smith was twice called to serve as its acting director (1941–46, 1950–52). In 1954 he became its permanent executive head. During World War II he was also consultant to various branches of the armed services, and some of his police principles found expression in military applications— for example, he transferred 350 Army Air Force colonels from desk jobs to the field.

Smith contributed many reports and articles to professional journals and penned the standard entries on police administration for the *Americana, Britannica,* and *Collier's* enyclopedias and for the *Encyclopedia of Social Sciences.* His last, unfinished book was a study of British police organizations. An avid sailor, in 1955 Smith suffered breathing difficulties aboard his yacht, the *Lucifer.* He died of a heart attack in a Southampton, New York, hospital a few days later, at the age of 63.

Further reading: Smith, Bruce, *Police Systems in the United States* (New York: Harper & Brothers, 1940, 1949).

Smith, Sir Sydney Alfred (1883–1969) The author of classic textbooks on firearms and gunshot wounds, forensic scientist Smith was an early and influential advocate of the comparison microscope. His research and study made significant contributions to several specializations in his field.

Born in Roxburgh, New Zealand, on August 4, 1883, Sydney Alfred Smith apprenticed with a pharmacist there before moving to Wellington, where he found work with a chemist and studied medicine part-time at Victoria College. His savings bought him steamship passage to Scotland, and in 1912 he graduated with honors (M.B., Ch.B.) from Edinburgh University. At this point, Smith was lured from a previous interest in ophthalmology by a paid assistantship to the well-known master of forensic medicine, Professor Harvey Littlejohn. With this financially attractive twist of fate, the young scientist's life's work began. The following year Smith's crucial testimony in identifying the much-decayed corpses of two young boys found in a Houpton quarry led to the prosecution of their father, Patrick Higgins, and to the establishment of Smith as a promising forensic authority.

Earning his medical degree and public health diploma in 1914, Smith returned to New Zealand to become medical officer of health in Dunedin. He served as a major in the New Zealand Army Corps during the First World War, and in 1917 he traveled to Cairo to teach medicine and to accept a position as medical-legal expert for the Egyptian government. In Cairo, increasing violence in the revolutionary struggles between nationalists and supporters of English rule presented Smith with an on-the-job immersion course in gunshot and shell wounds. Over time, his knowledge of ballistics grew to exceptionally advanced expertise. In 1924, reading of WAITE and GRAVELLE's New York experiments with a dual-objective microscope (which allowed the simultaneous comparison of two bullet specimens), Smith improvised a working model for his own laboratory. Only weeks later, when the sirdar—Sir Lee Stack, commander of the Anglo-Egyptian Army—was assassinated, Smith successfully applied his new instrument to solving the murder. During this period, the busy scientist completed his textbook *Forensic Medicine* (1925), a much-studied reference that earned him the Swiney Prize a few years later.

When Professor Littlejohn died in 1927, Smith was invited to succeed his former mentor as Edinburgh University's regius professor of forensic medicine. This he did, and he taught there for 25 years, becoming dean of the medical facility in 1931. His work in toxicology, ballistics, and microscopy became known worldwide, and he traveled as far afield as Australia and Ceylon to serve as forensic investigator and expert witness. He was appointed to the General Medical Council in 1936, served as a consultant during World War II, was knighted for his achievements in 1949, and continued to write and edit for his professional peers. But as accomplished as he was in many distinct and difficult areas of the medico-legal field, Smith was among the first forensic scientists to acknowledge and exploit the increasing specialization of modern medical knowledge, often assigning and orchestrating a team of experts to handle diverse aspects of a single case.

After he retired from Edinburgh as professor emeritus and rector in 1953, the university awarded him an honorary doctorate in law. He then worked as consultant to the World Health Organization, founded the British Association in Forensic Medicine, and penned his memoirs, which remained long in print. He died at 85, on May 8, 1969.

Further reading: Smith, Sydney Alfred, *Mostly Murder* (London: Harrap, 1959).

Smith, Tom (?–1892 or 1893) Wyoming range detective from Texas who led an unsuccessful attempt to incite a range war against enemies of the cattle industry.

A Texas native, Tom Smith worked as a lawman in various parts of the West, wearing a badge in Texas, Wyoming, and the Indian Territory (Oklahoma). Smith first gained prominence during the Jaybird-Woodpecker War of Fort Bend County, Texas, in 1888–90. The Jaybirds represented better than 90% of the white population of Fort Bend County, while the Woodpeckers consisted only of about 40 current and former public officials who were the beneficiaries of black votes. After mild outbreaks of violence, enforcement of the Fourteenth Amendment, explicitly extending citizenship to former slaves, allowed the Woodpeckers to regain control, but the county was polarized into two armed camps. The situation came to a head at the so-called battle of Richmond on August 16, 1889, when a savage firefight broke out, resulting in the deaths of leaders on both sides, as well as bystanders. Smith, serving as deputy sheriff, sided with the Woodpeckers and raked the Jaybird lines with carbine fire, killing several and effectively neutralizing the Jaybird faction in Fort Bend County.

Following the "war," Smith thought it wise to leave Texas and journeyed north to Wyoming, where he found work as a range detective for the Wyoming Stock Grower's Association. In that position, he vigorously pursued all enemies of the association, from small-time ranchers to rustlers to sheepherders. In the spring of 1892, the association commissioned Smith to gather a small army of gunfighters to begin a range war in an attempt to exterminate some 70 enemies of the association, who were mostly based around Johnson County, Wyoming. Smith returned to Texas to recruit approximately 25 hired guns, who were paid $5 a day and a $50 bonus for every assassination they carried out.

Taking their first crack at the association's "hit list," the self-proclaimed "Regulators" thoroughly botched the job and were eventually captured by the U.S. cavalry. Due to the political influence of the association, however, no charges were brought and all were released. Smith was killed the following summer in a gunfight on a train.

Snyder, LeMoyne (1899–1975) A leading forensic pathologist in the United States and a firm proponent of autopsies and the use of forensic medicine as an investigative tool.

A native of Lansing, Michigan, LeMoyne Snyder attended Harvard Medical School, graduating as a surgeon and going on to serve his internship at New York City's Fifth Avenue Hospital. His practice brought him into contact with the police and numerous victims of crime. As a result, Snyder became fascinated with the role of medicine in the law and in criminal investigation. Leaving New York, Snyder returned to Lansing and opened his own practice, specializing in criminal injuries and frequently testifying as an expert witness in court.

After Snyder frequently found himself at a disadvantage under cross-examination by crafty attorneys, he decided to enroll in law school and earned his law degree from Michigan State University while working as an official consultant to the Michigan State Police. These duties eventually supplanted his private practice, which Snyder finally abandoned in order to devote himself wholly to the investigative side of medicine. He was one of the few persons ever to hold membership in both the American Medical Association and the American Bar Association.

Snyder constantly stressed the fact that the body yielded clues to crime only if these were sought in the correct manner. He developed the dermalnitrate test, which detects minute powder traces on the skin and can determine if a subject has fired a gun recently. He was the first person in the United States to use the process of making plaster casts of tire tracks, wounds, and even the faces of unidentified dead.

Aware that many crimes were going unsolved in the United States for want of forensic and investigative expertise, Snyder, along with five other criminal investigators, formed the Court of Last Resort, a volunteer investigative team, which could be called into certain investigations when all other means of crime detection had failed. In many cases, the most basic items had been overlooked, including the fact that a crime had been committed in the first place; many physicians were hesitant to declare murder as a cause of death. Snyder worked to make physicians conscious of homicide, and at a 1958 medical conference, he implored doctors always to consider murder as a possible cause of death, citing that more than 20% of all deaths were the result of homicide.

Söderman, Harry (1903–56)   One of the original founders of INTERPOL; also founded Sweden's National Institute of Technical Police.

Born in Stockholm, Sweden, Harry Söderman was interested in police work and criminology from his youth. After graduating from the Chemical Institute of Malmö with honors and another two-year program in legal chemistry at the Technical Institute of Altenburg, Germany, Söderman embarked on a career in law enforcement. He began, at the age of 22, by setting out on an around-the-world journey to visit and observe police forces in all corners of the globe. To support himself, Söderman wrote articles along the way for the *Swedish Police Journal*. His odyssey ultimately consumed more than two years, and by the

time of his return to Stockholm, he had amassed a wealth of information available to no other law enforcement official in the world.

After studying at the French State Police Laboratory in Lyons, while simultaneously earning his doctorate from the University of Lyons, Söderman began teaching police science at the University of Stockholm. He also founded the National Institute of Technical Police, Sweden's version of the FBI, known around the world for its superior crime lab.

Near the end of World War II, Söderman was involved in securing the release of thousands of political prisoners held by the Nazis in occupied Norway. When word of the German capitulation was announced, Söderman rushed to the prison, proclaimed the men free, then essentially took over the country for a time. With the Nazis fleeing, Söderman commandeered the radio station and arrested the Oslo police commissioner, who was suspected of being a traitor. Söderman was subsequently decorated by the king of Norway.

Soon after the end of the war, Söderman laid the foundation for INTERPOL, which, based in France, developed into a powerful international crime-fighting organization.

Sparks, Richard F. (1934–88)   Studied the effectiveness of the local prison systems in England.

A native of Ironton, Ohio, Richard Sparks attended college in Evanston, Illinois, at Northwestern University, earning his bachelor's degree in 1955 before beginning his doctoral studies in Great Britain, at Cambridge University, where he received his Ph.D. in criminology. During the late 1950s and the 1960s, Sparks wrote on the effects of violent crime on perpetrators as well as victims. His most influential work was *Local Prisons: The Crisis in the English Penal System*, which detailed what he identified as the decline in penal effectiveness at the local level. Sparks argued that the linchpin of the penal system of any nation is the local prison. When that breaks down, all other elements of the system follow in domino fashion.

Spencer, John C. (1915–78)   Professor of social administration at the University of Edinburgh, Spencer was an expert in crime and delinquency, with special emphasis on the relationship between military service and crime.

Spencer held academic appointments in a number of British universities and served as a probation officer, as a London Juvenile Court magistrate, and as an officer in the British Army during World War II. His first major academic appointment in the field of sociology and criminology was at the University of

Toronto, where he served as professor on the faculty of social work and on the faculty of the Institute of Criminology. In 1967, he became chairman of the Department of Social Administration at the University of Edinburgh.

Spencer was an expert on juvenile delinquency and on the relation between military service and crime. His expertise in the latter area resulted in a groundbreaking 1954 book, *Crime and the Services*, which was the first full-scale study of crime within the army and navy and criminal activity among those discharged from the services. It is a key document in postwar sociology.

Further reading: Spencer, John C., *Crime and the Services* (London: Routledge & Kegan Paul, 1954).

Spilsbury, Sir Bernard Henry (1877–1947)   Combining his talents for practical pathology and criminological deduction with an articulate and convincing poise on the witness stand, this British forensics expert was lauded as "the greatest medical detective of the century."

The son of a chemist, Bernard Spilsbury was born at Leamington Spa, Warwickshire. He studied physiology at Magdalen College, Oxford, and graduated second in his class in 1899. At the medical school of St. Mary's Hospital in Paddington, he found his professional direction with the help and inspiration of three notable teachers, forensic medical pioneers Arthur Pearson Luff, Augustus Joseph PEPPER, and William WILLCOX. After graduation, Spilsbury became their colleague in the post of resident assistant pathologist. In 1908 he joined the Medico-Legal Society, later serving as its president.

The 1910 trial of Dr. Hawley Harvey Crippen, who was accused of murdering his wife, Cora, put Spilsbury's name in the newspaper headlines. The young scientist impressed the court—and deeply embarrassed careless experts for the defense—with his patient and thorough exposition of subtle medical evidence. Politely inviting jurors to join him at a benchside microscope, he explained the intricacies of a contested abdominal scar, and this necessary proof of the mutilated victim's identity promptly sent Crippen to the gallows. Even more important, Spilsbury's presentation contributed to a new public confidence in the enlightening and judiciary value of "the beastly science," as his field was then known.

Before long, Spilsbury was the predominant authority in British forensics, a junior honorary pathologist to the Home Office, and the "murder man" on whom one called when probing a hard-to-prove poisoning death or other crime with few workable clues. In the "Brides in the Bath" case of 1915, he demonstrated how George Joseph Smith had overpowered a succes-

sion of girlfriends while they were bathing; Spilsbury's exhibition proved more than amply realistic when his courtroom model, a St. Mary's nurse, nearly drowned.

In 1920 Spilsbury moved to St. Bartholomew's Hospital to accept a lectureship in morbid anatomy and histology, and three years later he was knighted for his increasingly venerated public service. In 1924, he was called to examine the butchered, incinerated, and much-decayed remains of an unfortunate victim in Sussex, and his appalled observation of barehanded local detectives prompted him to establish a standardized "murder bag," containing rubber gloves, medical compass, and other tools essential for those who deal with corpses. After solving the Sussex case and seeing it through conviction, Spilsbury performed a postmortem on the executed killer, Patrick Mahon; the autopsy—a world precedent—led to technical improvements in capital punishment—most immediately a swifter gallows technique.

At one point in his career, Spilsbury began to lose his much-relied-on sense of smell. Although the diminishment of this faculty allowed him to work for hours under otherwise unendurable conditions, Spilsbury missed the assistance of this previously invaluable, finely tuned instrument of detection. He adopted a practice of stepping outdoors periodically to rejuvenate his olfactory sensitivity, returning to the autopsy table to quickly "sniff out" additional clues before his nose deadened again.

In his waning years, Spilsbury's much-vaunted (though never self-proclaimed) reputation for infallibility met severe challenges in court, and the belated confessions (and repeat offenses) of acquitted suspects further undermined the accuracy of his findings at previous trials. Arthritis began to impinge on his famous dexterity in the morgue, and in 1934 he retired from full-time hospital and academic work, consulting only occasionally as honorary pathologist for the Home Office. After a minor stroke in 1940, Spilsbury faced a succession of tragedies, losing two sons and a sister within a few years. He grew ever more reclusive, and, at the age of 70, Spilsbury took his own life, gassing himself in his laboratory at the pharmacology department of University College, London. When his files were opened, researchers discovered meticulous records documenting all 25,000 autopsies he had conducted over the course of his career. Although only a tiny fraction of these involved murder cases, those gruesome bludgeonings, poisonings, shootings, and stranglings had made Sir Bernard Spilsbury a British household name.

Spitzka, Edward Anthony (1876–1922)   Brain anatomist who successfully refuted the long-held belief that criminality was the result of physical deformation of the brain.

Growing up in New York City, Edward Spitzka was graduated from the College of Physicians and Surgeons of Columbia University and became assistant demonstrator of anatomy at Columbia before moving to Philadelphia's Jefferson Medical College as professor of general anatomy. Spitzka was fascinated by the physiology and anatomy of the brain and made a lifelong study of the brains of noted individuals, both famous and infamous, looking for significant anatomical features.

Many successful people, including Dr. William Pepper, the soft drink magnate, left their brains to Spitzka for postmortem examination. Spitzka's fame rested, however, on his examination of criminal brains, his most famous postmortem study being that of the brain of Leon Czolgosz, the assassin of President William McKinley. Spitzka's work was more notable for what it did not find than for what it discovered. In all of his cranial autopsies, Spitzka kept diligent notes and made detailed drawings, none of which reveal any special physical characteristics in the brains of exceptional persons or in criminals. Spitzka therefore concluded that, despite the commonly held belief to the contrary, neither criminals nor geniuses had physically extraordinary brains. Spitzka declared: "Many criminals show not a single anomaly in their physical or mental makeup, while many persons with marked evidences of morphological aberration have never exhibited the criminal tendency."

Spurzheim, Johann Christoph (1776–1832) One of the early 19th-century criminologists who espoused the pseudoscience of phrenology, believing that it could detect certain malevolent traits.

Born near Trier, Germany, on December 21, 1776, Johann Spurzheim intended to become a clergyman, and his early education was undertaken toward that end. In 1799, he moved to Vienna to become a private tutor, and there he met Franz Joseph GALL, a leading physiologist and phrenologist. Gall persuaded Spurzheim to enter the medical field, and from 1800 to 1804, Spurzheim studied medicine at the University of Vienna.

His medical degree was not officially conferred until 1813, at which time Spurzheim was licensed in London by the Royal College of Physicians. Spurzheim did not so much practice medicine as continue to develop Gall's theories, particularly in regard to phrenology.

Before the turn of the century, Gall had popularized phrenology, the interpretation of the correspondence between the size and shape of the brain and various aspects of human behavior. Spurzheim refined Gall's work, dividing the brain into 35 different faculties, which amounted to almost 35 separate brains, each responsible for different behavioral and emotional patterns. Spurzheim further theorized that behavioral and emotional patterns could be detected by the physical contours of the brain, which were evident in the shape of the skull itself. He distinguished in particular certain features that denoted a tendency toward criminal and violent behavior. Spurzheim believed that such behavioral and emotional patterns could be detected even before any violent act was committed. Thus an individual could be examined, identified as a potential murderer, and, through timely counseling— that is, an early form of psychotherapy—apprised of his tendencies and turned away from acting on them. Although Spurzheim gained a small and vocal following, his theories were repeatedly discredited, even in his own lifetime.

Stalin, Josef (1879–1953) One of the most brutal dictators in a century of brutal dictators; a master architect of the police state.

Born Josef Djugasvili on December 21, 1879, in the Russian province of Georgia, Stalin suffered the abuses of an alcoholic peasant father and was doted upon by his mother, who pushed him into religious training at a seminary, which he entered at the age of 14. The young man quickly chafed under the harsh discipline of the priests and became involved in radical political activity against the czarist government. In 1899, he left the seminary to agitate against the government in earnest, and within a short time he was a member of the Georgian branch of the Social Democratic Party, touring the country, stirring up revolutionary activity, and organizing strikes. He came to the attention of Vladimir Iliych LENIN, who enrolled him in the Bolshevik wing of the growing Communist Party.

Stalin was one of the moving forces in the Communist Party. Although he was a taciturn and even inarticulate man, Stalin was a great organizer, establishing cells seemingly everywhere and financing the party through a series of daring robberies. After he was arrested and exiled in 1913, he returned from Siberia for the failed revolution in the summer of 1917. After the exile of Lenin following that event and the arrest of Leon Trotsky, Stalin worked to reorganize the party, and much of the credit for the success of the October Revolution must go to him. Stalin served Lenin loyally and ruthlessly and, following the Bolshevik leader's death in 1924, Stalin readily engineered his promotion as Lenin's successor.

Stalin quickly set the tone for his regime by pointedly departing from Lenin's leftist ideals and aligning himself with the radical right, ruthlessly eliminating his old colleagues. Having accomplished this, he then turned against the right and did the same thing to them, successfully eliminating potential rivals in both party factions. This was only a prelude. In the service of establishing and maintaining the communist state and his own position within it, Stalin greatly discounted the value of human life. In his attempt to collectivize the agricultural system in Russia, he viciously suppressed any who opposed him and his plan. Worse, the collectivization program came at a time of great famine. Stalin literally starved agricultural Russia in an effort to feed industrial Russia. While industrialization did proceed at breakneck speed, the cost was the deaths of at least 25 million people, who were either executed by Stalin's secret police or simply starved.

With the help of the OGPU, later reorganized as the KGB, the security and terror arm of the party, Stalin moved to suppress all opposition. When a rival arose with some popular support, Stalin directed his secret police to assassinate him, then blamed the assassination on high-ranking party officials and officers of the Red Army, whom he arrested for treason or conspiracy. Using his terror force, Stalin caused the execution of more than 65% of the central committee members and 55% of the congressional delegates in 1939. With the zealous cooperation of Lavrenti BERIA, the KGB head who often carried out executions personally, Stalin unleashed the terror on the general population, "purging" millions of citizens who may or may not have ever done anything against the party. Less directly, Stalin's police state policies caused even more death and suffering, since, in the years immediately preceding World War II, he executed most of the Red Army's senior officer corps, leaving his armed forces virtually leaderless and wholly vulnerable to the German juggernaut.

While his disastrous policies exposed the Soviet Union to near annihilation in the opening months of World War II, Stalin quickly recovered and showed himself as a great and inspiring war leader. With the end of the war, however, he renewed his purges, claiming that Nazi sympathizers abounded in Russia and in the eastern European nations that were now Soviet vassals. With the spread of communism into eastern Europe, the KGB assumed paramount importance in ferreting out underground resistance and brutally repressing it.

Stalin was on the verge of what promised to be the biggest internal purge yet when, fortunately for the Russian people, he died on March 5, 1953. His reign of terror had become so institutionalized during his long regime that people were afraid to criticize him even decades after his death.

Further reading: Knight, Amy W., *The KGB: Police and Politics in the Soviet Union* (Boston: Allen and Unwin, 1988).

Stalker, John (1939–) Deputy chief constable of Greater Manchester who was sent to Northern Ireland to investigate the 1982 shooting deaths of unarmed civilians by the police. He uncovered a British shoot-to-kill policy against suspected IRA terrorists.

John Stalker was born April 14, 1939, in Manchester, England, and was graduated from the Police Staff College (1969) and the Royal College of Defence Studies (1983). He joined the Greater Manchester Police in 1958 as a detective officer, serving until 1977, when he was made head of detectives of the Warwickshire County Police. In 1980, he was appointed deputy chief of the Greater Manchester force, serving until 1987, when he resigned in protest, complaining that his superiors would not allow him to conclude an inquiry into the 1982 police shootings of unarmed civilians in Northern Ireland.

Stalker had been removed from the inquiry after he charged that six unarmed men were deliberately shot to death by British police in Northern Ireland during a five-week period. Stalker further charged that authorities conspired to cover up the shootings and to obstruct the investigation Stalker had been assigned to conduct.

Following his resignation from the police force, Stalker published *The Stalker Affair* (1988), which compelled many in Great Britain to examine critically their government's treatment of nationalist activists in Northern Ireland.

Further reading: Stalker, John, *The Stalker Affair* (New York: Viking, 1988).

Standley, Jeremiah ("Doc") (1845–1908) One of the great lawmen of the Old West; deputy sheriff and sheriff of Mendocino County, California, during much of the last quarter of the 19th century.

Born in Andrew County, Missouri, on August 20, 1845, Jeremiah Standley went to California with his parents when he was eight years old. Stopping first in Petaluma, the family finally settled in Ukiah in 1858, where they operated a cattle ranch and a hotel. While he was still a boy, Standley doctored a sick cow back to health and thereby earned the nickname he bore for life: "Doc."

Standley leased his own ranch when he was 16, attending school in his spare time. In 1864, when he was 19, he was appointed deputy sheriff of Mendocino County, earning a reputation as a manhunter after he successfully tracked Jerry Bailey, a local outlaw. However, it was his investigation of the murder of one Catherine Strong in 1874 that fully established

Doc Standley's reputation as a crime solver and as a champion of justice. Not only did he identify and apprehend the woman's murderers, he also successfully defended his prisoners against an enraged lynch mob.

Standley was elected sheriff in 1882, serving until 1892. During these 10 years, he amassed a remarkable record. Between 1887 and 1892, for example, there were 14 stagecoach robberies in the county. Standley tracked, arrested, and convicted the perpetrators of 13 of them. After retiring as sheriff, Standley joined the gold rush to the Klondike and settled in Nome, Alaska, where he mined, ran a freighting operation, and served as deputy sheriff. In 1902, Standley and his wife returned to Ukiah, then returned to Alaska after 1903, when he failed to secure a much-desired appointment as the warden of California's Folsom Prison. In 1908, Standley was badly injured in a fall down a staircase. His family was taking him back to California, when he died, in Portland, Oregon, on July 8.

Stas, Jean-Servais (1813–91)   Refined the practice of forensic toxicology by developing a technique for determining the presence of vegetable alkaloids in dead tissue.

A native of Louvain, Belgium, Jean-Servais Stas was born on August 21, 1813. Entering the University of Louvain in 1832, Stas quickly absorbed all the faculty could teach him and received his M.D. in 1835. After joining the staff of the university, he began experimenting with apple trees and was able to isolate a crystalline glucoside, which he called phlorizin. Stas also refuted a commonly accepted theory regarding the determination of an element's atomic weight as a whole multiple of the atomic weight of hydrogen.

In 1837, Stas moved to Paris, where he continued to conduct experiments, and in September 1840 he was appointed to a chair in chemistry at the Royal Military Academy in Brussels. There he gained fame for his toxicological work in a murder case. Suspecting a victim had been poisoned, Stas was able to demonstrate the presence of a vegetable alkaloid in dead tissue. Through a process of repeated filtration and the use of alcohol solutions, he proved that any alkaloid could be detected in dead tissue.

In 1868, Stas became professor emeritus at the academy and served in that capacity until his death.

Steele, Sir Samuel Benfield (1849–1919)   Commander of the Royal Mounted Police during the Yukon Gold Rush at the end of the 19th century; helped develop that institution into the world-renowned force it is today.

Born in the province of Ontario, Samuel Steele joined the military at the age of 17 in 1866, enlisting first in the local militia and then in the Ontario Rifles. While he was with this outfit, he served in the Red River Campaign of 1870–71 in combat with Indians, and in 1873 was the first to enlist in the Royal Canadian Artillery, the first unit of the permanent Canadian Army. After racking up an impressive record as commander of Battery A in the RCA, Steele was named sergeant-major of the newly formed North West Mounted Police (subsequently the Royal Northwest Mounted Police and then the Royal Canadian Mounted Police).

Steele set out to mold the Mounted Police into a resilient and durable unit. During his first two years in command, Steele and his troops traveled almost 2,000 miles, setting up remote outposts, dealing with Indians, and mediating disputes between settlers and trappers. The Mounted Police were instrumental in developing a relatively peaceful relationship with the Indians (in strong contrast to the situation at the same time in the United States) and maintaining a degree of law and order on the frontier.

In 1885, Steele was promoted to superintendent and commanded his own body of troops during the Northwest Rebellion that same year. He was soon promoted to the rank of major. With the discovery of a major gold strike in the Yukon region in 1897, the provincial government in Ottawa was fearful of the sort of lawlessness and vigilantism that had prevailed in the mining towns of British Columbia and California during similar rushes. The government moved to establish authority, and the Mounted Police were hastily assigned to the region. Steele quickly set up a skeletal municipal infrastructure using the Mounted Police not only as a security force, but also as postal workers, tax collectors, and experts in Indian relations. Most visible, though, was the record Steele's men compiled for solving crimes. Soon the Mounties—as they became known popularly—could claim with considerable justification that they "always got their man."

Stein, Robert J. (1912–94)   The first medical examiner of Cook County, Illinois; gained international fame for his expertise in forensic pathology.

Robert Stein immigrated to the United States from his native Russia as a young child and grew up in Brooklyn, New York. Returning to Europe for medical study, Stein went to the University of Innsbruck in Austria, earning his degree in 1950. After returning to the United States, he earned an additional medical degree at Northwestern University. Stein then began working as a forensic pathologist in Chicago, and when Cook County converted the political patronage office of coroner to the professional merit position of medical examiner, Stein was named the county's first chief medical examiner in 1976.

As CME in one of the nation's largest counties, Stein investigated some 20,000 deaths in the Chicago area over 17 years. Some of his highest-profile cases included the DC-10 airplane crash at O'Hare Airport in 1979, which killed 279 people, and the examination of 33 bodies unearthed in the backyard of mass murderer John Wayne Gacy in December 1978. Stein's work in these and other cases gained him an international reputation for meticulous investigation and general excellence in forensic pathology.

Stone, Harlan Fiske (1872–1946)   Attorney general and, later, chief justice of the Supreme Court; appointed J. Edgar HOOVER to head the FBI.

A direct descendant of Massachusetts Bay Colony settlers, Harlan Fiske Stone grew up in Amherst, attended Amherst College, and earned his bachelor's degree there in 1896. After graduation, he went to work teaching high school to earn money for law school. He moved to New York and entered Columbia Law School, supporting himself as necessary by teaching. After graduating in 1898, he was admitted to the bar and began a private practice.

Stone enjoyed success as an attorney, but left to accept an appointment as dean of the law school of his alma mater and built it into a revered institution. In 1923, Stone abruptly resigned as dean to return to private practice, but the following year he was appointed attorney general by President Calvin COO-LIDGE, a friend from his student days. As attorney general, Stone became one of the president's closest advisors.

At the time of Stone's appointment, the Department of Justice was in a shambles, beset by scandals and generally inept management. Stone vowed to clean house and began doing so immediately. Under Warren G. Harding's attorney general, Harry Daugherty, the department had been rife with criminals and thugs who continued to prosecute the anti-radical campaign initiated by Woodrow WILSON's attorney general, A. Mitchell PALMER. Stone fired the head of the Bureau of Investigation, William BURNS, who was implicated in severe misuses of bureau resources, not the least of which was attempting to gain revenge against a senator who was opposed to him. In Burns's place, Stone hired a 29-year-old division chief from within the bureau named J. Edgar Hoover. Young Hoover promised to rid the bureau of political hacks, streamline it, and make it the finest investigative force in the land. He did that—and, for better or worse, more.

Hoover and Stone became very close, and Stone, highly impressed by Hoover's performance, named him permanent director after seven months. The relationship would continue, though not on the same terms, since Coolidge nominated Stone to a vacant Supreme Court seat only 11 months into his tenure as attorney general. As a Supreme Court associate justice, Stone gained a reputation for being methodical and leaning toward the safeguarding of individual rights while being tough on big business. Although Stone was a lifelong Republican who wrote opinions against much of Franklin Delano ROOSEVELT's New Deal legislation, FDR nominated Stone as chief justice in 1941. Stone died five years later.

Further reading: Ungar, Sanford J., *The FBI: An Uncensored Look Behind the Walls* (Boston: Little, Brown, 1976).

Stoudenmire, Dallas (1845–82)   Hard-drinking lawman and former Texas Ranger who had a reputation as the toughest lawman in Texas during the late 1800s.

Texas lawman Dallas Stuodenmire earned a reputation for hard drinking and even harder justice. (Courtesy of the Western History Collections, University of Oklahoma)

Dallas Stoudenmire became marshal of the "shooting gallery" Texas frontier town of El Paso in 1881. There he engaged in a long-standing and well-known feud with the Manning brothers, saloon owners. Stoudenmire quickly developed a reputation as the meanest lawman in Texas. His shoot-first-ask-questions-later policy split the residents of El Paso into pro- and anti-Stoudenmire factions, forcing the boisterous lawman to resign at one point in May 1882, only to return two weeks later as deputy U.S. marshal.

Stoudenmire's quick return rekindled his feud with the Manning brothers, and it came to a head on September 19, 1882, in a barroom gunfight between Doc Manning and the deputy marshal. Doc Manning fired first, wounding Stoudenmire, who responded by shooting Manning in the arm. Suddenly, brother James Manning appeared, shooting and killing the six-foot-four lawman as he struggled to get up.

The Mannings were acquitted of murder on the grounds of self-defense.

Further reading: Metz, Leon C., *Dallas Stoudenmire: El Paso Marshal* (Austin, Texas: Pemberton Press, 1969).

Stringham, James S. (1775–1817)
The first lecturer in the field of medical jurisprudence in the United States and considered by many to be the founder of the field in this country.

A native of New York City born at the start of the American Revolution, James Stringham early on considered becoming a clergyman. He graduated from Columbia University in 1793 with a degree in theology, but soon abandoned religion for medicine. He began study under noted physicians in New York, then traveled to Edinburgh University in Scotland, receiving his degree in 1799

After returning from Edinburgh, Stringham accepted a position at Columbia University in 1802 as a professor of chemistry. In 1813, he accepted the position of professor of medical jurisprudence in Columbia's College of Physicians and Surgeons. Stringham served in this department from 1813 until his death in 1817 and was the first to lecture on the subject in the United States. It is for this reason that many regard him as one of the founders of the discipline in this country.

Sutherland, Edwin Hardin (1883–1950)
The originator of the term "white collar crime," Sutherland held that crime was learned through interaction with others.

Edwin Sutherland was born August 13, 1883, in Gibbon, Nebraska, the son of a college professor. He attended nearby Grand Island College, earning his degree in 1904 before journeying north to teach at Sioux Falls College in South Dakota. In 1909 he re-

turned to Grand Island, remaining two years before moving on to the University of Chicago to earn his Ph.D. in sociology in 1913. For the next 40-plus years, Sutherland progressed from professorship to professorship, teaching at William Jewel College in Missouri and the universities of Illinois, Minnesota, Chicago, and Indiana.

While at Illinois in 1924, Sutherland published a book that gained him considerable recognition in the field of criminology (which he never considered a discipline in its own right, but, rather, a subdivision of sociology). The book, *Criminology* (revised in 1960 with Donald R. CRESSEY as *Principles of Criminology*), developed the concept of differential association, the proposition that criminal activity is learned behavior, acquired from association with others whom one identifies as socially similar to one's self, much in the way that any other behavioral patterns are learned. For this reason crime is often concentrated in pockets, criminals learning criminal behavior from other criminals.

While he was teaching at Indiana, Sutherland published *White Collar Crime* in 1949, which extended the definition of "criminal" beyond the traditional violent figure from the lower economic strata. In this book, Sutherland modified his theory of differential association to account for white-collar crime by shifting the focus from social deprivation as a causative factor to the concept of the development of the will to commit a crime.

Sutherland continued to write about the theory of criminality until his death, from a stroke, on October 11, 1950.

Sylvester, Richard (active 1898–1915)
Chief of the Washington, D.C., police department, president of the International Association of Chiefs of Police from 1901 to 1915, and an advocate of professionalism among law enforcement officers.

Before becoming chief of the police force of the nation's capital in 1898, Richard Sylvester had been a law student and a journalist. He then served as an official of the Ute Indian Commission, after which he became chief clerk of the Washington, D.C., police department. In 1894, he wrote an official history of the District of Columbia police and, four years later, was promoted to major and superintendent of the department—effectively, the city's police chief. Sylvester succeeded Webber S. SEAVEY as president of the National Chiefs of Police Union in 1901, which was renamed the International Association of Chiefs of Police a year later.

Sylvester introduced important new topics into the business of the IACP, including an emphasis on crime prevention, the value of probation, and strategies for the control of prostitution. He encouraged the efforts of Philip DIETSCH, chief of the Cincinnati police, to reform police training methods and to introduce high technology into crime detection and intervention.

In 1910, Sylvester wrote "A History of the 'Sweat Box' and 'Third Degree,'" chronicling the use of torture to extort confessions from accused criminals. Sylvester was able to secure a unanimous IACP resolution against the "third degree" and similar brutal police methods. Under Sylvester, the IACP became involved in work to improve the public image of police departments and police officers, waging a high-profile campaign against the fledgling movie industry for the "degrading" portrayal of law enforcement officials presented in director Mack Sennett's "Keystone Kops" series. This campaign was the first of many official and semi-official assaults on the nation's film industry as a potential corrupter of morals and a contributor to juvenile delinquency.

T

Tamm, Quinn (1910–86)   Director of the International Association of Chiefs of Police (IACP) during the turbulent 1960s and early 1970s; credited with making the organization the preeminent police association in the world.

Born on August 10, 1910, in Seattle, Washington, Quinn Tamm was educated at the University of Virginia, graduating with a B.A. in 1934. In that year, he joined the Federal Bureau of Investigation as a messenger, subsequently becoming assistant chief technician of the crime laboratory and, in 1938, chief of the Identification Division. Later, he became assistant director of the FBI in charge of the crime lab, then (successively) in charge of the Identification Division and the Training and Inspection Division.

Tamm left the FBI in 1960 and became director of the Field Service Division of the IACP in January 1961. Five months later, when executive director Leroy E. Wike was incapacitated by illness, Tamm became acting executive director of the IACP and was confirmed as Wike's permanent replacement in October 1961.

During Tamm's tenure, the nation's police agencies were under increasing attack by civil libertarians and others who clamored for reform and for greater police responsiveness to the social and ethnic needs of an increasingly diverse America. Tamm took the IACP from a relatively limited service organization of 4,500 members to an internationally recognized professional association of 10,500. The IACP evolved into a guiding force for America's beleaguered police agencies and an advocate organization for them.

Tamm stepped down in January 1975. He died at his home outside of Washington, D.C., on January 23, 1986.

Tarde, Gabriel (1843–1904)   Anticipating such later writers as the American Edwin SUTHERLAND, Tarde emphasized the importance of the physical environment on the creation of criminality.

Educated in a Jesuit school at Sarlat, France, Gabriel Tarde, like other thinkers of his day, chafed severely under the stifling atmosphere and discipline of the church. Tarde proved quite adept at mathematics and probably would have gone on to higher study in the field were it not for an eye disease that severely impaired his ability to read. Instead, he enrolled at Toulouse and studied law, apparently less demanding on the eyes than the study of mathematics.

After completing his legal studies, Tarde held a series of judicial posts that enabled him to study and write extensively in the field of sociology and criminology. It was in the field of criminology that Tarde gained his reputation. He theorized that the "criminal mind" was most heavily influenced by the physical environment around it, specifically the example of other criminal behavior. Tarde argued that professional criminals learned their "trade" by means of an unofficial apprenticeship, and he feared that, if society failed to intervene, the "profession" would grow, exposing the population at large to patterns of criminal behavior and thereby greatly expanding criminality.

Further reading: Sylvester, Sawyer, ed., *The Heritage of Modern Criminology* (Cambridge, Mass.: Schenkman Publishing Co., 1972).

Taylor, Alfred Swaine (1806–80)   A noted author on medical jurisprudence who published the definitive 19th-century work on the subject in England.

Educated privately in Hounslow, England, Alfred Taylor was apprenticed to a medical practitioner in 1822. After a year of apprenticeship, he became a student at the Hospital of Guy's and St. Thomas. He spent the summer of 1825 in Paris and received his medical degree in 1828. He next traveled extensively, attending lectures and studying with the most prominent physicians of the day. After completing his travels and various internships, Taylor was named a member of the Royal College of Surgeons in 1830. That same summer, he returned to Paris for short time during the revolution that preceded the July Monarchy of Louis-Philippe. It was on this occasion that Taylor had the opportunity to study gunshot wounds extensively. Upon his return to London in 1831, he accepted the first professorship of medical jurisprudence at Guy's Hospital (Guy's and St. Thomas having become two separate institutions). His initial lectures were the first ever given in England on the subject and were widely attended by numerous judicial officials.

As his reputation grew in the field, Taylor was frequently called to the witness stand to give expert testimony. He had the distinction of giving the clinching testimony in a poison-murder case that is believed to be the first case of murder committed to collect on a life insurance policy. Taylor also began writing his monumental *Elements of Medical Jurisprudence,* which became the cornerstone of 19th-century British thought on the subject and went through 12 editions in both England and the United States. Taylor later published *Principles and Practice of Medical Jurisprudence,* which was also received as a standard and was likewise published in 12 editions.

Taylor, Charles Anthony (1885–1965) Australia's preeminent criminal investigator; earned a near-legendary reputation for his ability to solve crimes with the aplomb of Sherlock Holmes.

A native of Australia's outback, Charles Taylor was nicknamed "the Cat," both for his investigative prowess and on account of his initials. Taylor graduated from the School of Mines and won a scholarship to the Teacher's Training College near Melbourne. He subsequently enrolled in Melbourne University to study medicine, but became enthralled with the process of chemical investigation instead. He established himself as one Melbourne's top chemical analysts.

In 1921, Taylor was appointed food analyst and deputy chief analyst of the Health Department. His expertise with the microscope and knowledge of the human body soon attracted the attention of the police department, which called upon him to investigate various crimes and to offer testimony at trials. Taylor was also an unimpeachable witness. His ability to present scientific evidence in a clear, exact, but easily understood way made him the cornerstone of any case. It was said that none of Taylor's evidence was ever ruled inadmissible in court. He soon gained a reputation for solving crimes that left all other

investigators baffled. Toward the end of Taylor's life, the director of the Victoria Police Department's forensic laboratory summed up Taylor's accomplishments by observing that, long before the development of specialized toxicology, chemistry, and other branches of investigative science, Taylor "did it all by himself."

Taylor, Creed (1820–?) Texas Ranger (and relative of General Zachary Taylor) and a ruthless Indian fighter.

Creed Taylor moved with his family from Tennessee to southwestern Texas in 1824. His father, Josiah Taylor, was an explorer who helped the Mexicans fight the Spanish in their battle for independence. After his father's death in 1830, Creed Taylor was sent by his mother to Gonzales, Texas, for schooling. Shortly thereafter, the Mexican government barred further American immigration into Texas. Mexico's action sparked the Texas war of independence. In 1835, elements of the Mexican Army marched on Gonzales to confiscate the cannon that was positioned there. Taylor, along with several of his classmates, turned the cannon on the Mexicans, helping to defeat them at the battle of Gonzales. Following the incident, young Taylor joined a Texas infantry unit and fought in several key battles, most notably the decisive battle of San Jacinto, which brought the surrender of the Mexican dictator, General Santa Ana.

When Texas declared itself a republic that same year, Taylor remained in its service, combating Indian "depredations" on the Texas prairie. Some time around 1841, Taylor joined the Texas Rangers and continued to serve in that organization after Texas was annexed by the United States in 1845. When the Mexican War broke out in 1846, Taylor served in every major battle from Palo Alto through Buena Vista.

Teare, Robert Donald (1911–79) One of the famed "Three Musketeers" of British pathology, Teare was a dominant force in the establishment of the autopsy as a matter of investigative importance in criminal cases.

Born on the Isle of Man on July 1, 1911, Donald Teare was educated at King William's College on the island before moving to the mainland, where he attended Gonville and Caius College, Cambridge, to study medicine. He continued his studies at St. George's Hospital, earning his degree there and staying on as a consultant pathologist.

Shortly before the outbreak of World War II, Teare met Francis CAMPS and Keith SIMPSON, also pathologists, and the three of them became close friends. When the war broke out, several doctors were needed on the front, leaving Teare, Camps, and Simpson, shortly to be known as the Three Musketeers, as three of the few remaining pathologists in London. Among them, they handled the bulk of the autopsies performed in London during the war. After work they were frequently seen at a Soho restaurant together, carousing and talking shop.

Of the three, Teare was the least well known but, many say, the best pathologist. He was a fierce proponent of the autopsy as a matter of course and even came to the United States in the late 1960s to speak at a conference on the issue. He had an ability to explain the most complex features of the human anatomy in the simplest of terms, and, for that reason, he was a favorite witness of both prosecution and defense lawyers in London. His testimony was the linchpin in several notable murder cases.

After several decades, the Three Musketeers parted company, Teare accepting a position as lecturer in forensic medicine at St. Batholomew's Hospital Medical College. In 1963, he became reader in forensic medicine at Charing Cross Hospital Medical School. He was appointed professor in 1967 and retired, as professor emeritus, in 1975.

Thomas, "Heck" (Henry Andrew) (1850–1912)
Wild West lawman and member of the famed "Three Guardsmen."

Heck Thomas was born in Georgia and, at age 12, served under Confederate general Thomas "Stonewall" Jackson during the Civil War. In 1875, Thomas moved to Texas and distinguished himself as a guard for the Texas Express Company. Promoted by the company to detective, Thomas captured and killed several members of the notorious gang of outlaw Sam Bass. In 1885, Thomas was appointed deputy U. S. marshal, reporting to "hanging judge" Isaac PARKER. Thomas joined fellow lawmen Chris MADSEN and Bill TILGHMAN to form the "Three Guardsmen" in the 1890s for the express purpose of rounding up the Bill DOOLIN gang. Celebrated for their skill, courage, and incorruptibility, they also apprehended the Barker Gang (whose matriarch was the infamous "Ma" BARKER).

Thomas was credited with personally tracking and killing Bill Doolin, but the (perhaps apocryphal) story goes that the outlaw was already dead when Thomas found him. The lawman shot him anyway, collected the reward money, and then gave it to the outlaw's penniless widow. Later in his life, Heck Thomas could be seen hunting with no less than Teddy Roosevelt in the Oklahoma Territory. He died on August 15, 1912, in Lawton, Oklahoma.

Further reading: O'Neal, Bill, *Encyclopedia of Western Gunfighters* (Norman: University of Oklahoma Press, 1979).

Thompson, Benjamin (1843–84)
Gunfighter, outlaw, gambler, and lawman; considered the deadliest shot in the West.

Born in England and raised in Austin, Texas, Benjamin Thompson fought for the Confederacy during the Civil War and in the service of Napoleon III's puppet emperor of Mexico, Maximilian, during the Mexican-French War of 1861–67.

Following his military career, Thompson took up as an itinerant gambler, making the circuit from cow town to cow town and quickly developing a reputation as a prolific and skilled gunslinger. With Phil Coe, he opened the Bull's Head Saloon in Abilene, Kansas, in 1870 and immediately ran afoul of maverick lawman Wild Bill HICKOK, who subsequently shot and killed Coe but declined to confront the quick-handed surviving partner.

Thompson left Abilene and joined his brother Billy in Ellsworth, Kansas, around 1872. The following year, Billy killed Sheriff "Happy Jack" Morco, and Ben had

Deputy marshal Heck Thomas, one of Oklahoma's famed Three Guardsmen (Courtesy of the Western History Collections, University of Oklahoma)

Ben Thompson—considered the deadliest shot in the West (Courtesy of the Western History Collections, University of Oklahoma)

to spirit his trigger-happy brother out of town. Ben Thompson spent most of the balance of the 1870s in and around Dodge City, Kansas, working briefly as a hired gun for the Santa Fe Railroad in the so-called Right-of-Way War for Royal Gorge in 1879. One of his partners on the Santa Fe job was Bat MASTERSON, who claimed that Thompson was the most dangerous man with a gun among all the "badmen" he knew.

In 1880, Thompson returned to Austin, where—despite or because of his reputation—he was elected the town's marshal. During his tenure, the rough-and-tumble town's crime rate dropped to an unprecedented low. However, in 1882, Thompson's characteristically reckless behavior, contemptuous of the law he supposedly served, forced his resignation. Two years later, Thompson and a new partner, noted gunfighter John King Fischer, were ambushed and killed at the Vaudeville Variety Theatre in San Antonio. Thompson had fired only once, but nine bullets were extracted from his body. For his part, Fischer had not fired at all, and 13 slugs were recovered from his

corpse. Nevertheless, the notorious reputation of the two men was sufficient for their assailants to gain acquittal on grounds of self-defense.

Further reading: Floyd, Benjamin S., *The Complete and Authentic Life of Ben Thompson: Man With a Gun* (New York: Frederick Fell, 1957).

Thorn, Benjamin Kent (1829–1905)   Celebrated as the "Law of Calaveras County," this sheriff tracked down some of California's most notorious outlaws and subsequently became the county's powerful and controversial political boss.

Benjamin Kent Thorn was born in Plattsburgh, New York, on December 22, 1829, and moved with his family to Chicago when he was four years old. Thorn grew up in Ottawa, Illinois, and at age 16 taught school locally. In 1849, aged 20, he trekked to California, like so many others, in search of gold. Thorn worked claims in Calaveras County during the 1850s, and in 1855 was appointed deputy sheriff of this most lawless region. A few months after his appointment, he collared the infamous gang of Jess Miller and "Longhair" Sam Brown, which immediately established his local reputation. That fall, he successfully ran for the office of constable of Township No. 5, still retaining his appointment as deputy sheriff.

Thorn developed a wide network of friends, informants, and contacts throughout the county, which enabled him to keep tabs on local criminal activity. In 1859, Thorn married Anna Meeks and presented her with a magnificent 13-room house in San Andreas. Thorn claimed that the structure had been financed with money from his mining claims, but it is more likely that he embezzled taxes he collected as constable. Despite the shadow of suspicion that fell over him, Thorn was elected to the newly created post of tax collector and also served as undersheriff from 1860 to 1864 and deputy sheriff from 1866 to 1868, during which time he continued to amass a remarkable record for apprehending criminals.

By 1868, still more evidence of Thorn's ongoing embezzlement had emerged, yet voters nevertheless put him in the sheriff's office that year. He served until 1875, when the Democratic Party, embarrassed by his extravagance and increasingly bold embezzling activity, dropped him as a candidate. Thorn was absent from the sheriff's office for the next four years, although he was frequently hired by Wells, Fargo detective James HUME to assist in tracking and apprehending stage and train robbers. In 1879, Thorn regained the sheriff's post, having run as an independent, and he remained in office for the next 23 years. Thorn was among those who participated in the manhunt for the legendary stage robber Black Bart.

Thorn suffered a paralytic stroke in November 1902, served out his term, then retired on January 5, 1903. His beloved wife died the following year, and Thorn died on November 15, 1905.

Thrasher, Frederic Milton (1892–1962) Undertook pioneering and comprehensive studies of gang behavior and youth criminality.

Frederic Thrasher was a graduate of DePauw University, where he earned a B.A. in 1915. He went on to the University of Chicago and its famed School of Sociology, taking a master's degree and, in 1926, a Ph.D. Elaborating on his doctoral dissertation, Thrasher undertook an extensive study of Chicago area youth gangs, including the social structure of the gangs and their allure, as well as defining the social gap that gangs fill. The published result was *The Gang: A Study of 1,313 Gangs in Chicago* (1963), which represented more than six years of research and personal observation, and endures as one of the most frequently quoted works on the subject in American sociology.

After completing his Ph.D., Thrasher joined the nascent Educational Sociology Department of New York University, where he embarked on his most ambitious project. Over the course of nine years, Thrasher studied the effects of the New York City Boy's Club on juvenile delinquency. He included almost everything within a community that could affect a child—public schools, movie houses, libraries, churches, neighborhood candy stores, and so on. His work revealed that children are exposed to a myriad of informal education processes on a daily basis, many of which present conflicting values and create conflicts within children. In conjunction with this broad study, Thrasher also undertook a more specialized study of the effects of movies on children—a pioneering inquiry.

Tilghman, Bill (1854–1924) Member of the legendary group of lawmen known as "The Three Guardsmen," Tilghman brought to the Wild West a uniquely personal style of law enforcement.

Born on July 4, in Fort Dodge, Iowa, Bill Tilghman first became a deputy in Dodge City, Kansas, in 1877, rising to the position of chief of police in the 1880s. It was Tilghman, not the better-known Wyatt Earp, who banned guns from the tough cow town of Dodge.

Tilghman left Dodge City in 1892 to become a deputy U.S. marshal and teamed up the following year with fellow lawmen Chris MADSEN and Heck THOMAS to form "The Three Guardsmen" with the express purpose of apprehending the notorious Bill DOOLIN Gang. By this time, Tilghman had earned a reputation as a courageous and uncorruptible agent

Deputy marshal Bill Tilghman, one of Oklahoma's famed Three Guardsmen (Courtesy of the Western History Collections, University of Oklahoma)

of the law. Uncharacteristically of western lawmen, he practiced professionalism and restraint, never shooting unless absolutely necessary. His commitment to fair play saved his life on one occasion, when he had cornered Doolin's outlaw gang in Arkansas. Gang members concealed behind some curtains had a clear shot at Tilghman, but Doolin himself, out of respect for the lawman, ordered them not to fire.

As a U.S. marshal, Tilghman was credited with apprehending such noted outlaws as Bill Raidler, Kid Donner, Jennie "Little Britches" Stevens, "Cattle Annie" McDougal, and Bill Doolin (who was later slain by fellow "Guardsman" Heck Thomas).

After his stint as marshal, Tilghman served as sheriff and chief of police in various Oklahoma communities until his retirement in 1914. Summoned out of retirement to "clean up" Cromwell, Oklahoma, in 1924, the 70-year-old lawman answered the call. After two productive months on the job, Tilghman was shot in the back by a drunken Prohibition agent, whom he was helping walk to jail.

Toch, Hans (1930–)

One of the first to study the social structure of prisons and its effect on inmates; wrote *Mosaic of Despair: Human Breakdowns in Prison.*

Born in Vienna, Austria, Hans Toch immigrated to the United States with his family at a very young age. After earning his undergraduate degree from Brooklyn College and his Ph.D. from Princeton University, Toch concentrated on the study of social psychology, soon specializing in deviancy. Toch was less interested in the concept of deviancy from social structure than in the social structure within deviancy itself. This led to his 1993 landmark work on prison life, *Mosaic of Despair.*

Toch concluded that, perhaps to a greater degree than anywhere else in American society, prison is ordered and rigid in its social structure. Each prisoner is alike in his desire and primal need to maintain a certain level of self-respect. Because of this, prison actually fosters something very similar to a law-abiding social order rather than the potential anarchy it is often assumed to be. Insofar as prison society is structured and maintains values, Toch argues, the social and emotional foundation exists for rehabilitation.

Toma, David (1933–)

A detective in Newark, New Jersey, who became nationally famous for his imaginative use of deep-cover disguises and stratagems, inspiring two popular television series, "Toma" and "Baretta."

David Toma was born on March 7, 1933, in the tough New Jersey city of Newark. Slightly built, Toma was nevertheless a talented athlete, declining a baseball scholarship to Duke University in order to play farm-league ball in Canada and for the Philadelphia Phillies. Later, he served a stint in the Marine Corps, becoming middleweight boxing champion of the Parris Island training camp. Following his discharge, he joined the Newark Police Department and, after walking a beat for three years, was promoted to detective, charged with enforcing narcotics, gambling, and prostitution statutes. Toma developed a highly idiosyncratic style of working alone, penetrating criminal rings through deep-cover tactics, which included a vast range of disguises and thoroughly developed identities: hippie, derelict, priest, even female prostitute. He was also a singularly compassionate cop, who spent a great deal of time with those he arrested, trying to help them turn their lives around.

But it was the undercover work and disguises that captured the popular imagination, especially in view of the arrest record Toma amassed: some 10,000 arrests during 17 years on the force. His conviction rate was an astounding 98%—and, in the course of all those arrests, he never fired his service revolver. (Indeed, while working in disguise, he carried neither a gun nor a badge.)

Toma's exploits inspired two television series, "Toma," which premiered in 1973, starring Tony Musante, and on which David Toma sometimes appeared in bit parts and contributed to scripts; and "Baretta," premiering in 1975 with Robert Blake in the title role. Characteristically, Toma's only complaint about the two series is that they were too violent. He himself became the author of several books, including *Toma, the Compassionate Cop* (1974), *Toma Tells It Straight—With Love* (1981), and *Turning Your Life Around: David Toma's Guide for Teenagers* (1992), all of which emphasize his concern with helping and rehabilitation. In the first book, he also discussed his own addiction to heroin and how he overcame it. Toma hosted a popular radio talk program and toured the United States as a youth counselor and lecturer.

Further reading: Toma, David (and Michael Brett), *Toma, the Compassionate Cop* (New York: Putnam, 1974).

Torrio, John (Johnny) (1882–1957)

Laid the foundation for the national crime syndicate formed by Charles "Lucky" LUCIANO and others in the United States during early 1930s.

Born in Osara, Italy, in February 1882, Johnny Torrio immigrated to New York with his mother in 1884. His father, a laborer, died just before his wife and two-year-old child sailed. Beginning as a local street thug, Torrio showed an early genius for organizing and leading. He quickly rose to gang boss in New York, then overlord of crime in Chicago, ultimately becoming a revered and feared "elder statesman" of organized crime in the United States, having laid the foundation of a multibillion-dollar industry of illegal activity. Although hundreds of rival gangsters were killed at his behest, not to mention an untold host of innocent victims, Torrio was never arrested for any major crime. He thoroughly insulated himself from his deeds and swore his lieutenants to absolute secrecy.

In 1904, using money accumulated from robberies and burglaries as a member of the notorious James Street Gang, Torrio, using the alias of J. T. McCarthy, opened a saloon in the slums of Lower Manhattan. He transformed the upper floors of the building and the neighboring building into a thriving bordello and hired a dozen James Street Gang toughs to protect his enterprise. He soon expanded operations, opening up a string of gambling dens, and was persuaded by Paul Kelly (Paulo Vaccarelli), the most powerful gangster in New York, to join his Five Points Gang in 1905.

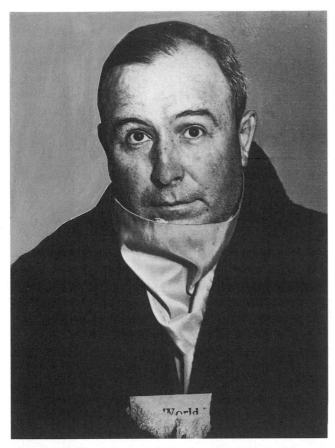

Johnny Torio laid the foundation on which Lucky Luciano, Meyer Lansky, and others built the national crime syndicate. (Courtesy of the Library of Congress)

As Kelly's chief lieutenant, Torrio developed a "rising generation" of criminals (some as young as 10) that included Al CAPONE, who was destined to succeed Torrio as a national crime figure. Torrio quickly grew wealthy and cultivated the image of a prosperous businessman, like Kelly, wearing conservative suits and displaying a polished manner. When a vicious gang war erupted between Kelly's organization and that of Edward "Monk" Eastman in 1908, Torrio left Manhattan for Brooklyn and opened a new saloon with Frankie Yale, establishing it as the headquarters of the Torrio-Yale gang. The following year, James "Big Jim" Colosimo invited Torrio—who was his nephew—to come to Chicago to manage his extensive brothel and gambling operations.

Colosimo had thoroughly corrupted Chicago politicians and enjoyed immunity from police harassment, but he was being challenged by elements of the Mafia, and Torrio's first assignment was to eliminate the Black Hand extortionists. Torrio's men gunned down three of the top lieutenants of James "Sunny Jim" Cosmano, who promptly retired from the Chicago crime scene. Thereafter, Torrio was a greatly feared and respected Chicago crime figure. By 1912, he estab-

lished his own headquarters at 2222 South Wabash Street, the Four Deuces. In 1919, he summoned Capone from New York to serve as his personal bodyguard, bouncer, hitman, and "enforcer." He also served Colosimo as the manager of what had become a brothel empire.

Torrio and Capone tried to persuade Colosimo to gear up for the impending implementation of Prohibition, which (the gangsters saw) would open up enormous potential for illegal profit. Big Jim declined, however, and Torrio, reasoning that the smaller Chicago gangs would seize the Colosimo territory for their own bootlegging operations, dispatched Capone to murder his mentor and uncle. Torrio took over Colosimo's empire and, with Capone as his right-hand man, divided the city into two major "territories." He took the South Side for himself and gave the North Side to Charles Dion O'BANNION. Their main business would henceforth be the illegal production and distribution of beer and hard liquor. "Organized crime" was born.

Not that the organization went smoothly. Rivalries were frequent, and Chicago erupted into a series of brutal gangland wars. Despite the urging of Capone, Torrio repeatedly favored "diplomacy" over violence, but when O'Bannion set him up for arrest on May 19, 1924, Torrio decided to act. He arranged for a hit on November 10, 1924, carried out by Frankie Yale and two others in O'Bannion's own flower shop. The O'Bannion killing touched off the bloodiest gang war in Chicago history. On January 24, 1925, Torrio was himself the victim of a hit, gunned down by Hymie WEISS and George "Bugs" MORAN. Torrio recovered and, true to the gangster's code of silence, refused to reveal the names of his attackers.

In February 1925, Torrio was sentenced to serve nine months in the Waukegan County Jail as a result of the arrest O'Bannion had arranged. With the cooperation of the prison's corrupt warden, he continued to conduct his criminal operations unimpeded, lived in luxury, and was fully protected from warring rivals. His incarceration also prompted him to think. The only way to escape death in the ensuing gang wars was to quit the rackets. Accordingly, he summoned Capone and informed him that he was turning over to him his entire criminal empire. "I'm through. It's all yours, Al. I'm going back to Italy . . . if I can get out of this city alive," he reportedly said.

After Torrio's release, Capone escorted him and his wife to an Indiana train station and a train bound for New York, whence the couple set sail for Naples, Italy. They returned to New York in 1928 when Italian dictator Benito Mussolini began waging war against the Mafia. Setting up in a luxurious Manhattan apartment, Torrio invested legitimately in New York real estate and also formed an illicit partnership with Charles "Lucky" LUCIANO, Abner "Longy" Zwillman, and Meyer LANSKY to establish an elaborate liquor distribution system extending from New York to Florida. Torrio commanded universal respect among gangsters and had so efficiently established his business interests that, after the repeal of Prohibition, his liquor distribution operations became even more profitable.

On April 22, 1936, Torrio was arrested for income tax evasion, fined, and sentenced to two-and-a-half years in the Leavenworth federal penitentiary. Paroled in 1941, he went into semi-retirement, and on April 16, 1957, he suffered a heart attack while in a barber's chair.

Trenchard, Viscount Hugh Montague (1873–1956)   The founder of Great Britain's Royal Air Force (RAF) was also a controversial commissioner of the Metropolitan Police.

One of a long line of Trenchards dating back to William the Conqueror's invasion of England, Hugh Trenchard was born on February 3, 1873. As a child, he was educated at home and received no conventional schooling whatsoever. This later proved an obstacle when he attempted to enter the military and failed both the navy and army entrance exams as well as the militia exam twice, before barely passing it on his third and final try in 1893. He was commissioned a second lieutenant in the Royal Scots Fusiliers and posted to India for five years.

When the Boer War broke out in 1898, Trenchard was transferred to South Africa and promoted to captain, where he led a mounted company. Gravely wounded in the chest, he was not expected to survive. Partially paralyzed and with his left lung collapsed, he was sent back to England where, determined to recover, he underwent a rigorous program of physical therapy. To the amazement of all but himself, Trenchard recovered fully and returned to South Africa.

When the conflict in South Africa ended, Trenchard considered retirement, but was persuaded to join the nascent Royal Flying Corps in 1912, where he was licensed as a pilot after logging barely an hour's flight time. With the outbreak of World War I, he was given command of No. 1 Air Wing in France and developed his theory of strategic bombing.

During the war and immediately after, Trenchard constantly fought to keep the army or navy from getting control of the Flying Corps, which he sought to maintain as an independent military service. His fervor and loyalty to the corps attracted the attention of the prime minister, Ramsay MacDonald, who was looking for someone to reform the Metropolitan Police. After several hesitations, Trenchard accepted,

wading into the problem immediately. Trenchard sought to reorganize the inefficient force along military lines. His two ways of accomplishing this drew stiff criticism. He proposed a police college to develop trained staff officers, similar to officers' school in the military, and he proposed 10-year enlistments for constables. In this way, he hoped to develop a trained hierarchy with permanent subordinates. His critics said that the college was just a way to cheat uneducated but hardworking career policemen out of advancement and promotion. They also said that the enlistment idea would create havoc by increasing turnover.

Unable to enact his principal proposals, Trenchard did manage to eliminate some of the corruption that plagued the Metropolitan Police by evaluating high-level personnel and firing many whom he felt were not up to their jobs. He also did away with the practice of listing unwitnessed robberies as "property missing, suspected stolen." This kept the publicized crime rate in London low, but when he subsequently reversed the policy, the publicized number again skyrocketed, and his critics blamed him.

He resigned as commissioner in 1935, feeling he had done all he could, and spent the rest of his life and career championing the creation of the RAF and fighting for its independent status among Great Britain's military forces. Trenchard died on February 10, 1956.

Further reading: Allen, H. R., *The Legacy of Lord Trenchard* (London: Cassell, 1972).
Boyle, Andrew, *Trenchard* (London: Collins, 1962).

Trojanowicz, Robert C(hester) (1941–94)   Professor of criminal justice at Michigan State University and an advocate of the community policing concept.

Robert Trojanowicz was born in Bay City, Michigan, on May 25, 1941, the son of a police detective. He was educated at Michigan State University, from which he earned a B.S. (1963), M.S.W. (1965), and Ph.D. (1969). He taught at the university throughout his career, beginning as an assistant professor (1969–71) and then receiving an appointment as associate professor of juvenile delinquency, deviant behavior, and the community, in which capacity he served beginning in 1971. Trojanowicz was appointed dean of the College of Social Sciences in 1973 and also served as director of the School of Criminal Justice.

In 1983, Trojanowicz founded and became director of the National Center for Community Policing, the culmination of his research in and advocacy of the community policing concept: taking police officers out of their cars and putting them on foot patrol in neighborhoods, to help prevent crime rather than merely react to it. In 1975, Trojanowicz published

Community Based Crime Prevention, a collaborative work, and in 1982 he issued *An Evaluation of the Neighborhood Foot Patrol in Flint, Michigan.* His other books include works on juvenile delinquency, criminal justice and the community, and the training of police personnel. Trojanowicz's career was cut short by a fatal heart attack on February 11, 1994.

Twain, David (1929–91)   Helped spearhead the federal effort to study the causes of crime and delinquency.

David Twain grew up in Atlantic City, New Jersey, and attended Pennsylvania State University as an undergraduate and graduate student, earning a doctorate in psychology. The focus of Twain's career was the formulation of a model that would give insight into crime and delinquency. From 1958 to 1961, he was chief of psychological services of the Federal Bureau of Prisons, investigating the psychological effect of incarceration on inmates. In 1961, he was named to head the Center for Studies of Crime and Delinquency of the National Institutes of Mental Health in Bethesda, Maryland. While at the center, Twain garnered enough political support to begin a federal effort toward the study of the causes of crime and delinquency. Partially as a result of Twain's campaigning, in the mid-1960s President Lyndon JOHN-SON pushed a massive crime bill through Congress, which included funding for the study and prevention of crime.

After leaving the Center for Studies of Crime and Delinquency, Twain became director of the Research and Developmental Center of the Jewish Board of Guardians, and in 1974 was a founding member of the school of criminal justice at the Newark, New Jersey, campus of Rutgers University. His *Creating Change in Social Settings: Planned Program Development* (1970) discussed the need for planned programs of alternate activities for groups most likely to commit crimes.

Tyrrell, John F. (1861–1955)   Over the course of a career spanning more than a half-century, this examiner of questioned documents became so identified with his field that he was called "Mr. E.Q.D." and "The Wizard of the Pen" and testified in several of the era's most newsmaking criminal trials.

John F. Tyrrell grew up in Milwaukee, Wisconsin, and showed an early interest and talent in graphology and penmanship. After graduating from high school, he went to work at the Northwestern Life Insurance Company, where his first job was addressing envelopes for the company's correspondence. Tyrrell subscribed to *Penman's Art Journal* and began to contribute sketches and short essays to the publication, which was edited by one of the nation's few acknowledged handwriting experts, William Kinsley. In one issue of the magazine, Kinsley recreated a difficult graphological challenge that he himself had been presented with in a recent criminal case. This contest in handwriting identification produced two winners: Tyrrell and Albert S. Osborn of Rochester, New York. With Kinsley's initial encouragement and referrals, both went on to fame—and later collaboration—in court.

By now, Tyrrell had been promoted to clerk at Northwestern Insurance and was studying signatures on claims and other documents to detect forgeries for the firm. Among other discoveries, he found that sickly applicants for life insurance policies were sending healthier proxies to the prerequisite medical examinations; because the stand-ins were also obliged to sign forms at the clinics, Tyrrell readily outwitted the perpetrators of fraud.

In 1899, Tyrrell came to public attention in the trial of Raymond B. Molineux, who was being tried for sending poisoned Bromo-Seltzer to a hated foe. Although the recipient did not ingest the medicine, his landlady did, and she died of cyanide of mercury poisoning. Kinsley, Tyrrell, and Osborn all testified for the prosecution, but of the three experts, Tyrrell stole the show. He made large, freehand, charcoal-on-paper replicas of the disputed script samples and then pointed out minute idiosyncracies in the actual originals that showed those were all written by Molineux's hand. (This was the demonstration that inspired the press nickname "Wizard of the Pen." Tyrrell's testimony addressed psychological aspects of handwriting analysis as well, an area that increasingly figured in the subsequent development of graphology.) The poisoner was convicted, but because of unrelated legal errors, a mistrial was declared, and since the next judge had no faith in handwriting testimony, the prosecution's case was debilitated and Molineux was acquitted. After attempting homicide again, the man ultimately died in an insane asylum.

After the century turned, Tyrrell consulted in a colorful case involving identical twin brothers—Lloyd and Leon Longley, genetically blessed forgers extraordinaire. The Milwaukee siblings looked alike, dressed alike, spoke alike, wrote alike, and, together, specialized in passing bad checks. One would cash a rubber check—signed L. Longley—while the other cemented a concrete alibi far across town. Tyrrell was the first to determine that two L. Longleys existed, deducing the fact from slight recurring differences among the check signatures. Tyrrell went on to prove in court that both brothers were guilty of paper crime, and the twins went on to separate jails.

The Milwaukee examiner of documents played a leading role in many other, even more sensational criminal investigations. He helped convict the lawyer of William Rice, who had poisoned the Texas millionaire and then forged his will; the perpetrator had erred by tracing a single sample of his employer's signature four times, producing too-perfect, inhumanly identical results. The lawyer was convicted, and Rice University was founded with the legacy retrieved.

But handwriting was only a part of the examiner's expertise. Tyrrell also worked wonders with the microscopic and chemical scrutiny of papers and inks, and sometimes linguistic knowledge came into play. In a Marshfield, Wisconsin, bombing murder case in 1922, Tyrrell worked with nothing more than a charred fragment of wrapping paper, but its partial address was misspelled in a Swedish-looking way. Tyrrell's hunch led police to a certain Mr. Magnuson, and a search of his house turned up a fountain pen whose corroded nib and particular ink matched those used on the dynamite package. Confronted with this evidence, the bomber confessed.

Tyrrell also knew typewriters, and in the notorious Leopold and Loeb case, his tracking of the kidnappers' ransom note to a particular machine was the event that convinced defense attorney Clarence DARROW to enter a guilty plea on his young clients' behalf as the only means of saving their lives. In other investigations, the examiner was able to distinguish between the "touch" of keystrokes produced by different typists working on the same typewriter. Tyrrell was among a host of graphologists summoned to study the ransom letters in the LINDBERGH baby kidnapping; the examiner later poked fun at the jealously secretive methodology of the other handwriting experts in this high-profile case.

With Albert Osborn, a founder of the American Society of Questioned Documents, Tyrrell actively consulted until his death at age 94.

U

Uhlenhuth, Paul Theodore (1870–1957) One of the pioneers of modern forensics; discovered a serum that enabled investigators to distinguish between human and animal blood.

Born in Hannover, Germany, Paul Uhlenhuth served as a German military surgeon. In 1900, the young physician was assigned a post as an assistant at the Institute for Infectious Diseases in Berlin—a world-renowned facility headed by tuberculosis pioneer and bacteriologist Dr. Robert Koch. It was through his working relationship with Koch that Uhlenhuth became interested in serology, the study of blood. Before the end of his first year at the institute, Uhlenhuth had discovered a characteristic protein that differed in the blood of different animals. The following year he published his findings in a paper entitled, "A Method for Investigation of Different Types of Blood." Valuable for medical science generally, the paper was a groundbreaker in the field of forensics. Uhlenhuth had given forensic investigators a means of distinguishing between animal and human blood, even when available evidence existed only in the form of a stain.

The first practical test of Uhlenhuth's work came after the arrest of a suspected serial killer in northern Germany. Ludwig Tessnow had terrorized northern Germany for several years. The journeyman carpenter had been tried for molesting, then butchering two children in 1898, but he was acquitted because police officials were unable to determine if bloodstains on his clothing were human or, as Tessnow claimed, animal. It was a common alibi; untold numbers of accused murderers had gone free because the suspects claimed bloodstains found on them were from butchered animals.

About 1900, in another north German town, two more children were murdered in the same brutal fashion as in 1898. Tessnow, who was again seen in the area, was again arrested. Although he had bloodstains on his clothing, the clever criminal had slaughtered sheep following his crime in order to confound the authorities once again. This time, however, the murderer appeared before a magistrate who had read about Uhlenhuth's work and appealed to the scientist to test Tessnow's clothing. In this first use of Uhlenhuth's serum in a trial, the doctor proved not only the existence of human blood on Tessnow's clothing from the most recent murders, but, testing the surviving evidence from the 1898 case, demonstrated the existence of human blood there as well. Tessnow was convicted, and forensic medicine had a new, powerful, and proven tool.

Ulasewicz, Anthony (1918–) Ex–New York City cop who was one of the chief "bagmen" for Richard NIXON's Watergate coverup.

A typical big-city private detective, Anthony Ulasewicz got his start working with the New York Police Department before becoming a private investigator. While he was establishing his firm, Ulasewicz met John Ehrlichman, the future chief counsel to Richard Nixon. After Nixon was elected president in 1968, Ulasewicz was employed by the Nixon administration in various of its undercover political investigations. Ehrlichman hired Ulasewicz as one of the group that would later be termed "The Plumbers"—assigned to plug information leaks in the administration.

Ulasewicz investigated those on Nixon's infamous "Enemies List," which consisted of what Nixon aide John Dean called, in an August 1971 memo to Ehrlichman and H. R. Haldeman, "persons known to be active in their opposition to our Administration." The list included several obvious targets, such as Edward Kennedy, George McGovern, and Walter Mondale, but it also included the likes of Steve McQueen, Paul Newman, and Joe Namath. Dean's memo talked of using the federal machinery available to the president to "screw" the administration's enemies. It was another Plumber, Donald Segretti, an attorney, who code named this activity "rat-fucking." Ulasewicz's mission was to gather damaging information, which Segretti, ex-CIA agent G. Gordon Liddy, and others would use against those on the list. Methods included blackmail, releasing damaging information to the press, and outright fabrication.

As Dean and Ehrlichman came increasingly to trust Ulasewicz, he was assigned a more important task: delivering hush money to the first wave of defendants following the Watergate break-in. On June 28, 1972, Dean approached Herbert Kalmbach, Nixon's personal attorney, about secretly raising funds for the defense of the Watergate burglars. Dean instructed Ulasewicz to make covert payments of $25,000 to the seven defendants by means of an elaborate system of pay-telephone phone messages and public locker drop-offs. Ulasewicz made so many calls from pay phones that he later testified to having armed himself with a bus driver's coin changer. Ultimately, Ulasewicz was convicted of nothing more than income tax evasion for having failed to report the funds received during the years he worked at the White House. He was sentenced to a year of unsupervised parole.

Ur-Nammu (reigned ca. 2278–ca. 2260 B.C.)   The legal codes of this Sumerian ruler, dating back to the end of the third millennium B.C., are the earliest known.

At the turn of the century, numerous Sumerian tablets were excavated and placed on display in the Istanbul Museum of the Ancient Orient. Among these were the law codes of the first ruler of the Third Dynasty of Ur (ca. 2278–2170 B.C.), Ur-Nammu. It was not until 1952 that three tablets, which had been largely ignored up to that time, were translated. Once they were deciphered, it was apparent that Ur-Nammu's codes predated the far more familiar codes of HAMMURABI by over 350 years.

Ur-Nammu's codes consist of three parts: a prologue, a text, and an epilogue. The text of the fragmentary clay tablets tell of a form of trial by water, includes a section on returning slaves to their rightful owners, and defines a class of criminal called "grabbers," presumably thieves.

Further reading: Kramer, Samuel Noah, *From the Poetry of Sumer: Twenty-five Firsts in Man's Recorded History* (Berkeley: University of California, 1979).

Woolley, Sir Charles Leonard, *Sumerians* (New York: W. W. Norton, 1965).

V

Valachi, Joseph Michael (1904–71)   A Mafia turncoat, Valachi revealed the existence of Cosa Nostra—the Mafia, or the Mob—to a Senate committee in 1962.

Joseph Valachi was a so-called "foot soldier" in the syndicate. Faced with conviction for a string of murder charges, this Mafia hitman violated the Mob's time-honored code of silence and testified in 1962

The 1962 Senate committee testimony of Mob hitman Joseph Valachi exposed details of the organization of the Mafia in America. (Courtesy of the Library of Congress)

before the McClellan Committee, spearheaded by Robert F. KENNEDY and investigating organized crime and labor racketeering.

Valachi not only confirmed the existence of the Mafia, but also called Cosa Nostra, but provided authorities with detailed organizational charts. Valachi's testimony marked the beginning of the modern era in the fight against organized crime in America. He died in prison in 1971.

Further reading: Maas, Peter, *The Valachi Papers* (New York: Pocket Books, 1986).

Valentine, Lewis Joseph (1882–1946)   Although Valentine's reputation as an "honest cop" made a seesaw of his career on the early-20th-century New York City police force, his ethical stance was vindicated in later years. Appointed commissioner by reform mayor Fiorello LaGuardia, he became famous for his clean-up of internal corruption in the NYPD.

An Irish-American born in Brooklyn, Lewis Valentine considered becoming a priest before his family's financial need prompted him to quit high school and work for the Abraham & Straus department store. He was quickly promoted from errand boy to delivery depot manager, but, thinking of his future, Valentine took civil service exams for the fire and police departments, passing both.

Valentine chose to become a policeman and in 1903 began pounding beats in Manhattan and in the Flatbush district of Brooklyn. It took 10 years before he made sergeant; his well-known resistance to graft was a hindrance to upward mobility in the department's notoriously crooked chain of command. Having finally gained his stripes, Valentine went on to become a lieutenant on the "confidential squad," a unit established earlier by "Honest Dan" Costigan to ferret out bribetaking and other abuses among members of the department.

When George V. McLaughlin was made police commissioner in 1926, he moved Valentine up to captain, then to deputy inspector, and the former shoo-fly was ordered to go after the city's network of gambling operations. This he did, and thoroughly. The inspector didn't restrict his investigation to the lowest levels of the underworld. He also busted the elite clubhouses of Tammany Hall politicians and other city bigwigs. Valentine's impartial approach to law enforcement cost him his rank when another commissioner, Grover Whalen, came to power. The inspector was demoted to captain and exiled to the city's outer boroughs once more, far from interference with the backroom betting of the powerful Manhattan bosses. Years later, Whalen's administration was disgraced for a number of illegal links, including a lucrative weekly arrangement with the gambling and prostitution empire run by Lucky LUCIANO.

Judge Samuel Seabury called Valentine back to the municipal fray with a subpoena to testify at the 1931 corruption inquiry scrutinizing Mayor James ("Gentleman Jim") WALKER and his Tammany Hall cronies. Valentine's courtroom deposition was instrumental in dismantling a decades-old city grafting machine.

Two years later, Fiorello LaGuardia was elected mayor and began to make good on his campaign promise of sweeping reforms. Valentine was named chief inspector under Commissioner John F. O'Ryan, and when mayor and commissioner fell out over the handling of a taxi strike in 1934—LaGuardia vetoed O'Ryan's plan to use billy clubs against the demonstrating drivers—the latter resigned, and LaGuardia brought Valentine to the top.

Valentine earned public appreciation that very year for the law enforcement protection he offered voters in the November election. The night before, police rounded up scores of well-known thugs whose extortionary "vote-getting" methods had made so many previous elections a sham, and on the day itself, for the first time in years, polling places themselves were guarded from disruption. Valentine's popularity continued to grow with his reduction of another public danger—traffic deaths—which he decreased by improving the city's street signage, papering the town with safety posters, and making personal calls on community groups to discuss the issue.

Addressing internal affairs, Valentine didn't just weed out corrupt members of the force, he slashed and burned a small forest of bad wood. In his first six years in office he fired some 300 officers, formally reprimanded 3,000, and fined 8,000 in all. But Valentine was far more ferocious where crooks were concerned. Very early in the commissioner's tenure, a station-house tirade—following the shooting of a patrolman friend of Valentine's—was leaked to the press; the chief had exhorted his men to "draw quickly and shoot accurately" when apprehending murderers, assuring them of his support "no matter what you do, if what you do is justified." While warning them not to fire at "innocent people" or use brutality for reasons of political bias, the chief freely suggested that "with the criminals, racketeers, and gangsters, the sky is the limit."

This tough talk, off the record, alarmed some citizens as a potential carte blanche for uniformed brutality, and when Valentine was offered a chance to clarify his position, he told the New York Times that he would repeat again what he'd said the day before. After a spell of criticism from the public and from law enforcement leaders in other cities, that particular controversy blew over, but throughout Valentine's career, his "mark 'em and muss 'em up" policy toward wrongdoers continued to spark criticism that Valentine was undermining civil liberties and the pretrial presumption of innocence.

The public's picture of Valentine was further colored after he prohibited news reporters from access to crime and emergency scenes. The disenfranchised and vindictive New York press thereafter made the most of remarks like "I'll promote the men who kick these gorillas around and bring them in." Valentine finally quit speaking to reporters altogether, and writers were forced to collect secondhand quotes from other sources in the department. At one point the chief did break his silence to deny press-mongered implications that he was personally responsible for inspiring several suicides among members of the force.

All the same, Valentine's anti-corruption stance and his success in crime reduction meant that New Yorkers generally approved of his "rough on rats" administration. Valentine's open and stubborn harassment of gangsters and racketeers caused sufficient pressure to elicit the surrender of Murder, Inc.'s Louis Lepke BUCHALTER, long hunted by J. Edward HOOVER. During the 1945 mayoralty campaign, all three leading candidates assured voters that they would retain Valentine as police commissioner. But following the victory of William O'Dwyer, the 63-year-old Valentine decided to retire from the city police, and he took another, presumably less stressful, job as consultant to and commentator on a weekly, reality-based radio show called "Gang Busters."

The next year Valentine was called back to government duty when General Douglas MacArthur invited him overseas to supervise postwar reform of the police, fire, and prison systems of Japan and South Korea. Valentine went to Asia and wrote a 283-page report; its recommendations included one patriotic but perhaps impractical suggestion that all Japanese rookies be sent to the States for training.

Valentine returned to America—and to radio—the same year, and kept a busy pace. The former chief appeared in several movie shorts on crime prevention and served on the editorial board of a magazine called *True Police Cases*. Valentine also volunteered his time as chief investigator of the state's Election Fraud Bureau, promoted the idea of a National Crime Prevention Week, and wrote his autobiography, titled *Night Stick*. He died of liver disease on December 16, 1946.

Further reading: Limpus, Lowell M., *Honest Cop: Lewis J. Valentine* (New York: E.P. Dutton, 1939).

Vambrey, Rustem (1871–1948) Hungarian minister to the United States and a noted jurist who organized the International Penitentiary Congress in Budapest in 1905 and later lectured in the United States on penology and criminology.

Vambrey was born in Budapest, the son of a famed Hungarian Asiatic explorer and the godson of Edward VII, the future king of England. He was educated at the universities of Budapest, Halle, and Geneva, and was admitted to the bar in Budapest in 1896. He served with the Hungarian Ministry of Justice, then became a public prosecutor and, finally, a judge of the Court of Appeal. Vambrey was one of the principal authors of Hungary's progressive Juvenile Court Law, as well as laws governing the rehabilitation of criminals and the decrees putting into effect the Code of Criminal Procedure. In 1905, Vambrey was a key organizer of the important, reforming International Penitentiary Congress, held in Budapest, and two years later he chaired the Anti-Alcohol Congress in that city. In 1918, Vambrey was appointed to a professorship at the University of Budapest.

Following the *Anschluss*—Adolf Hitler's annexation of Austria in 1938—Vambrey fled to the United States to escape the Nazi regime. He lectured on criminology and penology at New York's New School of Social Research from 1939 to 1944. During this period, he contributed articles to distinguished national journals and worked vigorously to restore democracy to Hungary. In 1947, he was appointed Hungarian minister to the United States, but resigned within a year because he believed that his government had no intention of improving relations with the United States. Vambrey died shortly after his resignation, on October 25, 1948.

Van Waters, Miriam (1887–1974) An American pioneer in penal reform for delinquent girls and women.

Miriam Van Waters was born on October 4, 1887, in Greensburg, Pennsylvania, to the family of an Episcopal minister. From her father, Van Waters imbibed a strong spirit of social awareness and responsibility. After the family moved to Portland, Oregon, Van Waters attended a school begun by her father and then attended the University of Oregon, graduating with a degree in philosophy (1908) and returning for a master's degree in psychology (1910). In 1913, she received a Ph.D. in anthropology from Clark University in Worcester, Massachusetts. Her dissertation, "The Adolescent Girl Among Primitive Peoples," anticipated the work of such famed anthropologists as Ruth Benedict and Margaret Mead.

While she was pursuing her academic studies, Van Waters also became interested in social reform. Beginning in 1911, she observed the causes and effects of juvenile delinquency in Boston, and in 1913 she was appointed an agent of the Boston Children's Aid Society. In this capacity, she became aware of the special nature of female delinquency. In the early part of the century, most female offenses were of a sexual nature, and courts generally judged such offenders "morally insane"—by definition beyond rehabilitation.

After working for the Children's Aid Society in Boston, Van Waters returned to Portland, Oregon, in 1914 to become head of Frazer Hall, a juvenile detention center. Almost immediately, however, she was diagnosed with tuberculosis, and her career was interrupted for three years. Van Waters relocated to Los Angeles, and in 1917 was appointed superintendent of the county juvenile home. Two years later, she also became director of an experimental county home for delinquent girls, which Van Waters christened a "preventorium." This institution soon attracted nationwide attention and, most important, funding from a Chicago philanthropist named Ethel Sturges Dummer, who financed Van Waters's national study of schools for delinquent girls. The study resulted in widespread reform, and Van Waters went on to complete two major books on juvenile delinquency, *Youth in Conflict* (1925) and *Parents on Probation* (1927).

In 1932, Van Waters was appointed superintendent of the Massachusetts Women's Reformatory at Framingham, which she liberalized by emphasizing rehabilitation, calling inmates "students," adding extensive programs of psychological counseling, and allowing some inmates to keep their children in the institution's nursery. In 1947, an inmate's suicide prompted a sensational investigation and allegations that Van Waters condoned lesbianism within the institution. As a result, Van Waters was removed as superintendent in 1949, but was quickly returned to office by order of a special governor's commission. She remained superintendent until 1957. Following her retirement, she continued to write and lecture on female penal reform.

Venard, Stephen (1824–91)   Nevada City, California, peace officer during the lawless days of the gold rush.

Stephen Venard was born in 1824 on a farm southwest of Lebanon, Ohio. Educated at the Waynesville Academy, he moved to Newport (now Fountain City), Indiana, and took a job as a schoolteacher. A committed abolitionist, he became involved in the Underground Railroad movement, then fled west when Southern slaveholders put a price on his head. He reached the gold-mining town of Nevada City, California, in 1850, opening up a grocery store there in 1853 and becoming deputy sheriff under W. W. "Boss" Wright in 1855. The following year, Wright was shot to death. Since the new sheriff, William Butterfield, did not get along with Venard, the latter resigned as deputy. Venard stood against the notorious Henry PLUMMER in the 1857 election for city marshal and was defeated. When Plummer left Nevada City, Venard was elected to the post of marshal in 1864.

In 1866, Venard achieved overnight celebrity throughout Northern California—and, by stories carried in national magazines, all of America—for putting an end to the career of a vicious gang of "road agents" (stagecoach robbers) headed by George Shanks. He managed to fell three of the gang members with four bullets. *Harper's Weekly* declared that "No romance could depict greater bravery."

Venard went on to an appointment as deputy sheriff at Meadow Lake City, a particularly lawless mining boomtown near Donner Pass in the High Sierra. After the boom went bust in 1869, Venard became a top guard for Wells, Fargo, then a Nevada City police officer in 1871. Shortly afterward this, he was rehired by Wells, Fargo to hunt down a band of road agents led by John L. Houx and Elisha William Andrus, who was better known as "Bigfoot" because of the oversize shoes he wore to confuse would-be trackers. Through skillful frontier detective work, Venard brought the gang members to justice.

Venard served as a constable and a police officer in Nevada City until 1886, when he retired to become a prospector, establishing the Detective Mine in 1888. The enterprise failed, and in 1891 he contracted a kidney ailment. He died, penniless, on May 20 of that year.

Vidocq, Eugène François (1775–1857)   Founder of the Sûreté, the French detective police.

Vidocq was the son of a baker in Arras, which he left at a very early age, having stolen 2,000 francs from his father to finance a voyage to America. En route, Vidocq himself was robbed and, reduced to abject poverty, eked out a living as a clown and acrobat. At length he returned to Arras, where his father pardoned him—on condition that he enlist in the Bourbon Regiment of the French army. This he did, but he soon fell to quarreling with his superior officers and deserted, only to join a regiment of chasseurs. However, afraid that he would be tried for his original desertion, Vidocq fled France for Austria, where he joined the Kinski Cuirassiers. He fared no better with that regiment; when he was about to receive a whipping for some offense, he deserted the Kinski and returned to France, where he rejoined the chasseurs. Wounded in battle in 1793, he went back to his hometown of Arras, where he married and was elevated to the rank of chevalier (the French equivalent of a knighthood). When he discovered that his bride had been unfaithful, he once again embarked on a life of adventuring and rejoined the army.

Posted to Belgium, Vidocq fell in with a gang of petty swindlers and by 1796 had amassed enough money to move to Paris, where he lived for a time in high style until he had entirely dissipated his ill-gotten fortune. He next traveled to Lille, where he was condemned to a prison term for severely beating a military officer who had seduced his girlfriend. In prison, Vidocq forged an order of release for a farmer who was serving time for theft. The forgery was detected, and Vidocq was sentenced to eight years at hard labor. Sent to a prison in Brest, he staged a daring escape by wearing a stolen policeman's uniform. He was subsequently recaptured, but once again escaped—this time by leaping from a prison watchtower. Indeed, until 1809, Vidocq's life was a series of captivities and escapes. In that year, he presented himself to police headquarters in Paris and offered his services as a thief catcher in a city overrun with criminals. He persuaded the authorities of the truth of the old adage that, to catch a thief, it takes a thief.

Vidocq was pardoned and hired—on condition that he first spend some time in the prison of La Force, where he devoted himself to a study of the character and customs of his fellow inmates. Vidocq was then released and placed in command of a brigade of freed convicts christened the Sûreté and charged with penetrating the world of thieves and criminals of all kinds. Vidocq took to the work instantly, and his brigade grew from four, to six, to eight, 12, 18, then 24 men—all former criminals and all expert at apprehending lawbreakers. Vidocq not only helped bring a measure of order to the lawless streets of Paris, he also amassed a considerable fortune. His salary was a modest 5,000 francs per year, but he was allowed to keep whatever he could take from those he apprehended—a benefit of the job known as the *tour du baton,* or "swing of the truncheon."

Vidocq sent his men into prison to infiltrate the underworld, and he sent them into the streets to do undercover work. He built up an extensive and systematic archive, replete with criminal dossiers, which soon required a veritable army of clerks to maintain.

In 1833, Henri Gisquet became prefect of police and objected to the Sûreté on the grounds that it was made up entirely of former convicts. When Gisquet proved intractable in his objections, Vidocq resigned from the force and invested his now considerable fortune in a paper-making factory, which he staffed with ex-convicts. The enterprise failed, and Vidocq set up a private detective agency—almost certainly the very first in the world. His legacy to French law enforcement was, in effect, the germ of the French criminal police, which included a brigade of specially trained operatives, a vast archive of criminals and criminal activity, and a set of undercover methods for investigating and even preventing crime.

Further reading: Edwards, Samuel, *The Vidocq Dossier: The Story of the World's First Detective* (Boston: Houghton Mifflin, 1977).

Vincent, Howard (1849–1908)

First director of the London Metropolitan Police Criminal Investigative Division (CID), from 1878 to 1908; expanded the detective force of Scotland Yard from about 250 to 800 men, established the credibility of the agency, and created the world's first anti-terrorist agency.

In the wake of a scandal involving three top detectives in Scotland Yard during the 1860s, a committee of inquiry was set up to reorganize the discredited agency. Howard Vincent was an upstart young lawyer with no police experience, but he had studied the French detective system at the behest of the committee. Deciding that he was the right man for the job of CID director, he lobbied hard and won the newly created position in 1878.

Opposition to Vincent came almost immediately. His attempt to incorporate French ideas and practices into a British system aroused ingrained prejudices and alienated many detectives. Worse yet, Vincent hired many detectives directly from civilian ranks rather than promoting them from the corps of beat cops. Despite friction and protest, Vincent enlarged the CID. But the preferential treatment given to Vincent's operatives—no less than Vincent's own often obnoxious aggressiveness—continued to produce grumbling and jealousy within Scotland Yard.

In this atmosphere of dissent and discontent, the CID got its first opportunity to prove itself during the 1880s. Between 1883 and 1885, radical Irish nationalists—members of the Sinn Fein—set off no fewer than 22 bombs in London. In response, Vincent established within the CID the world's first anti-terrorist squad, the "Special Irish Branch," which quickly proved highly successful in arresting the perpetrators.

Despite his personal abrasiveness and lack of traditional police experience, Howard Vincent molded the CID into an effective agency, and his innovative Special Irish Branch survives today as the CID's "Special Branch," charged with working to maintain the internal security of the state.

Further reading: Scoli, David, *The Queen's Peace* (London: Hamish Hamilton, 1979).

Vollmer, August (1876–1955)

Considered the father of the modern professional police force; introduced many reforms startling to contemporaries but now standard elements of American police work.

August Vollmer was born in New Orleans, orphaned young, and then raised in Germany. After finishing his education abroad, Vollmer returned to the United States and settled in Berkeley, California. He served in the Philippines during the Spanish-American War and was twice decorated for conspicuous acts of gallantry. Upon his return to the States, he was elected marshal of Berkeley in 1905, and in 1909 he embarked on his life's work when he achieved election as chief of the Berkeley Police Department, a position he was to hold for the next 24 years.

As police chief, Vollmer's goal was to professionalize his force, beginning with a requirement that his officers be college graduates. This shocked the police community and public alike; in the early 20th century, many urban police officers could barely speak, read, and write English. In conjunction with the Berkeley campus of the University of California, Vollmer instituted a police training program that amounted to a police academy—though it differed from a formal academy in two ways. First, the instructors were not police officers but University of California faculty members. Second, the curriculum did not consist of police procedure but the investigative applications of chemistry, biology, psychology, sociology, and other disciplines. Vollmer knew that such a high level of education would do much to foster the professionalism he sought.

Vollmer was extremely interested in any new technology that could be adapted to police work. Before the invention of the two-way wireless radio, there was no effective means of communicating with officers in the field. To facilitate communications, Vollmer set up throughout the city a system of blinking lights, controlled from police headquarters, to alert patrolmen to call in for instructions. Vollmer was an

August Vollmer, who pioneered scientific investigation in American law enforcement, in retirement (Courtesy of the National Archives)

advocate of lie-detection technology as well. His endorsement and support of early devices helped lead to the development of the modern polygraph. Vollmer argued for universal acceptance of systematic fingerprint identification. Keen on criminal psychology, he initiated the "modus operandi" concept of investigation, the study of a suspect's method of operation as an essential step in tracking, locating, and apprehending criminals. Vollmer recognized that the "M.O." could be as distinctive a signature of a particular criminal as his fingerprints.

Within a few short years, Vollmer's reputation as an innovator spread throughout the country and, soon, the world. The Berkeley Police Department became a progressive model, and Vollmer received invitations from cities in America and abroad to consult on the reform and restructure of their police departments. By the end of his career, he had been instrumental in restructuring the police forces of many cities, including Chicago, Los Angeles, New York, and Havana, Cuba. Perhaps the greatest mark he made on American police forces was his legacy of chiefs. By the time of his retirement in 1932, 25 of his own former officers had become police chiefs in other cities around the country.

Vucetich, Juan (1858–1925)   The work of this Argentine fingerprint pioneer led to Argentina's police agency becoming the first in the world to adopt dactyloscopy (fingerprinting) as a primary means of criminal identification in 1896.

A child prodigy with a particular gift for mathematics, Juan Vucetich entered the Argentine police agency, where he became head of the police statistical bureau. After reading Sir Francis GALTON's work on fingerprinting, the young Argentine was inspired to develop his own system of print classification. Convinced of the superiority of fingerprinting over the prevailing anthropometrical identification methods, Vucetich spent his own savings in an effort to convince the government of his findings, financing the publication of two books and the establishment of his own laboratory.

It was not until the gruesome murder of two small children that Vucetich's efforts finally paid off. Vucetich's analysis of bloody thumbprints on a part of a door implicated the children's mother, who was previously unsuspected. Confronted with the evidence, the woman confessed. Moved by this dramatic demonstration of the effectiveness of fingerprint identification, by 1896, Argentine police officials had made "dactyloscopy" their primary means of criminal identification.

Although this acceptance was a personal triumph for Vucetich, worldwide adoption of fingerprintng was slow to follow.

W

Waite, Charles E. (ca. 1874–1926)   One of the first ballistics experts; cataloged the telltale characteristics of thousands of firearms and was able to establish the uniqueness of each weapon.

Charles Waite was intrigued with firearms most of his life, but his interest grew into a veritable obsession when a convicted but innocent man was nearly sent to New York's electric chair on the basis of inaccurate ballistics testimony. Working as a government investigator in the New York state prosecutor's office, Waite was called upon in 1917 to help investigate the murder conviction of two years earlier. After studying the evidence in detail, and with a little luck, Waite proved the man's innocence. Motivated by a desire to ensure that the same kind of error would never recur, Waite vowed to perfect the study of ballistics and bring it to the level of an exact science.

He first set out to visit every American gun factory, soliciting the specifications and features of all small arms manufactured in the United States. This required considerable leg work, especially since the plants kept information only on recent models. An avid researcher, Waite nevertheless tracked down hundreds of notebooks full of the decades-old information; in this quest, he secured the assistance of lifelong foremen and others long familiar with the plants. After acquiring thousands of firearms himself and cataloging the information he gained from the plants, Waite had amassed a comprehensive, tested compilation of all manufactured characteristics of every American-made firearm, including direction and angle of twist, spacing in the grooves, and shell markings.

Then the bottom fell out.

While visiting friends at the New York Police Department, Waite watched department officials destroying captured firearms. He was dismayed to note that more than two-thirds of them were not American

made, but cheap foreign imitations of American brands. After further inquiry, he learned that over half a million weapons were brought into the country in 1922. At first, it seemed to Waite that all of his work was now virtually useless. But he decided not to despair and, instead, started from scratch in Europe.

At the end of 1922, he toured every gun factory in the major European cities, a pilgrimage that took more than a year, but, when it was over, he had the information he sought.

Realizing that he was still unable positively to trace a bullet to a specific firearm—as opposed to a particular model and year—Waite sought to prove the "firearm fingerprint" theory that would become the foundation of modern ballistics studies. After speaking with countless gunsmiths and machinists, he learned that, on a microscopic level, every gun barrel was marked by the tool that made it, a marking that changed with every gun, as the cutting and machining tools wore down, were sharpened, and wore down again. Each barrel, in effect, bore a machined "fingerprint" and would, in turn, impart that fingerprint to every round fired from it.

Before Waite could progress with the microscopic aspect of ballistics, he died. But his assistants carried on the work he had begun, so that he is justly considered the founder of the science of ballistics as it is practiced today.

Walker, James John (Gentleman Jimmy) (1881–1946)   The so-called "Night Mayor," Gentleman Jimmy Walker was the most important municipal chief executive ever brought down on corruption charges.

Jimmy Walker was born on June 19, 1881, in New York City and was educated in Catholic schools there. After attending college, he became involved in Democratic politics under the tutelage of his father, a state assemblyman, and of perennial presidential candidate Al Smith. By 1909, he had been elected to the state assembly representing the same Greenwich Village district his father had served. Walker served in the assembly until 1914, when he was elected to the state senate, serving there until 1925, when he was elected mayor.

As mayor, Walker, an affable and gregarious individual with a fondness for night life and an eye for the ladies, was popular and well liked by almost everyone. His popularity was founded in part on legislation he had introduced during his days in the assembly authorizing professional baseball on Sundays and legalizing prizefighting in New York. As mayor, he expanded the city's subway system and authorized construction of the Manhattan elevated expressway (West Side Highway). He spent his evenings on Broadway, visible to all his constituents, enjoying New York's famed night life, and gaining himself the nickname "Night Mayor."

Although Walker often had the good of his city at heart, it is also true that he put his hands into as many pockets as he could get them into. When Judge Samuel Seabury headed a state inquiry into corruption at the municipal level, it was discovered exactly how many pockets the mayor was into, including those of the Luciano-Costello Mafia crime family. These and other revelations forced Seabury to send the case to the governor, but before the investigation could continue, Walker abruptly resigned on September 1, 1932, and left for Europe in self-imposed exile.

Walker did not return until 1935, and he found his reputation little tarnished. Indeed, New Yorkers were willing to forgive their good-natured and charming ex-mayor, writing off his misdeed to business as usual and, in the depths of the Great Depression, even fondly associating his administration with the flush times of the Roaring Twenties. When Walker died in 1946, he was remembered, for the most part, with fondness.

Further reading: Walsh, George, *Gentleman Jimmy Walker: Mayor of the Jazz Age* (New York: Praeger, 1974).

Wallace, William Alexander Anderson ("Bigfoot") (1817–99)   One of the Texas Rangers' most colorful figures.

In 1836, during the Texan War of Independence, after his brother and a cousin were slain by Mexicans in the Goliad Massacre, Wallace left his native Virginia for La Grange County, Texas, moving on to Travis County in 1840, and then to San Antonio in 1842. Along the way, he exacted revenge against Mexicans he encountered, then joined the Texas Rangers and

subsequently fought in the Mexican-American War (1846–48).

In 1858, Wallace became a captain in the Texas Rangers, fighting both Indians and outlaws with equal ferocity and developing near-legendary expertise in tracking fugitives—especially escaped slaves—in west Texas. To augment his income during this period, Wallace rode shotgun on the San Antonio-El Paso stagecoach lines, which often resulted in spectacular shoot-outs with would-be robbers.

Having accumulated modest wealth, he bought a ranch in Frio County, and lived there until his death on January 7, 1899.

Walling, George (1823–91)   As captain of New York City's Metropolitan Police, Walling's attempted arrest of Mayor Fernando WOOD set off the bloody riots of 1857 between the Metropolitan and the Municipal forces.

A former captain of New York's notoriously corrupt Municipal Police, which was wholly controlled by the commensurately corrupt mayor of the city, Fernando Wood, George Walling accepted captaincy of the new Metropolitan force, which had been formed in 1857 by state authority to replace the Municipal force. When Mayor Wood refused to disband the Municipal Police and accept the state-mandated Metropolitan force, Captain Walling was sent to effect the mayor's arrest.

The result was a series of unprecedented police riots between the Metropolitan forces and the Municipal forces, which amounted to warfare that lasted more than a year.

The Metropolitan Police prevailed, and by the 1860s Walling's agency was freely practicing violent methods of law enforcement that included a brutal strong-arm squad. Many citizens felt it was just what was needed to combat the civil unrest that swept the city in 1863: the so-called Irish Riot and the Draft Riot (a protest over Civil War conscription that also became a race riot pitting Irish immigrant elements against the city's African-American residents). In one encounter, Walling led a squad of 80 men, who dispersed more than 2,000 rioters, and the captain claimed credit for personally clubbing a man to death.

After the Metropolitan force was dissolved in 1870, Walling was appointed police superintendent of the newly reformed Municipal Police, serving in that capacity until 1885.

Further reading: Walling, George, *Recollections of a New York Chief of Police* (New York: Caxton Book Concern, 1888).

Wambaugh, Joseph (Aloysius, Jr.) (1937–)   A Los Angeles police officer and detective, from 1960 to

1974, who became perhaps the most successful cop-turned-novelist in America.

Joseph Wambaugh was born on January 22, 1937, in East Pittsburgh, Pennsylvania, the son of a police officer. He was educated at Chaffey College (A.A., 1958) and at California State College (now University), from which he received a B.A. in 1960 and an M.A. in 1968. Wambaugh joined the Los Angeles Police Department in 1960, rising to the rank of detective sergeant before he retired from the force in 1974 to devote himself to writing full-time.

Wambaugh first became known as a novelist, publishing *The New Centurions* in 1971, which depicted police work with gritty realism and was especially sensitive to the emotional stress inherent in the life of an officer. As one critic said, Wambaugh's fiction "takes us into the minds and hearts, into the nerves and (sometime literally) into the guts of other human beings." This best-selling novel was followed by others, including *The Blue Knight* (1972), *The Onion Field* (1973), *The Choirboys* (1975), *The Black Marble* (1978), *Finnegan's Week* (1993), *Fugitive Nights* (1992), *Secrets of Harry Bright* (1985), *The Delta Star* (1983), *The Glitter Dome* (1981), *Lines & Shadows* (1984), *Golden Orange* (1990), *The Blooding* (1989), and *Echoes in the Darkness* (1987).

Wambaugh's success as a novelist led to the filming of most of his works and to a career in television, as the creator of and consultant to such successful series as "Police Story" and "The Blue Knight," both for NBC.

Further reading: Wambaugh, Joseph, *The Black Marble* (New York: Delacorte, 1978).
———, *The Blue Knight* (New York: Atlantic-Little, Brown, 1972).
———, *The Choirboys* (New York: Delacorte, 1975).
———, *The New Centurions* (New York: Atlantic-Little, Brown, 1971).
———, *The Onion Field* (New York: Delacorte, 1973).

Ward, Benjamin (1926–) Controversial New York City police commissioner from 1984 to 1989; tackled the big city drug problems of the 1980s with the slogan "Give the streets back to the people."

After a distinguished decade in his law enforcement career that included positions as New York City Department of Corrections Services commissioner (1975–78), Housing Authority chief (1979), and commissioner of the Department of Corrections (1979–83), the 1965 graduate of Brooklyn Law School was appointed by Mayor Edward Koch to the position of commissioner of the 23,000-member New York Police Department in 1984.

As commissioner, Ward was faced with rising crime rates and a shrinking law enforcement budget. Ward,

a hands-on administrator and self-described "action person," was not afraid of tackling difficult issues head on, including police brutality and racial inequality within the department.

Ward heightened police presence in New York neighborhoods by reinstituting foot patrols. He recruited larger numbers of minority officers and, in a controversial program, emphasized promotion of African-American and Hispanic officers to administrative and command roles. During six years as commissioner, Ward activated over 2,000 new police officers and raised the educational requirement for new recruits. His Community Patrol Officers Program, introduced in 1984, was a breakthrough in community-based policing. Ward also established a "steady shift" rotation designed to regularize officers' often unpredictable and, therefore, highly stressful schedules.

While many New Yorkers living in neighborhoods plagued by chronic and seemingly random violence would not conclude that Ward had given the streets back to the people, the commissioner did leave to the city a better-educated, better-paid, more ethnically diverse and representative, and more community-oriented department when he retired in 1989.

Warren, Sir Charles (1840–1927) Army veteran who had the misfortune of being commissioner of the London Metropolitan Police during the Jack the Ripper murders.

Sir Charles Warren was trained at Sandhurst, the British military academy, and served in the army with great distinction until 1886, when Queen Victoria appointed him commissioner of the London Metropolitan Police. Two years after he took office, Jack the Ripper began terrorizing London's East End, and the police, under Warren, seemed utterly powerless to stop him. Warren drew criticism not only from the press and public, but even Queen Victoria expressed her displeasure.

Indeed, the techniques Warren employed in the case were ludicrous and easy targets for public disdain. He rented a pair of bloodhounds (Barnaby and Burgho) to sniff out the Ripper. Not only did they fail in this, they became lost in one of the capital's infamous fogs, and a large search party had to be dispatched to recover them. Warren's other proposal was that police officers trade in their hobnailed boots for rubber-soled shoes—the better to sneak up on Jack the Ripper. At times, Warren's actions were worse than merely laughable. He clumsily destroyed evidence—most notably obliterating a message supposedly written by the Ripper on the wall of a building: "The Juwes are not the / men that will be blamed / for nothing." Warren wiped out the message because he feared it would spark anti-Semitic riots.

Having failed to solve the Ripper case, Warren resigned as police commissioner and resumed his military career. He later—privately—expressed the opinion that Jack the Ripper was "an Irish maniac." He apparently also believed that Montague Druitt, an early suspect in the killings who had committed suicide in the Thames, was, in fact, Jack the Ripper.

Warren, Earl (1891–1974)   One of the most influential chief justices in United States history moved the Supreme Court away from the self-restraint of Oliver Wendell HOLMES Jr. and brought it toward judicial activism.

Growing up in Northern California, Earl Warren attended the University of California and graduated with a law degree in 1920. After graduation, he took a job in the office of the district attorney of Alameda County. Within five years, he was himself elected D.A. for Alameda County, serving until 1938. In a 1931 survey of D.A.s nationwide, Warren was judged the best in the country, "without hesitation." His success in Alameda County easily won him the attorney general's job for the state of California in 1938, and in 1942 he was elected governor.

In many ways, Warren is responsible for the establishment of California as a "super" state, especially by helping to bring the aerospace industry to California during and following World War II. Warren appreciated the consequences of his state's rapid growth, telling his staff that "We have to prepare for another ten thousand people every Monday morning." He provided an extensive highway system to help connect the northern and southern parts of the state, promoted a modern hospital system, revamped the state's correctional facilities, and provided a system of extensive welfare benefits.

Warren was the only three-time elected governor in the history of the state, but did not serve his third term because President Dwight D. Eisenhower nominated him to the Supreme Court in 1953.

While many consider Warren's tenure on the court nothing short of brilliant, Eisenhower, a Republican and a conservative, later commented that the nomination was one of the worst mistakes of his presidency. Warren used his position as chief justice to mold the court and take it in a liberal direction. He did this through careful manipulation of his prerogatives as chief justice, which included controlling conference discussions in which cases are voted on. The chief justice leads the discussion and determines the priority of cases discussed. During the course of his tenure, the Supreme Court was popularly called the "Warren Court."

The Warren Court was characterized by judicial activism, with the court involving itself directly in social change, especially where civil rights and individual liberties were involved. This was a radical departure from the precedent set by Chief Justice Oliver Wendell Holmes Jr., who urged judicial self-restraint. Perhaps Warren's most momentous decision came in *Brown* v. *Board of Education of Topeka, Kansas* (1954), which overturned the previous decision in *Plessy* v. *Ferguson* that had established the doctrine of separate but equal public facilities for African Americans and whites. The decision of the Warren Court held that separate was inherently unequal and therefore mandated an end to segregation, not only in education, but also in all aspects of American life.

While *Brown* v. *Board of Education* would profoundly affect law enforcement—since the police and court system would now be actively involved in enforcing desegregation—the Warren decision with more direct impact on the nation's law officers was that in *Miranda* v. *Arizona* (1966), which overturned the rape conviction of Ernesto MIRANDA because the defendant had confessed without having been advised of his Fifth Amendment rights. The Warren Court ruled that defendants must be made aware of their rights to counsel and that anything they say can be used against them in a trial. Out of this decision came the so-called Miranda law, which requires law enforcement officers to read his rights to each arrested person before questioning.

The Miranda decision profoundly affected law enforcement in the United States. But, in a nation rocked by the social unrest of the 1960s and reeling under a burgeoning crime rate, the decision created such outrage, especially among police officers and officials, that Warren decided it was in the best interests of the court to resign, which he did in June 1968. However, President Lyndon JOHNSON's nominee, Abe Fortas, received such intense scrutiny during his confirmation hearings, that Johnson asked Warren to remain on the bench until the controversy was resolved. Earl Warren stepped down in 1969.

Webster, William H. (1924–   )   Career law enforcement official who served as director of the FBI and the CIA.

Growing up in the suburbs of St. Louis, Missouri, William Webster spent much of his early youth on his father's cattle ranch and adjacent farmland. He attended Amherst College on full scholarship but interrupted his studies to join the navy at the outbreak of World War II. After the war, he returned to Amherst and earned his degree in 1947. Returning home to St. Louis, Webster enrolled in Washington University Law School, taking his degree in 1949. Just as he was about to join a private firm, Webster was recalled to active naval duty during the Korean War. He was assigned to the legal staff and soon faced a major test of his character. Detailed to represent a client who had not been advised of his rights, Webster insisted that the sailor answer no further questions. Webster's superiors pressured and threatened him, but the young officer stood his ground, an action that eventually earned him a commendation and resulted in a significant revision of the Uniform Code of Military Justice.

After his release from the navy, Webster became active in politics and was appointed United States attorney by President Dwight D. Eisenhower in 1960. In 1971, he was named district court judge by President Richard M. NIXON. In 1978, President Jimmy Carter named him to head the Federal Bureau of Investigation, which had been without a permanent director since the death of J. Edgar HOOVER in 1972.

It was no enviable task to follow the legendary Hoover, who had run the bureau with absolute dictatorial authority, but Webster compiled an impressive record in his own right, aggressively investigating organized crime (which Hoover had done only grudgingly) and making the first significant federal progress against it. Webster's biggest success was the arrest of the five heads of the largest crime "families" in New York City. The FBI also stepped up its efforts against espionage and treason, which resulted most notably in the arrest and conviction of John Walker, an American accused of leaking vital security information to the Soviets.

When President Ronald Reagan sought a new head of the Central Intelligence Agency in 1987 following the disabling illness of William Casey, Webster was an obvious choice, due to his solid record of public service and his successful stewardship of the FBI. By this time, the so-called Iran-Contra affair had cast the CIA into public disrepute. It was a complicated scheme, apparently originating at the highest levels of the administration, in which the CIA was employed to circumvent Congress in order sell arms to Iran in return for its aid in freeing U.S. hostages held in Lebanon; the profits from these arms sales would, in turn, be used secretly to supply the anti-Communist rebels (the Contras) in their fight against the pro-Communist Sandinista government of Nicaragua. President Reagan saw in Webster a man who could rehabilitate the image of the beleaguered agency. Following investigations of the CIA's role in the Iran-Contra affair, Webster announced on December 17, 1987, that two senior officials had been dismissed and several others had been disciplined.

The highlight of Webster's career at the CIA came during the administration of Reagan's successor, President George Bush. During the 1991 Persian Gulf War against the forces of Iraq's Saddam Hussein, the CIA played a key role in amassing the kind of intelligence data that contributed to the swift and overwhelming victory of U.S.–led "coalition" forces. Webster retired in May 1991.

Weiss, Earl (born: Earl Wajcieckowski, alias: Hymie; Perfume Burglar) (1898–1926) A ruthless killer who paid the ultimate price for opposing Al CAPONE.

Weiss was born in Chicago of Polish Catholic parents. He committed his first burglary at age 10 and earned the unwanted sobriquet of the "Perfume Burglar" some years later, when he was arrested while robbing an apothecary shop. Perfume had spilled on him, and one of the cops, taking a sniff, asked, "Are you some sort of a pansy, fella?" Much to Weiss's dismay, the Chicago press corps picked up on the remark and dubbed Weiss the Perfume Burglar. Also early in his career, Weiss, a faithful adherent of the church, met the equally devout Charles Dion O'BANNION while both were at worship. The two became partners in strong-arm robbery and, with the introduction of Prohibition, went into bootlegging, along with George "Bugs" MORAN, Frank and Peter Gusenberg, and Vincent "Schemer" Drucci. These men formed the core of the O'Bannion-led North Side Gang.

Weiss's fortunes quickly rose with Prohibition, and he enthusiastically took to the life of a gangster, dressing to the nines and always carrying at least $10,000 in cash on him. Of course, he also carried a gun, a semi-automatic pistol, which he used freely. His favored method of execution was to drive his victim to a remote rural location and shoot him to death. It is Hymie Weiss who is generally credited with having invented the fixture of gangland life known as the "one-way ride."

Given the rivalry between O'Bannion's North Siders and Capone's South Siders, warfare soon broke out between Capone and Weiss as well, beginning early in 1924 when Capone violated territorial understandings with the North Side gangsters. On November 10 of that year, when Capone rubbed out O'Bannion, Weiss swore vengeance and struck against Capone on January 12, 1925. With Moran and another gangster, Vincent Drucci, Weiss sprayed a Capone hangout at State and 55th streets with machine-gun fire. Only Capone's driver was hurt. On January 20, the trio hit Capone's mentor, Johnny TORRIO, seriously wounding him and, more important, sending him fleeing from Chicago. Next came Angelo Genna, another associate of Torrio and Capone, whom Weiss murdered on June 13, 1925.

In response to the onslaught, Capone spent $26,000 on a custom-designed armored car, and he ordered

Earl Weiss, better known as "Hymie," was one of Al Capone's early rivals, ruthlessly eliminated. (Courtesy of the Chicago Historical Society)

hits against Weiss, who twice found himself the target of assassins. That the gunmen twice missed Weiss served only to escalate the war. On September 20, 1926, Weiss, Drucci, and others unloaded some one thousand machine-gun rounds at Capone in a crowded hotel lobby. Miraculously, the gangster escaped unscathed, but Capone got the message and attempted to make peace with Weiss. The truce overtures proved unsuccessful, and Capone sent Frank Nitti, Frank Diamond, John Scalise, and Albert Anselmi to do away with Weiss once and for all. They patiently staked out Weiss for several days, setting up an outpost in a rented room overlooking Holy Name Cathedral. On October 11, 1926, Weiss, his three bodyguards, Benny Jacobs, Sam Peller, and Paddy Murray, and his lawyer, William W. O'Brien, drove up to the church and prepared to enter it. The assassins opened fire from the second-story windows of their room, instantly killing Murray and Weiss and wounding Peller, O'Brien, and Jacobs.

Wells, Alice Stebbins (active 1910–1920s)   The first sworn female police officer in the United States—possibly in the world—traveled from city to city lecturing on the benefits of hiring female officers.

Born in Kansas, Alice Wells attended public schools there, graduating from high school before moving to New York, where she settled in Brooklyn, becoming an assistant to a Congregational minister. She then studied for two years at the Hartford Theological Seminary in Connecticut. After leaving Hartford, Wells toured the country, giving lectures on Christian propriety and the modern-day application of the teachings of Jesus and the Prophets. In both Maine and Oklahoma, she became the first woman to hold a pastorate of her own, before finally moving to Los Angeles.

On the West Coast, Wells worked diligently on behalf of prison reform, lecturing frequently on the subject. Hoping that, with "applied Christianity," she could ameliorate social ills as well as crime, Wells petitioned to have herself hired as a police officer. After she obtained the signatures of 100 prominent citizens, the city council was forced to oblige in September 1910, making her the first sworn woman police officer in the country, possibly in the world.

She carried no firearm but was empowered to make arrests—13 in her first year on the force. While many of her duties were those now performed by social services workers, Wells did frequently serve as an undercover officer in such places as arcades, skating rinks, and other public venues.

Hoping to get other women involved in the profession, Wells began traveling the nation, giving lectures on female police work and inspiring hundreds of other women to work in law enforcement. Back in Los Angeles, she began the first police training program for women at UCLA, and she also formed the International Association of Policewomen in 1915, an organization that has come to include thousands of women from police forces around the world.

Westley, William A. (1920–   )   This sociologist's pioneering 1970 study of the police subculture, *Vio-*

lence and the Police, was groundbreaking and influential.

William Westley received his Ph.D. from the University of Chicago in 1951 and took a professorship at McGill University in Montreal, Quebec. *Violence and the Police,* his 1970 study of the Gary, Indiana, police department, was the first to examine in depth the various dimensions of police subculture. Westley concluded that the subculture of the policeman reinforces traditions of secrecy and violence. He identified what he called a "sophistication-lag" in police management practices, and he believed that the current forms of police management lacked the tools necessary to adapt and change with the times. In essence, modernization, while essential, was impossible under current management models. Westley therefore advocated change in the departments through democratization and decentralization, and he further recommended the enlistment of the community in the direct management of the local police.

Westley's work was in the vanguard of the new school of sociological police research and remains valuable for analyzing and coping with the problems facing many of today's police departments in the United States.

Further reading: Westley, William A., *Violence and the Police: A Sociological Study of Law, Custom, and Morality* (Cambridge, Mass.: MIT Press, 1970).

White, Isaac Deforest (Ike) (1864–1943) One of the greatest crime reporters of all time; worked for the *New York World* from 1886 to 1931.

A Yale graduate and authority on libel law, Ike White devoted his career to crime reporting, becoming something of an embarrassment to New York police officials because of his uncanny ability to solve crimes that baffled them. White's most celebrated "case" involved an attempt to bomb financier Russell Sage in 1891. The would-be assassin—known only as the "bearded stranger"—was foiled only because he accidentally blew himself up, and the police were unable to identify him. White, on the scene, retrieved a button from the dead man's trousers and traced it to the tailor who had cut the pants. While the police were bewailing the fact that lack of evidence prevented their identifying the attacker, the *New York World* ran a headline broadcasting the assailant's name.

In another case, White discovered the key evidence that convicted prestigious physician Robert Buchanan of murdering his wife.

In 1913, publisher Joseph Pulitzer appointed Ike White head of the *World*'s Bureau of Accuracy and Fair Play. White's long and distinguished career ended with his retirement in 1931 to his Mount Kisco, New York, home.

Whitley, Herman C. (ca. 1821–ca. 1880) Named chief of the Secret Service shortly after its inception, Whitley developed the force into a centralized and highly efficient bureaucracy.

A Northern veteran of the Civil War, Colonel Herman Whitley returned to his native Lynchburg, Virginia, following the war to become the assistant tax assessor for the Internal Revenue Bureau in his district. While reading the newspaper one Sunday morning, he noticed what he thought was a typographical error: "Col. H. C. Whitley Selected for Chiefship of the Secret Service." He decided to contact the newspaper to rectify the error, but before he could do so, he received a telegram from the secretary of the treasury notifying him of his appointment and asking him to come to Washington at once.

After being assured there was no mistake, Whitley took over his new job with relish, declaring, "I'd rather be Chief of the Secret Service than President of the United States." He immediately fired most of the hired convicts and other underworld characters put on the service payroll as informants under the previous direction of William WOOD, first chief of the bureau. He also abolished the $25 bounty agents received for turning in counterfeiters. He then began a process to turn the federal government's only law enforcement agency into an integrated force with a working bureaucracy. He coordinated intelligence and information on criminal movements with local police, compiled criminal records on anyone the service came in contact with, and demanded detailed reports from both field agents and their offices.

Within three years, Whitley had turned the service into an efficient and professional federal agency—some 50 years before the Federal Bureau of Investigation came into existence.

One of the first problems other than counterfeiting to face the service was the rise of the Ku Klux Klan in the South and the continued postwar harassment of freed blacks. The Klan threatened, beat, and lynched hundreds of African Americans before President Ulysses S. Grant sent field agents from the Secret Service to deal with the problem. Within three years, more than a thousand Klansmen were convicted of civil liberties violations, and overt Klan operations nearly ceased, for a time.

When Whitley resigned in 1874, he left behind an expanded agency with expanding directives.

Whitney, Chauncey Belden ("Cap") (1842–73) A frontier gunfighter and lawman, and the first constable of the cattletown of Ellsworth, Kansas.

Born in New York, Chauncey "Cap" Whitney fought for the Union as an enlisted man in the Civil War. After the war, he moved west, settling in the newly established railhead cattletown of Ellsworth, Kansas, where he was named the town's first constable in August 1867. Whitney built Ellsworth's first jail and in November ran unsuccessfully for sheriff. In August 1868, an expedition was mounted to hunt down a renegade band of Cheyenne warriors led by Roman Nose. Whitney and approximately 50 of General George Alexander Forsyth's scouts were brutally routed at the battle of Beecher's Island. Whitney was among the survivors.

Returning to Ellsworth, Whitney again ran for sheriff and was again defeated. However, in July 1869, he was called to active duty in the Kansas state militia and commissioned a lieutenant in the continual fight against the Indians. Released from service the following November, he was named marshal of Ellsworth in July 1871. Whitney was finally elected sheriff in November of that year. In April 1873, while attempting to mediate a fight between one Billy Thompson and two gamblers, he was fatally shot.

Wiener, Alexander (1906–76)   The codiscoverer of the Rh blood factor was also a serologist who pioneered the study of blood and other bodily fluids as a method of criminal investigation.

Growing up in Brooklyn, New York, Alexander Wiener attended Boy's High School before moving on to Cornell University. He enrolled in medical school at the State University of New York, took his medical degree in 1930, and interned at the Jewish Hospital of Brooklyn. By this time he had already published his original findings on blood groupings and their transmission by heredity.

After finishing his internship, Wiener went into private practice in Brooklyn, also serving at Jewish Hospital as the head of its blood transfusion division. During this period, Wiener continued his research on blood and its myriad variations. In 1901, Dr. Karl LANDSTEINER had ascertained that there were four basic blood groups: A, B, AB, and O. Using some of Landsteiner's research and working with rhesus monkeys, Wiener, in conjunction with Landsteiner and Dr. Philip Levine, discovered that within each blood type was a factor—which they christened the Rh factor, after the rhesus monkeys—that multiplied the blood classification categories from four to eight. It has been estimated that each year this discovery saves an average of 10,000 people, who would otherwise die from faulty blood transfusions. Wiener also soon discerned the forensic possibilities of Rh blood typing. In 1938, he was named head of the serology and bacteriology department of the New York City medical examiner's office.

Dubbed the "blood cop" by reporters, Wiener advanced criminal investigation by extracting incredible amounts of data from bodily fluids. His work also raised the standards of crime scene investigation, which now demanded great meticulousness, since even the slightest trace of blood or saliva was of potential value. Through further research and advances in microscopy, Wiener was eventually able to distinguish some 500 different blood classifications. Today, that number is in excess of 5,000, making blood typing a very impressive means of identification.

Wiener frequently testified for the prosecution in murder cases, but no testimony he gave was more important than that given before the New York state legislature in 1935 and 1952, convincing that body to uphold the admissibility of blood evidence in paternity and criminal cases.

Wigmore, John Henry (1863–1943)   Founding father and first president of the American Institute of Criminal Law and Criminology; wrote a massive 10-volume *Treatise on the Anglo-American System of Evidence* in 1904.

John Wigmore practiced law in Boston from 1887 to 1898. In 1901, he became dean of the faculty of law at Northwestern University, Evanston, Illinois, a position he held until 1929. During his tenure at Northwestern, Wigmore published his 10-volume *Treatise on the Anglo-American System of Evidence* (1904) and, in 1909, organized the first National Conference on Criminal Law and Criminology in Chicago. Assembled at the convention were some of the greatest minds in the fields of criminology and law. Out of this historic assembly, the American Institute of Criminal Law and Criminology was formed, with Wigmore as president. Another result of this first national organization was the creation of the prestigious *Journal of the American Institute of Criminal Law and Criminology*. As president of the institute, Wigmore commissioned translations of important foreign works in the field of criminology.

John Henry Wigmore continued to figure as an important scholarly voice in American criminology and criminal law until his death in 1943.

Further reading: Millar, Robert Wyness, "John Henry Wigmore," *The Journal of Criminal Law, Criminology and Police Science*, 46:1 (May–June 1955).

Wild, Jonathan (1682–1725)   "Prince of Robbers" and a professional "thief-taker" (bounty hunter); organized one of the most notorious crime syndicates in London during the early 18th century and became the subject of a novel by Henry FIELDING.

Before the existence of a professional police force in London and vicinity, the apprehension of highway robbers, bandits, burglars, and murderers was left to

Jonathan Wild organized one of the most notorious crime syndicates in eighteenth-century London. (authors' collection)

a disreputable cadre of bounty hunters called thief-takers, who captured the malefactors, then handed them over to the authorities in return for a fee. The most famous of London's thief-takers was Jonathan Wild. After arriving in London in 1704, Wild set up shop as a recoverer of stolen goods. Crime was so rampant in London that citizens were compelled to surrender items to gangs almost at will. Wild's business was in recovering such goods, but it was likely that he stole his share of them in the first place. During the day he would receive respectable Londoners and—for a substantial fee—help them locate their property, while at night his apartments in the Old Bailey would be filled with the gangsters and crooks who, in effect, constituted his criminal syndicate.

In order to maintain his public reputation more effectively, Wild graduated from being a recoverer of stolen property to becoming a thief-taker. Indeed, he was credited with having sent more than a hundred criminals to the gallows. Of such persons he had a virtually unlimited supply. Wild's underworld connections provided a steady stream of criminals to turn in—the very criminals who also fattened Wild's

coffers with the bribes Wild demanded in return for allowing them to operate in the city.

Inevitably, Wild made some serious enemies. One such was Jack Shepherd, a small-time criminal boss whose associate, known only as Blueskin, slit Wild's throat in the 1720s. Wild survived the murder attempt, but his luck was beginning to wear thin, and in 1725 he was arrested himself and tried for violation of the Act of 1717, which dealt with receiving stolen property. His trial was decided before it began, and Wild, aware that a hangman's noose surely awaited him, attempted suicide by drinking a large dose of laudanum (a popular medicinal opiate) but survived to stand trial, suffer conviction, and be hanged at Tyburn on May 24, 1725.

Wild's life was the subject of a satirical novel by Henry Fielding, who was not only England's first great fiction writer, but also one of the architects of the modern concept of a profesional police force. Fielding wrote the book in large part as a means of exposing the lawlessness of London and dramatizing the need for a professional police force.

Further reading: Fitzgerald, Percy, *Chronicles of Bow-Street Police Office* (London: Chapman and Hall, 1888).

Pringle, Patrick, *Hue and Cry: The Story of Henry and John Fielding and the Bow Street Runners* (New York: Morrow, 1955).

Wiley, Harvey Washington (1844–1930) Chief of the U.S. Department of Agriculture's Bureau of Chemistry at the turn of the century, scientist Wiley uncovered widespread and potentially hazardous adulteration of factory-produced foods. He organized an all-volunteer "poison squad" to test the effects of ingesting chemical additives, and the bureau's report helped bring about the passage of the first food and drug legislation in 1906. Thereafter, Wiley's staff were charged with investigating and enforcing the new product safety and purity requirements.

Born, raised, and even home-schooled in a Kent, Indiana, log cabin, Harvey Wiley entered Hanover College in 1863. The Civil War intervened, however, and the following year he served as a corporal with the 137th Indiana Volunteers. After completing his B.A. at Hanover (1867), the young scientist taught for a year, then earned his M.D. at the Medical College of Indiana in Indianapolis (1871). During this time Wiley continued to lecture, teaching Greek and Latin at Northwestern Christian University, soon to be renamed Butler College. In 1873 he earned a bachelor of science degree at Harvard University.

Wiley returned to Indiana, taught at Butler and at his medical alma mater, and accepted a professorship in chemistry at Purdue University in Lafayette. At the same time, he was made state chemist for Indiana. He held both posts for nine years. Wiley spent 1878 in Berlin, where he undertook advanced training in chemistry, physics, and pathology, and began his first studies of food adulteration in association with the German Imperial Health Office.

In 1883 Wiley's scientific reputation and specific expertise in sugar chemistry gained him an appointment as chief chemist at the USDA. After 1899, Wiley also taught as a professor of agricultural chemistry at George Washington University. While continuing to explore new processes in sugar and syrup technology, he discovered substantial product adulteration by the nation's syrup manufacturers. He began to look into the practices of other food industries, and his research soon became a vocal crusade for "pure food" reforms. At the time, refrigeration techniques were scant and many factories bothered little about hygiene; Wiley reported that processors routinely depended on untested, potentially dangerous chemical additives to keep their products from spoiling. Furthermore, thoroughly unqualified "doctors"—patent medicine hucksters—were selling useless cancer "cures," morphine-laced potions to "soothe" crying infants, and other highly addictive "elixirs" and tonics. Wiley sounded alarms about these issues repeatedly in Washington, but his legislative proposals gained no ground in Congress, where protection of commercial interests held sway.

In 1902 Wiley began a much-publicized, yearlong experiment in which a group of volunteers ate nothing but food prepared with controlled doses of many preservatives then common: boric acid, formaldehyde, saccharin, benzoate of soda, salicylates, and copper salts. The human guinea pigs were dubbed the "poison squad" by the press, who provided regular updates on their chemical menu. Wiley himself became known as "Old Borax." By the time the Bureau of Chemistry announced its conclusions—that many preservative agents might indeed be harmful to one's health—public consciousness about the ubiquity of the additives had already risen to levels of concern. The uncovering of scandals in the meat-packing and patent medicine trades further fanned the flames of consumer rebellion. A bitter political struggle ensued, as food producers fiercely contested Wiley's findings. Citizen pressure won out, however, and on June 30, 1906, President Theodore Roosevelt signed the first Federal Food and Drugs Act.

Finding it necessary to mollify the indignant protests of the bureau's powerful commercial opponents, Roosevelt appointed a Referee Board of Consulting Scientific Experts to repeat the poison squad's research and make its own determination. Much to the satisfaction of industrial supporters—and to the skepticism of a now-wary public—Ira Remsen's Referee Board reported the additives safe, at least in small quantities. But Wiley's motto—"Tell the truth on the label and let the consumers judge for themselves"—had now become law, and when the labels began to appear, the public stayed away from certain chemicals in droves. Charged with enforcing the new standards of hygiene and purity, the Bureau of Chemistry hurried to design laboratory methods for testing food samples and assembled the first team of inspectors.

In 1907, 28 investigators began work, armed at first with little more than string shopping bags, suspicious minds, and a lot of pluck. But soon the agents had found their footing and were hoofing their way through America's food distribution network, from neighborhood groceries to oyster fishing wharves, from farms to mills to canning plants. Undercover investigators dressed in rags and haunted a local dump in Hackensack, New Jersey, to prove that racketeers were collecting dead horses meant for fertilizer plants and shipping the meat abroad for human consumption. Some agents posed as workers or delivery drivers to infiltrate suspect operations. In the West, inspectors sometimes discussed arsenic spraying over the barrel of an apple-grower's gun. But other missions were educational. Bureau officers would visit food processors to explain better methods of sanitation, refrigeration, and chemical-free preservation.

The more the investigators did, the more they knew had to be done. Stricter, more specific laws were needed for hygiene and labeling, and penalties needed more bite. The drug market was expanding with new and untried compounds, and some of them were even lethal. Therapeutic devices and cosmetics were still unregulated, despite their potential for permanent harm. And dirty-dealing producers and merchants were finding loopholes to slip through when they couldn't hide in plain sight, while court decisions nibbled away at the more vague edges of the law. Eventually, the Herculean task of enforcement was passed from the Bureau of Chemistry to a separate agency within the agriculture department (and, later, to the Department of Health, Education, and Welfare), but it was not until passage of the Food, Drug, and Cosmetics Act of 1938 that many of these issues were addressed.

Although he had built up a staff of over 500, Wiley was understandably frustrated by insufficient numbers of personnel, persistent government obstacles, and judiciary limitations on his bureau's enforcement powers. He faced additional difficulties in 1912, when he was falsely accused of misusing organizational funds. Although a congressional committee cleared his name of these charges, Wiley quit his post in disgust.

Apart from his "pure food" investigations, the bureau scientist had made valuable contributions to research in soils, agricultural analysis, standardization of laboratory apparatus, the establishment of climatic crop boundaries, and the improvement of road construction chemistry during his 29 years of service. He moved on to direct the Bureau of Foods, Sanitation, and Health for *Good Housekeeping* magazine, where he wrote monthly articles and a question-and-answer column. In these and in his many lecture engagements, Wiley attempted to further his cause through consumer education. He retired from his professorship at Georgetown University in 1914, and over the next few years he added several more books to his author credits, including *Not By Bread Alone* (1915), *The Lure of the Land* (1915), *Health Reader* (1916), and *Beverages and Their Adulteration* (1919). A well-regarded and witty public speaker, he was pressed more than once to run for governor or to seek nomination as a vice presidential candidate. Perhaps because of his USDA experiences, Wiley repeatedly shunned invitations to political office.

The recipient of awards, medals, and honorary degrees, Wiley helped found the Association of Official Agricultural Chemists in 1884 and served as its president two years later. The scientist also presided at the American Chemical Society (doubling its membership in his term, 1893–94), the Indiana Academy of Science (1901), the United States Pharmacopoeia Revision Committee (1910–20), and the American Therapeutic Society (1910–11). For his help in revising the pure food laws of France in 1907, Wiley was named a chevalier in the Legion of Honor.

Active until his death, on June 30, 1930, Wiley was buried at Arlington Cemetery.

Further reading: Wiley, Harvey, *Harvey W. Wiley—An Autobiography* (1930; reprint ed., New York: Arno Press, 1976).

Wilkie, John Elbert (1860–1934)

Wilkie, John Elbert (1860–1934)   Chief of the Secret Service who ferreted out the enemy spy network operating during the Spanish-American War and worked to reform the Secret Service.

A native of Chicago, John Wilkie first began work as a newspaperman with the *Chicago Times* in 1877, but then moved to the rival *Chicago Tribune* in 1881. His star rose at the *Tribune,* and he became city editor by 1893, when he went to London to work in the steamship business and in banking. Upon his return to the United States in 1896, he went back to the *Tribune* as a special investigator.

In the 1890s, the most successful counterfeiting ring in U.S. history was operating with seeming impunity. The head of the Secret Service was fired because he could not break the ring, and Wilkie was appointed to replace the departed chief in 1898 and personally oversee the "Monroe Note" investigation. After microscopic investigation of the phony notes, Wilkie and his men were able to trace the counterfeiters and arrest them twice—the second time while they were continuing to counterfeit from within prison!

With the outbreak of the Spanish-American War in 1898, an extensive foreign spy network was operating in Washington, D.C. Wilkie organized a special Secret Service task force to expose the spies, eventually deporting almost all Spanish diplomats in the country at the time as well as arresting their best operatives and driving the rest into hiding and inactivity.

Wilkie also sought to reform certain practices of the Secret Service, especially its investigative techniques regarding counterfeiters. While the agents balked at his prohibition of stool pigeons, their chief source of information, Wilkie was able to abolish the appointment of agents on the basis of political cronyism.

Wilkie stepped down from the Secret Service post in 1913 to become vice president of the Chicago Rail System.

Willcox, William Henry

Willcox, William Henry (ca. 1878–1941)   A pioneer toxicologist who established the physical properties in vegetable and cadaveric alkaloids, and who developed a method for determining the level of toxic material in a cadaver.

Although European pathology and forensic medicine were becoming well established by the turn of the 20th century, acceptance of the science greatly lagged in England. William Willcox, along with Augustus Joseph PEPPER and, later, a newcomer named Bernard SPILSBURY, worked at the prestigious St. Mary's Hospital in London, where, with other colleagues, they studied pathology, soon gaining a limited local reputation for their work in the field. When the widely publicized and horrifically brutal Crippen murder case came before Scotland Yard, officials quickly recruited the St. Mary's crew as Home Office pathologists to deal with the case.

Since toxicology was the least well defined aspect of forensic medicine at the time, Willcox was up against an even greater obstacle than his colleagues faced. Nevertheless, using a new method—heating an alkaloid crystal specimen and determining its identity by its melting point—Willcox was able to identify the kind of poison used to kill Cora Crippen. Building on this method, Willcox went on to establish another method for identifying the presence of vegetable or cadaveric alkaloids.

The Crippen case established Willcox as an authority in the developing field of toxicology, but his greatest professional moment was yet to come. As chief toxicologist of the Home Office, he was called to examine the body of Eliza Barrow, who had died of arsenic poisoning in 1911. Due to the vast presence of arsenic in almost everything in English society at the time, ranging from wallpaper to many medications, it was important to determine precisely just how much arsenic the victim had ingested in order to establish if hers was a gradual environmental death or, in fact, a case of murder.

After establishing the crystalline weight of arsenic, Willcox weighed each part of the victim's body that contained arsenic. By taking small sections of each body part, determining the amount of arsenic present, then multiplying it by the percentage of the organ used as the specimen, Willcox could determine how much arsenic was present in the stomach, liver, and so on, and then determine how much arsenic was present in the entire body. Although his method left room for error, it proved quite successful and was the first time the presence of poison was actually measured in a cadaver.

Williams, Alexander S. ("Clubber") (1839–1910)

One of the crookedest cops in the history of law enforcement; retired in 1895 with more than a million dollars he claimed to have saved from his $3,500 annual salary.

Alexander S. "Clubber" Williams was born in Nova Scotia, Canada, and arrived in New York at age 27. After serving two years with the city's Metropolitan Police, he was assigned to patrol the vicinity of Broadway and Houston Street, the focus of some of the most brutal gangs in the gang-ridden city.

Williams approached his assignment with gusto, seeking out the toughest gang members and summarily subjecting them to a severe beating with his nightstick. It was for such deeds that the officer earned his nickname. Indeed, Williams was known to have engaged in at least one fight each day for the four years he patrolled the Houston and Broadway beat.

In 1871, Clubber was promoted to captain and placed in charge of the 21st Precinct, the infamous Gas House District. Once again, Williams took to the streets, clubbing any thug he ran across. He also assembled a strong-arm force assigned quite literally to beat back the district's crime and criminals.

Clubber relished his power but did not exercise it in the selfless service of the people of New York.

Inspector Alex "Clubber" Williams stands on the far right of fellow commanders in the New York police department of the 1890s. (Photo by Jacob A. Riis, courtesy Jacob A. Riis Collection, Museum of the City of New York)

Instead, Williams highhandedly solicited graft money from businesses—both legitimate and illegitimate—in return for his special brand of "protection." In the meantime, as his unofficial career prospered, so did his official standing within the department. In 1876, Williams was promoted to the 29th Precinct, on which he himself bestowed the name "Tenderloin," signifying a territory juicy with opportunities to savor graft money.

During his tenure in the Tenderloin, Williams amassed a personal fortune from the brothels, saloons, and gambling joints he permitted to operate in the area. By the mid-1880s, Williams had been accused some 18 times of taking bribes or dishing out brutality, but he was so influential that he was, on each occasion, cleared of all charges. Still, such items of personal indulgence as a summer retreat in Connecticut and a $30,000 dock to accommodate his new yacht continually aroused the suspicions of those who grasped the fact that such things were beyond the reach of a man earning a police captain's $3,500 yearly salary.

At last, the Lexow Committee, formed to investigate New York City police corruption and spearheaded by a reform-minded Theodore ROOSEVELT—at the time president of the Board of Police Commissioners—pushed Clubber Williams into involuntary retirement on May 24, 1895. Certainly, Roosevelt would have had precious little patience with the likes of Clubber, but it is rumored that President Roosevelt's often-quoted dictum of foreign policy—"Speak softly and carry a big stick"—was inspired by his dealings with Clubber Williams. (Roosevelt, however, identified it as a West African proverb.)

Williams, Edward Bennett (1920–88)   One of America's premier defense lawyers; gained a reputation for defending a wide range of clients, all presumed guilty and all socially distasteful.

A child of the Great Depression, Edward Bennett Williams began working at a gas station in high school to help his family pay the bills. He won a scholarship to Holy Cross College in Worcester, Massachusetts, from which he graduated summa cum laude in 1941. After a brief stint in the navy during World War II, Williams entered law school at Georgetown University in Washington, D.C. Throughout his legal career, he was guided by a single principle: Everyone is entitled to legal counsel as guaranteed by the Sixth Amendment.

Williams drew both criticism and praise for the wide range of clients he defended. He counseled rabid anti-communist Senator Joseph McCarthy during his censure hearings before the Senate, yet he also defended Hollywood writers that McCarthy and his ilk had accused of communist affiliations. Williams

spectacularly defended Teamsters union president Jimmy Hoffa on bribery charges. Hoffa had been found with the proverbial smoking gun—incriminating documents—on his person. The case against Hoffa was so strong that Attorney General Robert F. Kennedy declared, "I'll jump off the Capitol Dome if I lose this case."

He lost, and Williams offered him a parachute.

In the Hoffa case, Williams demonstrated his brilliance in cross-examination and illustrated his policy of never asking a question to which he did not already know the answer. Williams grilled the government's chief witness for six days, eventually so discrediting him that the jury had no choice but to acquit. Asked later about the tactic, Williams said that witness query should never be to gather information but only to illustrate a point. Otherwise, the lawyer loses control of testimony if he or she doesn't know what the answer will be.

Williams was often criticized for defending known criminals, including Mafia boss Frank COSTELLO, but remarked, "The Sixth Amendment guarantees the right of legal counsel to *everyone*. It does not say to everyone except people like Frank Costello."

Williams, George Henry (1820–1910)   United States attorney general during the post-Civil War Reconstruction period; supported the Radical Republicans in their efforts to clamp down on Ku Klux Klan activity.

Born in New York on April 26, 1820, George Williams studied law and was admitted to the bar in 1844 at the age of 24. He then moved to the Iowa Territory to begin practice, and when Iowa was admitted to the Union in 1847, Williams was elected a district judge, serving until 1852. In 1853, President Franklin Pierce appointed him chief justice for Oregon Territory. There he rendered a decision in favor of a freed slave who petitioned to obtain custody of his three children from his former master.

Retiring from the bench in 1857, Williams set up private practice in Portland, Oregon, and supported Stephen A. Douglas in the 1860 presidential election. Williams was named a delegate to the state convention; after Oregon was admitted in June 1862, he was elected as a Republican senator in 1864. As a member of the Joint Committee on Reconstruction, Williams introduced the Tenure of Office Act, which would later be used to impeach President Andrew Johnson. In May 1871, President Ulysses S. Grant appointed him attorney general, and for the next two years Williams attempted to impose Reconstruction on an unwilling South.

Like other Radical Republicans, Williams refused to appreciate the depth of racial hatred that motivated

Southern whites. The authority of the North to enforce the provisions of Reconstruction was wholly dependent on the presence of federal troops. In their absence, enforcement collapsed. Williams and the other Republicans never made an effort to address the social and emotional aspects of racist resentment, but instead merely prosecuted the most blatant acts of violence directed against blacks, especially acts perpetrated by the Klu Klux Klan. Thus, in a noble but ultimately misguided effort to legislate morality, Williams devoted most of his energies as attorney general to dispatching more and more federal army units to protect his U.S. marshals in their legal war against the Klan.

In 1873, Grant nominated Williams to succeed Salmon P. Chase as chief justice of the U.S. Supreme Court, but the nomination failed when a past impropriety was discovered. In the so-called "stolen election" of 1876, when Rutherford B. Hayes defeated Samuel J. Tilden for the presidency, Williams was sent to Florida with General Lew Wallace to sort out the disputed election returns. But this good Republican perceived his mandate as really being to "save the state for Hayes." And he did just that.

With the end of Reconstruction in 1877, Williams retired to Portland and his law practice. He died in that city on April 4, 1910.

Williams, Willie L. (1943–   )

The first African-American police chief of Los Angeles, hired after the tumult following the police beating of Rodney King and the three-day South-Central riot that followed the acquittal of the officers involved.

The son of a Philadelphia meat cutter, Willie Williams grew up a sickly child, in and out of the hospital four times and given last rites three times before his 18th birthday. After working briefly with his father in a meat-packing plant—until he was injured on the job—Williams took a position with the Philadelphia Park Guards, an unarmed patrol force designed to protect the city's parks. Initially derided by the police department, the Park Guards were later incorporated into the police department in 1972. In this way, Williams entered the police department, excelled on his civil service exams, and moved up in the department through sergeant, detective, and eventually captain.

After completing an associate degree at Philadelphia College of Textiles and Science in 1982, Williams became a top candidate for police commissioner. However, he chafed under the tough—many have said racist—administration of Mayor Frank RIZZO, and it was not until June 1988 that Williams was named commissioner by Rizzo's successor, Wilson Goode. Williams helped transform a police department scarred by racial tension and poor community rela-

tions. He opened special substations in the neighborhoods hardest hit by crime, and when community relations problems surfaced, he rushed to deal with them openly and honestly.

Williams was exactly the type of officer the Los Angeles Police Board and Mayor Tom BRADLEY were looking for to replace Daryl F. GATES in the wake of the Rodney King beating. In March 1991, a bystander had captured on videotape the brutal beating of motorist Rodney King by four white police officers. Even after the tape was released to the news media, along with police radio transcripts replete with racial slurs by the police, Gates refused to discipline the officers, citing the department's policy of "managed and controlled use of force." Amid public outcry, the district attorney brought criminal charges against the four, who were, astoundingly, acquitted. Three days of rioting, looting, arson, and murder ensued.

After a period of defiance, Gates agreed to retire on his own terms, and Williams was brought in to replace him in July 1992, the first African-American police chief in the city's history and the first chief brought in from outside the department in 43 years.

Williamson, Adolphus Frederick ("Dolly") (fl. 1846–86)

Nineteenth-century superintendent of Scotland Yard who is considered by many as the greatest manhunter of his time.

Dolly Williamson was popularly called the "philosopher" of Scotland Yard. He combined a shrewd investigative technique and an easy familiarity with criminals and kings to make himself a legend in the agency he directed. Williamson was appointed superintendent of Scotland Yard after a distinguished 20-year career as a detective, which saw him solve such baffling crimes as the great Bullion Heist. As superintendent, Williamson molded Scotland Yard into an internationally recognized police agency with a reputation for efficiency and tenacity.

Unfortunately, in the 1880s, three of Williamson's top detectives were implicated in a bribery scheme that rocked Scotland Yard, forcing Williamson to resign from the agency in 1886 after 40 years of service.

Further reading: Gribble, Leonard, *Great Manhunters of the Yard* (New York: Roy, 1966).

Scoli, David, *The Queen's Peace* (London: Hamish Hamilton, 1979).

Wilson, Frank J. (1887–1970)

This Treasury Department agent built the basis of the income tax evasion case that sent the ever-elusive Al CAPONE to federal prison in 1931.

Frank Wilson joined the newly formed Treasury Department Intelligence Unit in 1920. For the next quarter century, he would make his mark on the department as one of the most ambitious and thorough of its investigators. In 1930, Wilson was chosen by Elmer IREY, head of the Intelligence Unit, to help devise a plan to indict and convict the elusive gangster Al Capone. Over the next year, Wilson followed a twisting paper trail that revealed the sources of the gangster's income and his extraordinary wealth— funds on which he had never paid taxes.

Feeling the heat, Capone sought to eliminate the probing Treasury agent, who had several narrow escapes. Despite Capone's efforts to stop him—one way or another—Wilson completed his investigation, and the gangster was indicted in October 1931 on charges of income tax evasion to the tune of $215,030.48. It was conviction on this charge that took the notorious Capone off the streets.

Wilson's next high-profile case was the LINDBERGH baby kidnapping in 1932. It was Wilson who suggested that the serial numbers of the gold certificates paid as ransom money be accurately recorded. Two years later, this information proved critical in the conviction of Bruno Richard HAUPTMANN, and the use of serial number records to tie money to criminals has been common practice ever since.

Wilson's star continued to rise in 1936, when he was appointed head of the Secret Service. As director of the Treasury Department's top police agency, Wilson was credited with virtually wiping out the counterfeiting plague rampant at the time in the United States through an innovative nationwide education program. Also, policies he established still figure today in the standard procedures followed by the Secret Service in ensuring presidential security.

Wilson retired from the Secret Service and public life in 1947.

Further reading: Spiering, Frank, *The Man Who Got Capone* (Indianapolis: Bobbs-Merrill, 1976).

Wilson, Sir (James) Harold (1916–) Prime minister of England during the 1970s; a founding member of the Trevi Group, which established international guidelines against terrorism.

Born in Huddersfield, England, on March 11, 1916, Harold Wilson received a classic English education, first at Huddersfield, then in secondary school at Cheshire, and finally at Oxford University. Upon graduating from Oxford in 1937 with first class honors, he took a lecturing position there in economics. After two years at Oxford, Wilson turned to politics, where he became involved in establishing the economic policies of the government.

In 1956, Wilson was appointed to the cabinet, the youngest since the junior PITT, and in 1963 he became head of the Labour Party. When that party returned

to power in 1964, he was elected prime minister by the slimmest of margins.

Although he was reelected in April 1966 by a more comfortable margin, his economic policies were severely hampered by external circumstances, and the Labour Party was ousted in 1970. At that point, Wilson assumed leadership of the opposition and regained residency at 10 Downing Street when the Labour Party returned to power in 1974.

During his second stint as prime minister, Wilson founded the Trevi Group in December 1975 in Rome, to deal with the ever-increasing problem of international terrorism. Prior to the Trevi meeting, terrorism was seen as a political crime and therefore not subject to extradition.

The Trevi Group was a conglomeration of European Community (EC) leaders and justice and interior ministers brought together under the direction of Wilson to create a unified front against international terrorism. The group first met in Luxembourg in June 1976 and passed a number of resolutions, including one to exchange freely technical information among members of the EC and to share police information relating to terrorist activity. Where necessary, police personnel would operate on exchange programs in order to share knowledge and tactics more effectively. The Trevi Group also investigated airport security and baggage handling. Many of the group's initial resolutions are now considered necessary steps against terrorism, especially those relating to airport security.

Further reading: Roth, Andrew, *Sir Harold Wilson: Yorkshire Walter Mitty* (London: Macdonald and Jane's, 1977).

Wilson, O(rlando) W(infield) (1900–72) Police chief, superintendent, consultant, professor, and author who was a prominent, frequently provocative leader in 20th-century American law enforcement.

Wilson was born in Veblen, South Dakota, but his Norwegian-American family moved to California when Wilson was in his teens. His father, a lawyer, set high standards for his children's educational development. After graduating from San Diego High School, Wilson majored in criminology at the University of California, Berkeley (B.A., 1924), and while still a student, he served as a patrolman for the progressive, trend-setting Berkeley Police Department. City police chief August VOLLMER became a mentor to Wilson, inspiring the young officer to commit himself to the field and work toward its improvement.

Fresh out of college, Wilson was offered a position as chief of police for a southern California town, but his tenure as head of the Fullerton force turned out to be very brief. The forward-thinking official alarmed the community with his academically progressive overview of crime and its origins, once publicly recommending birth control as a systemic deterrent to the concentric social—and criminal—pressures that result from overcrowding. Pressure was placed on Wilson, and he was crowded out of town; his less-than-voluntary resignation gracefully cited a lack of administrative experience.

Wilson worked as a detective for the Pacific Finance Corporation for two years thereafter, until Vollmer suggested his name to the authorities of Wichita, Kansas. The police chief there had been fired under a cloud of scandal, and bootleggers were out of control. Having once been burned, Wilson was twice shy about taking a commissioner's job, but Vollmer persuaded him, and he started work in 1928. Wilson stayed away from excess rhetoric this time, while reorganizing the department completely, introducing clearly marked police vehicles, mobile crime labs, lie detectors, and other modern innovations. He also hired college students as part-time patrolmen, and clamped down hard on the liquor lords. Within five years, Wilson had earned a national reputation for his cleanup of the police force and town. But Wichita was now so clean its vice operators and political community began to squeak, and the chief was once again pressured to step down. He took a leave of absence in 1936 to teach at Harvard University's Bureau for Street Traffic Research, and, following a change in city managers three years later, Wilson departed from the Wichita post permanently.

After a stint with Chicago's Public Administration Service, surveying municipal police organizations, Wilson was asked to return to Berkeley to succeed the retiring Vollmer as professor of police administration at the University of California. He did so, while continuing to consult to cities around the country. In 1943 he joined the U.S. Army as a lieutenant colonel in the military police, serving in Italy and England as chief public safety officer. He was awarded the Bronze Star and the Legion of Merit and attained the rank of full colonel before discharge in 1946. Wilson remained overseas as a civilian administrator with the War Department and showed typical stringency and vigor as the chief public safety officer in charge of "denazification" in the U.S. zone of occupied Germany. He also wrote a public safety manual for Germany and the liberated territories.

In 1947 Wilson resumed teaching at Berkeley, and in 1950 he was made dean of the School of Criminology there. A terse lecturer unpopular with students, Wilson also weathered faculty criticism for his lack of an advanced degree. Nonetheless, he successfully defended the criminology school's university status, which was under fire, and made it a leading educa-

tional facility of its kind. Wilson carried on with his consulting work as well, surveying and offering reform suggestions to police departments in many North American cities, among them Dallas, Nashville, Vancouver, Hartford, and Birmingham.

While heading a police chief selection board for Chicago in 1960, Wilson himself was ultimately recommended for the job by the four other members of the advisory panel. Before accepting the position, Wilson secured official guarantees of a free rein with the city's notoriously corrupt department—some of whose officers had recently been implicated in a series of burglaries—and its business-as-usual reputation for graft, racism, and other abuses. Over the next seven years Wilson's hard-line approach to efficiency and ethical conduct offended many, as always, but his programs also earned him accolades.

He radically reduced the number of Chicago's police districts, thereby destroying the fiefdoms of longtime captains and disconnecting local networks of patronage and bribery; and he created a much-resented Internal Investigation Division that was a hundred officers strong. Wilson thoroughly screened all new applicants to the force, obtained significant salary increases for police personnel, and reinstituted a promotions examination system to allow talented younger officers a chance for speedier advancement. He hired women as school crossing guards and hundreds of civilian clerks to free more than a thousand fully trained officers for active duty. He installed a $2 million police radio network, doubled Chicago's fleet of patrol cars, founded Operation Crime Stop—a telephone clearinghouse for citizen tips and eyewitness reports—and created a special task force of 600 officers dedicated to crime prevention in high-risk areas of town.

Wilson made efforts to racially integrate the police department, and he earned public acknowledgment from Dr. Martin Luther King Jr., who visited Chicago to highlight housing discrimination there in 1966. King later contrasted Wilson's out-of-the-ordinary invitation to police headquarters—to discuss security for the civil rights leader and his party—with the harassment he'd received from Southern police. The same year, Wilson was lauded for his department's next-day apprehension of Richard Franklin Speck, who had brutally murdered eight student nurses in their South Chicago hospital dorm, but the commissioner was also soon lambasted for his outspoken pretrial declarations of the (ultimately convicted) suspect's guilt.

Wilson retired in 1967, ending a distinguished, if controversial, career. Author of several books, he saw his *Police Administration* (1950, 1963, 1972), coauthored with Roy C. McLaren, through three editions and a number of foreign translations. He also edited *Parker on Police* (1956), a collection of writings and remarks by Los Angeles chief William H. PARKER. President of the American Society of Criminology (1941–49) and a life member of the International Association of Chiefs of Police, Wilson was recognized with numerous citations and annual awards, as well as honorary doctorates from several colleges and universities. He died of a stroke in Poway, California, in 1972.

Further reading: Bopp, William J., *"O. W.": O. W. Wilson and the Search for a Police Profession* (Port Washington, N.Y.: Kennikat Press, 1977).

Wilson, O. W., *Police Planning* (Springfield, Ill.: C.C. Thomas, 1952, 1957).

Wilson, (Thomas) Woodrow (1856–1924)

As 28th president of the United States, Wilson is best remembered for committing the nation to World War I, but he also coped with the police strikes of 1919, strengthened international law, and extended executive privilege over the Secret Service and the FBI.

A professor of jurisprudence, a Ph.D., president of Princeton University, and a prolific author, Woodrow Wilson entered political life in 1910, when he was elected as a reform governor of New Jersey. Two years later, Wilson became president of the United States and would serve two terms.

Wilson was president during one of the more turbulent periods in the history of the United States and the world. Friction with Mexico's rebel hero Pancho Villa and the agonizing decision to enter the Great War were just two of the daunting problems that faced the former educator. An advocate of a strong executive branch of government, Wilson set several precedents in the field of law.

When the United States entered World War I, Wilson removed restrictions on the Bureau of Investigation (later renamed the Federal Bureau of Investigation) and the more established Secret Service, giving them authority to carry out counterespionage operations and to bypass Congress in the process, thereby greatly extending executive privilege and the potential authority of federal police agencies.

Following the war, Wilson was faced with the nationwide police strikes of 1919. Police strikers protested low pay, and policemen were leaning toward affiliation with organized labor. Wilson, who was in general anti-union, denounced the strikes as "a crime against civilization," and used the full authority of his office to pressure would-be labor organizers among the police into abandoning the idea of unionizing.

Perhaps Woodrow Wilson's most enduring effect on law and law enforcement came in connection with his advocacy of the League of Nations following World War I, which involved defining principles of international law and international jurisprudence and creating agencies to enact and enforce these principles. Despite Wilson's efforts, the United States declined to join the League of Nations, which was therefore greatly weakened. However, many of the principles of international law for which Wilson was directly or indirectly responsible remained effective and influential, particularly after the creation of the United Nations following World War II.

Further reading: Nordholt, Jan, *Woodrow Wilson: A Life for World Peace* (Berkeley: University of California Press, 1991).

Winchell, Walter (1897–1972)

Perhaps the most famous and influential gossip columnist ever; played a role in law enforcement because of his public visibility, his influence with the mob, and his personal friendship with J. Edgar HOOVER.

After an early career in vaudeville, Walter Winchell began publishing a single-page, three-column Hollywood gossip sheet that came to the attention of Glenn Condon, the editor of *New York Vaudeville News*. Winchell became Condon's West Coast correspondent during the key years of Hollywood's emergence as the center of the entertainment industry. In 1922, Winchell moved back to New York City and took a full-time position with the *Vaudeville News*. His career took off from there, eventually earning him a syndicated newspaper column and a syndicated radio program that commanded a devoted nationwide audience of 20 million.

Walter Winchell not only invented the modern gossip column, he played footsies in public with the mob and with J. Edgar Hoover. He is shown here with actress Simone Simon. (Courtesy of the Museum of Modern Art Still Film Archive)

Winchell's following included figures from all walks of life, among them FBI director J. Edgar Hoover and several prominent members of the Mafia, most notably some of the members of Murder, Inc. His familiarity with both sides of the law sometimes got Winchell into trouble, as when he would intimate the possibility of gang warfare on his radio show or in his column—with amazing accuracy.

Winchell's most sensational role in law enforcement was his part in the surrender of Louis "Lepke" BU-CHALTER, the founder of Murder, Inc. The FBI classified Lepke as Public Enemy Number One for more than two years, but had been unable to apprehend him. In their efforts to bring Lepke to justice, however, the bureau had severely crimped mob operations by continually tailing Mafiosi. To ease the pressure, the mob in August 1939 persuaded Lepke to surrender himself, but he feared that he would be shot on sight by some overzealous cop or executed by rival Mafia factions.

Whom did Lepke trust?

Walter Winchell. Mob officials arranged a meeting in which Winchell would pick up Lepke and take him directly to Hoover.

By the end of the Depression, the public's infatuation with the "glamorous" gangster was coming to an end, and it was no coincidence that Winchell's influence diminished as well. Winchell's legend was sufficiently powerful, however, to prompt the producers of the popular television series "The Untouchables," loosely based on the exploits of federal agent Eliot NESS, to hire Winchell as the show's voice-over narrator.

Further reading: Winchell, Walter, *Winchell Exclusive: "Things That Happened to Me—and Me to Them"* (Englewood Cliffs, N.J.: Prentice-Hall, 1975).

Gabler, Neal, *Winchell: Gossip, Power and the Culture of Celebrity* (New York: Alfred A. Knopf, 1994).

Wines, Enoch Cobb (1806–79) One of the leading agitators for prison reform in the United States; headed the Prison Association of New York, as well as the National Prison Association.

After studying at Middlebury College in Vermont, from which he graduated in 1827, Enoch Wines began a successful career as a teacher, moving from Washington, D.C., to New Jersey, and then to Virginia. After publishing some works on educational methods, Wines accepted a position as professor of classical languages at Washington College in Pennsylvania in 1853. He continued to move about, getting all the way to St. Louis as president of the city university there before coming east again.

It was in 1862 that he was named the secretary of the New York Prison Association. From that point on,

Wines dedicated himself to the study and reform of the penal system. He journeyed around the Northeast, visiting every prison and reformatory in the region, making notes on positive and negative aspects of the current systems. In 1866, he and a colleague gave wide attention to CROFTON's "Irish system" of prison reform, which called for graded degrees of incarceration, depending on the offense and the parole system, and which had first been publicized in the United States by Samuel Gridley Howe. Wines espoused much of Crofton's system, as well as adapting it to include reformatories for younger offenders, rather than prison.

Hoping to effect national reform, Wines called for a national prison reform convention in 1870 to be held in Cincinnati. That convention formed the National Prison Association and named Wines its secretary. Wines continued to advocate prison reform, even traveling abroad and beginning an international congress on the issue before his death in 1879. Wines's son, Frederick Howard WINES, became a noted penologist.

Wines, Frederick Howard (1838–1912) Son of pioneer American prison reformer Enoch Cobb WINES, this penologist was instrumental in prison reform and advocated the separation of the mentally ill from the criminal element in American prisons.

Frederick Howard Wines was born April 9, 1838, in Philadelphia. Frederick attended Washington College (later Washington and Jefferson College) in Pennsylvania—where his father had taught—and graduated at the head of his class in 1857. He began seminary study the same year but was forced to withdraw when an eye infection hindered his studies. After the Civil War, he enrolled at Princeton and earned his seminary degree, becoming a pastor in Illinois.

With the creation of the Illinois State Board of Public Charities in 1869, Wines was appointed secretary, a position he held for the next 30 years. As effective head of one of the few such commissions of its time, Wines was charged with not only administering a program but also defining its policy. Much of the commission's success was due to Wines, and he picked up where his father had left off in his national and international advocacy of prison reform, organizing a National Conference of Charities and Correction, as well as serving as a delegate to the International Penitentiary Congress in Stockholm.

Wines published several books on the public stewardship of both criminals and the mentally ill, including *Punishment and Reformation* (1919), which was considered a standard work for many years. He also advocated more humane treatment of the mentally ill, arguing that they were not criminals and should not be treated as such, with chains and other physical restraints.

Witthaus, August Rudolph (1846–1915) The preeminent toxicologist in the United States and perhaps the world at the turn of the 19th and early 20th centuries.

August Witthaus was born on August 30, 1846, and raised in New York City. After graduating from Columbia University in 1867, he journeyed to Europe to study at the Sorbonne, remaining there for three years before returning to the United States to take his master's degree at Columbia. He again journeyed to Europe for another year of postgraduate study at the Sorbonne. Upon his return home, he enrolled at New York University and received his M.D. in 1875.

After a period at New York University as an associate professor of chemistry and physiology, he was also appointed professor of chemistry and toxicology at the University of Vermont and was appointed to a similar position on the faculty at the University of Buffalo. He journeyed among these three schools from 1882 until 1900, when he accepted a position at Cornell University in chemistry and physics, retiring as professor emeritus in 1911.

Witthaus's most valuable contributions were in the field of legal medicine, especially toxicology. He wrote copiously on the subject, publishing at least seven different works, including the highly acclaimed four-volume *Medical Jurisprudence: Forensic Medicine and Toxicology*, written in collaboration with T. C. Becker (Witthaus wrote the entire fourth volume on his own). Witthaus, who became recognized as the preeminent toxicologist in the country, was an invaluable asset to New York-area prosecutors, who frequently called on him as an expert witness. He testified in some of the more sensational murder trials of his day, and, it seemed, always succeeded in providing the evidence and interpretation that turned the case in favor of the prosecution.

Wolfgang, Marvin Eugene (1924–) Educator and criminologist who has published widely on crime and delinquency.

Marvin Wolfgang was appointed chairman of the Department of Sociology and Criminology at the University of Pennsylvania in 1960. Known for his strong empirical approach, Wolfgang has published works that include *Patterns in Criminal Homicide* (1958) and *The Measurement of Delinquency* (1964), *Subculture of Violence: Towards an Integrated Theory in Criminology* (1967, 1982), and *Delinquency in a Birth Cohort* (1972). Since 1960, he has also served as president of the Pennsylvania Prison Society.

Wood, Fernando (1812–81) One of 19th-century New York's most corrupt mayors, Wood was notori-

ous for maintaining the city police force as a kind of private palace guard.

Born in Philadelphia on June 14, 1812, Fernando Wood moved to New York and became a prosperous merchant and real estate developer in the expanding city. He became a leader in the city's machine-politics headquarters, Tammany Hall, and served a term in Congress (1841–43). Suffering defeat in his first bid for New York mayor in 1850, he won election in 1854, 1856, and 1859. During his terms, Wood introduced a number of reforms and did much to begin the development of the city's Upper West Side as well as Central Park. However, he was personally corrupt, accepting huge sums in graft. (Ironically, his own party accused him of being, in effect, insufficiently corrupt by failing to award a sufficient number of political patronage positions.) The Republican state legislature intervened in 1857, ordering his second term shortened by half and taking over a number of city functions, among them the police department. Abolishing the municipal police as it was constituted at the time—a veritable palace guard appointed by patronage and answerable directly and only to Fernando Wood—the state legislature created a police force that reported to a state board. When Wood resisted the state's efforts at forced reform, the city was appalled by the spectacle of two rival police

Mayor Fernando Wood helped to make New York City synonymous with corruption. (Portrait by Thomas Hicks, courtesy of the New-York Historical Society)

forces battling it out, mainly with their clubs, in front of City Hall. Finally, the governor called out the Seventh Regiment of the National Guard, which surrounded the building and put an end to the battle. Wood submitted to arrest, and the reform and professionalization of the New York City police began.

Despite the incident and despite his corruption—or, perhaps, because of it—Wood achieved reelection in 1859. With the outbreak of the Civil War, he briefly supported Abraham Lincoln and the Northern cause, but soon became a leader among the Copperheads, Northerners who opposed the war and demanded negotiation with the South. Indeed, at one point Wood proposed that New York City secede from the Union but not join the Confederacy; instead, he proposed that the city set itself up as a neutral city-state and enjoy a lucrative trade with both combatants. Wood served in Congress from 1863 to 1865 and from 1867 until his death in 1881.

Wood, William P. (1824–1903)   The first chief of the U.S. Secret Service was unscrupulous and unethical and freely transgressed the Constitution, but he was also highly successful at catching counterfeiters.

After serving with distinction in the Mexican-American War, William Wood adroitly made the political jump from the Whig Party to the new Republican Party in the 1850s, along with the likes of Abraham Lincoln. With the election of Lincoln in 1860 on the Republican ticket, Wood found himself with a sponsor in the form of Lincoln's secretary of war, Edwin Stanton, for whose law firm Wood had once perjuriously testified in an action involving the patent rights to the McCormick reaper. Wood and Stanton quickly became close friends, and when Wood failed to receive the coveted post of federal marshal of the District of Columbia during the Civil War, Stanton appointed him warden of the Old Capitol Prison, where Confederate spies (and others) were incarcerated.

Wood hardly devoted his full time to the administration of the prison, as he was constantly bombarded with requests from both Stanton and Lincoln to engage in investigative actions involving fraud against the government. Wood used his position as warden to gather all sorts of information, setting up a network of informants, some of whom were compensated for their trouble and some not. Wood also began running a Confederate mail service from Richmond to Washington. While the mail was actually delivered, it was also intercepted, read, and resealed.

When the problem of counterfeit federal currency grew out of control toward the end of the war, Secretary of the Treasury Hugh McCulloch declared that the only way to cope with the problem was to establish a full-time federal agency. The obvious choice to head the new Secret Service was Wood, who already had contacts in the underworld and had been successful in his previous efforts to investigate war-related fraud against the government. He distributed 30 agents in 15 cities, telling them that their "service belonged to the government 24 hours a day."

From a constitutional standpoint, Wood's methods were routinely scandalous. He frequently detained suspects for days at a time until he got the information he needed—usually the location of engraving plates. Wood's high-handed and illegal methods undeniably got results. He made more than 200 arrests in one year and sharply curtailed trafficking in bad federal currency. When Wood stepped down in 1869, the Secret Service was well established in dealing with counterfeiting.

Woodcock, Sir John (1932–)   Her Majesty's "Top Copper" was chief inspector of constabulary, responsible for Great Britain's 43 police forces, from 1990 to 1993.

Woodcock was born on January 14, 1932, in Preston, Lancashire, and he was educated in the elementary schools there and at Preston Technical College. He joined the constabulary at Lancashire and graduated from the police academy in 1947. In 1950, he left civilian police work for a two-year stint in the Army Special Investigation Branch, then returned to the Lancashire Constabulary, serving from 1952 to 1965 and rising to the rank of chief inspector. There followed a series of appointments to high-ranking posts in various constabularies until 1983, when Woodcock was named Her Majesty's inspector of constabulary for Wales and Midlands. In 1990, Woodcock became HM chief inspector of constabulary for all of Great Britain. He was knighted in 1989.

Having risen from the ranks, Woodcock was popular with his officers. He emphasized rehabilitation of the public image of the police, instituted minority recruitment programs, and heightened police sensitivity to the needs and feelings of the public.

Woods, Arthur (1870–1942)   Harvard-educated New York City police commissioner from 1914 to 1917; established the first school for patrolmen, which became the basis for the city's modern police academy.

Arthur Woods is considered one of the greatest administrators in the history of the New York Police Department. During his tenure as commissioner, the former educator stressed the need for reshaping the role of the police officer. Woods had made a study of police techniques and policy in Scotland Yard, and his ideas were strongly influenced by the so-called London School, which was based on an approach to law enforcement grounded in sociological and scien-

Arthur Woods, New York City's Harvard-educated police commissioner from 1914 to 1917, established the first school for patrolmen, which became the basis for the city's modern Police Academy. (Portrait by Pach Bros., courtesy of the New-York Historical Society)

tific principles and stressing selfless service to the public interest over personal advancement, political patronage, and departmental favoritism.

Woods's progressive approach produced the city's first school for patrolmen and inculcated an attitude of fairness and humanity among those charged with enforcing the law.

Woods had come to a department that was virtually held hostage by Tammany Hall bosses. His tenure was a welcome respite from the corruption and patronage so long associated with the police department of the nation's leading city. However, Woods's ability to enact reform was dependent on support from the city administration, and when Tammany candidate John "Red Mike" Hylan defeated Woods's supporter,

Mayor John Purroy Mitchel in 1917, the reform movement collapsed.

After resigning as commissioner, Woods continued to lecture on police reform. His 1918 book, *Policeman and Public,* distilled Woods's ideas on the role of a police department acting solely in the public interest. Woods also went on to distinguish himself in the national political arena, serving as assistant secretary of war in 1919, head of President Herbert Hoover's unemployment commission, and chairman of the education board of Rockefeller Center.

Wooldridge, Clifton (1850–1915) Among the most colorful law enforcement officers in American history, Wooldridge was the bane of Chicago's turn-of-the-century underworld.

Little is known of Clifton Wooldridge's early years. He joined the Chicago Police Department when he was 38, in 1888, and made detective within the year. During his ensuing 22 years on the force, Wooldridge made 19,500 arrests, averaging almost three a day for his entire career and earning him the street nickname of "that damned little flycop." He specialized in combating vice, and his record included personally closing more than 100 houses of prostitution and rescuing as many girls from brothels and white slavery rings. Wooldridge was shot at 44 times and wounded in the line of duty on 23 occasions.

Wooldridge's methods of law enforcement differed sharply from those of his contemporaries. Although he was an expert marksman, he never shot to kill, proclaiming, "A policeman's duty is to preserve order, not to kill." When a knife-wielding pimp, who had scarred several women, threatened to do the same to Wooldridge, the "damned little flycop" not only subdued and arrested him, but also forced the thug to carry him up Michigan Avenue—on his back—to police headquarters.

Wooldridge earned the reputation of closing bawdy houses no one else could and of making arrests no one else dared. In one instance, a South Side brothel owned by Big Susan Winslow had been ordered closed many times, but because Winslow weighed in excess of 450 pounds, she could never be arrested simply because no officer could fit her through the door. Wooldridge unhinged the back door, sawed out a two-foot section of the wall, then tied Winslow to a horse and yanked her clean through the wall of her establishment. When Wooldridge retired in 1910, a newspaper remarked that "His retirement marks the end of one of the most amazing and accomplished records in the history of the police system. It is also sad to see the end of such a source of levity in the grim business of crime battling."

Y

Yehudai, Yosef (1947–89)   As chief of police in Jerusalem, Yehudai was forced to deal with rising Arab militancy in the Israeli-annexed sections of the holy city.

A native of Romania, Yosef Yehudai immigrated to Israel in 1961 at the age of 14. In 1964, he began serving with the paramilitary Israeli border guards and shortly thereafter began service with the regular police in Israel. In 1986, he was appointed chief of police in Jerusalem, but in December 1987 Arab extremists, under the direction of the Palestine Liberation Organization, sparked outbreaks of violence in the Arab sectors of the city.

The Palestinian uprising left the Arab sectors all but a no-man's land, and Yehudai was forced, in January 1988, to secure emergency powers allowing him to impose strict curfews on the Arab sectors. Working in conjunction with the military, Yehudai managed to quell the Palestinian uprising with a relative minimum of bloodshed.

Yochelson, Samuel (1906?–76)   Psychiatrist who was an internationally recognized authority on the criminal mind.

Samuel Yochelson was born in Buffalo, New York, received his undergraduate training at the University of Buffalo, and went to Yale University for doctorates in psychology and medicine. During World War II, he served as a major in the U.S. Army Medical Corps, heading the neuropsychiatric service at Fort Meade, Maryland. After leaving the army, he returned to Buffalo, where he set up a practice in psychiatry, then in 1961 became director of research on criminal behavior at St. Elizabeth's Hospital in Washington, D.C., also serving as clinical professor of psychiatry and behavioral sciences at the George Washington University Medical School.

From 1961 until his death in 1976, Yochelson conducted the most ambitious and comprehensive study of criminal behavior ever undertaken by an independent researcher. The results of this research were published in a multivolume work entitled *The Criminal Personality*, coauthored with Stanton E. Samenow. The first volume appeared in 1976, the year of Yochelson's death.

Yochelson concluded that individual personalities and individual value systems are as important as social environment and other outside elements in understanding the criminal.

Z

Zacchias, Paolo (1584–1659)   Physician to the Vatican and the first to publish an expert work on what may be identified as a precursor to forensic medicine.

One of the founders of forensic medicine, Paolo Zacchias first came to notice with the publication of his landmark 11-volume work, *Questions of Legal Medicine*. The book is the first systematic compilation of expert medical opinion regarding forensic procedures, particularly autopsy. Zacchias argued numerous problems facing canon, civil, and criminal law, as well as public hygiene.

His work earned Zacchias the respect of his contemporaries, not only for the groundbreaking nature of his theories, but also for the meticulousness and detail with which he described specific case studies. The work also contained an exceptional amount of legal material as it relates to medicine. This was one of the first efforts to link the practice of medicine and the law.

Zacchias's case studies encompass such seemingly modern aspects of forensics as the examination of wounds and the investigation of sexual crimes, including analysis of bodily fluids. Zacchias's work remained a standard source for more than a century.

Zeisel, Hans (1905–   )   University of Chicago law professor who collaborated with Harry KALVEN to write the first comprehensive study of juries and the process of the jury trial.

A native of Czechoslovakia, Hans Zeisel immigrated to the United States shortly before the outbreak of World War II. Working as an instructor at Rutgers University, Zeisel taught economics and statistics before leaving to become director of research and development at a private firm. He returned to academia in 1953, accepting a position at the University of Chicago as professor of law and sociology. It was a post he would hold well into his nineties.

At Chicago, Zeisel began working with Harry Kalven, a fellow law professor who shared Zeisel's interest in the process of the jury trial. The work the two produced showed that, in 80% of the cases, juries reached the same verdicts as judges. Juries, however, were free to look beyond the letter of the law in handing up their decisions. This latitude, Zeisel and Kalven concluded, was potentially good, since justice is not always a matter of strict interpretation of the law. However, it also left room for potential abuse.

Paulo Zacchias, the pope's physician, was one of the founders of forensic medicine. (Courtesy of the Boston Medical Library)

INDEX

This index is designed to be used in conjunction with the cross-references within the A-to-Z entries. The main A-to-Z entries are indicated by **boldface** page references. The general subjects are subdivided by the A-to-Z entries. *Italicized* page references indicate illustrations.